DEMYSTIFYING CHINA'S ECONOMIC EMERGENCE

Origin, Model, and Characteristics
— A Festschrift in Honor of Professor Jun Zhang

DEMYSTIFYING CHINA'S ECONOMIC EMERGENCE

Origin, Model, and Characteristics — A Festschrift in Honor of Professor Jun Zhang

Editors

Y. Y. Kueh
Lingnan University, Hong Kong, China

Qu Feng
Nanyang Technological University, Singapore

Zhao Chen
Fudan University, China

World Scientific

NEW JERSEY • LONDON • SINGAPORE • BEIJING • SHANGHAI • TAIPEI • CHENNAI

Published by

World Scientific Publishing Co. Pte. Ltd.
5 Toh Tuck Link, Singapore 596224
USA office: 27 Warren Street, Suite 401-402, Hackensack, NJ 07601
UK office: 57 Shelton Street, Covent Garden, London WC2H 9HE

Library of Congress Control Number: 2025017054

British Library Cataloguing-in-Publication Data
A catalogue record for this book is available from the British Library.

DEMYSTIFYING CHINA'S ECONOMIC EMERGENCE
Origin, Model, and Characteristics — A Festschrift in Honor of Professor Jun Zhang

ISBN 978-981-98-1523-4 (hardcover)
ISBN 978-981-98-1524-1 (ebook for institutions)
ISBN 978-981-98-1525-8 (ebook for individuals)

For any available supplementary material, please visit
https://www.worldscientific.com/worldscibooks/10.1142/14367#t=suppl

Desk Editors: Eshak Nabi Akbar Ali/Yulin Jiang

Typeset by Stallion Press
Email: enquiries@stallionpress.com

This book is a Festschrift presented to celebrate the 60th birthday of Professor Jun Zhang

https://doi.org/10.1142/9789819815241_fmatter

PREFACE

Since 1978, China's economy has maintained an average annual growth rate of more than 9%. This growth increased China's per capita GDP from less than US$200 in 1978 to about US$10,000 in 2020. Considering that China has a population of nearly 1.4 billion, this makes China's total GDP about US$14 trillion, which means that its share of the world economy has increased from 1.8% in 1978 to roughly 17% today. China is now the world's second-largest economy, only behind the United States. In 2010, China surpassed Germany as the world's top exporter of goods, and as a globally important manufacturing power, China is now continuing to rise in the global value chain, not only with a significant increase in the added value of its exports and accelerated technological progress but also in its transformation from a technology follower to an technology innovator.

Scholars of the Chinese economy have long tried to understand the major historical phenomenon of China's successful economic rise by observing the changing incentives for economic decision-making, the evolution of fiscal decentralization, and especially the interaction between policy and the market economy. The market reforms promoted by Deng Xiaoping were instrumental in facilitating the China's transition from a planned economy to a market economy with a private sector. These reforms not only changed the pattern of economic development in mainland China after 1978 but also achieved unprecedented success.

It is undeniable, however, that promoting the marketization of the economy is only one necessary condition for the successful rise of the Chinese economy. Cross-country studies show that there are many additional conditions in addition to the market economy for a country's successful economic development; it is otherwise impossible to explain why so few countries (and regions) have actually managed to overcome the low- and middle-income traps. China undoubtedly has those conditions. Most current low-income countries have long been unable to achieve economic growth, probably not because they are ignoring the opportunities of economic marketization and opening up but because they lack the support of a national system.

Professor Y. Y. Kueh has published a number of research papers and books since 2000, which shows that he realized early on the necessity of investigating the model for China's economic rise. Unlike most economists, Professor Kueh believes that economists need to have a broader, historical perspective to understand that there should be a coherent rather than disconnected logic behind China's successful economic rise. He keeps reminding us that the foundation laid by the state over a long period in terms of human capital and industrialization (including the planned economy period prior to the reform and opening up) was a key contributor to the success of the reform and opening up under Deng Xiaoping, and that streamlining the state system and maintaining state order developed over a long period were even more significant.

Professor Jun Zhang, a renowned economist in the field of China's economy, agreed with Professor Kueh and wrote to exchange views. Professor Zhang is currently a senior professor of liberal arts at Fudan University, Dean of the School of Economics, and Director of the China Center for Economic Studies at Fudan University, where he has conducted superb research on China's economic issues and provided unique insights. Professor Kueh himself once thought of further promoting such relevant major research, but unfortunately, "he is unable to do what he hopes to do," and he has put his hopes on Professor Zhang and other like-minded economists.

Professor Zhang and Professor Kueh have known each other for nearly 30 years, and they are colleagues and close friends. Professor Zhang has visited Hong Kong many times and was once a visiting scholar at Lingnan University in Hong Kong. He also visited Professor Kueh's home in Hong Kong to talk with him about his research and interests, and these scenes are still fresh in Professor Kueh's mind today. In Professor Kueh's words, Professor Zhang not only possesses a profound research background and achievements related to the Chinese economy but has also actively promoted academic exchanges at home and abroad for many years, which has supported key brainstorming for Chinese economic research.

In 2010, Professor Zhang had just recovered from a serious illness and returned home to Pudong, Shanghai, to recuperate. To strengthen his confidence and courage, Professor Kueh and his wife, Dr. Cathie Kueh, came from Hong Kong to visit him, and on that day Professor Kueh said, "All that is well that ends well. When you celebrate your 60th birthday in the future, I will follow the tradition of German universities and publish a commemorative volume to celebrate your birthday." Professor Zhang celebrated his 60th birthday in January 2023, which also coincided with the 35th anniversary of his teaching career. Professor Kueh wanted to take this opportunity to invite leading Chinese economic researchers at home and abroad to take the time to write special articles to be compiled into a special volume, titled *Demystifying China's Economic Emergence: Origin, Model, and Characteristics*, as a gift to Professor Zhang to mark these two important milestones. Such volumes are quite popular in European and American academia and are customarily called a *Festschrift* in German universities, where they are a long-standing academic tradition.

Such a topic on China's economic emergence has also been one of Professor Zhang's main research directions in recent years. It's noteworthy that in 2021, Professor Zhang led the project *Towards a National Theory of Economic Development*, which was approved as a Legendary Project on Humanities and Social Sciences at Fudan University (XM04221238) and a Major Project of the Philosophy and Social Sciences Research of the Ministry of Education

(2023JZDZ018). In this project, Professor Zhang advocates placing the phenomenon of China's economic emergence within the context of China's national history. To achieve this, he proposes that efforts should be made to construct a national theory of economic development, an angle that Western development economics has long overlooked. The volume *Demystifying China's Economic Rise: Origin, Model, and Characteristics* naturally becomes one of the outcomes of this research project.

Against this backdrop, a feast of Chinese economic thought was eagerly anticipated! In 2021, Professor Kueh therefore sent invitations to the Chinese economics community and overseas colleagues working on China's economic issues, which received enthusiastic responses from many of Professor Zhang's academic friends and disciples. Over the course of a year, nearly 30 economists contributed papers to the Festschrift. An international symposium based on these papers was carefully organized by the current and former students of Professor Zhang. On September 17, 2022, a high-end symposium on "the Origin and Model of China's Economic Emergence," hosted by the Economics Division at Nanyang Technological University, Singapore, was successfully held online and broadcast live. More than 67,000 people watched the symposium, which was unprecedented.

The symposium was a grand event in the Chinese economics community in recent years. Professor Kueh personally delivered the opening speech, and he fondly recalled his cross-generational friendship with Professor Zhang and thanked his fellow scholars and colleagues for their active participation. He noted that he expected the symposium to produce fruitful academic results and promote the development and progress of economics in China. He expressed his hopes that the Festschrift would be a successful publication to celebrate the 35th anniversary of Professor Zhang's teaching career as well as his 60th birthday. Professor Qu Feng, a former student of Professor Zhang, then delivered an opening speech on behalf of the organizer, the Economics Division, Nanyang Technological University, Singapore. Professor Feng spoke highly of Professor Kueh's academic contributions and thanked him for personally initiating the preparation of the Festschrift and the symposium. He also recalled his own relationship with his teacher, Professor Zhang, and deeply thanked Professor Zhang for his guidance, cultivation, and encouragement. He observed that he was looking forward to working with the scholars of the symposium to share the latest research on China's economic development and to jointly promote transnational academic cooperation and theoretical development.

The opening ceremony of the symposium also featured a commemorative video specially produced by Professor Zhang's current and former students. The video took a closer look at their mentor's rich academic life from the perspective of two current students of the School of Economics at Fudan University, through their visits to three young faculty members. The video also reviewed Professor Zhang's outstanding contributions in academic research, international cooperation, and teaching, as well as the important achievements that he has made in leading the development of the school as its dean.

After the opening ceremony, Professor Justin Yifu Lin, a good friend of Professor Zhang and a famous economist and dean of the Institute of New Structural Economics at Peking University, was invited to give the opening speech. The title of Professor Lin's speech was "China's Economic Development from the Perspective of Structure Endogeneity." Professor Lin analyzed the internal mechanism of China's economic rise based on the conceptual framework of New Structural Economics and the new perspective of endogenous structure. He then looked into the future of China's economic development and suggested that China should utilize the joint role of "effective market and facilitating government" to achieve high-level development in accordance with its comparative advantages. He predicted that from 2019 to 2049, China would maintain an annual growth rate of 4.5%, thus becoming an advanced industrialized country and achieving the great goal of national rejuvenation.

A total of 18 economists were invited to share their latest works from their different research perspectives in four sessions. They are Yew-Kwang Ng (Monash University); Wan-wen Chu (Academia

Sinica); Yang Yao (Peking University); Mary-Françoise Renard (Université Clermont Auvergne); Ligang Song (the Australian National University); Tomoo Marukawa (the University of Tokyo); Deqiang Liu (Kyoto University); Yanrui Wu (the University of Western Australia); Shiyi Chen (Fudan University); Zhao Chen (Fudan University); Zheng Michael Song (The Chinese University of Hong Kong); Fung Kwan (University of Macau); Ying Fang (Xiamen University); Ziying Fan (Shanghai University of Finance and Economics); Naoki Murakami (Nihon University); Guiying Laura Wu (Nanyang Technological University); Xinxin Ma (Hosei University); and Zhiwei Xu (HSBC Business School of Peking University). Professors Qu Feng from Nanyang Technological University; Hongsheng Fang from Zhejiang University; and Zonglai Kou, Xiaohuan Lan, Changyuan Luo, Yuan Zhang, Qi Zhang, Hong Song, and Xican Xi from Fudan University were also invited to discuss the papers of the presenters. The symposium also attracted the participation of many senior economists from the international economics community, including Professor Kwok Hon Leonard Cheng, president of Lingnan University; Professor Lok Sang Ho, former head of the Department of Economics of Lingnan University; and Professor Ping Lin, former professor of Lingnan University and dean of the School of Economics of Shandong University. After the meeting, Professor Ho was also invited to contribute to the Festschrift.

Professor Jun Zhang was invited to give a closing speech. Professor Zhang first thanked Professor Kueh for his proposal and initiation, and also thanked the many friends and students in the field of economics at home and abroad for spending the whole day participating in the symposium engaged in wonderful sharing and discussion. Professor Zhang then made his academic presentation for the symposium about the origin of the model for China's economic rise. He first introduced the efforts of his research team in trying to analyze the theoretical framework of economic development based on the internal relationship of order–innovation–size. Historically, he said, industrialization first took place in modern Europe because Europe first solved the problem of compatibility between the political order and the innovative activities of business.

It then formed an economic system that was later strongly promoted by new institutional economists; this system was exported to other parts of the world through maritime trade and colonial expansion, but very few regions succeeded in economic development. The new institutional economics thus did not provide much help to the economic development of most countries in the postwar period. Changing the topic, Professor Zhang noted that the economic success of East Asia and the economic rise of China as a big country took place without the Western economic system. He reminded us that there should be a strategic component of catching up with the pioneers of industrialization in the East Asian development model. This catch-up strategy must meet the minimum requirements for system quality and be executable. One development strategy that meets these two conditions is the processing trade strategy. According to Professor Zhang, it is no coincidence that the pursuit of an export-oriented strategy is the common logical starting point for the economic rise of East Asia and China. Based on this analytical framework, Professor Zhang briefly introduced his basic views on the economic development and institutional changes of latecomers. Finally, he also noted that the continued rise of the economy of China, as a large country, would bring about profound changes in the theory of economic development. He noted that he looked forward to working together with friends from all walks of life at home and abroad to make greater contributions to the development of Chinese economics.

The symposium started at 8:30 a.m. and lasted until 6:30 p.m. Many of Professor Zhang's academic colleagues from home and abroad met with each other, exchanged ideas, and discussed the latest achievements in China's economic research. Taking this opportunity, colleagues in the academic community expressed their deepest wishes for Professor Zhang's upcoming 35th anniversary of teaching and his 60th birthday. In the words of Professor Lin, the fact that guests from all over the world were able to spend 10 uninterrupted hours participating in this symposium is a very rare phenomenon, which shows that theoretically exploring the model and origin of China's successful economic rise is indeed a very worthwhile academic activity. Professor Lin expressed his hopes that colleagues in the academic community would take the symposium as an opportunity to continue to hold high-end conferences on the topic and that they would be able to make new discoveries related to China's economic success that have not yet received attention in modern economics.

The present volume contains 24 papers from the symposium, which deal with the major issues of China's economy, including the historical evolution and practical challenges of economic growth, the national development strategy, modernization of national governance, institutional reform, industrial policy and market economy, fiscal policy transition, local government behavior, state-owned enterprise reform, innovation models, entrepreneurship and intellectual property protection, corporate financing constraints, carbon neutrality and energy transition, fusion marketization, the Internet and self-employment, a comparative analysis of the development models of East Asia, and China's impact on Africa's industrialization. This volume includes papers that put forward new insights, new evidence, and new theories for the study of China's economic issues, as well as carefully and systematically exploring the origins, model, and characteristics of China's economic rise.

Looking back at the grandeur of this symposium, we are inspired with firm confidence in the modernization, internationalization, and independent development of Chinese economics. The story of mutual understanding and respect among academics and the passing of the torch from teachers to students will surely inspire those who come after to devote themselves to the study of China's economic transformation and change: "A time will come to ride the wind and cleave the waves; I'll set my cloud-white sail and cross the sea which raves." As Professor Lin and Professor Zhang said in their summary of the symposium, let's join together to make new contributions to the great era of development in Chinese economics! With this symposium and this album, we would like to celebrate the 35th anniversary of Professor Zhang's teaching career and his 60th birthday. We wish Professor Zhang the best of health and hope that he continues to play a leading role in advancing the development of economic research in China!

https://doi.org/10.1142/9789819815241_fmatter

ABOUT THE EDITORS

Y. Y. Kueh is an internationally renowned expert on the Chinese economy. He was born in Simanggang, Sarawak, studied in New Asia College, Hong Kong and obtained his Ph.D. degree from Marburg University, Germany. Before he joined Lingnan University as Chair Professor of Economics and Dean of Social Sciences, he was a Professor of Economics at the Chinese University of Hong Kong, and had served as founding Director of the Centre for Chinese Political Economy at Macquarie University, Sydney. Prof. Kueh has authored multiple papers at *China Quarterly* and edited over 10 books covering different aspects of the Chinese economy. His monumental work on *Agricultural Instability in China* elucidated the influence of weather on China's food production from 1930s to the 60s. In *China's New Industrialization Strategy*, he attempted to answer the fundamental question: Was Chairman Mao really necessary in the modernization of Chinese economy? Among his other books are: *The Chinese Economy under Deng Xiaoping, PAX SINICA Geopolitics and Economics of China's Ascendance*, and *Xi Jinping: Negating Mao Zedong Will Result in Chaos* (Xi Jinping: Fou Ding Le Mao Zedong Tian Xia Hui Da Luan).

Qu Feng is the Head of Economics Division, and associate professor, School of Social Sciences, Nanyang Technological University (NTU), Singapore. He joined NTU after obtaining his Ph.D. in economics at Syracuse University in 2009. He is also a senior associate editor of *Singapore Economic Review*, a journal of the *Economic Society of Singapore.* His research interests include Chinese economy, financial markets and econometrics. His research papers appear in *Journal of Econometrics, Journal of Development Economics, Journal of Applied Econometrics, Journal of Economic Behavior and Organization,* etc. Dr. Feng was honored at NTU Convocation Ceremony 2013 for inspirational teaching and mentorship, and was nominated for the Nanyang Award for Research Excellence, NTU, 2012 and 2021, respectively. He received China Finance Review International Research Excellent Award in 2024.

Zhao Chen is Professor of Economics and Deputy Director, China Center for Economic Studies, Fudan University, China. His current research interest covers industrial polices and environment regulation. He teaches Principles of Economics and Economics of Information at Fudan University. He used to be Senior Associate Member at St. Antony's College, Oxford University, visiting scholar at IDEI, University of Toulouse I, France and visiting scholar of UNU-WIDER at Helsinki, Finland. He has published papers on Chinese economy in international journals such as *American Economic Review, Journal of Comparative Economics, Journal of Environmental Economics* and *Management and Review of Economic Studies.*

https://doi.org/10.1142/9789819815241_fmatter

LIST OF CONTRIBUTORS

Chong-En Bai, Tsinghua University
Haolin Bai, HSBC Business School of Peking University
Shiyi Chen, Fudan University
Zhao Chen, Fudan University
Wan-wen Chu, Academia Sinica
An Dong, Nanyang Technological University
Ziying Fan, Shanghai University of Finance and Economics
Hongsheng Fang, Zhejiang University
Qu Feng, Nanyang Technological University
Ying Fang, Xiamen University
Lok Sang Ho, Lingnan University
Chang-Tai Hsieh, the University of Chicago and the National Bureau of Economic Research
Wen-Quan Hu, Zhejiang University of Finance and Economics
Wing Lok Hung, Chinese University of Hong Kong
Kabinet Kaba, Université Clermont Auvergne
Fung Kwan, University of Macau
Xiaohuan Lan, Fudan University
Justin Yifu Lin, Peking University
Deqiang Liu, Kyoto University
Changyuan Luo, Fudan University
Xinxin Ma, Hosei University
Tomoo Marukawa, University of Tokyo
Naoki Murakami, Nihon University

Mary-Françoise Renard, Université Clermont Auvergne
Xiang Shao, Fudan University
Ruhua Shi, HwaBao Securities Co. Ltd.
Shuo Shi, Fudan University
Ligang Song, the Australian National University
Zheng Michael Song, the Chinese University of Hong Kong
Mei Tao, Fudan University
Xin Wang, the Chinese University of Hong Kong
Qiang Wen, Sichuan University
Yanrui Wu, the University of Western Australia
Zhiwei Xu, Fudan University
Yang Yao, Peking University
Xufei Zhang, Zhejiang University of Finance and Economics
Yuan Zhang, Fudan University
Shihao Zhou, Nanyang Technological University
Xiaochang Zhou, Shanghai University of Finance and Economics
Yixiao Zhou, the Australian National University

https://doi.org/10.1142/9789819815241_fmatter

CONTENTS

https://doi.org/10.1142/9789819815241_0001

Chapter 1

CHINA'S ECONOMIC DEVELOPMENT FROM THE PERSPECTIVE OF STRUCTURE ENDOGENEITY*

Justin Yifu Lin

Institute of New Structural Economics, Institute of South–South Cooperation and Development, and National School of Development, Peking University, Beijing, China
justinlin@nsd.pku.edu.cn

In recent years, I have advocated for new structural economics generalized from the experiences of economic development in China and other developing countries. In this chapter, I would like to discuss the ups and downs and eventual emergence of China's economy in the 20th century from the perspective of the endogeneity of economic structure within the framework of new structural economics.

The dramatic ups and downs of China's economy since the 19th century constitute a major event in the world's history. China

*The author thanks Dr. Shuo Shi, who helped organize this talk based on the keynote speech at the International Symposium on "the Origin and Model of China's Economic Emergence" on September 17, 2022.

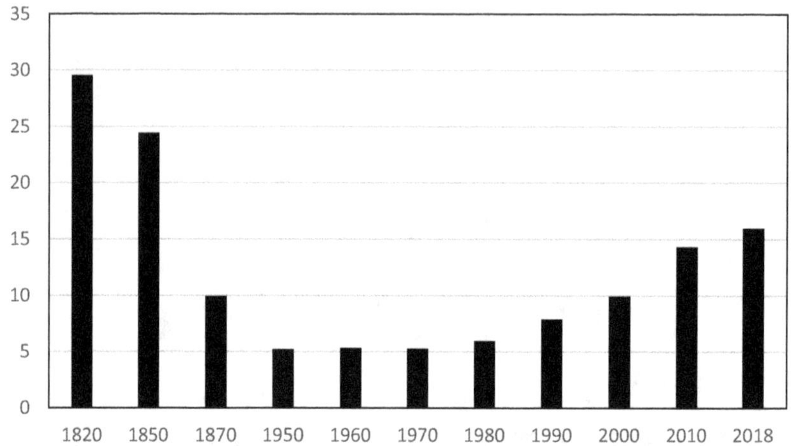

Figure 1. China's GDP as a share of the world GDP (%).
Source: Maddison Project Database (MPD) (2020).

was a historically prosperous civilization, but after the Industrial Revolution in the second half of the 18th century, its global economic status declined sharply. Figure 1, created using data from the Maddison Project, shows that China's GDP accounted for 30% of the world's total GDP in 1820, after which it fell rapidly and continuously. It did not rise again until the country's reform and opening up in the late 1970s.

The economy is the foundation of a country, and a decline in economic status is accompanied by the weakening of national power. In the Sino-British Opium War in 1840, China was defeated by Britain, marking the beginning of a humiliating century of ceding territories and paying indemnities. Chinese intellectuals have always taken the rise and fall of their motherland as their own responsibility. After the Opium War, several generations of intellectuals worked tirelessly to rejuvenate the Chinese nation. For example, Zeng Guofan, Li Hongzhang, and Zuo Zongtang promoted the Westernization Movement. Kang Youwei, Liang Qichao, and Tan Sitong engaged in the Constitutional Reform Movement of 1898. Sun Yat-sen, Huang Xing, and Song Jiaoren fostered the bourgeois democratic revolution. Chen Duxiu, Li Dazhao, and Hu Shi promoted the New Culture Movement and the May Fourth Movement. The generation after the

May Fourth Movement participated in the Northern Expedition, the War of Resistance, and the Socialist Revolution. Despite the unremitting efforts of these four generations, China's economic weight declined from being 30% of the world's GDP in 1820 to only 5.2% in 1950. After the founding of the People's Republic of China, the country's economy increased slightly to 5.9% of the world's total economy by 1978. For these generations, the rejuvenation of the nation was an unattainable dream.

Many people today are members of the sixth generation who entered universities after the reform and opening up in 1978 and who have worked hard for the great rejuvenation of the Chinese nation. Compared with the previous five generations, I think our generation is the most fortunate. Since its reform and opening up in 1978, China has achieved an average annual growth rate of 9.2% for more than 40 years. In the whole history of the world, no country or region has experienced economic growth at such a rapid pace and for such a long time. As a result, China's economic status in the world has risen sharply. China's economy increased from 5.9% of the world's GDP in 1980 to 16.0% in 2018. Now, China is closer to realizing the goal of national rejuvenation than at any time in its history.

To support national rejuvenation, we should examine the experiences of setbacks and successes of several generations of Chinese people in China's economic development so as to understand the principles, theories, and philosophies behind them. New theories come from new experiences. This is the theoretical basis of the new structural economics I am advocating. Therefore, I would like to briefly introduce the basic ideas of new structural economics. I analyze why China achieved miraculous economic growth after the reform and opening up and why China's economy was stagnant before the reform and opening up from the perspective of endogeneity of economic structure. Finally, I provide an outlook for the future development of China's economy.

New Structural Economics

Modern economics became separated from philosophy and evolved into an independent social science after Adam Smith published

The Wealth of Nations in 1776. From then until Keynes in the 1930s, the United Kingdom was the center of global economics research. The majority of economists who proposed pioneering theories during that period were generally British or people working in the United Kingdom. Economic theories advanced by economists in other regions were rare. From World War II to the present, economists leading the new theoretical trends were either Americans or people working in the United States. Again, leading economists from other regions were extremely rare.

Economic theory is generated from social and economic phenomena, where its proponents explore and summarize the reasons behind those phenomena. A theory follows simple causal logic. The proponent of a theory abstracts a variable from the numerous economic, social, political, and cultural variables that he believes are important determinant factors causing the observed phenomenon in the society or country of interest, and he uses this as the explanatory variable while neglecting[1] many other secondary variables to construct a theory that explains the phenomenon. Therefore, any theory is embedded in the economic, social, political, and cultural variables in the country where the theory was proposed, and these structural variables become the implicit premise of the theory. If the embedded structural variables change substantially or if some secondary variables change from unimportant factors to more influential parameters than the original dependent variables, the original theory will not be able to explain new phenomena. It will be replaced by a new theory established on new variables.

Theories originating in developed countries often neglect the differences in the structures of countries with varying levels of economic development. Generally, when there are differences in the economic, social, political, and cultural structures between developing and developed countries, they are considered distortions in developing countries that lead to resource misallocation and poor development performance.[2]

After World War II, many developing countries shed their colonial and semi-colonial status and began to pursue industrialization and modernization. At that time, a new sub-discipline, *development economics*, emerged in mainstream economics. The original theory of development economics was called *structuralism*. Structuralists acknowledge the differences in the industrial structure between developed and developing countries. For example, in the two-section model proposed by Arthur Lewis, high income levels in developed countries is attributed to a modern manufacturing industry in the production structure, while developing countries have low income levels because their production structure is dominated by traditional agriculture and other natural resource industries.[3] Although structuralism recognizes the structural differences between developing and developed countries, it considers such differences to be exogenous. This is the status quo of mainstream economic theory.

Based on my observation of the recent history of China's economic development and the rapid development of East Asian economies after World War II, I developed a novel theory called *new structural economics*. Like structuralism, new structural economics notes that there are differences in the structure of countries with varying economic levels. New structural economics adopts the "rational person hypothesis" of neoclassical economics and the mechanism of income (budget) and substitution (relative price) effects to study the causes and effects of structural differences and changes in countries of varying economic levels. Since the "structure" is treated as the research object, my theory is called "structural economics." To distinguish it from structuralism, I call it new structural economics.[4]

The core idea of new structural economics is that countries with different economic levels have different structures, i.e., structural heterogeneity. There is an endogenous reason for this heterogeneity. The endowment structure of an economy at a given time endogenously determines a production structure with comparative advantages and the lowest production cost at that time, and then the production structure endogenously determines an infrastructure (e.g., electricity and roads) and a superstructure (e.g., finance, education, law, regulation, ethics, and values), which will fully release the production structure's productive potential by making transaction costs sufficiently low.[5] For each economy, the factor endowment and its structure are given at any specific time and are changeable over time. Countries with different economic levels have different endowment structures. For example, developed countries have accumulated capital since the Industrial Revolution, and their capital is relatively abundant but labor is relatively scarce. Developing countries are the opposite, as they are usually relatively short on capital and relatively abundant in labor or natural resources. If an economy's industries and the technology used by every industry at each time point follow the comparative advantage determined by the given endowment structure at that time point, then the cost of the products produced by those industries will be the lowest both internationally and domestically compared to the costs of products in other industries. Therefore, we can say that such a production structure is optimal.

Countries with different economic levels have different industries in their production structure, different technologies in each industry, different economies of scale, different demands for capital, and different risk characteristics. Because economies of scale are not the same, the scope of the market varies. Therefore, the infrastructure that enables the market to operate, such as roads and ports, will have different requirements. In addition, there must be different capital requirements, risks, and transaction characteristics and thus different requirements for the superstructure, including educational, financial, legal, and normative institutional arrangements, to reduce risks and enable transactions to proceed smoothly.

Therefore, from the perspective of new structural economics, the endowment structure, production structure, infrastructure, and superstructure of each economy are interrelated. Specifically, the production structure is endogenous to the endowment structure, and the production structure endogenously determines the infrastructure and superstructure. This is the main idea of new structural economics.[6]

Since Adam Smith, economists have focused on the topic of how a country develops. This is also the focus of new structural economics. Various production structures, infrastructures, and superstructures are all endogenous to an economy's endowment structure, given at a specific point in time and changeable over time. For income to grow and the country to develop, the level of productivity must be continuously improved, industries in the production structure must be upgraded, and technologies must be innovated. However, since the production structure is endogenous to the endowment structure, to upgrade a production structure from low-productivity, land-intensive, or labor-intensive industries to high-productivity, capital-intensive industries and technology, the endowment structure must first shift from one of relatively abundant resources or labor to one of relatively abundant capital. This is a simple inference from the perspective of new structural economics.

How can a country's endowment structure be quickly upgraded to a relatively capital-abundant structure? From the perspective of new structural economics, the best way is to develop industries and technologies for production at each time point according to the production structure endogenously determined by the endowment structure at that time point. In this way, the production cost of the country will be the lowest among countries that produce similar products. Moreover, if the country has an infrastructure and a superstructure that meet the needs of the industry and technology in the production structure, the transaction costs will also be the lowest. Since production costs and transaction costs are both at a low level, the products will be the most competitive in domestic and international markets. Manufacturers will obtain the maximum profits, and the entire economy can create the largest surplus that can be used for savings. The rate of return on investments will be the highest, and so capital accumulation will be the fastest. The endowment structure will change to a capital-rich structure at the fastest speed, thereby bringing the fastest change in comparative advantages and in the upgrade of the production structures. To have a smooth upgrade, the infrastructure and superstructure must change according to changes in comparative advantages and production structures.

Therefore, according to new structural economics, there are two institutional prerequisites for a country's economic development to be successful. The first is an efficient market. Because entrepreneurs are the main driving force behind production activities in an economy, they will decide what industries to develop and what technologies to use in those industries according to the principle of profit maximization. The choices of entrepreneurs comprise the production structure of the economy. For the entrepreneur's spontaneous selection to conform to the principle of the optimal production structure proposed earlier, it requires that the relative costs of the factors at a given time point reflect the relative scarcity of various factors in the economy. Such a pricing system can only be obtained when the exchange of factors and products is carried out in a competitive market. Therefore, an effective market is the institutional prerequisite for economic development in accordance with comparative advantages.

The second institutional prerequisite is a facilitative government. Economic development is not a static, effective allocation of resources but rather a process of dynamic changes in various structures. The upgrade of the production structure according to the changes in the endowment structure requires pioneering entrepreneurs to start new industries and adopt new technologies. Success also requires improvement of the infrastructure (such as electricity and roads) and superstructure (such as finance, education, and law). Structural change is bound to be accompanied by market failure, which requires a facilitative government to help entrepreneurs overcome market failures. First, if an entrepreneur is the first to enter an industry that does not have comparative advantages, he/she will not succeed. The other entrepreneurs can avoid the same mistakes. If the first entrepreneur succeeds, then other entrepreneurs will follow. Therefore, regardless of whether the entrepreneur who moves first fails or succeeds, he/she will provide valuable information to other entrepreneurs. Hence, the entrepreneur who moves first needs to be compensated. Moreover, even if the production structure adopted by the entrepreneur is consistent with the comparative advantages determined by the endowment structure, to be competitive in the domestic and international markets, improvements to the infrastructure and superstructure are required to reduce transaction costs and have a lower total cost than in other countries. The improvement of the infrastructure and superstructure requires a facilitative government.

The question of the appropriate role of the market and the state has been debated. As Lewis said, there is no country that has developed successfully without positive stimulus from an intelligent government, but there are numerous stories of economic failure caused by government intervention.[7] From the perspective of new structural economics, having a facilitative government is a prerequisite for an efficient market because, in the process of structural upgrading, there will inevitably be market failures that need to be overcome by the government. However, the goal of a facilitative government is to make the market efficient. Moreover, due to the heterogeneity of development stages and structures in countries with different economic levels, market failures may occur in different forms. Therefore, the role of the government is also different. New structural economics provides an analytical framework for governments in countries with different economic levels without causing under- or over-interventions.

From the perspective of new structural economics, countries with different economic levels will have different production structures, infrastructures, and superstructures determined by the endowment structure at that time point. Heterogeneity will lead to differences in the principles of economic development, transition, and operation in countries with different economic levels. Endogeneity and heterogeneity can provide a logical and theoretical explanation for China's slow development before the transition and the rapid economic growth thereafter. The framework also provides an explanation for the slow growth of developing countries after they gained political independence after World War II and their difficult economic transition since the 1980s.

China's Rapid Economic Growth after the Reform and Opening Up

For the economy to grow and income to increase, productivity must be continuously improved. This concept is true for both developed and developing countries. Productivity improvement requires continuous technological innovation in the production structure and the adoption of increasingly capital-intensive technologies. At the same time, industrial upgrading is required to relocate various production factors from industries with a low added value (e.g., agriculture) to those with a high added value (e.g., manufacturing). The manufacturing industry itself also needs to upgrade from being relatively labor-intensive to being relatively capital-intensive. In other words, technological innovation and industrial upgrading are the mechanisms that any country must follow to achieve economic development.[8]

From the perspective of new structural economics, there is a structural difference between developed and developing countries. Developed countries have a high level of income and a high level of labor productivity. Their industries and technologies are at the world's frontier. To achieve technological innovation and industrial upgrading, they must invent new technologies and industries. This is the endogenous economic growth model proposed by Paul Romer in the mid-1980s.[9] Developed countries rely on endogenous economic growth. From the middle of the 19th century to the present, their average annual per capita GDP growth rate has been about 2%. Coupled with population growth, the annual GDP growth rate in developed countries has been about 3% in the past century.[10]

Developing countries also need technological innovation and industrial upgrading. However, low income levels and low labor productivity levels in developing countries mean that their industries and technologies are behind the world's frontiers. Due to such differences, there are two possibilities for technological innovation and industrial upgrading in developing countries, in addition to indigenous inventions similar to those in developed countries. The first possibility is the "advantage of backwardness" proposed by Alexander Gerschenkron. In a developed country, to implement a newly developed technology, it must abandon the old technology, whereas, during the upgrading of an industry in developing countries, this new technology can be adopted without abandoning an old technology. Therefore, there is an advantage of backwardness, i.e., the opportunity cost of adopting a new technology is lower in developing countries than in developed countries.[11]

In new structural economics, I emphasize a different concept: the latecomer advantage. The industries and technologies used in the production structures of developing countries are not at the world's frontier. In addition to the advantage of backwardness proposed by Gerschenkron, mature technologies that have been used in developed countries can be used as a source of technological innovation, and industrial upgrading can also involve entering a mature industry with higher added value. It does not require the adoption of the latest technology or entering cutting-edge industries. In this way, developing countries have a latecomer advantage where technological innovation and industrial upgrading are at a lower cost and risk than inventing new technologies and industries.[12]

Out of more than 200 economies, only 13 exploited the latecomer advantage after World War II. These economies achieved an annual growth rate of 7% or higher, which is twice or more than that of developed countries and has lasted for over 25 years. Consequently, these developing economies have substantially narrowed the gap and even caught up with developed countries.[13]

After China implemented the reform and opening-up policy in 1978, it became one of these 13 economies. The main reason for an average annual growth rate of 9.2% for more than 40 years and a per capita GDP growth rate of 8% in China is the latecomer advantage resulting from low-cost and low-risk technological innovation and industrial upgrading due to differences in the production structure compared to developed countries.

Slow Economic Growth before 1978

If the latecomer advantage is the main reason for China's rapid economic growth after 1978, there have been industrial and technological gaps between China and developed countries since the Industrial Revolution. Why did it fail to develop rapidly in the past? Before the founding of the People's Republic of China, China was suffering from internal and external political, economic, and social instabilities that hindered its economic development. After 1949,

China ushered in a period of peaceful nation-building. Why did it only achieve rapid development after the reform and opening up in 1978? According to the new structural economics, this is mainly an issue of development idea, which ignores the endogenous nature of the production structure in economic development.

To catch up with the developed countries and for the sake of national defense, China prioritized the development of capital-intensive heavy industries under the condition of a relatively extreme scarcity of capital in the endowment structure. Developed countries have comparative advantages in those capital-intensive industries relative to poor agrarian countries. Therefore, the development strategy violated the comparative advantages determined by the endowment structure. Enterprises have no viability in an open and competitive market.[14] Even with normal management, they cannot obtain an acceptable profit, and understandably, entrepreneurs did not enter the industry spontaneously. Therefore, to develop such industries, the government gave various protections and subsidies to industry, including granting market monopoly status, not allowing similar foreign products to enter China, and allowing companies in targeted industries to set high product prices. Moreover, the input prices of various factors, including capital, foreign exchange, raw materials, and labor, were artificially lowered, allowing companies to run at a relatively low cost. This price distortion led to a supply shortage. The government had to use administrative means to allocate resources to the priority industries.[15]

The distorted pricing system and administrative resource allocation allowed China to quickly build up capital-intensive heavy industries in a poor agrarian economy, enabling China to test atomic bombs in the 1960s and launch satellites in the 1970s, thus establishing an independent national defense system. However, the industries that were established lacked competitiveness in an open market and failed to be profitable. The industries that had comparative advantages, however, did not obtain the necessary resources to develop. Therefore, the upgrading of the endowment structure and industrial structure was slow, resulting in slow economic and income growth. In 1978, China's per capita GDP was only US$156, which was less than one-third of the average GDP of sub-Saharan African countries. From the perspective of per capita income, the gap between China and developed countries was constantly widening.

After the reform and opening up, the government changed its development strategy. Earlier, China had the same development strategy as other socialist countries and developing countries, with similarly poor development performance and the same problems. Compared with other countries in economic transition, such as the former Soviet Union and those in Eastern Europe, the biggest difference in China's reform and opening up is that China has achieved stability and rapid growth and avoided economic collapse, stagnation, and crises. This difference lies in the different paths of transition. The former Soviet Union, Eastern European countries, and other developing countries followed the Washington Consensus, which promoted marketization, privatization, and liberalization at the same time through the "shock therapy" advocated by mainstream neoliberalism. China, however, adopted a gradual dual-track reform strategy referred to as the "old people follow the old way, new people follow the new way."[16]

The so-called "old people's old way" is to realize that various administrative interventions and distortions in the original economy are endogenous to the needs of giving those non-viable enterprises in priority industries protection and subsidies. Before the endogenous reasons are eliminated, that is, if those protections and subsidies are canceled when the enterprises are not yet viable, there will be the situation of eliminating the "second best," rather than returning to the "first best," which will lead to a worse situation.[17] During the transition period, the Chinese government realized this and therefore continued to provide the necessary protections and subsidies to the old enterprises to ensure their continued survival, thus maintaining economic stability.

The Chinese government also adopted the "new people's new way" to liberalize access to labor-intensive industries consistent with China's comparative advantages, while the government has also played an important facilitation role, not only actively promoting foreign investment but also establishing industrial parks and export zones, as well as infrastructure (e.g., electricity, roads, drainage, and telecommunications) and superstructure that met the needs of industrial development with comparative advantages. These industries quickly became the core of China's competitive advantages in domestic and foreign markets. Because of this latecomer advantage, China achieved rapid economic growth.

This pragmatic approach not only allowed China to maintain economic stability and high-speed growth during the transition but also created the necessary endowment structure for it to gradually eliminate the various distortions from the planned economy era. Various administrative interventions and distortions were needed to protect the old industries in the planned economy period and in the early stages of the transition because the old industries that were prioritized violated China's comparative advantages at that time. Therefore, these enterprises lacked viability. During the transitional period, China enjoyed 30–40 years of rapid economic growth. Capital accumulation occurred at a rapid pace, and the per capita GDP increased from only US$156 in 1978 to US$10,000 currently. In the endowment structure, capital gradually became relatively abundant. The comparative advantages and production structures were upgraded from labor-intensive to capital-intensive industries and technologies. Many industries that violated comparative advantages at the initial stage of transition became China's comparative advantages, as determined by the endowment structure. Enterprises in these industries became viable and obtained acceptable profits in a competitive market. Typical examples of these enterprises include the steel and machinery industries. The protections and subsidies during the transition period changed from "providing charcoal in the snow" (i.e., providing support to those who needed it) to "putting icing on the cake" (i.e., doing something that looks good but is not essential). The "icing on the cake" is not only unnecessary to maintain economic stability and development but also results in rent-seeking, corruption, and unfair income distribution. Therefore, this measure can be given up. As for a few industries relating to national defense and economic security that violate China's comparative advantages, the government can directly subsidize them, as is done in developed countries. By following this approach, China will have an effective market.[18]

Suggestions for Future Economic Reform and Development

Now, we are closer to the great rejuvenation of the Chinese nation than ever in modern history. The ultimate realization of this goal depends on an economy developing faster than that of developed countries. From the perspective of new structural economics, the government should carry out the transition and upgrading of the production structure and the improvement of the corresponding infrastructures and superstructures in accordance with the changes in the endowment structure and comparative advantages. With China's rapid economic development in the past decades, some of its industries, such as household appliances, photovoltaic equipment, and steel, are already at the world's frontier. Further technological innovation and upgrading of these industries depends on endogenous growth through indigenous research and development. Additionally, China's current per capita GDP is only about a quarter of that of the United States, which means that most of China's industries are still in the stage of catching up. In this process, China needs to fully utilize its latecomer advantage to conduct technological innovation and industrial upgrading to achieve faster and more sustainable development than developed countries.

As a large country with a population of 1.4 billion, the rapid rise of China's economy after the reform and opening up has brought about major changes unseen in the world in a century. The United States, which has been the largest and strongest economy in the world since the end of the 19th century, initiated trade and technological wars against China to maintain its hegemony in the world, restricting the normal market exchanges of many high-tech Chinese companies in an effort to curb China's development. However, most of the high-tech industries in which China does not have comparative advantages exist not only in the United States but also in other developed countries. Trade is a win-win game. Small economies benefit more than large economies. China is now the world's largest economy in terms of purchasing power parity. As long as China maintains rapid growth and openness, other developed countries (e.g., Germany, France, Switzerland, Japan, and South Korea) will not have incentives to sacrifice the benefits of trade with China to maintain the hegemony of the United States. Therefore, except for those high-tech products that are only available in the United States and not in other developed countries, China needs to provide direct fiscal subsidies to support indigenous inventions to overcome technological challenges. For other products, the principle of comparative advantage should be followed to accelerate economic development by relying on both domestic and international markets and resources. I predict that China will still have significant development potential in the future. According to statistics from the 10th edition of the *World Table* released by the University of Pennsylvania, China's per capita GDP in 2019 was only 22.6% of that of the United States in terms of purchasing power parity, which is equivalent to the gap between the United States and Germany in 1946, Japan in 1956, and South Korea in 1985. These three countries have maintained an average annual growth rate of more than 8% in per capita GDP for 16 years. Therefore, from the perspective of latecomer advantage, China should achieve an average annual growth rate in per capita GDP of at least 8% before 2035.

In addition, compared to Germany, Japan, and South Korea when they were at China's current development level, China has another advantage. When those countries were in this development stage, there was no new economy, which entails elements such as big data and artificial intelligence. The research and development cycle of this new economy is extremely short. The main input is human capital, which is composed of acquired education and innate talent. There is actually little difference in human capital between developing countries and developed countries for developing countries that place emphasis on education, giving them the possibility of overtaking developed countries in the new economy.[19] China's capital endowment is relatively scarce compared to developed countries that have developed since the industrial revolution. China does not yet have a comparative advantage in many traditional capital-intensive industries. However, it not only stands on the same "starting line" as developed countries in the new economy but also has the advantages of a large number of gifted people, a large domestic market, and more complete industrial sectors than other countries. Therefore, combining the latecomer advantage of the traditional economy with the advantage of the new economy, China should still have an annual growth potential of no less than 8% before 2035. Using the same analysis, China has the potential to grow at a higher rate than developed countries by 2049.

In 2019, China's per capita GDP in terms of purchasing power parity was 22.6% of that of the United States. Over the past 50 years, the average annual growth rate of per capita GDP in the United States has been 1.8%. It is likely to maintain this growth rate in the future. If China can maintain an average annual growth rate in per capita GDP of 2.7 percentage points higher than the United States from 2019 to 2049, which is 4.5%, then by 2049, China's per capita GDP will reach 50% of that of the United States. Since China's population is about four times that of the United States, China's economy will inevitably be twice that of the United States at that time. By then, the per capita GDPs of Beijing, Tianjin, Shanghai, and the five advanced eastern coastal provinces with a population of more than 400 million people are likely to reach the same level as that of the United States. This advanced region's productivity, industry, and technology will also be at the same level as the United States, thus eliminating the possibility of the United States hindering China's growth by embargoing advanced technology. Moreover, in bilateral trade, the United States will gain more than China. By that time, the United States will maintain friendly relations with China for its own development and employment. As such, the world is likely to emerge from a century-long upheaval caused by the great power rivalry and enter a new and stable phase.[20]

There are now 70 high-income economies in the world, and 28 of them are advanced countries with a per capita GDP of 50% or more than that of the United States. In addition to some small oil-producing countries and small countries like Monaco that rely on gaming or financial industries, these include old industrialized countries in Europe and America, as well as new industrialized countries in Asia, such as Japan, South Korea, Singapore, and Israel. It is estimated that by 2049, if China's per capita GDP can reach half of that of the United States, it will also become an advanced industrialized country and realize its goal of national rejuvenation.

Conclusion

Since Adam Smith, the center of the world economy has also been the world center of economics research and the place from where the masters who lead the theoretical thinking in the world have come. New theories come from new phenomena. The robust rise of China's economy after a century of decline is a new economic phenomenon. China's future development will also proceed under conditions that are different from the experience on which the existing theories from developed countries are based. China's experience will be a gold mine for theoretical innovation. When China achieves national rejuvenation and succeeds the United Kingdom and the United States to become the largest and most important economy in the world, it should also become the world center of economic research and theoretical innovation and the place from where the masters come, just like Britain in the past and the United States in the present. To make this hope a reality, researchers in the economic community need to use scientific methods to study indigenous phenomena in China and advance new, original theories. The higher China's economic status in the world is, the more important China's empirical phenomena are in the world, and the more influential the theoretical innovations from China will be. Chinese economists who propose such theories will also lead the new economic thinking in the world,[21] and I hope that young researchers will seize this opportunity.

Endnotes

1. *Neglection* and *abstraction* are philosophical terms. *Abstraction* means that the theory's proponent extracts important dependent variables from many social and economic variables and uses them in his theory to explain the observed social and economic phenomena. *Neglection* refers to the theory's proponent disregarding variables that are considered unimportant for the sake of logical simplicity.
2. For instance, when new institutional economists study the institutions of developed countries, they generally regard institutions as endogenous. However, when studying developing countries, they regard the institutional differences between developing and developed countries as exogenous distortions. The book Acemoglu and Robinson (2011) is a masterpiece in this regard. The World Bank's Doing Business and World Governance indicators, as well as the indicators used in the *World Competitiveness Report*, are all based on this idea.
3. Lewis (1954).
4. This naming principle is a common practice in modern economics. For example, when North used neoclassical economics to study institutions and institutional changes in the 1960s, he should have used the name *institutional economics*. However, to distinguish the idea from institutionalism at the end of the 19th century and the beginning of the 20th century, it was called *new institutional economics*.
5. "Infrastructure" is commonly expressed as "basic structure" in Chinese, and "superstructure" refers to a top-level structure.
6. The new structural economics takes the endowment structure as the starting point of endogenous analysis of an economy, which is in line with the principle of the primacy of material in Marxist materialist dialectics. It indicates that the endowment structure endogenously determines the production structure, and the production structure endogenously determines the infrastructure and superstructure, which reflects the spirit of Marxist historical materialism. Factor endowment is the total budget of an economy at a given point in time. The endowment structure determines the relative price of elements in an economy at that point in time. Therefore, factor endowment and its structure endogenously determine the production structure through budgetary and relative cost effects and then endogenously determine the infrastructure and superstructure. This method unifies

the analytical paradigms of Marxism and neoclassical economics. For a more detailed introduction to new structural economics, please refer Lin and Fu.

7. Lewis (1955).
8. Kuznets (1966).
9. Romer (1986).
10. Maddison (2006).
11. Gerschenkron (1962).
12. During technological innovation and industrial upgrading in a developing country, if the latest technology has a comparative advantage as determined by its endowment structure, then the latecomer advantage is equal to the advantage of backwardness. Therefore, the latecomer advantage includes the advantage of backwardness. However, the advantage of backwardness excludes the possibility of adopting mature technology as a source of technological innovation. Many developing countries have misused the concept of the advantage of backwardness and adopted the latest technologies, which violates the comparative advantage when they do not have a comparative advantage. This has led to the disadvantage of backwardness, requiring various government distortions and interventions. For more details, refer Lin (2016).
13. Commission on Growth and Development (2008).
14. Lin and Tan (1999).
15. Lin *et al.* (1994) and Lin (2018).
16. See the books Lin Yifu (2008, Chinese version) and Lin (2009, English version) published based on my talk given in 2007 at Oxford University, and Lin (2014).
17. Lipsey and Lancaster (1956).
18. Lin (2021b).
19. Lee (2013).
20. Lin (2021a).
21. Lin (1995).

References

Acemoglu, D. and Robinson, J. 2011. *Why Nations Fail.* Cambridge, USA: MIT Press.

Commission on Growth and Development. 2008. *The Growth Report: Strategies for Sustained Growth and Inclusive Development.* Washington, DC: World Bank.

Gerschenkron, A. 1962. *Economic Backwardness in Historical Perspective: A Book of Essays*. Cambridge, Mass.: Belknap Press of Harvard University Press.

Kuznets, S. 1966. *Modern Economic Growth: Rate, Structure and Spread*. New Haven and London: Yale University Press.

Lee, K. 2013. *Schumpeterian Analysis of Economic Catch-up: Knowledge, Path Creation, and the Middle-income Trap*. Cambridge: Cambridge University Press.

Lewis, A.A. 1954. Economic development with unlimited supplies of labor. *The Manchester School* (May).

Lewis, A. 1955. *Theory of Economic Growth*. London: Allen and Unwin, p. 376.

Lin, J.Y. 1995. Localization, standardization, and internationalization: Congratulations on the 40th anniversary of the founding of the journal. *Economic Research*, 10, pp. 13–17.

Lin, J.Y. 2014. The Washington consensus revisited: A new structural economics perspective. *Journal of Economic Policy Reform*, 18(2): 96–113.

Lin, J.Y. 2016. The latecomer advantages and disadvantages: A new structural economics perspective. In Andersson, M. and Axelsson, T. (eds.), *Diverse Development Paths and Structural Transition in Escape from Poverty*. Cambridge: Cambridge University Press, pp. 43–67.

Lin, J.Y. 2021a. China's new development paradigm and prospect of future economic development in the great change that has been unseen over the last one hundred years. *Journal of Peking University (Philosophy and Social Sciences)*, 5: 32–40.

Lin, J.Y. 2021b. State-owned enterprise reform in China: The new structural economics perspective. *Structural Change and Economic Dynamics*, 58(September): 106–111.

Lin, J.Y. and Fu, C. 2023. New structural economics. *Handbook of Chinese Economics*. Beijing: China Social Sciences Press.

Lin, J.Y. and Tan, G. 1999. Policy burdens, accountability, and the soft budget constraint. *American Economic Review*, 89(2); *Papers and Proceedings of the One Hundred Eleventh Annual Meeting of the American Economic Association*, May, pp. 426–431.

Lin, J.Y., Cai, F., and Li, Z. 1994. *The Miracle of China: Development Strategy and Economic Reform*. Shanghai Sanlian and People's Publishing House.

Lin, Y. [林毅夫]. 2008.《经济发展与转型》(*Economic Development and Transition*). Peking University Press (Chinese version); Lin, J.Y. 2009.

Economic Development and Transition: Thought, Strategy and Viability. Cambridge: Cambridge University Press (English version).
Lin, Y. 2018. *Interpreting China's Economy*. Beijing: Peking University Press.
Lipsey, R.G. and Lancaster, K. 1956. The general theory of second best. *Review of Economic Studies*, 24(1): 11–32.
Maddison, A. 2006. *The World Economy*. Paris: Organization for Economic Cooperation and Development.
Romer, P. 1986. Increasing returns and long-run growth. *Journal of Political Economy*, 94(5): 1002–1037.

https://doi.org/10.1142/9789819815241_0002

Chapter 2

CHINESE-STYLE MARKET ECONOMY: PERSPECTIVE OF INDUSTRIAL DEVELOPMENT

Wan-wen Chu

Adjunct Research Fellow, RCHSS,
Academia Sinica, Taipei, Taiwan
wwchu@gate.sinica.edu.tw

After China's swift rise in the new century, there have been numerous discussions about its global impact. The relations between the US and China have often been described as a great power game, or a Thucydides' Trap, along with various other ways using criteria such as relative strength, growth prospects, or respective strategies. However, viewing US–China relations purely from a great power game perspective makes them highly uncertain and not easily subject to concrete analysis, which may not be helpful for us to understand the reality.

China's economic strength relative to that of the US no doubt matters a great deal in the overall great power rivalry. How should we evaluate China's economic position in the world? This chapter proposes a particular approach that narrows the focus to the condition of the industries. Moreover, we will not carry out a concurrent comparison of China's current conditions in industries to those of the US at the present time. Instead, the comparison will be between the current conditions of China's industries and those of the US at the end of the 19th century. The latter was the time when the US began to overtake Britain in economic terms. That is, it was the beginning of the long process of the US replacing Britain as the new hegemon in the world. Because China is now considered to be the candidate to replace the US as the hegemon in the future, it is appropriate to choose the time frame as proposed above instead of a concurrent comparison.

Changes in Hegemonies

In this new century, we have observed a swift rise in China's share of global GDP (in current US dollars), from a mere 4% in 2001 to 17% in 2020 (see Figure 1). The ratio of China's GDP (current US dollars) to that of the US rose sharply from 13% in 2001 to 70% in 2020[1] (see Figure 2). The speed of change has been astonishing, which clearly shows that China is experiencing a renaissance. Though China is catching up with the US in terms of GDP, it does not imply that China will challenge or even replace US' hegemony in the future.

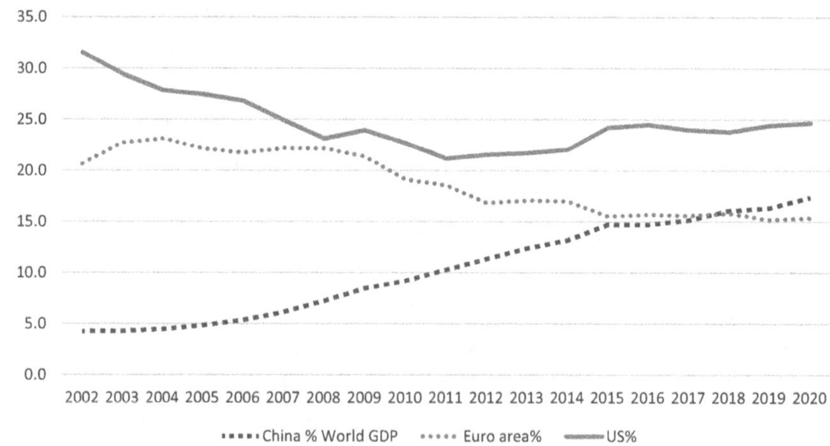

Figure 1. Changes in global GDP distribution, 2001–2020.

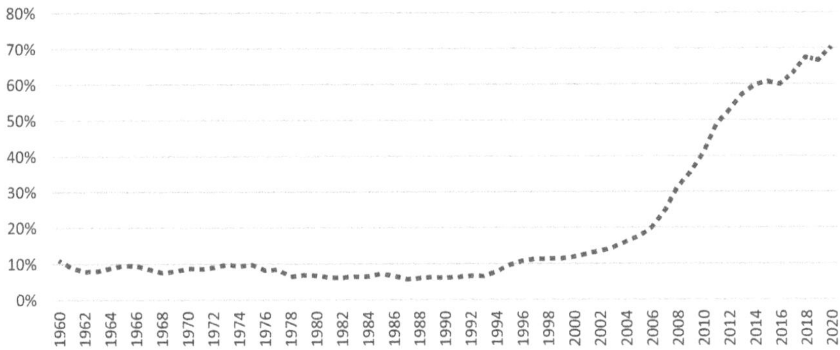

Figure 2. Current GDP ratio: China/US.

Note: GDP ratio — 13% in 2001 and 70% in 2020.

Source: From World Bank databank.

Judging from the overall level of industrial competitiveness, China is clearly behind and still trying to catch up with the leaders in the West. Some Chinese firms may have come close to or even reached the world frontier in some sectors, but the Chinese industry, in general, is still not there yet. Moreover, this chapter will not delve into an assessment of this kind. Instead, it compares the current conditions of China's industries to those of the US at the end of the 19th century. The reasons for adopting this approach here are inspired by Giovanni Arrighi's work.

Arrighi (2010) establishes a theory of the hegemonic cycles of world capitalism in his important book, *The Long Twentieth Century: Money, Power, and the Origins of Our Times*. Arrighi does not think that the latest trend of "financialization" in world capitalism, starting from the 1970s, is a new development; rather, he sees it as a recurrent phenomenon. World capitalism has cycles. When competition intensifies, profits fall below normal levels, and an increasing mass of capital shifts to financial areas. Every phase of capitalism has ended in financialization and a change in hegemonies. He also sees capitalism's origins in the fusion of state and capital, and identifies four hegemonies, or systemic cycles of accumulation: the Genoese, Dutch, British, and American. Following its precursor, each hegemony imitates and innovates in terms of its organizations and global structures. Each hegemonic success also contains the germs of its demise because it always inspires imitation and challenges.[2] Genoa and Holland set up long-distance trade and finance regimes; and Britain combined them with industrialization. The US hegemony comprised military and political dominance, with the multinational corporation as the organizational innovation. Historically, these successive regimes have exhibited increasing scope, greater complexity, and shorter durations.

The change of guard in hegemony is a complicated process and takes time. By the end of the 19th century, Britain had reached its financialization phase, which signaled the beginning of the decline of its hegemony. The rise of Germany and the US presented challenges. Nonetheless, the British provided a large amount of capital to finance the US' industrialization in the 19th century, similar to how Dutch capital helped finance the British rise in the 18th century. Germany lacked the necessary conditions to take over Britain's place, but its military challenge in the form of the two World Wars was enough to wear down Britain. By supplying capital and supplies to Britain during the wars, the US gradually took over Britain's place. It should be noted that there was no supposedly inevitable Thucydides' Trap between the two. The change of guard in hegemony is usually associated with wars, but not necessarily between old and new hegemons.

The US hegemony began its decline in the 1970s, which was the time when its financialization phase began. At the same time, East Asia became the global economic powerhouse. First, there emerged Japan, then the East Asian Tigers, and then China. The unusual part of this development is the bifurcation of military and economic power. The US still retains military superiority, while the new economic power, instead of being financed by the old hegemon, helps finance the US' excesses. Arrighi examines this new development in his subsequent work, *Adam Smith in Beijing: Lineages of the Twenty-First Century* (Arrighi, 2007), which will not be discussed here.

Let us look briefly at the US' economic standing at the end of the 19th century. According to Maddison (2010), the US' GDP level surpassed the UK' in 1872, when its per capita GDP was only 77% of the UK'. Nonetheless, the US economy progressed rapidly, and its GDP became 88% larger than that of the UK in 1901; by that time, the US had caught up with the UK in per capita GDP and manufacturing productivity.[3] According to Arrighi, Britain entered its financialization phase, and its hegemonic decline began around 1870. In these critical last three decades of the 19th century, the US not only grew faster than Britain but also gradually overtook it in leading the global industrial competition.

After the Civil War ended, the US not only greatly expanded its territory but also quickly integrated the national market across the continent. There were waves of mergers, acquisitions, and rationalizations in its industries. New industrial firms arose by consolidating the large US domestic market, realizing economies of scale and scope, and quickly globalizing. In reaction to the rise of the resulting large conglomerates, there emerged an antitrust movement in the US, which led to the passage of the Sherman Antitrust Act of 1890, the Clayton Act of 1914, and the Federal Trade Commission Act of 1914. These acts mainly aimed to promote competition, prohibit monopolies, and mostly focus on horizontal markets. Therefore, large firms turned to vertical integration. A new type of multi-unit, vertically integrated enterprise developed in this environment. It internalized the market, which Chandler (1990) terms the "visible hand," and accumulated organizational capabilities in technology, production, and marketing. It also became multinational almost immediately. Though the US became the leader in the global industrial sector, it was not yet ready to challenge Britain's hegemony because it still lagged far behind in the military, financial, and ideological spheres. The change of guard was not completed until the end of World War II.

Comparing Conditions in Industries: The US Then and China Now

China is now considered the only likely candidate to challenge the US' hegemony. The US began to challenge Britain at the end of the 19th century. As noted above, at that time, the US had already built up advanced industries, which were dominated by advanced firms. The leading firms were oligopolistic and multinational, and many are still present today.

On the other hand, at the present time, China's industrial productivity still lags far behind that of the US. As a proxy for overall productivity, China's GDP per capita was a mere 3% of the US' in 2001. Though it rose rapidly to 17% of the US' in 2020, it was nevertheless slightly below the world average.[4] Actually, China's current economic standing relative to that of the US, in terms of GDP and GDP per capita, is similar to that of the year 1900.[5] That is, in both cases, China's large GDP is driven by its large population, but this is countered by a relatively low level of GDP per capita. The difference is that China then was on the decline but, after more than one hundred years, is now on the rise. Apparently, development momentum and prospects matter most.

The Chinese economy is growing fast, though at a relatively low level. Therefore, it is important to explore its likely future development path. As noted above, Chinese industry is still in the catching-up stage, though conditions vary across sectors. Rather than examining the size of the productivity gap between China and the West, this chapter examines China's present industrial structure and compares it to that of the US in 1900. Using the US' industrial transformation at the end of the 19th century as a reference, we explore whether the Chinese domestic or national market will integrate further, its industrial development will exhibit the same concentration tendency, and advanced firms will emerge from market integration.

From the US example, it is usually assumed that the leader's manufacturing sector emerges by consolidating the large domestic market, realizing economies of scale and scope, and quickly globalizing. Major industries become oligopolies, dominated by a small number of advanced firms. It is supposed that an integrated national market is a natural outcome of development and a necessary condition for progress. It was relatively easy for the US to achieve integration due to its short history. Will the same logic apply to China? That is, will integration lead to the subsequent concentration and emergence of advanced firms?

It is not possible to offer an overall evaluation of the Chinese industrial structure here. Instead, some cases of important industries are discussed.

Case 1: Steel industry

When China began its reform era, its steel industry was relatively small, and its share of global steel output was about 5% in 1980. Four decades later, after feverish rounds of construction, its share of global crude steel output reached 56.7% in 2020.[6] Privatization led to a decrease in the output share of state-owned enterprises (SOEs), which was greater than 80% in 1998 and is now less than 40%. The local steel industry undoubtedly became very active in the first two decades of this century, and entry and exit rates averaged around 20–30% per year, much higher than those of other countries (5–10%). The industry has been highly competitive, but excess capacity persists. In 2019, the concentration ratio of the top four firms (CR4) was 22%, while that of the top ten firms (CR10) was 37%.[7] Moreover, the concentration level has remained relatively stable and shown no increasing trend.

On the other hand, the US steel industry's path of development was different. It experienced fierce price competition at the end of the 19th century but soon turned oligopolistic after several rounds of mergers. When the leading firm, the US Steel Corporation, was formed in 1901 through mergers, it controlled 65% of the market. Thereafter, in 1904, the US steel industry's CR(4) was 74%. That ratio declined somewhat in later decades but still reached 64% in 1950 and 47% in 1984.[8]

Case 2: Automobile industry

The Chinese government began to promote the automobile industry, mainly after the reforms that began at the end of the 1970s. It adopted a strategy of relying upon joint ventures, and the industry has become one dominated by joint ventures with foreign firms since then. However, the market structure of the Chinese automobile industry has been changing substantially since this century began. Chu (2011) discusses how the government policy toward the auto industry changed from allowing only joint ventures to also allowing indigenous development in 2004. Around that time, some indigenous auto firms were set up with help from local governments without heeding the central government's guidelines. They successfully gained market share by selling cheap, imitative small cars, and their success induced the policy change.[9]

The Chinese auto market has been booming since then. The annual auto output increased from 2 million units in 2000 to close to 30 million units in 2020. Nonetheless, the share of local brands in the Chinese market has stabilized at around 40% after the initial surge in the early 2000s. In addition, the local firms found it difficult to gain market share in the sedan segment and hence focused on the utility vehicle sector instead. In 2018, local firms accounted for 18% of the sedan segment, 63% of the utility vehicle segment, and 41% of the total auto market.[10] In a way, the local firms have been struggling to maintain their limited market share. The market for new energy vehicles is still developing, with many new firms entering the industry. It is fair to say that the concentration level for the local firms has been relatively low, at least for now.

The US automobile industry began to develop in the 1890s and soon overtook Europe and became the world leader. By 1913, there were 31 firms, and the top two firms, Ford and GM, already had 52% of the market. Henry Ford pioneered mass-production techniques and greatly expanded the industry in the 1910s. By 1937, the number of firms was reduced to 12, and the top three firms, at that time including Chrysler, owned 89% of the market. The number of firms dropped further to four in the 1970s.[11] That is, the US auto industry's concentration level rose quickly at the beginning of its development, soon reached a high level, and stayed there.

The structure of the Chinese auto industry is still evolving, and it is not certain how it will turn out. Nonetheless, its development path certainly looks quite different from that of the US.

Other sectors

Do most of China's manufacturing industries exhibit low concentration values? Due to a lack of relevant studies, it is difficult to know the answer. From cursory observations, it can be seen that some important mid-tech industries, such as steel, are more likely to show this pattern. These industries face increasing and widespread demand and do not have high barriers to entry. Moreover, for example, for new internet-related industries, the administrative boundary has become less important, as has the role of the local government.

In many developing countries, some sectors, such as utilities and heavy industries, are often monopolistic or oligopolistic by policy design. Chinese utilities and strategic sectors are also monopolized by SOEs. However, China must be unique in that some of its mid-tech industries show no apparent tendency toward concentration. We shall see whether China does indeed have a different model of industrialization.

Case 3: Lack of monopoly/monopsony power?

Now, let us discuss another issue, using iron ore as an example. Does China lack market power even when it is the largest buyer? As noted above, the Chinese steel industry has been growing rapidly since the new century began and reached a production share of about 56% of the global steel output in 2019. Because China produces little iron ore itself, its import dependence ratio has now reached 80%. It has imported about 65% of the world's iron ore every year in recent years and is now the dominant buyer in the market. However, it is widely believed that China lacks price-setting power.

Why does it lack price-setting power in the case of iron ore? On the one hand, 80% of imports come from a few large mining companies in Brazil and Australia. And less than 10% come from overseas mines owned by Chinese firms. On the other hand, there are very many steel firms in China, large and small, which need to import iron ore.

Is this case of iron ore unique? Probably not. Prior to 2001, it was common for advanced firms to exercise monopsony power to set commodity prices when the number of purchasing firms was small, leading to a declining trend in prices. However, at the turn of the century, rising demand from China for various commodities, including iron ore, reversed this trend, and their prices increased during 2001–2011. Did China's lack of price-setting power help raise commodity prices and spread gains from growth?

Using World Bank commodity price data, Figure 3 shows that the annual non-energy commodity price indices (setting 2010 prices at 100 in real 2010 US dollars) started at 96.7 in 1960, continued to decline, and reached a low of 55.7 in 2001. The indices then began to increase and reached a high of 107.7 in 2011, except for a dip during the crisis year 2009. It again started to decrease after 2011, when China's growth began to slow.

It should be noted that the downward trend in real commodity prices can be traced back much earlier and lasted for a long period. According to one study, real commodity prices declined by 1.3% annually from 1862 to 1999.[12] That is consistent with the Prebisch–Singer hypothesis.

There is no doubt that China's lack of market power is due to the fact that there are simply a great number of small firms in most sectors. Will this phenomenon end as the concentration level gradu-

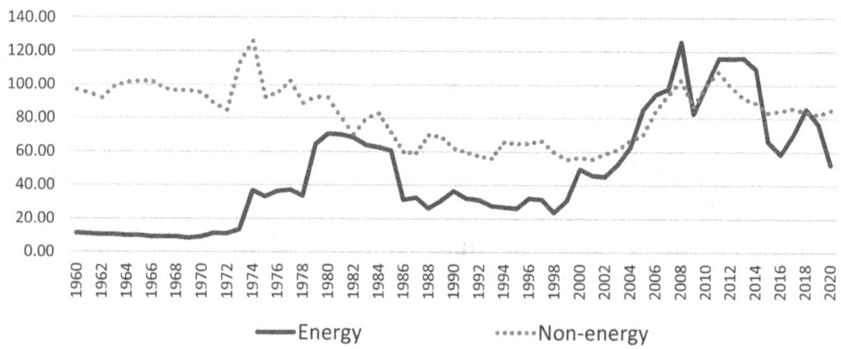

Figure 3. World Bank commodity price indices, 1960–2020 (annual indices, 2010 = 100, real 2010 US dollars).

Source: World Bank Commodity Price Data.

ally increases in most markets when the Chinese economy gets more "mature"? Or has this been the norm in China?

China in the 18th-Century

Arrighi (2007) views the traditional Chinese economy as closely fitting Adam Smith's "natural" market economy. That is, it was introverted and highly commercialized, the domestic market was highly integrated, and labor mobility was high. In contrast, the "unnatural" European path had characteristics including extroversion, embeddedness in the global market, and a synergy between capitalism, industrialism, and militarism, which were driven by interstate competition.

Piketty (2020) also thinks that the old China fit Adam Smith's ideal well, with the corresponding institutions: low taxes, a balanced budget and thus little public debt, respect for property rights, and raising debt only when forced to pay reparations to the West. Qing China's tax burden was only about 1–2% of GDP, while Europe's averaged 6–8% of GDP during the same period. Europe also had high government debt ratios in the past few centuries.

Could there be possible historical continuity? Arrighi (2007) certainly thinks so and perceives, or wishes, that China would replace the US as the hegemon but lead the world on to a hybrid, non-capitalist, and market-based development path.

After the 15th anniversary in December 2016 of China's entry into the WTO, there emerged a debate on China's "market economy" status. The Western countries denied that there was an implicit promise to automatically change the designation of China from a non-market to a market economy 15 years after its entry. The US argued that China is still not a market economy based on criteria concerning currency convertibility, free labor, capital liberalization, and the extent of government intervention. The relatively high share of SOEs and the extent of government intervention are of particular concern. Nonetheless, what criteria are appropriate? As noted above, it is widely recognized that markets in China are highly competitive, though they coexist with excess capacity. There is indeed diversity in ownership types, including hybrid ones. The central and local governments intervene differently. The whole pattern may not be approaching the Western path, but whether it is suitable to apply the US definition of market economy to evaluate China's status is certainly debatable. It is not only a normative issue but also concerns how we understand China's economy, its past, and its prospects. It is a tremendous challenge.

Industrial Policy with Chinese Characteristics

Chu (2011, 2017) offers another explanation of the excess capacity problem of some Chinese industries, viewing the Chinese industrial policy as operating in a multilayered framework. Mainly due to its huge scale, there has always been a division of labor between the central and local governments. The central government formulates policies, and local governments implement them. Local governments have incentives to promote industrial development and support local firms, which entail increases in tax revenue, employment, and cadre performance. The downside is that the local governments may also want to protect the local firms, even when they are inefficient and making losses. The center and local governments may have conflicts concerning overall long-term industrial development at the national level. Consolidation to weed out the less efficient may prove to be difficult. The central government also seeks to have more balanced regional development.

The needed "reform" on this front seems to be difficult by design. Local governments are responsible for promoting industrial development and hence may try to protect local firms from going bankrupt regardless. The effects of industrial policy are inevitably uncertain. Therefore, it is challenging to find a way to provide incentives for a local government to allow failing firms to fall without taking away its duty to promote industrial development.

Prospects

China is now considered the only likely challenger to US' hegemony. To evaluate the prospect of this hegemonic change, this chapter briefly compared today's China with the US around 1900 from the perspective of industrial development. That was the time when Britain's hegemony started its decline and the US began to surpass Britain in industrial might. However, it is found that China may now be catching up to the US in terms of scale but not yet in terms of industrial competitiveness. Though China is rapidly closing the gap in productivity, the gap is still substantial. It is the speed of catching up that has alarmed the West.

The Chinese industries in general are still in the catching-up stage, certainly nowhere near the leading position achieved by the US in around 1900. Its industrial structure is far from being as oligopolistic as that of the US then. The US' hegemony has clearly started to decline. Nonetheless, compared to the time around 1900, the hegemonic change in terms of industrial strength had not taken place, at least not yet.

Moreover, the above discussion shows that the US industrial development model may not be the right guide. With its long historical political tradition, China differs from the US that emerged around 1900 in various ways. A market economy has long existed in China's extended history, though in an environment unlike that of the West. China's multilayered framework of industrial policy may imply that the integration of the domestic market could be a complicated and prolonged process. China's economic growth surely will continue, but the model of hegemonic change from the Western past may not be the guide. We need new tools and theories to better understand China and the world. The prospects are uncertain, but we no doubt need more understanding.

Endnotes

1. From World Bank databank.
2. Ingham (1996, p. 1473).
3. Maddison (2010). All these are measured in real 1990 International G-K dollars. It is estimated that China's GDP level was almost twice the size of the US in 1870, while its per capita GDP was only 22% of the US'.

4. China's GDP per capita was $10434.8 (current US dollars), while the world average was $10910 in 2020 (World Bank databank).
5. According to Maddison (2010), measured in real international K-P dollars, China's GDP was 70% of the US, and its GDP per capita was 13% in 1900. These deflated measures usually give higher estimates than those based on current values for the less developed economies due to their relatively lower price levels.
6. World Steel Association (2021).
7. Jiang *et al.* (2021) and Sun (2007).
8. Adams (1986, pp. 74–80).
9. Chu (2011) calls it "the Chinese model of industrial policy propelled by the catch-up consensus" and considers it a successful case of industrial policy.
10. Chu (2020, p. 75); originally from Fourin China (2019).
11. Adams (1986, pp. 126–128).
12. Cashin and McDermott (2002).

References

Adams, W. (ed.). 1986. *The Structure of American Industry*, 7th edn. New York: MacMillan.

Arrighi, G. 2007. *Adam Smith in Beijing: Lineages of the Twenty-First Century.* London: Verso.

Arrighi, G. 2010. *The Long Twentieth Century: Money, Power and the Origins of Our Times.* London: Verso.

Cashin, P. and McDermott, C.J. 2002. The long-run behavior of commodity prices: Small trends and big variability. *IMF Staff Papers,* 49(2): 175–199.

Chandler Jr., A.D. 1990. *Scale and Scope: The Dynamics of Industrial Capitalism.* Cambridge: Belknap Press.

Chu, W.-W. 2011. How the Chinese government promoted a global automobile industry. *Industrial and Corporate Change,* 20(5): 1235–1276.

Chu, W.-W. 2017. Industry policy with Chinese characteristics: A multilayered model. *China Economic Journal,* 10(3): 305–318. October 2017.

Chu, W.-W. 2020. *The Development Model of China's Industries: Exploring the Role of Industrial Policy.* Taipei: TRQSS Series-21 (in Chinese).

Fourin China. 2019. *Beijing Fourin's Monthly Report on the Chinese Automobile Industry.* Beijing: Fourin China (various issues).

Ingham, G. 1996. Review of the Long Twentieth Century. *American Journal of Sociology,* 101(5): 1472–1474.

Jiang, F.-T., *et al.* 2021. *Understanding China's Industrial Policy*. Beijing: CITIC Press (in Chinese).

Maddison, A. 2010. Historical Statistics of the World Economy: 1-2008 AD. https://www.rug.nl/ggdc/historicaldevelopment/maddison/?lang=en.

Piketty, T. 2020. *Capital and Ideology*. Translated by Arthur Goldhammer. Cambridge, Mass.: The Belknap Press of Harvard University Press.

Sun, P. 2007. Is the state-led industrial restructuring effective in transition China? Evidence from the steel sector. *Cambridge Journal of Economics*, 2007, 31: 601–624.

World Steel Association. 2021. *2021 World Steel in Figures*. https://worldsteel.org/world-steel-in-figures-2021/. World Steel Association, Brussels, Belgium.

https://doi.org/10.1142/9789819815241_0003

Chapter 3

THE PATH OF CHINESE MODERNIZATION AND ITS WORLD SIGNIFICANCE

Yang Yao

National School of Development and China Center for Economic Research, Peking University
yyao@nsd.pku.edu.cn

At the juncture of the centennial of the Chinese Communist Party's (CCP's) founding, how to understand the relationship between the Party and China's modernization remains an important issue for contemporary Chinese intellectuals. This chapter examines the centennial history of the CCP within the framework of the modernization of late-developing countries and explores the path of Chinese modernization pioneered by the Party and the significance of this path for the world, especially for other late-developing countries.

In all countries, modernization consists of two dimensions: transition and development. In terms of transition, modernization means the abandonment of the rigid and oppressive social, political, and economic systems of traditional societies and their replacement by the more open and freer systems of modern societies; in terms of development, modernization means the continuous increase in people's income and national strength. The two do not always go together and may indeed constrain one another. The challenge is even greater for late-developing countries, which have to complete their transition and development in an even shorter period of time, given their dual goals of catching up with the social, economic, and political development of the developed countries as soon as possible while, at the same time, having to face the challenges and perhaps even invasions of those same developed countries.

The CCP was born in the process of Chinese intellectuals' search for a total solution that would allow China to achieve transition and development, with the initial aim of changing the political, social, and economic structure of China by means of class struggle and thus creating a new and equal society. In the first 30 years after the founding of New China, the Party led the people of the entire nation in a dual process of socialist revolution and socialist construction, setting the pace for China's transformation and development. After reform and opening up, the Party reconciled with Chinese tradition in terms of practice, drawing on the best elements of that tradition to provide important philosophical and institutional guarantees for China's economic takeoff. In so doing, the Party has led China on a unique and globally significant path toward modernization.

Specifically, the global significance of this path is made up of four aspects. First, China managed to carry out a process of peaceful transition and development in a large late-developing country, pioneering a new path toward modernization for the world; second, this path prioritized human development and improved the education and health of the general public; third, the path was pragmatic and down to earth in its engagement with economics and institution-building; fourth, the ruling party has been broadly representative, relatively neutral in its relation to society, and concerned with the long-term development of the country as a whole.

The Birth of the Chinese Communist Party

If we begin with England's Glorious Revolution in 1688, the modernization of the world has been underway for more than 300 years; if we take the post–World War II era as the end-point of Western modernization, the latter has also been going on for more than 200 years. However, the modernization of late-developing countries cannot go through the same lengthy process because the results of modernization are staring them in the face. In terms of economic development, the point is to catch up. The developed economies essentially got where they are by following a basic script relying on a market approach to build their economies, but late-developing countries hoping to catch up with the living standards of the developed world may well have to think outside the box. Still, catching up is very hard to do. In the 70 years following World War II, only 11 economies were able to leave behind their status as middle-income or low-income countries and join the developed world. This includes Japan and certain countries in southern Europe. The only countries to have genuinely transformed their poor economies into developed economies are the Four Asian Tigers (South Korea, Taiwan, Hong Kong, and Singapore). This suggests that catching up in economic terms is an extremely difficult process, with a small probability of success.

Alongside the challenge of economic development is that of social and political change, which is even greater. Traditional societies were hierarchical societies, and the upper classes were in no hurry to give up their privileges. Traditional societies were also intellectually rigid societies, and those classes enjoying intellectual dominance would not easily abandon their positions. Although traditional Chinese society was marked by a high degree of mobility, its institutions and ideas were still rigid. Of course, the most important features of modern societies are their open systems and freedom of thought. The conflict with traditional societies is inevitable, and the transition from traditional to modern society is bound to be very painful.

In European history, countries such as England or France, large countries at the start of these historical processes, went through revolutions before starting the modernization process, while countries that did not experience revolutions suffered in other ways. Germany, for example, was the most successful economy of the 19th century in terms of catching up with England and France, but this occurred in the absence of a social revolution, and Germany's eventual slide toward militarism had much to do with this. Japan, the Germany of the 20th century in economic terms, had the same problem.

China began its trek toward modernization in 1860. According to Li Hongzhang (1823–1901), a high official who was much involved in this process, China, at the end of the 19th century, experienced its greatest change in three thousand years. Chinese civilization, which has a written history of some three thousand years, had never encountered such a huge challenge as that of Western civilization. The other major foreign challenge China had faced was the introduction of Buddhism, which took China roughly one thousand years to completely digest. The impact of Western civilization was even more vast and penetrating than that of Buddhism, and Chinese scholars at the time worried that it would take even longer for China to completely absorb it.

Between 1860 and 1919, China's modernization went through three stages. The first stage was the Foreign Affairs Movement. The Foreign Affairs Movement was not without its successes, one of which is that, on the eve of the Sino-Japanese War in 1895, China had the largest fleet in Asia, the Beiyang Fleet. China's defeat in the war led those with vision to realize that technology alone was not enough and that the system had to be changed, which led to the second stage of modernization. At this point, two different forces appeared, one advocating revolution and the other reform. The former was led by Sun Yat-sen and his Revive China Society, and the latter was led by Kang Youwei (1858–1927) and his Hundred Days' Reform. The reform ended in failure, and the revolution ultimately ended with the establishment of the Republic of China. The victory of the revolution did not achieve the expected results, however, as Yuan Shikai (1859–1916), the interim president, sought to proclaim himself emperor, militarists divided the country between them, and the foreign powers continued their abuse and oppression.

Around the time of the Hundred Days' Reform in 1898, social Darwinist ideas began circulating in China, the result of Yan Fu's

(1854–1921) translation of Thomas Huxley's *Evolution and Ethics* and Liang Qichao's (1873–1929) writings in newspapers such as *Qingyi Bao* and *Xinmin Bao,* printed in Japan, and became one of the dominant trends among Chinese intellectuals for more than a decade. Since the revolution had not allowed China to take its rightful place in the world, intellectuals had to come up with something else. This was the background of the New Culture Movement in the 1910s and 1920s. The third stage began.

Given that technological development and institutional reforms had both failed, intellectuals who launched the New Culture Movement decided that the problem was China's culture, so they began to focus on the transformation of the people's minds and culture. One of the themes was opposing tradition, hence the slogan "Down with Confucius." The May Fourth Movement further radicalized the New Culture Movement, and radical intellectuals such as Chen Duxiu (1879–1942) and Li Dazhao (1888–1927) began to introduce Marxism into China. The victory of the October Revolution in Russia in 1917 made them realize that a socialist revolution might offer a total solution for building a strong China.

Having experienced the First World War, Western intellectuals began to entertain pessimistic views about Western culture, a trend which also influenced Chinese intellectuals. Marxism emerged as the antithesis of mainstream Western culture, which merged well with the critical attitude of Chinese radical intellectuals toward the West; the cultural revolution already underway in China was in need of a radical doctrine to take command, which means that Marxism came in at just the right moment. The sinification of Marxism began at that point.

The CCP's acceptance of Marxism was both idealistic and instrumental, with the latter becoming more important in practice. Class struggle was the Party's tool for social transformation, and whenever the situation permitted, the Party attempted to carry out social transformation through class struggle. From the point of view of modernization, the class struggle of that era was a means to an end in the transition toward modernization and transformation. The objects of class struggle were those in power who represented the political, social, and economic order of traditional society, and the outcome of the class struggle was the establishment of a new modern order.

Why did the Nationalist Party — the Kuomintang — fail to shoulder the responsibility of China's transition to modernity? Because, from the outset, the Kuomintang did not have such qualities and abilities. For Sun Yat-sen, revolution started out with nationalism, but he later came up with the Three People's Principles with an eye toward merging the Tongmenghui with the later Kuomintang. During the United Front period, when Sun allied with the Communists between 1923 and 1927, he believed that his principle advocating "people's livelihood" was consistent with Communism because both were about improving the lives of the common people, which meant that the Three People's Principles could accommodate Communism. He used this explanation to convince rightists in the Kuomintang to cooperate with the Communists. But Sun was always strongly opposed to the idea of class struggle in China because he believed that there were basically no differences between the classes in China. Here, we see that Sun lacked historical vision and did not realize that the CCP's advocacy of class struggle was actually meant to use this struggle as a weapon to overthrow the old system.

Sun's successor, Chiang Kai-shek, initially supported Soviet Communism, was sympathetic to the Russian Revolution, and once led a study tour to Russia. His transformation away from this stance was a complicated process. First, there was the conflict with the CCP over the Canton Coup of 1926, when Chiang purged certain Communist members in the Nationalist army. Second, his victories in the Northern Expedition in 1927 fueled his desire for power. Third, the CCP's land reform in the countryside and power grabs in the cities stirred his conservative instincts. The Shanghai Massacre of April 12, 1927, allowed Chiang Kai-shek to finally take control of the Kuomintang and eliminate the Communists from its ranks; however, in the long run, it also made the Kuomintang into a counter-revolutionary movement, which cost them the support of progressive youth who yearned for something else. So, by the

Yan'an period (1936–1945), patriotic young people flocked to the Communist headquarters in Yan'an instead of the Kuomintang capital in Chongqing. Those who went to Chongqing went to escape the war, while those who went to Yan'an were seeking a glorious and completely new China. In the eyes of the progressive youth, the Kuomintang was already corrupt. In this sense, the Kuomintang had lost its status as the leader of the Chinese revolution and the promoter of Chinese modernization.

According to Li Zehou[1] (1930–2021), the period from 1919 to 1949 was marked by the two themes of Enlightenment and national salvation, and national salvation ultimately won out over Enlightenment. However, characterizing this period as "Enlightenment" seems incomplete; instead, we should look at it from the perspective of modernization. Enlightenment is merely one part of modernization; and the revolution, the goal of which was to start a social transformation, was the more important part. Consequently, national salvation not only prevailed over Enlightenment but also over the revolution. The revolution could only be completed once New China was established.

The Socialist Revolution and Its Significance

After setting up its new regime, the CCP began to try to realize the original ambitions of the early period of the PRC, which meant carrying out a socialist revolution whose contents included land reform (and the later collectivization, including the People's Communes set up during the Great Leap Forward), the socialist transformation of industry and commerce, the emancipation of women, and the construction of a new socialist culture. In addition, the Party was committed to universal education and the improvement of public health. All of these changes greatly advanced China's modernization process, although the collectivization of agriculture and the transformation of industry and commerce served the ends of building socialism more than modernization, as discussed in the following section.

Land reform

Some people have used partial data to argue that land relations in old China were not all that problematic. However, according to a survey conducted by the National Resources Commission in the early 1930s, the percentage of farmers who owned and worked their own land was only 41.7% nationwide and was even lower in the south, at 27.2%. Among the farmers who did not till their own fields, there were more hired laborers in the north and more tenant farmers in the south. This suggests that land relations in old China were indeed very problematic. The significance of breaking these archaic land relations was twofold.

The first point was to liberate the productive forces. There were two reasons that the land situation constrained these forces. First, the peasants had no control over either the land or the fruits of their labor and thus were less motivated to produce. The hired laborers had no land at all and lived on the pitiful wages paid by the landlord, so they naturally had little motivation; tenant farmers generally had to give 50% of their harvest to the landlord, which also affected their incentive to work. Second, tenant farmers have very little wealth and have very little ability to assume risk, but they have no choice but to bear the risk of natural disasters, especially under fixed lease contracts, according to which they bear all the risks of a reduced harvest, which is a blow to their work incentive. Carrying out a program of providing "land to the tiller" would completely eliminate the efficiency loss due to the first factor and also greatly reduce the efficiency loss due to the second.

The second element is that the old land relationships created personal attachments. Both hired laborers and tenant farmers had relationships of personal dependency on the landlord, as in the case of Bai Jiaxuan and his long-time worker Lu San in the novel and television drama *White Deer Plain*.[2] These various political, social, and economic relationships of personal dependence are the very opposite of modernization. In an agrarian society, land is the most basic factor of production, and land relations determine other social relations; consequently, breaking the old land relationships is a crucial step toward the modernization of an agrarian society.

Studies have shown that land reform is a significant determinant of a country's (or a region's) long-term economic growth. The extremely unequal distribution of land in Latin American countries, where agriculture is dominated by large plantations and where the early politics of these countries was dominated by the owners of these *haciendas*, severely hindered the development of these countries. In contrast, South Korea and Taiwan both experienced thoroughgoing land reforms that greatly contributed to industrial development in both places. Land reform in mainland China was much deeper and more extensive and played a crucial role in increasing food production and promoting the modern transition in rural areas.

Women's emancipation

In almost all traditional societies, the status of women was very low. Women's liberation in developed countries followed a long path, with most countries not granting women the right to vote until after World War I. Late-developing countries needed to achieve women's emancipation in a much shorter period of time. The CCP accorded considerable importance to women's emancipation in the early period of the regime. During the Soviet period[3] between 1927 and 1936, the Party mobilized women to participate in labor to make up for the labor shortage created by men's participation in the war. During the Yan'an period from 1936 to 1945, women's liberation focused on women's literacy and political participation. Research has shown that these measures have had a long-term impact, in that counties that belonged to Soviet areas had a more balanced gender ratio and higher female labor force participation rates than other surrounding counties several decades later, and in the Shaanxi-Gansu-Ningxia border area, the female educational level was higher than the male education level in the present day.

After the founding of New China, the Party advanced the cause of women's emancipation through revolution. Even before the Constitution was promulgated, the Marriage Law was enacted, which abolished the evil customs that had damaged the status of women in the past, such as foot-binding, arranged marriages, and concubinage, thus using legal means to establish equal rights for men and women within the family. On the other hand, women were mobilized to participate in local political activities, which greatly improved women's social status and had a long-term impact. In counties with a high percentage of female party members in the 1950s, women's education levels were higher, and there was a more balanced gender ratio even in the 1980s. Under the commune system, female labor force participation rates increased substantially, a tradition that was retained even after the implementation of the responsibility system during reform and opening up. Although the female labor force participation rate has declined somewhat over the past two decades, it remains over 60% today, well above the world average of 50%.

Building a new socialist culture

Traditional Chinese society was a society based on place and blood ties, and with the exception of the literati, the vast majority of people interacted within the boundaries of the relationships determined by place and kinship. As the anthropologist Fei Xiaotong pointed out, the social relations of Chinese people are like the ripples created by a stone thrown into a pond, the stone in the middle representing the individual, whose relations to the "ripples" are determined according to their proximity in terms of locality and kinship.

Chinese social relations were centered on the individual, and beyond the ties of place and kin, traditional Chinese society had few functioning social organizations. This is very different from the West. In the West, religion occupies a central place in people's lives, and the role of religious groups is very clear in the connections people make with one another. Religious beliefs touched a much wider range of people than place and kinship, creating a greater possibility that even strangers could come together as a community. China was different. For the vast majority of people, "China" had only a cultural meaning, not a political one. At the grassroots level, social governance relied entirely on village and kin ties, and the role of the state was merely to defend against foreign invasion and to maintain domestic peace. For this reason, Chinese "collectivism" is collective in the Hobbesian sense: the state is a Leviathan that protects the people's tranquility, and the people approve of what the state does. The common people did not see the state as an organic part of society but as an external authority to which they had to submit.

Modern society is the polar opposite of traditional Chinese society; modern states can contain any number of cultures, and ties between people grow out of a common political identity and a unified government built on the basis of that identity. One of the major tasks of Chinese modernization has been to mold the political identity of the Chinese people and to build the country according to a unified popular idea of politics and government. The CCP accomplished this task by building a new socialist culture and forging a national identity for the Chinese people within the framework of socialism. The institutional changes brought about by the socialist revolution were themselves part of this process.

Never before in Chinese history has there been a radical social transformation like that produced by the socialist revolution. The Party reached into every corner of society through its tight organization and brought all Chinese into the process of modernization. In his comparison of the Kuomintang and the Communist Party, the historian Ray Huang (1918–2000) profoundly pointed out that the Kuomintang governed the country in a top-down manner, while the Communist Party did so in a bottom-up manner. The Party-led socialist revolution overturned the soil of Chinese society, radically changing the structure and function of society at the grassroots level, greatly advancing the political identification of the Chinese general public with the state. On this basis, the Party further strengthened the people's national political identity through the propaganda system, the educational system, and literature. The following is a discussion of how the Party constructed people's political identity through literary works, using the film *The Five Jin Huas*[4] as an example.

The Five Jin Huas is a 1959 technicolor film about a young man of the Bai ethnic minority group named Ah Peng who is looking for his beloved, a woman named Jin Hua. One year later, Ah Peng is on his way to the Third Month Fair and meets the beautiful Jin Hua at the Butterfly Spring. The next year, Ah Peng comes to the Butterfly Spring once again, bringing the love pledge given to him the previous year by Jin Hua, and searches in vain for her throughout the Cang Mountain and Er Lake areas around Dali, Yunnan. In the course of looking for her, he meets four other young women, also named Jin Hua, each of whom is an activist in her commune, before finally finding his own Jin Hua, who is the vice president of the commune. The lovers finally marry, and the film ends happily. The film is beautifully shot, and some of the songs are still sung to this day. For the purpose of this chapter, what is most important is the political message the film conveys.

First of all, the film's two main characters are both Bai, and the film's message promoting China's multi-ethnic family is obvious. The southwestern region had long been under the rule of the Tusi kingdoms and had a very weak identification with the Chinese state. The scenery of Dali, the strong Bai boy, and the beautiful Bai girl in the film give the audience from the rest of China a good impression of the minority region and naturally inspire the people's enthusiasm for ethnic unity. Second, as it follows Ah Peng's search for Jin Hua, the film presents the joyful changes brought by the people's communes to people's lives. Regardless of the context of the time, such a presentation subconsciously encourages the audience to identify politically with the country. Third, the five Jin Huas Ah Peng meets are all active members of the commune, highlighting the depth and breadth of women's emancipation in ethnic minority areas. The constraints on women in ethnic minority areas are not as severe as those in Han areas, and each of the five Jin Huas in the film is cheerful and lively, far more daring and open than Han women. Although such a portrayal romanticizes ethnic minorities to a certain extent, the romanticism plays a positive role in promoting women's emancipation. Women's emancipation is an important part of socialist cultural values, and the film promotes the idea of women's emancipation in a romantic form that has significance beyond women's emancipation itself and has a catalytic effect on the country's political identity.

In the process of socialist revolution and construction, interpersonal relationships have undergone significant changes. The fact that strangers came to address one another as "comrades" can be seen as a representative manifestation of these changes. "Comrade" is used by people who share the same ambition and vision and was originally used only within the Party. The use of the term "comrade" among strangers meant that strangers shared a common ideal or goal, which at that time was to build a socialist China. The use of "comrade" thus became an important expression of national political identity at the individual level. Today, strangers rarely use "comrade" to address one another, which might also be a sign that China's national political identity is complete.

Socialist Construction

Industrialization

With the founding of New China, the Party's socialist revolution was accompanied by a vigorous campaign of socialist construction, establishing a path of industrialization led by heavy industry. There were various reasons for choosing this path at the time. One was the lesson of history. Beginning with the Foreign Affairs Movement, several generations of Chinese intellectuals and leaders firmly believed that underdevelopment invited exterior aggression and that to avoid this required building China's own industry. Mao Zedong was no exception.

Second, the international environment at the time was not conducive to China's participation in the worldwide division of labor. The West imposed an embargo on China, which left China's economy largely isolated from the West. At the same time, the Soviet Union tried to position China as an agricultural country within the socialist camp, which Mao firmly opposed, and he ultimately convinced the Soviet Union to provide assistance for China's industrialization.

Third, the popular advice to developing countries in international academic and policy circles at the time was also to implement a policy of import substitution, allowing them to develop their own industries. Development economics had just taken shape as a discipline, and one of its central concerns was economies of scale in industrial development. This logic suggested that enterprises need to reach a minimum scale of production in order to survive, which gave rise to the policy known as "protection of infant industries." At the same time, the economist Raúl Prebisch's (1901–1986) center–periphery hypothesis emphasized the differences between central countries, which are dominated by manufacturing, and peripheral countries, which are dominated by the production of raw materials. According to general principles, technological progress in manufacturing in the center should improve the terms of trade of the peripheral countries, thus benefiting them, but Prebisch did not find this to be the case. This hypothesis later developed into dependency theory, meaning that peripheral countries fall into the trap of producing raw materials and, over time, become dependent on the central countries. New China, being at the forefront of anti-imperialism and anti-colonialism, readily accepted such a theory.

Soviet aid to China played an important role in China's industrialization in the 1950s, and the 156 Soviet-aided civic projects laid the foundation for China's heavy industry, some of which continue to play an important role today. But domestic capital accumulation was even more important. Soviet aid to China was mostly in the form of loans, and China itself had to accumulate the capital needed for industrialization. Circumstances at the time dictated that the only possible source of capital was the rural areas. As the Soviets had done before, China took the approach of depressing the prices of agricultural products. This was an important part of the background leading to collectivization and unified purchase and marketing. Given that farming was decentralized, it was difficult for the state to control agricultural production and prices; collectivization unified agricultural production, and unified purchase and marketing centralized the purchase and sale of agricultural products, thus controlling prices. Once capital was available, its use had to be concentrated in strategic sectors approved by the state, and the socialist transformation of industry and commerce was meant to serve this purpose.

In general terms, China's industrialization strategy was focused on catching up to an unusual degree. What should we make of this strategy? In 2008, my Ph.D. student Zheng Dongya and I published a quantitative simulation study to answer this question. The starting point for our research is that heavy industry has technological externalities affecting other industries, and technological progress in heavy industry can reduce production costs in other industries. Given the existence of such externalities, the government should subsidize heavy industry. We calculated the optimal subsidy rate and the optimal amount of time the subsidies should continue and found that the optimal subsidy rate is 33%, while our model showed that the actual rate in practice was 36.7%, which is not a big difference; however, we calculated that the optimal subsidy time was 12 years, while in reality subsidies continued for 25 years, which is a big difference. This means that there was nothing wrong with the catch-up strategy itself; rather, the problem was that the policy was followed for too long. Moreover, in the process of carrying out the catch-up strategy, the Party also made rash mistakes such as the Great Leap Forward, which should serve as lessons for future generations.

Human development

While promoting economic construction, the Party also focused on universal access to education and public health improvements. Studies show that the correlation between the education level of people born in the late 1940s and 1950s and that of their parents is the weakest among the birth cohorts between 1930 and 1985, suggesting that the focus of attention in the first three decades of New China was to spread education to the general population and enhance intergenerational educational mobility. In terms of public health, the commune-based primary healthcare system made basic medical care available to the general population and reduced

Table 1. Comparisons of China and India in 1978.

	China	India
Per-capita GDP (constant 2000 US dollars)	155.0	206.0
Adult literacy rate (%)	65.5	40.8
Tertiary school enrollment (% gross)	0.7	4.9
Life expectancy	66.0	54.0
Infant mortality rate (%)	54.2	106.4
Share of manufacturing in GDP (%)	40.0	17.0
Share of manufacturing in employment (%)	17.3	13.0

Note: China's literacy rate is for 1982 and India's literary rate is for 1981.
Source: The table is from Yao (2014).

infant mortality, and patriotic health campaigns and vaccinations eradicated many infectious diseases and steadily increased the life expectancy of the people.

Table 1 offers a comparison between China and India in around 1978, which gives a good indication of China's achievements in promoting modernization. China and India are comparable in many ways. India gained independence in 1947, while New China was established in 1949, and the two countries have almost the same population. In addition, like China, India implemented import substitution policies and developed its own industries. However, the table tells us that, with the exception of per capita income and enrollment in higher education, India lagged significantly behind China in terms of literacy, infant mortality, life expectancy, and industrial development. The fact that India's per capita income was higher has to do with China's lower starting point and the concentration of most of China's accumulation in heavy industry. By 1992, China's per capita income had surpassed that of India. That India's rate of enrollment in higher education was much higher than China's had to do with the fact that college entrance exams had just been reinstated in China, but it also showed that India was more concerned with higher education, while China was more concerned with basic education. Given the low income levels and high illiteracy rates in both countries at the time, basic education should clearly have been a national priority, and with hindsight, it is clear that the development of basic education in China played an important role in the development of an export-oriented economy after reform and opening, while India's lower level of education has been a constraint on its industrial development.

Reform and Opening Up: Reconciling with the Chinese Tradition

The socialist revolution took China by storm and transformed it, bringing the country to the threshold of modernization. The purpose of the revolution was to build a better country, and the revolution prepared the conditions for national construction: the hierarchical structure of Chinese society was destroyed, social and political equality reached high levels, and the national political identity of the population was enhanced; at the same time, socialist construction laid the foundation for industry and improved the education and health of the population.

After the beginning of reform and opening up, the Party shifted its focus to economic construction, and abandoning the radical ideas and practices of the socialist revolution became the obvious choice. At this point, the Party also began to reexamine its relationship with tradition. Two factors deserve attention here. First, the socialist revolution functioned primarily at the political, social, and economic levels without touching the family or the private sphere associated with the family. In rural areas, the family raises poultry and livestock on the land allocated to it; in urban areas, although the family does not have its own property, it is still, as in rural areas, a complete social unit. Traditional Chinese culture is carried forward by the family. Economic construction requires motivating individuals; respect for traditional culture and the individual behavior patterns derived therefrom is a necessary condition for such motivation.

Second, having abandoned radical ideas and practices, the Party had to find new intellectual resources and practical models in which to anchor its actions. Being in China, it was a natural thing to turn toward the best parts of the Chinese tradition. The Party returned to the best of Chinese traditions in three specific areas: pragmatism, meritocracy, and the market economy. By combining these traditions with the long-established theories and practices of a Marxist party, the Party laid the philosophical and political foundations for the economic takeoff that followed reform and opening up.

Pragmatism

At the ground level, the most striking feature of Chinese culture is pragmatism. From the daily lives of the people to political practice, pragmatism was the most prominent feature of traditional China. The most important reason for the emergence of pragmatism in China is that it had no indigenous religion; our ancestors were concerned with life as lived on earth from the very beginning. The *Book of Songs* is a product of the early Western Zhou period and shows that our ancestors were already singing about love, while Greece at the time was still in what we call the mythological age. The Battle of Troy was fought over a kidnapped woman, while our ancestors had already established a model of peaceful living in the same territory where they sang of love and of life on earth. This is a particularity of Chinese civilization.

On a philosophical level, pragmatism expresses itself in two basic principles. First, the desirability of the ends to be achieved reasonably lends legitimacy to the means to be employed. One of the prerequisites of revolution is to distinguish enemies from friends, which dictates an emphasis on the means, hence the slogan "I would rather have socialist grass than capitalist seedlings." Pragmatism starts with the ends, and as long as the end can be achieved, the means may be justified. Deng Xiaoping's (1904–1997) theory that "[i]t doesn't matter if a cat is black or white, so long as it catches mice" is a graphic description of this principle. Here, reason is very important. When inferring the legitimacy of the means, a person must think in terms of his own knowledge system, moral standards, and logic; otherwise, unscrupulous things will result.

Second, there is no eternal truth, and practice is the sole criterion of truth. The Chinese do not believe in an eternal existence, and a very important idea in traditional Chinese philosophy is that the only constant law in the universe is that everything is in flux. The Chinese believe that practice produces true knowledge and that only practice can determine whether knowledge is true knowledge. The Chinese word *shijian* is generally translated as "practice," but this is inaccurate. "Practice" means that a model already exists and that you train yourself according to this model until you become skilled. *Shijian* is different. It involves a cycle of "explore — build a theory — apply the theory — explore again," for which there is no exact equivalent in English.

Pragmatism opens the door to reform and drives the process forward. Imagine if we were still stuck in the middle of debates over "isms" and "truths" — which of our reforms would have gotten off the ground? Whether we are talking about rural reforms, reform of state-owned enterprises, or price reform, all are at odds with the theoretical truths held in the past. Deng Xiaoping's stance of "let's not debate" led the Party to a results-oriented philosophy of action, under which the legitimacy of a system is no longer determined by how the system is labeled, but by whether it can promote the development of productive forces and the great rejuvenation of the Chinese nation. This is what made institutional reforms possible.

Meritocracy

China has a long tradition of meritocracy. As early as the Western Zhou period, there was already an "Imperial Academy" whose purpose was to nurture talent. Meritocratic practices were institutionalized under Emperor Han Wudi (156–87 BCE); the Sui dynasty (581–618) invented the imperial examination system, providing the sons of the common people with a vehicle of social mobility. The philosophical foundation of meritocracy is found in the pre-Qin Confucian view of human nature. Unlike the Western view, which sees human nature as fixed, pre-Qin Confucianism believed that human nature was diverse, fluid, and malleable and that the level of merit one could achieve depended on one's efforts and the surrounding environment. Since political positions are limited and economic development needs to incentivize the population, the political structure must adopt the principle of selecting the worthy, and the economic structure must reward merit.

At the practical level, the Mohists[5] made an even greater contribution to meritocracy. By the time Confucianism became dominant in the Western Han period, Confucianism had absorbed Mohist ideas, and eventually, through the doctrines of Dong Zhongshu[6] (179–104 BCE), meritocracy became a constitutional principle of the Chinese bureaucratic empire. From today's perspective, this constitutional principle can serve as an alternative to the vote as practiced in electoral democracies, correcting some of the problems of these systems, particularly their tendencies toward populism and the creation of demagogues who incite the people for their own selfish purposes.

During reform and opening up, the Party took up this meritocratic tradition. Beginning in the early 1980s, with the launch of the policy of "four transformations,"[7] the Party has emphasized the training and selection of cadres. Many studies have shown that the Party's cadre selection system is in line with meritocratic principles. More capable officials are more likely to be promoted and to achieve more over the course of their careers; the Party also attaches importance to cadre training, among other measures, by assigning cadres to different positions to enhance their abilities over time.

Meritocracy as a constitutional principle also has significant theoretical and practical significance today. The CCP is composed of pioneering members of China's population, according to meritocratic principles, which lends constitutional legitimacy to the leadership of the Party. The Party puts forward major policies and legislative ideas, and the People's Congress is the place where the Party generates consensus. The sovereign role of the People's Congress is carried out when this body deliberates and votes on the Party's personnel nominations and major political policies, as well as when it passes legislation based on the Party's proposals.

The return to the market economy

Deng Xiaoping said that the market economy is not unique to capitalism. Nor is the market economy unique to the West. China had already built a market economy by the time of the Northern Song dynasty at the very latest. By that point, China's market economy was already relatively complete, with the development of private land ownership, industry, commerce, and a commodity economy — and even the invention of paper money and securities trading, which marked the beginnings of finance. The main characteristic of Western capitalism was not the market economy but steam-powered mass production and the almost unconstrained accumulation of capital that resulted therefrom. When China began to embrace the market economy after reform and opening up, it seemed at the time that it was copying the West, but in fact it was returning to the Chinese tradition. To a great extent, China's market economy has distinctly Chinese characteristics, highly related to our stage of development and the cultural psychology of the population; in other words, the Party led the nation toward China's own version of a market economy.

The market economy carries out factor-based distribution,[8] rewards diligence and punishes laziness, and ensures the survival of the fittest, which are necessary principles to ensure the efficiency of the market economy. This is also consistent with China's meritocratic traditions, and at the same time, it does not contradict the principle of "to each according to his labor." On the one hand, factor-based distribution includes "to each according to his labor" because labor is a productive factor; on the other, factor-based distribution is, in the end, "to each according to his labor," because capital is essentially also a product of labor.

The meaning of the revolution reexamined

When future historians write about Deng Xiaoping's historical achievements, they will naturally talk about reform and opening up, but scholars with a sense of historical depth will surely emphasize that his main contribution was to "bring the Party back to China." The birth of the Party was a product of the West's coming to China, a party constructed by radical Chinese intellectuals during the May Fourth period who chose radical Western ideas. As described earlier, the Party consciously became an instrument of Chinese modernization, bringing China into the modern world in a great tumult. Here, we meet the great issue of Chinese culture's absorption and integration of Western culture.

During the revolutionary period, the Party was to a great degree practicing a Western theory of revolution, but as a political party rooted in the soil of China, the Party had to eventually face the great issue of the integration of China and the West. At present, this issue is unfolding within the framework of the sinification of Marxism, but more important for future historians will be that Deng Xiaoping led the Party back to China, initiating the process of China's casting off a century of cultural importation.

In terms of "techniques," reform and opening up sought to learn from the West, but in terms of China's "path," they initiated the process leading to China's return to Chinese tradition. It should not be forgotten that the planned economy also came from the West, so reform and opening up meant merely a switch from copying one Western thing to copying another, but in the learning process of reform and opening up, the Party's guiding ideology and mode of behavior have been completely Chinese. In this sense, we are returning to the stance of "Chinese learning for substance, Western learning for application 中体西用." For a civilization with three thousand years of written history, it is a perfectly understandable and perhaps inevitable choice to cling to one's "substance." However, China's current "substance" is different from that of more than a century ago, having separated the wheat from the chaff and adopting value systems and behavioral logic appropriate to the times in the process of "applying" Western learning. Consequently, since reform and opening up, "Chinese learning for substance, Western learning for application" must be a fusion of Chinese tradition and modern Western value systems instead of the two completely different entities as understood during the Foreign Affairs Movement.

This leads to yet another question: Given this final return to China, was the 20th-century revolution a mistake? The answer is no. First, the revolution sped up the modernization of China, bringing it from a stubbornly traditional society to the threshold of modernity in a relatively short period of time. Second, the return to Chinese tradition today is a return at a higher level. The revolution swept away the corrupt parts of Chinese tradition, allowing today's return to lighten the load and select the best parts of the tradition to be inherited and carried forward. Third, international comparisons reveal that those late-developing countries where no revolution occurred have had a very difficult transition to modernization that has delayed their economic catch-up.

A typical example of this is the Philippines, whose per capita GDP in 1980 was more than five times that of China, while by 2020, China's per capita GDP was almost four times that of the Philippines, a huge reversal in merely four decades. How did the Philippines fail? Since the fall of the Marcos dictatorship in 1986, Filipino democracy has continued uninterruptedly and seems to have the capacity to correct mistakes, as witnessed by the impeachment of President Estrada. However, Filipino democracy is still based on an unchanged social structure, as several Filipino scholars have lamented: "Thus has emerged the great Philippine paradox: an extremely lively play of electoral politics unfolding above an immobile class structure that is one of the worst in Asia."[9]

The Filipino class structure is based on the plantation economy left behind by the Spanish colonizers, with big plantation owners being the dominant economic and political force, and to this day, Filipino politics still bears strong traces of family politics, where party affiliation is unimportant and loyalty to the politically powerful is all that matters. Since 1988, with the exception of the impeached Estrada (a famous actor before his election) and one more president (a former defense secretary), the other presidents have had deep family backgrounds, with the recently elected president being the son of Marcos Sr. and the vice president being the daughter of the recently departed Duterte. This is exactly the kind of clientelistic politics that the political scientist Francis Fukuyama believes has led to the downfall of democracy, the latter being one of the main obstacles to economic growth because it leads to nepotism in the economy and allows a small number of people to monopolize economic opportunities and resources.

Revolutions are painful, but short-term pain can be traded for long-term peace. The vast majority of late-developing countries have a history of colonization, and the colonizers left them with tools of electoral politics, meaning that they have had no choice but to transform their societies within the framework of democracy ever since. Democracy always results in compromise among various forces, while social transformation means depriving certain powerful groups of their power and interests. The two are in conflict, so social transformation in post-colonial countries is exceptionally long and difficult.

For example, land reform in the Philippines was started under US occupation but was not completed until the first decade of this century, and the land was sold — rather than given — to landless peasants. Land reform in India has proven to be even more difficult. The Land Reform Act was passed in India immediately after independence, but it was barely implemented for 70 years, and even in West Bengal, where the Communist Party has been in power for decades, more than 30% of farmers are still landless. One of the great paradoxes of modern transformation is that a genuine social transformation must be completed through violence to be successful in the short term. China is an example of success, while many post-colonial countries are examples of failure.

The Global Significance of the Chinese Path

Returning to the dilemma of transition and catching up raised at the beginning of this chapter, it would seem that the Chinese path provides an answer to this dilemma. From the perspective of the interaction between transition and catching up, we can identify three types of countries in the past two hundred years: for the first type, transition lagged behind catching up; in the second, the two occurred together; and in the third, there was neither transition nor catch up.

Germany and Japan before World War II are typical examples of the first category of countries. Germany was the most successful catch-up country in the 19th century, and Japan was the most successful catch-up country in the 20th, but both countries eventually moved toward militarism because they did not succeed in carrying out a transition. In fact, their economic success was a major reason for delaying their failure to achieve political and social transition. Germany's economic as well as military successes ignited a sense of German national pride. For the Germans, Russian culture was base, French culture was corrupt, and British culture was at best sly; only German culture represented the sublime and the glorious, which meant that Germany should be the master of Europe. The Germans were angry at the European "disrespect" for Germany, and this is particularly true of Kaiser Wilhelm II. He coveted the wealth of Paris and, at the same time, resented the contempt of his mother's country of birth, England, for Germany, and hoped through war to take Paris and earn the respect he "deserved."

In essence, Japan followed exactly the same path as Germany. After the Meiji Restoration, Japan's power increased dramatically, and it easily defeated its former teacher, China, in the Sino-Japanese War, as well as Russia, the "steamroller of Europe,"[10] in the Russo-Japanese War. Japan subsequently thought it could represent the yellow race in a war against the white race and went so far as to see itself as the true representative of Chinese civilization, while China was no better than "Shina 支那."[11] In the end, both countries ruined themselves in war. The reason for this is that while they had joined the front ranks of the modern economy, in terms of ideas, politics, and society, they remained somewhere between tradition and modernity. When the most advanced technology is harnessed to the logic of pre-modern thinking and behavior, the result will certainly be anti-modern.

The Four Little Dragons, especially South Korea and Taiwan, are representatives of the second category of countries (or regions). Japan intentionally suppressed the industrial and commercial elites of Korea and Taiwan during the colonial period, and both regions implemented agrarian reform after World War II, resulting in very egalitarian societies, eliminating powerful groups that impeded change, and providing the political and social conditions for the government to initiate economic growth. Singapore is a city-state, and coupled with Lee Kuan Yew's rational and intelligent governance, the social structure was rapidly modernized and transformed, greatly contributing to economic growth. What these examples have in common is that social transformation came first, creating the basis for a neutral exercise of government power.

Most developing countries fall into the third category. In these countries, slow political and social transformation is the main reason why they cannot catch up quickly enough. Most developing countries were European and American colonies, and prior to colonization, they were traditional, or even primitive, societies. Instead of changing their traditional or primitive social structures, the colonizers took full advantage of them and exploited them for their own ends, thus solidifying the social and political structures of these countries.

When the colonizers departed, they left these countries with a modern system of electoral democracy, which greatly reduced their space for social change. They could only hope to achieve social and political change through market forces in the process of development, but in so doing, these countries entered a close-end cycle: the lack of political and social transformation constrained economic development, and the lack of economic development, in turn, constrained political and social transformation.

However, Germany and Japan seem to be two counterexamples. The reason may be that both Germany and Japan had a strong state that could accumulate resources to accomplish economic catch-up in the short term, while most developing countries have not produced such a state. In developing countries, transition and economic catch-up must both evolve out of the process of social development, and both will demand a long historical process.

China is more like the Four Little Dragons, where transition and catch-up occurred simultaneously. But China is a large country, and its modernization path has greater global significance. In concrete terms, the Chinese path has the following meanings.

First, it made the transition from tradition to modernity relatively quickly. The British Revolution lasted more than half a century, and the French Revolution and the shocks it released lasted more than a hundred years. If we do not count the period of the Japanese invasion, the 20th-century Chinese Revolution (including the socialist revolution) also lasted half a century, which is not long in comparative terms. Just as the British Revolution and the French Revolution brought those countries into the modern era, so did the Chinese Revolution.

In terms of economic catch-up, the revolution allowed China to establish an egalitarian society without class distinctions, providing a necessary guarantee that China could achieve economic takeoff. Although we do not expect other developing countries to complete their political and social transition through revolution, they must make the promotion of equality a central task of political reform; otherwise, they will have difficulty achieving long-term and stable economic growth.

Second, focus on human development. As the summary of the table in section "Socialist Construction" shows, during the period of socialist revolution and construction, the Party focused on improving the educational level of the general population and the health of the entire population. In comparing the different economic performances of China and India, Amartya Sen particularly emphasized that China was better prepared than India in terms of human development. People are the first productive force, and education and health are the main measures of people as productive forces; to improve education and health is to improve human productivity. Compared to other developing countries, China has placed greater emphasis on the education and health levels of ordinary people, which both reflects the egalitarian philosophy of the CCP and is consistent with the general logic of economic development, meaning that in the early stages of economic development, improving the capabilities of the majority is more likely to promote economic growth than improving the capabilities of a minority.

Third, make pragmatism the basic philosophy guiding your actions. National pride is an important intellectual source of national unity, but many developing countries take it to the extreme and reject actions that would lose "face" for the nation. In terms of economic development, this is reflected in the refusal to develop labor-intensive industries and the pursuit of high-class industries, because the elites of developing countries believe that labor-intensive industries are undignified and exploitative and that the development of high-class industries is the only way to put their countries on a par with developed countries. In terms of institution building, they are unwilling to compromise with national conditions and insist on what they call the "best" systems, whether they work or not.

China is different. In the early period of its economic takeoff, China readily accepted labor-intensive industries outsourced from developed economies, thus accumulating capital and technology, which paved the way for building up one of the world's largest and most resilient manufacturing systems and finally entering the world's forefront in many technological fields. In terms of institution-building, we did not pursue a perfect system, but adopted a gradual approach, first establishing a "useful" system and then improving it in practice. As a result, China's institutional transformation has avoided the painful institutional transformation of the Soviet Union and Eastern Europe and has provided the conditions for smooth economic development. China's pragmatic attitude and successful experience thus have an important meaning in the global context.

Fourth, the ruling party plays the role of the backbone of society. With its broad representation and its current 90 million members from all walks of life, the CCP has become the place where social consensus is forged. Guided by the principle of democratic centralism, the Party brings together the views of different classes and representative groups of people to form the country's general policies. As a result, the Party and the government can stand above the interests of other social groups, remaining disinterested and impartial in the face of possible conflicts of social interest and working for the long-term development of China as a whole. In other developing countries, governments tend to be biased, either swayed by interest groups or held hostage by populism, and resources are not allocated to where they are most effective.

Although most countries do not have a strong ruling party like the CCP, this does not mean that they cannot learn from China's experience of disinterested government, which is possible to construct through rational institutional arrangements even in electoral democracies. The neutrality of the state is something that Adam Smith began to emphasize in his *Wealth of Nations*, and the Chinese state is a state in Smith's sense, which is why the sociologist Giovanni Arrighi (1937–2009) gave the title *Adam Smith in Beijing* to his magnum opus on the world system.

China is still following the path toward modernization; the next 30 years will be a sprint to modernize China. If, by 2049, the 100th anniversary of the founding of New China, we can complete our political and social transformation and catch up with the income levels of developed countries, we will have not only completed the great rejuvenation of the Chinese nation but will have also created a modernization path that is both Chinese and has significance for the world. So far, China is the only large country that has not engaged in external expansion when it hastes to modernize, and when future historians write this chapter of history, they should pay particular attention to this fact. In the future, China will adhere to the path of peaceful development and continue to make greater contributions to the world.

Endnotes

1. Translator's note: Li Zehou was a philosopher who focused on aesthetics and ethics, as well as a public intellectual who had an immense impact on China's "second Enlightenment" in the 1980s.
2. Translator's note: *White Deer Plain* is a novel written by Chen Zhongshi, published in 1993. Anhui TV developed into a television series, broadcast in 2017.
3. Translator's note: After the rupture of the United Front between the Nationalists and the Communists in 1927, most Communists abandoned China's cities, where they had been attempting to organize the working class, for the countryside, where they founded "Soviets" and

sought to mobilize the peasants. This choice, forced on them by the Nationalists' decision to end the United Front and brutally purge the Communists, led to a fundamental change in the nature of the CCP.

4. Translator's note: The title of the film is an untranslatable play on words; the literal meaning is "five bouquets of golden flowers," because the translation of the female lead's name — Jin Hua — is "golden flower," and there are five characters named Jin Hua that appear in the story.
5. Translator's note: Mozi (470–391 BCE) was a thinker during China's "axial age" who opposed Confucius's emphasis on family and hierarchy and preached instead that "one ought to be concerned for the welfare of people in a spirit of 'impartial concern' (jian'ai) that does not make distinctions between self and other, associates and strangers, a doctrine often described more simplistically as 'universal love.'" For more information, see here.
6. Translator's note: Dong Zhongshu (179–104 B.C.E.) was a scholar-official credited with having convinced emperor Han Wudi to adopt Confucianism as China's state ideology.
7. Translator's note: The "four transformations" aimed to train cadres who were more "revolutionary," younger, better educated, and more specialized. The idea was to produce a new corps of public servants more in line with a modernizing China and to replace both the stereotypical Maoist cadre — a poorly educated worker or peasant — as well as those ideological opportunists who joined the Party or the government during the Cultural Revolution.
8. Translator's note: "Factor-based distribution 按要素分配", opposing "to each according to his labor 按劳分配" derived from Carl Marx's labor theory of value, is part of the discourse of China's "early stage of socialism," in which the productive forces must be encouraged to produce the material base necessary to achieve a "moderately prosperous" country. In practice, what this means is allowing the entrepreneurial to become wealthy and allowing the wealthy to accumulate more wealth, before proceeding to a more equitable distribution of income once society is richer.
9. Bello *et al.* (2005).
10. Translator's note: Russian military power was greatly overestimated by certain European nations in the early 20th century, chiefly due to the

impressive size of Tsarist armies. The nickname "Europe's steamroller" came from this.

11. Translator's note: This was a pejorative, racist term used by Japan to refer to China, particularly during the Sino-Japanese War.

References

Bello, W., de Guzman, M., Malig, M.L., and Docena, H. 2005. *The Anti-Development State: The Political Economy of Permanent Crisis in the Philippines.* Manila: Zed Books, p. xvi.

Yao, Y. 2014. Chapter 7: The Chinese growth miracle. In Durlauf, S. and Agion, P. (eds.), *Handbook of Economic Growth,* Vol. 2B. Amsterdam: North Holland, pp. 943–1032.

https://doi.org/10.1142/9789819815241_0004

Chapter 4

"SPECIAL DEALS": THE INFORMAL INSTITUTIONAL FOUNDATION OF CHINA'S ECONOMIC GROWTH*

Chong-En Bai[†,¶], Chang-Tai Hsieh[‡,||], Zheng Michael Song[§,**], and Xin Wang[§,††]

[†]*School of Economics and Management, Tsinghua University, Beijing, China*
[‡]*University of Chicago, Chicago, USA*
[§]*Chinese University of Hong Kong, Hong Kong*
[¶]*baichn@sem.tsinghua.edu.cn*
[||]*chsieh@chicagoBooth.edu*
[**]*zheng.michael.song@gmail.com*
[††]*xwang@surgery.cuhk.edu.hk*

Introduction

China's economy has experienced extraordinary growth over the past four decades, with the development of private enterprises playing a crucial role. Some data, however, suggest that China's formal economic institutions are still not well established. For instance, according to the World Bank's "Doing Business" report, before

*This chapter is based on two of the authors' papers (Bai *et al.*, 2020a, 2020b).

2015, China consistently ranked around 90th out of nearly 190 economies worldwide in terms of its overall business environment. Moreover, the specific subindicator "Starting a business" ranked China even lower, at around 150th.

Given the considerable deviation from the Washington Consensus, how did China achieve rapid economic growth in the absence of a well-established formal economic system? We think that the answer lies in a series of informal institutions that emerged in the early 1990s, which collectively are referred to as the "special deals" system. The main feature of this system is that it allows local governments to help specific private enterprises bypass unfavorable regulations within the formal structure. As a result, these enterprises gain the ability to commence their operations, endure challenges, and ultimately expand their business. To test this hypothesis, it is essential to address two fundamental questions:

- Countries with inadequate formal systems have a prevalence of similar informal institutions. Extensive evidence suggests that the advantages obtained by certain enterprises through these institutions are largely negated by the expenses incurred by other enterprises.[1] As a result, overall social welfare does not increase, and the economy does not grow substantially. This being the case, why is China an exception?
- Informal institutions often exhibit strong locality and lack the universality seen in formal systems. Another suspicion regarding China's "special deals" system is that the government can assist only a limited number of enterprises (e.g., a municipal party secretary may support at most a few dozen enterprises, whereas an average prefecture-level city has around 100,000 enterprises). How does this theory explain the extensive growth of private enterprises in China?

Regarding the first question, three key reasons explain why the "special deals" system in China likely yields benefits that outweigh its costs. First, China's local governments possess robust administrative capabilities, enabling them to extend a helping hand to selected enterprises. Second, local officials have a strong incentive to support this system, driven by their responsibility to promote local economic development or by their desire to gain recognition and career advancement.[2] Third, fierce competition among local governments to attract investment effectively limits the potential damage caused to other enterprises as a result of preferential treatment. These factors are discussed in detail in the section "Why Does 'Special Deals' Work in China?", along with supporting evidence.[3]

Regarding the second question, by studying the establishment of joint ventures between state-owned and private enterprises nationwide and between private enterprises, we found the following: (1) The largest private owners often have joint ventures with state owners, which may serve as their primary mode or prerequisite for receiving "special deals." More importantly, (2) these private owners can partially extend the benefits of the "special deals" to more private owners by forming joint ventures, thus enhancing the latter's operating environment. This mechanism can continually extend to a larger number of relatively smaller private enterprises. In Figure 1 (a), red circles represent state owners, blue circles represent private contributors, connections indicate joint ventures between them, and d represents the distance we define between private and state owners (a detailed definition is provided in the following). Through a similar hierarchical structure, the scope of enterprises benefiting from the "special deals" system has significantly expanded.

Figure 1 (b) shows the growth in the number of private owners directly benefiting ($d = 1$) from "special deals" and those indirectly benefiting ($d \geq 2$) between 2000 and 2019. The number of direct

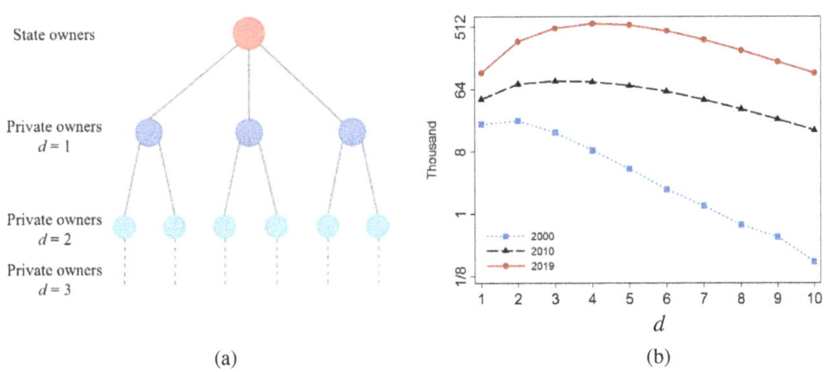

Figure 1. Expansion of the scope of the "special deals" system: (a) schematic diagram; and (b) China data, 2000–2019.

beneficiaries increased approximately 5.5 times, and indirect beneficiaries saw a nearly 60-fold increase. As measured by registered capital, the proportion of private enterprises benefiting from this system rose from 16% of the entire economy in 2000 to 35% in 2019. Section "How Does the 'Special Deals' Approach Benefit a Large Number of Private Enterprises?" provides an overview of this research.[4]

Understanding the "special deals" system also aids in comprehending the challenges China currently faces and will confront in its future development. Notably, issues relating to factor allocation distortion, financial risks, and trade disputes stemming from this system have become increasingly prominent in recent years. Section "Risks and Challenges" discusses these concerns.

Why Does "Special Deals" Work in China?

Similar informal institutions, such as the "special deals," are prevalent in countries with inadequate formal systems. The essence of such systems lies in certain enterprises receiving government assistance and protection, resulting in their benefits, whereas other enterprises often suffer because of the preferential treatment given to the former. In many cases, the gains of the former are essentially offset by the costs borne by the latter, leading to no overall improvement in societal welfare.

Three reasons, however, might explain why the benefits of the "special deals" system in China could potentially outweigh its costs.

First, compared with many countries with imperfect formal systems, China's local governments possess strong administrative capabilities that they can use to extend assistance to selected enterprises. Among other measures, this assistance includes breaking through existing unfavorable rules (which is the essence of the term "special deals"), improving local infrastructure, enhancing operational efficiency, providing land at preferential prices, relaxing credit constraints, and preventing competitors from entering. Apart from measures that may decrease societal welfare, such as preventing competitors from entering, many other actions contribute to enhancing productivity and fostering economic growth. For instance, local governments actively assist enterprises in entering industries that were traditionally dominated by state-owned enterprises.[5]

Second, local officials have strong incentives to support the "special deals" system. Based on our observations, local governments often exhibit impressive dedication to attracting and supporting private enterprises, with a significant portion of top officials' time devoted to this endeavor. The support for private enterprises from local officials may stem from their sense of responsibility and achievement in local economic development or from the desire to gain achievements and promotion opportunities.[6] Therefore, given limited time and resources, if the cost of providing the "special deals" treatment to each enterprise is roughly the same, local officials tend to prefer supporting enterprises with higher productivity, a larger scale, and better growth prospects.

Third, competition to attract investments is intense among local governments. This competition effectively limits the damage caused to other enterprises because of the protection given to certain companies. Under the "special deals" system, local governments can protect only their chosen enterprises from competition locally, and they cannot extend this protection to other regions. As a result, less efficient enterprises may continue to exist because of the protection they receive, but they are confined to specific local markets. Meanwhile, more efficient enterprises can survive and thrive in other regions. The competition among local governments also provides businesses with more choices, especially when they encounter officials who cannot address issues or engage in corrupt practices.

Under the combined influence of these three factors, the "special deals" system has emerged as a primary driving force behind China's economic growth over the past four decades. The following supporting evidence aligns with this finding.

Enterprises with higher productivity are more likely to receive assistance

Given limited time and resources, local governments are more inclined to grant "special treatment" to more productive (and larger-scale) companies. As such, the shifting significance of large

Table 1. Sales share of top 1% companies.

Industrial enterprises above designated size (%)		All industrial enterprises (%)	
1998	25.2	1995	31.6
2002	28.9	2004	37.5
2007	33.3	2008	45.1

Source: China Industrial Enterprises Database, Economic Census Data (1995, 2004, and 2008).

enterprises has been observed. Table 1 displays changes in the production share of industrial companies that are in the top 1% in terms of employment scale. The left column uses data from large-scale industrial enterprises, in which the sales share of the top 1% of companies increased from 25% to 33% between 1998 and 2007. The right column uses data from all industrial enterprises in the economic census. A similar rising trend shows that the sales share of the top 1% of companies increased from 32% to 45% between 1995 and 2008.

Correspondingly, relevant evidence can also be provided at the city level. Specifically, if a city has a high proportion of highly productive private enterprises, more companies will receive assistance from the local government under the "special deals" system. Consequently, this support results in faster economic growth for the city. Figure 2 shows a scatter plot of the average annual employment growth rate from 1998 to 2007 for each city (*Y*-axis, representing economic growth rate) and the initial employment share of private enterprises with more than 500 employees in 1998 (*X*-axis, representing the proportion of highly productive private enterprises). A clear positive correlation can be observed between the two. After controlling for the city's initial employment level, provincial fixed effects, and the distance to the nearest port, the estimated coefficient of the initial employment share of large private enterprises on the employment growth rate remains significantly positive.[7]

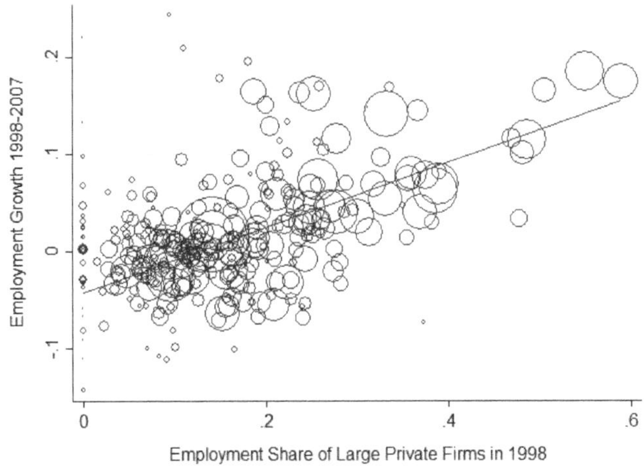

Figure 2. Employment growth and initial employment share of large private enterprises.

Source: China Industrial Enterprises Database.

Land supply

Local governments may also offer land to companies granted "special deals" at prices below market cost. Land sale data for 2000–2014 were obtained from the Ministry of Land and Resources.[8] Each transaction provides information on the plot area, geographic location, sales price, and land use (residential, commercial, or industrial).[9]

Table 2 illustrates the price disparity in land for different uses after controlling for a series of location factors. In the first column, which does not control for any location factors, the average price for industrial land is only 18% of that for residential land.[10] The second column shows a regression controlling for the fixed effects of the district where the land is located, which causes the price disparity to slightly decline. This suggests that districts with cheaper land allocate more land for industrial use, but within the same district, industrial land remains cheaper than residential land. The third column controls for the district's fixed effects and the distance from the plot to the district center, but this has almost no impact on

Table 2. Prices of commercial and industrial land relative to residential land.

	(1)	(2)	(3)	(4)
Commercial land	−0.37	−0.25	−0.24	−0.20
	(0.00)	(0.00)	(0.00)	(0.00)
Industrial land	−1.72	−1.51	−1.47	−1.46
	(0.00)	(0.00)	(0.00)	(0.00)
Control variables				
County fixed effects	No	Yes	Yes	No
Distance from county center	No	No	Yes	No
Community fixed effects	No	No	No	Yes

Note: The sample units are the parcels of land sold by local governments (land sale data between 2000 and 2014 from the Ministry of Land and Resources; sample size: 979,206). The figures in the table are the coefficients (and standard errors) from regressing the log value of the price per hectare on dummy variables for commercial and industrial land (relative to residential land). All regressions control for year fixed effects.

the price gap. Finally, the fourth column looks at the price gap at a narrower community level, comparing the prices of land with different uses within the same community.[11] The results show that the average price for industrial land is only about a quarter of that for residential land. The lower price for industrial land essentially acts as a subsidy for the users of such land.

Local protection and corporate export behavior

Under the "special deals" system, some less-efficient firms might survive and occupy a market in a certain region because of local government protection. More efficient firms can exist and develop only in other regions. Consequently, local protection disrupts the relationship between firm productivity and domestic sales — more efficient firms should hold a larger domestic market share. When considering a firm's exports in an open economy, note that local governments cannot extend similar protective actions to international markets. Therefore, these relatively efficient firms focus only on exports, resulting in their low domestic market sales ratios.

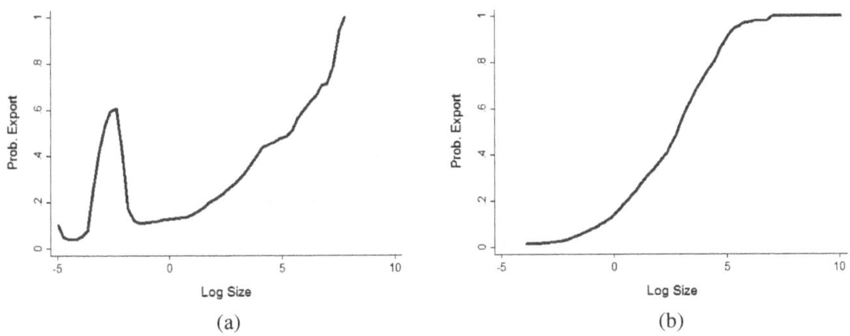

Figure 3. Proportion of export enterprises divided by scale: (a) China; and (b) the United States.

Figure 3(a) illustrates the relationship between the likelihood of manufacturing firms exporting and their domestic sales volume (in log values and average values subtracted) using data from industrial firms above a designated scale in 2007.[12] It is evident that a significant and predictive feature is that a group of firms with low domestic sales are simultaneously exporting to foreign markets. More than half of these firms have an export share exceeding 50%. For comparison, Figure 3(b) presents data from US manufacturing firms, which do not exhibit a similar feature.[13] The export ratio of US firms is monotonically positive with the scale of the firm, and the domestic sales ratios of exporting firms are not high, approximately around 20%.

How Does the "Special Deals" Approach Benefit a Large Number of Private Enterprises?

In the previous section, we examined why the informal system of "special deals" is effective in the Chinese context. Given the limited resources and time of local governments and officials, however, they can provide assistance to only a limited number of private enterprises. Thus, an unanswered question remains: How does this theory explain the massive growth of private enterprises in China?

The response to this question is whether or not the "special deals" mechanism outlined in section "Why Does 'Special Deals' Work in China?" are confined to interactions between local governments and selected private enterprises. It expands to additional enterprises through those that have already received such "special deals" from the local government. This hierarchical structure, illustrated in Figure 1 (a), enables the "special deals" system to benefit a wider range of private enterprises.

The equity network centered on state owners

The noted findings are inspired by observing a number of "special deals" examples. It has been observed, for example, that a private enterprise commonly employs certain strategies when attempting to enter a monopolized market. These strategies include seeking to establish a joint venture with local governments that control key resources or attempting to form joint ventures with large state-owned enterprises that possess production licenses or certain monopolistic powers. Similar stories frequently appear in finance articles or books that describe corporate history. Some private enterprises have established joint ventures with state-owned enterprises or units to gain listing quotas. More private enterprises have adopted similar strategies for more convenient financing.

These observations have sparked our thinking; that is, establishing joint ventures (creating equity connections) with state-owned sectors could be the preconditions or primary mode to facilitate such "special deals" arrangements. This approach provides us with a new perspective for studying the "special deals" system.

Firm registration data from the State Administration for Market Regulation allow us to investigate equity links more broadly between the private and state sectors. The data provide information on every registered enterprise in China, including those already deregistered, such as the establishment date, deregistration date, geographic location, industry, registered capital, direct shareholders, and contribution ratios.[14] The data also include information on all enterprises in the economy. Therefore, when a situation arises in which the shareholder of one enterprise is another enterprise — a common scenario in enterprise groups — it is possible to delve into this equity structure and identify shareholders at a higher level from this layer of shareholders. Thus, for each enterprise, this process can be followed until the ultimate shareholder is identified.[15]

The ultimate shareholders are classified into two categories: state owners and private owners. State owners can be governments at any level (central, provincial, city, or county), and different departments of the same local government are considered to be a single investor.[16] Large state-owned enterprises directly and wholly owned by a certain level of government are regarded as independent state owners, which reveals their influence comparable to that of local governments. Private owners, mostly natural persons, also include companies registered overseas and nonenterprise organizations registered domestically. With enterprise registration data from 2019, about 40,000 state investors and 63 million private investors were identified, owning 21% and 79% of the registered capital in the country, respectively. Unless specifically indicated otherwise, the findings in this report are based on firm registration data from 2019.

The subsequent phase delves into an investigation of equity links among ultimate owners. This method, to a certain degree, can be interpreted as examining the "special deals" system from the viewpoint of corporate conglomerates rather than individual entities.[17] Focusing on ultimate owners has two benefits. First, it eliminates interference from potentially complex equity structures within a single enterprise, many of which are likely unrelated to the "special deals" system under study. Second, this approach considers that resources can be relatively easily allocated among companies that belong to the same ultimate owner, thereby making it a more reasonable way to study the benefits that the "special deals" system brings to private enterprises.

The definition of equity connections among ultimate owners is described as follows: when two ultimate shareholders form a joint venture, an equity connection is deemed to exist. This joint venture can be established through either direct investment or indirect investment that spans several companies.[18] For instance, if a private owner's business group and a large local state-owned enterprise jointly establish a new company, an equity connection is established between the private owner and the state-owned enterprise.

Upon constructing the equity connections between ultimate owners, a clear hierarchical structure emerges, as shown in Figure 1(a). At the top of this hierarchy are state owners, notably the largest ones. Each state owner has equity connections with multiple private owners. The following evidence shows that these are the largest private owners and are referred to as private owners directly connected with state investors, with the distance d defined as 1. Next, although some private investors do not have equity connections with state owners, they do have equity connections with private owners at $d = 1$. Their distance d is defined as 2. Finally, private owners at $d \geq 3$ can be found, and along with private owners at $d = 2$, they are collectively referred to as private owners indirectly connected with state owners.

Distance from state owners and characteristics of private owners

Table 3 reveals a common equity connection among the largest owners. Among the top 100 owners, 63 are state owners, each of whom has at least one equity connection with a private owner. Of the remaining 37 private owners, 31 are directly connected to state owners and 3 are indirectly connected. As the number of investors decreases, the proportion of those with equity connections decreases

Table 3. Equity links of the largest owners.

	Owners ranked by size			
	Top 100	Top 1,000	Top 10,000	Top 100,000
State Owners	63	458	2,438	6,826
Has equity connections with private owners	63	452	2,305	5,243
Private owners	37	542	7,562	93,174
Directly connected	31	358	3,466	17,236
Indirectly connected	3	73	1,953	37,360

Note: The size of the owner is measured by the sum of the registered capital of all companies owned by the owner, weighted by the proportion of the owner's contribution in the respective companies.

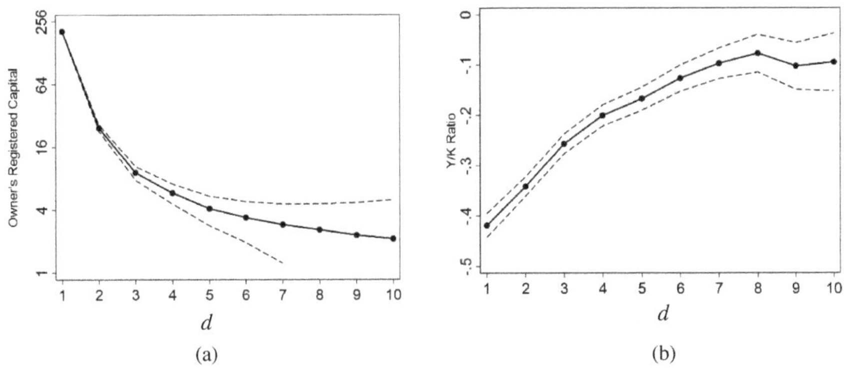

Figure 4. Distance to state owners and characteristics of private owners: (a) registered capital; and (b) capital productivity.

correspondingly. Among the top 100,000 investors, approximately 93,000 are private owners, with 17,000 directly connected to state owners and another 37,000 indirectly connected.

Observing the relationship between the distance *d* from state owners and several key characteristics of private investors, as illustrated in Figure 4, provides clearer insight into the hierarchical structure depicted in Figure 1(a).

Figure 4(a) demonstrates the relationship between the size of private owners (measured by their registered capital) and the distance *d*.[19] Evidently, the most substantial private owners (where $d=1$) maintain a direct connection with state investors. On average, their registered capital is approximately 200 times that of private owners who do not have direct or indirect equity connections with state owners. This aligns with the findings given in the previous section, which suggested that local governments are more willing to provide special arrangement to more productive (i.e., larger-scale) private enterprises. As the distance *d* from state owners increases, the average size of the private owners decreases correspondingly. It is evident, however, that private owners with direct or indirect equity connections with state owners, on average, are larger in size (greater than 1) than those without equity connections.

Figure 4(b) illustrates the relationship between the capital productivity of enterprises owned by private owners and the distance *d*.[20]

Private owners directly connected to state owners (d = 1) have a capital productivity in their enterprises that is on average around 40% lower than the industry median. These results suggest that these enterprises can secure financing at lower costs than median enterprises. As the distance d increases, the capital productivity of enterprises owned by the corresponding private owners gradually increases. However, all private owners, whether directly or indirectly connected to state owners, own enterprises with capital productivity below the industry median. The figure does not show that the capital productivity of enterprises owned by state owners is, on average, around 50% lower than the industry median.

Figure 4 conveys this information to us: the mechanism of "special deals" is not limited to local governments and private enterprises that receive special treatment (d = 1). Similar mechanisms exist widely among private enterprises that receive "special deals" treatment and other private enterprises connected to them through equity ($d \geq 2$). The former can pass some benefits of the "special deals" to the latter. In other words, through the hierarchical structure shown in Figure 1(a), the system of "special deals" benefits a wider range of private enterprises to varying degrees.

Figure 5 provides further evidence for this viewpoint from another angle. As mentioned in the previous section, due to time and resource constraints, each local government can offer "special

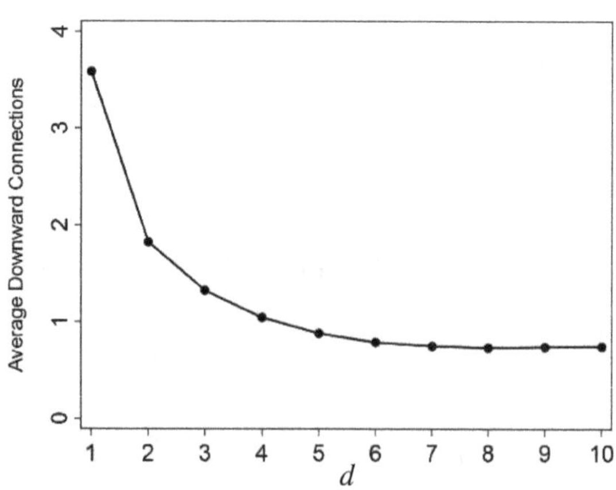

Figure 5. Average number of connections to the next layer.

deals" treatment to only a limited number of private enterprises. Based on 2019 data, each state owner with equity ties to at least one private owner is connected to an average of 15 private owners. The benefits of "special deals" may weaken as they trickle down the hierarchical structure illustrated in Figure 1(a). If we assume that the cost of implementing this mechanism stays roughly constant across all levels, then the anticipated outcome is a decrease in the average number of connections each owner provides to the next level. This outcome aligns with the results presented in Figure 5.

Another implication of the results shown in Figures 4 and 5 is that under the "special deals" system, the boundaries between state-owned and private enterprises are not clear-cut. The differences among private enterprises (such as between private owners with $d = 1$ and those with no equity connections) are far greater than those between certain private enterprises ($d = 1$) and state-owned enterprises. Future academic research and policy discussions need to delve deeper into this situation to avoid oversimplifying the binary division between state-owned and private economies.

Expansion of equity connection network

The previous sections noted that the "special deals" system can benefit a wider range of private enterprises through the hierarchical structure shown in Figure 1(a). An intriguing question arises regarding the development of this system in the past two decades. Utilizing the 2013 version of the firm registration data, an exploration was conducted tracing the equity connection between state and private owners in 2010 and 2000.[21] This investigation enabled a clear observation of the expansion of the equity connection network between state and private owners from 2000 to 2019. Such an observation contributed significantly to the understanding of the changes in the scope of enterprises benefiting from the "special deals" system.

Figure 6(a) shows a consistent increase in the proportion of state owners with equity links to private owners, rising from about 12% in 2000 to 25% in 2019. At the same time, the average number of connections per state owner to private owners also continued to increase, as shown in Figure 6(b), from less than 6 in 2000 to

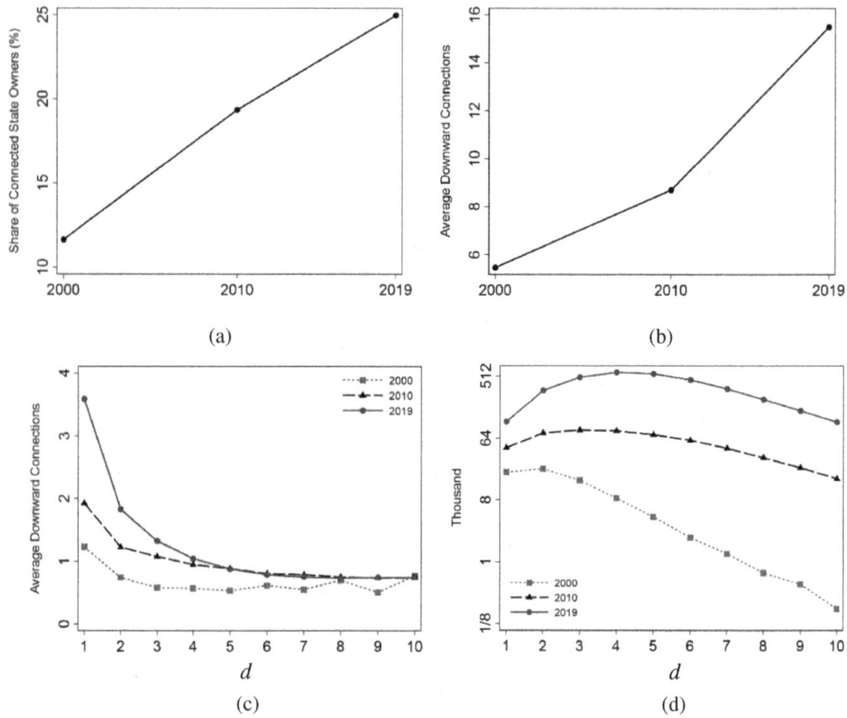

Figure 6. Expansion of the equity connection network. (a) Proportion of state owners with equity links to private owners; (b) Average number of connections per state owner to private owners; (c) Number of private owners directly connected with state owners; and (d) Number of private owners indirectly connected with state owners.

approximately 15 private owners in 2019.[22] These two factors have led to an increase in the number of private owners that have direct equity connections with state owners. As depicted on the horizontal axis $d = 1$ of Figure 6(d), there has been approximately a 5.5-fold increase from 2000 to 2019.

As shown in Figure 6(c), each private owner ($d = 1$) directly linked to state owners has equity links with a larger number of smaller-scale private owners ($d = 2$). This further helps a greater number of private owners to connect indirectly with state owners. From 2000 to 2019, the number of private owners indirectly connected with state owners has increased nearly 60 times, as shown in Figure 6(d).

Table 4. Proportion of registered capital of connected owners, 2000–2019.

	State owners with equity connections to private owners (%)	Private owners		
		All (%)	Directly connected (%)	Indirectly connected (%)
2000	33.0	64.2	10.3	5.6
2010	28.0	70.6	13.6	11.3
2019	20.8	78.6	16.7	18.7

Note: The size of the owner is measured by the sum of the registered capital of all companies owned by the owner, weighted by the proportion of the owner's contribution in the respective companies.

Table 4 presents a summary of the changes in the proportion of registered capital from private owners who are directly and indirectly connected with state owners from 2000 to 2019. In 2000, the registered capital of directly connected private owners made up 10.3% of the entire economy, and this proportion increased to 16.7% in 2019. In 2000, the registered capital of indirectly connected private owners represented 5.6% of the total economy, and this percentage rose to 18.7% in 2019. The growth of private owners, whether directly or indirectly connected with state owners, acts as a primary driving force for the expansion of the private economy. By 2019, the registered capital of private enterprises that benefited from the "special deals" system made up 35% of the entire economy and 45% of the entire private economy. Although the state-owned sector has seen growth during this period, its share within the overall economy has been on a continual decline.

A model was established to better understand the impact of the expansion of the equity connection network from 2000 to 2019 on economic growth. In this model, private investors can choose the distance d from state owners. The benefits they receive (such as improvements in productivity) γ_d, the costs paid for equity connections, and the number of connections that can be provided to the subsequent tier of private owners are all determined by d. Data from 2000, 2010, and 2019 were used to conduct a structural estimation of this model. The results indicate that the rise in γ_d was a determining factor in the expansion of the equity connection network during this period.

Furthermore, a series of counterfactual analyses were carried out. These analyses hypothesize that all other parameters remain the same during a certain period, with only γ_d varying, to observe the impact of an increase in γ_d on economic growth. The first row of Table 5 shows the growth rate of the GDP of the private economy in actual data, and the second row shows the impact of the expansion of equity connection networks brought about by the increase in γ_d (for all d) on total output. From 2000 to 2019, the expansion of the equity connection networks drove an average annual increase of 4.2% in the total output of the private economy, which accounted for almost half of the current growth rate of the private economy's GDP. The contributions of the network expansion were 3.4% and 5.1% for the periods 2000–2010 and 2010–2019, respectively.

In the third and fourth rows of Table 5, we decompose this impact into the influence on total output from the increase in benefits

Table 5. The impact of equity connection network expansion on economic growth, 2000–2019.

	2000–2019 (%)	2000–2010 (%)	2010–2019 (%)
Annual growth rate of private economy GDP (actual data, %)	10.2	11.6	8.6
Annual growth rate of total output (model, %):			
$\Delta\gamma_d$, $d \geq 1$	4.2	3.4	5.1
$\Delta\gamma_d$, $d = 1$	2.4	2.4	2.3
$\Delta\gamma_d$, $d \geq 2$	1.9	1.1	2.8
Annual growth rate of total output (model, %)			
Directly connected private owners	2.5	2.4	2.5
Indirectly connected private owners	2.4	1.5	3.4

Note: The average annual growth rate of the private economy GDP in the actual data is derived from the 2019 "China Statistical Yearbook" and the 2019 "Statistical Bulletin on National Economic and Social Development." This rate also considers our calculations of the proportion of the private economy for the respective year.

directly connected to state owners (γ_1) and the increase in benefits indirectly connected (γ_d, $d \geq 2$). The contribution of the increase in γ_1 to the growth of total output accounted for two-thirds in 2000–2010 and almost half in 2010–2019. During this period, the increase in γ_1 was smaller than other γ_d's. The reason for such a large contribution is that the increase in γ_1 increased the number of private owners directly connected with state owners, which in turn increased the number of indirectly connected private owners ($d \geq 2$), which we call the "multiplier effect" of the equity connection network. The last two rows of Table 5 decompose the growth of total output into the growth of output from private owners who are directly and indirectly connected. From 2000 to 2019, both directly and indirectly connected private owners accounted for approximately 50% each of the total output of growth. After 2010, however, the growth of output from indirectly connected private owners made a larger contribution.

In this section, we present evidence from the perspectives of equity connections between state and private owners, as well as those between private investors. The results not only show that the "special deals" mechanism exists between local governments and private enterprises directly obtaining the special treatment but also that enterprises receiving assistance can distribute some of these benefits to a broader scope of private enterprises through equity connections. Consequently, the range of private enterprises benefiting from the "special deals" system has substantially broadened, although the benefits received by private enterprises within this scope do vary. Evidence indicates a significant expansion in the range of enterprises benefiting from the "special deals" system through equity connections from 2000 to 2019. According to our model, the increased benefits from establishing equity connections are the driving force behind this phenomenon. The counterfactual analysis results reveal that from 2000 to 2019, the expansion of the range of enterprises that benefit from the "special deals" system propelled an average annual growth of 4.2% in the private economy. This represents approximately half of the growth of the private economy during this period.

Risks and Challenges

In this chapter, we presented a novel point of view that the exceptional economic growth and rapid development of the private economy in China since the early 1990s have been driven primarily by an informal system referred to as "special deals." A principal feature of this system is its operation within a context in which formal institutions are still under development. Local governments facilitate certain private enterprises to circumvent some of the restrictive rules imposed by formal institutions. This supportive role played by local governments allows these enterprises to establish themselves, endure challenges, and eventually thrive.

The study progresses by examining two primary questions. First, considering the powerful administrative capacity of the Chinese government, the potent incentives prompting officials to back this system, and the competition among various local governments that mitigates potential negative outcomes, it is apparent that the "special deals" system in China yields benefits that outstrip any losses incurred by a few enterprises. As a result, this system significantly contributes to propelling the overall economic growth in China. In other countries where formal institutions are imperfect, however, similar institutional arrangements may not be effective.

Second, enterprises that directly benefit from government assistance can transmit part of the benefits of "special deals" to a broader spectrum of private enterprises through the equity connection network. This transmission mechanism allows a more diverse array of businesses to enjoy varying degrees of benefits from the "special deals" system.

This does not imply, however, that the "special deals" system's role in promoting China's economic growth is sustainable. The formation of well-developed formal institutions is a very difficult and time-consuming process, and the "special deals" system is a "second-best" solution to perfect formal institutions. As highlighted in this chapter, the "special deals" system has indeed proven to stimulate economic growth under certain conditions. As China's economy develops and various circumstances evolve, however, the assortment of issues accompanying this system have grown increasingly prominent in recent years.

For instance, before 2008, the help that local governments offered to businesses primarily consisted of reducing institutional costs, which promoted economic growth. However, beginning in 2009, local governments received large amounts of funds through local financing vehicles. As a result, these local governments could directly provide additional resources to businesses receiving the "special deals." According to Bai *et al.* (2016), this approach might lead to a significant distortion in the allocation of economic resources and subsequently inhibit growth.

In addition, noticing the potential benefits under the "special deals" system, some businesses transfer a portion of their shares to local state-owned enterprises. They then obtain substantial loans in the name of the state-owned subsidiary and illicitly transfer funds to their associated companies.[23] Even more alarmingly, some leverage their affiliation with peripheral business units or equity connections with state-owned enterprises to masquerade their private firms as state-owned entities. This guise is used to provide guarantees for private equity fund products issued by affiliated enterprises. Recent instances of these funds falling overdue have been observed.[24] These practices led to significant losses for the relevant state-owned enterprises and investors and could introduce substantial risks to China's still-developing financial market.

Third, the "special deals" system can potentially create tension between China and its trade partners. When foreign businesses investing in China are not eligible for the "special deals," they are likely to find themselves at a competitive disadvantage against Chinese firms receiving similar benefits. Their intellectual property rights and contracts may lack sufficient protection within the existing formal structures.

Probably recognizing the drawbacks of the "special deals" system, the Chinese government has taken significant steps in recent years toward creating a more balanced, transparent, and inclusive formal economic system. In November 2013, during the Third Plenary Session of the 18th Central Committee of the Communist

Party of China, a significant resolution called the "Decision on Some Major Issues Concerning Comprehensively Deepening Reform" was ratified. This resolution promoted the idea of "allowing the market to decisively direct resource distribution." It emphasized the importance of "ensuring equal legal usage of resources for all economic sectors, irrespective of ownership type, and their fair participation in market competition." The resolution also "advocated a strong stand against illegal favoritism, local protectionism, monopolies, and unfair competition." As a result of these and other initiatives, since 2016, China's overall ease of doing business ranking has seen a steady rise. The 2020 "Ease of Doing Business Report" ranks China overall at 31st place, with a specific rank of 27th for "starting a business."

In the context of the long-established "special deals" system, achieving these ambitious goals is a daunting and intricate task that comes with many challenges. For instance, tax incentives — a common component of the "special deals" approach employed by local governments — is one such area. A document published by the State Council in November 2014 discussed the advantages and disadvantages of tax incentive policies, echoing the same complexity identified in this chapter's analysis of the "special deals" system. The document underscored that "in certain regions and departments, preferential policies have been introduced relating to tax, non-tax income, and fiscal expenditures for specific companies and their investors (or administrators). These measures have, to an extent, promoted the growth of investment and industrial concentration." However, "it also acknowledged that some of these tax incentives have disrupted the market order, ... and might even contradict our commitments to external entities, potentially triggering international trade disputes." As such, it recommended "an extensive review and cleanup of all local and departmental tax incentive policies, especially those linked to contracts, agreements, memos, and case-by-case requests, reports, and approvals. ... It also emphasized that all preferential policies that violate national laws and regulations should be discontinued immediately."[25] However, in a surprising twist, the State Council issued another document in May 2015, putting a hold on this rigorous cleanup process. The document suggested that "prevailing preferential policies should continue to be implemented as per their given timelines; those without an outlined duration and needing adjustments ... should be upheld through a transitional phase."[26] As of the completion of this study, no further policy announcements have been made about the recommencement of this cleanup initiative.

Several factors may account for the difficulties in implementing measures to eliminate tax incentives. First, the "special deals" system has been in place for almost 30 years, creating deeply ingrained benefits. An abrupt discontinuation could harm those who have profited from this system, including local governments, officials, and enterprises, leading to potential obstacles. Second, ending this system before a formal economic system is fully developed could negatively affect short-term economic growth, creating additional resistance to reform. Third, on a practical level, some arrangements under the special treatment system are already formalized through contracts between local governments and businesses. Immediate termination could involve credibility and legal issues for the government. Thus, transforming the "special deals" system and genuinely establishing an equitable, transparent, and universal formal economic system remains a monumental task.

Endnotes

1. Hallward-Driemeier and Pritchett (2015) document the widespread use of similar informal system arrangements in countries with weaker formal systems.
2. A large body of literature, such as the works of Li and Zhou (2005) and Jia *et al.* (2015), provides empirical evidence showing a significant association between the promotion of local officials in China and regional economic growth.
3. Related discussions are also available in existing research. Xu (2011) posits that economic decentralization empowers local governments by giving them significant motivation to stimulate the growth of private enterprises. Concurrently, a cadre system with relative centralization proves advantageous as it fosters local competition and mitigates potential issues arising from such decentralization. Yao Yang (2018) believes that the neutral central government, local decentralization,

and the meritocratic official selection system are the politicoeconomic reasons for China's economic achievements. Zhou Li'an's "promotion tournament model" and the "bureaucracy + market" theory developed on this basis (Zhou Li'an, 2018) describe the interaction model between local officials and enterprises in their jurisdiction. Nie Huihua (2020) explains China's rapid economic growth and the simultaneous occurrence of various problems (such as mine disasters and environmental pollution) from the perspective of government–business relations (collusion or cooperation). Similar to these studies, the significant role of local governments in stimulating economic growth has been emphasized. The uniqueness of this paper lies in the observation and emphasis that the support extended by local governments to private enterprises typically takes the form of "special arrangements for special cases." This approach can provide benefits to certain enterprises while potentially causing losses for others. This observation underscores China's unique stage of development and institutional context over the past three decades. It suggests that the benefits derived from such "special treatment for special cases" probably outweigh their associated drawbacks, thereby catalyzing swift, comprehensive economic growth.

4. The definition of "owner" is explained in section "How Does the 'Special Deals' Approach Benefit a Large Number of Private Enterprises?"
5. These industries include, for example, the aluminum and automotive industries.
6. Of course, in some cases of corruption, local officials gain economic benefits.
7. The coefficient estimate is 0.196, and the standard error is 0.029.
8. The specific transaction information for each plot of land totals 979,206 records.
9. Approximately 50–60% of the new land is used for industrial purposes.
10. The natural constant e to the power of -1.72 is approximately 0.18.
11. A community is defined as a 9 km^2 block.
12. Export-processing enterprises have been excluded from the sample for this analysis. The same characteristics can be observed in data from other years as well.
13. The data come from the 1987 U.S. Manufacturing Census.
14. The data used for this analysis do not include individual businesses (*Ge Ti Hu*).

15. Some companies might have complex ownership structures, requiring the tracing of more than 20 layers of shareholders to identify their ultimate owners.
16. For example, the Shandong Provincial Department of Finance and the Shandong State-Owned Assets Supervision and Administration Commission are regarded as the same state owner, i.e., the Shandong Provincial Government. However, the Shandong Provincial Government and the Jinan Municipal Government are still two different state-owned investors.
17. The remaining discrepancy is that one corporate group might correspond to multiple ultimate owners. Future research could consider how to identify and consolidate ultimate owners belonging to the same corporate group.
18. The study further requires that the two ultimate shareholders each hold more than 10% of the shares in the joint venture company.
19. The average registered capital of private owners who are unconnected with state owners serves as a reference point and is normalized to one.
20. Capital productivity is calculated using the ratio of a firm's sales to its net fixed assets, which is then divided by the median of the four-digit industry and subsequently log-transformed. As the firm registration data do not provide information on sales or fixed assets, we used the 2013 China Industrial Enterprise data, which were then matched with the 2013 version of the firm registration data to obtain the results shown in Figure 4(b).
21. This tracing exercise assumes that a firm's direct shareholders remain constant over time. In real-world scenarios, however, changes in direct shareholders are possible. The firm registration data reflect the status of direct shareholders at specific time points, such as at the end of 2013 or the end of 2019. As a result, a series of robustness tests were carried out. The findings from these tests largely affirm the conclusions outlined in this study.
22. The number of state owners did not change significantly from 2000 to 2019, with about 35,000, 32,000, and 41,000 state owners identified in 2000, 2010, and 2019, respectively.
23. See the article Caixin Weekly (2019).
24. See the article Caixin Weekly (2020).
25. See the Guo Fa [2014] No. 62.
26. See the Guo Fa [2015] No. 25.

References

Bai, C.-E., Hsieh, C.-T., and Song, Z.M. 2016. The long shadow of China's fiscal expansion. *Brookings Papers on Economic Activity*, 47(2): 129–181.

Bai, C.-E., Hsieh, C.-T., and Song, Z.M. 2020a. Special deals with Chinese characteristics. *NBER Macroeconomics Annual*, 34(1): 341–379.

Bai, C.-E., Hsieh, C.-T., Song, Z.M., and Wang, X. 2020b. Special deals from special investors: The rise of state-connected private owners in China. NBER Working Paper w28170.

Caixin Weekly. 2019. Shaanxi JinKong proxy-held private enterprises to collect management fees, scammers ran away with the money. August 9, 2019. http://weekly.caixin.com/2019-08-09/101449156.html?p0#page2.

Caixin Weekly. 2020. China railway's fake state capital raised 4 billion yuan involved in illegal fundraising, 10 people were arrested. June 19, 2020. http://finance.caixin.com/2020-06-19/101570036.html?utm_source=.

Guo Fa. 2014. No. 62. Notice of the state council on cleaning up and regulating preferential policies on taxes and other items. November 27, 2014.

Guo Fa. 2015. No. 25. Notice of the state council on relevant matters concerning preferential policies on taxes and other items. May 10, 2015.

Hallward-Driemeier, M. and Pritchett, L. 2015. How business is done in the developing world: Deals versus rules. *Journal of Economic Perspective*, 29(3): 121–140.

Jia, R., Kudamatsu, M., and Seim, D. 2015. Political selection in China: The complementary roles of connections and performance. *Journal of the European Economic Association*, 13(4): 631–668.

Li, H. and Zhou, L.-A. 2005. Political turnover and economic performance: The incentive role of personnel control in China. *Journal of Public Economics*, 89(9–10): 1743–1762.

Nie, H. 2020. From political-business collusion to political-business cooperation: A preliminary dynamic analysis framework of political-business relations. *Academic Monthly*, (6): 1–14.

Xu, C. 2011. The fundamental institutions of China's reforms and development. *Journal of Economic Literature*, 49(4): 1076–1151.

Yao, Y. 2018. The political economy reasons for China's economic success. *Economic and Management Research*, (39): 3–12.

Zhou, L.-A. 2018. "Bureaucracy + Market" and the Chinese growth story. *Society*, (2): 1–45.

https://doi.org/10.1142/9789819815241_0005

Chapter 5

CHINA'S ECONOMIC TRANSFORMATION UNDER THREE-SECTOR DUALISM*

Fung Kwan

Department of Economics and Asia-Pacific Academy of Economics and Management, University of Macau, Taipa, Macao
fungkwan@um.edu.mo

Introduction

China's economic growth has been extraordinary, with an annual per capita output growth of 8.2% between 1978 and 2020.[1] While there exist several paradigms enlightening its structural change,[2] this chapter intends to offer an alternative proposition of China's structural transformation during this period by applying and extending conventional dualism. More fundamentally, such change reflects the resource reallocation that promotes output growth and improves living standards.

*Special thanks to Annie Wei, Yanrui Wu, Yang Zhang, and Shuaihe Zhuo for co-authorship of previous papers; and Min Yang, Lu Zhang, and Fei Zhao for their excellent research assistance. The usual disclaimers apply.

The analytical logic begins with the ample exogenous unskilled workers, characterized by their extremely low productivity. They could migrate to activities other than their original low value-added production without a significant increase in cost. This process continues until it reaches the so-called turning point. Thus, examination of this point is essential for us to judge whether the course of structural change might end. Even more importantly, understanding whether such a reallocation process could benefit productivity growth in different sectors is crucial to many developing nations, including China.

We first apply the Lewis–Fei–Ranis dual economy framework to examine the labor reallocation in China by measuring the size of surplus agricultural labor and comparing the marginal product of labor and wages in agriculture. Then, such reallocation impacts on productivity growth, based on Temple and Wößmann (2006), are assessed.

Our results reveal that the huge labor reallocation from primary production to other non-agricultural activities in both rural and urban areas significantly contributed to the economic transformation during the 1980s and 2010s. China might have moved into another growth pattern toward the end of the 2010s. Our findings provide important policy implications for the growth of highly populated developing economies through industrialization.

We contribute to the literature by focusing on understanding China's structural change in various dimensions. First, our alternative measure of surplus labor in agriculture by examining technical inefficiency is methodologically more precise to quantify the workload distribution in rural China. Second, the extension of two-sector dualism is theoretically more applicable to the reality of China's labor market by examining the meticulous resource flows among sectors. Third, we prove rural industrialization in highly populated developing economies is an alternative policy for promoting productivity growth. Fourth, the choice of system GMM is considered an econometrically better approach to identifying causality in our empirical growth regression, initially proposed by Mankiw *et al.* (1992).

The reminder of this chapter is organized as follows. We first discuss the dualistic economic framework. Then, the size of surplus labor is estimated before we examine the turning point. After introducing our three-sector model for labor reallocation, we explore China's experience compared to other developing nations. We finally conclude our analysis.

The Lewis–Fei–Ranis Dualism

The Lewis–Fei–Ranis framework is largely a combined version of Lewis (1954) and Ranis and Fei (1961).[3] In brief, a developing economy could roughly consist of two parts: a traditional segment[4] with a sizeable labor surplus whose marginal productivity is very low for subsistence consumption, and a modern segment[5] with capital accumulation for profit maximization. By assuming that all profits are reinvested, firms will demand labor from the traditional segment to meet their expanded production. This labor absorption process ends with all surplus labor exhausted. Then, the competition of labor and capital between the two segments leads to the convergence from a dual-economy structure to a conventional neoclassical economy. The Lewis turning point is then the key assessment criterion of such transformation for most development economists.

More precisely, this point is the second turning point in the Lewis–Fei–Ranis framework, named "full commercialization," signifying the rough equalization of wages and marginal productivity of labor in the traditional segment.[6] To measure this turning point in China's case empirically,[7] we estimate the volume of surplus labor in agriculture and apply the criterion of comparing agricultural wages with the marginal product of labor proposed by Minami (1968).[8]

Surplus Agricultural Labor

The notions of "surplus labor," "inefficient labor," and "redundant labor" have frequently been used interchangeably. A precise estimate of the scope of surplus labor in rural China is empirically difficult for a number of reasons. First and foremost, the quantitative approach to derive such a surplus varies across practitioners. Kwan (2009) summarized major economic and non-economic techniques of measuring China's surplus labor and found that the estimated figures could be very different, from 75 million to 135 million between 1980 and 2005 at the national level. The second reason is mainly conceptual, referring to whether the surplus labor consists of those in the rural area (with both agricultural and non-agricultural activities) or those in agricultural production (with farming and non-farming) only. Empirically, the major source of surplus is from cultivation, as labor's marginal productivity of this activity is very low. The third reason is the limitation of data. China's National Bureau of Statistics (NBS) presents labor statistics based on the household registration unit *hukou*, which could overreport the number, as quite many of them are not fully engaged in agricultural production. Without precise particulars of peasants' production activities, surplus labor estimation could be misleading. An alternative measure of agricultural labor based on the information on cost and revenue for different products is presented in Appendix 1.

We apply the production efficiency approach to estimate the theoretical labor requirement for different agricultural products with a given level of technology and output and subtract it from our alternatively estimated agricultural labor to acquire the surplus labor in the Chinese rural area. Since our estimated input frontier could be viewed as the best hypothetical labor required for producing output under the pre-conditioned technology, this criterion satisfies the condition of the turning point, where wages are equal to the marginal product of labor in the subsistence sector. In fact, the difference between the estimated labor requirement and our alternatively estimated agricultural labor is regarded as a surplus, with labor's marginal productivity between zero and the equilibrium wage. In other words, the amount of surplus labor in our measure is able to capture all those with marginal products below wages.

Theoretically, labor is considered part of the factor input in producing different outputs. The conventional production function implicitly imposes a neoclassical assumption of any single decision-making unit (DMU) operating at a technically efficient level. Experiences from many developing economies show that agricultural production is possibly working below full capacity. To include potential inefficiency, which is unobservable and either varying or invariant over time but could be estimated empirically, an additional parameter to capture technical inefficiency is integrated into the production function. Intuitively, deviations from a production frontier may be regarded as under-produced output due to inefficient factor-input utilization. This output-oriented measure of technical efficiency could be otherwise translated into an input-oriented measure by asking how much input quantity could be reduced without changing the output quantity. Particularly, under the production technology facing constant returns to scale, both input- and output-oriented frontier analyses are expected to yield the same results.[9]

Our labor-use model originates from Diewert (1974), Aigner *et al.* (1977), and, more recently, Kumbhakar and Hjalmarsson (1995).[10] This chapter is largely based on the modification of the stochastic frontier model developed by Battese and Coelli (1995) with the following Cobb-Douglas specifications:

$$L = f(Y)\, e^{v+u} \tag{1}$$

where f (.) is a labor requirement function, Y is the agricultural output, v is the standard white noise to capture factors such as weather and other uncontrollable elements, and u is the non-negative random term associated with the technical inefficiency. L here is the minimum requirement for producing different agricultural products.

If labor is fully efficient during production, i.e., the technical inefficiency u is zero, then the labor requirement function L^* is written as

$$L^* = f(Y)\, e^{v} \tag{2}$$

where L^* denotes the optimal level of labor in producing Y. Inefficient labor, or surplus labor, L^s, is defined as the difference between observed labor input and optimal labor input:

$$L^s = L - L^* \tag{3}$$

The empirical estimate of the optimal labor input L^* is presented in Appendix 2. Using equation (3), the annual size of surplus labor for each product of farm and animal husbandry is calculated. The sum of all individual surplus labor is the national total surplus labor. We divide the calculated surplus labor by our estimated agricultural labor to obtain the labor surplus ratio across years, with the assumption that there is negligible surplus labor in fishing and forestry.

Our estimated size of national surplus agricultural labor and its ratio are reported in Table 1. The average surplus is 29.7 million laborers for the sample period, with around 40 million in 2001 and around 26 million in 2013. The inefficient labor from farming was 72% of the total surplus. The share stood at 82% in 2001 but dropped to 58% in 2005. However, the ratio went up again to the highest in 2013, being 84% of the total. Although our estimated inefficiency scores are similar to many others, such as those reported by Kwan *et al.* (2013) and Guo (2007), the absolute size of surplus labor is smaller during our sample period, with our

Table 1. Estimated national surplus agricultural labor in China, 2001–2013.

	Animal husbandry	Farming	Total surplus	Estimated labor	Surplus ratio
2001	725.5	3,309.5	4,035.0	22,741.5	17.7
2002	747.7	3,014.9	3,762.6	22,204.5	16.9
2003	799.9	2,540.8	3,340.8	22,619.9	14.8
2004	1,172.8	2,198.1	3,370.9	22,730.6	14.8
2005	1,259.3	1,760.5	3,019.8	23,455.6	12.9
2006	1,130.1	1,775.0	2,905.2	22,494.0	12.9
2007	985.6	1,608.4	2,593.9	21,371.5	12.1
2008	847.5	1,767.8	2,615.3	22,148.8	11.8
2009	779.8	1,729.4	2,509.2	19,936.8	12.6
2010	614.0	1,827.9	2,441.8	19,630.7	12.4
2011	601.5	2,082.8	2,684.3	18,722.6	14.3
2012	596.9	2,156.0	2,752.8	18,509.2	14.9
2013	399.0	2,183.3	2,582.3	18,486.0	14.0
Average	820.0	2,150.3	2,970.3	21,157.8	14.0

Note: In 10,000 persons except the "surplus ratio" in %.

alternatively-derived observed agricultural labor being smaller than the NBS figures.

China's Turning Point

The turning point in China is assessed by the trends of surplus labor in agriculture and the empirical comparison between agricultural wages and corresponding labor productivity. Regarding the size of the labor surplus in agriculture, the above estimates indicate that it has been declining steadily at the national level. This is consistent with the criterion of moving toward the turning point.

We now examine the relationship between agricultural real wages (*LW* and *HW*) and the marginal product of labor (MPL), a criterion set forth by Minami (1968). Appendices 3 and 4 detail our calculation of wages and marginal productivity, respectively, using the available official statistics. We consider that the economy has taken off or has at least entered a window period of the turning point when agricultural MPLs rise above *LW*. If agricultural MPLs exceed *HW*, then we regard the economy as having passed (the window period of) the turning point, and the economy is on a self-sustained growth path. Our analysis starts at the national level and proceeds to the four macroeconomic regions, along with their included provinces.

As shown in Figure 1, at the national level, agricultural MPL was around RMB 1,700 in China in 1996. It started rising in the late 1990s, when surplus labor began to migrate from agriculture to the modern sector. Agricultural MPL exceeded *LW* at RMB 1,850 in 2002 and then fluctuated around *HW* between 2004 and 2009. By the end of the period under investigation, agricultural MPL had converged to the same level as *HW* at RMB 2,950. It seems to indicate that China has passed the turning point. However, this interpretation is proven to be an illusion, as revealed by the following regional analysis.

China's eastern region has long benefited from its proximity to sea-based trade and various preferential government policies. Its urbanization and industrialization are well above the national average. Apart from Hainan, the MPLs surpassed the lower-bound agricultural wages in other eastern provinces. Those in Shandong,

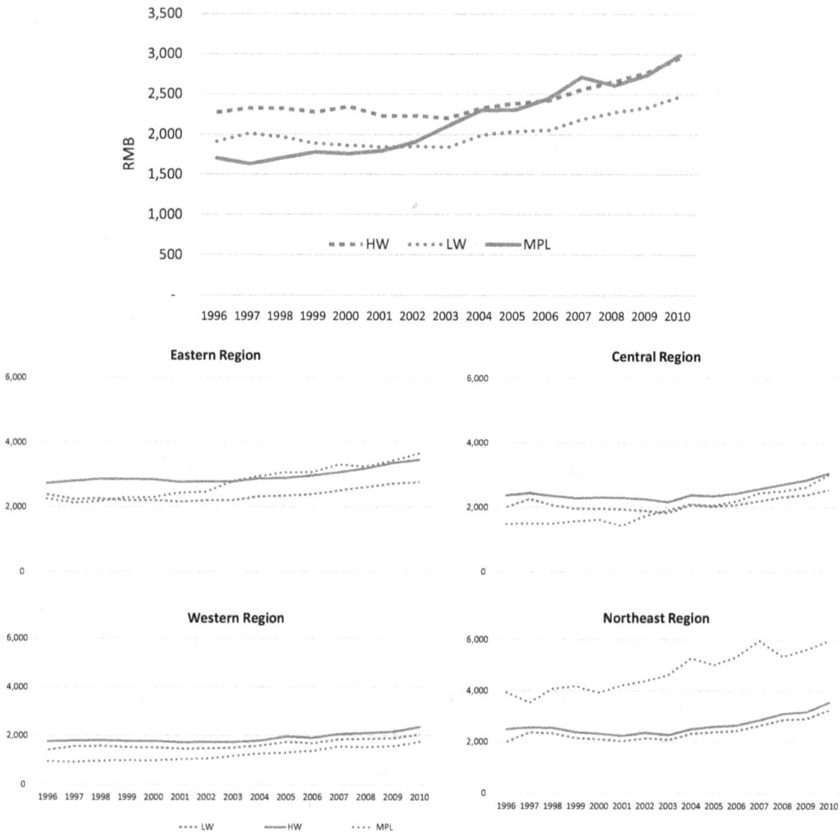

Figure 1. Agricultural wages versus MPLs in China, national & regional levels, 1996–2010.

Source: Authors' Calculations.

Guangdong, and Hebei were even higher than the upper bound. Correspondingly, the eastern region has passed the turning point. In the central region, only Hunan's agricultural labor productivity surpassed HW in 2003, while Henan and Hubei exceeded LW in 2002. Being an important food grain producer, Anhui is a mysterious case, with its marginal labor productivity well below both the HW and LW during our sample period, though it is next to Zhejiang and Jiangsu. Overall, this region is marginally entering the lower bound of the turning point. Being the poorest region, our results show that none of the six provinces in western China has passed the turning point, indicating that this region is still at the stage of having an unlimited supply of labor. In northeastern China, agricultural labor productivity is not only considerably higher than in any other region but also remains above both wage rates, even before the start of the period under investigation. Historically, labor outmigration has been phenomenal. This region may have passed the turning point. Table 2 presents the provincial comparison between labor productivity and wages.

The issue of the timeframe for China to approach the turning point suggested by the Lewis–Fei–Ranis model remains controversial in the current literature. This turning point with the equalization of the marginal product of labor and wages for subsistence activities

Table 2. Agricultural marginal products of labor (MPLs) versus wages in China's macroeconomic regions and provinces, 1996–2010.

Regions	Provinces	By which year MPL > *LW*	By which year MPL > *HW*
Eastern	Shandong	1998	1999
	Guangdong	1997	2002
	Hainan	No	No
	Hebei	2003	2006
	Jiangsu	2003–2010, fluctuating	No
	Zhejiang	2002–2010, fluctuating	No
Central	Jiangxi	No	No
	Henan	2002	No
	Hubei	Close to 2010	No
	Hunan	2002	2003
	Anhui	No	No
Western	Sichuan	2007–2010, fluctuating	No
	Guizhou	No	No
	Yunnan	No	No
	Shaanxi	2010	No
	Guangxi	No	No
	Gansu	No	No
Northeast	Jilin	Before 1996	Before 1996
	Liaoning	Before 1996	Before 1996

Note: Provincial figures on the trends of MPLs and real wages can be provided on request.

signifies the transition from traditional dualism into the standard neoclassical development path in such a hugely populated economy. This could also produce substantial macroeconomic impacts on China's continuing economic transformation (Garnaut, 2010; Song and Zhang, 2010). Broadly, the changes in wages and the labor's productivity in the traditional sector are at the core of the debate.

According to Lewis (1954), earnings are for survival purposes in the traditional sector. If family-run agriculture dominates the traditional sector, output is mostly shared among the household members for subsistence consumption, and wages are, thus, equal to the labor's average product (rather than marginal productivity). A continuous increase in wages might suggest a departure from production for subsistence purposes and thus movement toward the turning point. Against this criterion, many attempted to examine whether a persistent and considerable increase in wages in rural China was observed. Cai and Du (2011), Golley and Meng (2011), and Zhang *et al.* (2011) are examples to support this claim, and their results indicate that a successive increase in urban wages and migrant wages was confirmed in the 2010s. Although these non-agricultural wage increases might be indirectly related to the corresponding rise in agricultural wages, factors such as labor demand and supply conditions in manufacturing production and the differences between skilled and nonskilled labor could possibly alternate the non-agricultural wages in China. More importantly, the gradual implementation of minimum wage policy has imposed an important burden on urban wages: the nominal minimum wage has increased from RMB 299 in 2000 to RMB 848 in 2010 (Kwan *et al.*, 2013).

The presence of an extremely low marginal labor productivity reflects the major characteristics of the traditional sector in the Lewis model. The marginal productivity being zero, negligible, or well below the subsistence wage is largely due to the oversupply of labor relative to land and other fixed capital in the traditional sector. A demographic transition could eventually change the supply of labor and thus its marginal productivity. Cai (2010) and Li *et al.* (2013) examined the overall demographic trends and concluded that China has reached the turning point. However, the reduction in population in the traditional sector could push labor productivity to increase, but it does not necessarily reach the subsistence wage. Minami (1968) tested the relationship between labor's marginal productivity and wages in the subsistence sector to approximate the arrival of the turning point. Accordingly, studies including those by Erolani and Wei (2011), Islam and Yokota (2008), and Minami and Ma (2011) attempted to find out whether or not China's real wages in agriculture are determined by labor's marginal productivity. Their empirical findings cannot confirm the turning point time period in China yet.

All existing studies provide some evidence to support or argue against China reaching its turning point. While many studies focused on wages and labor productivity, we provide an alternative scenario of the current debate by measuring the size of inefficient labor in the traditional agricultural sector for the period 2001–2013, a time when heavy attention is drawn to the onset of China's turning point.

Here is our argument. If China has already reached the turning point in Lewis' sense, its surplus labor in subsistence production is expected to decline and become unimportant.

It is believed that marginal productivity of labor and subsistence wages are well-incorporated into the concept of surplus labor. If the measured extent of surplus is still relatively large compared to the labor supply in the traditional sector, its marginal product has to be very low and still far below subsistence wages. Correspondingly, the economy is in the first stage of transition in the Lewi–Fei–Ranis framework. If the size of the surplus is getting smaller relative to its previous stage, the gap between labor productivity and wages is getting smaller, and the economy is moving into the second stage of transition after the shortage point. Finally, if the economy is moving toward commercialization, with marginal productivity being almost the same as wages, all the surplus labor will be exhausted.

Our estimated size of surplus labor is, on average, 29.7 million (14.0% of agricultural labor) during the period 2001–2013, with a steady decrease over the years. Since our alternatively measured observed labor in agriculture is meaningfully smaller than that of the NBS, our quantified size of the surplus labor is smaller than other estimates for the 1980s and 1990s. This reduced observed agricultural labor could be due to measurement errors and the essential demographic changes in the 2010s.

Demographic changes have been particularly phenomenal in the countryside during the past decades. The rural population has been decreasing rapidly, and thus the labor supply has reduced from 490 million persons in the late 1990s to around 380 million in the mid-2010s (a fall of 22%) while total labor employment increased by 8%. Largely due to the decline in total fertility rate, China's rural labor share was less than its urban counterpart's in 2014 for the first time.[11] The United Nations even forecasted China's population would peak by 2030, and the working population might even reach its maximum before 2020 (UN, 2009, 2015).

An equally important debate is about the coexistence of surplus labor and wage increase in China. Many believe this is counterintuitive to the Lewis model. By using 2002 and 2007 household data, Knight *et al.* (2011) estimated migration functions to examine the probability of non-migrants in rural areas. With different measures of potential migration, they confirmed that a considerable supply of migrants in rural China is still accessible. Our findings appear consistent with theirs by gauging the surplus labor and showing its decreasing size during the period 2001–2013.

It is also important to note that the measured extent of surplus in our chapter is that of subsistence agriculture in rural China. With the constant relaxation of the household registration system allowing more peasants to work in urban areas, one would expect that some of those migrant workers might be earning subsistence wages only due to their level of skill and training, especially in informal production activities.

In sum, our analysis shows that China might have reached the turning point period around the mid- to second half of the 2000s, with the surplus labor in agriculture amounting to some 20 million, or 13% of our alternatively estimated agricultural labor. Coincidentally, China resumed its WTO membership in 2001, following 15 years of accession negotiations. This move is a milestone for China to further reallocate labor and capital to gradually generate productive activities and significantly reduce the national poverty level, although the analysis is beyond the scope of this chapter.

The Emergence of Three-Sector Dualism

One feature of China's industrialization that has not been addressed in the literature is the rapid expansion of non-agricultural production in the countryside. As indicated in Table 3, production in rural China has become more diversified since the 1980s, and agriculture and the countryside are no longer synonymous. This points to a growing and important rural non-agricultural sector, which needs to be considered in labor reallocation models, with the following concerns.

First, labor productivity in the Chinese agricultural sector changed significantly when non-cultivation agricultural activities developed quickly after the agricultural reform of the late 1970s. Fishing, forestry, and animal husbandry experienced higher labor productivity growth than cultivation. Second, a considerable number of peasants in rural China have been employed by different non-agricultural sectors since the 1980s, initially by rural enterprises

Table 3. Sectoral composition of GDP in China (1980–2014, selected years).

	Rural agriculture	Rural industry	Rural service	Urban industry	Urban service
1980	29.1	4.5	3.3	42.4	20.7
1985	28.4	8.6	6.7	34.5	21.8
1990	27.1	11.3	9.7	30.4	21.6
1995	20.5	20.7	10.4	28.1	20.3
2000	15.1	21.1	12.2	24.8	26.8
2005	12.1	21.6	12.2	25.8	28.3
2010	10.1	21.2	12.6	25.5	30.7
2011	10.0	21.1	12.2	25.5	31.1
2014	9.2	19.1	13.0	23.5	35.2

Note: All numbers are in percentage terms. Urban agriculture accounts for less than 1% of total output.

Source: Chinese Academy of Social Sciences and National Bureau of Statistics (various issues).

(mainly the township and village enterprises TVEs) and later by formal and informal production in the countryside. Admittedly, more TVEs have become privatized since the late 1990s.[12] Due to sectoral variation, the marginal product of labor in agriculture is likely to be notably different from that of rural non-agriculture. Third, because of the household registration system (HRS, *hukou*), the workforce engaged in urban formal and informal production includes a large number of rural workers with the status of temporary migrants in cities.[13] They have had more choices in the urban job market, especially since China's WTO membership was reconfirmed in 2001.

Therefore, we establish a three-sector model to incorporate labor reallocation from rural agriculture to rural non-agriculture and from rural agriculture to the urban sector. Conceptually, our sectoral division is more suitable for capturing Chinese reality than those of Brandt *et al.* (2008) and Wu (1995). As indicated in Appendix 5, in comparison with others, we focus more on labor reallocation across geographical regions due to differences in output and productivity than on variation in ownership structure. In our model, labor flows across production entities, regardless of ownership, with different geographic area classifications potentially having different effects on TFP growth.

Accordingly, China's dual economy framework is characterized by a *three-sector dualism*: the traditional sector, composed of rural agriculture (and possibly informal urban production) and adopted largely for subsistence purposes, and the modern sectors, composed of rural non-agriculture and urban non-agriculture and adopted purely for profit maximization. China's three-sector dualism allows its modern sectors to grow continuously by optimally absorbing surplus agricultural labor, while the expansion of the modern sector is driven by rural non-agricultural production due to the practice of HRS.

The formal derivation of our three-sector model is an extension of the model proposed by Temple and Wößmann (2006), and Kwan *et al.* (2011, 2018) give the full details. We derive an empirical model consistent with equation [11] by Kwan *et al.* (2018), adopting the following aggregate production function:

$$Y_t = K_t^{\alpha} H^{\rho} (A_t L_t)^{1-\alpha-\rho} \tag{4}$$

where α and ρ are the factor shares of physical capital and human capital, respectively. This labor-augmented production function is subject to the Cobb–Douglas specification. Based on Mankiw *et al.* (1992), we can derive the following equation by taking the logarithmic change of output per worker:

$$\ln\frac{Y_t}{L_t}-\ln\frac{Y(0)}{L(0)}=\theta\ln A(0)+gt+\frac{\theta\alpha}{1-\alpha}\ln s-\frac{\theta\alpha}{1-\alpha}\ln(n+g+\delta)$$
$$+\frac{\theta\rho}{1-\alpha}\ln H-\theta\ln\frac{Y(0)}{L(0)} \tag{5}$$

where all (0)s stand for the initial values, g is the growth rate of technology, n is the growth rate of population, δ is the depreciation rate, s is the saving rate, t is time, and θ is a parameter that captures the speed of convergence. In the empirical estimation, $g+\delta$ is set to 5%, as suggested by Mankiw *et al.* (1992). Equation (5) implies that the economy will converge to the steady state in the initial year. When there is no structural change, TFP growth in the Solow model is expressed as

$$\frac{\dot{Z}}{Z}=\frac{\dot{A}}{A}=\left(1-S_b-S_m\right)\frac{\dot{A}_a}{A_a}+S_b\frac{\dot{A}_b}{A_b}+S_m\frac{\dot{A}_m}{A_m}=g \tag{6}$$

In the Mankiw *et al.* (1992) model, the TFP growth rate g is assumed constant. After introducing the structural change terms, the TFP growth rate includes additional variables. Assuming $\ln A(0)$ and *ln s* are constant across provinces, our empirical model for cross-section regression is

$$\ln\frac{Y_t}{L_t}-\ln\frac{Y(0)}{L(0)}=\text{constant}+\frac{\theta\alpha}{1-\alpha}\ln s-\frac{\theta\alpha}{1-\alpha}\ln(n+g+\delta)$$
$$+\frac{\theta\rho}{1-\alpha}\ln H-\theta\ln\frac{Y(0)}{L(0)}$$
$$+\frac{t\phi(\kappa_1-1)}{1-\alpha}GROWTH_b+\frac{t\phi(\kappa_2-1)}{1-\alpha}GROWTH_m$$
$$+\frac{t\phi\kappa_1}{\varphi_1(1-\alpha)}DISEQ_b+\frac{t\phi\kappa_2}{\varphi_2(1-\alpha)}DISEQ_m \tag{7}$$

To transform equation (5) into our empirical dynamic panel data structure, we largely follow Bond *et al.* (2001):

$$y_{it} = \alpha y_{it-1} + \beta X_{it} + \gamma_i + \delta_t + v_{it} \tag{8}$$

where X_{it} s are a set of independent variables, including saving rates, population growth, $GROWTH_b$, $GROWTH_m$ $DISEQ_b$, $DISEQ_m$, and human capital; y_{it-1} is the previous per capita output; γ_i is the cross-section unobservable effect; δ_t is the time unobservable effect; and v_{it} is a random error term. More details on estimation techniques are covered in Appendix 6.

Our results reveal that labor reallocation from rural agriculture to rural non-agriculture and from rural agriculture to urban non-agriculture are both significant. By further checking the magnitudes of the two structural change terms, it appears that the impact of labor reallocation on economic growth is stronger for the case of labor movement from agriculture to rural non-agricultural sectors: 4.384 vs. 2.790. By further imposing the Cobb–Douglas assumption on *MGROWTH* and *DISEQ*, the effect of labor reallocation shows a stronger effect on economic growth. For example, the coefficients $MGROWTH_b$ and $MGROWTH_m$ are 11.080 and 5.114 in Table A6.2, but only 4.384 and 2.790 in Table A6.1, respectively.

Our results also show that regional variations matter. We pool the total observations into coastal and noncoastal sub-samples.[14] The estimation results in Table A6.3 show that the more developed provinces in the coastal region enjoy a greater impact on economic growth of labor reallocating to rural non-agriculture and urban sectors, as indicated by both bigger coefficient values (5.260 and 3.658 for *MGROETHs* in coastal provinces) and a higher level of significance (1% level).

China's Experience and Its Implications for Developing Economies

Dualism, featuring the coexistence of traditional and modern sectors, is still fundamental to understanding economic development in many developing countries LDCs. Inter-sectoral resource transfer from low- to high-productivity activities, especially labor reallocation, is an important driving force of economic growth. Indeed, different parts in each sector are not methodologically disturbing and are analytically convenient (Basu, 1997) since wages and marginal productivity differentials are crucial for reallocating labor across parts of each sector and across sectors.

Our three-sector framework supplements the orthodox two-sector dualism. For economies with a relatively high ratio of population to available land and inadequate human capital, non-agricultural production in the countryside appears to be an alternative strategy of industrialization, supplementing the commonly promoted rural-to-urban migration. China's migration restriction policy under the HRS has been the real cause of its high man–land ratio, apart from political movements such as the Cultural Revolution (Kwan, 2011). Against this background, our new model successfully captures the rapid growth of rural non-agricultural labor since the 1980s, when the *hukou* system remained in place. Our model reflects the reality that rural labor left farm work but stayed in the countryside (*litu bu lixiang*) for non-agricultural activities (*jinchang bu jincheng*). Recent years have seen the growth of rural-urban fringe areas, which provide informal job opportunities in both rural and urban areas but further complicate the issue of labor migration as land holding is introduced.[15]

Countries with a high man–land ratio, such as India and Bangladesh (Table 4), could consider China's pattern of industrialization driven by labor reallocation to both rural non-agriculture and urban non-agriculture. By promoting non-agricultural activities in the countryside, unskilled labor employment and output expansion are likely to industrialize these LDCs in the long run.

We believe that our results also shed light on other aspects of LDCs. First, countries which lack sufficiently advanced institutions to allocate resources optimally can still improve efficiency through rural industrialization. Such industrialization best occurs through the combined efforts of the private sector, marketization, and state policy. Supported and encouraged by local governments, the initial non-agricultural firms in rural China produced output without a widespread free-market mechanism. These combined efforts

Table 4. Population–land ratio of the economies with the largest populations.

Country	2010	2000	1990	1980	1970
Brazil	11.2	12.5	16.2	18.7	21.7
China	130.9	154.2	165.1	184.7	180.0
India	470.5	417.5	359.3	298.5	249.6
Indonesia	220.0	271.0	283.8	309.2	255.6
Bangladesh	1160.2	1053.4	812.7	687.4	637.3
Pakistan	421.6	358.6	299.3	228.9	183.5
Nigeria	106.0	99.2	87.6	76.7	63.4

Note: The man–land ratio is measured as the number of rural population per squared kilometer of agricultural land.
Source: World Bank (various years).

considerably increased the supply of consumable goods and extended the consumption horizon of individuals in both the cities and the countryside while giving local governments access to tax revenue from the enterprises.

Second, the exploitation of comparative advantage is essential for directing resources toward their most productive employment. In China, labor-intensive industrialization has been consistent with its factor endowment in its countryside. Toward the end of the 1990s, China produced and exported vast quantities of manufactured goods to the global market thanks to its comparative advantage. The identification of comparative advantage of resource endowment in different developing economies is thus important for reallocation to generate output growth.

Third, even without a completely free market, governments can nurture a market-friendly environment by allowing some departure, directing limited resources to productive sectors. China has gradually transferred non-agricultural production from the TVEs to private firms in rural areas. To keep the pressure of migration to the cities under control, China has not, so far, abolished the HRS. The development of non-agriculture in rural areas increases peasants' income and minimizes the flow of the rural workforce from agriculture to urban sectors. In the meantime, the continuous improvement of social welfare in cities for migrant workers allows for greater stability and a smoother transition between rural and urban areas. Such a process is theoretically and empirically supported by our three-sector setting.

Epilogue

This chapter intends to supplement the existing works by explaining China's structural change since 1978 neoclassically by studying the welfare impact of excess labor reallocation across sectors geographically. The major policy implication has been how a suitable industrialization strategy might be adopted by those populated nations under the constraint of limited market power with dynamic government-led policies.

There are several agendas for further scholarly consideration. While our three-sector dualism expounds on Chinese development over four decades, the spectacular growth beyond the so-called turning point is still puzzling. Certainly, the WTO re-accession empowers China to further shift its production frontier. Did China face the so-called middle-income trap or not? How does the recent COVID-19 impact China's short- and long-term economic development? In terms of lessons for other LDCs, there is still debate over the qualification of the China model for other low-income economies because of its unique political and social systems. How should the policy frameworks of the small developing countries be made, especially those in Africa? Perhaps the most important lesson from this chapter is the application of three-sector dualism based on the specific factor endowment of individual countries, with the objective of achieving long-term economic growth and stability.

Endnotes

1. Measured by per capita GDP (in RMB, deflated by the implicit per capita GDP deflator, 2000 = 100).
2. Such as the arguments of "growing out of the plan" by McMillan and Naughton (1992) and Nee (1989, 2000), "state-led reform" by Oi (1995), and "local dynamics" by Qian and Weingast (1997) and Xu (2011).

3. There are later supplements by Lewis (1972), Fei and Ranis (1997), and Ranis (2012). Usually, the literature uses the term "the Lewis model" to cover the main idea of any dual economy model.
4. Practically, it is referred to as agriculture with unskilled labor, though some small-scale processing industries (especially those operated by families) are part of the traditional segment.
5. Mainly manufacturing, but also those profit-oriented services employ huge unskilled workers.
6. After passing this turning point, the equilibrium wage is determined by labor's marginal product.
7. The term "turning point" in this chapter refers to the "full commercialization" point.
8. The other four criteria are correlation between real wages and marginal productivity of labor in the subsistence sector, movements in real wages in the subsistence sector, changes in the wage differentials between the two segments, and elasticity of labor supply in the subsistence segment.
9. These two measures can also be applied to either increasing- or decreasing return-to-scale technology with further expression. See Coelli *et al.* (2005), pp. 52–57.
10. Bhattacharyya and Parker (1999) used this model with modifications.
11. 393.1 million urban labor and 379.4 million urban labor in 2014 (NBS, 2015a).
12. Since then, the direct capital contributions of local governments to TVEs have become insignificant, and certain TVEs can now raise funding from the stock market. Some TVEs have obtained capital through foreign investment.
13. The practice of *Hukou* allows no permanent migration into cities (unless one can change his/her status). There are workers in urban non-agricultural production from the cities and rural areas. In other words, the urban workforce is supposed to be larger than just the urban-based labor. The conventional two-sector model pools urban migrant workers with urban workers and therefore cannot account for this group properly.
14. Coastal provinces include Beijing, Fujian, Guangdong, Guangxi, Hebei, Jiangsu, Liaoning, Shandong, Shanghai, Tianjin, Zhejiang; while non-coastal provinces include Anhui, Gansu, Guizhou, Heilongjiang, Henan, Hubei, Hunan, Jiangxi, Jilin, Ningxia, Qinghai, Shaanxi, Shanxi, Sichuan, Xinjiang, Xizang, Yunnan.

15. Complications include the management of agricultural and non-agricultural *hukou*, land management and development, administrative regions between rural and urban, and arrangements for the future of peasants' statuses.
16. Due to data unavailability of forestry and fishing and the relatively small proportion of the two sectors in total agricultural output and employment, only farming and animal husbandry will be focused.
17. *Danwei yonggongliang* in Chinese. "Unit" is measured by *mu* for farm or head for animal husbandry. "Workday" refers to the production effort of eight hours a day for one middle-aged peasant in rural China. Middle-aged peasants (including household members and employed individuals) refer to those who are aged 18–50 (male) or 18–45 (female). When calculating the unit workday requirement, all other types of working individuals will be converted into middle-aged equivalence.
18. Using 180 workdays as a benchmark, Appendix Table A1 provides estimates of annual national agricultural labor and surplus labor under different workday assumptions: 200, 160, and 120 workdays for readers' reference.
19. For example, Knight *et al.* (2011) analyzed 2008 CHIP data and estimated that the average number of workdays by farmer was 183 days. The RUMiCI survey (the rural household survey part) defines those who work for nine or more months as having an agricultural job (Golley and Meng, 2011). This definition gives an estimate of 190 workdays (= 270–72–8 are calculated on the basis of nine months (270 days), 72 Saturdays and Sundays, and 8 public holidays).
20. Farming includes rice (early indica rice, medium indica rice, late indica rice, and keng rice), wheat, corn, peanut, rapeseed, cotton, flue-cured tobacco, tomato (open-field, greenhouse), cucumber (open-field, greenhouse), cabbage (open-field, open-field celery), and apple.
21. Animal husbandry includes pigs (backyard, small scale, median scale, large scale), beef cattle, dairy cows (free-range, small, middle & large scale dairy cows), sheep, and chicken (small-, middle-, & large-scale chickens and broilers).
22. Our data are sourced from the annual RHS for the 1996–2010 period. Since 2011, rural and urban household surveys have been combined into the *China Yearbook of Household Survey*. The RHS is conducted by the Household Survey Office at China's NBS. In total, 74,000 households are selected from 7,000 villages within 896 counties in rural areas across 31

Chinese provinces. The household sample is selected by using the probability proportional to size, two-stage sampling method. At the first stage, counties are drawn from each province, and then villages are selected from those counties. At the second stage, households are selected by multi-stage, multi-phase, stratified systematic sampling methods.

23. The RHS reports both gross and net incomes of rural households. The net income is the gross income less the expenses of FAM, tax payment, allowance for depreciation on fixed assets, and internal transfers.
24. In the RHS, the four sources of income are respectively *Jiating jingyingxing shouru*, *Gongzixing shouru*, *Caichanxing shouru* and *Zhuanyixing shouru* in Chinese.
25. As the RHS only reports the *gross* FAM income from primary production for each province, we calculate the *net* FAM income from primary production by multiplying net FAM incomes from total production by the share of gross FAM incomes from primary production in gross FAM incomes from total production.
26. This deflator is better at reflecting the expenditure patterns of rural households than the overall CPI used by Islam and Yokota (2008) or the ratio of nominal GDP to real GDP of the primary industry, as used by Minami and Ma (2011).
27. FAM incomes are reported in *per capita* terms in the RHS. We convert it into *per worker* terms using the equation $W_i = \frac{G_i N}{L}$, where W_i denotes per worker income of household i, G_i signifies per capita income of household i, and N and L respectively refer to the average number of persons and workers in household i.
28. Alternatively, we can weight provincial-level agricultural wages by the proportion of the number of agricultural workers in a province to the total number of agricultural workers in that region to calculate LW and HW for each region. We find that the results are similar to those by arithmetic averages. For simplicity, the national or regional averages reported in this chapter are all calculated by using the arithmetic average of provincial-level values.
29. We distinguish the two specifications of the production function by using the log-likelihood ratio test (466.63 at 5% level) and the F-test (9.48 at 5% level), indicating that the translog form is preferred and the joint significance of its quadratic and interactive terms.

30. Our dataset covers 232 prefectures in 19 provinces, representing 74% of the total number of prefectures in China. The data are sourced from the NBS provincial-level statistical yearbooks.
31. The Breusch & Pagan Lagrangian multiplier test follows a chi-squared distribution with its statistic being 10045.70, significant at the 1% level.
32. More details of the data in this part could be found in Kwan *et al.* (2018).
33. Although the two-step system GMM estimators are more efficient, their asymptotic standard errors may be biased downward and thus signal an unreliable guide for reference (Bond *et al.*, 2001). Moreover, the Monte Carlo studies and Ding and Knight (2009) showed that the results of one-step and two-step estimates are very close to each other.
34. The *p*-value of 0.409 suggests no series problem with the validity of instruments.

References

Aigner, D., Lovell, C., and Schmidt, P. 1977. Formulation and estimation of stochastic frontier production function models. *Journal of Econometrics*, 6: 21–37.

Anderson, G. and Ge, Y. 2009. Intercity income inequality, growth and convergence in China. *Journal of Income Distribution*, 18(1): 70–89.

Arellano, Y. and Bond, S. 1991. Some tests of specification for panel data: Monte Carlo evidence and an application to employment equations. *Review of Economic Statistics*, 58(2): 277–297.

Basu, K. 1997. The structure of a dual economy. In *Analytical Development Economics: The Less Developed Economy Revisited.* Cambridge, Massachusetts: MIT Press, pp. 151–161.

Battese, G. and Coelli, C. 1995. A model for technical inefficiency effects in a stochastic frontier. *Empirical Economics*, 20: 325–332.

Bhattacharyya, A. and Parker, E. 1999. Labor productivity and migration in Chinese agriculture — a stochastic frontier approach. *China Economic Review*, 10: 59–74.

Bond, S., Hoeffler, A., and Temple, J. 2001. GMM estimation of empirical growth models. CEPR Discussion Paper 3048.

Bosworth, B. and Collins, S.M. 2008. Accounting for growth: Comparing China and India. *Journal of Economic Perspectives*, 22(1): 45–66.

Brandt, L., Hsieh, C., and Zhu, Z. 2008. Growth and structural transformation in China. In Brandt, L. and Rawski, T. (eds.), *China's Great Economic Transformation*. New York: Cambridge University Press, pp. 683–728.

Cai, F. 2010. Demographic transition, demographic dividend, and Lewis turning point in China. *China Economic Journal*, 3(2): 107–119.

Cai, F. and Du, Y. 2011. Wage increases, wage convergence, and the Lewis turning point in China. *China Economic Review*, 22: 601–610.

Caselli, F., Esquivel, G., and Lefort, F. 1996. Reopening the convergence debate: A new look at cross-country growth empirics. *Journal of Economic Growth*, 1(3): 363–389.

Coelli, T., Rao, P., O'Donnell, C., and Battese, G. 2005. *An Introduction to Efficiency and Productivity Analysis*, 2nd edn. New York: Springer.

Diewert, W.E. 1974. Functional forms for revenue and factor requirements functions. *International Economic Review*, 15(1): 119–130.

Ding, S. and Knight, J. 2009. Can the augmented solow model explain China's remarkable economic growth? A cross-country panel data analysis. *Journal of Comparative Economics*, 37: 432–452.

Easterly, W., Loayza, N., and Montiel, P. 1997. Has Latin America's post-reform growth been disappointing? *Journal of International Economics*, 4(3–4): 287–311.

Ercolani, M.G. and Wei, Z. 2011. An empirical analysis of China's dualistic economic development: 1965–2009. *Asian Economic Paper*, 10(3): 1–29.

Fei, J.C.H. and Ranis, G. 1997. *Growth and Development from an Evolutionary Perspective*. Malden MA: Blackwell; England: Oxford.

Garnaut, R. 2010. Macro-economic implications of the turning point. *China Economic Journal*, 3(2): 181–190.

Golley, J. and Meng, X. 2011. Has China run out of surplus labour? *China Economic Review*, 22: 555–572.

Guo, J.X. 2007. The estimation of surplus labour in Chinese agriculture in 1996–2005: A stochastic frontier approach. *Nankai Economic Studies*, 4: 72–81 (in Chinese).

Herrerias, M.J. 2012. Weighted convergence and regional growth in China: An alternative approach (1952–2008). *Annul Regional Science*, 49: 685–718.

Islam, N. and Yokota, K. 2008. Lewis growth model and China's industrialization. *Asian Economic Journal*, 22(4): 359–396.

Knight, J., Deng, Q., and Li, S. 2011. The puzzle of migrant labour shortage and rural labour surplus in China. *China Economic Review*, 22: 585–600.

Kumbhakar, S. and Hjalmarsson, L. 1995. Labour-use efficiency in Swedish social insurance offices. *Journal of Applied Econometrics*, 10(1): 33–47.

Kwan, F. 2009. Agricultural labour and the indicence of surplus labour: Experience from China during reform. *Journal of Chinese Economic and Business Studies*, 7(3): 341–361.

Kwan, F. 2011. China's macroeconomy: Global-local interaction. In Chan, L.H, Chan, G., and Kwan, F. (eds.), *China at 60: Global-Local Interactions.* Singapore: World Scientific, pp. 117–138.

Kwan, F., Zhang, Y., and Zhuo, S.H. 2011. Rural labour reallocation and productivity growth in China. *International Journal of Business Studies,* 19(1): 109–124.

Kwan, F., Wu, Y.R., and Zhuo, S.H. 2013. Re-examination of the surplus agricultural labour in China. *China Agricultural Economic Review*, 5(2): 197–213.

Kwan, F., Zhang, Y., and Zhuo, S.H. 2018. Labour reallocation, productivity growth and dualism: The case of China. *International Review of Economics and Finance*, 57: 198–210.

Lau, C.K. 2010. New evidence about regional income divergence in China. *China Economic Review*, 21: 293–309.

Lewis, A.W. 1954. Economic development with unlimited supplies of labor. *Manchester School*, 22: 139–191.

Lewis, A.W. 1972. Reflections on unlimited labor. In Di Marco, L. (ed.), *International Economics and Development.* New York: Academic Press, pp. 75–96.

Li, H., Huang, J., Luo, R., and Liu, C. 2013. China's labour transition and the future of China's rural wages and employment. *China and World Economy*, 21(3): 4–24.

Mankiw, N.G., Romer, D., and Weil, D.N. 1992. A contribution to the empirics of economic growth. *The Quarterly Journal of Economics,* 107: 407–437.

McMillan, J. and Naughton, B. 1992. How to reform a planned economy: Lessons from China. *Oxford Review of Economic Policy*, 8(1): 130–143.

Minami, R. 1968. The turning point in the Japanese economy. *The Quarterly Journal of Economics*, 82: 380–402.

Minami, R. and Ma, X. 2011. The Lewis turning point of Chinese economy: Comparison with Japanese experience. *China Economic Journal*, 3(2): 163–179.

Ministry of Agriculture. 2009. *New China's Agricultural Statistics for 60 Years.* Beijing, China: China Agricultural Press.

National Bureau of Statistics (NBSa). 2015. *China Statistical Yearbook.*

National Bureau of Statistics (NBSb). 2015. *China Rural Statistical Yearbook.*

National Bureau of Statistics (NBS). 2015a. *China Statistical Yearbook 2015.*

National Bureau of Statistics (NBS). Various years. *Quanguo Nonchanpin Chengben Shouyi Ziliao Huibian* (*Compilation of National Cost and Revenue of Agricultural Products*).

Naughton, B. 2015. Inside and outside: The modernized hierarchy that runs China. *Journal of Comparative Economics,* 44: 404–415.

Nee, V. 1989. A theory of market transition: From redistribution to markets in state socialism. *American Sociological Review,* 54(5): 663–681.

Nee, V. 2000. The role of the state in making a market economy. *Journal of Institutional and Theoretical Economics,* 156(1): 64–88.

Oi, J. 1995. The role of the local state in China's transitional economy. *The China Quarterly,* 144: 1132–1149.

Pedroni, P. and Yao, J.Y. 2006. Regional income divergence in China. *Journal of Asian Economics,* 17: 294–315.

Qian, Y.Y. and Weingast, B. 1997. Federalism as a commitment to preserving market incentives. *Journal of Economic Perspectives,* 11(4): 83–92.

Ranis, G. 2012. Labor surplus revisited. Center Discussion Paper No 1016, Economic Growth Center, Yale University.

Ranis, G. and Fei, J.C.H. 1961. A theory of economic development. *American Economic Review,* 51: 533–565.

Song, L.G. and Zhang, Y.S. 2010. Will Chinese growth slow after the Lewis turning point? *China Economic Journal,* 3(2): 209–219.

Temple, J. and Wößmann, L. 2006. Dualism and cross-country growth regressions. *Journal of Economic Growth,* 11: 187–228.

United Nations (UN). 2009. *World Population Prospects: The 2008 Revision.*

United Nations (UN). 2015. *World Population Prospects: The 2015 Revision.*

Wu, Y.R. 1995. Productivity growth, technological progress, and technical efficiency change in China: A three-sector analysis. *Journal of Comparative Economics,* 21: 207–229.

Xu, C.G. 2011. The fundamental institutions of China's reform and development. *Journal of Economic Literature,* 49(4): 1076–1151.

Zhang, X.B., Yang, J., and Wang, S.L. 2011. China has reached the Lewis turning point. *China Economic Review,* 22: 542–554.

Appendix 1: Alternative Measure of Agricultural Labor in China

We attempt to derive an alternative measure of China's agricultural labor force by using the information of production cost and revenue (NBS) for farming and animal husbandry.[16] Specifically, we first identify the "unit workday requirement"[17] of each farm and animal husbandry product. We then find out the sown area of different farm products and the number of heads of different animal husbandry products. Each peasant is assumed to participate in agricultural work for 180 workdays annually.[18] This assumption is consistent with the statistics reported in several key sources.[19] Finally, the amount of farm and animal husbandry labor in the *i*th province for the *m*th farm product[20] or the *n*th product of animal husbandry[21] is calculated using the following equations:

$$L_F = \sum_i \sum_m \frac{U_{im} SA_{im}}{D} \tag{A1.1}$$

$$L_A = \sum_i \sum_n \frac{U_{in} H_{in}}{D} \tag{A1.2}$$

where D is the standard workday per annum, U_{im} and U_{in} are the standard workdays per mu or per head, SA_{im} and H_{in} are sown area or number of slaughter. L_F and L_A are the estimated total farm labor and the total animal husbandry labor.

There are several findings based on our newly derived China's agricultural labor series, which are presented in Table A1.1. First of all, according to official statistics, total labor employment has increased by 5.6% from 728 million in 2001 to 770 million in 2013 (5.6 percentage points, or a 42 million increment), while the agricultural employment figure has decreased by 33.6 percentage points, or a 122 million decrement. Our alternative measures show a slower pace of decrease from 227 million to 185 million for the same period, a decrease of 43 million, or 18.7 percentage points. Second, it is found that the difference between our estimates and the official figures had narrowed over time, from 136 million to 57 million (or 37.5% to 23.5%) during 2001–2013. It is not sure at

Table A1.1. Estimated China's agricultural labor, 2001–2013.

	[1]	[2]	[3]	[4]	[5]	[6]	[7]	[8]
	Estimated	Estimated	Estimated	Estimated	NBS	NBS		
	Farm	Animal husbandry	Others	Agriculture	Agriculture	Total	[4]/[6]	[5]/[6]
2001	20,020.1	2,253.7	467.7	22,741.5	36,398.5	72,797.0	31.2	50.0
2002	19,376.4	2,371.4	456.7	22,204.5	36,640.0	73,280.0	30.3	50.0
2003	19,228.1	2,926.5	465.2	22,619.9	36,204.4	73,736.0	30.7	49.1
2004	18,456.1	3,806.9	467.5	22,730.6	34,829.8	74,264.0	30.6	46.9
2005	18,269.2	4,703.9	482.4	23,455.6	33,441.9	74,647.0	31.4	44.8
2006	17,853.2	4,178.1	462.7	22,494.0	31,940.6	74,978.0	30.0	42.6
2007	17,399.0	3,532.9	439.6	21,371.5	30,731.0	75,321.0	28.4	40.8
2008	16,759.0	4,934.2	455.6	22,148.8	29,923.3	75,564.0	29.3	39.6
2009	16,468.5	3,058.2	410.1	19,936.8	28,890.5	75,828.0	26.3	38.1
2010	16,138.0	3,089.0	403.8	19,630.7	27,930.5	76,105.0	25.8	36.7
2011	15,339.7	2,997.8	385.1	18,722.6	26,594.0	76,420.0	24.5	34.8
2012	15,102.7	3,025.8	380.7	18,509.2	25,773.0	76,704.0	24.1	33.6
2013	15,120.3	2,985.4	380.2	18,486.0	24,171.0	76,977.0	24.0	31.4

Note: All are in 10,000 persons except % for columns [7] and [8]. Annually, 180 workdays are assumed.

Sources: [1]–[4] are authors' calculations, and [5]–[6] are from NBS (2015a).

this point whether the smaller gaps are due to various adjustments after the two waves of the agricultural census and the economic census. Third, our alternative estimates further reduce the share of agricultural employment to total employment in the first decade of the 21st century. In 2001, 31% of labor worked for primary production against the official figure of 50%. In 2013, agricultural employment took up 24% of the total, against the official figure of 31%. In other words, our estimates reflect a smoother decline of agricultural employment with an average of −1.6% change annually, while the NSB figures show a more rapid change of −3.3% per annum. Fourth, an international comparison of agricultural employment places China as a case between the lower-middle-income countries and the upper-middle-income countries. With the official data,

China's agricultural employment was clearly comparable to the lower-middle-income countries until around 2006. With our data, the agricultural labor share of China was already very similar to that of the upper-middle-income nations in 2001 and 2002. Nevertheless, China's share was getting closer to the world's average in 2010: 26% vs. 19.8%.

Appendix 2: Estimates of the Chinese Surplus Agricultural Labor

Empirically, we estimate the following labor requirement frontiers for 17 farm products and 13 animal husbandry products individually for the period 2001–2013:

$$\ln \mathrm{L}_{it} = \alpha_0 + \alpha_1 \ln \mathrm{Y}_{it} + \alpha_2 t + \alpha_3 t^2 + \sum \partial_i D_i + \mathrm{v}_{it} + \mathrm{u}_{it} \qquad \text{(A2.1)}$$

u_{it} is a time-varying function to capture the inefficient labor use:

$$u_{it} = \lambda z_{it} + \varepsilon_{it} \qquad \text{(A2.2)}$$

where z_{it} are province-specific exogenous variables which vary over time to influence inefficiency. Specifically,

$$\mathrm{u}_{it} = \beta_0 + \beta_1 t + \beta_2 t^2 + \sum \mu_i D_i + \varepsilon_{it} \qquad \text{(A2.3)}$$

with the following distributional assumptions: $v_{it} \sim \text{iid}\, N(0, \sigma_v^2)$, $u_{it} \sim \text{iid}\, N^+(z_{it}\lambda, \sigma_u^2)$, and $\varepsilon_{it} \sim \text{iid}\, N(0, \sigma_u^2), \varepsilon_{it} \geq -\lambda z_{it}$. Provincial dummy variables are included in both $f(.)$and $\mathrm{u}(.)$. Each labor requirement function is estimated by the maximum likelihood using Frontier 4.1.

Unlike Kumbhakar and Hjalmarsson (1995), using multiple outputs in $f(.)$, we estimate the labor-use equations for all farm and animal husbandry products separately. Individual estimates allow us to obtain the technical inefficiency scores for each product. In addition, our relatively large sample with provincial data for each product across 13 years makes it possible to produce asymptotic robust results. There are in total 17 and 13 farming and animal husbandry labor-use equations, and their regression results are presented in Tables A2.1 and A2.2.

Table A2.1. Labor-use models for China's farm production, 2001–2013.

Product	Constant	Y	t	t^2	u[constant]	u[t]	u[t^2]	σ^2	γ	Obs
Early indica rice	3.524***	–0.246	–0.116***	0.010***	–0.083	–0.113***	0.021***	0.013***	0.988***	112
Medium indica rice	3.294***	–0.138***	–0.121***	0.011***	0.204***	–0.106***	0.018***	0.013***	0.999***	135
Late indica rice	1.646***	0.119*	–0.140***	0.012***	0.234***	–0.130***	0.018***	0.015***	0.999***	115
Keng rice	2.629***	0.025	–0.098***	0.009***	0.199***	–0.063***	0.013***	0.018***	0.997***	185
Wheat	1.420***	0.060	–0.050***	0.002*	–0.131	0.006	0.016**	0.058***	0.967***	235
Corn	1.108***	0.110***	–0.059***	0.004***	0.248***	–0.033***	0.007***	0.015***	0.997***	262
Peanut	1.734***	0.146***	–0.035***	0.003***	–51.405	0.081**	–0.010	0.047***	0.946***	159
Rapeseed	1.723***	0.103**	–0.054***	0.003**	0.737***	–0.035	–0.002	0.035***	0.879***	200
Cotton	2.671***	0.098***	–0.040***	0.004***	0.058	–0.059***	0.015***	0.016***	0.999***	167
Flue-cured tobacco	2.875***	0.225***	–0.053***	0.002***	0.864***	–0.066***	0.006**	0.021***	0.999***	246
Open-field tomato	2.213***	0.270***	–0.091***	0.012*	0.564**	–0.106	0.018	0.050***	0.998***	261
Greenhouse tomato	0.085	0.512***	–0.046**	0.003	0.131	–0.053	0.009	0.162***	0.999***	203
Open-field cucumber	3.762***	0.070	–0.057***	0.003	0.474**	–0.056	–0.004	0.062***	0.998***	255
Greenhouse cucumber	–0.192	0.527***	–0.037	0.002	–0.035	–0.075*	0.016	0.086***	0.998***	179
Open-field cabbage	3.738***	0.035	0.003	–0.002	0.141	0.028	0.006	0.063***	0.944***	234
Open-field celery cabbage	1.434	0.150	–0.093	0.016	0.054	–0.122	0.029	0.059	0.850	280
Apple	3.274***	0.099*	–0.012	0.000	0.291*	–0.088***	0.015***	0.030***	0.996***	108

Note: ***, **, * are 1%, 5%, and 10% level of significance, respectively;
Y: output, t: time, σ^2: sum of variances of v and u, v: two-sided random error, u: technical inefficiency, γ: $\frac{\sigma_u^2}{\sigma_u^2+\sigma_v^2}$, obs: number of observation; Provincial dummy variables are omitted.

Table A2.2. Labor-use models for China's animal husbandry production, 2001–2013.

Product	Constant	Y	t	t^2	u[constant]	u[t]	u[t^2]	σ^2	γ	Obs
Backyard pigs	1.676	0.513**	–0.320***	0.022***	1.808***	–0.241***	0.016**	0.020***	0.999***	238
Small-scale pigs	–0.482	0.404*	–0.043	0.000	0.182	–0.078	0.010	0.090	0.827	344
Middle-scale pigs	–2.661***	0.895***	–0.127***	0.007	1.101***	–0.204*	0.015	0.096***	0.999***	364
Large-scale pigs	1.937**	–0.096	–0.101***	0.005*	1.089***	–0.128***	0.008	0.059***	0.999***	362
Free-range beef	8.418***	–0.439**	–0.309	0.042	1.871*	–0.410	0.054	0.168***	0.999***	67
Free-range sheep	0.093	0.560***	–0.048***	0.002*	0.959***	–0.280***	0.029***	0.061***	0.999***	93
Small-scale broiler	–2.012**	0.664***	–0.107**	0.010	0.374	–0.484***	0.062**	0.167***	0.998***	119
Middle-scale broiler	2.450***	–0.083	–0.176***	0.013***	1.774***	–0.335***	0.026***	0.077***	0.999***	204
Large-scale broiler	–1.088	0.695***	–0.273***	0.016***	2.237***	–0.243**	0.006	0.159***	0.997***	128
Free-range dairy cow	–4.589***	1.069***	–0.123***	0.009***	–0.752	–0.251**	0.020*	0.047***	0.999***	135
Small-scale dairy cow	2.490**	0.205*	–0.186***	0.012	0.884	–0.190	0.014	0.081***	0.987***	199
Middle-scale dairy cow	4.042***	0.044	–0.206***	0.018***	1.789***	–0.354***	0.038***	0.087***	0.999***	194
Large-scale dairy cow	1.647*	0.291**	–0.110	0.005	0.677	–0.065	0.002	0.157***	0.999***	254

Note: ***, **, * are 1%, 5%, and 10% levels of significance, respectively;

Y: output, *t*: time, σ^2: sum of variances of v and u, v: two-sided random error, u: technical inefficiency, γ: $\frac{\sigma_u^2}{\sigma_u^2+\sigma_v^2}$, obs: number of observation; Provincial dummy variables are omitted.

Overall, 17 individual farming labor-use equations estimated (94% of total) have a highly significant value of γ, defined as $[\sigma_u^2/(\sigma_u^2+\sigma_u^2)]$, denoting that most variations of composite errors in equation (10) are due to technical inefficiency rather than measurement errors or random noise. More than half of the estimated coefficients of different farm outputs are statistically significant. The negative and significant time trends in $f(.)$ for 14 products indicate labor productivity increases overtime. The time trends in the inefficiency specification show that labor became more efficiently used in 10 products, and almost all of them can maintain this efficiency improvement, as indicated by the positive sign of their quadratic terms. In particular, rice, corn, cotton, and apple show this pattern strongly. Except the small-scale pigs, all other animal husbandry labor-use equations (92% of total) also have highly significant γ. More than two-thirds of the estimated coefficients of animal husbandry outputs are statistically significant. The negative and significant time trends in $f(.)$ for 10 products indicate labor productivity increases across the sample period. Efficiency improvement in labor use is confirmed in the production of backyard pigs, large-scale pigs, free-range sheep, small- and medium-scale broilers, and medium-scale dairy cows.

Appendix 3: Agricultural Wages in China

We review the provincial-level data on the real agricultural wage from the Rural Household Survey (RHS)[22] covering the 1996–2010 period. In China, rural households rely on net incomes[23] from four possible sources: incomes from family-run primary production and other business activities (FAM), wages and salaries, property incomes, and transfer incomes (including public and private transfers, e.g., remittances).[24] The net FAM income is and has always been a dominant source of earnings for Chinese rural households, although its share has been gradually declining, as more farmers participate in profit-driven production activities in local villages and thereby earn wages and salaries. As shown in Figure A3.1, the net FAM income accounted for more than half of household net income between 1995 and 2012. Other sources of household income were increasing during that period, particularly from wages and salaries, but accounted for relatively small proportions. Incomes from these

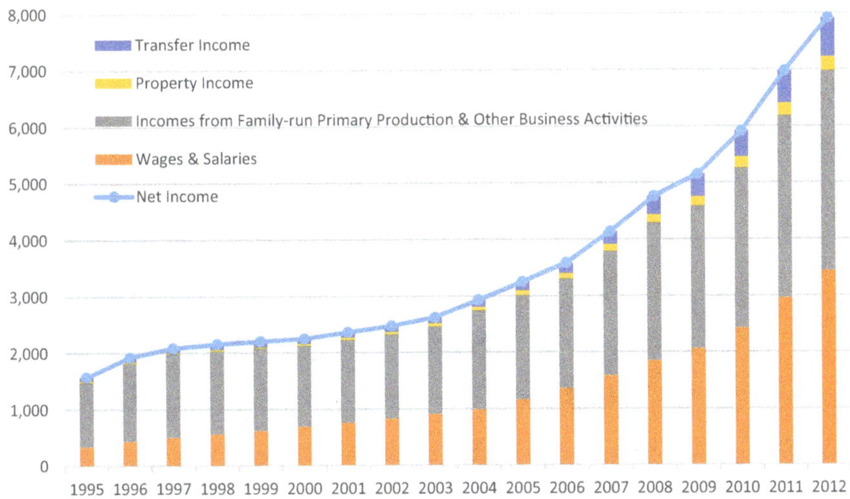

Figure A3.1. Net incomes and their composition in China's rural households, 1995–2012.

Note: All amounts are in nominal per capita RMB.
Source: NBS (2013).

sources may vary remarkably across households, depending on economic conditions or government policies. Hence, the net FAM income refers to the earnings that support subsistence living among rural households, especially when other sources of income are not in place, or they account for disproportionally small amounts. Moreover, FAM income is usually shared within a household — a typical application of the conventional sharing rule, assumed by Lewis for wage determination in the traditional sector. Thus, the net FAM income is a better proxy for the agricultural real wage rate defined in our analysis than those used in previous literature.

It is worth noting that FAM income is mainly generated by primary production, which refers to farming, fishery, forestry, and animal husbandry. As shown in Figure A3.2, it may also be generated by secondary and tertiary production activities, when rural households are involved in some family-run business activities, such as food processing, ecological tourism, restaurants, hotels, and petty trade. Although FAM incomes from secondary and tertiary production account for a small proportion, they still increase farmers'

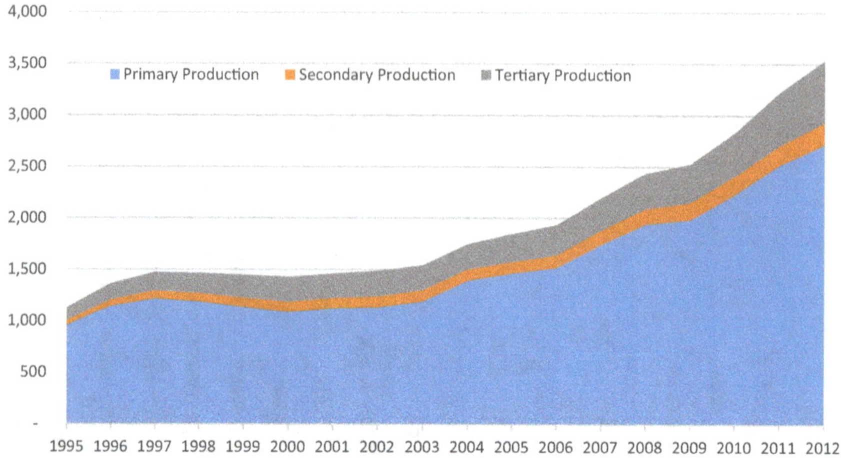

Figure A3.2. Sectoral composition of rural household incomes from FAM, 1995–2012.

Note: All amounts are in nominal per capita RMB.
Source: NBS (2013).

incomes. We use the net FAM income from primary production[25] to capture the lowest level of the real agricultural wage rate (*LW*), while the net FAM income from total production captures the highest level (*HW*). Both wage measures are deflated by the rural consumer price index (CPI),[26] converted to the year 2000 prices and expressed in per worker terms[27] to match the agricultural productivity measured per worker. *LW* and *HW* help define a range to which the true value of agricultural wages may belong.

The agricultural wages in the four macroeconomic regions are derived as the arithmetic averages[28] of provincial-level agricultural wages, as shown in Figure A3.3.

Increments in agricultural wages show that the minimum standard of living for Chinese farmers has generally improved. This could be a result of technological advancements in agriculture, with possible wider applications of greenhouses, bio-techniques, and fertilizers. It may also be due to the increase in terms of trade against industry, when surplus labor emigrates and agricultural productivity increases (Lewis, 1972). However, it does not necessarily mean that the agricultural wage rate has started to be determined by labor's marginal productivity.

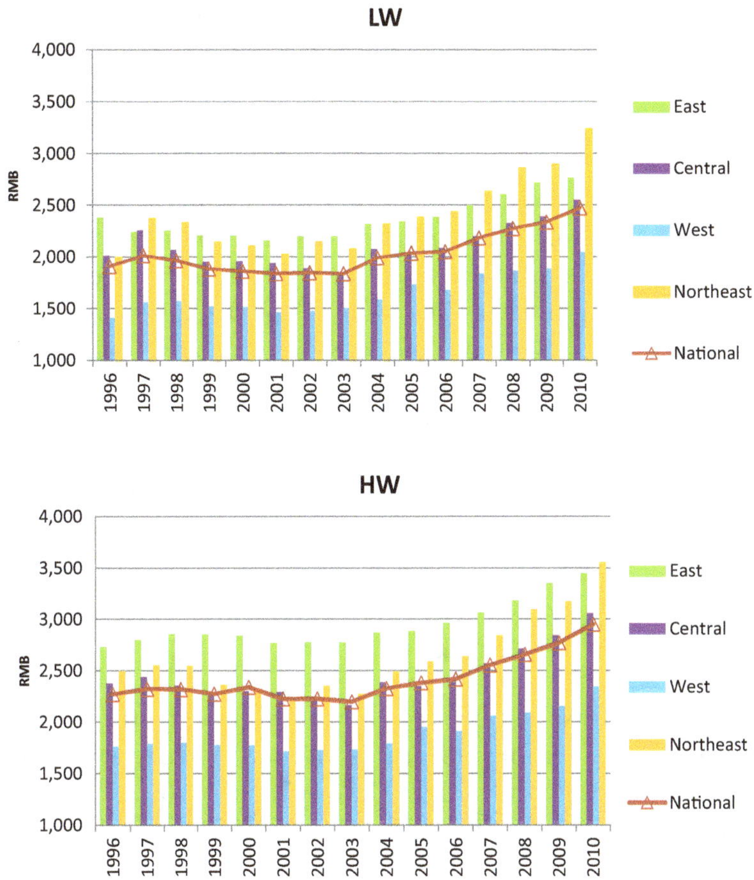

Figure A3.3. Agricultural wages across China's macroeconomic regions, 1996–2010.

Note: The data for LW and HW are compiled at the aggregate level and for the four macroeconomic regions, respectively.
Sources: NBS (1996–2010).

Appendix 4: Agricultural Labor Productivity in China

The agricultural labor's marginal productivity is the product of the average output of labor and the output elasticity with respect to labor, estimated by the transcendental logarithmic production function:

$$\ln Y_{it} = A + \sum_{i=1}^{n} \alpha_i \ln x_{it} + \frac{1}{2}\sum_{i=1}^{n}\sum_{j=1}^{n} \beta_{ij} \ln x_{it} \ln x_{jt} + T + \sum_{k=1}^{n-1} \gamma_k D_k + \varepsilon_{it} \quad \text{(A4.1)}$$

Where Y_{it} represents the gross output value of agriculture in prefecture I at time t and is deflated by the rural CPI at the year 2000 prices. A is a constant, and ε_{it} is the error term. Inputs x_{it} and x_{jt} include labor, capital, land, and fertilizers. Labor is the direct measure of workers in primary production. Capital is measured by the power generated from machinery, while chemical fertilizers are measured by their net contents and considered intermediate inputs. A time trend, T, is included to capture technical change over time. Equation (1) is estimated[29] by OLS (Cobb–Douglas and translog) and GLS (translog FE and translog RE) with a panel of prefecture-level data between 1996 and 2010.[30]

Table A4.1 shows different estimates of the production function. Since the random effect model is more efficient in accommodating time-invariant provincial heterogeneity of agricultural production,[31] column (3) results are used to compute the output elasticities:

$$\frac{\partial Y_{it}}{\partial x_{it}} = \left[\frac{\partial \ln Y_{it}}{\partial \ln x_{it}}\right]\left[\frac{Y_{it}}{x_{it}}\right] = \left[\alpha_i + \sum_{j=1}^{n} \beta_{ij} \ln x_{jt}\right]\left[\frac{Y_{it}}{x_{it}}\right] \qquad \text{(A4.2)}$$

Table A4.2 lists the values of elasticities by taking the averages of estimated elasticities for prefectures within a province to obtain provincial elasticities. At the national level, China's output elasticity with respect to labor was around 0.21 during 1996–2010, which is in line with other studies (such as Islam and Yokota, 2008; Minami and Ma, 2011). We observe a declining trend in the elasticities, suggesting that the use of agricultural labor in China has diminishing marginal returns.

By multiplying the provincial-level output elasticities regarding labor by the average product of labor in a particular province, we obtain the MPLs for each province. Again, we take the average values of provincial MPLs to obtain regional and national values. As reported in Table A4.3, at the national level, agricultural MPL remained relatively stable until 2002 and then started to increase at a rate of 5.6% per annum. In 2010, China's agricultural productivity was 175% of that in 1996 in real terms. This rising trend is also observed in the four regions. The MPL in the central region

Table A4.1. China's agricultural production function, 1996–2010.

Y	(1) CD OLS	(2) Translog OLS	(3) Translog RE	(4) Translog FE
L	0.209***	0.629***	0.393***	1.217***
	(0.014)	(0.064)	(0.083)	(0.080)
N	0.271***	–0.574***	0.103	–1.052***
	(0.015)	(0.074)	(0.111)	(0.094)
F	0.222***	0.140***	0.226***	0.253***
	(0.011)	(0.041)	(0.047)	(0.048)
M	0.198***	0.582***	0.191***	0.488***
	(0.012)	(0.053)	(0.057)	(0.061)
T	0.026***	0.004	0.027***	–0.006
	(0.001)	(0.009)	(0.006)	(0.012)
L*L		0.000	0.000*	0.001*
		(0.000)	(0.000)	(0.000)
N*N		0.089***	0.045***	0.045**
		(0.014)	(0.011)	(0.017)
F*F		0.186***	0.097***	0.193***
		(0.013)	(0.014)	(0.016)
M*M		0.090***	0.024***	0.080***
		(0.007)	(0.007)	(0.009)
T*T		–0.001	–0.024***	–0.044***
		(0.005)	(0.004)	(0.005)
L*N		–0.139***	–0.153***	–0.225***
		(0.018)	(0.020)	(0.024)
L*M		–0.007	0.083***	0.105***
		(0.013)	(0.014)	(0.016)
L*F		–0.052***	0.002	–0.067***
		(0.013)	(0.011)	(0.016)
L*T		–0.004	–0.008***	–0.009**
		(0.002)	(0.001)	(0.003)
L*M		–0.219***	–0.134***	–0.280***
		(0.019)	(0.017)	(0.024)
N*F		0.026	0.036**	0.139***
		(0.016)	(0.014)	(0.019)
N*T		0.014***	0.008***	0.019***
		(0.003)	(0.002)	(0.004)

(*Continued*)

Table A4.1. (*Continued*)

Y	(1) CD OLS	(2) Translog OLS	(3) Translog RE	(4) Translog FE
M*F		0.041***	0.023**	0.041**
		(0.011)	(0.009)	(0.013)
M*T		−0.011***	−0.002*	−0.014***
		(0.002)	(0.001)	(0.003)
F*T		−0.000	−0.000	0.001
		(0.001)	(0.001)	(0.002)
Constant	-1.570***	-0.898***	−0.849**	0.095
	(0.103)	(0.179)	(0.306)	(0.173)
Provincial dummies	Yes	Yes	Yes	N/A
R squares	0.915	0.925	0.638	0.844
Observations	3480	3480	3480	3480

Note: The dependent variable is Y, the gross value of agricultural output. L: Labor. N: Adjusted land. F: Chemical fertilizer. M: Agricultural machinery *, ** and *** represent the significance at the 10%, 5%, and 1% levels, respectively. CD and Translog are Cobb–Douglas and Translog specifications. OLS, FE, and RE are ordinary least squares, fixed effect, and random effect models, respectively.

Table A4.2. Agricultural output elasticities with respect to labor in China, 1996–2010.

Year	National	East	Central	West	Northeast
1996	0.224	0.232	0.215	0.211	0.311
1997	0.225	0.227	0.215	0.220	0.307
1998	0.223	0.221	0.210	0.223	0.303
1999	0.221	0.218	0.210	0.219	0.299
2000	0.214	0.213	0.207	0.210	0.291
2001	0.205	0.214	0.179	0.208	0.284
2002	0.206	0.208	0.197	0.202	0.279
2003	0.207	0.210	0.199	0.202	0.273
2004	0.204	0.207	0.197	0.195	0.285

Table A4.2. (*Continued*)

Year	National	East	Central	West	Northeast
2005	0.201	0.204	0.194	0.194	0.269
2006	0.198	0.197	0.196	0.191	0.265
2007	0.196	0.196	0.191	0.189	0.262
2008	0.193	0.190	0.191	0.186	0.259
2009	0.191	0.191	0.185	0.185	0.254
2010	0.186	0.182	0.179	0.184	0.250
Average	0.206	0.207	0.198	0.201	0.279

Note: Elasticities reported in this table are the arithmetic averages of the prefectural-level elasticities estimated, based on those reported in Column (3) of Table A4.1.

Table A4.3. Agricultural marginal products of labor (MPLs) in China, 1996–2010.

	Agricultural MPLs				
Year	National	East	Central	West	Northeast
1996	1701.31	2257.24	1492.68	945.29	3937.07
1997	1633.53	2131.40	1500.21	925.76	3545.41
1998	1706.89	2176.82	1495.91	960.73	4090.65
1999	1778.43	2291.15	1572.57	993.91	4182.99
2000	1757.03	2295.67	1622.70	981.02	3945.33
2001	1794.57	2432.31	1435.61	1040.18	4218.96
2002	1906.97	2466.42	1730.64	1054.98	4380.02
2003	2104.78	2789.53	1919.03	1168.82	4624.02
2004	2300.28	2951.66	2106.64	1268.82	5272.49
2005	2304.66	3060.53	2058.51	1298.33	5018.75
2006	2442.91	3073.50	2191.23	1375.66	5332.28
2007	2708.08	3306.52	2450.47	1554.31	5957.02
2008	2609.66	3244.15	2510.69	1530.12	5341.01
2009	2740.15	3432.56	2623.68	1567.89	5611.90
2010	2985.91	3649.92	3016.81	1746.24	5962.78
Averages	2165.01	2770.63	1981.83	1227.47	4761.38
	Average annual growth rates of MPLs (%)				
1996–2010	4.02	3.43	5.03	4.38	2.97
1996–2002	1.90	1.48	2.47	1.83	1.78
2003–2010	5.60	4.90	6.95	6.30	3.86

Note: The agricultural MPLs reported in this table are the arithmetic averages of the prefectural-level MPLs, calculated based on equation (3).

experienced a speedy increase: 7% per year during the 2003–2010 period. Among the four regions, MPLs are higher in northeastern and eastern China but much lower in western China.

Appendix 5: Comparisons of Labor Flows in Selected Three-Sector Models

Kwan *et al.* (2018)	From *Rural Agriculture* to *Rural Non-Agriculture* From *Rural Agriculture* to *Urban Non-Agriculture*
Wu (1995)	From *Rural Agriculture* to *Rural Industry* From *Rural Agriculture* to *Urban SOE (Industry)*
Brandt *et al.* (2008)	From *Rural Agriculture* to *Non-SOEs* From *Rural Agriculture* to *SOEs*
Lewis-Fei-Ranis (1954, 1961)	From *Traditional Sector* to *Modern Sector*

Note: Wu (1995): the three sectors account for around 80% of total output, w/o the service sectors in both rural and urban areas.

Appendix 6: The Three-Sector Model

All data for our empirical analysis are at the provincial level, mainly from the China Statistical Yearbook and the China Rural Statistical Yearbook published by the National Bureau of Statistics of China (NBSa and NBSb), with the agricultural statistics coming from the Ministry of Agriculture (2009). The sample period starts from the earliest available year of data and ends in 2010, long enough to capture China's economic changes during the reform period.[32]

Using OLS to estimate equation (8) may lead to a biased and inconsistent estimation because geographic, demographic, and other unobserved time invariant individual specific effects might be correlated with the regressors. Furthermore, the lagged dependent variable y_{it-1} is possibly endogenous to the error term via v_{it}, invalidating the use of the OLS technique. The issue of endogeneity of X_{it} could be serious for two possible reasons. Economic growth is likely to have a two-way interaction with the level of education and other factor inputs. In addition, labor might move to either the rural non-agriculture or urban sectors if the economy experiences strong output expansion. To obtain consistent parameter estimates with potential endogeneity and measurement errors on the right-hand side of equation [16], we follow the procedure suggested by Arellano and Bond (1991). This methodology was further refined by Caselli *et al.* (1996) and has become increasingly popular for studying economic growth (such as Easterly *et al.*, 1997).

In brief, equation (8) is first differenced and then the lagged levels of variables on the right-hand side are treated as instruments in the first-differenced equation. We use the one-step system GMM technique to estimate our dynamic panel data model.[33]

Table A6.1 presents the initial results of the three-sector model. The conventional input variables (except for population) are all statistically significant, although the sign on initial per capita income is not as expected. The two newly introduced structural change terms are jointly significant (as demonstrated by the Joint F tests, such as 38.141 for the system GMM model), though the two nonlinear terms are not individually significant. Including more independent variables could potentially over-specify any dynamic panel data model; however, the Sargan tests suggest that there is no evidence of overidentification.[34]

According to Temple and Wößmann (2006), countries going through larger structural change will experience a greater impact on their output growth, captured by the convex relationship between output growth and the extent of structural change. In China, provinces with larger wage differentials are expected to observe a bigger effect of labor transfer to either rural non-agriculture or urban non-agriculture, as indicated by the two nonlinear structural change terms specified in equation [16]. Our empirical results show that the $DISEQ_b$ terms are negative but not statistically significant at the 10% level.

Econometrically, in addition to the statistical significance of individual parameters, the high Joint F values provide support for the overall stability of the models we test. The *p*-values of Arellano–Bond tests on AR1 and AR2 confirm the non-existence of first-order serial correlation across models, indicating that the instruments in our models are valid with system GMM estimation.

Table A6.1. Three-sector model.

	OLS	Fixed effect	System GMM
$\ln(y_{i,t-1})$	0.047***	0.054***	0.059***
	(0.009)	(0.015)	(0.016)
$\ln(S_{it})$	0.251***	0.364***	0.417***
	(0.052)	(0.073)	(0.094)
$\ln(n_{it} + g + \delta)$	–0.091**	–0.040	–0.035
	(0.032)	(0.035)	(0.027)
$\ln(h_{it})$	0.004	0.012	0.022*
	(0.008)	(0.008)	(0.010)
$GROWTH_b$	5.373***	4.459***	4.384***
	(0.623)	(0.666)	(1.092)
$GROWTH_m$	1.742**	1.984**	2.790***
	(0.580)	(0.594)	(0.648)
$DISEQ_b$	–5.009*	–1.317	–1.691
	(2.160)	(2.207)	(1.123)
$DISEQ_m$	12.523*	5.972	6.637
	(5.225)	(5.345)	(5.850)
Constant	–0.497***	–0.455***	–0.508***
	(0.103)	(0.126)	(0.112)
Sargan			171.587
Sargan p			0.409
AR1 p			0.006
AR2 p			0.682
Joint F	27.998	31.989	38.141

Note: The model is based on equation [16]. The three-year interval provincial panel data are used for estimation; $y_{i,t-1}$: lagged per capita output; S_{it}: saving rates; n_{it}: population growth rate; h_{it}: human capital; g: productivity growth; δ: depreciation; Heteroskedasticity-consistent standard errors are in parentheses; AR1 p and AR2 p denote the *p*-values of first order and second order serial correlations, respectively; Joint F is test for overall significance; Sargan and Sargan P are test and its *p*-value for over-identification; ***, **, * are 1%, 5%, & 10% levels of significance, respectively; $y_{i,t-1}$ and h_{it} are treated as pre-determined variables; S_{it}, n_{it}, *MGROWTH*, and *DISEQ* are treated as endogenous variables; $g + \delta$ is assumed to be 5%.

Table A6.2. Three-sector model in Cobb–Douglas method.

	OLS	Fixed effect	System GMM
$\ln(y_{i,t-1})$	0.058***	0.075***	0.071***
	(0.009)	(0.015)	(0.018)
$\ln(S_{it})$	0.290***	0.364***	0.455***
	(0.052)	(0.071)	(0.088)
$\ln(n_{it} + g + \delta)$	–0.097**	–0.044	–0.036
	(0.031)	(0.034)	(0.026)
$\ln(h_{it})$	0.010	0.020*	0.031**
	(0.008)	(0.008)	(0.009)
$GROWTH2_b$	12.622***	10.636***	11.080**
	(1.492)	(1.589)	(3.154)
$GROWTH2_m$	2.748	3.350*	5.114**
	(1.500)	(1.507)	(1.706)
$DISEQ2_b$	–25.711*	–7.305	–8.567
	(10.275)	(10.452)	(5.197)
$DISEQ2_m$	33.022*	17.654	21.808
	(13.933)	(13.966)	(14.252)
Constant	–0.612***	–0.627***	–0.631***
	(0.105)	(0.129)	(0.130)
Sargan			177.750
Sargan p			0.288
Hansen			21.542
Hansen p			1.000
AR1 p			0.004
AR2 p			0.645
Joint F	28.269	33.539	38.578

Note: The model is based on equation [16]. The three-year interval provincial panel data are used for estimation; $y_{i,t-1}$: lagged per capita output; S_{it}: saving rates; n_{it}: population growth rate; h_{it}: human capital; g: productivity growth; δ: depreciation; Heteroskedasticity-consistent standard errors are in parentheses; AR1 p and AR2 p denote the *p*-values of first order and second order serial correlations, respectively; Joint F is test for overall significance; Sargan and Sargan P are test and its *p*-value for over-identification; ***, **, * are 1%, 5%, & 10% levels of significance, respectively; $y_{i,t-1}$ and h_{it} are treated as pre-determined variables; S_{it}, n_{it}, *MGROWTH*, and *DISEQ* are treated as endogenous variables; $g + \delta$ is assumed to be 5%.

Table A6.3. Three-sector model in two regions.

	Coastal	Noncoastal
$\ln(y_{i,t-1})$	0.044	0.084**
	(0.024)	(0.029)
$\ln(S_{it})$	0.449***	0.264
	(0.073)	(0.128)
$\ln(n_{it} + g + \delta)$	–0.070*	–0.037
	(0.024)	(0.050)
$\ln(h_{it})$	0.012	0.019
	(0.012)	(0.013)
$GROWTH_b$	5.260***	3.995
	(0.906)	(1.895)
$GROWTH_m$	3.658***	1.870*
	(0.623)	(0.745)
$DISEQ_b$	–1.264	–9.964
	(0.774)	(33.590)
$DISEQ_m$	–0.594	19.170*
	(2.997)	(6.789)
Constant	–0.502*	–0.614***
	(0.185)	(0.146)
Sargan	95.751	157.390
Sargan p	0.904	0.228
AR1 p	0.085	0.033
AR2 p	0.935	0.903
Joint F	18.394	43.030

Note: The model is based on equation [16] estimated by system GMM. The three-year interval provincial panel data are used for estimation; $y_{i,t-1}$: lagged per capita output; S_{it}: saving rates; n_{it}: population growth rate; h_{it}: human capital; g: productivity growth; δ: depreciation; Heteroskedasticity-consistent standard errors are in parentheses; AR1 p and AR2 p denote the *p*-values of first order and second order serial correlations, respectively; Joint F is test for overall significance; Sargan and Sargan P are test and its *p*-value for over-identification; ***, **, * are 1%, 5%, & 10% level of significance, respectively; $y_{i,t-1}$ and $h_{i,t}$ are treated as pre-determined variables; S_{it}, n_{it}, *MGROWTH* , and *DISEQ* are treated as endogenous variables; $g + \delta$ is assumed to be 5%.

In addition to the effect of labor reallocation on growth, this study also provides empirical evidence of the use of conventional variables in explaining growth in the dualistic Chinese economy. Savings are considered essential in mobilizing resources for productive activities, and our results show that the saving rates are statistically significant at the 1% level in every model that we estimate (excluding the noncoastal regression). Another important variable for modern economic growth is the stock of human capital. Our modified human capital data fit both the two-sector and three-sector frameworks well: 0.031 in the three-sector Cobb-Douglas setting and 0.036 in the two-sector framework. It is worth noting that including both the saving rate and human capital in the Cobb–Douglas three-sector model enhances the explanatory power of the two structural terms.

The Solow-type neoclassical model predicts that poor economies can catch up thanks to faster economic growth under proper market functioning. Many studies examine the speed of inter-provincial growth convergence in post-reform China, and some point to growing regional disparities in recent years. Bosworth and Collins (2008) find that Chinese provinces may converge in the long run but diverge over the short term. After controlling for the population and economic size of individual provinces, Herrerias (2012) finds that Chinese regions are growing at different speeds. Anderson and Ge (2009) conclude that the evidence on convergence in the economy is mixed, with a convergence in the center of the distribution but divergence at the extremes. Similar to Pedroni and Yao (2006) and Lau (2010), our empirical findings of positive per capita income growth suggest increased disparities across provinces in China between 1980 and 2010 rather than convergence.

https://doi.org/10.1142/9789819815241_0006

Chapter 6

WHY CHINA'S ECONOMY GREW RAPIDLY? AN INVESTIGATION BASED ON THE EAST ASIAN MODEL

Deqiang Liu

Kyoto University
liu.deqiang.4z@kyoto-u.ac.jp

Introduction

Since the implementation of the reform and opening-up policy in China in 1978, its economic development has been remarkable. Its GDP per capita increased from US$200 in 1978 to US$12,300 in 2021. It is expected that China will soon become a high-income country. The size of China's economy surpassed Japan's in 2010 to become the world's second-largest economy. It is expected to overtake the United States (US) as the largest economy in the world by 2030 (Nikkei Center, 2020).

What is the main driving force behind China's rapid economic growth?[1] This question has long been debated by economists. A common view is that the rapid growth of China's economy has benefited from (1) the reform and opening-up policy in 1978,

(2) globalization, (3) the effective utilization of market mechanisms, (4) moderate government intervention, and (5) orderly and progressive reforms (Liu, 2012). This theory comprehensively reflects the important factors that were in play during China's economic growth. However, it does not specify the exact mechanism of such rapid economic growth.

A more convincing theory is that China adopted the comparatively advantageous development strategy after the reform and opening up. Before 1978, China prioritized the development of heavy industry. Such a development strategy went against China's comparative advantages and hindered its economic development. Since the implementation of the reform and opening-up policy in 1978, China has implemented a comparative advantage strategy that was in line with its own factor endowment, which took advantage of cheap labor and being a latecomer, and led to economic acceleration (Lin, 2012). This theory presents a promising explanation as to why China did not develop before the reform and opening up, yet it does not explain why other countries without prioritization of heavy industry did not experience such rapid growth.

Another theory states that one way for developing countries like China to take advantage of their latecomer advantage is to introduce advanced technology from developed countries. Since advanced technologies are often embodied in machinery and equipment, importing the latter from abroad is an important pathway to introducing advanced technology. Since 1978, not only the quantity but also the proportion of machinery and equipment has increased significantly among China's imported products, which has greatly improved the technological level of China's manufacturing industry and accelerated its economic development (Zhang, 2013). This theory explains more concretely and clearly the source of China's rapid economic growth, but it does not touch on why China is able to massively import advanced technology and equipment from abroad.[2]

Stiglitz (2013) believed that exports played a critical role in China's economic development; that is, the rapid growth in the past three decades was export-driven. As in other East Asian countries, exports played an important role in providing a platform for innovation, enhancing competition, and eliminating excess capacity. Moreover, Stiglitz also emphasized the role of foreign exchange reserves in preventing financial crises. However, Stiglitz's discussion was mainly focused on the contribution of exports at the macro level without examining the mechanism by which exports and foreign exchange earnings promote China's economic growth.

In addition to the above theories, there are some other views with unique perspectives. For instance, Zhang (2009) proposed the theory of county-level government competition, Lu (2022) developed the basic structure theory of a great power, and Zhu (2016) applied the theory of Confucianism to explore the reasons for China's rapid economic growth.

In summary, each of the above studies was able to explain the question from one or several aspects, which provided insights for solving the mystery of China's rapid economic growth. However, we believe that this mystery is still not completely solved. This is because none of the existing studies have answered the following question: How can we solve the problem of insufficient foreign currency that is often faced by developing countries? In order for a lagging economy to take advantage of its latecomer advantage, imports from developed countries are necessary, including advanced technologies, machinery and equipment, and other factors that contribute to economic growth. However, imported products cost money (foreign currency). The higher the development goals of the government, the more foreign exchange it needs and the greater the constraints it is subject to. Therefore, whether to adopt a development strategy of rapidly increasing foreign exchange income is a key factor in the success of economic development in such countries.

In the current study, we examined the economic development processes of some East Asian countries/regions, including Japan, South Korea, Taiwan, and China. The following conclusions were obtained: (1) China's rapid economic growth is because of the export-oriented industrialization strategy. This strategy has enabled China to expand exports, increase its foreign exchange reserve, and eliminate the foreign exchange constraints caused by importing foreign technologies. (2) The smooth implementation of export-oriented industrialization in China is due to the marketization and privatization reforms in China. (3) China's economic development model is in line with the East Asian model.

The rest of this chapter is organized as follows: the second section presents the common development strategies adopted by developing countries in order to provide basic concepts and frameworks for subsequent discussions. The third section describes the development strategies of East Asian economies and the reasons and conditions for the adoption of such strategies. The fourth section introduces the process and results of the export-oriented industrialization strategy in China. The fifth section briefly summarizes several unique factors that are conducive to China's economic development. The last section presents the conclusions and prospects of this study.

Industrialization Strategies

Factors affecting economic growth

For an agricultural country, economic development usually means industrialization. Unlike traditional agricultural production, industrial production not only requires the traditional investment of land and labor but also other production materials such as capital, raw materials, and energy. Moreover, since the economic growth of the least-developed countries is actually a process of continuously adopting various advanced technologies and advanced institutions, technologies and institutions are also indispensable input factors. In addition, the market size of a country will also restrict its economic growth. Therefore, to study the economic development of the least-developed countries, various factors need to be taken into consideration.

Further, the labor required for production includes not only physical labor but also a large amount of intelligent labor in terms of technological support and management. Similarly, the funds or capital needed for production include not only the general capital used to build factories and purchase various raw materials, machinery, and equipment but also the foreign exchange required for the purchase of these input factors from abroad. For an undeveloped agricultural country, almost all the factors needed for industrialization, such as advanced technology, machinery, and equipment, are purchased internationally. In essence, the so-called industrialization is the process of continuously importing, digesting, and absorbing foreign advanced technologies.[3] This process usually requires a large amount of foreign exchange.

To put it another way, the economic development of a country is directly restricted by the above factors. The factor endowment status of developing countries is usually characterized by a lack of capital and foreign exchange, a lack of technology and talents, a lagging system and poor infrastructure, an underdeveloped market, and a low-efficiency government. Resources that are abundant are land and labor. Industrialization under such factor endowment conditions will be heavily subject to various constraints. Among them, foreign exchange constraints are the most severe. Hence, increasing foreign exchange earnings is an important measure for accelerating the country's economic development.

Importance of foreign exchange

For a developing country, insufficient funds are a major constraint. However, what is more serious than insufficient funds is the shortage of foreign exchange. This is because the shortage of funds can be relatively easily resolved through some domestic policies, such as raising interest rates, encouraging savings, issuing treasury bonds, and even creating inflation. However, easing foreign exchange constraints requires the cooperation of foreign institutions, which is much more challenging.

In general, the main method for the industrialization of developing countries is to import advanced technologies from developed countries. Advanced technologies usually mean advanced equipment. Therefore, introducing advanced technologies means importing advanced equipment from developed countries. In a sense, the speed of economic growth depends on the speed of importing advanced technologies and equipment, which in turn depends on the speed of foreign exchange earnings of a country.[4]

There are usually four ways for developing countries to obtain foreign currency. The first one is to seek financial aid from foreign governments and international institutions. The second is to borrow from foreign financial institutions. The third is to attract direct foreign investment, and the last one is to earn foreign exchange through exports. A country will usually not be able to secure sufficient foreign currency for industrialization through the first way. The second method is affected by the solvency of the country, and it is generally difficult if there is no other way to obtain foreign exchange. Even if it can be done, the cost and risk are very high. The third way, i.e., foreign investment, is the most straightforward and safest. However, this depends on the country's international credibility and government policies, and it can be a lengthy process. This is because the infrastructure and institutional environment in developing countries are often very poor and do not meet the requirements of multinational enterprises. In the end, the most feasible way is to earn foreign exchange through exports. Only when a country has the ability to earn foreign exchange from exports can it be easier to obtain international loans and direct investment. The main export products of agricultural countries are usually primary products. Unless the country is rich in mineral resources, it is often difficult to obtain the foreign exchange needed for industrialization by exporting agricultural goods alone.

Conversely, if a country can obtain enough foreign exchange by itself, then all the resources needed for industrialization can be easily obtained from the international market, and the various constraints can also be eliminated more easily. In addition to constraints in capital, other constraints, such as advanced technology, high-end technical and management personnel, and energy and raw materials, can also be easily resolved. A country that has just started the industrialization process can only use low-quality domestic resources if there is no foreign exchange reserve. However, if foreign exchange is available, it can directly use relatively high-quality resources from all over the world. Hence, foreign exchange is critical to the successful economic growth of developing countries. Therefore, in the early stages of industrialization, how to increase foreign exchange earnings as soon as possible is a question of decisive significance to a country's economic growth.

Three industrialization strategies

After World War II (WWII), many former colonial countries gained political independence and started the process of industrialization. However, more than 70 years have passed, and there are only a handful of cases where a traditional agricultural country has become a developed industrial country. The vast majority of developing countries have yet to achieve industrialization and escape poverty. The reason is that different countries have adopted different development strategies or development models.[5] The development strategies and models adopted in developing countries can roughly be divided into three categories (Table 1).

Table 1. Comparison of three development strategies.

Development strategy	Priority industries	Necessary factors of production	Factors of production in shortage
Import substitution industrialization I	Heavy industrial products	Capital, foreign exchange, technology, management, labor, raw materials and components, and market	Capital, foreign exchange, technology, management, raw materials, and components
Import substitution industrialization II	Light industrial products	Capital, foreign exchange, technology, management, labor, raw materials and components, and market	Foreign exchange and market
Export-oriented industrialization	Light industrial products	Capital, foreign exchange, technology, management, labor, raw materials and components, and market	

The import substitution industrialization strategy is a development strategy often used by developing countries. In this approach, a country restricts the import of some important industrial products by adopting measures such as high tariffs, import quantity restrictions, and foreign exchange controls to support and protect the development of local industrial sectors. The purpose of this strategy is to replace imported products with domestically produced industrial products to reduce the country's dependence on foreign products, reduce scarce foreign exchange expenditures, balance international payments, and promote the development of national industries. According to the types of import substitution products, this strategy can be further divided into import substitution industrialization strategy I, which targets heavy industrial products, and import substitution industrialization strategy II, which targets light industrial products. The other development strategy is the export-oriented industrialization strategy. In this approach, the focus of economic development is placed on expanding exports, through which the country promotes the growth of the entire national economy.

Import substitution industrialization strategy I

Import substitution industrialization strategy I prioritizes the development of the heavy industry. The production technology of heavy industrial products, such as steel, automobiles, and mechanical equipment, is typically capital- and technology-intensive. It requires a large investment of capital, advanced technology, and a large number of technical and management personnel, as well as high-quality raw materials and components. Because countries in their initial stage of industrialization often do not have any industrial capabilities to manufacture machinery, raw materials, and components, considerable amounts of foreign exchange are needed to import those from abroad. Almost all factors needed for industrialization are insufficient in the least-developed countries, especially foreign exchange.[6] Therefore, it is quite challenging for the least-developed countries to pursue this industrialization strategy. Since this development strategy is against the country's comparative advantages, to develop these industries, it must first restrict the import of foreign products through measures such as high tariffs and protect local industry through low-interest loans, financial subsidies, and factor price distortion. State-owned enterprises (SOEs) are also established to promote the development of local industries (Lin, 2012). Even so, these protected industries may not survive. Since the production surplus of agriculture and light industry is forcefully transferred to heavy industry, it is difficult for agriculture and light industry to develop. As a result, the industrialization of countries adopting this strategy mostly ends in failure.

Import substitution industrialization strategy II

The import substitution industrialization strategy II is a strategy that converts imported light industrial products into domestic production to meet domestic consumption. Light industrial products, represented by textiles and daily groceries, are labor-intensive and capital-saving industrial products which comply with the factor endowment status of the least-developed countries. Moreover, the requirements of such industries for technology and management are not high, so it is relatively easy to realize. The development of such industries is beneficial to increasing the employment rate, accumulating capital, promoting the degree of industrialization, and improving people's lives.

However, this development strategy has the following problems:

(1) Foreign exchange constraints. Since the protected light industrial products are based on the needs of the domestic market and the machinery and equipment, raw materials, and components required for the production process are usually imported, the more the production, the more foreign exchange is needed, which will result in insufficient foreign exchange.
(2) Low enterprise efforts. Since the products are protected by high tariffs and there is a lack of competition with similar foreign products, the product quality is not comparable to foreign

products. However, the protected industries tend to establish a relationship with the government so as to obtain favorable benefits, such as tax relief, instead of making profits from product innovation, which reduces the enterprises' competitiveness with regard to international peers.

(3) Constraint in the size of the domestic market. Since the products are only traded on the domestic market, the expansion of the domestic market depends on the growth of people's income, which, in the least-developed countries, is usually a lengthy process, and it is difficult to achieve rapid development of the industry.

(4) Unable to take advantage of the international division of labor. Under this development strategy, the domestic economy needs to be self-sufficient, and every industry has to repeat the same development path and face the same problems mentioned above. Therefore, although this development strategy can better promote economic growth than import substitution industrialization strategy I, the development speed is slow and the cost is high when compared with the export-oriented industrialization strategy.

Export-oriented industrialization strategy

Export-oriented industrialization is a strategy to achieve industrialization by expanding the export of industrial products to international markets. In the early stages of industrialization, a few light industrial products (such as textiles) with strong competitiveness are usually selected and produced for export. The government provides financial, tax, and information support for the production and export of these products and implements an exchange rate policy favoring exports so as to help the industry enter the international market. Since the least-developed countries have a large amount of low-cost labor, they have obvious advantages in the production of labor-intensive products. These products typically do not have high requirements for capital and technology and can be produced even with outdated technology and equipment. The important point is that after obtaining foreign exchange, advanced technology and equipment can be imported, and high-quality and cheap raw materials and other intermediate inputs can be purchased from the international market, which can further improve the international competitiveness of these products and expand exports. As this positive cycle reinforces, these products will become the dominant products of the country. As long as they are accepted by the international market, the products or the industry can continue to grow until the international market is saturated or domestic wages rise, which causes the industry to lose its competitive advantage. By this time, the country had already made great achievements in its industrialization progress.

The export-oriented industrialization strategy has obvious advantages compared to import substitution industrialization strategy II, which also targets light industrial products, and import substitution industrialization strategy I, which targets heavy industrial products. Specifically: (1) it eliminates the foreign exchange constraints, and advanced technology, machinery and equipment, and other production elements can be imported from abroad quickly, maximizing the latecomer advantage. (2) By taking full advantage of the international division of labor, the country can only focus on some of the most advantageous products and industries and form industrial clusters in some regions, thereby further improving the efficiency of the division of labor. In this way, the international competitiveness of the products will further increase, resulting in export expansion and foreign exchange earnings. (3) More foreign direct investment can be attracted. This is because the labor-intensive industries in developed countries usually produce products for the markets of developed countries that they are familiar with, rather than for the markets of developing countries. Therefore, the enterprise's interests can only be realized when the products produced in developing countries can be exported to developed countries on favorable terms. This goal is only possible under the export-oriented industrialization strategy. This strategy is a low-cost and high-efficiency development strategy for developing countries, and countries adopting it are more likely to achieve rapid economic growth compared to those that do not.

Characteristics of the East Asian Model

To explore the reasons for China's rapid economic growth and the characteristics of its development model, it is necessary for us to look at the successful development experiences of various East Asian economies around China. In the early 1980s, when China first began implementing its reform and opening-up policy, it sent high-level government delegations to Japan and Singapore to study their approaches. China's development model has been heavily influenced by the successful development experiences of other East Asian economies, such as Japan and Singapore.

Among East Asian countries/regions, Japan and the Four Asian Tigers (South Korea, Taiwan, Hong Kong, and Singapore) are examples of economies whose per capita GDP has reached the level of developed countries. They are well-deserved success stories. Among them, Hong Kong and Singapore are very small in terms of territory and population, and both are highly urbanized economies, with more than 90% of their populations living in urban areas. They are far behind China in terms of territory and population. Therefore, we only focused on the economies of Japan, Taiwan, and South Korea in this study.

Japan started its industrialization process after the Meiji Restoration in 1867, and its economic development spanned two completely different historical periods separated by WWII. South Korea and Taiwan developed rapidly after WWII and thus have more reference value for China. Figure 1 shows the changes in GDP per capita in purchasing power parity terms for these economies. It can be seen that all three economies experienced rapid economic growth during this period, with Japan's per capita GDP reaching the level of developed countries in the 1970s. Taiwan surpassed Japan after the 2008 financial crisis, and South Korea followed closely behind, entering the ranks of developed countries/regions.

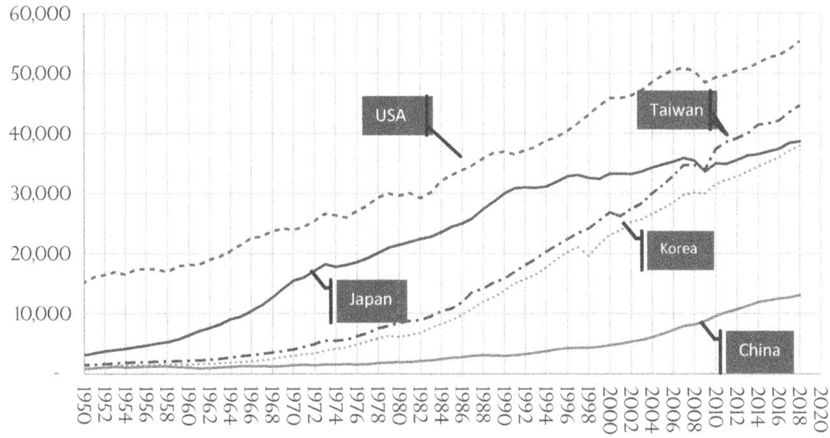

Figure 1. Per capita GDP of East Asian countries/regions (1950–2018, PPP, 2010 prices, international dollar).

Source: Data from Maddison Project Database (2020). https://www.rug.nl/ggdc/historical development/maddison/releases/maddison-project-database-2020?lang=en.

The East Asian model refers to the development model of some East Asian economies that have successfully achieved industrialization and modernization and entered the ranks of developed countries. The World Bank (1993) summarized the characteristics of this model into eight categories: (1) rapid economic growth, (2) reduction in distributional inequality, (3) rapid increase in agricultural production and productivity, (4) rapid growth in industrial exports, (5) rapid decline in birth rate, (6) high capital growth rate supported by high savings rate, (7) rapid growth of human capital in the early stage, and (8) rapid improvement of production efficiency. The World Bank particularly praised the simultaneous realization of rapid economic growth and equitable income distribution, calling it the "East Asian Miracle" (World Bank, 1993), because it challenges the conventional wisdom that economic growth and distributional fairness are incompatible goals. In the East Asian model, these two goals are achieved simultaneously, making it a valuable model for other economies to emulate.

However, it is not difficult to observe that some of these eight characteristics given by the World Bank are the results of economic growth rather than the causes. Those that may be used to explain industrialization or economic growth in whole or in part are: (3) rapid increase in agricultural production and productivity, (4) rapid growth in industrial exports, (6) high capital growth rate supported by a high savings rate, and (7) rapid growth of human capital in the early stage. The rapid growth in industrial exports is the most important factor, which can have a direct or indirect impact on other characteristics. Therefore, the core feature of the East Asian model is rapid growth in industrial exports, which is brought about by the export-oriented industrialization strategy.

Export-oriented industrialization strategy

As mentioned in the previous section, the export-oriented industrialization strategy is more suitable for developing countries. By adopting this strategy, developing countries can solve the most prominent problem of foreign exchange shortages in the process of industrialization, especially in the early stages of economic development. Hence, we first use the trade dependence ratio to analyze the importance of foreign trade in the economic development of Japan, South Korea, and Taiwan.

The trade dependence ratio is the ratio of a country's total trade to the country's GDP. Generally, the higher the ratio, the greater the country's economic dependence on international trade, and the higher the degree of participation in the international division of labor. Other related concepts include the export dependence ratio and the import dependence ratio. The former is the ratio of a country's total exports to the country's GDP, and the latter refers to the ratio of the country's total imports to its GDP.

Figure 2 shows the variation of South Korea's trade dependence ratio. At the start of South Korea's industrialization in 1962, the trade dependence ratio was only 15%, and the export dependence ratio was even lower, at 2%. This means that the Korean economy at that time was focused on the domestic market.[7] However, with the implementation of the first five-year plan promoted by the South Korean government, especially after the implementation of the export-oriented industrialization strategy in 1964, South Korea's

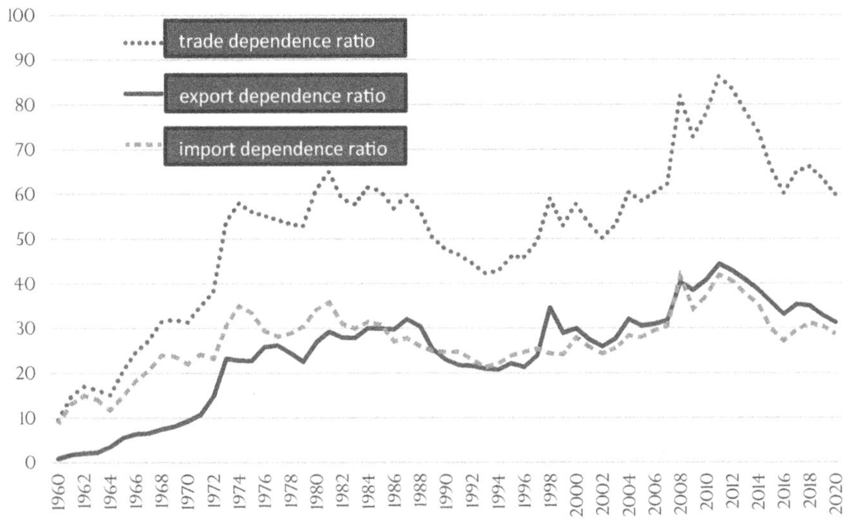

Figure 2. Variations in South Korea's trade dependence ratio (1960–2020, %).
Source: Data from World Bank Database. https://data.worldbank.org/indicator.

trade dependence ratio increased rapidly, from 12% in 1964 to 31% in 1968. The number further increased to 58% in 1974 and 65% in 1981. In this period, the export dependence ratio also increased, reaching 23% in 1973 and 32% in 1987. With the increase in the export dependence ratio, South Korea's import dependence ratio also increased to 36% by 1981.[8]

Figure 3 shows the variation of Taiwan's export dependence ratio since 1951. As can be seen, in the late 1950s, like South Korea, Taiwan also had a very low export dependence ratio, which was close to the world average. After 1962, the ratio increased rapidly, reaching about 45% in 1973 and 57% in 1986. Later, it declined for a certain period and then rose again after 1991, eventually reaching 70% in 2010. It can be seen that Taiwan's export dependence ratio is much higher than the world average. Similar to South Korea, Taiwan's economic development has obvious characteristics of export-oriented industrialization.

From Figure 3, we can also see the changes in Japan's export dependence ratio after WWII. Surprisingly, Japan's export dependence ratio after 1960 did not increase with economic growth; it was

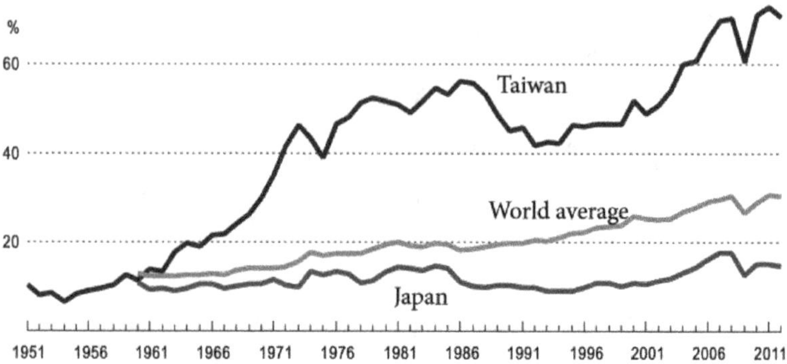

Figure 3. Variations in Taiwan's export dependence ratio (1951–2011).
Source: Wu (2016).

low and even declined for a period of time after 1985. Japan's export dependence ratio after WWII has been even lower than the world average level. Does this mean that the export-oriented industrialization strategy is not working as expected in Japan? The answer is "no." Figure 4 shows the changes in Japan's trade dependence ratio after the Meiji Restoration, from which two characteristics can be obtained:

(1) From 1886 to 1937, when WWII began, Japan's trade dependence ratio increased from 10% to over 50%. This demonstrates that foreign trade also played a leading role in Japan's industrialization process before WWII. From this point of view, Japan's industrialization strategy was consistent with that of Taiwan and South Korea, that is, an export-oriented industrialization strategy. The "flying geese" (FG) pattern of economic development was actually proposed by the famous Japanese economist Akamatsu (1962) based on the industrialization process of pre-war Japan.
(2) During the recovery period after WWII, the Japanese economy saw a rapid increase in the trade dependence ratio, from 5% in 1946 to 30% in 1951. The rapid increase during this period also demonstrates the dominant role of trade in Japan's economic development.[9]

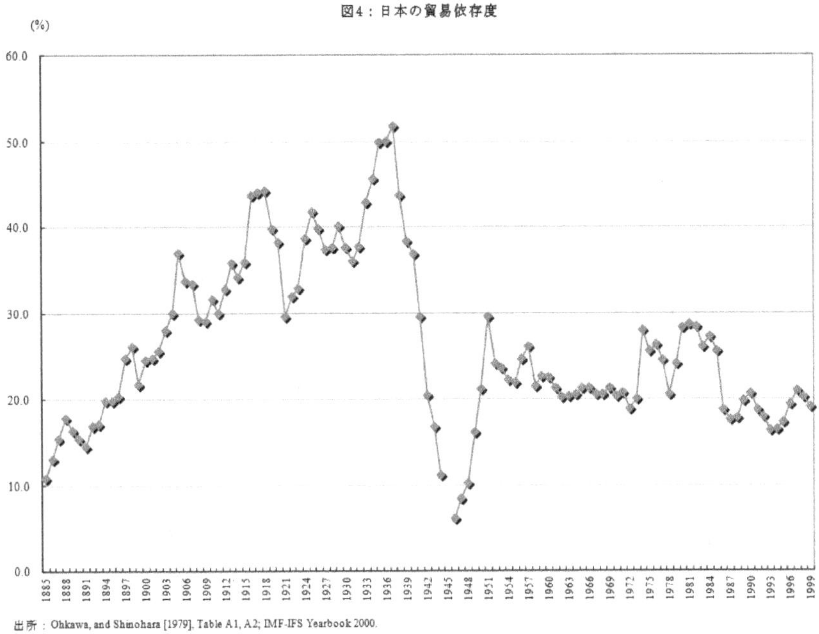

Figure 4. Variations in Japan's trade dependence ratio (1886–2000, %).
Source: Hirohisa Kohama (2007).

It can be concluded from the above analysis that Japan, South Korea, and Taiwan have all implemented export-oriented industrialization strategies in their industrialization process. Because the pre-war international environment for Japan was quite different from that after WWII, we only focus on the implementation of the export-oriented industrialization strategy in South Korea and Taiwan.

Reasons for the implementation of the export-oriented industrialization strategy

After WWII, like many other politically independent developing countries, South Korea and Taiwan sought an independent economic development path. Since both economies were facing severe national security issues, the export-oriented industrialization strategy that relies heavily on the international market was not their first choice but a last resort.

South Korea

When Korea was under Japanese rule, most of the investments on the Korean peninsula were concentrated in today's North Korea, and South Korea's industrial infrastructure was very poor. Beginning in 1950, South Korea experienced the Three Years' War, which made the already poor economy even worse. After the Korean War, South Korea, like other developing countries, implemented an import substitution industrialization strategy. The cotton textile industry and milling industry were the two important industries of import substitution, followed by the chemical fertilizer and sugar industries. Beginning in 1954, the government restricted the import of these products by raising import tariffs and implementing regulations. The government provided support to these industries through preferential allocations of foreign exchange and preferential loans. Under these conditions, these industries developed to a certain extent, yet South Korea's exports have not increased.[10] The Syngman Rhee regime felt the pressure of the foreign exchange shortage and took some measures. However, under an export structure dominated by primary products, the measures resulted in little effect. Hence, Korea relied on US aid. However, US aid declined from US$380 million in 1957 to US$200 million in 1961 (Lee, 2013). This forced South Korea to find another way to improve its economy. In 1960, South Korea's per capita income was only US$80.[11] The proportion of the GNP attributed to the manufacturing industry was only 14%, and that attributed to the agricultural industry was 37%. South Korea was a typical agricultural economy (Kim, 2009).

After the establishment of the military regime in 1961, the government prioritized economic development and implemented the first five-year plan (1962–1966) with the goal of "realizing economic self-reliance." This was also an import substitution industrialization strategy. The import substitution industries included not only traditional labor-intensive industries but also capital- and technology-intensive industries such as steel, automobiles, televisions, and watches.

To promote the development strategy, the South Korean government actively attracted foreign investment and implemented emergency monetary measures in June 1962 to mobilize domestic capital and implement a large-scale investment plan. However, some important products in this plan, such as steel, automobiles, televisions, and watches, required the import of a large amount of advanced equipment and technology from abroad, as well as a large number of raw materials and components, which would also consume significant foreign exchange. These investment plans were either abandoned or reduced due to insufficient foreign exchange and other reasons. With the first five-year plan in danger of failing, the South Korean government adjusted the five-year plan in 1964, terminated the inflationary policy of mobilizing domestic capital, and abandoned many projects that relied heavily on foreign exchange. Instead, South Korea implemented a financial stabilization policy and adopted a series of policies to encourage exports.

First, foreign exchange marketization reform was carried out. In May 1964, the South Korean government lowered the overvalued official exchange rate from 130 won to US$1 to 256 won to US$1 and adopted the variable exchange rate. In March 1965, a single variable exchange rate was implemented. After August 1965, the exchange rate between the Korean won and the US dollar stabilized at US$1 to 270 won. This laid the foundation for the implementation of the export-oriented industrialization strategy. Second, preferential policies were implemented to encourage exports. The Korean Ministry of Commerce and Industry implemented a comprehensive export promotion plan in 1965. This plan included: (1) preferential export credits, (2) exemption from domestic indirect taxes on intermediate products used for export production and export sales, and (3) reduction and exemption of direct taxes on exports and foreign exchange earnings. The implementation of these measures has contributed to a sharp increase in South Korea's exports. In 1966, the last year of the first five-year plan, exports

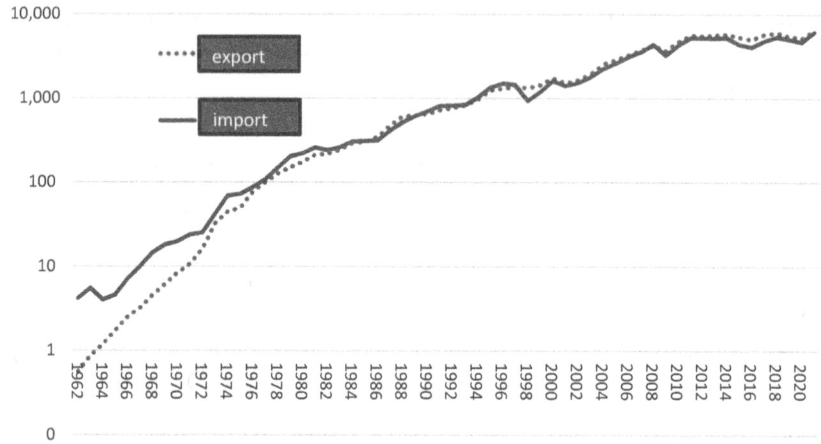

Figure 5. Growth of foreign trade in South Korea between 1962 and 2020 (in 100 millions of US dollars).

Source: Data from World Bank Database. https://data.worldbank.org/indicator.

exceeded the original projection of US$137 million to reach US$250 million. The unexpected increase in foreign exports ensured the realization of South Korea's economic growth goals. The average economic growth rate target during the first five-year plan was 7.1%, but it actually reached 7.8%. The complete success of the first five-year plan laid a solid foundation for South Korea's economic development in the following decades (Cho, 2005). Figure 5 shows the growth of Korea's foreign trade. The rapid growth of foreign trade has greatly supported the rapid economic development of South Korea.

Taiwan

In the early 1950s, the Kuomintang began to focus on economic development. Taiwan at that time was also a typical agricultural economy, with agricultural products, such as sugar, as the dominant export products, and the foreign exchange earnings were very low. After the outbreak of the Korean War in 1950, the US resumed its economic aid to Taiwan, which became Taiwan's main source of foreign exchange.[12] In 1953, Taiwan implemented its first four-year plan, which mainly focused on the electricity industry and fertilizer production while protecting the original light industries such as textiles, food, paper, and chemicals. This was import substitution industrialization strategy II, conforming to Taiwan's comparative advantages. To develop Taiwan's local industries, the government restricted the import of these products by overvaluing the exchange rate of the Taiwanese dollar, raising tariffs, and implementing import quotas. The government also encouraged the production of these products locally by implementing priority allocations of funds and foreign exchange for manufacturers of these products. A multiple exchange rate system was also implemented (Asamoto, 2007). However, the implementation of this development strategy was not smooth, and there were many problems.

First, the strategy was not only detrimental to exports but also encouraged imports, which exacerbated the foreign exchange shortage. The development of the electricity industry, chemical fertilizer industry, and other light industries requires the importation of a large amount of machinery, equipment, and raw materials from abroad. This made it difficult to improve Taiwan's balance of payments and restricted the development of these industries. Second, because these industries were protected and their products did not face competition from foreign products, business owners were not interested in improving quality and reducing costs but spent more time and energy obtaining preferential terms from the government, resulting in a low production efficiency of such products. Third, the development of these light industries was constrained by the domestic market, making it difficult to achieve rapid growth and promote the development of the entire economy. At that time, Taiwan's per capita GNP was only US$100, and the population was only 12 million. Once the domestic market was saturated, it was difficult for the economy to continue to grow (Asamoto, 2007).

A key factor driving Taiwan's economic policy is the cessation of aid from the US to Taiwan, which was essentially a foreign exchange issue. From 1951 to 1960, the US accumulatively aided Taiwan with US$900 million. In the mid-1950s, the US informed Taiwan that it would halt aid.[13] This forced Taiwan to rely on its own efforts to earn foreign exchange. Under such circumstances, a series of policies were initiated.

First, the foreign exchange policy was adjusted. In April 1958, Taiwan abolished the multiple exchange rate system that was unfavorable to exports, especially the export of light industrial products, and changed to a dual exchange rate system. In September 1963, the single exchange rate was implemented, and the exchange rate was lowered from US$1 to 24.78 New Taiwan dollars to US$1 to 40 New Taiwan dollars. Taiwan implemented 19 financial and economic reform measures to promote an export-oriented industrialization strategy, including the foreign trade reform in 1958, government budget equalization, relaxation of economic control, tax system consolidation, export promotion, incentives for personal savings and investment in 1959, and investment incentive regulations in 1960. These measures greatly promoted Taiwan's export trade.

To attract foreign capital and expand exports, Taiwan creatively established an export processing zone in Kaohsiung in 1966, which provided a favorable production and export environment for all investment enterprises. Because of the great success of the Kaohsiung Export Processing Zone, the government established two more export processing zones in Nanzi and Taichung in 1971, which further expanded Taiwan's export trade. The export processing zones were the first of their kind, and the system was later adopted by countries/regions such as Singapore, Hong Kong, and the Philippines, and eventually mainland China.

It is worth emphasizing that for capital-scarce developing countries, attracting foreign capital is important for alleviating a capital shortage, especially a foreign exchange shortage. For this reason, Taiwan had formulated relevant policies in 1952 to attract foreign capital, although their effect was not promising. The primary reason is that the import substitution industrialization strategy was not conducive to exports and did not encourage the influx of foreign capital. However, after Taiwan shifted its industrialization strategy to an export-oriented strategy, foreign capital poured into Taiwan. From 1951 to 1960, Taiwan had a total of 86 cases of accumulative foreign capital projects with a value of US$36 million. After the policy change, foreign capital soared to US$523 million from 1961 to 1970 and further increased to US$2.16 billion from 1971 to 1980 (Gu and Chen, 2003). The entry of foreign capital brought not only scarce foreign exchange but also various resources needed for development. Therefore, the export-oriented industrialization strategy can not only promote the rapid development of domestic-funded enterprises but also crucially attract foreign funds and foreign exchange to accelerate the development of an economy.

From the economic trajectories of South Korea and Taiwan, it can be seen that both economies, like other developing countries at the time, first chose the import substitution industrialization strategy. However, the shortage of foreign exchange brought about by this strategy seriously affected the industrialization process, which promoted them to turn to the export-oriented industrialization strategy.[14] In the export-oriented industrialization strategy, earning foreign exchange through exports is the top priority. Once foreign capital is obtained, various problems restricting economic development can be easily solved. This is the true mechanism of this strategy. It is precisely because of this that South Korea once boasted of the slogan "All For Export" in the 1960s, and similarly, Taiwan had the slogan "Export First." This demonstrates that exporting played a prominent role in the initial stage of industrialization in South Korea and Taiwan.

Institutional basis of the export-oriented industrialization strategy

Japan, South Korea, and Taiwan successfully implemented the export-oriented industrialization strategy, which enabled the three economies to achieve rapid growth. What is the institutional basis for the success of the export-oriented industrialization strategy implemented by these economies? A logical answer is private enterprise and the market economy.

In the research on the economic growth of East Asian countries, there are many discussions on the relationship between the state and the market, yet little has been discussed regarding the role of the market economy and private enterprise in the implementation of the export-oriented industrialization strategy (The World Bank, 1993). This is because most East Asian countries developed on the basis of a market economy and private enterprise. When evaluating the economic development experience of East Asian countries, attention is often paid to the degree of government intervention and the presence or absence of public enterprises, rather than the presence or absence of a market economy and private enterprises. While the former focuses more on the role of the government, the latter focuses more on the role of the market economy and private enterprise.

From this perspective, the three economies developed on the premise of a market economy and a private enterprise system. Before and after WWII, Japan's economic system was based on private ownership and a market economy. Private property has always been strictly protected (except during WWII). After the Meiji Restoration, to accelerate the industrialization process, the Japanese government invested in some SOEs, but they were later sold to the private sector due to poor management and financial reasons.[15]

In South Korea, although the Park Chung-hee government implemented strong intervention policies in some heavy industries, he did not promote nationalization in the manufacturing industry, nor did he establish a large number of SOEs, except for a few basic industries. Instead, he developed the economy on the premise of private enterprise. According to Jo (2005), South Korea followed five principles in its economic development:

(1) Achieving economic development through industrialization: The focus was on the light industries in the early stages. With the progression of industrialization, the focus shifted to the heavy chemical industry.
(2) Economic development is carried out under government control and management The government determined the policy according to the economic development plan. Part of the development goal was carried out through the market, and the other part was through the government's investment and

financing. The government supported some important industries through off-market measures.

(3) In principle, enterprises are privately owned and operated by the private sector. For important investments, the government can supplement or replace private sector decision-making.

(4) Using foreign capital as the source of economic development: To increase employment and repay foreign debts, increasing exports was considered the most important economic task.

(5) Prioritizing economic growth. The income gap and regional development imbalance were eliminated through economic growth, and inflation brought about by rapid economic growth was tolerated.

The above five principles were embedded in the economic development process of South Korea in the 1960s and 1970s (Cho, 2005). Although the second and third principles emphasize the role of the government, the economic system of South Korea is still based on a market economy and private enterprise. The government was only making some interventions, even when the interventions were strong.

Unlike South Korea, Taiwan once faced the dilemma of institutional choice. In the early 1950s, Taiwan's government was ideologically more inclined to implement a state-capitalist regulated economy than a free market economy. One reason for this approach was that the "Three Principles of the People" advocated by Sun Yat-sen included the idea of "restricting capital" (i.e., developing state capital and restricting private capital). The Kuomintang government, which had the "Three Principles of the People" as the foundation of its party, naturally wanted to use this idea in specific economic policies. Another reason was that Keynesian economics was the mainstream form of economics at that time, and it emphasized government intervention. In addition, Taiwan was still in a state of war, and strengthening armaments was a top priority. All these prevented Taiwan from becoming a market economy. Under such circumstances, Taiwan practiced a planned economy in the early 1950s.

During this period, liberal scholars who came to Taiwan with the Kuomintang began to reflect on the Kuomintang's rule over the mainland. Friedrich Hayek's book *The Road to Serfdom* caused strong reactions in Taiwan. Liberal intellectuals, represented by Hu Shi, called for a market economy. The thinking also influenced a group of technocrats in the government, such as Zhongrong Yin, which resulted in a major turning point in Taiwan's economic policy. A series of market-oriented policies, such as foreign exchange marketization, implementation of the export-oriented industrialization strategy, privatization of SOEs, and encouragement of private entrepreneurship, were proposed by Zhongrong Yin and his team. According to Guoding Li, who had long followed Yin and participated in the formulation of economic policies, Yin's ideas on economic development are as follows (Li, 1963):

(1) It is necessary for the government to participate in economic development, yet it is not necessary for it to directly control enterprises.
(2) Only by restoring the market mechanism can the economy develop normally and rapidly.
(3) With the goal of the overall development of the economy, the government should flexibly determine the mode and order of economic development of various industries.
(4) The order of economic investment should be determined according to its economic effects.

The first point highlights the indispensable role of the government in economic development, but it also affirms that private enterprises are the main body of economic activities rather than public enterprises. The second point emphasizes the decisive role of the market economic system. Therefore, private enterprises and the market economy are the basic economic systems for Taiwan's post-war development, and various strategies and policies were implemented on this basis.

The logic behind the export-oriented industrialization strategy

The reason why Japan, South Korea, and Taiwan could smoothly implement the export-oriented industrialization strategy is precisely because of the market economy and private enterprise system. Without this economic system, a country cannot effectively implement the export-oriented industrialization strategy, but only the import-substitution industrialization strategy. This is because, under the market economy and private enterprise system, the enterprise owners will maximize the integration of various resources and use them in the most efficient way to pursue maximum profit, for instance, by importing advanced products, technologies, knowledge, and more efficient management models from abroad. By maximizing the quality of the products and minimizing the cost, the international competitiveness of the products is improved. Compared with the small domestic market, the international market will bring more profits. As long as it is profitable, private enterprises will continue to expand production and create jobs. The natural result is the development of the domestic economy.

Is it possible for a country to implement an export-oriented industrialization strategy under the planned economy and public enterprise system? The answer is "no." Under the planned economic system, the state monopolizes all resources, the prices of production factors (including foreign exchange) cannot be reasonably determined, and inefficient resource allocation will stifle the international competitiveness of enterprises. More importantly, the government will try its best to eliminate uncontrollable factors to ensure the smooth implementation of the economic plan.[16] For the planning department, the dependence of enterprises on the international market for raw materials and products is an uncontrollable factor. Even in peacetime, any change in the foreign market may disrupt the economic plan of the country, which is unacceptable to the government. Therefore, the planned economy can only exist in the form of a self-sufficient closed economy, and the suitable development strategy for this system is the import substitution industrialization strategy. Such countries do not make plans based on the international market, but rather control national production to satisfy the domestic market.[17]

Is it possible for public enterprises in the market economic system to become the main body of export-oriented industrialization? The answer is also "no." This is because it is difficult for public enterprises to overcome the lack of responsibility. Whether it is the workers and managers of the enterprise or the authorities of the SOEs, they will not and cannot be responsible for the enterprise's operation. This results in high costs and low efficiency in these public enterprises, making it difficult for them to become internationally competitive.[18]

From this perspective, the premise of export-oriented industrialization is that the domestic economy is based on the market economy and private enterprises. Without this institutional condition, it is extremely challenging to implement this strategy.

Influence of international relations on export-oriented industrialization

Another indispensable condition for export-oriented industrialization is peaceful and stable international relations. For a long time, developed countries in Europe and the US have been the leading forces in the world economy. These countries not only have a large GDP but are also in a leading position in terms of knowledge, technology, and management. Therefore, if a developing country attempts to implement export-oriented industrialization and participate in the international division of labor, it must establish mutual trust and benefit with these developed countries. Let us consider Japan as an example: before WWII, it achieved export-oriented industrialization thanks to its good relations with Western countries. However, as Japan became hostile to major countries in Europe and the US during WWII, it was eventually removed from the international market. Under such circumstances, Japan had to implement import substitution industrialization. After the war, with Japan's return to the international community, an export-oriented industrialization strategy became possible again. In the post-war period, although Japan's trade dependence ratio was much lower than that of other East Asian countries, a lack of foreign exchange was not the main factor restricting Japan's economic growth. Most industries in Japan had the ability to produce high-quality products by importing advanced technologies, especially patents. Therefore, Japan did not need to import large amounts of machinery and equipment like other developing countries in the early stages of industrialization.

South Korea and Taiwan have always been members of international organizations led by the US and other Western countries. Their economic industrialization was not constrained by international relations; it was rather a self-chosen decision. Therefore, people tend to not focus on the influence of international relations on the economic development of South Korea and Taiwan. However, to study China's industrialization strategy, international relations are an important factor.

China's Industrialization Strategy

Looking back on China's economic development trajectory in the last four decades, it is easy to see that although China's development trajectory was different from Japan, South Korea, and Taiwan, they all ended up in the same position, i.e., using export-oriented industrialization. Before the implementation of the reform and opening-up policy, China implemented a planned economic system that was different from other mainstream economies. After going through many problems, it finally entered the fast export-oriented development track.

Import substitution industrialization strategy

After 1949, China imitated the former Soviet Union to implement a development strategy that gave priority to the heavy industries. This is essentially an import substitution industrialization strategy (i.e., import substitution industrialization strategy I). In China, there was scarce capital but abundant labor at that time. Prioritizing the capital-intensive heavy industries was against China's comparative advantages and hindered its industrialization process. As a result, after nearly three decades of economic development, China's per capita GDP did not increase much, and people's living standards were not substantially improved.[19]

Nonetheless, China did not immediately turn to the export-oriented industrialization strategy. In the early stages of economic reform and opening up, China was still implementing the import substitution industrialization strategy. This was manifested in two aspects. First, policies prioritizing the development of heavy industries still existed. In fact, the Chinese government has never officially announced the abandonment of the Heavy Industry Priority Development Strategy. After the end of the Cultural Revolution, to realize the goal of the "Four Modernizations," the Chinese government restarted the "Ten-Year Planning Outline (1976–1985)" that was originally formulated in 1975. According to this plan, China would introduce 22 large-scale investment projects from Europe, the US, and Japan in the fields of iron and steel, petrochemicals, chemical fibers, and chemical fertilizers. The total investment would be worth US$7.8 billion. In fact, contracts worth US$3.1 billion were signed in the last 10 days of 1978 (Ju, 2021). It can be seen that even in the early stages of economic reform and opening up, the Chinese government had not abandoned its priority of the development of the heavy industries. Baoshan Iron & Steel, built with the efforts of the whole country, is the most representative example.

However, after the reform and opening up policy was adopted, China unconsciously implemented an import substitution industrialization strategy targeting light industrial products (i.e., the import substitution industrialization strategy II). At the end of the 1970s, since the unsustainable low-efficiency planned economy was in its last days, the government had to allocate lands to each household in rural areas and allow SOEs to have partial operating autonomy in cities. Fortunately, these last resort reform measures became a historic turning point for the Chinese economy.

After the division of lands in rural areas, a potential surplus labor force became apparent. However, the government did not allow farmers to migrate into cities: they were required to "leave the land and never leave the village." As a concession, the government gave up the original restrictions on the business activities of rural enterprises.[20] As a result, a large number of township and village enterprises (TVEs) that were not directly controlled by the state emerged in rural China. Although these enterprises are called collective enterprises, their interest structure is close to that of private enterprises, and they are an enterprise form between state-owned and private enterprises. Even though the property rights of this enterprise system were not clear, it had a significant institutional advantage compared to the public enterprises under the planned economic system because it incorporated elements of private enterprises. Their products quickly occupied the Chinese rural market and gradually entered the urban consumer goods market. The TVEs became a critical source of China's economic growth in the 1980s and constituted an important part of China's economy. Although these TVEs made contributions to China's exports during this period, their role was still essentially import substitution. All kinds of consumer goods and production materials (such as steel, cement, and agricultural machinery) that were insufficiently produced by SOEs were provided by TVEs.

The reform of SOEs during this period also created favorable conditions for the development of TVEs. Beginning in 1978, SOEs underwent a series of reforms to expand operating autonomy and the contract system. The government started to allow SOEs to independently produce and sell some products outside of the national plan. These measures partially introduced market mechanisms into SOEs. From a microscopic perspective, this reform improved the production and operation efficiency of SOEs to a certain extent. On a macro level, it has a much more significant effect. Specifically, it provided the necessary conditions for the development of TVEs and other private enterprises. Various important production materials, such as steel, coal, machinery, and equipment that were unavailable to rural enterprises under the planned economy, could then be obtained from the market. With the continuous expansion of the unplanned production of SOEs, TVEs gained more space for development, which not only generated the requirements but also created the conditions for the implementation of the export-oriented industrialization strategy.

Implementation of the export-oriented industrialization strategy

Due to ideological reasons, China was still wary of the Western world in the early stages of economic reform and opening up.[21] China wanted to obtain foreign capital and advanced technology, but it was worried about being controlled by other countries. It was a forced decision to implement the export-oriented industrialization strategy. An important factor driving this decision was the foreign exchange shortage, which was also faced by South Korea and Taiwan in their early stages of industrialization.

In 1977, the year before the reform and opening up, China started a plan to import advanced technology and equipment on a large scale. However, as shown in Table 2, China's total exports in 1978 were less than US$9.8 billion, and its foreign exchange reserve was almost zero. This plan overwhelmed China's financial resources

Table 2. China's foreign trade and foreign exchange reserves (1970–1990, in 100 millions of US dollars).

	Total trade	Total export	Total import	Trade balance	Trade balance/total export (%)	Foreign exchange reserves
1970	45.8	23.1	22.7	0.4	1.6	0.9
1971	49.1	27.8	21.3	6.5	23.5	0.4
1972	65.4	36.9	28.5	8.4	22.8	2.46
1973	110.8	58.8	52.1	6.7	11.4	-0.8
1974	149.0	71.1	77.9	**-6.8**	**-9.6**	**0**
1975	156.2	76.9	79.3	**-2.4**	**-3.1**	**1.8**
1976	136.0	69.4	66.6	2.8	4.1	5.8
1977	146.6	75.1	71.5	3.6	4.8	9.5
1978	206.4	97.5	108.9	**-11.4**	**-11.7**	**1.6**
1979	292.4	136.1	156.2	**-20.1**	**-14.7**	**8.4**
1980	381.4	181.2	200.2	**-19.0**	**-10.5**	**-13.0**

Table 2. (*Continued*)

	Total trade	Total export	Total import	Trade balance	Trade balance/total export (%)	Foreign exchange reserves
1981	440.2	220.1	220.2	−0.1	0.0	27.1
1982	416.1	223.2	192.9	30.4	13.6	70.0
1983	436.2	222.3	213.9	8.4	3.8	89.0
1984	535.5	261.4	274.1	−12.7	−4.9	82.2
1985	696.0	273.5	422.5	**−149.0**	**−54.5**	**26.4**
1986	738.5	309.4	429.0	**−119.6**	**−38.7**	**20.7**
1987	826.5	394.4	432.2	**−37.8**	**−9.6**	**29.2**
1988	1027.9	475.2	552.8	**−77.6**	**−16.3**	**33.7**
1989	1116.8	525.4	591.4	**−66.0**	**−12.6**	**55.5**
1990	1154.4	620.9	533.5	87.4	14.1	110.9

Source: Data from CEIC China Premium Database.

and exceeded China's ability to pay the foreign exchange. Therefore, it had to be abandoned in April 1979, shortly after its implementation. Following this, the adjustment and consolidation of the national economy began.[22] Between 1978 and 1980, China had a significant trade deficit. China's foreign exchange reserve dropped to an unbelievable −US$1.3 billion in 1980.

Baoshan Iron & Steel is the most representative project in this plan. During Deng Xiaoping's visit to Japan in October 1978, he asked Japan to help China build a steel plant as advanced as the Kimitsu Steel Works operated by Nippon Steel Corporation. After the order contract was signed, the Chinese government unilaterally terminated the contract, which caused a negative international response. The project was able to restart with a commercial loan from Japan, and it was completed in 1985. However, the project created a large trade deficit. As shown in Table 2, China's trade deficit in 1985 was as high as US$15 billion, more than half of China's total exports that year. The ensuing years were also marked by large trade deficits until the economic adjustment in 1990. In conclusion, a foreign exchange shortage has always been a critical restricting factor that hindered China from importing advanced technologies and economic development.

According to the memoirs of then Vice Premier Tian Jiyun, when Deng Xiaoping met with then premier minister Zhao Ziyang in June 1986, he talked about three strategic issues of great significance to China's development, namely, the agricultural issue, the political system reform issue, and the foreign exchange issue. Here's what he said:

> The second is the foreign exchange issue. Will the shortage of foreign exchange and the deficit in foreign trade hold us back? China has a lot of products to export. It is necessary to study various ways to open up the international market, including the markets of Hong Kong, Southeast Asia, and Japan ... The key to opening up the export market is to improve product quality. If the product quality is not high, they will not be competitive. Reducing the foreign trade deficit year by year is a strategic issue. Otherwise, sustained and stable economic development is impossible, and the economy will eventually shrink. (Tian, 2008)

In addition to the huge trade deficit, China was also facing serious domestic problems at that time. With the reform of China's SOEs and the rapid development of TVEs, the development strategy focusing on domestic resources and markets had the following problems: (1) there was a large amount of surplus labor in inland areas; (2) a large number of enterprises in the coastal areas had insufficient raw materials and energy; and (3) there was excess capacity in some light textile products due to the domestic market.

To solve these problems, the Chinese government put forward the export-oriented industrialization strategy in 1987, which was also referred to as the "Coastal Area Development Strategy" or "International Economic Cycle Strategy." Learning from Taiwan, Singapore, and Hong Kong, export processing industries were vigorously developed in coastal areas. With imported foreign product design and raw materials, they were processed by cheap labor in China and then sold in the international market. According to the words of Tian Jiyun, then vice premier of the State Council, who was in charge of the implementation of the plan, the characteristics of this strategy can be summarized as "both ends (of production) are outside (China), large scale of imports and exports, mutual support between imports and exports, and integration of imports and exports" (Tian, 2015). Specifically, "both ends (of production) are outside (China), and large scale of imports and exports" are the means, and "mutual support between imports and exports" is the goal. Through large exports, foreign exchange that is needed to import advanced technology, equipment, raw materials, and parts could be obtained. They will further improve product competitiveness and increase exports and foreign exchange further. The implementation of this strategy not only solved the problem of surplus labor in rural China but also played an important role in eliminating the bottlenecks of technology, capital, raw materials, the domestic market, and foreign exchange. In a sense, the market reforms, the development of private enterprises, and the implementation of export-oriented development strategies in the 1980s laid a solid institutional and strategic foundation for the subsequent rapid economic growth. Therefore, the implementation of the Costal Area Development Strategy is a historical turning point in China's economic development.

After Deng Xiaoping's southern tour speech was published in 1992, a new wave of reform and opening up emerged in China. The prices of important production materials, including iron, steel, and coal, were almost completely liberalized, which marked a decisive step in the market-oriented reform. SOEs also shifted from the contract system to the ownership reform, and a large number of small- and medium-sized SOEs were converted into private enterprises in various ways. Rural TVEs also accelerated the pace of ownership reform. Against such a background, foreign investment poured into China (Figure 6).

A series of fiscal, financial, and foreign exchange reforms was implemented in 1994, which had a much more significant impact on China's export-oriented industrialization. The fiscal and taxation system changed from the original fiscal and taxation contract system to a tax-sharing system, and a value-added tax of up to 17% was

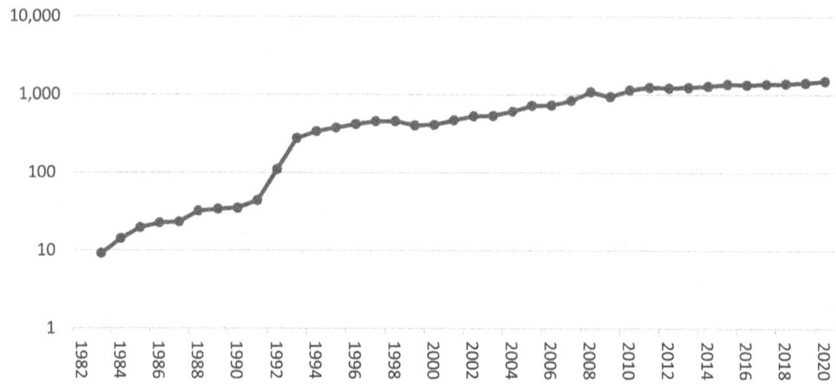

Figure 6. Variations in foreign direct investment (1983–2020, in 100 millions of US dollars).

Source: Data from CEIC China Premium Database.

introduced, which increased the government's fiscal and taxation. In the meantime, export tax rebates were given to export enterprises, which greatly encouraged the export industry. Moreover, the government significantly lowered the exchange rate of RMB against the US dollar, from 5.7 RMB to US$1 to 8.7 RMB to US$1. Similar to the situation in South Korea and Taiwan, the exchange rate reform removed the obstacles to expanding exports, and the Chinese economy officially embarked on the track of export-oriented industrialization. After 1994, China's foreign trade no longer ran a deficit. The era when China's economic growth was restricted by insufficient foreign exchange came to an end.

However, the international factors that restricted China's exports still existed. Since China was not a member of the World Trade Organization (WTO), it could not enjoy the privileges that other member countries offered to each other in terms of exports. Developed countries such as the US could still restrict China's exports in accordance with relevant regulations. Since the US is China's largest export market, Congress reviews every year whether to grant China the most-favored-nation status. This increased uncertainty and restricted the growth of Chinese exports. However, as China officially joined the WTO at the end of 2001, the US market was fully opened to China, and the international

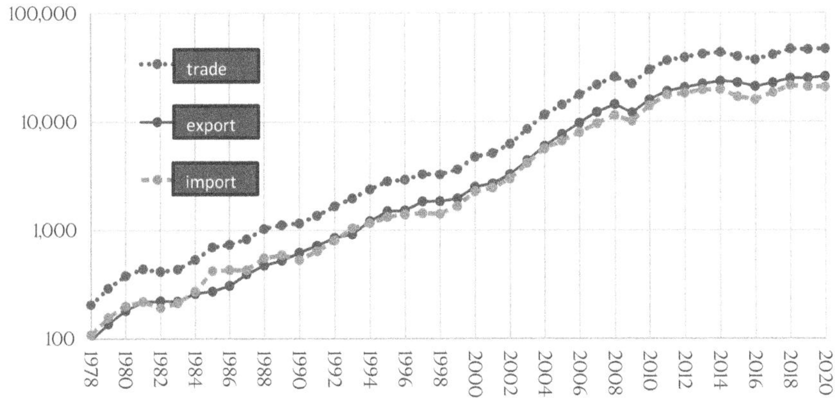

Figure 7. Growth of foreign trade in China (1978–2020, in 100 millions of US dollars).

Source: Data from CEIC China Premium Database.

market factors that restricted China's foreign trade were finally eliminated. At the same time, international capital, full of expectations for the Chinese market, further entered China on a large scale (Figure 6), bringing about a golden age of economic development. From 2001 to 2011, the average annual growth rate of China's exports was as high as 22%, which is extremely rare in the history of world trade (Figure 7). Such an export growth rate is beyond the reach of the import substitution industrialization strategy. In this sense, China's rapid economic growth is another successful case of the export-oriented industrialization strategy.

Trade structure and trade dependence ratio

With the implementation of the export-oriented industrialization strategy, how exactly did China achieve its achievements in foreign trade? Figure 8 shows the changes in China's trade structure. In 1993, general trade and processing trade with supplied materials accounted for almost half of China's total exports. Since China did not have any processing trade before 1978, this portion undoubtedly developed in the 14 years between 1978 and 1993. Processing trade is the primary form of trade in the export-oriented industrialization

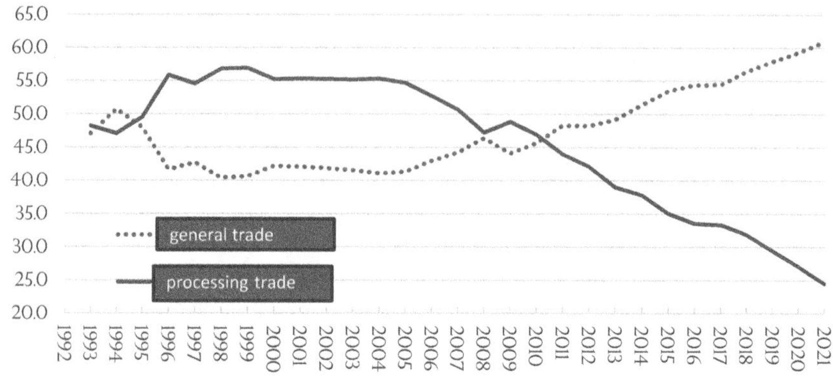

Figure 8. Export structure 1993–2021 (%).

Source: Data from CEIC China Premium Database.

strategy, and it is an effective way to increase domestic employment and foreign exchange. The increase in the proportion of processing exports in total exports indicated that China's export-oriented industrialization reached a high level in 1993. The number was increased further, reaching 55% in 1996, and continued to increase until 2005, after China's accession to the WTO. Then, with the rapid development of the domestic manufacturing industry, the proportion of processing trade with supplied materials began to decline. In the meantime, the export of domestic products, i.e., general trade, started to rise and exceeded 60% by 2021.

To a large extent, changes in the trade structure reflect changes in the trade entities. As shown in Figure 9, SOEs accounted for 44% of the export trade in 1995, almost the same as foreign-funded enterprises. Since the proportion of foreign-funded enterprises was nearly zero in the early stages of reform and opening up, it can be concluded that the proportion of exports from SOEs dropped sharply after 1978, whereas that of foreign-funded enterprises continued to rise and reached a peak of 54.7% in 2004. China's export-oriented industrialization relied heavily on foreign-funded enterprises, including Hong Kong, Macao, and Taiwan enterprises. Until 2004, China's economic development can be considered export-oriented industrialization led by foreign capital. This is similar

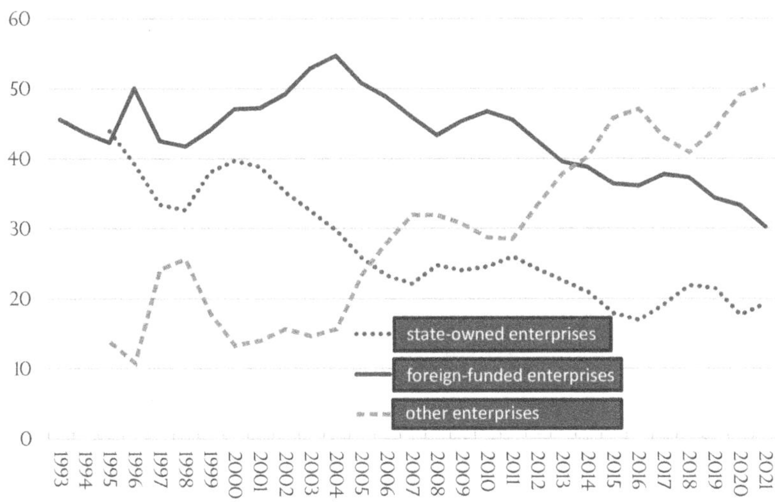

Figure 9. Variations of export entities 1993–2021 (%).

Source: Data from CEIC China Premium Database.

to some countries in Southeast Asia, such as Malaysia. However, after 2005, the proportion of foreign-funded enterprises began to decline, and other private enterprises emerged and became a leader in China's exports. Their exports increased from 15% in 2004 to more than 50% in 2021.

A direct consequence of the export-oriented industrialization strategy is the increase in the trade dependence ratio. Japan, South Korea, and Taiwan have experienced such an increase, and China is no exception. As shown in Figure 10, China's trade dependence ratio was about 10% in the planned economy era and only increased slightly in the 1950s when there were trades with the former Soviet Union and Eastern European countries. During the early period of the Cultural Revolution, when self-reliance was emphasized, the ratio dropped to as low as 6% and then returned to about 10% after easing relations between China and major Western countries, such as the US and Japan. After the implementation of the economic reform and opening up policy, the trade dependence ratio climbed from 10% to 33% in 1992 and remained at 30–40% until the end of the 1990s. After joining the WTO in 2001, the ratio increased

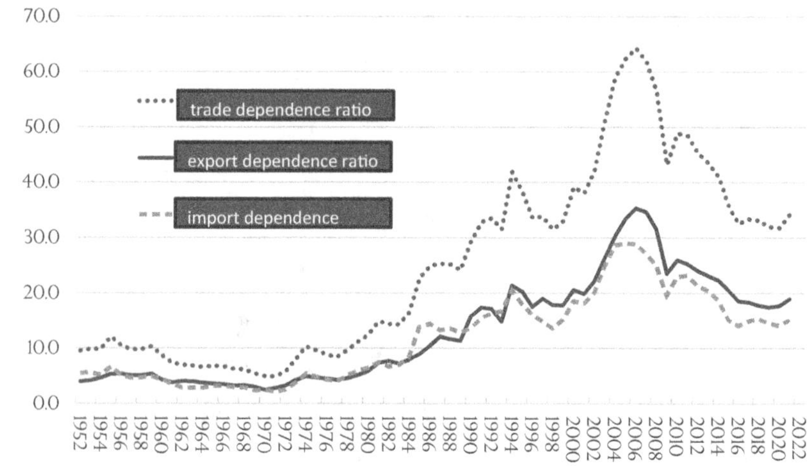

Figure 10. Variations in China's trade dependence ratio 1952–2020 (%).
Source: Data from CEIC China Premium Database.

rapidly again, reaching 64.2% in 2006. After that, with the expansion of non-trade sectors such as the real estate industry and the tertiary industry, China's trade dependence ratio showed a declining trend, falling to 33% in 2021. Nonetheless, China's trade dependence ratio is still much higher than that of Japan and other developed countries. Export-oriented industrialization is still playing an integral role in China.

From the analysis in this section, it can be concluded that: (1) China's rapid economic growth is due to the implementation of the export-oriented industrialization strategy. This strategy was originally implemented in the late 1980s, deepened in the mid-1990s, and fully launched at the beginning of this century. (2) Foreign-funded enterprises played a critical role in the strategy. (3) The successful implementation of this strategy is due to a favorable international environment and the reform and opening up policy as well as the reforms of privatization and marketization, with the latter playing a decisive role. Without these reforms, it would have been impossible for China to smoothly integrate into the international community.

Commentary on China's Rapid Economic Growth

China's economic achievements are regarded as "miracles" by many researchers. Through a comparison with East Asian economies, it is easy to see that China's success is very similar to that of other East Asian economies, in terms of both development strategies and results. So, how can we evaluate the rapid economic development in China in the past 40 years? Let us first consider several unique factors that promoted China's economic growth.

China's unique favorable factors

(1) **One-child policy:** To reduce the negative effect of population growth on economic development, the Chinese government implemented a strict one-child policy in 1979. It lowered the birth rate and increased the ratio of the productive population. This policy was beneficial for improving the quality of the population and increasing savings and investment. According to official estimates, the implementation of the one-child policy reduced China's population by 400 million (National Health and Family Planning Commission, 2013). Although this strict policy may lead to many issues in China's future development, it was undoubtedly a favorable factor in the initial stage of economic development.

(2) **Public ownership of lands:** Land is the most basic factor in economic activities. Not only does agricultural production but also infrastructure (e.g., railways and roads) as well as production and residential facilities (e.g., factories and houses) require a large amount of land. In countries with private ownership of land, purchasing land from landlords not only involves a large cost but also requires time to obtain the landlord's consent. Undoubtedly, this would increase the construction cost, prolong the construction cycle, and reduce the rate of economic growth. In China, since the land is *de facto* owned by the state and individuals have no ownership, the government can expropriate the needed land in a very short period of time and at a

much lower price than that of the market. This resulted in a high speed in the construction of public facilities and enterprises, which consequently accelerated China's economic development. In the 1980s and 1990s, many local governments sold land at very cheap prices (or even free) to attract foreign investments to grow their local economies. When the price of land increased, the local government purchased land from farmers and resold it to real estate developers at a much higher price, generating significant income which was used for administrative expenses and building public facilities.

(3) **Household registration system:** The household registration system was initially implemented during the planned economy period. It was adjusted significantly after the implementation of the reform and opening up, yet it still has not been abolished. The household registration system artificially widened the income gap between urban and rural residents, creating a labor force group unique to China called "migrant workers," who earn low wages and have minimal benefits. The existence of hundreds of millions of migrant workers not only reduced the cost of various construction projects in China but also ensured the international competitiveness of China's export products to a certain extent, resulting in the rapid growth of China's economy. Moreover, in times of economic crisis, it is also possible to reduce the pressure on the government by requiring migrant workers to return to their hometowns.

(4) **Chinese nationals living in Hong Kong, Macao, Taiwan, and overseas:** In the 1980s and 1990s, the international community still lacked trust in China's systems and policies. At this time, the people who invested in China were mainly Chinese from Hong Kong, Macao, Taiwan, and overseas. Hong Kong has played an indispensable role in this process. As an international financial center and a bridge linking China and the world, Hong Kong took the lead in developing economic relations with mainland China. Many businessmen from other countries were lobbied to invest in China. The success of Shenzhen,

China's largest special economic zone, benefited from Hong Kong. Before China's accession to the WTO, Hong Kong was not only China's largest export destination but also China's largest investor.[23] Hence, China's successful implementation of the export-oriented industrialization strategy is inseparable from Hong Kong's contribution.

(5) **Large population:** A large population is usually a burden to a country in its early stages of economic development. With a limited amount of land and other resources, the larger the population, the fewer resources per capita, and the more difficult it is to realize capital accumulation. This was also part of the reason why China implemented a strict one-child policy.[24] Once the economy improves under the export-oriented industrialization strategy, the large population means a large production capacity and a huge market. China is often referred to as a "world factory" and has the most complete industrial chain in the world; this, in fact, has a lot to do with China's large population size.

Undoubtedly, each country has some favorable or unfavorable factors unique to that country. China is no exception. However, the above factors are unique to China. In China's four-decade development trajectory, these factors have all played a promoting role during a certain period.

"Miracle" or "Normality"?

China's economic growth is often the subject of comparison with that of the former Soviet Union and Eastern European countries. Some scholars believe that the economic collapse of the former Soviet Union and Eastern European countries was due to radical market-oriented reform measures recommended by some international organizations, such as the International Monetary Fund. However, the Chinese government flexibly solved individual problems in the process of economic development. It not only maintained domestic political and social stability but also achieved rapid economic growth. This reform is called "progressive reform," and China's rapid economic growth is called "the China miracle."

It is indeed remarkable that China was able to smoothly transform from a planned economy to a market economy and achieve rapid economic growth. However, if the rapid economic growth is attributed to "progressive reforms" or the effective control of the economy by the government, it would be impossible to identify the true reason for China's economic development. In fact, the reason for the effective progressive reforms is the orderly release, rather than an explosion, of the growth momentum suppressed by the original public ownership and planned economic system. However, if China had continued implementing the import substitution industrialization strategies (I or II), even though the progressive reforms were successful, China's economy would not have been able to achieve high-speed growth. This is because capital accumulation under such strategies would take a long time, and the foreign exchange constraint would always hinder the import of advanced technologies and equipment. Only when an export-oriented industrialization strategy is implemented can these constraints be eliminated and high-speed growth be achieved. The rapid growth of East Asian economies, especially South Korea and Taiwan, provides solid proof.

As shown in Figure 11, Japan's economy returned to the pre-war level in 1955 and then entered a period of rapid growth. From 1955 to 1973, when the first oil crisis broke out, the average annual growth rate of Japan's GDP was as high as 9.4%. Over an 18-year period, Japan's per capita GDP reached the level of developed countries, and Japan also became the second-largest economy in the world.

South Korea experienced 34 years of rapid economic growth, from its first five-year plan in 1962 to the Asian financial crisis in 1996. Its GDP growth rate during the period was 9.4%. Especially during the Park Chung-hee regime, South Korea's modern industrial production capacity increased from almost zero to an era of

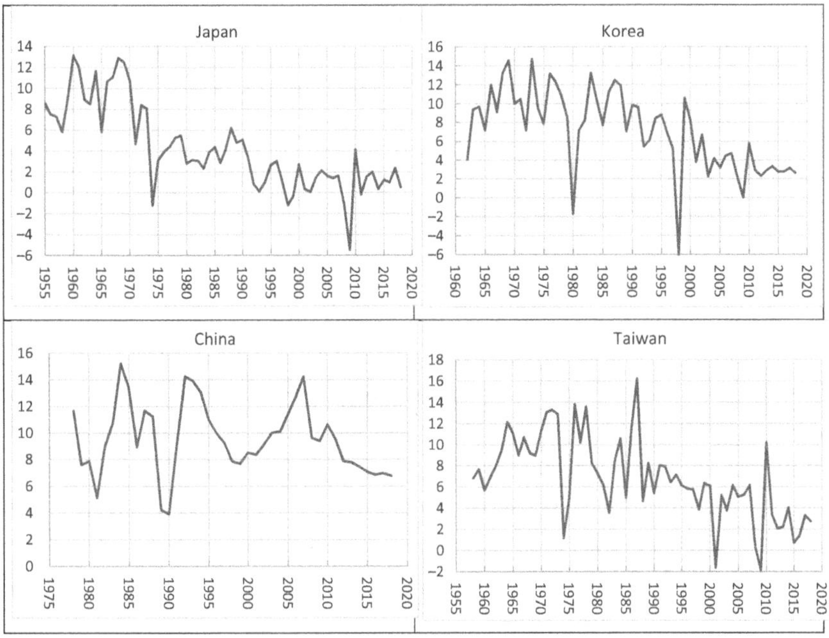

Figure 11. Variations in the economic growth rates of East Asian countries and regions.

Source: Japan, South Korea, and Taiwan: Maddison Project Database (2020); China: National Bureau of Statistics. For Japan, South Korea, and Taiwan, the purchasing power parity in 2011 prices was used to evaluate GDP, and for China, the real GDP was used.

heavy industrialization. The economic growth during this period was often called "the miracle on the Han River."[25] After 60 years of economic growth, South Korea's per capita GDP caught up with Japan, and it became a developed country. Taiwan's economic development was almost in sync with that of South Korea. Between 1958 and 1994, the average GDP growth rate was 8.9%.[26] Like South Korea, Taiwan's per capita GDP also reached the level of developed countries.

In terms of China's economic growth, according to official statistics, the average GDP growth rate from 1978 to 2012 was 9.8%, close to that of the above economies.[27] After 2013, the GDP growth rate dropped to around 6%, and China entered a stage of steady growth. It is worth noting that, unlike Japan, South Korea, and Taiwan,

China's per capita GDP still lags far behind that of developed countries. If the international and domestic environments do not undergo major changes, there will likely be rapid growth in the future.

From the above discussion, it can be concluded that countries/regions implementing the export-oriented industrialization strategy are more likely to achieve rapid economic growth. According to the latecomer advantage theory, the economic growth rate of latecomers is usually higher than that of "early comers." China's economic growth rate has only maintained a level similar to that of Japan, South Korea, and Taiwan. Even putting aside the huge income gap, China's economic growth can hardly be called a "miracle" in terms of economic growth rate alone and is a normal case under the export-oriented industrialization strategy. In particular, China enjoyed various advantages, as mentioned above, that other countries did not have.

Conclusions and Prospects

In this study, we discussed the driving factors behind China's economic growth by comparing it with that of Japan, South Korea, and Taiwan. We obtained the following conclusions.

First, the rapid economic growth in China was mainly due to the implementation of an export-oriented industrialization strategy. Compared to the import substitution industrialization strategies targeting heavy industrial products during the planned economy period and light industrial products in the early stages of reform and opening up, the export-oriented industrialization strategy takes full advantage of cheap labor, and by adopting labor-intensive technologies, products are sold on the international market. This strategy solves various problems restricting economic development, such as a foreign exchange shortage, insufficient capital, insufficient talent, and outdated management, and it grows the economy in a low-cost manner. The heavy industrialization strategy implemented during the planned economy period was constrained by almost all production factors, with the exception of land and labor. As a result, not only did it fail to develop the heavy industry, but it dragged down the entire economy. The import substitution industrialization strategy targeting light industrial products (although it alleviated, to a certain extent, the constraints of various factors of production and brought about relatively rapid economic growth) was still subject to foreign exchange and domestic market constraints; hence, it was difficult to take full advantage of the cheap labor and achieve rapid economic growth. Only the export-oriented industrialization strategy can eliminate various constraints to the greatest extent, realize efficient utilization of domestic and foreign resources, and ultimately achieved rapid economic growth.

Second, the preconditions for the implementation of the export-oriented industrialization strategy are domestic privatization, market reforms, and opening-up policies. This strategy requires mutual trust and benefit between China and the international community. Without such a relationship and the acceptance of the international community, unilateral opening up will have a very limited effect. Moreover, the strategy requires the implementation of a market economic system based on private ownership. Without private ownership and a market economy, it would be impossible to produce entrepreneurs who can lead economic growth, entrepreneurship that brings disruptive innovation, or the division of labor and enterprise cooperation (especially industrial clusters) that improve the international competitiveness of products. Consequently, it is difficult to achieve rapid growth in exports, capital accumulation, and production expansion. The export-oriented industrialization strategy in China was gradually implemented after certain developments in the private enterprise and market economic systems. With the deepening of privatization and marketization, the advantages of this strategy are finally maximized.

Third, the Chinese model of economic development has not yet been formed. Among the factors that promoted China's rapid economic growth, many were also seen during the economic growth of Japan, South Korea, and Taiwan (e.g., increase in exports, introduction of foreign capital, privatization, marketization, infrastructure construction, establishment of a macroeconomic system, and moderate industrial policies). China's economic development model does not quite have unique elements but is rather an example of the East Asian model. If one must present a summary based on China's development experience in the past 40 or 70 years, it is that the export-oriented industrialization strategy is critical to the successful industrialization of developing countries. This model works not only in small economies like South Korea and Taiwan but also in large countries like China, which has the largest population in the world. This model will have certain implications for other countries with large populations. However, it is undeniable that some unique factors have played a role in promoting China's economic development, such as the public ownership of land, the one-child policy, and the household registration system. But these favorable conditions all emerged under China's political and historical conditions at the expense of national welfare, especially the welfare of farmers. They are neither sustainable nor replicable and cannot be promoted in other developing countries.

Fourth, the government plays an important role in formulating the correct development strategy, choosing a reasonable development model, and creating a fair market environment. This is probably more important than formulating specific policies. From the experience of East Asian countries, the most critical factor for economic growth is the selection of the correct development strategy, that is, the export-oriented industrialization strategy. Economic policies and government intervention based on this strategy will accelerate the country's economic development. However, if policies and government intervention are against this strategy, economic development will be hindered. China has introduced many industrial policies so far, but few are effective. An obvious example is the policies related to the automobile and semiconductor industries. Policies or interventions that promote fair market competition and entrepreneurship will contribute to economic development. Therefore, we should have an objective understanding of the government's ability to formulate and implement policies and let the market play a decisive role in the allocation of resources.

After more than four decades of rapid growth, China is no longer what it used to be. Both the domestic economic structure and the international status have undergone profound changes, which in some respects have brought unprecedented favorable conditions to China and, at the same time, challenges. Under such circumstances, China's development strategy should also keep pace with the times and make corresponding adjustments. However, the fundamental development model should remain unchanged, that is, to eliminate the current and future development bottlenecks and seek economic development in the competitive international market. Today, China is facing challenges brought about by potential decoupling from the international community and the stagnation of marketization and privatization reforms, all of which could seriously impact China's economic development. Considering that there is still a significant gap in the per capita GDP between China and developed countries, the introduction of foreign advanced technology and systems will remain a critical issue for a long time. Therefore, maintaining good international relations, deepening reforms, and continuing to open up are still the best choices for China.

Endnotes

1. In strict terms, economic development and economic growth are different concepts. Economic growth refers to the increase in a country's GDP, while economic development covers not only economic growth but also other issues accompanying economic growth, such as changes in the industrial structure, improvement of education level, income distribution, and urbanization. In this chapter, however, these two are not distinguished, unless otherwise specified.
2. Zhang (2013) argued that imports were more important than exports for China's economic growth. It is undeniable that foreign exchange earnings through exports are a prerequisite for imports. As we discussed, foreign exchange earnings determine the success of a country's economic growth, especially in the early stages.
3. Undoubtedly, advanced systems also need to be imported in the process of industrialization.
4. After importing advanced technologies, developing countries can convert expensive foreign technology into cheap applicable technology and produce it domestically, thereby reducing imports. This can reduce the demand for foreign exchange to a certain extent, but it

does not undermine the importance of foreign exchange in the early stages of industrialization.

5. In this chapter, both the development model and the development strategy refer to the set of policies used to achieve different development goals, unless otherwise specified.
6. Even if a country has abundant mineral resources that can be exported, the exploration itself also requires large amounts of capital, technology, and foreign exchange.
7. The excess of imports over exports is mainly due to aid from the US.
8. Before 1985, the import dependence ratio of South Korea was higher than its export dependence ratio. In addition to economic aid from foreign countries, labor exports and loans from foreign financial institutions have also increased South Korea's imports.
9. For a country like Japan that lacks resources, the trade dependence ratio did not continue to rise after WWII. A possible explanation is that before WWII, Japan's industrialization had reached a very high level. Japan was decoupled from the international market during WWII and had to implement import substitution in the entire industry in order to be self-sufficient. As a result, a relatively comprehensive industrial system was formed. Even in the post-war period, Japan no longer needed to rely heavily on the export of a few specific industries to drive the development of the entire economy as it did before the war.
10. South Korea's total exports were worth US$38.65 million in 1961, which was less than US$39.59 million in 1953 (Lee, 2013).
11. This income level was even lower than in some poor African countries at that time.
12. The amount of aid is approximately US$100 million per year.
13. In fact, the US ended up cutting off economic aid to Taiwan in 1965.
14. The same thing happened in other Southeast Asian countries such as Thailand and Malaysia. For example, Thailand began its industrialization in the late 1950s. At the beginning, the Thai government also implemented the import substitution industrialization model. In order to encourage economic development, the "Industrial Investment Incentive Act" was enacted in 1960. To solve the problem of insufficient capital, the "Industrial Investment Incentive Law" was amended in 1962 to encourage foreign direct investment. To increase domestic production and realize import substitution, the Thai government imported a large amount of advanced technology, machinery, and equipment, which brought about a shortage of foreign exchange.

Under such circumstances, the Thai government had to turn to the export-oriented industrialization strategy in the 1970s.

15. One of the most famous examples of this is the Tomioka Silk Mill.
16. In the planned economic system, it is also possible to establish closed export processing zones to earn foreign exchange. However, without a labor market, the flexibility of employment cannot be guaranteed. Therefore, it will not operate effectively.
17. Although there is an industrial division of labor between the member states of the former socialist camp, it is not a cooperation based on mutual interests but rather an expanded planned economy.
18. A large number of township and village enterprises emerged in China after the implementation of the reform and opening-up policy. Although these enterprises were collective enterprises, their operation was completely different from that of SOEs and urban collective enterprises and had more of the characteristics of private enterprises. According to the author's survey, foreign buyers were often more willing to order from these township enterprises because, compared with SOEs and urban collective enterprises, township enterprises had lower production costs and shorter lead times and were more flexible to meet buyers' requirements.
19. Although China's real GDP rose by 6.2% between 1952 and 1978, excluding the increase in population and the increase in heavy industry, the output that could be used to improve people's lives did not increase much. Hence, the living standards of the people basically did not improve during the planned economy period.
20. Prior to this, the government limited the business scope of the rural enterprises to agricultural production, farmers' lives, and urban large-scale industry.
21. The controversy over the Shenzhen Special Economic Zone is a good example.
22. This movement of importing machinery and equipment to develop China's economy was called the "foreign leap forward."
23. It is undeniable that since the beginning of this century, many foreign investments from Hong Kong have been roundabout investments by mainland Chinese enterprises.
24. This reason also indicates that China's decision makers at that time were still considering the import substitution industrialization strategy, especially for the heavy industries. As discussed in this chapter, in the export-oriented industrialization strategy, an increase in population means a greater future labor force, and the low wage advantage can last

for a long time. Under this strategy, a large number of women can be absorbed into labor-intensive export industries. This increases household income and the opportunity cost of raising children for women. However, it also raises women's awareness of social production, which eventually leads to a decline in the birth rate. Although no compulsory one-child policy like in China was implemented, the birth rates in Japan, South Korea, and Taiwan all dropped sharply along with economic growth.

25. Ezra Vogel believes that South Korea's development into an industrialized country was based on zero industrial technology, from handicrafts to heavy industry, from poverty to prosperity, from inexperienced leaders to modern economic planners, administrators, and engineers. No other country, including Japan, has completed this transition in such a short period of time (Yergin and Stanislaw, 1998).
26. The start and end times of Taiwan's rapid economic growth are not as clear as those of Japan and South Korea. Here, a period roughly in line with South Korea's growth is selected.
27. According to the 2020 Maddison Project Database, the average GDP growth rate in China from 1978 to 2012, calculated by purchasing power parity, was only 6.5%.

References

Akamatsu, K. 1962. A historical pattern of economic growth in developing countries. *The Developing Economies* (The Institute of Asian Economic Affairs), Preliminary Issue No. 1: 3–25. March–August 1962.

Asamoto, T. 2007. Economic policy and economic development. In Watanabe, T. and Asamoto, T. (eds.), *Introduction to Taiwan's Economy*. Tokyo: Keisoshobo (in Japanese).

Cho, S. 2005. *Dynamism of Korean Economic Development*. Tokyo: Hosei University Press (in Japanese). Translated by Hiroshi Fukagawa and Shogo Fujikawa.

Gu, Y. and Chen, T. 2003. Foreign direct investment and foreign capital introduction policy. In Liu, J. and Asamoto, T. (eds.), *The Industrial Policy of Taiwan*. Tokyo: Keisoshobo (in Japanese).

Kim, K.-S. 2009. Dynamism of industrial policy. In Cho, L.-J. (ed.), *The Age of Park Chung-hee: Modernization and Economic Development in South Korea. Watanabe Toshio, Carter Eckert*. Tokyo: University of Tokyo Press (in Japanese).

Kohama, H. 2007. Chapter 2: The political economy of the IMF. In Kunimune, K. (ed.), *Research Report on IMF and Developing Countries*. Asian Economic Research Institute (in Japanese).

Lee, S.-C. 2013. Industry breeding policy. In Hara, A. and Sun, J. (eds.), *South Korea's Path to Economic Development: Liberation, War, and Revival*. *Japan Economic Review* (in Japanese).

Li, G.-D. 1963. The Helmsman of Taiwan's economic development: Mourning Mr. Yun Jung-yong. *Free China's Industry*, 19(2) (in Chinese).

Lin, Y. 2012. *New Structural Economics: A Framework for Rethinking Development and Policy*. Beijing: Peking University Press (in Chinese).

Liu, H. 2012. Reasons for China's economic success and its future trends. *China Business Update*, 4, 2012 (in Chinese).

Lu, F. 2022. Why China's economy grows? *Social Sciences in China*, 1, 2022 (in Chinese).

National Health and Family Planning Commission. 2013. For more than 40 years of family planning, more than 400 million births have been lost in China. Central Government Portal. November 11, 2013. http://www.gov.cn/govweb/jrzg/2013-11/11/content_2525418.htm.

Nikkei Center. 2020. China's GDP will surpass that of the United States in 2028. *Nikkei Economic News*, December 10, 2020 (in Japanese).

Stiglitz. 2013. The core of China's development model. *Foreign Theoretical Trends*, 1, 2013 (in Chinese). Bao Jinze (translator).

The World Bank. 1993. *The East Asian Miracle*. Oxford: Oxford University Press.

Tian, J. 2008. Experience Deng Xiaoping up close. news.ifeng.com, January 3, 2008 (in Chinese). https://news.ifeng.com/history/1/200801/0103_335_351133_1.shtml.

Tian, J. 2015. Formation and implementation of development strategy in coastal areas. *Yanhuang Chunqiu*, 3, 2015 (in Chinese).

Wu, T.-M. 2016. From economic controls to export expansion in Postwar Taiwan: 1946-1960. RIETI Discussion Paper Series 16-E-028.

Yergin, D. and Stanislaw, J. 1998. *The Commanding Heights: The Battle Between Government and the Marketplace That is Remaking the Modern World*. New York: Simon & Schuster.

Zhang, J. 2013. How much longer can China's economy grow? https://www.aisixiang.com/data/64820.html (in Chinese).

Zhang, W. 2009. *The Economic System of China*. Beijing: CITIC Publishing House (in Chinese).

Zhu, T. 2016. *The Mystery of China's Growth*. Peking: Zhongxin Press (in Chinese).

https://doi.org/10.1142/9789819815241_0007

Chapter 7

THE NEXT PHASE OF ECONOMIC GROWTH AND DEVELOPMENT IN CHINA*

Ligang Song† and Yixiao Zhou‡

Arndt-Corden Department of Economics, Crawford School of Public Policy, The Australian National University, Canberra, Australia
†ligang.song@anu.edu.au
‡yixiao.zhou@anu.edu.au

Introduction

Since the reform and opening-up policies were introduced in 1978, China has experienced a high average annual growth rate of 9.3% between 1978 and 2021. The economy has been transformed from a planned to a market-based economy, accompanied by significant changes to economic activities and people's livelihoods. The urbanization rate rose from 19.4% to 64.7% over this period. The contribution of the primary industry to China's GDP decreased

*This chapter is based on a paper that was written in honor of Professor Zhang Jun from Fudan University, celebrating his 35 years of teaching economics and his 60th birthday in 2023.

from 27.7% in 1978 to 7.3% in 2021, while the tertiary industry accounted for 53.3% in 2021, a 29% increase from 1978, and the contribution of the secondary industry declined from 48% in 1978 to 39.4% in 2021. Between 1978 and 2021, real GDP per capita grew 29 times, and the average life expectancy rose by 12 years to 77 years in 2021. The number of people in China with incomes below US$1.90 per day (the International Poverty Line defined by the World Bank to track global extreme poverty) has fallen by nearly 800 million, contributing close to three-quarters of the global reduction in the number of people living in extreme poverty.

China's economic growth was driven significantly by productivity growth, both from institutional reforms and technological progress. The economy enjoyed three kinds of "dividends," which propelled rapid productivity growth over most of the reform period. The first is the reform dividends from marketization, decentralization, privatization, urbanization, literalization, and institution-building (Zhang, 2018). The second is the demographic dividends, which brought about higher savings arising from the high working-age population as a share of the total population (Cai, 2018). The third globalization dividends came from the global scale of resource allocation, technology spillover, and the subsequent gains from trade and technological progress after China's integration into global trade and investment systems (Song, 1996; Drysdale and Song, 2000). All three kinds of dividends have been weakening in recent years against the background of slow progress in reform in certain areas, population aging and deglobalization. With those headwinds facing the economy, China is compelled to adjust its strategies to meet the challenges in the new phase of growth and development.

Due to the three factors, as identified above, China has experienced a slowdown in real GDP growth since the 2007–2009 Global Financial Crisis (GFC) (Figure 1). When decomposing the growth rate of real GDP into four contributory factors, namely labor force (measured by employment), labor force quality (measured by human capital per worker), capital intensity (physical capital per worker), and total factor productivity (TFP), we could see that the

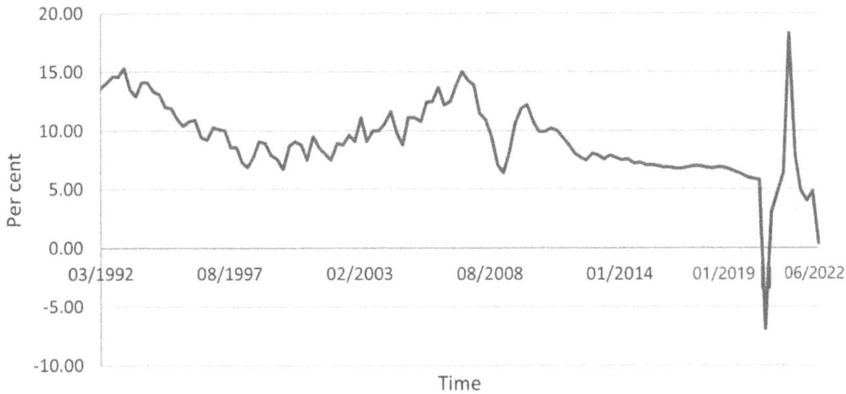

Figure 1. Quarterly real GDP growth rate of China, year on year, 1992Q1–2022Q2.
Source: Authors' construction using data from the CEIC Database.

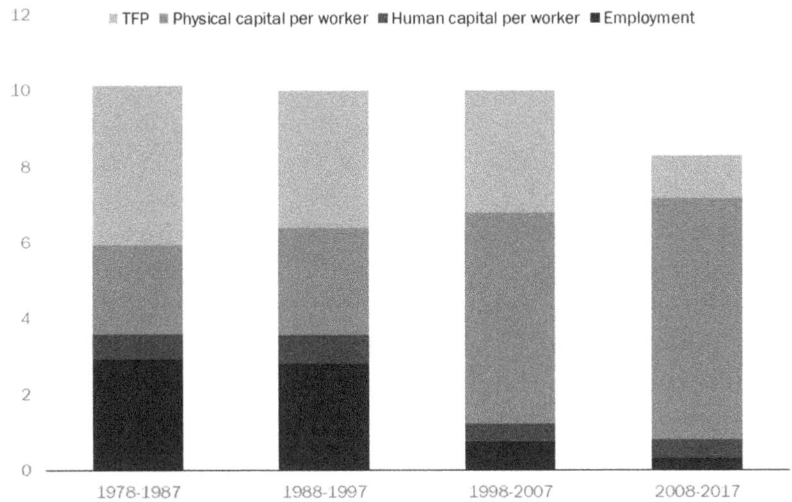

Figure 2. Drivers of economic growth in China.
Source: World Bank (2019) and Raiser and Soh (2019).

decline in TFP growth and employment growth were the main drivers behind slower economic growth, while physical capital per worker grew more rapidly and was a counteracting factor, and the growth of human capital per worker was relatively stable (Figure 2). Although weaker TFP growth in China has coincided with — and

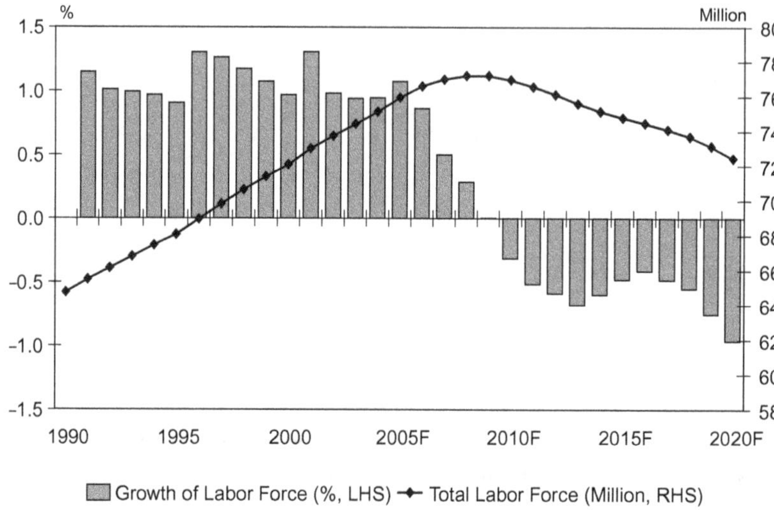

Figure 3. Total labor supply and its trend: 1990–2020 (Lewis turning point).
Source: Authors' construction using data from CEIC Database.

likely been affected by — the recent decline in world productivity growth, the deceleration in China has been sharper (Brandt *et al.*, 2020).

The above changes in the four contributing factors correspond to the main headwinds to economic growth in China. First, in terms of labor force growth, extremely low fertility rates caused the problem of population aging and a shrinking labor force (Figure 3). Second, in terms of TFP growth, the following headwinds are at work to put downward pressure on technological catch-up and economic dynamism and hence drag down TFP growth: the unfavorable global macroeconomic environment and financial conditions since the GFC and now with COVID-19; the increasing financial risks due to high leverages on parts of households, firms, and local governments; deglobalization with rising protectionism and economic and technological decoupling hampering the efforts for global and regional integration (Figure 4); challenges in adopting low-carbon development strategies; and the rising geopolitical tensions.

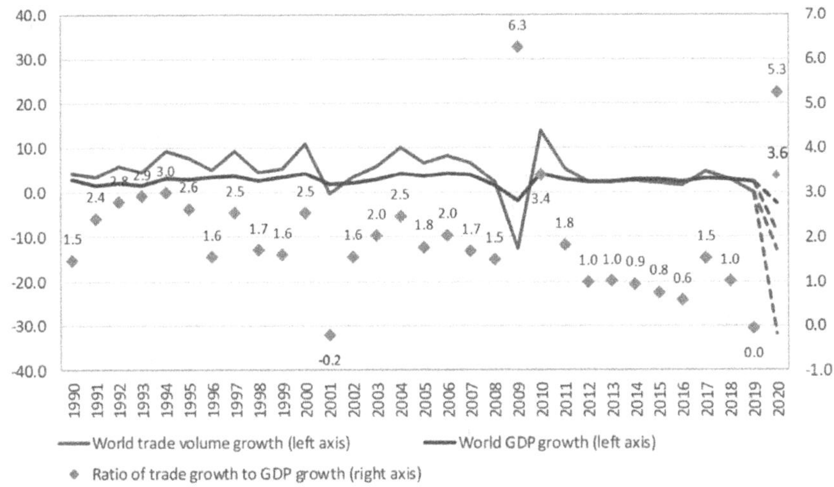

Figure 4. Ratio of trade growth to global GDP growth: 1990–2020 (%).
Source: The World-Trade-Organization (WTO) Global Trade Data Portal (1991–2021).

New Sources of Growth in the Next Phase of China's Economic Development: A Growth Accounting Perspective

Going ahead, what could be China's new sources of growth in the next phase of its economic development as a new entrant into the group of high-income economies? We explore in detail based on the four contributing factors of growth.

First, as growth theories have made clear that TFP growth is the ultimate driver of long-term economic growth, it is crucial to adjust policies and institutions to adapt to and nurture TFP growth as the economic structure evolves and to remove domestic factors and policy choices that contribute to the slowdown in TFP growth by deepening supply-side reform focusing on state-owned enterprises (SOEs), the financial sector, factor markets, and entrepreneurship. The government should continue to play a key role in leading the nation's drives to become more innovative, especially in those areas where uncertainties could prevent the private sector from investing in innovation.

Second, China's fertility rate continues to fall in recent years. China has already entered the age of aging society, as the share of the aged population (65 years and above) has surpassed 14%. The rapid pace of aging prompted the Chinese government to adopt a series of policies, including the two-child policy, hoping to raise the fertility rate and increase the labor force in the long run. It is likely that the government will remove the family planning policy altogether, returning rights to reproduce to the family, with the hope that some kind of balance in its demographic structure will be restored in the long term. However, loosening birth policies alone may not be sufficient, and other conditions need to be changed to incentivize higher fertility, including financial subsidies to families which have more children. However, one concern about such incentives is that the younger generations have had a low propensity to reproduce despite such subsidies, as also shown in the experiences of Japan and Korea.

Third, although China's has made significant achievements in enhancing education access and quality, there is still large room for catching up toward the education levels in advanced economies. Against the background of a falling labor force since 2012 (and soon the total population from 2023), policies should focus more on quality than quantity of labor force. It will require, apart from increasing government expenditure on education and training, the reform of its education system, including the reform of curricula for all levels of education and a boost in the development of vocational education. The former will help improve the employability of the graduates by resolving the issue of the mismatch between what has been learned at schools and universities and what is required in workplaces. The latter will not only fill in the gaps in educational provision but also equip young people with the necessary skills, making them more employable in the workplace.

There are two important areas as far as education policies are concerned. One is that China has a large labor force (around 800 million in total). Upgrading the skills of the existing labor force is critical for confronting the challenges of enhancing firms' productivity, carrying out the ongoing digital transformation of the economy, and achieving green growth. Enterprises should shoulder more responsibilities in contributing to such training, and they will reap the payoffs from doing so, as the quality of the labor being employed is improved as a result. The other is to address the urban–rural divide in educational provision as well as the quality of education by allocating more investment funds for education in rural and inland regions. Reforming China's fiscal system holds the key to securing such funding from local public finance. Private sector participation in education investment is also an option for filling the investment gaps in educational provision in China.

Fourth, since the GFC, the predominant driver of economic growth in China has been capital deepening, as seen in the contribution from capital intensity growth to real GDP growth in Figure 2. While capital deepening boosts labor productivity as well as technological progress as there are new embodied technologies in new investments, when TFP growth slows down and labor force expansion is constrained, continued capital deepening will encounter diminishing returns and hence become less effective in sustaining and boosting economic growth.

Another major concern is whether the resources are allocated to the most efficient use and hence generate maximum returns. In China's context, the comparison between the return on investment in the state economy and the return on investment in the private economy is important. While the state economy undertakes important functions such as maintaining employment stability, lowering income inequality, investing in infrastructure and research and development (R&D) projects with strong positive spillover effects, the relative productivity of the state sector versus the private sector is also an important consideration for the optimal resource allocation between the state sector and the private sector. Therefore, going ahead, to drive and sustain economic growth, capital deepening needs to go hand in hand with polices and reforms that boost TFP growth and efficiency in resource allocation. It becomes quite necessary given the fact down the track saving will become more scare due to the continued fall in labor force and population aging.

In the following, we expand on what the new sources of growth could be in relation to the four contributory factors discussed above.

In terms of TFP growth, there is potential for TFP growth through more rapid innovation in products, production processes, organizations, and governance, as well as the further expansion of a dynamic private sector through nurturing entrepreneurship. With a labor force that peaked in 2011 and an aging society, labor costs, caring responsibilities and demand for healthcare resources add to the cost of operating the economy. Counteracting forces include continued technological progress and labor-substituting/augmenting automation. New technological developments in artificial intelligence (AI) and digital transformation are important new sources of TFP growth in China, and the country is accelerating investments in automation technologies (Figure 5). In its report on *Artificial Intelligence: Implications for China*, McKinsey estimates that AI technology in China could add 0.8–1.4 percentage points to China's annual GDP growth (a target of 5% for 2022), depending on the speed of adoption. Furthermore, China now accounts for 42% of global e-commerce, boasts one-third of the world's most successful tech start-ups, and conducts 11 times more mobile payments than the United States (US) per year.

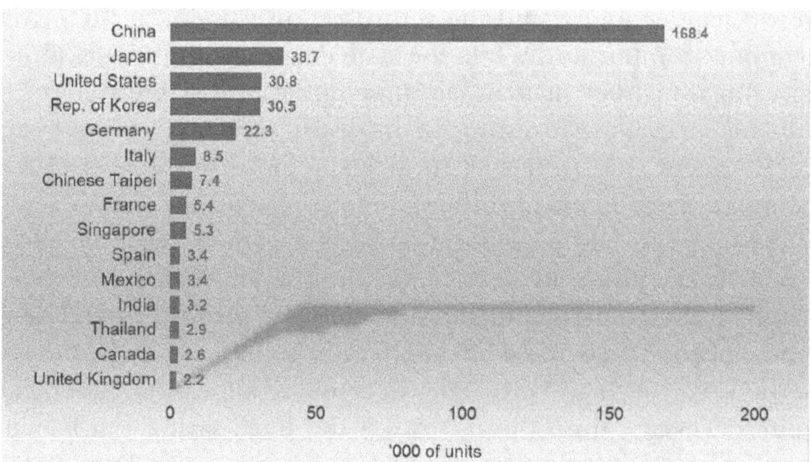

Figure 5. Annual installations of industrial robots, 15 largest markets (2020).
Source: International Federation of Robotics (2021).

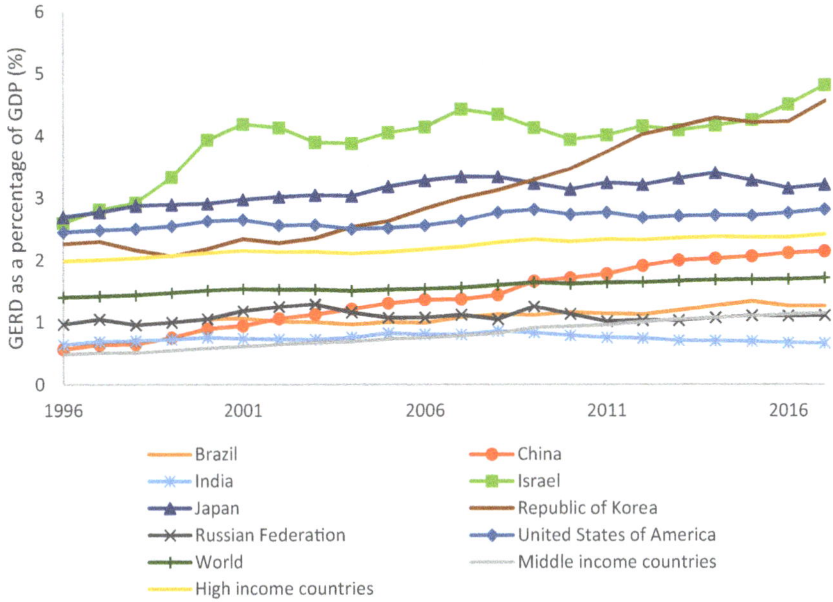

Figure 6. R&D intensity in various economies.

Source: Authors' construction from the OECD statistics.

China has made significant progress in both innovation inputs (Figures 6 and 7) and innovation performance (Figures 8 and 9). There is still a significant gap between China and advanced economies in key determinants of innovation performance. Closing these gaps will propel innovation activities in China further, raising TFP growth and economic growth in the long run. The areas requiring future efforts include the following: more basic research (research activities can be categorized into three types: basic research, applied research, and experimental development research) is needed for sustaining innovation and technological progress as China moves toward the world's technology frontier; more efficient allocation of innovation funds is needed between SOEs and private firms and between businesses, higher education institutions, and research institutions. Further improvement in institutional quality through supply-side reforms is needed to nurture more research and development (R&D) investments and innovation activities. The areas of improvement include strengthening IPR protection, improving the

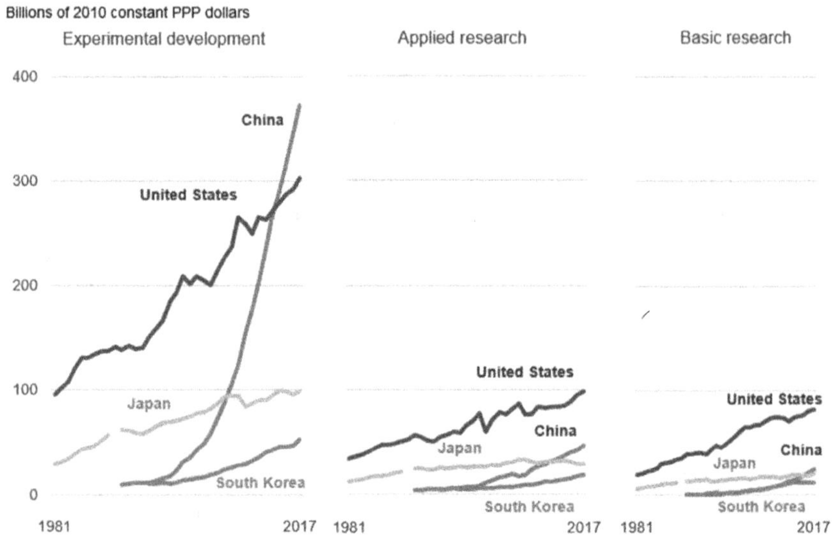

Figure 7. China leads the world in experimental development spending.

Source: NSF based on OECD Statistics. https://www.nsf.gov/statistics/2020/nsf20304/overview.htm.

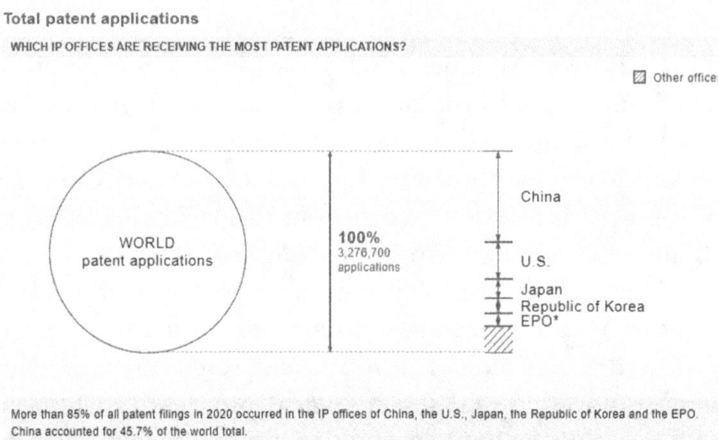

Figure 8. Major countries in patent application in 2020.

Source: WIPO Statistics Database.

Figure 9. Top 10 countries in terms of number of unicorns in 2019.

Note: A unicorn startup or unicorn company is a private company with a valuation over US$1 billion. As of August 2020, there are more than 400 unicorns around the world.
Source: Hurun Institute (2020).

business environment, and promoting fair competition, all of which help enhance the spirit of entrepreneurship and market-driven innovation. Lastly, improvement in the design of the national innovation system, e.g., incentives and wage structure of science and technology (S&T) workers, will incentivize more innovation activities as well.

China's commitment to peak carbon emissions by 2030 and achieving carbon neutrality by 2060 requires a dramatic change in output structure, energy mix, regional and industrial location, and production technologies. Moving along the pathway of decarbonization represents the beginning of the decline of the traditional ways of industrialization in China, which in the past have powered its industrialization with high investments, high resource and energy intensities, and high pollution. It also represents an opportunity for China to undertake the historical transformation of its economy toward more efficient and sustainable development. The combination of measures including structural reform, energy transformation, new technology, new patterns of international trade and wider cooperation offers hope that continued economic growth with greater environmental amenity and higher productivity will result (Song, 2022).

In terms of labor force quality growth, between 2000 and 2018, total enrolment in Chinese universities climbed from 7.4 million to more than 44 million. For comparison's sake, total higher education enrollment in the US peaked at just over 21 million students in 2011 and has been declining marginally ever since. The returns on education have been increasing. Compared to those with lower levels of education (junior high school and below), graduates from senior high school, technical school and college earned 4%, 7%, and 14% more, respectively, in 1998. By 2009, these amounts had increased to 18%, 32%, and 61%, respectively (Meng *et al.*, 2013). However, there is still great room for catch-up toward education levels in advanced economies such as the US, Japan, and Australia. Figure 10 shows the relationship between per capita income level and education level measured as mean years of schooling in a global context. The fitted polynomial curve based on cross-country data in 2020 shows that at relatively low-income levels, education level rises

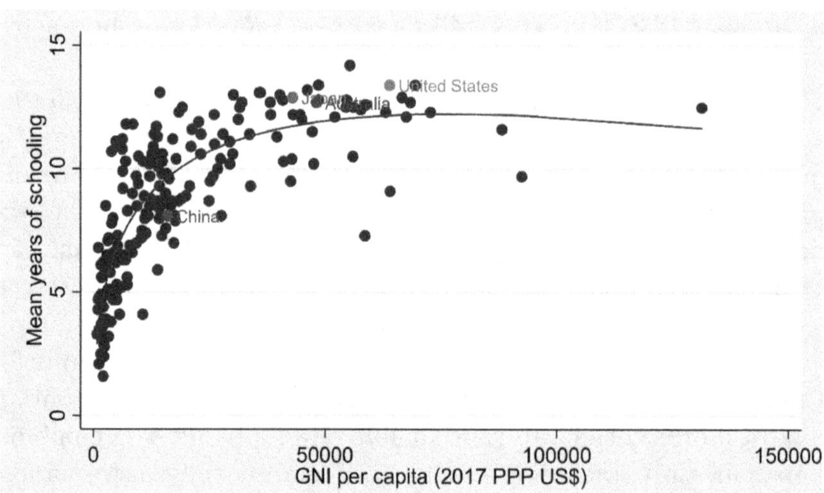

Figure 10. Income level and education level, cross-country data.

Source: Authors' own construction using data from the United Nations.

quickly as income level increases, but education level plateaus and does not grow further as income level rises after income reaches a certain threshold. The current position of China in the figure is far from the threshold, showing that there is still room for education level to rise in China to catch up to those in advanced economies.

According to the OECD, the nine-year free and compulsory education in China targets children from age 6 to age 15. It encompasses primary and lower secondary education. Despite the efforts to bring children to schools, the quality of the learning environment still needs to be improved in China. In 2013, in China, there were on average 38 children per class in primary school and 50 in lower secondary school, while the OECD averages were 19 and 21, respectively. Tertiary education has been expanding in the last few decades. In China, 28% of 18 year olds, 39% of 19 year olds and 40% of 20 year olds were enrolled in tertiary education in 2019 compared to 18%, 34%, and 39% on average across OECD countries.

There is a great disparity in the quantity and quality of education that urban and rural children receive. There is also a gap in the educational attainment of the children of migrant workers and the children of urban residents (Golley and Kong, 2013). The transmission of education from one generation of a household to another is a powerful phenomenon in reform-era China and has become stronger in recent years. It tends to reproduce educational inequality, and thus income inequality, over the generations (Knight *et al.*, 2013).

Third, to change the long-term trend of a declining labor force, measures that need to be taken also include delaying retirement ages and increasing labor participation. It is also important to provide support for women giving birth through an adequate childcare system so that they feel confident about returning to the workforce. Housing also needs to be redesigned to accommodate large families. Looking after the aged will be a big challenge for China, given the shortfalls in its pension funds and government budget constraints. One option is to introduce the system of forced savings (which is like the superannuation system in Australia) to gradually shift the burden of looking after the elderly from the government to individuals, allowing more government funds to be spent on the provision of public goods. The future growth of the Chinese economy needs to factor in this significant demographic change to achieve more balanced and sustainable growth.

Fourth, let's turn our attention to investment in capital as a driver of economic growth. China's economic growth is now challenged by overinvestment in low-return assets, causing the problem of overcapacity in some industries. One example is low-grade infrastructure. Based on Chinese provincial data for the period 1995–2011, Shi and Huang (2014) found that most of the western provinces in China overinvested in infrastructure in 2008 and that the nationwide large-scale infrastructure investments enacted by the government after the GFC are not socially optimal. Xu and Wang (2014) found that since 2009, government stimulus measures and infrastructure spending have generated US$6.8 trillion in wasted investment, approximately 37% of total investment.

However, the declining return on capital investment is a broader issue than low-grade infrastructure investment. Figure 11 presents the ratio of investment to GDP, and Figure 12 presents the incremental capital-output ratio (ICOR). ICOR is a measure of how much investment it takes to produce each additional unit of output in an economy, with investment as the numerator and additional GDP as the denominator. We can see that the ratio of investment to

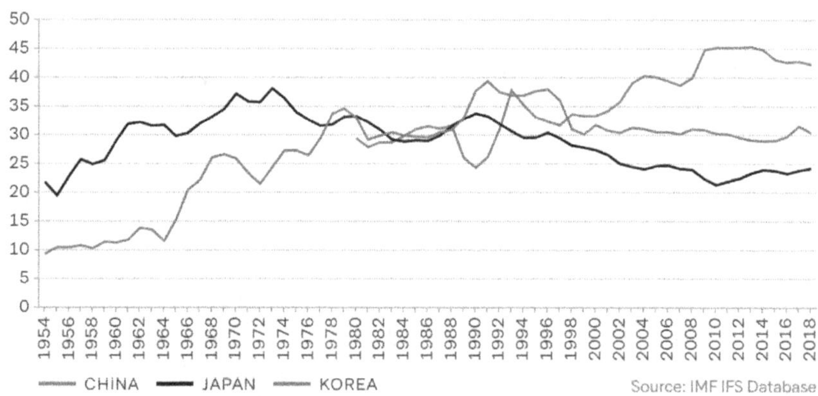

Figure 11. The ratio of investment to GDP (INV/GDP) in percent.

Source: IMF IFS Database.

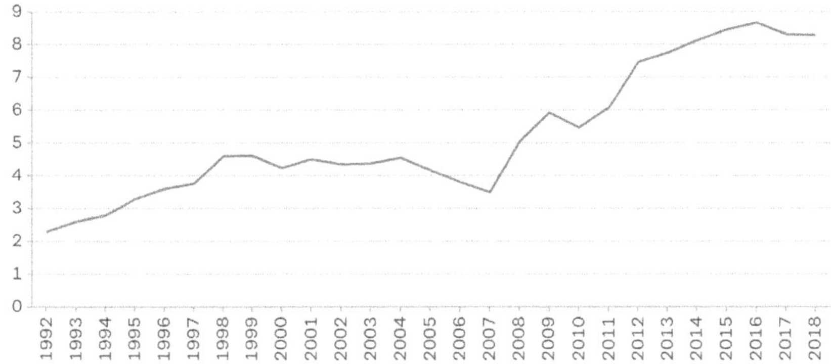

Figure 12. Incremental capital output ratio (ICOR).

Source: National Bureau of Statistics of China.

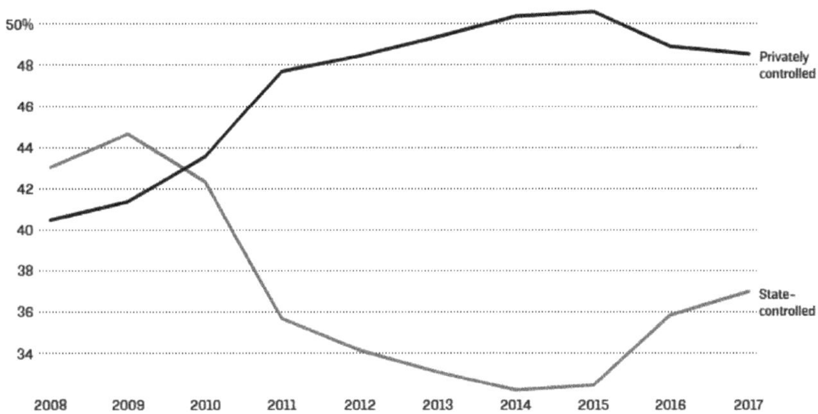

Figure 13. Fixed asset investment by firm type in China (percentage share).

Source: Huang (2021).

GDP in China is higher than that in Japan and South Korea, two economies that are intensive in manufacturing activities (Figure 11). The return on investment in China is deteriorating over time (Figure 12), and this could be explained by both the decline in relatively high-return private assets as a share of total investment (Figure 13) and the decline in return on private assets (Figure 14).

Since 2016, the share of private asset investment has been on the decline, while that of state assets has risen. Both the return on private assets and that on state assets have dropped, although the return

Figure 14. Return on assets (in percent).

Note: Orange line indicates SOEs, and blue line indicates private firms.
Source: China Statistical Yearbooks.

on private assets is still higher than that on state assets. Brandt *et al.* (2020) find that earlier reforms led to SOEs catching up to private sector productivity levels in manufacturing, but convergence stalled after 2007. Limited market entry and exit and a lack of resource allocation to more productive firms were associated with slower manufacturing TFP growth. Furthermore, the allocation of a larger share of credit and investment to infrastructure and housing led to lower returns on capital, a rapid buildup in debt, and slower growth.

Structural Problems to Be Tackled in the Next Phase of Growth

We point out three structural problems that need to be addressed to lower the risks to growth. The first structural problem is high debt and the associated financial risks, the second is high income inequality, and the third is the deepening of integration in the international market. China's overall debt was estimated to be 270.1% of gross domestic product (GDP) at the end of 2020 by China's National Institution for Finance and Development (NIFD), up from 246.5% at the end of 2019. Although lower than that of the US, China's debt-to-GDP almost doubled in the decade after the 2008 GFC. Current deleveraging is focused on the non-financial

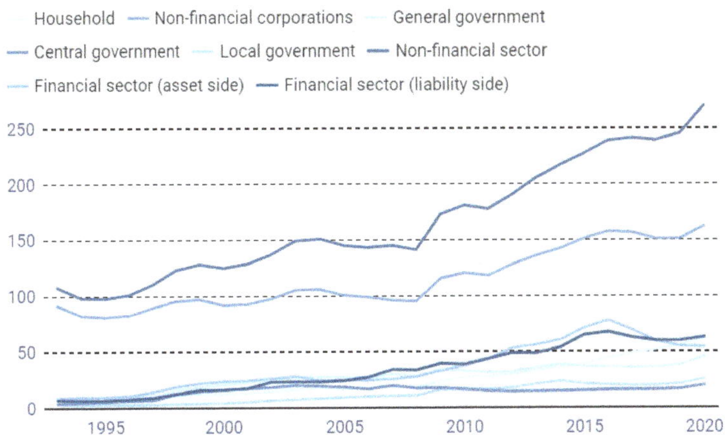

Figure 15. China's internal debt.

Source: Authors' construction based on data from the CEIC Database.

corporate sector, where it is expected to fall by 6.5 percentage points, according to the NIFD. Reducing the stock debt is just the first step to creating a more sustainable debt model. Another important step is to remove implicit government guarantees for large institutions and allow creative destruction to occur to reallocate resources from unproductive firms to more productive firms, thus enhancing the return on investment and economic growth and the ability to pay down the debt burden. This change could be seen in the recent Evergrande debt crisis that started in 2021.

The second structural problem is high income inequality (Figure 16). Piketty *et al.* (2019) found that China's inequality level used to be less than Europe's in the late 1970s, close to the most egalitarian Nordic countries, while it is now approaching US levels. The rapid increase in income inequality has put China among the most unequal countries in Asia and indeed the world. China is now one of the least equal 25% of countries worldwide, a group to which very few Asian countries belong. With the Gini coefficient at 0.47, China's level of income inequality is similar to that of several high-inequality Latin American countries (Sicular, 2013) and approaching that of the US (Piketty *et al.*, 2019). Income inequality has become an economic, political, and social problem for China.

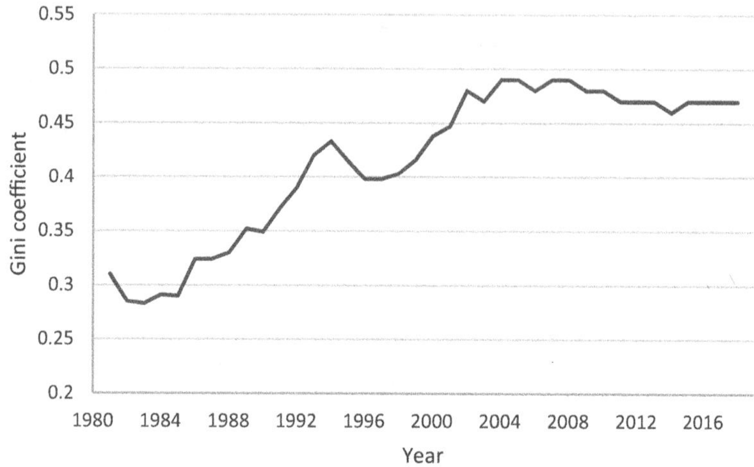

Figure 16. Gini coefficient in China, 1981–2018.

Source: Zhou and Song (2016). Gini coefficients for the years 1981–2001 are from Ravallion and Chen (2007), 2002 from WIID, and 2003–2018 from the National Bureau of Statistics, China.

Income inequality rises along with the increase in per capita income and may fall after a country reaches a certain level of per capita income. This pattern of changes in inequality in relation to changes in income is commonly referred to as the inverted Kuznets U-curve (Kuznets, 1955). This implies a causal relationship running from economic or income growth to income inequality. However, in reality, potential causes for income inequality can be very complex, involving factors such as technological and structural changes, political and economic institutions, social norms, cultural factors, and geography. It is even more so for China, as the country is not only a developing economy but also a transition economy. A transition economy emphasizes economic incentives but is still nurturing market means for allocating resources and the redistribution function of government policies.

Piketty quoted Charles Dunoyer (1845) as saying, "Reduce everything to equality and you will bring everything to a standstill" (Piketty, 2014, p. 85). However, there is evidence which shows that overemphasizing income equality at the expense of incentives and efficiency could compromise growth. Therefore, finding a right balance between efficiency and equity is one of the most challenging tasks for China's economic reform and public policy.

In order to develop sound policies that could alleviate income inequality, it is important to identify the roles and evolution of various drivers of income inequality, such as the urban–rural income gap, within-urban and within-rural income gap, income gap due to incomplete economic reforms such as wage income gap between workers employed in monopolistic industries and workers employed in more competitive sectors, regional inequality attributed to different levels of trade liberalization, fiscal decentralization and marketization in various regions in China, and wage income gap due to different skill and education levels.

Besides rising income inequality, wealth concentration in China has sharply increased over the last few decades. The top 10% wealth share rose from 40% in 1995 to 67% in 2015, while the middle 40% and bottom 50% wealth shares collapsed. As a result, while wealth inequality used to be much lower in China than in the Western world in the mid-1990s, it is now between European and American levels. The Chinese top 10% wealth share (67% in 2015) is getting close to that of the United States (72%) and is much higher than in a country like France (50%). The bottom 50% wealth share is now barely higher than in rich countries, where it is usually around 0–5%. According to Piketty *et al.* (2019), saving flows explain 50–60% of the rise in the wealth-income ratio since 1978, while the increase in relative asset prices accounts for the remaining 40–50%. That is, equity and housing prices have increased above and beyond the rise in consumer prices. These causes of rising inequality present a big challenge for China in pursuing the policy of "common prosperity," by which a more equal outcome from growth and development can be achieved.

The third structural problem is how China could integrate further with the international markets. China has grown into a world manufacturing powerhouse, propelled by the lowering of institutional barriers for international trade and technological change that leads to declining transportation and communication costs and facilitates global value chains. In the future, China may move beyond being a manufacturing powerhouse toward becoming a financial powerhouse as well. The economic fundamentals suggest that there are economic rationales for this to happen, and this change is beneficial for long-term growth in China, but institutional challenges are still not small.

Economic fundamentals favor a portfolio adjustment to China's market. First, let us look at the economic fundamentals. As China's exports to international markets become more uncertain in prospect due to trade conflicts resulting from rising protectionism, it needs to rely more on domestic investment and consumption to drive economic growth. However, this switch in GDP composition is faced with headwinds, including an aging demographic structure. Population aging has caused China's domestic saving ratio to decline continuously, from the peak of 50% in 2010 to 45% in 2019. This decline contributes to the fall in the net export to GDP ratio post the GFC as well as the tighter availability of investment funds and declining rates of domestic investment. As discussed in section "New Sources of Growth in the Next Phase of China's Economic Development: A Growth Accounting Perspective", to counteract these downward forces on investment, one possibility is for China to undertake reforms to boost the efficiency of fund allocation and thus raise investment returns. These reforms would go beyond financial market reforms and involve enhancing competitive neutrality and balancing out market forces and government intervention in investment decisions. The other possibility is for China to have further financial opening-up and integration with the world capital market, which could lead to global portfolios balancing toward the Chinese financial market and greater foreign capital inflow to fund investment in China.

It may be an opportune time now for China to implement financial integration as a long-term growth strategy. Aided by Chinese bonds' inclusion in global benchmark indices and China's Bond Connect program, which allows foreign fund managers to trade in the country's debt markets without an onshore trading entity, there has been a strong pick-up in foreign buying of Chinese bonds and an increase in exposure to Chinese debt in recent months. Foreign

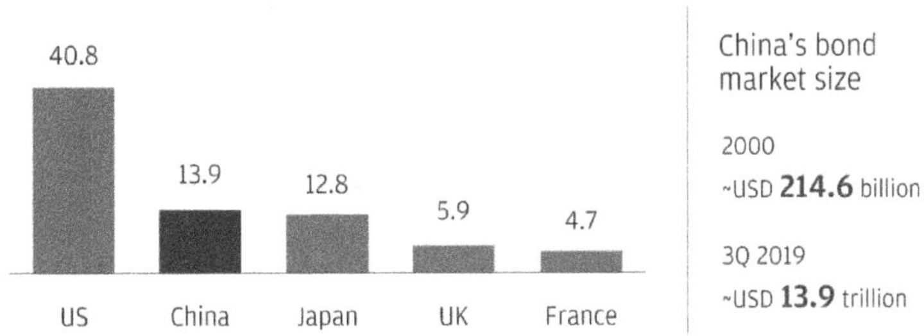

Figure 17. The world's top five bond markets (market size in USD trillion).
Source: JPMorgan (2021).

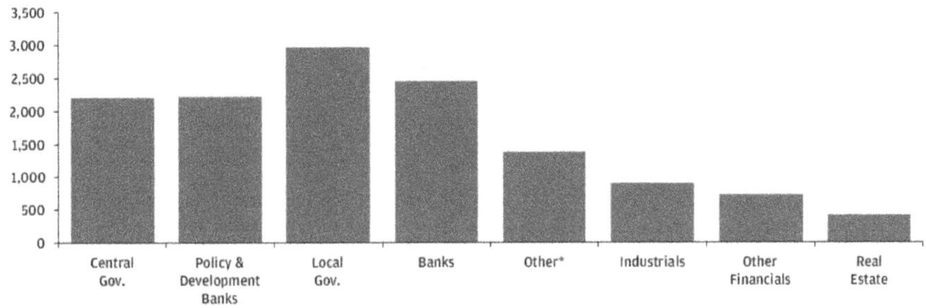

Figure 18. The government is the largest issuer of onshore bond in China.
Source: JPMorgan (2021).

investors accounted for about 12% of all purchases of Chinese government and policy bank bonds in 2020. China's onshore fixed income market is the second largest in the world, with a total of US$13.7 trillion in outstanding bonds as of December 2019, and the government is the major issuer of bonds (Figures 17 and 18).

China's bond market is still developing, and foreign investors still face challenges. First, onshore bond market trading lacks market-makers to facilitate buying and selling, and bonds are traded directly between parties in the interbank market. Although this could help preserve the lower volatility of traditional safe assets that are attracting foreign investors, it also means less liquidity compared to US Treasuries and more difficulty for investors to enter and exit the market quickly. Second, there is a conjecture that the acceleration of financial opening up is partly motivated by China's consideration to preempt possible US financial decoupling. With more integration into the global financial markets, it could be more difficult to have financial decoupling, and the leverage of financial decoupling decreases as well.

What does a financially integrated Chinese market mean for the global economy? Tyers and Zhou (2020) show that China's financial openness, as measured by cross-border flows and asset ownership, peaked during its growth surge in the 2000s, as did downward pressure on global interest rates and price levels. Globally, China's growth surge raised asset prices, reduced yields, and bolstered deflationary pressures while improving aggregate economic welfare. Therefore, greater financial integration between China and the world will amplify the impacts of China's economic growth on the global economy and, in the meantime, moderate the effects on China's domestic economy.

China's integration into the global financial system will require further financial reform and opening up, including its capital account liberalization and the full convertibility of RMB. At the same time, financial opening up involves risks. China can reduce the potential risks by allowing more flexibility in RMB exchange rates, building a more solid banking system with more stringent prudential regulations, reducing government debts at all levels through more stringent fiscal discipline, and maintaining a balanced position in its international balance of payment. The last task may prove to be difficult given the falling domestic saving ratios due to population aging. It may be too early now to predict the situation in which China becomes a net importer of capital, but such a prospect will have significant implications for China's long-term growth and development as well as the global macroeconomic balances with respect to the relationship between savings and investments (and therefore the determination of global interest rates).

Are Policymakers Looking in the Right Directions for New Sources of Growth in China?

The strategic goals that the Chinese government has set for China's economy include: to build a modern advanced economy by the mid-21st century; to build an integrated domestic market (through supply-side reform); to build an innovation-based economy centering on digital transformation of the economy and the use of new and renewable energies; to achieve more equitable development (common prosperity); to achieve carbon peak by 2030 and carbon neutrality by 2060; and to enhance global and regional economic reintegration by cementing China's position as a hub for global value and supply chains (by implementing the dual circulation strategy).

These goals are in line with the challenges and structural problems we identified in sections "New Sources of Growth in the Next Phase of China's Economic Development: A Growth Accounting Perspective" and "Structural Problems to Be Tackled in the Next Phase of Growth", but to realize these strategic goals, China must build more effective institutions to deal with business failures, absorb losses, and manage risks and uncertainty. In particular, China needs improved bankruptcy procedures, multilevel capital markets, an effective social-security system, reliable public housing, and a progressive tax regime that aims to reduce inequality. At the same time, to counter market abuses, China should introduce more robust competition laws, anti-corruption mechanisms, and stronger environmental regulations. China will need to phase out the hukou system, enhancing nation-wide mobility of people and other resources. This underlines the government's recent call for building a nation-wide, integrated domestic market which will unleash further productivity gains and add impetus to economic growth.

China also needs to develop a more comprehensive strategy for confronting all the challenges resulting from its significant demographic changes, considering those potential economic, political, social, and environmental impacts. This strategy will allow China to achieve its goals of long-term development without many disruptions. Again, policies of investing in human capital, enhancing fertilities, and automation hold the key.

As the second-largest economy and the largest trading nation in the world, it is in China's fundamental interests and those of others to continue to champion both regional and global economic reintegration in the post-COVID-19 pandemic world, which has led some countries to pursue a strategy for self-sufficiency in the name of safeguarding supply security. Resisting the attempts at economic and technological decoupling will be crucial to restoring the global trading order in the process of economic recovery from the pandemic (Song and Zhou, 2020). China should actively participate in regional economic cooperations and global efforts to push for changes in the multilateral trading system the World Trade Organization (WTO) to minimize the damage brought about by deglobalization and maximize the chances that international trade will continue to be an engine for global economic growth.

When these policies are successfully implemented, we can predict that the policy impact will help offset the weakening trend of the three dividends, as identified in the chapter. Together, the reform dividends, the new demographic dividends with human capital development at the center, and the dividends from the process of reglobalization will power the Chinese economy into the next phase of its economic growth and development.

References

Brandt, L., Litwack, J., Mileva, E., Wang, L., Zhang, Y., and Zhao, L. 2020. China's Productivity slowdown and future growth potential. *Policy Research Working Paper*, No. 9298. Washington, DC: World Bank.

Cai, F. 2018. Chapter 13: How has the Chinese economy capitalized on the demographic dividend during the reform period? In Garnaut, R., Song, L., and Cai, F. (eds.), *China's 40 Years of Reform and Development: 1978–2018*. Australian National University Press: Canberra, pp. 235–256.

Drysdale, P. and Song, L. (eds.). 2000. *China's Entry to the WTO: Strategic Issues and Quantitative Assessments*. Routledge: London and New York.

Knight, J., Sicular, T., and Yue, X. 2013. Educational inequality in China: The intergenerational dimension. In Li, S., Sato, H., and Sicular, T. (eds.), *Rising Inequality in China: Challenges to the Harmonious Society*. Cambridge, UK: Cambridge University Press.

Kuznets, S. 1955. Economic growth and income inequality. *American Economic Review*, 65(1), 1–28.

Meng, X., Shen, K., and Xue, S. 2013. Economic reform, education expansion, and earnings inequality for urban males in China, 1988–2009. *Journal of Comparative Economics*, 41(1), 227–244.

Piketty, T. 2014. *Capital in the Twenty-First Century*. Cambridge, MA: The Belknap Press of Harvard University Press.

Piketty, T., Yang, L., and Zucman, G. 2019. Capital accumulation, private property, and rising inequality in China, 1978–2015. *American Economic Review*, 109(7), 2469–2496.

Raiser, M. and Soh, H. S. 2019. To sustain growth, China can learn from previous transitions to high income. *Future Development* (The Brookings Institution).

Ravallion, M. and Chen, S. 2007. China's uneven progress against poverty. *Journal of Development Economics*, 82(1), 1–42.

Shi, H. and Huang, S. 2014. How much infrastructure is too much? A new approach and evidence from China. *World Development*, 56, 272–286.

Sicular, T. 2013. The challenge of high inequality in China. *Inequality in Focus*, 2(2), 1–5.

Song, L. 1996. Chapter 12: Institutional change, trade composition, and export supply potential in China. In Guitian, M. and Mundell, R. (eds.), *Inflation and Growth in China*. Washington DC: International Monetary Fund, pp. 190–228.

Song, L. 2022. Chapter 6: Decarbonizing China's steel industry. In Garnaut, R. (ed.), *The Superpower Transformation: Making Australia's Zero-Carbon Future*. Melbourne: La Trobe University Press, pp. 219–239.

Song, L. and Zhou, Y. 2020. The COVID-19 pandemic and its impact on the global economy: What does it take to turn crisis into opportunity. *China & World Economy*, 28(4), 1–25.

United Nations (UN). 2015. *The Millennium Development Goals Report 2015*. New York.

World Bank. 2009. *Innovative China: New Drivers of Growth*. Washington, DC: World Bank. https://openknowledge.worldbank.org/handle/10986/32351. License: CC BY 3.0 IGO.

Xu, C. and Wang, Y. 2014. Prevent resource waste due to inefficient investment. *Shanghai Securities News. (Shanghai Zhengjuan Bao)*, November 20, 2014, pp. A3.

Yue, X., Li, S., and Sicular, T. 2011. High incomes in monopoly industries: A discussion. *Social Sciences in China*, XXXII(2), 178–196.

Zhang, J. 2018. Chapter 12: China's price liberalization and market reform: A historical perspective. In Garnaut, R., Song, L., and Cai, F. (eds.),

China's 40 Years of Reform and Development: 1978–2018. Canberra: Australian National University Press, pp. 215–234.

Zhang, X. 2006. Fiscal decentralization and political centralization in China: Implications for growth and inequality. *Journal of Comparative Economics*, 34, 713–726.

Zhou, Y. and Song, L. 2016. Income inequality in China: Causes and policy responses. *China Economic Journal*, 9(2), 186–208.

Zhou, Y. and Tyers, R. 2019. Automation and inequality in China. *China Economic Review*, 58, 101202.

Zhou, Y., Gao, Y., Liu, Y., Wu, W., and Li, Y. 2018. Targeted poverty alleviation and land policy innovation: Some practice and policy implications from China. *Land Use Policy*, 74, 53–65.

https://doi.org/10.1142/9789819815241_0008

Chapter 8

FROM MORE GROWTH TO BETTER GROWTH: THE CHALLENGE AND THE WAY OUT

Lok Sang Ho[*,‡] and Wing Lok Hung[†,§]

[*]*Pan Sutong Shanghai-Hong Kong Economic Policy Research Institute, Lingnan University, Hong Kong*
[†]*School of Governance and Policy Science Chinese University of Hong Kong*
[‡]*lsho@ln.edu.hk*
[§]*winglokhung@cuhk.edu.hk*

Introduction

The Chinese economy's meteoric rise has caused alarm in the West. An article published online on the CNN website states, "China's rapid technological advances have also made it a strategic threat to the United States and its allies. It's steadily pushing American rivals out of long-held leadership positions in sectors ranging from 5G technology to artificial intelligence."[1] This, in truth, is the nature of the "threat" perceived by politicians in the West. It was also pointed out that "[u]ntil recently, some economists were predicting that China would become the world's biggest economy by 2030, unseating the United States."[2] If China is to continue to grow at three times the rate of the United States (US) on average, it will leave the US in the dust before long. This is the basis of the fear that worries American politicians. Another strand of the fear, of course, is the apparent inadequacy of the Western model of governance that is billed as democracy. American politicians, unable to address problems at home, turn to a strategy of "divide and rule": dividing the world between the "democratic camp" and the "totalitarian camp," creating fear among their constituents about an external enemy. All the talk about the China threat is in order that voters will turn their attention away from problems at home.

The CNN story, interestingly, did expose some fundamental problems within China. Citing Neil Thomas, a senior analyst for China and Northeast Asia at Eurasia Group, it correctly pointed out that the developmental path of China "had reached a point of significantly diminishing returns and was increasing economic inequality, financial debt, and environmental damage."[3] Since Xi Jinping took over the helm of the Communist Party of China and became the president of the country, he began to address all the concerns that had unfolded prior to his rule. This change in developmental path, however, is not entirely to his credit. His predecessor, Hu Jintao, in particular, was also aware of the need for China to change course. It was Hu who introduced the "scientific outlook of development" that would squarely address sustainability issues as well as the need for more balanced development that fit in with the laws of nature and the laws of the market.

It was Hu Jintao who announced that China was going to launch a 10-year poverty eradication campaign in 2011. His campaign to eradicate extreme poverty is not merely aimed at lifting the incomes of people above the bare minimum that is defined to mark extreme poverty. He announced that China would commit to achieving two bold goals, called "two assurances and three guarantees."[4] This means that by 2020, the rural poor will be assured of adequate food and clothing, as well as guaranteed access to compulsory education, basic medical services, and safe housing. In January 2021, the Chinese government, under the presidency of Xi Jinping, announced that these had finally been achieved. What is promised during the time of one generation of leaders is accomplished by the time of the next, unlike in the US, where a newly elected president may overturn what has been initiated by the former president. In contrast, the transition of leadership does not affect the continuity of policy in China.

A peaceful transition of the leadership is something that only the ballot box democracy is supposed to make possible. Readers from the West are likely to be surprised when someone writes about the transition of leadership in China, given that there is no political party rotation. Many commentators simplistically jump from China's unitary leadership and single-party political landscape to the conclusion that a meaningful transition of the leadership does not exist in China. The fact, however, is that the transition of leadership in China does take place regularly and has been peaceful for decades. The style of leadership does change from one generation of leaders to another. Xi Jinping's style is clearly different from that of Hu Jintao; Hu Jintao's leadership style is also clearly different from that of Jiang Zemin. But the desire to serve the country remains the same. As experience is gained and lessons are learned, it is expected that the Chinese leadership will learn and policy will evolve for the better, even if it stumbles sometimes.

Just as Xi Jinping delivered what Hu Jintao had promised on the poverty eradication front, so did he work on and deliver what Hu had promised on the environmental front. As China Dialogue noted, there had been "years of neglect," and in 2007, Hu Jintao, while "speaking at the opening of a study session for provincial and ministry-level cadres, spoke at unusual length about the 'ecological civilisation', a concept he first put forward in 2007."[5]

It must be admitted that the first three decades of strong economic growth had been achieved at significant environmental and social costs:

> China experienced its highest annual emissions of sulfur dioxide (SO_2) in 2007, nitrogen oxides (NOx) in 2012, and primary fine particulate matter (PM2.5) in 2006, at respectively 2.5, 4.6, and 1.5 times the corresponding values for 1990 in China. In 2017, approximately 70% of all 338 municipal cities in China still did not meet the National Ambient Air Quality Standard (NAAQS), with

> non-attainment of PM2.5 as the most prominent air pollution problem. China faces the dual pressures of the improvement of national air quality and the mitigation of climate change.[6]

As late as 2015, Beijing declared a first ever smog "red alert" for three days.[7] According to Wang Jinnan, the president of the Ministry of Ecology and Environment's Environmental Planning Institute, the cost of China's pollution damage roughly quadrupled from 2004–2013 and has accounted for up to 3% of annual GDP over the past decade.[8] Writing for *Lancet,* Chen Zhu of the Chinese Medical Association and Chinese Academy of Sciences estimated that 350,000–500,000 people died prematurely due to particulates in cities.[9] Before he stepped down, in 2012, Hu Jintao declared at the 18th National Congress that the environment must be a priority. He devoted an entire section of his speech to "environmental civilization" — a term he first coined in his address to the 17th party congress five years ago to describe his vision of growth and conservation.[10]

After Xi Jinping became President in March 2013, he soon led a major campaign to improve the environment, particularly air and water quality. In early 2022, it was reported that "climate advocates are hailing "extraordinary progress" in Beijing's fight against air pollution." For the first time ever, Beijing's air quality targets were achieved fully in 2021, almost a decade earlier than experts expected.[11] This achievement did not come fortuitously, but with massive inputs of labor and capital and a notable slowdown in economic growth. China's leaders opted for the quality of growth rather than the quantity of growth.

The Effort to Steer the Economy to High-Quality Growth

Better growth requires sacrifice, including, unavoidably, that of some vested interests who would naturally oppose or at least be inimical to the policies that directly or indirectly lead to personal economic losses. The key question is whether the sacrifice is worth it. Moreover, quality growth is multidimensional: it is not just about environment and ecology; it is also about eradicating extreme poverty and achieving common prosperity: health, education, safety, fighting corruption, and reducing regional disparity. Some evidence for more balanced growth in China can be presented: in 2020, a year of very weak growth, of the 20 provinces that outperformed the national economic growth rate of 2.3%, many were relatively backward provinces or autonomous regions. The list of 20 includes Tibet, Xinjiang, Guizhou, Yunnan, Hebei, Chongqing, Gansu, Ningxia, Sichuan, Guangxi, Jiangsu, Zhejiang, Shandong, Hainan, Fujian, Anhui, Hunan, Jiangxi, Shanxi, and Jilin. In the first half of 2022, the top five provinces in terms of GDP growth rate were Ningxia (5.3%), Shanxi (5.2%), Xinjiang (4.9%), Jiangxi (4.9%), and Tibet (4.8%), in that order.[12]

There is little doubt that in the fight for better growth, China sometimes stumbles and makes mistakes, meaning that the sacrifice could be bigger than the social gains. In a sense, this is unavoidable. With humility to learn from mistakes, however, China will correct these mistakes. In 2018, the "scientific outlook on development" that was proposed by Hu Jintao was enshrined and became part of the Chinese Constitution. This implies that China's development path should not be dictated by dogmas and must be based on the scientific and objective laws of nature. Mistakes are part of the cost of learning. The biggest mistake is refusing to admit mistakes and correct them.

One big mistake in the past has been the excessive emphasis on GDP growth. The limits of using GDP growth as an indicator of economic success are now well understood. For one thing, GDP growth completely ignores the loss of lives and erosion of social values simply because these do not carry a price tag. Crimes could boost GDP because people spend more on security systems and insurance against losses due to crimes, yet crimes obviously undermine national well-being. There has been a lot of talk about introducing the concept of "green GDP" over the years. Green GDP would deduct the costs due to environmental damage and include the benefits of improved health, among other things. Closely related to green GDP is a new metric called the Genuine Progress Indicator

(GPI), which starts with personal consumption spending and adds positives and subtracts negatives resulting from such things as volunteer work, crimes, and pollution.[13] Its proponents had worked out that over the entire period of record, the GPI in America has fallen by US$14.41 billion, a 7% decrease.

Xi Jinping is a strategist. Given the sheer size of the country and the differences in natural endowments and even customs from province to province and from county to county, he proposed a "targeted" approach to lift the last person from extreme poverty. He steered China to invest heavily in infrastructure so that even the remotest county will have access to markets, the use of electricity, and an adequate water supply. Many well-developed provinces paired up with poorer provinces or autonomous regions, while well-developed cities paired up with poor townships and villages to lend support. Many state-owned enterprises chipped in their effort. Sometimes, even private enterprises were called upon to work with the local governments to achieve identified goals. In January 2021, the Chinese government, under the presidency of Xi Jinping, announced that these had been achieved ahead of schedule.

A 2011 policy brief from the Food and Agriculture Organization commended this pairing exercise and described some background to the policy:

> This policy brief suggests that innovations focused on standardization, practicability, and operability of east-west pairing-off cooperation can further improve the approach's impact in reducing persistent poverty in China's western regions. Begun more than 12 years ago, east-west pairing's rich experience and results can be further strengthened by creating relevant policies and standards.[14]

The policy brief noted "China's remarkable achievements in poverty reduction and the tremendous development potential offered by east-west pairing-off cooperation." Still, in the beginning, there had been a lack of a central government policy on east–west pairing, a lack of institutional and financial commitments, as well as a lack of unified and standardized national guidance documents on cooperation arrangements. Since then, these inadequacies have been steadily addressed.

An example of such pairing up ventures is the pairing up of Kizilsu Kyrgyz Autonomous Prefecture, located in the west of the Xinjiang Uygur Autonomous Region, with various provinces in the country that are more advanced in development. According to a report from CGTN, then latest round of pairing assistance that started in 2010 "has involved ministries, 19 provinces and municipalities, which are economically advanced, to help all of Xinjiang's 14 prefectures and cities." Huge financial commitments were made. For example, since 2016, Jiangsu and Jiangxi Provinces have launched 221 projects and allocated 3.86 billion yuan (US$545 million) in this endeavor. Kizilsu Kyrgyz Autonomous Prefecture in the west of Xinjiang had a registered impoverished population of 250,962 at the end of 2019. It was allocated 110 projects and 802 million yuan (US$113 million). Hangzhou, the city that is the home of Alibaba and many leading high-tech firms, began offering pairing assistance in April 2021 and worked with 12 counties in the Tibetan Autonomous Prefecture of Garzê and six counties in the city of Guangyuan in western China's Sichuan Province. This drive happened after China declared success in eradicating extreme poverty in early 2021, suggesting that poverty eradication will continue to be an ongoing effort.[15]

To observers, China's economic growth in recent years has noticeably slowed down. Average growth in each of the decades, the 1980s, 1990s, and 2000s, have all been close to, and in the 2000s even exceeded, 10% per year. The arithmetic average of GDP growth rates from 2010 to 2019 fell to 7.7%. This is like losing a third of the growth which China had been used to. However, this decline is not because China could not grow as fast as before. China opted for quality growth: more balanced growth, more equality, cleaner water bodies, better air quality, more conservation and protection of endangered species, more reforestation, converting desert into arable land, fewer crimes, better healthcare, and more infrastructure development to improve people's livelihoods. Unsustainable development ultimately costs lives, health, and well-being and leads to the extinction of species. Sustainable development, however, requires sacrifice. This sacrifice includes direct spending to improve the environment and protect biodiversity, to improve water management, to build infrastructure that connects people and expands markets, to improve work safety and healthcare, to improve community amenities, etc. All this requires labor, capital, and land resources. There need not be, however, a commensurate increase in GDP. This leads to a fundamental flaw in methodology when researchers work out total factor productivity (TFP) growth based on aggregate data. Because the inputs such as labor input and capital input are measured, but the results in output may not show through a higher GDP figure, such TFP measures are extremely misleading.

A recent paper from the World Bank Group referred to the TFP slowdown in China, from 2.8% in the decade before the global financial crisis to 0.7% in 2009–2018.[16] But the TFP figures reported are based on aggregate data using the formula

$$\frac{\Delta Y}{Y} = \frac{\Delta A}{A} + \varepsilon 1 \frac{\Delta K}{K} + \varepsilon 2 \frac{\Delta L}{L}$$

where $\frac{\Delta A}{A}$ is growth of total factor productivity, $\frac{\Delta K}{K}$ is growth of capital, and $\frac{\Delta L}{L}$ is growth of labor, while $\varepsilon 1$ and $\varepsilon 2$ are the elasticities of output growth with respect to capital growth and that with respect to labor growth, respectively.

Given that GDP is such a flawed indicator that includes only what the market values but excludes things that are valuable to society but carry no market value, the estimate of TFP based on aggregate data will grossly understate true productivity. In the decade from 2009, a lot of factor inputs were plowed into improving the environment and the livelihoods of people. Although this effort has proved to bear fruit, as is witnessed in the improved air and water quality, these positive results are neglected in TFP estimates that rely on the GDP as an indicator of output. Since GDP does not include outputs not transacted through the market, no matter how valuable they are, it is not surprising that China's economic growth fell below

7% for the first time since 1991. This is merely a natural result of the reorientation from rapid growth to quality growth. The conclusion that "domestic factors and policy choices have contributed to the slowdown" is however correct.[17]

Our interpretation of the apparent productivity growth slowdown is supported by a recent study using sectoral data. Li and Lv estimated the TFP growth of Chinese industrial enterprises from 2007 to 2017 using the National Taxation Survey Database. Using this approach with firm level data, all inputs are inputs for the production of market goods.[18] Thus, such data should allow the researchers to better estimate TFP. They found that "the weighted TFP rose from 3.65 in 2007 to 4.69 in 2017, with an average growth rate of 2.58%." Moreover, they found that, while there are differences in industrial TFP among different enterprise sizes, industries, ownership types, export types, and regions, there is an apparent trend for TFP growth to converge. Interestingly, this converging trend corroborates with the result obtained by Brandt, who observed that there was a process of SOEs catching up to private sector efficiency.[19] Interestingly, the authors found that this process has recently stalled. The timing of this stalling is consistent with the need for SOEs to help with their "political mission" (*zhengzhi renwu*), i.e., to help with the new policy priorities identified by the Party. Given the reorientation of the development path, this "stalling" to catch up to private sector efficiency confirms that this is likely due to a deliberate switch to trade market-valued output for non-market-valued policy goals.

The Headwinds Facing China Today

China, in 2022, is facing challenges not seen in many years. Today, China appears to be well positioned, as it has modern infrastructure that is the envy of the world. It boasts the world's largest speed rail network, an excellent road network with remarkable bridges and tunnels across the country through intimidating terrains, the world's best 5G coverage, and internet access that extends to remote areas of the country. Life expectancy in China has exceeded that of the

US in 2021[20]. China's literacy rate, infant mortality, home ownership rate, low crime rate, and public hygiene are all remarkable, and it not only beats most, if not all, other developing countries but also many advanced nations. Yet, it is in serious trouble.

Externally, China is facing America's all-out strategy to contain the country's further advance. The US is not only continuing the trade war that was started by President Trump, but it is doubling down with sanctions and a long "entity list" of companies that are denied "access to American technology." The denials are applicable to suppliers all over the world, including ASML, the Dutch company that has a global monopoly in the supply of EUV lithography systems and cannot sell its machines to China. New US restrictions are preventing US employees of chip-related businesses in China from serving their Chinese clients. As a result of such restrictions, the stock prices of many chipmakers and that of ASML have plummeted. Even TSMC, which is the semiconductor foundry with the largest market share, has seen its stock price lose more than a third of its value in 2022. Since then, the stock price has recovered but continues to be sensitive to geopolitical factors. Huawei, the top company that the US wants to hit, was in "survival mode," but managed to regain profitability and vigor by 2024.

America was instrumental in igniting the Ukraine–Russia war that started early in 2022. It is inciting China to start a civil war to force Taiwan to reunite with its motherland. It has ganged up with a number of countries in the Western world and with Japan to contain China's rise, inventing pretexts such as genocide and forced labor in Xinjiang.

With the consecutive Federal Funds Rate raises in recent months to fight inflation, the US dollar had surged to new highs against practically all currencies, the RMB included. The RMB, however, has remained steady against a basket of currencies. As of February 14, 2023, the RMB has fallen only 3.3% since 2015 against the "benchmark basket" that includes the USD, the Euro, the RMB, the British Pound, the Japanese Yen, the Canadian dollar, and the Australian dollar.[21]

While China continues to attract an inflow of foreign direct investment, which has risen about 20% in USD terms year on year for the first eight months of 2022 to US$138.4 billion.[22] At the same time, however, overseas demand for China's goods is weakening, given increasing pessimism about the global economic outlook.

Apart from FDI, which is a bright spot, government spending on infrastructure remains strong, lending some support to economic growth in the medium term. But domestic private demand is weak. Business investment as well as household consumption are both weak. This is in part a result of the major correction in China's residential development sector. While the government has launched a number of policies to stabilize the market, the number of defaults on debt has grown significantly. In Henan, it was reported that protesters had gathered in front of the Zhengzhou sub-branch of the People's Bank of China, asking for help to recover frozen savings held in rural banks.[23]

The crisis with the real estate and banking sectors can be traced to the "three red lines policy" that was announced in 2020 and took effect in early 2021. The policy was intended to contain leverage in the sector, which had been thriving for years with debt accumulating at a pace that caused regulators to worry about excessive leverage. The three red lines require that: (a) developers' debt-to-asset ratio after deducting advance receipts should be no more than 70%, (b) net debt ratio should be no more than 100%, and (c) the ratio of cash to short-term debt should be no more than one.

The imposition of these three rules was a sudden change in the rules of the game that was entirely unanticipated and hit the cash flows of major developers hard. Without the necessary cash flow, projects could not be completed, and buyers, without the promise of getting the flats that they had bought, refused to continue with mortgage payments. This would cause serious problems with big lenders for homebuyers. The central government tried very hard to contain the spread of the crisis through the injection of funds into the banking system to revive stalling development projects. But given the magnitude of the problem, and with continuing defaults, it is still not clear that the crisis can be dissipated successfully.

A change in regulations from time to time is not uncommon and is not a problem. But a change in regulations that goes against long-held expectations about policy continuity is a problem. In general, regulators should inform market players about the basic principles in the rules of the game. Changes in regulations should not deviate from these basic principles. This is basic to investor confidence. If businesses are left with having to face new regulations from time to time that are not based on long-held principles, they would hesitate to invest over the longer term. Research and development, especially primary research, that matter in the long term for the "sea change" kind of innovations have typically long payoff periods.

The recent policy changes that hit multiple sectors since early 2021, with all their good intentions, have rocked business confidence hard. Apart from diffusing the crisis and hoping for a recovery before too long, the government will have to make it transparent to all market players that regulatory principles will not change over the medium to long term. This way, business confidence can be restored.

The Belt and Road Initiative and China's Role in Better Growth in the World

China in 2022 managed to grow at 3%. The sharp decline was of course not an intended trade-off of quantity for quality. The hostilities of the West toward China and weak demand from the rest of the world, along with problems at home such as a collapse in confidence and a besieged housing market and strict zero-COVID-19 measures, forced China's actual growth to fall short of target significantly.

President Xi was certainly aware of the rising hostilities of the US toward China when he became president of China. Joseph Nye wrote in 2011 of China's "misreading" of Obama's pivot to Asia as a "supposed US effort to contain it strategically."[24] Some people criticized President Xi for deviating from Deng Xiaoping's advice to "hide your strength and bide your time." But as the world transitions into the 21st century, China's economic prowess is like an elephant in the room. There is no way to "hide your strength." *Death by China: Confronting the Dragon — A Global Call to Action*, by Peter Navarro and Greg Autry, was published in 2011 before Xi became president.

The Belt and Road Initiative (BRI) can be seen as Xi's signature initiative to help other developing countries build infrastructure, embark on stronger, higher-quality growth, and, at the same time, expand China's market and secure China's access to resources, such as energy, that it needs. But in retrospect, whether by design or not, the BRI turns out to be an important strategy to counter America's containment policy.

Since the BRI was proposed in 2013, China's trade with and investment in BRI countries have increased sharply. Even in 2022, a year when world trade was severely battered by the COVID-19 pandemic, China's goods trade with countries along the Belt and Road hit another record, reaching 13.8 trillion yuan (US$2.05 trillion), up 19.4% year on year, 11.7 percentage points higher than China's overall trade growth. China's non-financial direct investment in BRI countries hit 141.05 billion yuan, while direct investment from BRI countries in China rose to 89.15 billion yuan, up 7.7%.[25] January 2022 also saw the Regional Comprehensive Economic Partnership (RCEP) come into effect. Data from the Ministry of Commerce (MOC) show that China's trade with the other RCEP signatories expanded 7.9% year on year to 11.8 trillion yuan (about US$1.69 trillion) in the first 11 months of 2022, accounting for 30.7% of China's total foreign trade value.[26] Both the RCEP and the BRI have certainly helped China achieve better-than-expected growth of 3% in 2022.

The BRI has also played an important role in the recent rebalancing of growth between western and coastal regions. The western region suffered in the past because of its long distance from any sea port. With the launch of the BRI and the construction of key railway links, the western region gained the benefit of proximity and access to markets in Europe, the Middle East, and even Africa.

Prashant Yadav and Vinika D. Rao at INSEAD, the well-known Swiss business school, noted the following:

> Not only is Africa the world's fastest-growing continent, but it is also demographically the youngest. In addition, recent trends

> suggest its growth is becoming more sustainable and equitable. Starting in the mid-2000s, the extractive industries such as oil and gas began declining as a share of overall FDI for the continent. A new trend of growth led by the service sector and manufacturing has emerged.[27]

The BRI is undoubtedly behind this development. Wenjie Chen found that, while China's share of the stock of foreign investment is small, it has been investing aggressively in recent years. Unlike investors from the West. who focus their investment in countries with better governance and on resource extraction, China's investments appear uncorrelated with the measure of rule of law and are more oriented toward manufacturing and services.[28] With the establishment of the African Continental Free Trade Area (AfCFTA) in 2021 and the expected concomitant decline of tariffs between African nations and other trade-liberalization measures, the GDP of most economies on the continent could rise by as much as 3%, according to the UN. [29] As of August 2022, China's official Belt and Road website lists 52 African countries that have signed an agreement or understanding with the One Belt One Road initiative. A recent report from the China-Africa Business Council, titled *Chinese Investment in Africa (2022): China-Africa Cooperation from a Supply Chain Perspective*, found that deeper Belt and Road cooperation between China and African countries "will play an important role in building a more integrated African continent as well as connecting Africa to global supply chains."[30]

The ASEAN overtook the EU as China's top trading partner in 2020, China's exports to ASEAN rose 14.2% year on year in 2023, while imports from ASEAN rose 5.2%.[31] Since China joined the World Trade Organization (WTO) in 2001, it has expanded trade with Latin America, which has been increasing at a striking 31% annual rate on average. As of December 2021, 20 out of 24 countries in Latin America and the Caribbean region have signed up with the BRI.[32] In December 2021, the China–CELAC Joint Action Plan for Cooperation in Key Areas (2022–2024) was signed, covering collaboration in areas such as political and security cooperation, pragmatic economic cooperation, high-quality infrastructure cooperation, cooperation in social, cultural, and people-to-people matters, and sustainable development.[33] China is now South America's largest trading partner.

Conclusions

It must be recognized that sustainable development is not just about protecting the environment and the habitats of all the species that now inhabit the Earth. Sustainable development also includes fiscal sustainability, secure supply chains, food security, and, above all, peace. The world cannot achieve peace without mutual respect and inclusive or common prosperity. All these goals cannot be possible if disinformation and imagined threats continue to thwart cooperation and communication. Scholars from Johns Hopkins University have demonstrated that the much hyped-up debt trap narrative about loans made by China to BRI countries is nothing but a myth.[34]

The US understands that China's role in combating climate change is indispensable. Climate change is the true existential threat facing the US and all of us. The Belt and Road Initiative is simply China's strategy to leverage the "China advantage" of being the foremost infrastructure builder in the world today and the conveyer of peace to make life better at home and elsewhere.

To end this chapter, let us quote from the first author's recent *China Daily* article:

> The US has tremendous sway on public opinion. If the US and China, the two leading countries in the world, are to work together to build a better world, fair play and mutual respect are paramount, and the US should help douse the toxic rhetoric. China has come a long way in the protection of intellectual property rights and private property rights. The West has never found any evidence of so-called "Huawei backdoors", "forced labor in Xinjiang", "genocide of Uyghurs", or "predatory lending" in the Belt and Road Initiative. So let us turn the tide, and let all take advantage of the "China advantage."[35]

Endnotes

1. He (2022).
2. *Ibid.*
3. He (2022).
4. Ministry of Foreign Affairs of the People's Republic of China (2021).
5. Si (2012).
6. Lu *et al.* (2020).
7. BBC News (2015).
8. Wang (2016).
9. Chen *et al.* (2013).
10. Li (2012).
11. Lo (2022).
12. Zhou (2022).
13. Hayes (2022); see also Cobb *et al.* (2015).
14. FAO (2011).
15. CGTN (2022).
16. Brandt *et al.* (2020).
17. *Ibid.*
18. Li and Lv (2021).
19. Brandt *et al.* (2020).

20 Hui, Mary (2022). China's life expectancy is non higher than that of the US, Sept 1, Yahoo!Tech.

21. Based on the quotations from the World Currency Unit website at Lingnan University. http://wcu.ln.edu.hk/en/quotation.php.
22. Huld (2022).
23. Li (2022).
24. Nye and Hitt (2021).
25. The State Council Information Office of the People's Republic of China (2023).
26. Xinhua (2023).
27. Yadav and Rao (2022).
28. Chen *et al.* (2016).
29. Yadav and Rao (2022).
30. Belt and Road Portal (2022).

31 See *China Briefing*, Aug. 9, (2024).

32. Chiodi and Nguyen (2022).
33. Ministry of Foreign Affairs of the People's Republic of China (2021).
34. Brautigam and Rithmire (2021).
35. Ho (2023).

References

BBC News. 2015. Beijing smog: Images before and after. December 7, 2015. https://www.bbc.com/news/world-asia-china-35028483.

Belt and Road Portal. 2022. Closer China-Africa cooperation boosting Africa's supply chain development: Report. August 25, 2022. https://eng.yidaiyilu.gov.cn/qwyw/rdxw/271001.htm.

Brandt, L., Litwack, J., Mileva, E., Wang, L., Zhang, Y., and Zhao, L. 2020. *China's Productivity Slowdown and Future Growth Potential, Handle Proxy.* Washington, DC: World Bank. June 1, 2020. http://hdl.handle.net/10986/33993.

Brautigam, D. and Rithmire, M. 2021. The Chinese "debt trap" is a myth. *The Atlantic.* April 12, 2021. https://www.theatlantic.com/international/archive/2021/02/china-debt-trap-diplomacy/617953/.

CGTN. 2022. How pairing assistance is helping a remote part of China shake off poverty. Accessed October 21, 2022. https://news.cgtn.com/news/2020-04-28/How-pairing-assistance-helps-a-remote-part-of-China-shake-off-poverty-Q1Pc1zjeo0/index.html.

Chen, W., Dollar, D., and Tang, H. 2016. Why is China investing in Africa? Evidence from the firm level. *The World Bank Economic Review.* https://doi.org/10.1093/wber/lhw049.

Chen, Z., Wang, J.-N., Ma, G.-X., and Zhang, Y.-S. 2013. China tackles the health effects of air pollution. *The Lancet,* 382(9909), 1959–1960. https://doi.org/10.1016/s0140-6736(13)62064-4.

Chiodi, L. and Nguyen, T. 2022. The Belt and Road initiative in Latin America: How China makes friends and what this means for the Region. *Latin American Focus Group.* March 21, 2022. https://blogs.eui.eu/latin-american-working-group/the-belt-and-road-initiative-in-latin-america-how-china-makes-friends-and-what-this-means-for-the-region/.

Cobb, C., Halstead, T., and Rowe, J. 2015. If the GDP is up, why is America down? *The Atlantic.* November 12, 2015. https://www.theatlantic.com/magazine/archive/1995/10/if-the-gdp-is-up-why-is-america-down/415605/.

Costanza, R., *et al.* 2014. Development: Time to leave GDP behind. *Nature,* 505(7483), 283–285. https://doi.org/10.1038/505283a.

FAO. 2011. Pro-poor policy options: East-West pairing-off cooperation for poverty reduction in China. https://www.fao.org/publications/card/zh/c/9e01aefa-b2aa-4d31-9301-5160b2f4140d/.

Global Times. 2021. China's decade of solid progress on emergency response. https://www.globaltimes.cn/page/202208/1274292.shtml.

Hayes, A. 2022. Genuine progress indicator (GPI): Definition, formula, vs. GDP. *Investopedia.* October 30, 2022. https://www.investopedia.com/terms/g/gpi.asp.

He, L. 2022. China's economy is 'in deep trouble' as XI heads for next decade in power. *CNN.* https://edition.cnn.com/2022/10/14/economy/china-party-congress-economy-trouble-xi-intl-hnk/index.html.

Ho, L. S. 2023. New year's wish: 'China advantage' is meant to benefit the entire world. *China Daily Hong Kong.* January 31, 2023. https://www.chinadailyhk.com/article/312502.

Huld, A. 2022. Foreign investment in China — August 2022 roundup and policy trajectory. *China Briefing News.* October 9, 2022. https://www.china-briefing.com/news/foreign-investment-in-china-august-2022-round-up/#:~:text=China%20FDI%20up%2020.2%20percent,the%20same%20period%20in%202021.

Li, J. 2012. Hu Jintao tells congress that environment must be a priority. *South China Morning Post.* November 8, 2012. https://www.scmp.com/news/china/article/1078152/hu-jintao-tells-congress-environment-must-be-priority.

Li, V. 2022. Protest in China over frozen bank accounts ends in violence. *The Guardian.* July 12, 2022. https://www.theguardian.com/world/2022/jul/11/china-violent-clashes-at-protest-over-frozen-rural-bank-accounts.

Li, Z. and Lv, B. 2021. Total factor productivity of Chinese industrial firms: Evidence from 2007 to 2017. *Applied Economics,* 53(60), 6910–6926. https://doi.org/10.1080/00036846.2021.1954592.

Lo, J. 2022. 'Extraordinary progress' — Beijing meets air pollution goals after coal crackdown. *Climate Home News.* January 5, 2022. https://www.climatechangenews.com/2022/01/04/extraordinary-progress-beijing-meets-air-pollution-goals-coal-crackdown/.

Lu, X., Zhang, S., Xing, J., Wang, Y., Chen, W., Ding, D., Wu, Y., Wang, S., Duan, L., and Hao, J. 2020. Progress of air pollution control in China and its challenges and opportunities in the ecological civilization era. *Engineering,* 6(12), 1423–1431. https://doi.org/10.1016/j.eng.2020.03.014.

Ministry of Foreign Affairs of the People's Republic of China. 2021. Kaselehlie Press publishes Ambassador Huang Zheng's article elaborating on Chinese government's white paper: Poverty alleviation: China's experience and contribution. May 17, 2021. https://www.

fmprc.gov.cn/eng/wjb_663304/zwjg_665342/zwbd_665378/202105/t20210519_9169671.html.

Ministry of Foreign Affairs of the People's Republic of China. 2021. China — CELAC joint action plan for cooperation in key areas (2022–2024). December 7, 2021. https://www.fmprc.gov.cn/mfa_eng/wjbxw/202112/t20211207_10463459.html.

Nye, J. S. and Hitt, D. 2021. Obama's pacific pivot. *Project Syndicate.* July 22, 2021. https://www.project-syndicate.org/commentary/obama-s-pacific-pivot-2011-12.

Si, M. 2012. An insight into the green vocabulary of the Chinese communist party. *China Dialogue.* May 14, 2012. https://chinadialogue.net/en/pollution/5339-an-insight-into-the-green-vocabulary-of-the-chinese-communist-party/.

The State Council Information Office of the People's Republic of China. 2023. China's trade with BRI countries hits record high. February 3, 2023. http://english.scio.gov.cn/pressroom/2023-02/03/content_85087409.htm.

Wang, J. 2016. Revive China's green GDP programme. *Nature,* 534(7605), 37–37. https://doi.org/10.1038/534037b.

Wu, H. 2022. Pairing assistance drives economic development in Western China. *SHINE.* https://www.shine.cn/biz/economy/2205195802/.

Xinhua. 2023. One year on, RCEP bears fruit for trade, industrial integration. January 1, 2023. https://english.news.cn/20230101/64cd775cbc254080876a1e0a9bfab254/c.html#:~:text=Data%20from%20the%20Ministry%20of,China's%20total%20foreign%20trade%20value.

Yadav, P. and Rao, V. D. 2022. How Africa could astonish the world. *INSEAD Knowledge.* August 16, 2022. https://knowledge.insead.edu/economics-finance/how-africa-could-astonish-world.

Zhou, Q. 2022. China's GDP across provinces in H1 2022: Top performers. *China Briefing News.* August 1, 2022. https://www.china-briefing.com/news/chinas-gdp-across-provinces-in-h1-2022/.

https://doi.org/10.1142/9789819815241_0009

Chapter 9

FROM IMBALANCE TO REBALANCING: UNDERSTANDING CHINA'S ECONOMIC DEVELOPMENT PATH

Yuan Zhang[*,†]

[*]*School of Economics, Fudan University, Shanghai, China*
[†]*China Center for Economic Studies, Fudan University, Shanghai, China*
zhangyuanfd@fudan.edu.cn

Introduction

Starting point of economic development in the People's Republic of China (hereafter PRC)

Under the leadership of the Communist Party of China (CPC), China faced the Second Sino-Japanese War and the War of Liberation. The PRC was then established. The PRC achieved independence and liberation, ended the fragmentation of old China, abolished unequal treaties imposed on old China as well as the privileges of imperialists in the country, and created the social conditions for national rejuvenation. After the founding of the PRC, however, the country was devastated and had an extremely weak economic foundation, manifested in the aspects described as follows.

China's total economic volume was insignificant, and agriculture dominated the economy. At the end of 1952, China's GDP was only 67.9 billion yuan, and the GDP per capita was only 119 yuan. By the end of 1949, China had a population of 541.67 million, of which 484.02 million were rural residents. At the end of 1952, 34.6 billion yuan of China's GDP came from primary industries, accounting for 51% of the total. Of the country's 207.29 million employed people, 182.43 million lived in the countryside, 173.17 million were employed in the primary sector, and only 15.31 million and 18.81 million were employed in the secondary and tertiary sectors, respectively.

Both urban and rural residents had extremely low standards of living, and the number of rural people in poverty was large. At the end of 1952, the per capita consumption level of urban residents was 154 yuan, while that of rural residents was only 65 yuan. In 1949, the number of civilian cars was only 50,900. In 1957, the per capita net income of rural residents was only 73 yuan, and the Engel coefficient of rural residents was as high as 65.7%. Even in 1978, the per capita residential building area in urban areas was only 6.7 square meters, while that of rural residents was 8.1 square meters. Low standards of living and disparities in urban and rural socioeconomic development led to a high incidence of rural poverty. According to an earlier standard set by the National Bureau of Statistics of the PRC, the poverty line in 1978 was an annual income of 100 yuan, according to which, even in 1978, there were still 250 million people living below the poverty line in rural China.[1] The rural population in 1978 was 790.14 million, and the corresponding poverty incidence rate was 31.64%.

Urban and rural infrastructure, as well as education and health conditions, were extremely weak, and the level of social development was extremely low. In terms of infrastructure, in 1949, China had 21,800 kilometers of railroad, 80,700 kilometers of road, 6,587 kilometers of water supply lines in cities, 1,039 kilometers of gas supply lines, 11,129 kilometers of urban streets, and 2,292 operating buses. In terms of health facilities, the number of various health institutions in 1949 was 3,670, including 2,600 hospitals, 9 maternal and child health centers, and 11 specialized prevention and treatment hospitals (institutes and stations). The number of personnel in various health institutions nationwide that year was 541,000, with only 0.67 professional (assistant) physicians per 1,000 people. The number of beds in all types of health institutions was 85,000, and the number of beds in hospitals and health centers per 1,000 people was only 0.15. The lack of medical resources led to generally low levels of public health, and the death rate of the population was as high as 20 per 1,000 at the end of 1949. In terms of education, in 1949, there were 205 general colleges and universities, 1,597 high schools, and 2,448 junior high schools. The number of full-time teachers in general colleges and universities was only 16,000, while that in high schools and junior high schools was 14,000 and 53,000, respectively. In 1949, there were 629 enrolled graduate students nationwide. In 1952, the net enrollment rate of primary school–age children was only 49.2%.

China's industrial base was weak, and the level of industrialization was extremely low. In 1949, the total output value of industrial enterprises was only 14 billion yuan, and in 1957, the number of industrial enterprises was only 169,500. In 1949, in terms of national output, raw coal was only 32 million tons; crude oil was 1.2 billion tons; power generation was 4.3 billion kilowatts; pig iron and crude steel were 2.5 and 1.6 billion tons, respectively; finished steel was only 1.3 billion tons; cement and sulfuric acid were 660 and 40 thousand tons, respectively; and chemical fertilizer was only 0.6 million tons. This weak industrial base led to an extremely low level of industrialization at the founding of the PRC, with the value added of industry accounting for only 17.6% of the national GDP in 1952.

Major development challenges for large countries

China is the world's most populous country and has the largest developing economy. In 2010, China became the second-largest economy in the world. Yet, right after the founding of the PRC, it was still a typical economy dominated by small peasants. As a result, China's development path faced challenges that were different from those of other small economies. According to Zhang and Yang (1999), large countries generally face five major development challenges: (1) the significant influence of historical heritage and cultural traditions; (2) heavy population pressure, severe employment problems, and low economic efficiency; (3) regional economic imbalances; (4) the contradiction between agricultural backwardness and coordinated industrial and agricultural development; and (5) the choice between endogenous development and external opening up. They argue that, unlike small countries, an important characteristic of large economies is that they are vast, and their national economies consist of multiple regional economies. Owing to different resource endowments, development bases, and human and technological conditions, there are great differences in the level and speed of development of each regional economy. Therefore, how to coordinate development among regional economies and develop the economies within each region is a difficult issue that must be properly handled by large countries when formulating economic development strategies and policies. If the government adopts a balanced growth strategy, although it can promote economic growth in backward regions and temporarily narrow economic gaps between developed and underdeveloped regions, this egalitarian approach can hinder developed regions and therefore be detrimental to the long-term, overall development of the national economy. Conversely, if the government adopts an unbalanced growth strategy tilted toward the developed regions, it can intensify polarization between regions, making the rich regions richer and the poor regions poorer. That's to say, when formulating regional economic development policies, large countries should not only recognize regional differences and avoid "one-size-fits-all" egalitarianism but also avoid polarization between regions. This is indeed a difficult problem.

The literature on balanced versus imbalanced urban–rural development

Development economists have recognized the importance of the agricultural sector for the economic advancement of developing countries. Some development economists believe there is a vicious circle in developing economies. Specifically, developing countries cannot industrialize because there is no market for their products; there is no market for their products because the income of the population is low; and the income of the population is low because there is no industrialization. To break this vicious circle and low level of equilibrium, it is necessary to synchronize the industrialization of all economic sectors. To do so, a "Big Push," or "Balanced Growth," strategy is needed (Rosenstein-Rodan, 1943; Nurkse, 1953; Scitovsky, 1954; Fleming, 1955). In this sense, development is a synergistic, synchronized, and balanced growth process across economic sectors. For example, Rosenstein-Rodan (1943) proposes the "Big Push" theory, which argues that the industrialization of developing countries must rely on government programs that target investment in complementary industrial sectors, with a particular focus on infrastructure and light industry, so they can gain access to external economies and absorb large amounts of surplus rural labor. Here, the capital needed for investment comes from not only domestic sources but also international investment and the importation of foreign capital. Similarly, Nurkse (1953), Scitovsky (1954), and Fleming (1955) argue that developing countries should invest in complementary industrial sectors simultaneously so that they support each other and achieve "balanced growth."

Most balanced-development theorists recognize the importance of the agricultural sector in economic development. Nurkse (1953), for example, argues that "everyone knows that the spectacular industrial revolution cannot have taken place without the agricultural revolution that preceded it." Ranis and Fei (1961) emphasize the importance of the balanced development of industry and agriculture based on the Lewis model, arguing that industry and agriculture do not achieve technological progress independently of each other. Rather, for successful modernization, the two sectors need to develop in a balanced way, while landlords can act as investors between the two sectors.

Balanced growth theory is positive in that it recognizes the organic linkages and coordination among industries and sectors in the national economy. However, most developing countries face the dilemma of capital scarcity, and a balanced strategy of the simultaneous advancement of multiple industries and sectors necessarily requires large amounts of capital investment. Thus, other development economists argue that with a shortage of capital, unbalanced point-to-area economic development is the norm. Perroux (1950), for example, proposes the "Growth Pole" theory from the perspective of spatial and regional development, arguing that priority can be given to the development of leading industries and industries with innovation capabilities. In this way, they can form "growth poles" and then spread outward to drive the development of the surrounding areas and the whole economy. However, this theory does not give much consideration to how cities can drive rural development. For example, Lewis's (1950) famous dual economy model focused on the effect of the transfer of surplus rural labor to the urban sector on economic growth and the urban–rural gap but ignored the need for the development of the agricultural sector itself. Myrdal (1957), meanwhile, proposes the principle of circular cumulative causation to explain the mechanism of uneven development in terms of the "backwash effect" and "spread effect." The former is the flow of production factors from backward regions to developed ones, attracted by the income gap. The latter is the expansion of production scale in developed regions, leading to an increase in production costs and a decrease in profit opportunities, which drives the spread of capital and technology to backward regions. In this framework, developing countries can take advantage of the backwash effect to take the lead in urban development and then use the spread effect to drive rural development. Hirschman (1958) also proposes the theory of unbalanced growth, arguing that developing countries should devote their limited resources to developing a few leading industries first, given the constraints of insufficient capital accumulation; then, these industries should create supply and demand after industrialization (so-called forward linkage and backward linkage) to drive the development of other related industries.

We can see that the core idea of the theory of unbalanced urban–rural development is that developing countries can realize the path of urban development, leading to rural development, by developing heavy industry first, which then leads to the development of light industry, which in turn leads to the development of agriculture, finally resulting in urban–rural integration.

Some Chinese social scientists also conducted early theoretical explorations of the urban–rural relationship. Before the establishment of the PRC, sociologist Wu (1933, 1934) had argued that developing industry to subsidize agriculture and urban development to relieve the countryside, supplemented by population control and other means, was the proper direction for China's rural development. By contrast, Fei (1939), in his book *Peasant Life in China,* points out that "it is not a matter of tightening the expenses of the peasants but of increasing their income. Let me therefore reiterate that the restoration of rural enterprises is the fundamental measure." He also describes the relationship between urban and rural areas as "mutual success and conflict." Here, "mutual success" means that urban and rural areas complement each other; "mutual conflict" means that urban and rural areas compete with each other. Moreover, the contrast between these two forces can change over the course of history. Fei goes on to emphasize the importance of the rural income industry for rural economic development and the resolution of urban–rural conflict, as well as the decline of rural handicrafts owing to competition from urban industry (Fei, 1947, 1948). Meanwhile, in his PhD thesis, the Chinese development economist Zhang Peigang (1949) recognizes that many developing countries misunderstood the connotation of industrialization, which led to the neglect of agriculture. He argues that industrialization should include the industrialization of both the industrial and agricultural sectors, not just the modernization of the industrial sector.

After the founding of the PRC, the strategy of prioritizing heavy-industry development was adopted, and urban heavy industry was subsidized by depriving agricultural profits in the form of a price scissor between industrial and agricultural products. This resulted in the unbalanced development of the urban and rural sectors and the continuous widening of the income gap between urban and rural residents. As a result, Chinese economists started to consider rural "industry feeding agriculture in return," an idea pioneered by Zhang and Yang (1992). They argue that the takeoff of rural industry leads to a relative scarcity of rural labor, thus putting forward requirements for promoting agricultural mechanization and moderate-scale operations. Meanwhile, the takeoff of rural industry generally increases the income of rural residents and the demand for secondary food, which constitutes external pressure for agricultural transformation. At this time, rural industries can promote agricultural modernization through "direct feeding" and "indirect feeding." Direct feeding involves extracting a sum of money from the profits of rural industries and using it directly for agricultural modernization. Indirect feeding refers to socially shared capital (e.g., power supply and transportation) being invested by rural industries in their own development, which also provides the necessary material conditions for modernized agriculture. Zhang and Yang argue that the development of rural industry can bring hope for the modernization of agriculture in developing countries.

Promoting Economic Growth by Creating Imbalances

Prioritized heavy-industry development strategy

Immediately after the founding of the PRC, the country's leaders faced the choice of which development path and management system to choose to stimulate economic development and rapidly rejuvenate the nation. Based on the international and domestic environment of the time, the PRC's leaders decided to adopt a planned economy and the accompanying strategy of prioritizing heavy-industry development to promote economic growth and social progress. The rationale for this strategy is that heavy industry is the foundation of light industry, the construction industry, and the agricultural machinery industry. Without the steel and chemical raw materials provided by heavy industry, light industry and other industries would lack the sources needed for development. However, heavy industry is a capital-intensive industry, and the prioritized development of heavy industry poses two major challenges for developing countries, especially for the PRC: how to solve the problem of capital accumulation needed for prioritized heavy-industry development and how to coordinate development processes between different industries. As noted by historian Chen Biao (1986), heavy industry involves large investment, has a long cycle, and is slow to yield results. The textile industry was the basis for the takeoff of British industry, followed by the industrialization of light industry, heavy industry, and transportation. The paths of the US, France, Germany, and Japan are basically similar. Germany, owing to the rise of Prussian militarism, saw an immediate climax of heavy industry, especially the military industry, at the beginning of industrialization. However, it had a unique background at that time, namely, the influx of large amounts of foreign capital from the Netherlands, Belgium, Britain, and France, which solved the contradiction of Germany's own lack of capital. Although this assertion by Chen ignores the fact that capitalist countries, such as the UK and the US, formed their original capital accumulation and promoted industrialization through colonial plunder, slave trade, and opium trafficking, it also speaks to the possible sequence of industrialization in noncolonial countries.

Soon after the founding of the PRC, national leaders had to consider how to deal with the relationship between heavy industry and other industries. For example, the first relationship noted by Mao Zedong in his speech to the Political Bureau of the Central Committee in April 1956, "On the 10 Relationships," was the relationship between heavy industry and light industry and agriculture. He argued that the proportion of investment in light industry and agriculture should be appropriately increased. Thus, Mao regarded the relationship between the development of different industries under limited resources as the first of 10 relationships that reflect the importance of this relationship and the overall situation. Liu Shaoqi further noted the following:

> Why should the process of industrialization in China take such steps? After restoring China's economy and making the best possible use of the existing production capacity, the first step in the plan to develop the economy should focus on the development of agriculture and light industry. Only the development of agriculture can supply industry with enough raw materials and food and expand the market for industrial development. Only the development of light industry can supply peasants with a large number of industrial goods in exchange for raw materials and food produced by peasants and accumulate funds for the continued development of industry. At the same time, on the basis of the development of agriculture and light industry, it is also possible to raise the low standard of living of the working people, which urgently needs to be raised, by a step, which is also very necessary to improve the health of the people and to further unite the whole people politically. And the establishment of some necessary and much-needed defense industries is indispensable for safeguarding the environment in which we build peace. Only after this step has been successfully completed will we be able to focus the greatest amount of money and effort on building all the foundations of heavy industry and developing it. Only after heavy industry is established will it be possible to develop light industry considerably, to mechanize agriculture, and to raise the living standards of the people considerably.[2]

The dilemma the PRC faced in implementing the strategy of prioritizing heavy-industry development was that the national savings rate at that time was extremely low, the government's financial resources were extremely limited, and there was almost no capacity for capital accumulation. At the end of 1952, for example, the national per capita savings balance was only 1.5 yuan. The GDP was 69.22 billion yuan,[3] according to the expenditure method of accounting, while the accumulated consumption of residents and government was as high as 54.63 billion yuan, but total capital formation was only 15.37 billion yuan. Meanwhile, the net export was −780 million yuan. In 1950, the total tax revenue of the country was only 4.898 billion yuan. In 1952, the government's gold reserve was only five million ounces, and the foreign exchange reserve was only 139 million dollars. Faced with the above dilemma of capital accumulation, the only thing the PRC could do was adopt an urban-biased policy. This refers to economic and social policies in developing countries that favor the urban sector. They aim to develop capital-intensive industries in the face of capital constraints to transfer agricultural profits to the industrial sector in the cities, thereby accelerating industrialization and economic takeoff.

Prioritized development strategy for the coastal areas

When China decided to shift from an import substitution strategy to an export-oriented strategy in the early 1970s, one of the first problems it faced was the need for production bases that could produce large quantities of goods for export to developed countries. Inspired by the "Four Asian Tigers," a natural choice for the country's leaders was to establish special economic zones, open cities, and open areas in the eastern coastal region (Wu, 2010). From the perspective of "New Economic Geography," the prioritized investment of limited resources in the eastern coastal region was in line with economic laws.

First, China's geography indicates a better historical foundation for infrastructure in the eastern region. The eastern coastal economy was more developed than the inland one even before the founding of the PRC. At the same time, the construction cost of providing infrastructure in the east was lower than in the central hilly areas and western mountainous areas.

Second, most of China's ports are concentrated in the eastern coastal region, which facilitates its participation in the international division of labor. Fuji and Mori (1996), for example, found that the advantage of transportation costs near a well-connected river, port, or transportation hub will allow a region to concentrate more economic activities and population. If a country's first city is also a port, its population will increase because of the major transportation effect. From the perspective of New Economic Geography, urban agglomeration of a certain scale will bring economies of scale through mechanisms such as shared investment, skill matching, and knowledge spillover, thus increasing production efficiency while attracting more enterprises and population agglomeration and increasing self-reinforcement. In addition, eastern coastal cities, such as Quanzhou and Guangzhou, have been traditionally engaged in international trade throughout the long history of China's agricultural civilization.

Third, China shifted its industrialization strategy from import substitution to export orientation in the 1970s. The production purpose of this export-oriented economy was mainly for international markets, especially for processing incoming materials in the early stages. Concentration in the eastern coastal region could save on the transportation costs of incoming materials and the export costs of products. For example, Krugman and Livas Elizondo (1996) observed that when Mexico opened up to the outside world in the 1980s, manufacturing industries that had been concentrated in Mexico City moved to the Mexico–US border. To explain this phenomenon, they developed a theoretical model to explore the relationship between international trade and urban concentration in developing countries: if a developing country implements an import-substitution industrialization strategy and manufacturing industries serve only a small domestic market, it will generate strong forward and backward linkages, and firms will relocate to where consumers and intermediate goods are concentrated, thus creating megacities; meanwhile, if a developing country implements trade liberalization policies, the forward and backward linkages will be weakened, and the incentive for firms to be concentrated in large inland cities will be reduced, and thus the megacities will shrink. The dynamics behind China's opening up to the outside world, leading to a shift of production centers to the eastern coastal region, are clearly consistent with the shift of manufacturing in Mexico City to the US–Mexico border.

Fourth, under Deng Xiaoping's idea of "letting some people and some regions get rich first, so that the rich first can lead others to become rich later," China historically chose "the eastern region to get rich first." Meeting with a delegation of senior American entrepreneurs in 1985, Deng proposed that "some regions and some people can get rich first to drive and help other regions and other people to gradually achieve common prosperity."[4] This idea drove China to choose the eastern region — which had a higher degree of economic vitality as well as an openness to the outside world — to take the lead in development and then help the central and western regions through radiation, demonstration, and driving effects. Similarly, on June 10, 2021, the Central Committee of the CPC and the State Council issued "Opinions on Supporting Zhejiang's High-Quality Development to Build a Common Prosperity Demonstration Zone." This opinion points out that Zhejiang Province has achieved obvious results in exploring solutions to the problem of unbalanced, insufficient development, and it has the foundation and advantages to construct a common prosperity demonstration zone. It also has some shortcomings and weaknesses, however, with a broad space for optimization and development potential. Thus, this opinion requires Zhejiang Province to achieve substantive progress in promoting high-quality development in the construction of a common prosperity demonstration area by 2025, establish the basic institutional mechanisms and policy frameworks for common prosperity, and form a number of replicable, promotable successful experiences.

How the development strategy prioritizing heavy industry and coastal zones promotes economic growth

Prioritizing heavy-industry development brought about rapid growth in China's heavy industry. Lin *et al.* (1994) calculated the leading index of heavy-industry growth (i.e., the average annual growth rate of heavy industry divided by that of light industry) and found that the leading coefficient of heavy industry was 1.47 during 1953–1978. Within that time period, it was 1.97 during the First Five-Year Plan period, rose sharply to 6.0 during the Second Five-Year Plan period, fell below 1 during 1963–1965, and rose to 1 during the Third and Fourth Five-Year Plan periods. The rapid development of heavy industry laid the foundation not only for national defense but also for China's rapid industrialization and its emergence as a world manufacturing power. Lin *et al.* suggest that China's strategy of prioritizing heavy-industry development and its corresponding economic system was able to raise the accumulation rate to more than 15% from a backward starting point and build a relatively complete industrial economy at a relatively fast pace. This rapidly transformed China from a country with predominantly agricultural output to an economy with predominantly industrial output. The following is a summary of the important contributions to China's socioeconomic development brought by the prioritized development strategy for heavy industry after the founding of the PRC from several different perspectives.

First, it laid a solid foundation for China's rapid economic growth, with its total national income having already "caught up" with the UK and being poised to "surpass" the US in the near future. Figure 1 shows a comparison of gross national income (GNI) data (current-year prices, USD) for China, the US, and the UK from 1970 to 2019. We can see that in 1970, China's GNI totaled US$9.62 billion, while that of the UK and the US was US$14.137 billion and US$107.436 billion, respectively; thus, China's GNI was only 68% and 8.95% of the GNI of the UK and the US, respectively. In 2006, China's GNI surpassed that of the UK, and in 2019, it was 65.97% of that of the US. This demonstrates China's extraordinary economic growth rate.

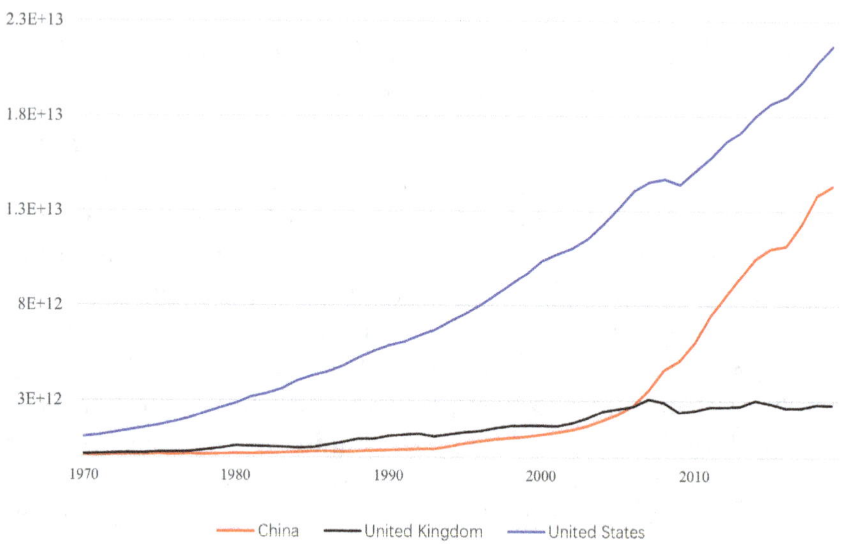

Figure 1. Comparison of GNI (current USD) in China, the US, and the UK (1970–2019).

Source: Data from World Bank WDI (2020).

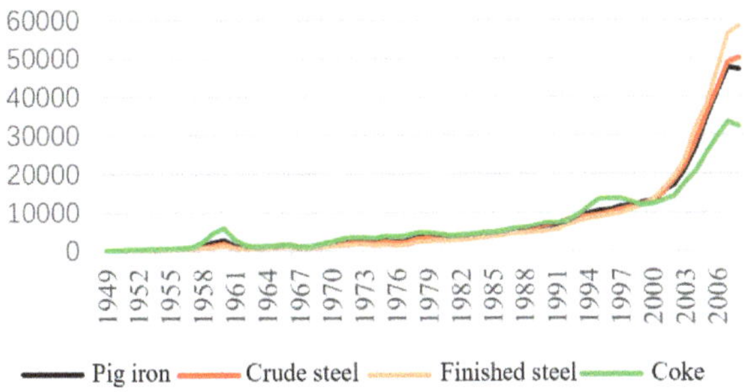

Figure 2. Production of heavy industrial products (e.g., pig iron, crude steel) in PRC.

Source: Data from *China Compendium of Statistics 1949–2008.*

Second, the strategy of prioritizing heavy-industry development has driven the rapid growth of heavy industry in China. Figure 2 shows the output growth of the four key heavy industrial products: pig iron, crude steel, finished steel, and coke. We can see that the growth rates of these four heavy industrial products have been very rapid, especially in the 21st century.

At a press conference of the State Council Information Office on September 20, 2019, Miao Wei, the Minister of Industry and Information Technology said:

> In 1949, China's steel production was only 158,000 tons, accounting for only 0.1% of the world's steel production in that year, and during the "Great Leap Forward" in 1958, we were still struggling to produce 10.7 million tons of steel. By 2018, China's steel production has exceeded 900 million tons, an increase of 5,799 times, having accounted for half of the world's steel for a long time.[5]

Third, it has driven the rapid growth of China's industry, and the industrial sector has grown much faster than the agriculture sector. The rapid growth of heavy industry has also laid the foundation for the growth of light industry, which led to the rapid growth of the industrial sector as a whole. For example, Figure 3 reports the value added of primary and secondary industries in China. We can see that the difference between the value added of the primary and secondary industries was not obvious at the founding of the

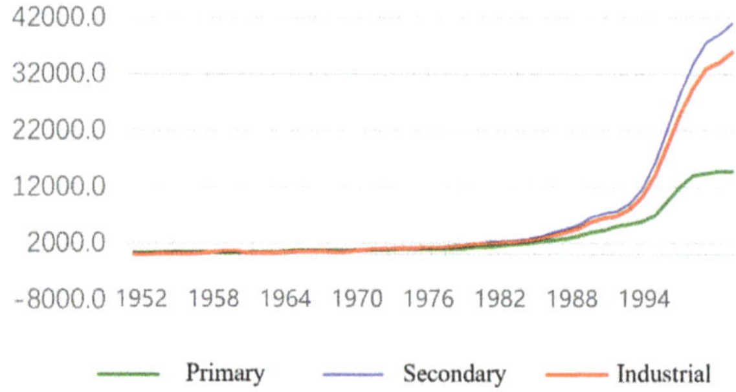

Figure 3. Comparison of the value added of secondary industry and value added of tertiary industry in China (1952–1998).

Source: Data from *China Compendium of Statistics 1949–2008*.

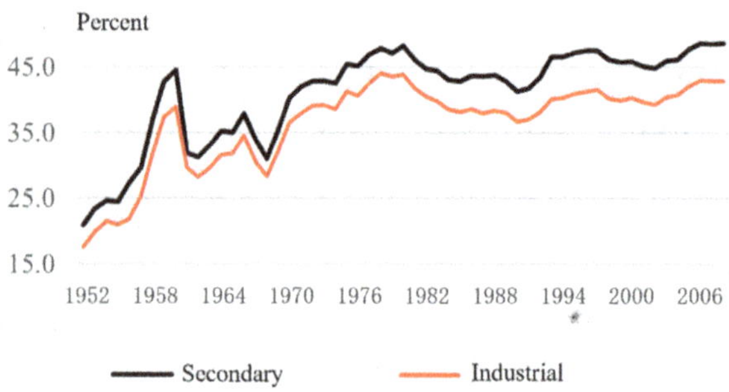

Figure 4. Industrialization process in China (1952–2008, as a percentage of GDP).

Source: Data from *China Compendium of Statistics 1949–2008*.

PRC, but with the implementation of the strategy of prioritizing heavy-industry development, the value added of secondary industries far exceeded that of primary industries. Especially after the 1990s, the gap between the value added of secondary industry and that of tertiary industry continued to increase rapidly.

Fourth, it has promoted the rapid rise of China's level of industrialization and its growth into a large, industrialized country. The rapid growth of heavy and light industries drove the growth of secondary industries and provided the impetus for China's rapid industrialization. Figure 4 reports the level of industrialization as measured by the share of secondary-industry GDP and industrial GDP in all GDP. We can see that the PRC experienced rapid growth in both indicators from its founding to the end of 1970. For example, while the share of industrial GDP was around 20% at the founding of the country, it exceeded 40% by the 1970s and has remained at around 40% since then.

Fifth, it has driven China to form a comprehensive industrial system that has enabled it to quickly become a global manufacturing power. Having a sound industrial system and a complete industrial chain in key manufacturing industries is important for the health and resilience of a country's overall economy. Based on its strategy of prioritizing heavy-industry development, the PRC quickly grew from a small farmer-dominated economy to an industrialized country with a full range of industrial sectors. Miao Wei, the Minister of Industry and Information Technology, said at the September 20, 2019, State Information Office conference that, in the 70 years since the founding of the PRC, China's industrial value added has grown more than 970 times, forming an independent and complete modern industrial system. In its industrialization process, China achieved in a matter of decades what other countries took hundreds of years to accomplish. After 70 years of development, the PRC, with 41 major industrial categories, 207 industrial categories, and 666 industrial subcategories, is the only country in the world that has all of the industrial categories listed in the UN Industrial Classification.[6] Industry in China has therefore achieved historic leaps. According to World Bank data, measured in US dollars, the value added of Chinese manufacturing exceeded that of the US for the first time in 2010, becoming the world's largest manufacturing country. In 2018, the value added of Chinese manufacturing accounted for more than 28% of the world's share, becoming an important engine driving global industrial growth.

Sixth, as suggested by Wu (2010), China's strategy of using special economic zones and other approaches to develop the eastern coastal region has four implications. First, these open areas can effectively utilize international resources and actively participate in international competition, becoming the pioneer zones of China's opening up to the outside world. Second, the opening up of these regions has strongly contributed to rapid economic development, making them the most dynamic high-growth areas in the regional economy. Third, these regions have performed the function of attracting foreigners and linking them to the domestic market, thus becoming a hub connecting the mainland and the international market. Fourth, and more importantly, these special zones and open economic zones have become the testing ground for establishing a modern market economy system. Drawing on the experience of developed market economies, they have boldly explored new economic systems and new systems of economic management, thereby accumulating experience, sorting out models, providing references for nationwide economic system reform, and becoming test zones for reform.

Table 1 reports the GDP shares of the eastern, central, and western regions in the national GDP from 1960 to 2005. We can see that in 1960, the eastern region already generated more than half of the national GDP. Over time, the GDP share of the eastern region in the national GDP remained largely stable until the mid-1980s, but since then it has continued to grow by 10 percentage points. By contrast, the share of GDP generated in the central and western regions has declined as a percentage of national GDP. This means that China's sustained rapid economic growth has been driven mainly by the eastern region, which has become the engine of China's rapid economic growth as a result of its prioritized development strategy.

Moreover, the strategy of prioritizing the development of the eastern coastal region can contribute to China's socioeconomic development through several channels. First, the eastern coastal region can contribute to the economic development of the mainland through channels such as industrial transfer, capital flow, and technology spillover. Second, the developed eastern region generates

Table 1. Share of GDP generated by different regions in China.

	1960 (%)	1965 (%)	1970 (%)	1975 (%)	1980 (%)	1985 (%)	1990 (%)	1995 (%)	2000 (%)	2005 (%)
Eastern part	53.28	49.66	50.81	51.96	52.36	53.15	54.24	59.33	60.40	61.66
Central part	32.29	32.96	33.41	32.00	31.17	31.06	29.66	26.54	25.93	25.39
Western part	14.43	17.38	15.78	16.04	16.46	15.78	16.10	14.12	13.67	12.95

Source: Calculated based on the GDP of each province provided in the *China Compendium of Statistics 1949–2008*.

more tax revenue and sends it to the central government, which then supports the mainland in the form of fiscal transfer payments. Third, the developed eastern regions also directly participate or assist in the economic growth of the central and western regions. For example, in the process of poverty alleviation, the developed eastern regions give various kinds of support to the central and western regions, send many cadres to those regions to support local construction, train grassroots cadres in those regions to improve their management skills, and transmit to them various advanced concepts and practices from the developed regions.

Urban–Rural Integration and Coordinated Regional Development: China's Rebalancing Strategy

Problems arising from the strategy of prioritizing heavy-industry development

Pursuing a catch-up strategy characterized by priority growth in heavy industry has been the main strategy for not only China but also other developing countries. However, while this strategy has laid a solid foundation for China's economic development, it is not without its drawbacks. It has distorted the efficiency of resource allocation, led to a loss of economic efficiency, and had far-reaching negative effects on China's balanced economic growth and social development (Lin *et al.*, 1994).

The urban-biased policy, which is in line with the policy prioritizing heavy-industry development, has played an important role in China's economic advancement but has also had negative effects on socioeconomic development.

First, urban-biased policies have exacerbated the urban–rural dichotomy in China's society and economy. Yang (1999), for example, argues that China's urban–rural divide is rooted in the centrally planned economy's strategy of prioritizing heavy industry, which necessitates the extraction of agricultural surplus to increase urban capital accumulation and subsidies to cities.

Second, it has led to slow agricultural growth and massive rural poverty. Carter (1997) argues that the negative effect of urban-biased policies on agricultural production is retarding the growth of agriculture and decreasing the efficiency of agricultural inputs. Yang and Cai (2000) similarly note that the distortions of production inputs and the resulting slow growth in agriculture have affected the growth of the entire economy. Knight and Song (1993) argue that the restrictions on urban–rural labor mobility under urban-biased policies have led to a predominantly rural poverty problem in China. Table 2 reports the incidence of poverty in both rural and urban sectors in China based on PovcalNet data. It is clear that the incidence of poverty in the rural sector is much higher than that in the urban sector, regardless of the poverty line adopted. Obviously, the urban-biased policy under the strategy of prioritizing heavy-industry development, which devoted more resources to the urban sector while extracting agricultural surplus to subsidize the urban sector, is an important source of China's "three rural problems."

Third, it has led to a widening of the income and development gaps between urban and rural residents. The urban-biased policy, on the one hand, pushes the urban sector to grow faster; on the other hand, it gives urban residents higher levels of welfare, which inevitably widens the income gap between urban and rural residents. Theoretically, such widening cannot be reduced until China's economy reaches the "Lewis turning point." Figure 5 reports the per capita disposable household income of urban residents and the per capita net household income of farmers from

Table 2. Incidence of poverty in China's urban and rural sectors.

		1981 (%)	1990 (%)	1999 (%)
US$1.9	Urban	59.18	32.01	10.88
	Rural	95.37	78.58	55.89
US$3.2	Urban	96.92	76.07	38.47
	Rural	99.92	95.05	84.36

Source: Data from PovcalNet at World Bank, http://iresearch.worldbank.org/PovcalNet/povOnDemand.aspx.

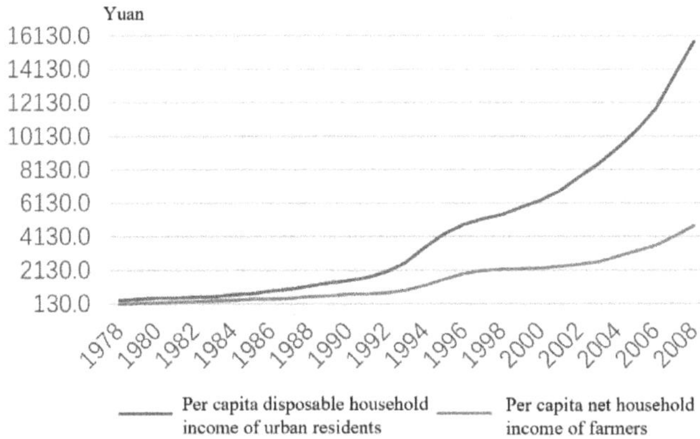

Figure 5. Comparison of urban and rural residents' income (1978–2008).
Source: Data from *China Compendium of Statistics 1949–2008.*

1978 to 2008. It shows that the gap between the two continues to widen: in 1978, the former was 2.57 times higher than the latter, decreasing to 1.82 times in 1983 and then rising continuously to 3.31 times in 2008.

Lu and Chen (2004) argue that the persistent widening of the urban–rural income gap in China is related to the overall urban bias of economic policies implemented by the Chinese government since the reform and opening up. Urban residents benefited more from the reform and opening up owing to the urban–rural division of governance and urban-biased economic policies. They confirm that urbanization is conducive to narrowing the urban–rural income gap, but this effect is limited by household registration management between urban and rural areas. Under the household registration system, rural residents with more money have more opportunities to become urban residents. Thus, the higher the cumulative share of the foreign population in a region, the larger the urban–rural income gap in that region. Lu and Chen also find that the opening up of the economy, the restructuring of the ownership of employment, the withdrawal of government from economic activities, and the restructuring of fiscal spending are all important factors related to widening the urban–rural income gap. The share of fiscal expenditures supporting agriculture and the share of agricultural loans for narrowing the urban–rural income gap show different degrees of decline across the board; thus, the widening trend of the urban–rural income gap has not been effectively controlled. In addition, Yang and Zhou (1999) and Tian (2001) suggest that the financial transfer programs implemented by the Chinese government in favor of the urban sector have also contributed to the urban–rural income gap since 1985. From 1986 to 1992, China experienced an average annual inflation rate of 8.5%, which was shared between urban and rural residents. Part of the reason for this inflation was the increase in government spending and investment, but much of this spending went to the urban sector. Similarly, Yao (2000) argues that the subsidies given to urban residents by urban-biased policies in areas such as housing, pensions, health, education, and food are also important factors in the urban–rural income gap. Zhang (2003) argues that inequalities in education and healthcare, in both rural and urban areas, are increasing as economic reforms proceed, due in large part to urban bias, with urban residents enjoying far more education and healthcare facilities than rural residents, which translates into large urban–rural disparities in social development processes.

Using an industry-feeding-agriculture approach to overcome rural poverty and narrow the urban–rural income gap

The strategy of prioritizing heavy-industry development and the accompanying policies of urban bias, planned economy in the urban sector, and collective economy in the rural sector caused many problems. The Chinese government therefore began to reverse these policies, or their effects, through various reforms after the economy took off.

With its economy continuing to grow rapidly, China has implemented policies to benefit farmers since the 10th Five-Year Plan. The 2004 Central Government Document No. 1 states that the "solution to the problems of agriculture, rural areas, and farmers (three rural issues) should be the top priority of the whole Party." To increase farmers' income, the first step is to abolish all kinds of taxes and fees for farmers. The second step is to adjust the production structure, encourage the production of more cash crops and less basic crops, and promote the development of the food-processing industry. From 2006 onward, all agricultural taxes, pastoral taxes, and agricultural special taxes, except for tobacco, were exempted nationwide. The "Proposal of the Central Committee of the Communist Party of China on the Eleventh Five-Year Plan for National Economic and Social Development" notes that "building a new socialist countryside is a major historical task in the process of modernization in China." In accordance with the requirements of "productive development, prosperous living, civilized countryside, neat and clean village, and democratic management," we should consider the actual situation of each place, respect the will of rural people, and steadily promote the construction of the new countryside. The construction of a new socialist countryside is the concrete realization of the policy of coordinating urban and rural development and implementing "industry feeding agriculture and urban supporting the countryside." Under the guidance of this strategy, governments at all levels have gradually rebuilt the medical and pension protection systems covering rural residents, referred to as the "New Rural Cooperative" and "New Rural Insurance." In October 2017, the 19th Party Congress put forward a strategy for rural revitalization, emphasizing that the solution to the "three rural issues" must be the top priority of the Party's work, the prioritized development of agriculture and rural areas must be adhered to, and the rural revitalization plan must be implemented. This can be regarded as a reversal of the policy prioritizing heavy-industry development since the founding of the PRC.

In 2012, the report of the 18th National Congress further stated that solving the "three rural issues" is a top priority and proposed that integrating urban and rural development is the best way to solve these problems. The report of the 19th National Congress also emphasizes solving the three rural issues, prioritizing the development of agriculture and rural areas, and pursuing the revitalization of rural areas. This "prioritized development of agriculture and rural areas" will lead China's economy into a new era.

With the abolition of agricultural taxes and fees, increased government investment in agriculture and rural areas, increased subsidies for agriculture, and the gradual consumption of surplus rural labor by industrialization and urbanization, farmers are increasingly benefiting from China's sustained economic growth. In particular, by the end of 2020, China had overcome absolute rural poverty, lifting the last remaining 100 million people out of poverty. Figure 6 depicts the incidence of rural poverty under different absolute poverty standards set by the Chinese government. We can see that the incidence of rural poverty in China continues to trend downward rapidly until it reaches zero, regardless of which absolute poverty line is used.

With the reversal of China's economic development strategy and the increase in government attention to and investment in the "three rural issues," agriculture, rural areas, and farmers have increasingly benefited from China's sustained economic growth, and the urban–rural development gap has begun to narrow. Figure 7 reports the income ratio between urban and rural residents, which can be regarded as a rough measure of urban–rural inequality. We can see that after the reform and opening up, the income gap between urban and rural residents tends to rise with fluctuations. After reaching a high of 3.33 in 2009, it starts to show an obvious downward trend.

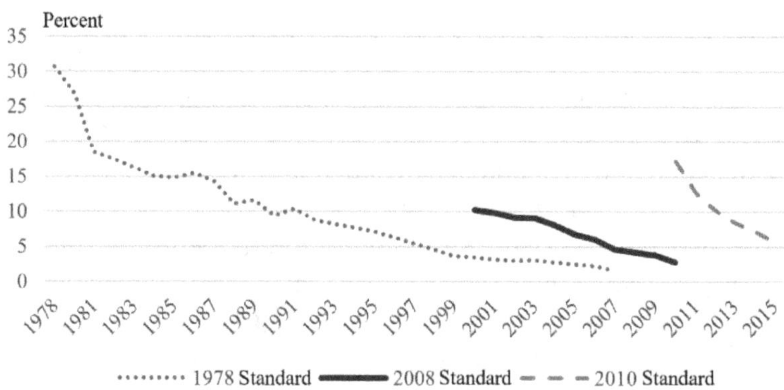

Figure 6. Annual rural poverty incidence and its changes in China (1978–2015).
Source: 1993 and 1996 data from *China Overcoming Rural Poverty: A World Bank Country Report*; data for other years from the *China Rural Poverty Monitoring Report, 2016*.

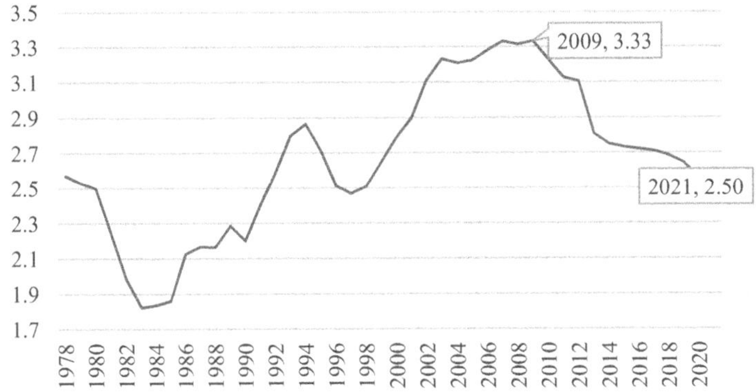

Figure 7. Ratio of income between urban and rural residents in China (1978–2021).

Note: The urban and rural survey systems were tabulated together in 2013, after which the net incomes of rural households were merged with urban households, and disposable income was used.

Source: Data from China Statistical Yearbooks for all years.

Problems arising from the strategy prioritizing eastern development

Despite creating a rapid economic growth pole in the eastern region and exerting a demonstration effect on the central and western regions, prioritized eastern development has led to the eastward migration of China's economic center and to a widening of the development gap between regions. Table 3 reports the per capita GDP levels of central and western China from 1960 to 2005. We can see that during the observed period, the per capita GDP of the eastern region grew from 446.27 to 25,190.08, a cumulative increase of 55.45 times, while the western region only grew by 45.75, showing that the per capita GDP growth rate of the western region was significantly slower than that of the eastern region. This naturally widened the gap in GDP per capita between the eastern and western regions. The data in Table 3 show that in 1960, the level of GDP per capita in the eastern region was 2.24 times higher than that in the west, which did not rise significantly until the 1990s but expanded significantly thereafter, to 2.71 times in 2005. The gap between the eastern and central regions also tended to widen over time.

Table 3. GDP per capita gap between different regions in China.

	1960	1965	1970	1975	1980	1985	1990	1995	2000	2005
East	446.27	339.82	449.82	581.73	811.58	1,393.75	2,594.42	7,984.17	13,367.25	25,190.08
Central	250.57	223.70	225.86	285.59	409.44	758.52	1,439.57	3,709.38	6,074.16	11,991.22
West	199.10	199.80	203.90	252.60	364.90	652.40	1,253.00	3,081.00	4,965.60	9,307.30
East/West	2.24	1.70	2.21	2.30	2.22	2.14	2.07	2.59	2.69	2.71
East/Central	1.78	1.52	1.99	2.04	1.98	1.84	1.80	2.15	2.20	2.10
Central/West	1.26	1.12	1.11	1.13	1.12	1.16	1.15	1.20	1.22	1.29

Note: The unit of GDP per capita is the yuan.
Source: Calculated based on the GDP per capita of each province provided by the *China Compendium of Statistics 1949–2008*.

Regional integration and narrowing the development gap between regions

To narrow the development gap between regions, China has successively implemented the "Western Development Strategy," "Central Rise Strategy," and "Northeast Revitalization Strategy."

In September 1999, the Fourth Plenary Session of the 15th Central Committee of the CPC proposed the Western Development Strategy. Then, in January 2000, the State Council established the Leading Group for the Development of Western Regions, with then-premier Zhu Rongji as leader, then-vice-premier Wen Jiabao as vice leader, and the main persons in charge of the State Council and relevant ministries and commissions as members. The Western Development Office of the State Council officially started operations in March 2000. The scope of this office includes 12 provinces and cities: Sichuan, Shaanxi, Gansu, Qinghai, Yunnan, Guizhou, Chongqing, Guangxi, Inner Mongolia, Ningxia, Xinjiang, and Tibet. It also includes three prefecture-level administrative regions: Enshi in Hubei, Xiangxi in Hunan, and Yanbian in Jilin. From January 19 to 22, 2000, the Western Region Development Leading Group of the State Council held a meeting in Beijing. It was noted that in the 50 years since the founding of the PRC, and especially in the 20 years since the reform and opening up, China's comprehensive national strength had increased significantly, people's lives were close to the well-off level, and the country had the ability to increase support for the central and western regions. In particular, the fiscal policy for expanding domestic demand could use more financial resources to support the development of the west. China had largely solved the national food problem, and there were even phases of food oversupply. This presented an excellent opportunity to implement in ecologically fragile areas a step-by-step return of farmland to forest (grass) to improve the environment. With China's accession to the World Trade Organization, its "opening up" had entered a new stage, and the central and western regions could also become more open, like the eastern coastal areas. The conditions for accelerating the development of the central and western regions were basically available, and the time was ripe. The implementation of western development was considered a large-scale system project and a difficult historical task.

The strategic objective of western development is to fundamentally change the relatively backward western region by the middle of the 21st century, when China basically achieves modernization. The aim is to build a new western region characterized by economic prosperity, social progress, and national unity. The main goals have been to make breakthroughs in the construction of infrastructure and the environment in the western region; further develop its economy and industries; accelerate the pace of development of key zones; strengthen science and technology education and health, culture, and other social undertakings; introduce a new "reform and opening up"; and further improve people's lives. To achieve these goals, the central government has provided support for and investment in five areas: accelerating infrastructure construction, strengthening environmental protection and construction, adjusting the industrial structure, developing science and technology and education, accelerating talent training, and increasing reform and opening up. In terms of deepening reform and expanding the opening up, the government has promoted some key areas of reform in the western region for early and pilot implementation and implemented the strategic concepts of the Belt and Road Initiative. Relying on key economic zones, the government has made efforts to build inland open economic highlands, such as Chengdu, Xi'an, Chongqing, and Nanning; cultivate central cities along the border provinces and regions to connect border crossings and economic corridors to neighboring countries and regions; support the accelerated construction of key development and opening-up pilot zones; and put forward relevant policy measures. It has also provided more favorable policies for industry access and taxation to absorb foreign investment in the western region, thus encouraging foreign investment. It has further deepened industrial cooperation between the east and west and considered the development of industrial cooperation and exchange platforms. The government also focused on organizing and preparing for the Western Expo and the Western Fair.

Wu (2010) suggests that this strategy is directly related to expanding domestic demand, promoting economic growth, fostering national unity and border consolidation, and coordinating east–west development to achieve common prosperity. The implementation of the Western Development Strategy has greatly improved the infrastructure conditions and the environment of the western region and has injected vitality into the industrial development of the region. Some studies have explored the positive effects of this strategy. However, limited by data availability, research that comprehensively and scientifically evaluates the effects of the strategy is rare. The GDP per capita gap between the eastern and western regions reported in Table 3 shows that the gap widened from 2.07 to 2.59 from 1990 to 1995, with a coefficient increase of 0.52. After the implementation of the strategy, however, the gap only increased from 2.69 to 2.71 from 2000 to 2005, with an increase of 0.02. This means the implementation of the strategy has curbed the expansion of the development gap between the central and western regions, thus helping to narrow the development gap.

Institutional Basis for China's Unbalanced Development Strategy

Achieving common prosperity is the essential characteristic of socialism with Chinese characteristics. The CPC has always taken it as its historical mission to lead the whole nation to achieve common prosperity. Marxist theory also concerns realizing common prosperity for all humankind. At the beginning of the founding of the PRC, Mao Zedong repeatedly raised the issue of common prosperity. For example, on July 31, 1955, he proposed that the road to socialism should be followed to "make all rural people rich together." On October 11 of the same year, he again proposed that "common prosperity" was the reason for the masses to believe in the Communist Party. Further, on October 27, 1955, Mao Zedong proposed in a talk with the industrial and commercial circles that "we should work together with everyone to become rich." Then, on October 29, he pointed out at a symposium on the socialist transformation of capitalist industry and commerce that "this common prosperity is certain, just as you know what to do tomorrow. The situation of not being able to control our own destiny should be gradually ended within a few five-year plans."

Since the early 1980s, when emphasizing that some people and regions should "get rich first," Deng Xiaoping has also continued to emphasize the relationship between getting rich first and getting rich together, reminding people that "the fundamental goal of our adherence to the road of socialism is to achieve common prosperity." On October 23, 1985, when meeting with a delegation of senior US entrepreneurs organized by Time Inc., Deng Xiaoping proposed that "some regions and some people can get rich first and drive and help other regions and other people to gradually achieve common prosperity."[7] In the 1992 Southern Tour Talks, Deng Xiaoping noted:

> The concept of common prosperity is proposed in this way: some regions have the conditions to develop first, some regions develop more slowly, and the regions that develop first will drive the regions that develop later to eventually achieve common prosperity. If the rich get richer and the poor get poorer, polarization will arise, and the socialist system should and can avoid polarization.

After the reform and opening up, China grew rapidly to become the world's second-largest economy. It completely eliminated absolute poverty under the current standards by 2020, thus becoming the first developing country to accomplish the UN Millennium Development Goals, thereby making great contributions to the cause of global poverty reduction. In a speech commemorating the centenary of the founding of the CPC, Xi Jinping proposed that more significant and substantial progress should be made in the new journey to promote comprehensive human development and common prosperity for all people. Based on the assertions of several national leaders mentioned above, we can see that the original intention and goal of the CPC is to lead the whole nation to common prosperity; therefore, all major socioeconomic development strategies formulated in China have necessarily focused on this goal.

China's national leaders have always attached great importance to the issue of balanced regional development. As early as the 1950s, Mao noted in the "Ten Relationships," regarding the relationship between coastal and mainland industries, that:

> ...about 70% of China's entire light and heavy industries are on the coast, and only 30% are inland. This is an unreasonable situation that has developed over the course of history. The coastal industrial base must be fully utilized, but, to balance the layout of industrial development, inland industry must be vigorously developed.[8]

On September 12, 1988, Deng Xiaoping, while listening to a report on preliminary proposals for price and wage reform, put forward the strategic concept of regional development "considering the two overall situations":

> The coastal areas should be opened up to the outside world faster so that this vast area with a population of 200 million people can

> be developed first, which is a matter of the overall picture. The inland should consider the overall picture. In turn, when development reaches a certain point, the coast is required to come up with more resources to help the development of the inland, which is also a big picture. At that time, the coast must also obey the overall picture.[9]

It can be said that this balanced regional development of the "two big pictures" and the proposal he made in 1985 for "letting some people and some regions get rich first" are completely consistent.

We can clearly see the lineage of China's economic development strategy by synthesizing the strategy prioritizing heavy-industry development and the regional development strategy. Facing the development challenges of a large country, the central government first adopted an unbalanced policy (prioritized heavy-industry development + prioritized coastal-area development) to launch industrialization and form a high-speed economic growth belt along the eastern coast. After economic growth reached a certain level, the central government then aimed to move toward common prosperity by "feeding agriculture with industry, leading rural areas with urban areas," and helping the central and western areas, as well as urban and rural areas, to achieve common levels of development. This strategy of moving from imbalance to balance has worked well for a large country like China, as shown by the results. Thus, an important question naturally arises: Why has this strategy been successful in China? We believe that Deng Xiaoping had already given the answer when he asserted the "one unity, two big pictures" concept for coastal and inland development:

> None of this can be done without the authority of the central government. With each one looking after its own, fighting with each other, and tearing each other apart, unification is not possible. Who can unify? The center! The center is the Party Central Committee and the State Council.[10]

Endnotes

1. Office of Household Survey, National Bureau of Statistics, *China Rural Poverty Monitoring Report, 2016*; National Statistics Press, 2017 edition.
2. From the People's website: http://www.people.com.cn/item/newlsq/zz/lxjx/lxjx001.html.
3. The expenditure method of accounting yields a 1949 GDP of 69.22 billion yuan, while the income method of accounting yields a 1949 GDP of 67.9 billion yuan, with the difference arising from calculation errors. See the footnote on p. 13 of the *China Compendium of Statistics 1949–2008.*
4. *Selected Works of Deng Xiaoping*, Vol. 3, p. 149.
5. https://xw.qq.com/amphtml/20190920006503/FIN2019092000650300.
6. This evaluation should also be viewed cautiously because if the 666 industrial subcategories are further subdivided, some of the more minor industrial categories are not available in China.
7. *Selected Works of Deng Xiaoping*, Vol. 3, p. 149.
8. *Selected Works of Mao Zedong*, Vol. 5, p. 270.
9. *Selected Works of Deng Xiaoping*, Vol. 3, pp. 277–278.
10. *Selected Works of Deng Xiaoping*, Vol. 3, p. 278.

References

Chen, B. 1986. The foreign affairs movement and the trend of modern industrialization in the world. *Monthly Journal of History*, 4, 53–59.

Department of Comprehensive Statistics of National Economy, National Bureau of Statistics. 2010. *China Compendium of Statistics 1949–2008*, 1st edn. Beijing: China Statistics Press.

Fei, X. 1939. *Peasant Life in China* (translated by Dai Kejing), 1986 edition. Nanjing: Jiangsu People's Publishing House.

Fei, X. 1947. Village — town — metropolis. *Ta Kung Pao* (Hong Kong edition) (April 27, 1947): 2.

Fei, X. 1948. About "village industry" and "gentry power". *Observation*, 4(4): 13.

Fleming, J.M. 1955. External economies and the doctrine of balanced growth. *The Economic Journal*, 65(258): 241–256.

Hirschman Albert, O. 1958. *The Strategy of Economic Development.* New Haven: Yale University Press.

Krugman, P. and Livas Elizondo, R. 1996. Trade policy and the third world metropolis. *Journal of Development Economics*, 49: 137–150.

Lin, Y., Cai, F., and Li, Z. 1994. *China's Miracle: Development Strategies and Economic Reforms*, 1st edn. Shanghai, China: Shanghai Sanlian Bookstore and Shanghai People's Publishing House.

Lu, M. and Chen, Z. 2004. Urbanization, urban-biased economic policies and urban-rural inequality. *Economic Research Journal*, 6: 50–58.

Myrdal, G. 1957. *Economic Theory and Underdeveloped Regions*. London: Gerald Duckworth and Co.

Nurkse, R. 1953. *Problems of Capital Formation in Underdeveloped Countries*. Oxford: Basil Blackwell.

Office of Household Survey, National Bureau of Statistics. 2017. *China Rural Poverty Monitoring Report-2016*. Beijing: National Statistics Press.

Perroux, F. 1950. Economic space: Theory and applications. *The Quarterly Journal of Economics*, 64(1): 89–104.

Ranis, G. and Fei, J.C.H. 1961. A theory of economic development. *American Economic Review*, 51(4): 533–565.

Rosenstein-Rodan, P.N. 1943. Problems of industrialisation of Eastern and South-Eastern Europe. *The Economic Journal*, 53(210/211): 202–211.

Scitovsky, T. 1954. Two concepts of external economies. *Journal of Political Economics*, 62: 143–151.

Tian, Q. 2001. China's new urban-rural divide and pitfalls for the Chinese economy. *Canadian Journal of Development Studies*, 22(1): 165–190.

Wu, J. 1933. The background of modern urbanization. *Tsinghua Journal*, 8(2): 80.

Wu, J. 1934. Developing the city to relieve the countryside. *Ta Kung Pao* (Tianjin edition) (September 9): 2.

Wu, J.L. 2010. *Tutorial on Economic Reform in Contemporary China*, 1st edn. Shanghai: Shanghai Far Eastern Publishing House.

Yang, D.T. 1999. Urban-Biased Policies and Rising Income Inequality in China. *American Economic Review*, 89(2): 306–310. *Papers and Proceedings of the One Hundred Eleventh Annual Meeting of the American Economic Association*, May 1999.

Yang, D.T. and Cai, F. 2000. The political economy of China's rural-urban divide. Working Paper No. 62 of Center for Research on Economic Development and Policy Reform, Stanford University.

Yang, D.T. and Zhou, H. 1999. Rural-urban disparity and sectoral labor allocation in China. *Journal of Development Studies*, 35(3): 105–133.

Yao, S. 2000. Economic Development and Poverty Reduction in China over 20 Years of Reform. *Economic Development and Cultural Change*, 43: 447–474.

Zhang, P. 1949. *Agriculture and Industrialization.* Mount Pleasant: Arcadia Press (2003).

Zhang, P. and Yang, J. 1999. *New Development Economics,* 2nd edn. (Revised edition). Zhengzhou: Henan People's Publishing House.

Zhang, X. 2003. Inequality in education and health care in China. *Economics* (Quarterly), 2(2): 405–416.

https://doi.org/10.1142/9789819815241_0010

Chapter 10

IS CHINA AN OPPORTUNITY FOR INDUSTRIALIZATION IN AFRICAN COUNTRIES?

Kabinet Kaba* and Mary-Françoise Renard†

CERDI, University Clermont Auvergne, France
**kabinet.kaba@uca.fr*
†m-francoise.renard@uca.fr

Introduction

Since the beginning of the 21st century, China's influence has been spreading around the world, now with a particular interest for countries associated with the Belt and Road Initiative and more broadly in developing countries. From a theoretical point of view, it is consistent with the defense of the superiority of South–South trade over North–South trade for the development of these countries.

The underlying arguments related to this type of international trade were mainly threefold (Greenaway and Milner, 1990; Lin, 2011):

First, a problem of export diversification: Since the comparative advantage of developed regions lies in industrial production, there will be a failure to diversify exports from developing countries because of their natural resource endowment. This reason is confirmed by Kaba *et al.* (2022), who show that the high concentration of exports from African countries explains the negative impact of trade openness on industrialization.

Second, a capture of gains from trade: Developed economies would capture a large part of trade gains due to their greater bargaining power and to the worsening terms of trade in developing countries. Advocates of South–South trade argue that intra-trade in developing countries would contribute to a more equitable distribution of trade gains.

Third, a crowding out effect: With their high technology, Northern producers have the capacity to produce good-quality products from new technologies. Since developing countries do not have access to some technologies, they will become simple consumers of many industrial products, which will prevent the creation of some categories of manufacturing firms.

As a result, the 2000s were marked by the emergence of intra-trade between developing countries, specifically trade between China and developing countries. China implemented an economic diplomacy targeting several dimensions: trade, financial flows, and special economic zones. China became the main trade partner of Africa. Over the past few decades, special attention has been paid to the role of Chinese emergence in other countries' economic prosperity, both in media headlines and in the scientific world. For example, for every 1% of economic growth in China, about 7.7 million people outside China would move out of poverty (Garroway *et al.*, 2012). A part of this growth could result from manufacturing sector expansion, highlighting the potential of China in the industrialization of Africa. Indeed, Lin explains that a reallocation of a small proportion of the 85 million labor-intensive manufacturing jobs in China to Africa will be a boon to African industrialization since manufacturing employment in that region is estimated at 10 million jobs.

This chapter studies the impact of trade with China on industrialization in Africa. In addition, we show the particularities of Africa compared to other developing countries (ODCs), including those in Asia. In the sample of ODCs, we consider countries classified by the International Monetary Fund as low-income economies and emerging economies. To the best of our knowledge, we are the first to make such a comparison that highlights a number of heterogeneities in South–South trade. Based on theoretical assumptions, we first discuss the conditions under which South–South trade can be a source of industrialization or deindustrialization. Second, descriptive statistics are utilized to understand the evolution and nature of Chinese trade in Africa and in ODCs. Third, empirical estimation is applied to study the effect of trade with China on industrialization in Africa and in ODCs. For this purpose, we consider 53 African countries and 98 developing countries excluding Africa (78 emerging economies and 20 low-income economies) during 1995–2021.

The impact of China's trade on the industrial sector of all developing countries depends on the content of these trade flows.[1] Therefore, international trade can have a positive or negative impact on industrialization. Indeed, we argue that commodity exports and imports of finished manufactured goods adversely affect industrialization. In contrast, exports of finished manufactured goods and imports of intermediate inputs, as well as physical capital, have a beneficial impact on industrialization. Regarding the negative impact of exports, the assumption is that African and ODCs' commodity exports to China crowd out the manufacturing sector. In the case of the negative impact of imports, we assume that manufacturing imports put competitive pressure on manufacturing firms in developing countries. From the perspective of technology transfer and lower production costs, the impact of manufacturing exports and input imports should be positive.

Our results show that trade with China is a source of deindustrialization in Africa on both the export and import sides. However, although it is a source of industrialization for ODCs on the export side, it is a source of deindustrialization on the import side. Thus, in terms of exports to China, our results show that Africa is a special case compared to ODCs. More precisely, we find that the impact of aggregate exports is through heavy dependence on commodity exports to China.

Finally, the rest of this chapter is organized as follows: the second section discusses how international trade can affect industrialization. The third section makes comparisons between the influence of China's trade and that of developed countries in Africa. The fourth and fifth section describe variables, data, and the empirical approach. The sixth section presents the results, and the last section concludes.

How International Trade with China can Affect Industrialization?

The aim of this chapter is to study how trade with China could affect industrialization in Africa and in ODCs. The question is how the two directions of trade (exports and imports) positively or negatively influence the process of industrialization. The nature of the impact of these two channels depends strongly on their content (raw materials, finished manufactured goods, intermediate inputs, and/or physical capital). Thus, this section discusses the negative and positive effects of exports and imports on industrialization.

Negative impact of international trade on industrialization

This section explains how international trade can negatively affect industrialization by presenting the negative impact of exports and imports on the manufacturing sector.

Negative impact of exports on industrialization

According to the Dutch disease and resource curse theories, an export boom in the resource sector leads to deindustrialization through several channels. Although both Dutch disease and the resource curse highlight the negative impact of commodity exports on industrialization, the transmission channels remain different. Since the resource curse theory is more general (referring to institutional determinants in addition to exchange rate appreciation as transmission channels), the Dutch disease is often considered a form of the resource curse rather than a specific theory. At the beginning of the 1980s, many theoretical papers studied the Dutch disease issue (Bruno and Sachs, 1982; Buiter and Purvis, 1980; Corden and Neary, 1982; Corden, 1984; Van Wijnbergen, 1984). Nevertheless, the Corden–Neary model is generally used as the theoretical basis for most empirical studies. Considering a small open economy with three economic sectors (resource sector, tradable sector, and non-tradable sector), a number of assumptions are made in the model.[2] The authors highlight two effects of the export boom in the resource sector, the spending effect and the resource movement effect.

Spending Effect: As a boom in natural resource exports generates additional income, the demand for tradable and non-tradable goods will increase. However, since supply is fixed in the short term and the price of tradable goods is set on the international market, this will result in higher prices for non-tradable goods and higher import demands for tradable goods. Moreover, knowing that the return on capital will increase in the non-tradable sector, wages will rise in both sectors (because of the perfect mobility of labor), leading to a fall in profits in the tradable sector. Thus, the main consequence of the spending effect is real exchange rate appreciation due to inflation, which in turn leads to export competitiveness deterioration involving a slowdown in the natural resources sector and a boom in the non-tradable sector.

Resource-Movement Effect: Since wages rise in the booming sector, there will be labor movement from the tradable and non-tradable sectors to natural resources. This will reduce output in the non-booming sectors (tradable and non-tradable sectors). The economy will thus be faced with a continuous decline in supply in the non-booming sectors, which will create a gap between supply and demand in these sectors. To restore the balance between supply and demand, the imports of tradable goods must increase, and prices will rise in the non-tradable sector because it is not substitutable with imports. This will create a new episode of inflation, which will lead to an appreciation of the real exchange rate. Real exchange rate appreciation will generate a new movement of labor from the tradable sector to the non-tradable sector, generating a process of deindustrialization.

The Corden–Neary model is based on the hypothesis of a short-term shock in resource exports that makes supply constant in the spending effect. However, specialization in resource exports can also have a deleterious impact on the long-term evolution of the manufacturing sector.

Long-Term Effect: As mentioned by Kaba *et al.* (2022), for developing countries with a weak manufacturing sector and a lack of infrastructure, exports of raw materials create an incentive for import activities. It becomes more profitable to import manufactured goods than to locally produce them because of their poor quality and the lack of infrastructure. At the same time, countries that use export rents to solve the infrastructure deficit should make manufacturing activity more profitable and thus encourage economic agents to enter this sector at the expense of import activities. Hence, the long-term negative impact of the specialization in natural resource exports to China will depend on how states invest the export revenues in improving the quality and availability of infrastructure.

Negative impact of imports on industrialization

Theoretically, if imports are mainly made up of finished manufactured products, they can have a negative impact on the local manufacturing sector. Indeed, competition from foreign products puts pressure on local manufacturing firms. As a result, less competitive firms may leave the domestic market or lose market share, leading to a decline in the share of manufacturing value added in GDP or total value added and employment in total employment. Empirically, a wave of literature has highlighted this impact through an exposure index of countries to Chinese trade. For the first time,

David *et al.* (2013) show that the more the United States (US) is exposed to the imports of manufactured goods from China, the more manufacturing employment declines in the US. Indeed, US exposure to the competition from Chinese manufacturing imports explained 33% of the decline in manufacturing jobs during 1990–2000, 55% during 2000–2007, and 44% during 1990–2007 (David *et al.*, 2013). Moreover, exposure to competition from Chinese manufactured product imports leads to a decline in manufacturing employment in France, Norway, and Spain (Malgouyres, 2017; Balsvik *et al.*, 2015; Donoso *et al.*, 2015). Precisely, a US$1,000 increase in the exposure index to Chinese imports per worker leads to a 6.2% drop in manufacturing employment growth in France (Malgouyres, 2017). In addition, exposure of the Norwegian labor market to competition from Chinese manufactured product imports explained more than 10% of the reduction in manufacturing employment during 1996–2007 (Balsvik *et al.*, 2015). In the case of Africa, between 2004 and 2008, 17 Nigerian manufacturing industries would have succumbed to competition from Chinese manufacturing imports, six of them employing more than 1,000 people (Bräutigam and Tang, 2014). In Ethiopia, many firms in the informal sector have suffered from Chinese import competition (Bräutigam and Tang, 2014). For ODCs such as Mexico and Chile, Mendez (2015) and Álvarez and Claro (2009) find that manufactured product imports from China increase the probability of exit and reduce manufacturing employment growth.

Positive impact of international trade on industrialization

This section explains how international trade could positively affect industrialization by presenting how exports and imports may positively impact the manufacturing growth process.

Positive impact of exports on industrialization

Unlike the case of commodity exports, if exports are mainly made up of manufactured goods, they can positively affect industrialization.

For an economy, exports represent the external sale of a part of domestic production. If foreign demand for domestic products increases or if the share of foreign-oriented domestic production increases for any reason, domestic exports, especially exports from the largest exporting sector, will increase. If exports are mainly made up of manufactured products, manufacturing output will increase relative to other sectors, leading to industrialization. The most illustrative example of the role of manufacturing exports in economies' industrialization process is the Asian miracle. Indeed, according to Page (1994), the eight most successful East Asian countries in terms of industrialization — Japan, Hong Kong, the Republic of Korea, Singapore, Taiwan, Indonesia, Malaysia, and Thailand — have all implemented exchange rate devaluation policies to support manufacturing export growth. The consequence of such a policy has been an increase in the share of East Asian countries in world trade. Indeed, these eight countries recorded an increase in their share of world exports, from 7.9% in 1965 to 13.1% in 1980 and 18.2% in 1990. The contribution of manufacturing exports to global export growth was the most important aspect of the trade performance of these countries. Between 1965 and 1990, Japan became the largest exporter of manufactured goods in the world, increasing its share from 8% to 12% between 1970 and 1980. The global share of manufacturing exports of the Four Tigers has increased almost four times faster than that of Japan. Indonesia, Malaysia, and Thailand also experienced similar increases in manufactured product exports.

Although the above discussion is based on macroeconomic analysis, a number of papers have carried out comparative studies between the performance of exporting and non-exporting companies. This second wave of literature is divided into two main work groups. The first, based on the US, Colombia, Morocco, and Spain (Delgado *et al.*, 2002; Isgut, 2001; Bernard and Jensen, 1999; Clerides *et al.*, 1998), concluded that manufacturing exporting firms are more productive than non-manufacturing exporters. Some authors argue that this difference in productivity is not explained by any advantage related to export activity but by the fact that it is the most productive firms that undertake export activities. There would therefore be self-selection because only companies that are sufficiently productive to be competitive in foreign markets and able to pay transport costs undertake export activities. In this context, industrialization will be explained by an increase in the number of companies sufficiently productive to invest in the manufacturing sector in order to export finished products. The second group of studies (Fafchamps *et al.*, 2007; Van Biesebroeck, 2005; Greenaway *et al.*, 2002; Aw *et al.*, 2000; Bigsten *et al.*, 2000; Kraay, 1999), focusing on China, Cameroon, Ethiopia, Ghana, Kenya, Morocco, Tanzania, the United Kingdom, Zambia, and Zimbabwe, concluded that exports generate a process of learning by doing. According to these authors, even if it is the most productive firms that export, exporting firms improve their productivity as soon as they start exporting. Exports improve firms' productivity through the adoption of international best practices, good production techniques, and interaction with customers in the countries to which they export (Van Biesebroeck, 2005).

Positive impact of imports on industrialization

Although in some cases they can fuel competition in the domestic economy and push some local manufacturing firms out of the market, in some other circumstances, imports can have a positive impact on industrialization. Theoretical studies such as those by Grossman and Helpman (1991), Markusen (1989), Romer (1987), and Ethier (1982) show that access to more varieties of intermediate inputs leads to productivity growth for firms importing these goods. Thus, two effects are to be noted. First, an expansion in the import of intermediate inputs to which the economy already had access increases the production of manufactured goods initially available in the domestic economy. Second, the access to new varieties of intermediate inputs initially unavailable in the economy leads to an increase in the production of new varieties of domestic finished products. Studies such as those by Halpern *et al.* (2015), Goldberg *et al.* (2010), and Amiti and Konings (2007) empirically establish the positive impact of intermediate input imports on productivity.

Indeed, the import of intermediate inputs accounted for 30% of total factor productivity growth in Hungary, and about 50% of this effect was explained by the increase in the productivity of importers (Halpern *et al.*, 2015). In the case of India, lower tariffs have led to higher imports of new varieties of inputs, which in turn have accounted for 31% of new varieties production (Goldberg *et al.*, 2010). This group of papers explains that trade openness allows access to new varieties of intermediate inputs, reducing the technological constraints of the local manufacturing sector. In the long run, progressive access to different varieties of high-tech input allows the domestic manufacturing sector to experience long-run productivity growth.

China's Trade Influence in Africa and the Nature of Africa–China and ODCs–China Trade

This section presents China's trade influence in Africa and the nature of trade between China and the two regions of interest. Before discussing the differences that result from the nature of trade between Africa–China trade and ODCs–China trade, it is important to analyze the evolution of China's trade influence in Africa. Indeed, the debate on the growing market share of China in Africa at the expense of Western countries is increasingly attracting the attention of policymakers in the three regions.[3]

China in Africa: Myth or reality?

The share of China in Africa's total exports and total imports increased from 1.09% and 2.52% in 1995 to 16.75% and 19.90% in 2021, respectively according to the statistics by the United Nations Conference on Trade and Development (UNCTAD). Thus, the objective of this part is to make comparisons between the evolution of developing and developed countries' trade influence in Africa, with emphasis on the case of China. In 1995, the share of developed countries in African commodity exports was about 80%, while that of developing countries was about 20% (Figure 1). In the same year, the share of developed

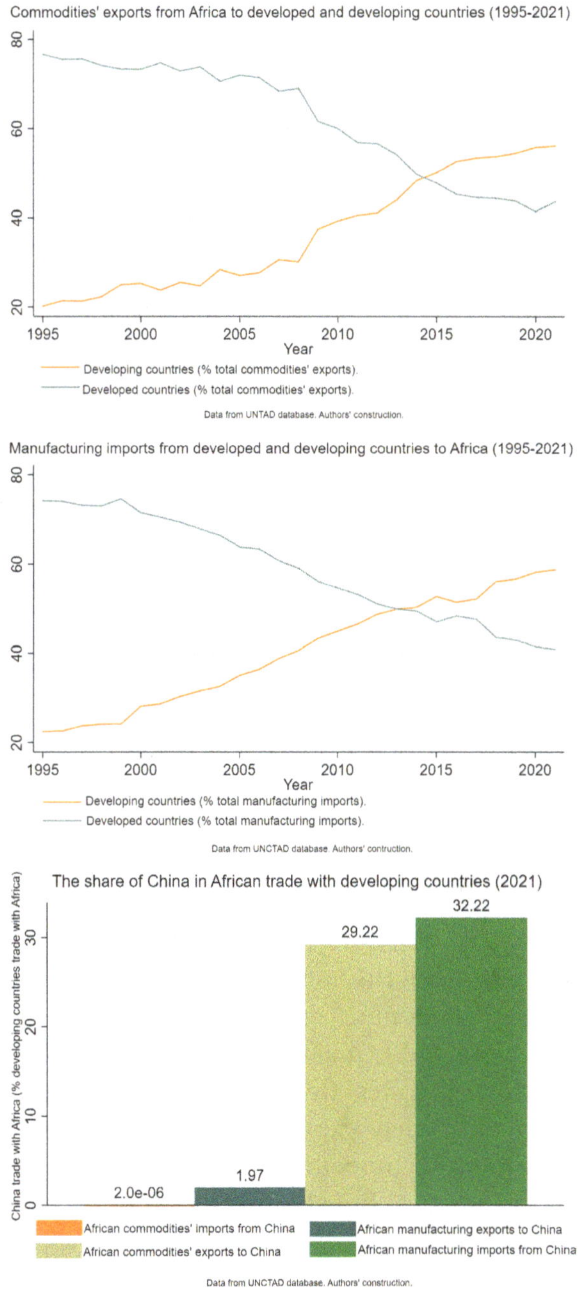

Figure 1. The share of developed and developing countries in African trade.

countries in African manufacturing imports was just under 80%, while that of developing countries was less than 30% (Figure 1). Over time, there has been a catching-up process: the share of developing countries in African trade has steadily increased in contrast to that of developed countries (Figure 1). In 2021, Africa traded more with developing countries than developed countries. So, what role does China play in the rise of trade between ODCs and Africa? Indeed, China accounted for more than 30% of African manufacturing imports from developing countries in 2021 (Figure 1). In addition, the share of China in African commodity exports to developing countries was 29% in 2021. It should be noted that the share of China in African manufacturing exports to developing countries is still very low.

Another way to understand China's trade influence in Africa is to compare it to that of the former colonizers of African countries. This comparison is relevant in the sense that, after their independence, most African countries maintained — sometimes several years after independence — economic and trade relations with their former colonial powers. Despite the historical connection, currently, China trades more with African countries than their former colonizers (Figure 2). Progressively, since the beginning of the 2000s, British, Belgian, and, finally, French colonies began to trade more with China than with the former colonial powers.

The nature of South–South trade: Is Africa a special case?

This section is the core of the analysis in this chapter. Indeed, one of the key arguments of South– South trade theory is the diversification of trade among developing countries. Thus, one would expect imports from China and exports from ODCs and Africa to China to be less concentrated. To test this hypothesis, it is important to analyze the content of Chinese exports and imports in relation to these two regions of interest. Indeed, not only the size of trade between Africa and China matters, but also the nature of that trade. In 2021, more than 90% of Africa's exports to China were made up of commodities, and more than 90% of its imports from China were made up of manufactured goods (Figure 3). This fact shows that in Africa–China trade, the first is fully specialized in commodity

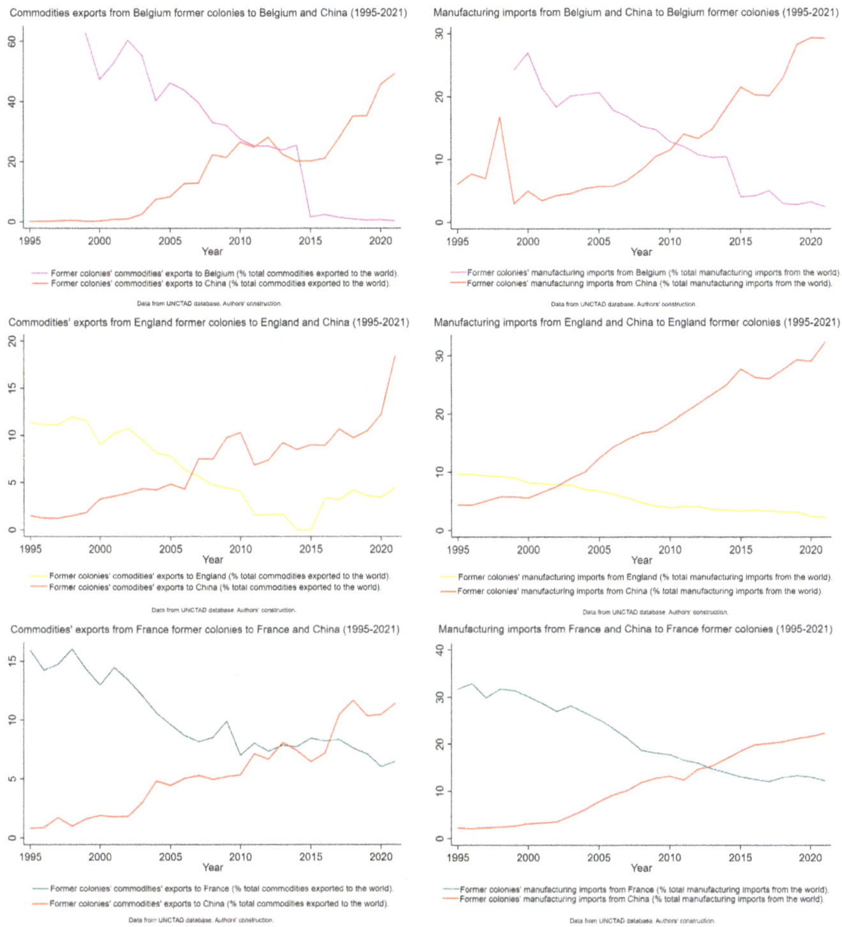

Figure 2. The share of China and former African colonizers in African trade (1995–2021).

exports and manufacturing imports. It should also be noted that commodity imports from China to Africa (7.24%) are higher than African manufacturing exports to China (6.32%). On the contrary, the share of manufactured products in exports from ODCs to China is almost 60%, while that of commodities is 40% (Figure 3). However, there is a similarity between Africa–China and ODCs–China trade in terms of imports. Similar to African countries, more than 90% of imports from China to ODCs are made up of manufactured goods. As a result, the exports from ODCs to China are more

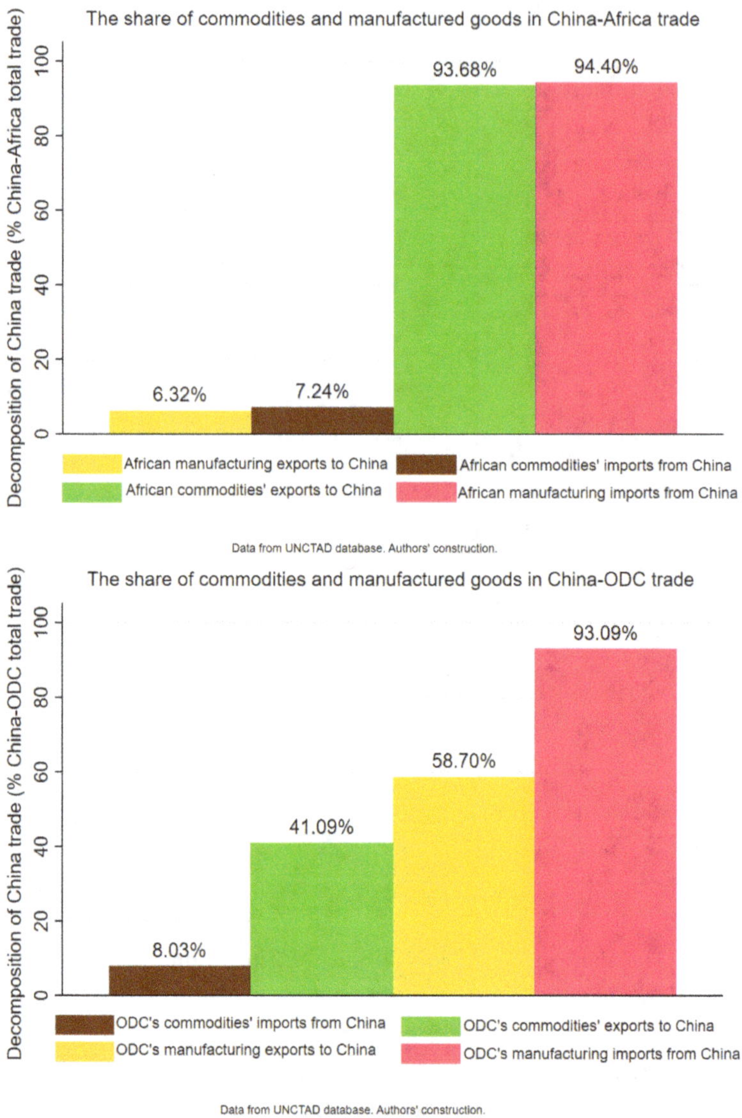

Figure 3. The nature of trade between Africa and China (2021) vs. the nature of trade between ODCs and China (2021).

diversified than those from Africa, as are Chinese imports to the two regions.

Taking China as the benchmark country of the South, the above statistics highlight two important facts. First, the theory that intra-trade in developing countries would diversify imports is neither verified in Africa nor in the ODCs. With the high concentration of Chinese exports of manufactured goods in Africa and in ODCs, imports from China could be a source of deindustrialization in the two regions. Second, South–South trade is diversified in terms of exports only in the case of trade between ODCs and China. For Africa–China trade, exports are still heavily concentrated in natural resources. This shows that Africa does not verify the South–South trade theory. One could therefore argue that Africa's exports to China would be a source of deindustrialization in Africa, while those from ODCs to China would be a source of industrialization, as over half of them are made up of manufactured products. Although the above data can show whether trade with China is diversified or not, they do not permit an empirical conclusion on whether Chinese trade is a source of deindustrialization or industrialization. Therefore, econometric estimates are made in the following to understand the link between Chinese trade and industrialization in Africa and in ODCs.

Variables and Data Description

Industrialization: Industrialization represents the dependent variable, and it is determined as the manufacturing value added share in total value added. In order to allow for comparison between countries and to control the effect of inflation, manufacturing value added and total value added are both in constant 2010 US dollar prices (United Nations Statistics Division, or UNSD, database).

Africa–China and ODCs–China Trade: The variables of interest are merchandise exports from Africa or ODCs to China and merchandise imports from China to Africa or ODCs. The variable "Exports" is the share of merchandise exports from Africa or ODCs to China (as a percentage of GDP). The variable "Imports" is the share of merchandise imports from China to Africa or ODCs (as a percentage of GDP). In order to study the channels through which exports and imports impact industrialization, we break down the two variables into commodity and manufactured product exports/ imports. Regarding commodities, the variable "Primary commodities, Precious Stones and Non-monetary Gold Exports" is used. It follows the standard international trade classification (SITC) and contains all the commodities in "SITC 0 + 1 + 2 + 3 + 4 + 68 + 667 + 971." For manufactured products, the variable "Manufactured goods," including all the manufactured goods in "SITC 5 to 8 less 667 and 68," is used (United Nations Conference on Trade and Development database).

Real exchange rate overvaluation: According to Rodrik (2008) and McMillan and Rodrik (2011), in developing countries, real exchange rate (RER) undervaluation and overvaluation positively and negatively impact the manufacturing sector's competitiveness, respectively. Referring to these authors, we study the impact of RER overvaluation on industrialization. To do so, the overvaluation index "overvalue" is constructed in three steps following Rodrik (2008). The "price level of GDP" from Penn World Table 9.1 is used as the RER measurement. Indeed, according to Rodrik (2008), this variable is equivalent to the RER, and it is expressed as one unit of local currency against an amount of dollar, which allows us to construct an overvaluation index rather than an undervaluation index, contrary to Rodrik (Penn World Table 9.1).

Market Size: According to Murphy *et al.* (1989), in developing countries, market size positively impacts industrialization if the national income is concentrated in the hands of the middle class, which is the class that consumes industrial products the most. Empirically, as in a number of papers on industrialization (Rodrik, 2016; Gui-Diby and Renard, 2015; Kang and Lee, 2011; Kaya, 2010; Rowthorn and Ramaswamy, 1999), we use GDP per capita and population as market size measures, represented by "Market size" (UNSD database).

Total Employment % Population: In addition to being important for industrialization in terms of factor of production, employment plays an important role in industrial specialization. For developing countries (including Africa) rich in low-cost labor, the comparative advantage is in the production of labor-intensive manufactured goods. To take into account this comparative advantage effect, the impact of employment is controlled (World Bank database).

Public investment: According to Newman *et al.* (2016), an important element of post- independence industrial strategy in Africa was massive public investment in state-owned industries. In addition, according to Dorosh and Thurlow (2014), public investment in cities positively affects structural change, leading to industrialization in some African countries. So, "Public investment" denotes the share of public investment in GDP and is used to take into account public intervention (International Monetary Fund database).

Private investment: According to the big push theory, the transition of firms from the traditional to the modern sector can take place if private investment is simultaneous with coordination provided by the state. Moreover, a number of empirical studies (Kang and Lee, 2011; Kaya, 2010; Rowthorn and Ramaswamy, 1999) find that investment has a positive impact on industrialization. However, in the Dutch disease context, resources are directed toward the natural resources sector. As an example, Gui-Diby and Renard (2015) find that investment negatively impacts industrialization in Africa. Thus, "Private investment," as a percentage of GDP, is used in the econometric model (International Monetary Fund database).

Trade protection and financial restriction polices: Developing countries, in their economic history, have often experienced two types of trade and financial policies. First, the end of the 1950s was marked by economic measures of self-reliance to ensure economic independence from former colonizers. Governments thus put in place trade protection and financial restriction policies. These trade and financial measures were intended to allow the creation and protection of local industries. While these economic measures effectively allowed the emergence of state-owned industries, their unsustainability led to inefficiency in the case of African countries (Newman *et al.*, 2016; Kaba *et al.*, 2022). Second, the 1980s were characterized by a wave of trade and financial openness in these countries. According to Meier *et al.* (1989), trade and financial openness in relation to the structural adjustment programs of international institutions led to deindustrialization in numerous African countries.

In this context, we use in our empirical model an indicator of trade protection policies consisting of the following measures: trade regulations, trade taxes, tariffs, and trade agreements. The indicator of financial restrictions is determined from the measures of investment restrictions, capital account openness, and international investment agreements. These two variables come from the KOF Swiss Economic Institute (Konjunkturforschungsstelle) database (trade globalization, de jure; financial globalization, de jure).

Agriculture value added in total value added: According to the structural change theory, the movement of resources from the traditional sector (agriculture) to the modern sector (manufacturing) leads to the growth of the manufacturing sector (Gui-Diby and Renard, 2015; Lin, 2011; Lewis, 1954). Thus, the effect of structural transformation is controlled by the share of agricultural value added in total value added (UNSD database).

Empirical Strategy

In this chapter, the ordinary least squares (OLS) with country and year fixed effects is used as the estimation approach to study the link between Chinese trade and industrialization in Africa and in ODCs. The OLS with country and year fixed effects is relevant in the sense that it allows us to consider one dimension of endogeneity, namely the issue of omitted variables. Controlling for country and year fixed effects helps capture the country- and year-specific characteristics that can affect industrialization. Not controlling for the country and year heterogeneities leads to an omitted variable bias since these variables will end up in the error term. If the omitted variables are correlated to the explanatory variables, it will result in a correlation between the error term and the variables of interest (endogeneity). To circumvent the other dimension of endogeneity, which is the reverse causality, we use lagged values ($t-1$) of all explanatory variables. In a macro-econometric model, variables (explained and explanatory variables) are explained by each other. As mentioned above, trade with China can either positively or negatively affect industrialization. However, manufacturing growth can promote trade with China, especially through the export of manufactured goods and the import of intermediate inputs. In addition, the expansion of the manufacturing sector due to local processing of raw materials may reduce commodity exports to China. To take into account these reverse causalities between industrialization and trade with China, we regressed instantaneous industrialization on trade one year ago. Also, we lag all of the explanatory variables by one year to ensure that a potential reverse causality between them and industrialization does not bias the estimates.

In addition to the endogeneity issue, the problem of spurious regression — due to the non-stationarity of variables in the model — can affect the quality of estimates from a panel with an important time dimension like ours. In fact, most of the macroeconomic variables are not stationary in level (they have unit roots in level). To avoid this problem, it is often recommended to consider the first differences of any variable in the model that contains unit roots in level. However, estimating a model with first-difference variables highlights the short-run effects of explanatory variables on the dependent variable. In our case, the aim is to study the long-run effects (variables in level) on industrialization. In this context, the spurious regression due to the existence of unit roots is addressed by considering a model that includes the lagged explanatory variables as well as the lagged explained variable. The model can be written as follows:

$$\begin{aligned} Industrialization_{i,t} = {} & \beta Exports_{i,t-1} + \sigma Imports_{i,t-1} + \gamma X_{i,t-1} + \\ & Industrialization_{i,t-1} + \delta_i + \theta_t + \nu_{i,t} \end{aligned} \tag{1}$$

The variable $Exports_{i,t-1}$ is the share of total exports to China one year ago in percentage of GDP, while $Imports_{i,t-1}$ is the share of total imports from China one year ago in percentage of GDP. To study the transmission channels, exports and imports are decomposed into commodities and manufacturing exports/imports. The vector $X_{i,t-1}$ represents the set of control variables (lagged). δ_i and θ_t are the country and year fixed effects, respectively, while $\nu_{i,t}$ is the idiosyncratic error term.

Results

This section presents the findings about the effects of trade with China on industrialization in Africa and in ODCs, namely low-income economies and emerging economies.

Table 1 reports the results for the African sample. In column 1, we consider only African exports to China and imports from China as explanatory variables. The control variables are introduced in column 2. Then, the explanatory variables that may be strongly correlated with trade with China are introduced gradually. Considering exclusively exports and imports, only African exports to China negatively and significantly affect industrialization (column 1). In the presence of control variables, the impact of exports remains negative and significant, while that of imports is insignificant though negative (column 2). From column 3 to column 6, with the introduction of trade protection policies, financial restrictions, and the agricultural value added, the coefficients of exports and imports are slightly modified. However, the effects of exports remain negative and significant, and those of imports become significant. Furthermore, by introducing industrialization delayed by one year (column 7), the coefficients of exports and imports fall sharply, although they remain significant.

Table 2 describes the results for the sample of low-income economies. As in Table 1, only exports have a significant and negative impact on industrialization in column 1. However, once the control variables are introduced, the effect of exports becomes positive and significant, while that of imports becomes negative and significant (column 2). Similar to Table 1, the coefficients of imports and exports fall drastically after the introduction of the industrialization

Table 1. The effects of China's trade on industrialization in Africa (% GDP).

	Africa						
	(1)	(2)	(3)	(4)	(5)	(6)	(7)
	Model 1	Model 2	Model 3	Model 4	Model 5	Model 6	Model 7
Exports % GDP (t–1)	–0.003*	–0.004**	–0.021***	–0.021***	–0.021***	–0.023***	–0.003**
	(0.002)	(0.002)	(0.003)	(0.003)	(0.003)	(0.003)	(0.001)
Imports % GDP (t–1)	–0.045	–0.076	–0.261***	–0.261***	–0.261***	–0.240***	–0.078**
	(0.036)	(0.047)	(0.052)	(0.052)	(0.051)	(0.051)	(0.035)
Market Size (t–1)		–0.000	–0.001***	–0.001***	–0.001***	–0.001***	–0.000
		(0.000)	(0.000)	(0.000)	(0.000)	(0.000)	(0.000)
Private Investment (t–1)		–0.079***	–0.033**	–0.036**	–0.035**	–0.041**	–0.015
		(0.022)	(0.016)	(0.017)	(0.017)	(0.017)	(0.010)
Public Investment (t–1)		0.091***	–0.008	–0.011	0.002	–0.009	0.021
		(0.029)	(0.031)	(0.031)	(0.032)	(0.033)	(0.016)
Employment (t–1)		0.737***	0.830***	0.816***	0.844***	0.819***	0.111**
		(0.108)	(0.109)	(0.110)	(0.110)	(0.116)	(0.047)
Population (t–1)		–0.370***	–0.406***	–0.399***	–0.426***	–0.420***	–0.047*
		(0.055)	(0.056)	(0.057)	(0.060)	(0.062)	(0.025)
Trade Protection Policies (t–1)			–0.064***	–0.067***	–0.067***	–0.068***	–0.003
			(0.010)	(0.009)	(0.009)	(0.009)	(0.007)

Financial Restriction Policies (t–1)				0.021*	0.017	0.017	0.006
				(0.011)	(0.011)	(0.011)	(0.007)
Overvalue (t–1)					–3.761***	–4.046***	–0.618
					(1.256)	(1.237)	(0.524)
Agriculture Value Added (t–1)						–0.049*	0.018
						(0.025)	(0.015)
Industrialization (t–1)							0.833***
							(0.030)
Observation	1186.000	1106.000	1040.000	1040.000	1040.000	1040.000	1040.000
F-stats	3.075	10.250	28.325	26.506	24.833	24.710	153.445
R^2	0.884	0.887	0.911	0.912	0.913	0.913	0.976
Country fixed effect	Yes	Yes	Yes	Yes	Yes	Yes	Yes
Year fixed effect	Yes	Yes	Yes	Yes	Yes	Yes	Yes

Notes: Robust standard errors are in parentheses: *** $p < 0.01$, ** $p < 0.05$, * $p < 0.1$.

Table 2. The effects of China's trade on industrialization in low-income developing economies (% GDP).

	Low-income countries						
	(1)	(2)	(3)	(4)	(5)	(6)	(7)
	Model 1	Model 2	Model 3	Model 4	Model 5	Model 6	Model 7
Exports % GDP (*t*–1)	–0.018*	0.045***	0.041***	0.060***	0.058***	0.111***	0.016***
	(0.010)	(0.011)	(0.012)	(0.013)	(0.013)	(0.014)	(0.005)
Imports % GDP (*t*–1)	–0.099	–0.253**	–0.326**	–0.505***	–0.505***	–0.349***	–0.060*
	(0.098)	(0.115)	(0.128)	(0.134)	(0.134)	(0.104)	(0.031)
Market Size (*t*–1)		–0.002**	–0.001	–0.001	–0.001	–0.006***	–0.001***
		(0.001)	(0.001)	(0.001)	(0.001)	(0.001)	(0.000)
Private Investment (*t*–1)		0.315***	0.304***	0.270***	0.268***	0.056	–0.004
		(0.061)	(0.064)	(0.059)	(0.058)	(0.038)	(0.015)
Public Investment (*t*–1)		0.231***	0.154*	0.000	–0.023	0.069	0.069***
		(0.083)	(0.086)	(0.089)	(0.094)	(0.076)	(0.023)
Employment (*t*–1)		0.592***	0.614***	0.566***	0.614***	0.764***	0.135**
		(0.191)	(0.191)	(0.182)	(0.186)	(0.160)	(0.061)
Population (*t*–1)		–0.170	–0.167	–0.111	–0.145	–0.140	–0.018
		(0.124)	(0.124)	(0.120)	(0.122)	(0.104)	(0.035)
Trade Protection Policies (*t*–1)			–0.044	–0.057	–0.058	–0.066***	–0.014
			(0.040)	(0.036)	(0.036)	(0.025)	(0.009)
Financial Restriction Policies (*t*–1)				0.151***	0.150***	0.031	–0.006
				(0.027)	(0.027)	(0.021)	(0.008)

Overvalue (t–1)					–3.906	–13.600***	–2.615**
					(3.420)	(3.144)	(1.217)
Agriculture Value Added (t–1)						–0.589***	–0.076***
						(0.053)	(0.028)
Industrialization (t–1)							0.846***
							(0.038)
Observation	417.000	308.000	295.000	295.000	295.000	295.000	295.000
F-stats	6.957	13.910	12.065	16.984	15.699	31.768	292.959
R^2	0.735	0.769	0.776	0.804	0.805	0.878	0.982
Country fixed effect	Yes	Yes	Yes	Yes	Yes	Yes	Yes
Year fixed effect	Yes	Yes	Yes	Yes	Yes	Yes	Yes

Notes: Robust standard errors are in parentheses: *** $p < 0.01$, ** $p < 0.05$, * $p < 0.1$.

variable lagged by one year (columns 3–7). As shown in columns 3–6, in the case of emerging economies, the effect of exports is significantly positive, whereas the effect of imports is significantly negative (Table 3). Considering the effects of industrialization lagged by one year, exports and imports no longer significantly affect industrialization in emerging economies.

From the above results, it appears that trade with China does not affect developing countries in the same way. Indeed, total exports to China are a source of deindustrialization in Africa (negative effect), whereas they are a source of industrialization in low-income economies and emerging economies (positive effect).[4] However, total imports from China appear to have negative and significant effects on industrialization in all three: Africa, low-income economies, and emerging economies. The difference between the effects of total exports in Africa and in ODCs may be explained by the nature of exports. As shown in Figure 3, more than 90% of exports from Africa to China are made up of commodities, while 60% of exports from ODCs to China are made up of manufactured goods. Thus, the concentration of African countries in commodity exports, crowding out the manufacturing sector, could explain why exports are a source of deindustrialization in Africa. Moreover, these results show that the argument that South–South trade diversifies exports to be a source of industrialization is not empirically valid in Africa, although it is in ODCs. This makes Africa a special case in South–South trade.

Since the negative effect of total exports from Africa to China is explained by the specialization of African countries in commodity exports, the overall exports are decomposed into commodity and manufacturing exports to China. Table 4 reports the results of the effects of commodity and manufactured product exports. From column 1 to column 4, the results show that the share of commodity exports to China in total exports to China has a negative and significant impact on industrialization in Africa, while that of manufacturing exports is not significant. The current results confirm previous analyses by showing that the negative effect of total exports on industrialization in Africa is due to specialization in

Table 3. The effects of China's trade on industrialization in emerging economies (% GDP).

	Emerging countries						
	(1)	(2)	(3)	(4)	(5)	(6)	(7)
	Model 1	Model 2	Model 3	Model 4	Model 5	Model 6	Model 7
Exports % GDP (*t*–1)	0.002	0.001	0.005***	0.006***	0.005***	0.006***	0.000
	(0.001)	(0.001)	(0.002)	(0.002)	(0.002)	(0.002)	(0.001)
Imports % GDP (*t*–1)	–0.027	–0.074**	–0.071*	–0.082**	–0.104***	–0.119***	–0.025
	(0.033)	(0.033)	(0.037)	(0.036)	(0.034)	(0.034)	(0.017)
Market Size (*t*–1)		–0.000	–0.000	–0.000	–0.000	–0.000	0.000
		(0.000)	(0.000)	(0.000)	(0.000)	(0.000)	(0.000)
Private Investment (*t*–1)		0.059***	0.063***	0.047**	0.032*	0.031*	0.006
		(0.019)	(0.020)	(0.019)	(0.017)	(0.017)	(0.010)
Public Investment (*t*–1)		0.022	0.027	0.036	0.009	0.007	0.005
		(0.027)	(0.031)	(0.030)	(0.027)	(0.028)	(0.012)
Employment (*t*–1)		–0.060***	–0.059***	–0.045***	–0.047***	–0.041**	–0.002
		(0.016)	(0.016)	(0.017)	(0.017)	(0.017)	(0.008)
Population (*t*–1)		0.026***	0.025***	0.021***	0.021***	0.016***	0.002
		(0.005)	(0.005)	(0.005)	(0.005)	(0.005)	(0.003)
Trade Protection Policies (*t*–1)			0.013	0.006	0.005	0.005	–0.000
			(0.008)	(0.008)	(0.008)	(0.008)	(0.003)

(*Continued*)

Table 3. (*Continued*)

	Emerging countries						
	(1)	(2)	(3)	(4)	(5)	(6)	(7)
	Model 1	Model 2	Model 3	Model 4	Model 5	Model 6	Model 7
Financial Restriction Policies (t–1)				0.035***	0.031***	0.029***	0.006**
				(0.007)	(0.006)	(0.006)	(0.002)
Overvalue (t–1)					–0.458***	–0.464***	–0.147***
					(0.075)	(0.075)	(0.022)
Agriculture Value Added (t–1)						–0.094***	0.002
						(0.035)	(0.024)
Industrialization (t–1)							0.885***
							(0.016)
Observation	1594.000	1315.000	1269.000	1269.000	1269.000	1269.000	1269.000
F-stats	1.251	12.013	11.250	12.768	17.241	15.947	424.836
R^2	0.902	0.921	0.913	0.915	0.918	0.919	0.986
Country fixed effect	Yes	Yes	Yes	Yes	Yes	Yes	Yes
Year fixed effect	Yes	Yes	Yes	Yes	Yes	Yes	Yes

Notes: Robust standard errors are in parentheses: *** $p < 0.01$, ** $p < 0.05$, * $p < 0.1$.

Table 4. The effects of Africa–China trade on industrialization in Africa (Transmission channels).

	(1) Model 1	(2) Model 2	(3) Model 3	(4) Model 4
Commodity Exports % Exports to China (*t*–1)	–1.40e –08***	–1.42e –08***	–1.43e –08***	–1.49e –08***
	(0.000)	(0.000)	(0.000)	(0.000)
Manufacturing Imports % Imports from China (*t*–1)	0.000	0.000	0.000	0.000
	(0.000)	(0.000)	(0.000)	(0.000)
Commodity Imports % Imports from China (*t*–1)	0.006	0.005	0.004	0.006
	(0.009)	(0.009)	(0.009)	(0.009)
Manufacturing Imports % Imports from China (*t*–1)	0.003	0.003	0.002	0.003
	(0.008)	(0.008)	(0.008)	(0.008)
Industrialization (*t*–1)	0.841***	0.839***	0.838***	0.841***
	(0.032)	(0.032)	(0.032)	(0.032)
Market Size (*t*–1)	–0.000	–0.000	–0.000	–0.000
	(0.000)	(0.000)	(0.000)	(0.000)
Private Investment (*t*–1)	–0.014	–0.015	–0.015	–0.013
	(0.010)	(0.011)	(0.011)	(0.011)
Public Investment (*t*–1)	0.010	0.008	0.009	0.013
	(0.019)	(0.020)	(0.020)	(0.018)
Employment (*t*–1)	0.065	0.062	0.067	0.074
	(0.046)	(0.045)	(0.048)	(0.050)
Population (*t*–1)	–0.022	–0.021	–0.025	–0.026
	(0.024)	(0.023)	(0.025)	(0.026)
Trade Protection Policies (*t*–1)	0.001	0.000	0.000	0.001
	(0.008)	(0.007)	(0.007)	(0.007)
Financial Restriction Policies (*t*–1)		0.008	0.007	0.007
		(0.008)	(0.008)	(0.007)
Overvalue (*t*–1)			–0.501	–0.375
			(0.551)	(0.545)
Agriculture Value Added (*t*–1)				0.017
				(0.014)
Observation	950.000	950.000	950.000	950.000
F-stats	109.709	101.290	93.891	87.884
R^2	0.975	0.975	0.975	0.975
Country fixed effect	Yes	Yes	Yes	Yes
Year fixed effect	Yes	Yes	Yes	Yes

Notes: Robust standard errors are in parentheses: *** $p < 0.01$, ** $p < 0.05$, * $p < 0.1$.

Table 5. List of African countries.

Country	Freq.	Percent	Cum.
Algeria	27	1.96	1.96
Angola	27	1.96	3.92
Benin	27	1.96	5.88
Botswana	27	1.96	7.84
Burkina Faso	27	1.96	9.80
Burundi	27	1.96	11.76
Cameroon	27	1.96	13.73
Central African Republic	27	1.96	15.69
Chad	27	1.96	17.65
Comoros	27	1.96	19.61
Congo	27	1.96	21.57
Djibouti	27	1.96	23.53
Egypt	27	1.96	25.49
Equatorial Guinea	27	1.96	27.45
Eritrea	27	1.96	29.41
Ethiopia	27	1.96	31.37
Gabon	27	1.96	33.33
Gambia	27	1.96	35.29
Ghana	27	1.96	37.25
Guinea	27	1.96	39.22
Guinea-Bissau	27	1.96	41.18
Kenya	27	1.96	43.14
Lesotho	27	1.96	45.10
Liberia	27	1.96	47.06
Libya	27	1.96	49.02
Madagascar	27	1.96	50.98
Malawi	27	1.96	52.94
Mali	27	1.96	54.90
Mauritania	27	1.96	56.86
Mauritius	27	1.96	58.82
Morocco	27	1.96	60.78
Mozambique	27	1.96	62.75
Namibia	27	1.96	64.71

Table 5. (*Continued*)

Country	Freq.	Percent	Cum.
Niger	27	1.96	66.67
Nigeria	27	1.96	68.63
Rwanda	27	1.96	70.59
Sao Tome and Principe	27	1.96	72.55
Senegal	27	1.96	74.51
Seychelles	27	1.96	76.47
Sierra Leone	27	1.96	78.43
Somalia	27	1.96	80.39
South Africa	27	1.96	82.35
Tanzania, United Republic of	27	1.96	84.31
Togo	27	1.96	86.27
Tunisia	27	1.96	88.24
Uganda	27	1.96	90.20
Zambia	27	1.96	92.16
Zimbabwe	27	1.96	94.12
Cote d'Ivoire	27	1.96	96.08
Democratic Republic of the Congo	27	1.96	98.04
Swaziland	27	1.96	100.00
Total	1,377	100.00	

Source: United Nations Statistics Division.

Table 6. List of low-income economies.

Country	Freq.	Percent	Cum.
Afghanistan	27	5.00	5.00
Bangladesh	27	5.00	10.00
Bhutan	27	5.00	15.00
Cambodia	27	5.00	20.00
Haiti	27	5.00	25.00
Honduras	27	5.00	30.00
Kiribati	27	5.00	35.00

(*Continued*)

Table 6. (*Continued*)

Country	Freq.	Percent	Cum.
Kyrgyzstan	27	5.00	40.00
Moldova, Republic of	27	5.00	45.00
Myanmar	27	5.00	50.00
Nepal	27	5.00	55.00
Nicaragua	27	5.00	60.00
Papua New Guinea	27	5.00	65.00
Solomon Islands	27	5.00	70.00
Tajikistan	27	5.00	75.00
Uzbekistan	27	5.00	80.00
Viet Nam	27	5.00	85.00
Yemen	27	5.00	90.00
Laos	27	5.00	95.00
Timor-Leste	27	5.00	100.00
Total	540	100.00	

Source: United Nations Statistics Division.

Table 7. List of emerging economies.

Country	Freq.	Percent	Cum.
Albania	27	1.28	1.28
Antigua and Barbuda	27	1.28	2.56
Argentina	27	1.28	3.85
Armenia	27	1.28	5.13
Aruba	27	1.28	6.41
Azerbaijan	27	1.28	7.69
Bahamas	27	1.28	8.97
Bahrain	27	1.28	10.26
Barbados	27	1.28	11.54
Belarus	27	1.28	12.82
Belize	27	1.28	14.10
Bosnia and Herzegovina	27	1.28	15.38
Brazil	27	1.28	16.67
Brunei Darussalam	27	1.28	17.95

Table 7. (*Continued*)

Country	Freq.	Percent	Cum.
Bulgaria	27	1.28	19.23
Chile	27	1.28	20.51
Colombia	27	1.28	21.79
Costa Rica	27	1.28	23.08
Croatia	27	1.28	24.36
Dominica	27	1.28	25.64
Dominican Republic	27	1.28	26.92
Ecuador	27	1.28	28.21
El Salvador	27	1.28	29.49
Fiji	27	1.28	30.77
Georgia	27	1.28	32.05
Grenada	27	1.28	33.33
Guatemala	27	1.28	34.62
Guyana	27	1.28	35.90
Hungary	27	1.28	37.18
India	27	1.28	38.46
Indonesia	27	1.28	39.74
Iran (Islamic Republic of)	27	1.28	41.03
Iraq	27	1.28	42.31
Jamaica	27	1.28	43.59
Jordan	27	1.28	44.87
Kazakhstan	27	1.28	46.15
Kuwait	27	1.28	47.44
Lebanon	27	1.28	48.72
Macedonia	27	1.28	50.00
Malaysia	27	1.28	51.28
Maldives	27	1.28	52.56
Marshall Islands	27	1.28	53.85
Mexico	27	1.28	55.13
Mongolia	27	1.28	56.41
Nauru	27	1.28	57.69
Oman	27	1.28	58.97

(*Continued*)

Table 7. (*Continued*)

Country	Freq.	Percent	Cum.
Pakistan	27	1.28	60.26
Palau	27	1.28	61.54
Panama	27	1.28	62.82
Paraguay	27	1.28	64.10
Peru	27	1.28	65.38
Philippines	27	1.28	66.67
Poland	27	1.28	67.95
Qatar	27	1.28	69.23
Romania	27	1.28	70.51
Saint Kitts and Nevis	27	1.28	71.79
Saint Lucia	27	1.28	73.08
Saint Vincent and the Grena	27	1.28	74.36
Samoa	27	1.28	75.64
Saudi Arabia	27	1.28	76.92
Sri Lanka	27	1.28	78.21
Suriname	27	1.28	79.49
Syrian Arab Republic	27	1.28	80.77
Thailand	27	1.28	82.05
Tonga	27	1.28	83.33
Trinidad and Tobago	27	1.28	84.62
Turkmenistan	27	1.28	85.90
Tuvalu	27	1.28	87.18
Ukraine	27	1.28	88.46
United Arab Emirates	27	1.28	89.74
Uruguay	27	1.28	91.03
Vanuatu	27	1.28	92.31
Venezuela	27	1.28	93.59
Bolivia	27	1.28	94.87
Russian Federation	27	1.28	96.15
Serbia	27	1.28	97.44
Turkey	27	1.28	98.72
West Bank and Gaza	27	1.28	100.00
Total	2,106	100.00	

Source: United Nations Statistics Division.

commodity exports. Note that our main objective is to understand the nature of the impact of trade with China. The low coefficients of commodity exports are due to the fact that, in addition to commodity exports to China, trade with many other countries affects industrialization in Africa.

Concluding Remarks

This chapter showed that the idea that South–South trade would contribute to export diversification for each trading partner involving their industrialization is not empirically validated in the case of Africa, although it is verified for ODCs. Indeed, we find that trade with China is a source of deindustrialization in Africa on the aggregate exports side, while it is a source of industrialization in ODCs. In the case of Africa, the underlying mechanism of aggregate exports impact is through heavy dependence on commodity exports to China. Thus, one of the challenges associated with Africa's industrialization is to transform the nature of its trade with China to make it a source of industrialization.

Given that trade with China is a source of deindustrialization in Africa, the question is how Africa can take advantage of this trade to industrialize. Africa could have both an advantage in its imports and exports with China. On the import side, African governments have to put in place trade policies aimed at reducing the cost of importing intermediate inputs and physical capital from China. This will reduce the costs of investment in manufacturing firms by reducing the part of investment's cost associated with capital and input. Consequently, the economic costs of the infrastructure deficit in these countries will be reduced. On the export side, African governments have two possibilities, which seem to be alternatives. First, the wage rate is increasing in China, so governments could attract Chinese firms to locally process commodities imported by China from African countries. However, in some economies on this continent, the quality of infrastructure and institutions generates production losses for industrial firms. Thus, African governments should provide incentives, such as special economic zones, in which all the conditions for manufacturing activities are satisfied. Second, as is already the case in some African countries, governments can trade commodities against the construction of road and electricity infrastructure by Chinese firms, which will eventually reduce the economic cost of investment in the industrial sector. However, such trade can be beneficial for African countries if the contracts are structured in such a way that the amount of raw materials extracted corresponds to the amount of investment in infrastructure by Chinese companies. Another condition is the equity between China and African countries in each contract. In any case, institutional issues (respect for the law, the fight against corruption, etc.) remain fundamental and are still far from being resolved.

Endnotes

1. In this chapter, the industrial sector represents only the manufacturing sector.
2. The hypotheses are related to the mobility of production factors (labor and capital), the equilibrium of trade, full employment, and the flexibility of real wages.
3. The three regions: Africa, China, and Western countries.
4. Note that for emerging economies, the positive and negative effects, respectively, of exports and imports are not significant.

References

Álvarez, R. and Claro, S. 2009. David versus goliath: The impact of Chinese competition on developing countries. *World Development*, 37(3): 560–571.

Amiti, M. and Konings, J. 2007. Trade liberalization, intermediate inputs, and productivity: Evidence from Indonesia. *American Economic Review*, 97(5): 1611–1638.

Aw, B.Y., Chung, S., and Roberts, M.J. 2000. Productivity and turnover in the export market: Microlevel evidence from the republic of Korea and Taiwan (China). *The World Bank Economic Review*, 14(1): 65–90.

Balsvik, R., Jensen, S., and Salvanes, K.G. 2015. Made in China, sold in Norway: Local labor market effects of an import shock. *Journal of Public Economics*, 127: 137–144.

Bernard, A.B. and Jensen, J.B. 1999. Exceptional exporter performance: Cause, effect, or both? *Journal of International Economics,* 47(1): 1–25.

Bigsten, A., Collier, P., Dercon, S., Fafchamps, M., Gauthier, B., Gunning, J.W., Habarurema, J., Oduro, A., Oostendorp, R., Pattillo, C., *et al.* 2000. *Exports and Firm-Level Efficiency in African Manufacturing.* Oxford: University of Oxford, Centre for the Institute of Economics and Statistics.

Bräutigam, D. and Tang, X. 2014. Going global in groups: Structural transformation and Chinas special economic zones overseas. *World Development,* 63: 78–91.

Bruno, M. and Sachs, J. 1982. Energy and resource allocation: A dynamic model of the Dutch disease. *The Review of Economic Studies,* 49(5): 845–859.

Buiter, W.H. and Purvis, D.D. 1980. Oil, disinflation, and export competitiveness: A model of the "Dutch disease". Technical Report, National Bureau of Economic Research.

Clerides, S.K., Lach, S., and Tybout, J.R. 1998. Is learning by exporting important? Micro-dynamic evidence from Colombia, Mexico, and Morocco. *The Quarterly Journal of Economics,* 113(3): 903–947.

Corden, W.M. 1984. Booming sector and Dutch disease economics: Survey and consolidation. *Oxford Economic Papers,* 36(3): 359–380.

Corden, W.M. and Neary, J.P. 1982. Booming sector and de-industrialisation in a small open economy. *The Economic Journal,* 92(368): 825–848.

David, H., Dorn, D., and Hanson, G.H. 2013. The China syndrome: Local labor market effects of import competition in the United States. *American Economic Review,* 103(6): 2121–2168.

Delgado, M.A., Farinas, J.C., and Ruano, S. 2002. Firm productivity and export markets: A nonparametric approach. *Journal of International Economics,* 57(2): 397–422.

Donoso, V., Martín, V., and Minondo, A. 2015. Do differences in the exposure to Chinese imports lead to differences in local labour market outcomes? An analysis for Spanish provinces. *Regional Studies,* 49(10): 1746–1764.

Dorosh, P. and Thurlow, J. 2014. Can cities or towns drive African development? Economywide analysis for Ethiopia and Uganda. *World Development,* 63: 113–123.

Ethier, W.J. 1982. National and international returns to scale in the modern theory of international trade. *The American Economic Review,* 72(3): 389–405.

Fafchamps, M., El Hamine, S., and Zeufack, A. 2007. Learning to export: Evidence from Moroccan manufacturing. *Journal of African Economies*, 17(2): 305–355.

Garroway, C., Hacibedel, B., Reisen, H., and Turkisch, E. 2012. The renminbi and poor-country growth. *The World Economy*, 35(3): 273–294.

Goldberg, P.K., Khandelwal, A.K., Pavcnik, N., and Topalova, P. 2010. Imported intermediate inputs and domestic product growth: Evidence from India. *The Quarterly Journal of Economics*, 125(4): 1727–1767.

Greenaway, D. and Milner, C. 1990. South-south trade: Theory, evidence, and policy. *The World Bank Research Observer*, 5(1): 47–68.

Greenaway, D., Girma, S., and Kneller, R. 2002. Does exporting lead to better performance? A microeconometric analysis of matched firms. GEP Working Paper (2002/09), University of Nottingham.

Grossman, G.M. and Helpman, E. 1991. Trade, knowledge spillovers, and growth. *European Economic Review*, 35(2–3): 517–526.

Gui-Diby, S.L. and Renard, M.-F. 2015. Foreign direct investment inflows and the industrialization of African countries. *World Development*, 74: 43–57.

Halpern, L., Koren, M., and Szeidl, A. 2015. Imported inputs and productivity. *American Economic Review*, 105(12): 3660–3703.

Isgut, A. 2001. What's different about exporters? Evidence from Colombian manufacturing. *Journal of Development Studies*, 37(5): 57–82.

Kaba, K., Lin, J.Y., and Renard, M.-F. 2022. Structural change and trade openness in sub-Saharan African countries. *The World Economy*, 45, 2101–2134.

Kang, S.J. and Lee, H. 2011. Foreign direct investment and de-industrialisation. *The World Economy*, 34(2): 313–329.

Kaya, Y. 2010. Globalization and industrialization in 64 developing countries, 1980–2003. *Social Forces*, 88(3): 1153–1182.

Kraay, A. 1999. Exportations et performances economiques: Etude d'un panel d'entreprises chi-noises. *Revue d'économie du développement*, 7(1): 183–207.

Lewis, W.A. 1954. Economic development with unlimited supplies of labour. *The Manchester School*, 22(2): 139–191.

Lin, J.Y. 2011. *From Flying Geese to Leading Dragons: New Opportunities and Strategies for Structural Transformation in Developing Countries.* Washington D.C: The World Bank, World Bank Policy Research Working Paper No. 5702.

Malgouyres, C. 2017. The impact of Chinese import competition on the local structure of employment and wages: Evidence from France. *Journal of Regional Science,* 57(3): 411–441.

Markusen, J.R. 1989. Trade in producer services and in other specialized intermediate inputs. *The American Economic Review,* 79(1): 85–95.

McMillan, M.S. and Rodrik, D. 2011. Globalization, structural change and productivity growth. Technical Report, National Bureau of Economic Research.

Meier, G.M., Steel, W.F., and Carroll, R.J. 1989. *Industrial Adjustment in Sub-Saharan Africa.* Oxford: Oxford University Press.

Mendez, O. 2015. The effect of Chinese import competition on Mexican local labor markets. *The North American Journal of Economics and Finance,* 34: 364–380.

Murphy, K.M., Shleifer, A., and Vishny, R. 1989. Income distribution, market size, and industrialization. *The Quarterly Journal of Economics,* 104(3): 537–564.

Newman, C., Page, J., Rand, J., Shimeles, A., Söderbom, M., and Tarp, F. 2016. *Made in Africa: Learning to Compete in Industry.* Washington, D.C: Brookings Institution Press.

Page, J. 1994. The east Asian miracle: Four lessons for development policy. *NBER Macroeconomics Annual,* 9: 219–269.

Rodrik, D. 2008. The real exchange rate and economic growth. *Brookings Papers on Economic Activity,* 2008(2): 365–412.

Rodrik, D. 2016. An African growth miracle? *Journal of African Economies,* 27(1): 10–27.

Romer, P.M. 1987. Growth based on increasing returns due to specialization. *The American Economic Review,* 77(2): 56–62.

Rowthorn, R. and Ramaswamy, R. 1999. Growth, trade, and deindustrialization. *IMF Staff Papers,* 46(1): 18–41.

Van Biesebroeck, J. 2005. Exporting raises productivity in sub-Saharan African manufacturing firms. *Journal of International Economics,* 67(2): 373–391.

Van Wijnbergen, S. 1984. The 'Dutch disease': A disease after all? *The Economic Journal,* 94(373): 41–55.

https://doi.org/10.1142/9789819815241_0011

Chapter 11

INDUSTRIAL POLICIES IN THE CONTEXT OF GREAT-POWER GOVERNANCE

Zhao Chen

China Center for Economic Studies, Fudan University, Shanghai, China
zhaochen@fudan.edu.cn

Introduction

China has implemented industry-specific policies to enable the faster and better development of certain strategic industries. The evolution of industrial policies, from the initial heavy industrial development strategy, which relied mainly on planning, to the current guiding industrial policies, such as the Five-Year Plans (FYPs) and industrial development strategies, can be considered a microcosm of China's "reform and opening up." Although China's industrial policies are still under constant adjustment, they have undergone a drastic change from the original state of "poverty and blankness" to the formation of a modern industrial system. This system has a full range of categories and a market-oriented technological innovation system, including firms as the main layers, along with a combination of industries, universities, and research institutes. Such a transformation represents a significant achievement in industrial development since the founding of the People's Republic of China. This achievement reflects the efforts of the Chinese people to pursue a better life, China's unique advantages of scale on its path of development, and the role of government policy in various areas, including science and technology, education, and health.

This chapter discusses the role of industrial policies in China and future directions for policy adjustment. More specifically, it discusses the rationality of industrial policies, who should implement them, and how they should be implemented, focusing on the goal of optimization. There is a wealth of research on specific industrial policies, along with broader analyses of industrial policies conducted from multiple perspectives.[1] At the same time, there remains an academic debate on industrial policies, especially regarding whether China really needs them.[2] The current work does not focus on the issue of whether an industrial policy is needed but focuses instead on how industrial policies can be optimally implemented. This work differs from existing studies in that it highlights two unique perspectives for understanding China's industrial policies. The first is a central–local government perspective, which is indispensable in the context of great-power governance. This perspective helps us understand possible deviations between central and local governments in terms of industrial policy goals and their implications for efficiency. The second concerns the general equilibrium effects of policies. This helps us recognize the possible unintended consequences of industrial policy implementation from the perspective of spillover effects. Both perspectives can facilitate a more comprehensive understanding of the effectiveness of industrial policies, highlighting, in particular, possible deviations from the overall goals of policy implementation.[3]

Next, starting with the concept of industrial policy, we first discuss theoretically the foundations and possible efficiency considerations of industrial policy. Then, we analyze the characteristics of industrial policy and possible deviations from overall development goals in the context of China's industrial policy practices. Finally, we discuss misconceptions and various experiences in industrial policy formulation, taking information asymmetry as the root cause, to propose guidelines for better policy implementation in the future.

Why is Industrial Policy Necessary?

What is industrial policy?

There are different definitions of industrial policy. In the author's view, simply put, any policy implemented for a specific industry can be called an industrial policy, which can be further divided into two main types.

The first type aims to promote the development of a specific industry and hence often contains a series of supportive measures. An example is the Decision of the State Council on Accelerating the Cultivation and Development of Strategic Emerging Industries (SC [2010] No. 32), issued by the State Council on October 10, 2010. This policy aimed to use supportive means to help seven major industries in China (i.e., energy saving and environmental protection, new-generation information technology, biology, high-end equipment manufacturing, new energy, new materials, and new-energy vehicles) achieve advanced global levels within 20 years.

The second type is industrial regulatory policy, which, as the name implies, is based on industry-specific regulatory measures and can be divided into competition policy and environmental regulatory policy. The purpose of competition policy is to maintain the competitive landscape of the market and to avoid the formation of monopolies, which can harm social welfare. For example, to prevent monopolistic behavior in the platform economy and guide operators to comply with laws and regulations, the State Administration for Market Regulation drafted the Antitrust Guidelines for the Platform Economy (Draft for Comments). This means that in the future, internet platform companies will be regulated by competition policy under the framework of the Antitrust Law. Environmental regulatory policy, meanwhile, aims to reduce environmental damage caused by firms' production activities. In recent years, the

Chinese government has attached increasing importance to environmental regulation. For example, since the 11th FYP, China has implemented a system for assessing the implementation of plans for controlling water pollution in key river basins and a strict verification system for reducing total pollutant emissions. Such measures have had effects on textile printing and dyeing, papermaking, and other water pollution-related industries.

By *industrial policy*, we often mean industrial support policy, which is the focus of this section. It should be noted, however, that policy boundaries are sometimes blurred. For example, China's innovation incentive policy provides policy incentives for firms' R&D investment in the form of tax incentives, which are available to all eligible high-tech firms. However, such a policy is more beneficial for certain industries with more intensive R&D investment. Another example is that China has widely implemented various economic zone policies, including economic and technological development zones, high-tech industrial parks, and export-processing zones. These policies are often called "place-based" policies because they are implemented in specific geographic areas. However, in the implementation of such policies, priority industries are often designated for development or attraction; thus, these policies have the characteristics of what we call "industrial support policies."

Theoretical foundations for industrial policy

What is the theoretical basis for industrial policy? In other words, why does the development of certain fields especially require the support of industrial policy? Simply put, there are two basic conditions: necessity and feasibility. We discuss necessity first and feasibility later.

One necessity of industrial policy arises from a lack of market coordination. If market coordination alone can facilitate the development of a specific industry, then industrial policy should not be implemented because, after all, there are costs associated with any policy implementation. Let us consider two real-world scenarios that may lead to a lack of market coordination.

The first scenario involves complementarity in production. For example, to attract investment, local governments today often try to bring in, as a package, firms that are important in the entire industrial chain. Such an approach is attractive to firms if a particular industry requires the spatial agglomeration of upstream and downstream firms. In this case, if the entire industry chain has not yet formed, relying solely on market mechanisms might require many firms to act alone. This would not only require high communication costs but also make coordination difficult owing to a lack of consensus among firms on whether the industry can take shape locally.

Such complementarity might manifest itself in other ways. For example, local governments might provide local public goods such as infrastructure for the construction of industrial zones. In this way, fixed costs can be better allocated, and the time for firms to be settled and put into production is greatly shortened. A typical phenomenon is that, to better attract investment, local governments often provide one-stop services. That is, the different functional departments involved are brought together to serve firms, which greatly improves the efficiency of government services and reduces firms' costs.

The second scenario involves the positive externalities of investment. If a part of the benefits of corporate investment is shared by other firms for free, then there are positive externalities to corporate investment. This leads to insufficient private investment by firms, thus requiring policy incentives for firms to further expand their investments. In reality, some cutting-edge technology areas often require firms to spend a great deal on R&D investment. For example, there are different potential technological paths — such as pure battery power, hybrid power, and fuel cell power — in the development of the new-energy vehicle industry, but which technological path is the most feasible? Firms are only able to answer this question after continuous investment in R&D. However, the first mover faces great risks. On the one hand, if a firm realizes that a certain technological path is not feasible after spending a lot of money, it will face great challenges in its operations; other firms, meanwhile, might learn from this firm, at little cost, that the technological path does not work. On the other hand, if a firm succeeds in its R&D, the new knowledge will benefit peer firms through imitation and learning. This knowledge-spillover effect becomes another important source of positive externalities for firms' innovation investments.

It is precisely because of these positive externalities that, from a society-wide perspective, individual firms' investment in innovation is likely to be inadequate, thus requiring incentivizing policies. In developing countries, less developed financial markets and poor interfirm credit systems may make government coordination all the more necessary and industrial policy thus more useful.

The other necessity of industrial policy pertains to social benefit. Is it necessary to have industrial policy support just because of insufficient market coordination? The answer is no. Because of limited resources, government support for certain areas will inevitably affect the development environment of other areas. For example, when the government supports the development of new-energy vehicles through industrial policies, more resources, such as talent and funds, will flow to new-energy vehicle companies, which will adversely affect the development of traditional automobile companies. Therefore, even if there is a lack of market coordination, policy support is only necessary when the development of a given industry has considerable social benefits. Taking R&D incentives as an example, only when the positive externalities are large enough can an industry truly grow via policies that incentivize R&D investment. There are at least two perspectives that can help us better understand the social benefits of industrial development.

First, there are industries with strong linkage effects. The so-called industrial linkage effect refers to the driving effect of the development of one industry on its related upstream and downstream industries through the input–output relationship. One reason the automobile industry has been favored by industrial policy is that it has a strong industrial linkage effect, which can have a strong driving effect on upstream raw material industries (e.g., steel, nonferrous metals, rubber, and petroleum) and other parts and components industries (e.g., instruments, accessories, and body and trim). Another typical example is the chip industry, which has strong linkage effects on downstream industries because chips are needed in an increasing number of manufacturing industries. Therefore, when the supply of high-end chips that China cannot produce is mainly controlled by the US, the chip industry becomes a "stranglehold" industry, which has a great effect on China's downstream manufacturing industry.

Second, there are forward-looking or emerging industries. Forward-looking industries are those that are currently in the nascent stage of the market but have great development potential in the future. The emergence of forward-looking industries is usually accompanied by the development and application of new technologies, so they often belong to emerging industries. Industrial policy favors this type of industry not only because of its huge market potential but also because the players are more likely to be on the same starting line, and it is easier to get a head start with policy support in the early stages. Similar considerations are behind China's increased efforts to build new infrastructure, such as 5G, the Internet of Things, industrial Internet, artificial intelligence, and data centers. Taking 5G technology as an example, since the first mention of 5G in a 2017 government work report, China has attached increasing importance to 5G in its national policies. The fact that Chinese firms are keeping pace with competitors and even leading the world in 5G technology provides support for the rationality of such industrial policies.

A lack of market coordination, coupled with significant social benefits, makes the implementation of industrial policies necessary. The next question is this: Can industrial policy be effective?

Comparative advantage and industrial policy

Theoretically, the industries supported by a country's industrial policies may be those in which the country has a comparative advantage as well as those in which the country does not. In the US, for example, the Endless Frontier Act, which was back in the public eye in 2021, aims to increase policy support for the innovation and development of key technology industries. The Act is a response to the concern in the US that its leadership in science and technology may be challenged. It is conceivable that the US government will pay more attention to the role of industrial policy in supporting key technology industries under the influence of the Act. Such industrial policies are often based on industries in which the US has a comparative advantage. Semiconductors, for example, are among the major areas in which investment will be increased under the Act — precisely an area in which China relies on supply from the US.

By contrast, industries supported by China as a developing country are often those in which it does not have a comparative advantage in the global context. In other words, the industrial policies of developing countries are usually focused on catching up with developed countries. Then, a question arises: Why do we not fully follow the comparative advantages of countries in the industrial division of labor? Is it possible, for example, to hand over production in high-tech areas to developed countries, such as the US, while China focuses on the production of labor-intensive products with more comparative advantage and then uses international trade for exchange with developed countries? Put differently, if China violates the division of labor principle by using industrial policies to support industries it does not have a comparative advantage in, will it be beneficial for China?

The US position on high-end chip manufacturing is the best answer to this question. For industrial areas such as chips, which have a great driving effect on downstream industries, if China is completely unable to produce alternative products with the resources it can mobilize, then China will be in an unfavorable negotiating position in the international division of labor. Therefore, to avoid being controlled by others, China needs to be able to integrate resources in the industrial chain to produce alternative products in such key areas. This does not mean that China must innovate key technologies, but that it should be able to compel foreign companies that do dominate key technologies to provide it with products at a reasonable price. When the key technologies are in the hands of only a few developed countries, however, it is likely that a reasonable price will be difficult to obtain. This is precisely why China has independently developed large aircraft, built its own space station, and strived to make breakthroughs in chip technology.

Such divisions of labor, which are seemingly set against comparative advantages, reflect strategic competition between countries and also make industrial policies more useful. The characteristics of China as a great power further enhance the rationality of the above-mentioned strategic competition. This is because, first, China has the strength to focus its resources on policy support for industries in which it does not have a comparative advantage yet. Second, when key areas are controlled by others, great powers need to pay higher prices for the huge market demand.[4] Third, a great power's economies of scale, or its huge domestic market, can better exert the scale effect and hence enable local firms to gradually foster their own comparative advantages.

While affirming the rationality of industrial policies in developing great powers, these considerations raise another question. In the case of China, for example, there are large developmental differences between regions. Therefore, which regions in a great power such as China should start developing the industries that are supported in violation of comparative advantage? Can the strategic division of labor between countries be equally applicable in this context? Here, we must emphasize an essential difference. Competition between countries reflects the interests of the respective countries, and there is no organization beyond countries that can truly coordinate or redistribute the interests of various countries. However, although competition between regions within a country also reflects the interests of various regions, there is the state — an overriding authority over local governments — that can coordinate or redistribute the interests of various regions. In other words, in the division of labor among regions within a country, there should not be a strategic division of labor that is against comparative advantages.[5] When choosing an industrial division of labor, the first thing local governments should consider is how to make the industry grow and expand — that is, to pursue the overall goal — which requires division of labor according to their respective comparative advantages, while the central government can perform the necessary coordination by means of, for example, transfer payments to take care of local interests.

In the practice of industrial policy, however, local governments may go against their local comparative advantages, leading to industrial policies that deviate from the maximization of long-term interests. Therefore, when discussing China's industrial policies, we need to place special emphasis on distinguishing such a central–local government perspective.

China's Industrial Policies

Here, we analyze China's industrial policies from both central and local perspectives.[6] In the 1950s and 1960s, Japan's industrial policies in areas such as automobiles and semiconductors appeared to be successful. Since the mid-1980s, China has also introduced industrial policies, often with specific regulations for the targeted industries, that need to be either developed or constrained. China's State Council has the power to make decisions about industrial policy formulation, and the National Development and Reform Commission (formerly the State Planning Commission and the State Development Planning Commission) leads the ministries and commissions in formulating specific industrial policies. Since the mid-1990s, various industrial policies have been promulgated separately in the form of a "catalog of industries," which is revised periodically, as the main basis for attracting investment.

In 1989, China promulgated the Decision of the State Council on the Key Points of Current Industrial Policies. Here, the term "industrial policies" is referred to directly in the title of the document. This decision clarified the priorities of encouragement or elimination/restriction in various areas of the national economy. Since then, industrial restructuring policies for various areas of the national economy have been successively issued. In response to various problems in China's economic development, the central government has also introduced policies to adjust and supplement the industrial structure. For example, the industrial policy for foreign direct investment clearly defined the areas in which foreign investment is encouraged or restricted. To help pillar industries catch up with developed countries and make gains in science, technology, and the economy, China's central government has issued industrial policies to encourage the development of basic or high-tech industries, along with place-based industrial policies intended to balance regional development. The central government has also issued policies to curb overcapacity, and in response to the 2008 financial crisis, it introduced policies specifically targeting certain industries. Table 1 lists the main types of industrial policies and the corresponding catalogs.

Industrial policies issued by the central government have two features that are worth mentioning. First, policies related to key industries account for the highest proportion of such policies.

Table 1. Types of industrial policies of the central government and their corresponding catalogs.

Policy type	Corresponding catalog
Industrial restructuring policy	Guidance Catalog for Industrial Restructuring
Industrial policy for foreign direct investment	Guidance Catalog for Foreign Investment Industries
Key industrial policy	Catalog of Major Technical Equipment and Products Supported by the State for Development
	Catalog of Imported Key Components and Raw Materials for Major Technical Equipment
	Guidelines for Key Areas of High-Tech Industrialization with Current Priorities
	Guidance Catalog of Key Products and Services in Strategic Emerging Industries
Place-based industrial policy	Guidance Catalog for Industrial Transfer (2012 Edition)
	Catalog of Encouraged Industries in the Western Region
Industrial policy to curb overcapacity	Catalog for the Elimination of Outdated Production Capacities, Processes, and Products
	Catalog for Preventing Duplicate Construction in Industrial and Commercial Investment (First Batch)

In terms of the time dimension, the central government issues key industrial policies in every FYP period, and their importance is becoming increasingly prominent. Second, industrial policies issued by the central government tend to have counter-cyclical characteristics; that is, if economic growth is in a trough, the central government is more likely to issue a large number of industrial policies. Thus, it seems that the central government aims to promote economic growth through the introduction of industrial policies.

In addition, under China's existing system, local governments have high motivation and autonomy to promote local economic development, and industrial policies have become an important means for local governments in this effort. Next, we examine the relationship between industrial policy and comparative advantage, considering the choice of key industries by the central and local governments in FYPs. This can help us to understand possible deviations from overall goals in the implementation of industrial policies from the perspective of central–local governance.

Industrial policies by the central government

Considering the slightly different purposes of formulating different types of industrial policies and the representativeness of key industrial policies, we focus exclusively on key industrial policies issued by central and local governments to study the patterns of the industrial policies themselves. We draw on the content of central and provincial FYPs for economic and social development to extract relevant information about key industrial policies. In the economic restructuring chapter of the FYPs, more than three-quarters of the content often pertains to key industry development, thus confirming the importance of key industries in industrial policies.

To sort out the key industries identified by the central government from the 9th to 12th FYPs, we extract industries and products involving the keywords "pillar industries," "advantage industries," "emerging industries," "vigorous development," "key cultivation," "active development," and "key development" from the chapters on economic restructuring in the FYPs. We then correlate them with the two-digit codes in the Industrial Classification for National Economic Activities to extract the key industries for the central government in each FYP period.

As shown in Table 2, the key industries during the 9th FYP period were basic industries that are related to the national economy and people's livelihoods and have a major driving effect on the national economy. The goal was to establish the pillar industries of the national economy. Since the 10th FYP period, the key industries have been similar. All are high-tech industries, reflecting an aim to be at the frontier of science and technology, foster a new economic growth engine, and achieve strong economic gains.

Next, we examine whether the key industries chosen by the central government have local comparative advantages in different regions of China. Whether a region has a comparative advantage in an industry might very well depend on whether the local resource endowment, institutional environment, and market size are more suited to the development of that industry. However, this is difficult to measure directly. An alternative approach is to look directly at the results, that is, to determine whether there is a comparative advantage based on the development status of different industries. If a certain industry in one region is more developed than the national average, we can assume this region has local comparative advantage — also known as explicit comparative advantage — in this industry, which

Table 2. Central government's key industries from the 9th to 12th FYP periods.

Period	Key industrial policy of the central government
9th FYP (1996–2000)	Machinery industry
	Automotive industry
	Electronics industry
	Petrochemical industry
10th FYP (2001–2005)	High-tech industry
11th FYP (2006–2010)	High-tech industry
	Equipment manufacturing industry
12th FYP (2011–2015)	Strategic emerging industries

can manifest as a higher-than-national-average proportion of employment or output in that industry in the local employment or output of all industries.

Using this method, we can examine whether different regions of China have comparative advantages in key industries identified by the central government. We find that, on average, at the beginning of each FYP period, no regions at the province level had comparative advantages in the central government's key industries. The reason is that the key industries chosen by the central government are often at the frontier of technology, and those industries are usually concentrated in a few developed regions at city level. Further investigation reveals that the central and western regions have never shown an obvious comparative advantage in key industries, while the eastern region has increasingly shown such an advantage.

Then, in terms of industrial policy implementation, which provinces in China should promote the key industries the central government wishes to develop? According to the above discussion regarding comparative advantage and division of labor, provinces should implement industrial policies in different ways according to their comparative advantages. Based on this logic, the developed eastern region should become the main area for promoting and implementing the key industrial policies of the central government. However, this is not necessarily the case in reality, as we illustrate in the following by examining the industrial policies of local governments.[7]

Industrial policies by local governments

To examine whether local governments choose and support industries suitable for local development according to their comparative advantages and local conditions, we sort out from provincial FYPs the local key industries in 30 provinces (excluding Tibet) in mainland China from the 9th to 12th FYP periods.

Table 3 shows the proportions of local key industries overlapping with central key industries. The proportion for the eastern region is higher than that for other regions. From the 9th to 12th FYP periods, local governments increasingly tended to take the key

Table 3. Proportions of local key industries belonging to central key industries.

	9th FYP	10th FYP	11th FYP	12th FYP
Eastern region	0.525	0.753	0.464	0.708
Central region	0.38	0.425	0.469	0.523
Western region	0.327	0.385	0.416	0.472

industries chosen by the central government as their local key industries for development. This was largely in line with local comparative advantage in the eastern region but was likely to deviate from local comparative advantage in the central and western regions.

With further comparison, we find that the key industries chosen by the central and western regions that also belong to the central government's key industries often do not have local comparative advantages. Meanwhile, the key industries chosen by the central and western regions that do not belong to the central government's key industries usually do have local comparative advantages. In other words, when local governments in the central and western regions follow the central government in choosing key industries, it is not because they are unable to correctly recognize their own comparative advantages. Why, then, do the central and western regions blindly follow the central government in choosing industrial policies?

One possible explanation is that doing so makes local governments more likely to receive policy resources from the central government. For example, local applications for national economic zones are more likely to be successful when they are oriented toward the central government's key industries. However, such behavior does not really foster new comparative advantages for local areas. While it might be theoretically possible that less developed regions could successfully foster new comparative advantages, the likelihood of this occurring is relatively low, making it misaligned with the principle of efficiency. The principles of comparative advantage and division of labor have already shown us that it is more costly for less developed regions to go against their comparative advantages when they could engage in other production activities in which they do have comparative advantages.

Broad industry-based policies

In addition to supportive industry-based policies, there are broad policies that are not called industrial policies but have the nature of industrial policy. In recent years, for example, China's central government has proposed to "accelerate the construction of new infrastructure such as information networks." This development idea emphasizes "new infrastructure" such as 5G networks and data centers, which are directly related to knowledge- or technology-intensive industries. As a form of public good, infrastructure usually has positive externalities. Compared with traditional infrastructure, new infrastructure is more likely to be the weak link in China's future economic development. Therefore, the government's emphasis on "new infrastructure" will also provide a favorable external environment for the development of knowledge- and technology-intensive industries, so that infrastructure construction is also industry based to some extent.

Economic zone programs might also have an industrial policy dimension. These are primarily place-based policies since they usually define a specific geographical area, and firms in those areas are eligible for the corresponding preferential treatment. There are various types of economic zones in China, including special economic zones, economic and technological development zones, high-tech industrial parks, and export-processing zones. Shenzhen and other special economic zones are typical examples of institutional pilots in the early stages of China's reform and opening up. The policies at that time were mainly exploratory and experimental. Later economic zones were more closely associated with specific industries. When the establishment of an economic and technological development zone, a high-tech industrial park, or an export-processing zone is approved, its key development directions are often specified (e.g., "automobiles and parts," "biomedicine," "green food," "industrial automation equipment," "electronic appliances"). As a result, development zone programs are also industry based and have the nature of industrial policies. Different from the early special economic zone pilots, subsequent economic zones have more often served to provide convenience and coordination for firms in addition to offering preferential policies. For example, on April 27, 2000, when the State Council approved the establishment of export-processing zones under the supervision of customs, the export-processing zones were located within the established economic zones to facilitate operations and provide customs clearance convenience.

What are the actual effects of economic zones? If establishing an economic zone only attracts firms from other places, then even if we see an increased number of firms in the development zone, as well as more local output and employment, we still cannot necessarily regard the zone as a promoter of economic growth. This is because the real effect is to merely redistribute the existing "pie" among different regions, not to make the pie bigger. If, to boost the local economy, local governments compete to attract investment by establishing economic zones, but they disregard their local comparative advantages and even lower the price of industrial land or relax environmental regulation, they will likely deviate from the principle of efficiency and end up with a heavy debt burden.[8] However, if the economic zone enables the spatial agglomeration of a large number of excellent firms while generating a multiplying effect with the help of more frequent interactions between firms and employees, then the pie is made bigger, which is an additional benefit generated by the construction of the development zone.[9]

Innovation policy in China also has the nature of industrial policy. Although China is a developing country, its government has always focused on the independent innovation and technological progress of firms, providing an important institutional guarantee for continued economic growth. As early as 1988, the Central Committee of the Communist Party of China (CPC) and the State Council implemented the Torch Program, which aimed to accelerate the development of China's high-tech industries. This spawned the emergence of various technology-based incubators for small- and medium-sized firms, national high-tech industrial development zones, and productivity promotion centers throughout the country. Because of its emphasis on high-tech industries, the Program has more likely benefitted industries such as electronic information, biomedicine, new materials, and energy conservation and new energy, making it, to some extent, oriented toward specific industries. Moreover, in these industries, we are more likely to see the characteristics of insufficient market coordination and greater social benefits related to the necessity of industrial policy.

Policies such as the Torch Program have had far-reaching implications for the transformation and upgrading of China's economy. Since the 1990s, and especially after 2008, Chinese firms' investment in innovation has grown rapidly. In 1996, China's R&D spending as a percentage of the GDP was lower than that of India, but by 2011, it had surpassed that of Canada and was approaching that of the US, which is an innovation leader. A number of outstanding firms have emerged in China whose innovation performance has made a mark in the international market. Chinese firms' innovation investment is inseparable from the incentivizing effect of innovation policies, especially the R&D incentive policy for high-tech firms, which provides large tax incentives for high-tech firms that meet certain R&D intensity standards. Although this is an innovation incentive policy, high-tech industries are the main beneficiaries, and their R&D investment has reached as high as 70% of that of all Chinese firms.

The theoretical foundation for innovation policies lies mainly in the fact that firms' innovation investment has positive externalities. That is, after a firm increases its R&D investment, it also enhances the efficiency of other firms in the industry.[10] Although this effect may be minimal for other firms in a single industry, as long as the innovation policy has a clear incentivizing effect on the R&D investment of all firms in the industry, the efficiency improvement of the whole industry will become significant under the joint promotion.

For a developing great power such as China, which has large regional disparities, innovation policies may deviate from optimality if there is a lack of coordination between regions. This further demonstrates the need to focus on the effective central government coordination of regions while leveraging the advantages a great power possesses. Such coordination is difficult, however. On the one hand, there is an information asymmetry between the central government and local governments. For example, local governments are more aware of the industries they have local comparative advantages in and are more likely to develop their economies according to local conditions; the central government, meanwhile, does not possess the same information. On the other hand, there are certain conflicts between the central government and local governments, with the former more concerned with overall development and the latter more concerned with local interests. In reality, therefore, their local industrial policies may be implemented against their own comparative advantages, thus deviating from the overall optimal goals, and the central government is not always able to effectively coordinate. For example, some areas have introduced various local financial support related to high-tech firms and have even linked the assessment of local officials with the performance of local high-tech firms. For some areas that did not already have comparative advantages in high-tech industries, this could place undue emphasis on firms' innovation investment, leading to misallocations in the investment of innovation resources.

Misconceptions and Experiences in the Implementation of Industrial Policies

Next, based on different industrial policy practices, we discuss possible misconceptions in policy implementation from a general perspective. We then summarize the experience gained and lessons learned from the design of specific policies.

Potential misconceptions in the implementation of industrial policies

Industrial policies are prone to the misconception that government intervention replaces the market mechanism. The existence of positive externalities does not necessarily require government intervention; it depends on whether the market can coordinate itself. In a large shopping mall, for example, the presence of well-known brands can have a traffic-attracting effect, making the entire mall more popular and thus creating positive externalities for other businesses. Since the well-known brands cannot charge other businesses directly, is government intervention needed to increase incentives for the well-known brands to move into the mall? The answer is, in fact, no. In reality, the large mall offers premium store space to well-known luxury brands with low rent to attract traffic, while other businesses pay the mall in the form of rent, thereby "internalizing" externalities by means of the market mechanism. In this case, we do not need to replace the market mechanism with government intervention.

Even with industrial policies, we should avoid situations where government intervention replaces market mechanisms. This is manifested by the fact that governments artificially choose specific firms as policy support targets when it would be more reasonable for policies to be oriented toward the entire industry, giving all potential firms equal opportunities to compete. Such policy misconceptions might also be evident in the fact that once policy support appears in the form of projects, it often involves the *ex post* acceptance of projects or evaluation of the effectiveness of the policy. In this case, the government may replace the market mechanism.

The importance of information in the implementation of industrial policies is reflected in the above policy misconceptions. Compared with entrepreneurs, the government often has little awareness of the complex information behind the development of firms and industries and, thus, is unable to make accurate judgments about firms' development status under policy support. In other words, if firms' development under policy support is not satisfactory, the government still does not know whether it is attributable to external market risks in the industry, to a lack of effort from the entrepreneur of the firms, or to insufficient firm capabilities.

From the implementation of the innovation-driven development strategy proposed at the 18th CPC National Congress to the 14th FYP, which proposed adhering to innovation-driven development and shaping new development advantages, it seems clear that China's industrial policies will increasingly emphasize policy support for corporate innovation in the future. The more innovation-intensive the field is, the less information advantage the government has, and the easier it is for industrial policies to fall into misconceptions. For example, in the field of chip technology, in which China is subjected to the stranglehold of the US, chip manufacturers have been established in many places under policy support. However, the government soon realized that industrial policy cannot count on enthusiasm alone and that it needs to rely more on rational mechanism design to introduce competition and regulate all aspects of policy implementation. This requires designing a reasonable policy framework for different industrial policies according to specific situations, which will be discussed in the following section.

Finally, we should emphasize that because the government lacks information advantages compared with the market or entrepreneurs in choosing industry directions, industrial policies cannot be limited to certain known targets; rather, they must leave sufficient room for the development of unknown industries. This is especially true for the development of emerging industries. Before the government forms consensus on the development of emerging industries, some entrepreneurs must be the first to make judgments about potential market opportunities and put them into practice. Therefore, what the government should focus on is providing a favorable market environment for the development of unknown emerging industries.

Information asymmetry and industrial policy design

In the design of industrial policy, the government must consider the difficulties that may arise from information asymmetry. For example, in the incentive policies for firms' R&D investment, the government cannot easily be informed about whether firms might engage in R&D relabeling; that is, it does not know whether the R&D investment is possibly exaggerated. This has long posed a difficult problem for researchers. It is known that firms must have engaged in R&D relabeling under preferential policies, but it is not clear how serious it is, and it is unknown whether the existence of R&D relabeling necessarily means R&D incentives are ineffective.

We need to first recognize that information asymmetry inevitably exists and cannot be changed. That being the case, it might not be optimal to completely eliminate R&D relabeling since it would require huge regulatory costs for the government, which would outweigh the gains. A more feasible policy goal would be to control R&D relabeling within a certain range with reasonable regulatory costs while also incentivizing firms to significantly increase their real R&D investment. This requires sound policy design by the government.

China's InnoCom program for high-tech firms is one such measure, which provides substantial corporate income tax cuts to firms that report R&D investment over a given threshold or "notch." Those firms usually have great innovation potential. Basically, this policy approach aims to invigorate large firms and relax control over small ones. By contrast, European and North American countries generally do not set such high policy thresholds and enable a wider range of firms to enjoy a certain percentage of tax credits after investing in R&D. In other words, the number of firms in Europe and the US directly affected by this policy approach far exceeds that in China. Policy simulations in a previous study by the author showed that under the models in Europe and the US, governments need to regulate a larger number of firms, which leaves individual firms less regulated and encourages R&D relabeling by firms, affecting the actual effectiveness of the policy. Under China's InnoCom program, the government can focus its limited regulatory power on a few innovative firms, which can more effectively reduce R&D relabeling and ultimately leverage more corporate R&D investment with lower financial costs.[11]

How to accommodate both overall and multidimensional goals in policy implementation

Difficulties related to information asymmetry in policy implementation can also appear in other forms. Next, in the context of specific policies, we consider two situations in which overall and multidimensional goals may be adversely affected. The presence of information asymmetry may cause industrial policies, whether for water pollution or new-energy vehicle subsidies, to fail to simultaneously cover all aspects. This again reminds us of the need to consider possible general equilibrium effects when formulating industrial policies, that is, the possible spillover effects of policies in different dimensions.

The first situation considers the water pollution regulatory policy, which is regulatory rather than supportive. We will see that the policy might have spatial spillover effects. That is, a policy implemented in one place might be effective locally but have unintended negative effects in other places. Thus, such a policy might fail to accommodate the overall goal.

In 2005, the central government acknowledged the serious challenges posed by water pollution and specified in the 11th FYP (2006–2010) emission-reduction targets for chemical oxygen demand (COD), a major water pollutant, with higher requirements for more polluted provinces. The government also linked the achievement of emission-reduction targets with the promotion of local officials, providing incentives for local officials to meet the targets.

However, by the end of the 11th FYP, water pollution remained severe in the Yangtze River Basin. According to data from the Ministry of Water Resources, the total discharge of industrial wastewater into the Yangtze River increased from 20.4 billion tons in 2005 to 22.7 billion tons in 2010. In addition, the extent of rivers in the basin that did not meet drinking-water standards increased from 27% in 2005 to 33% in 2010. Why did the water quality of the Yangtze River continue to deteriorate despite government efforts to reduce COD emissions? A previous study by the author found that it was likely due to differences in the stringency of water pollution regulation in cities along the Yangtze River, with generally less stringent regulations in upstream cities and more stringent ones in downstream cities. Thus, the production activities of water-polluting firms shifted from downstream cities to upstream cities, eventually leading to the limited improvement of water quality in downstream areas but a significant deterioration of water quality in upstream areas.[12]

The above example shows that coordination among regions needs to be considered in the implementation of industrial policies. Otherwise, even if the activities of polluters slow down and water quality improves in the developed downstream areas, the overall effectiveness of the policy is greatly reduced. More generally, if local governments in less developed regions have as their primary goal the pursuit of GDP, then different environmental regulations may cause less developed regions to become havens for pollution activities. To reverse this situation, the central government needs to consider regional differences when implementing policies and carry out the necessary coordination by means of its authority. Since the downstream areas of most developing countries are usually closer to major seaports, they are economically more developed than the upstream areas. Therefore, this analysis can provide general implications for water pollution regulation in developing countries and remind policymakers to avoid worsening the situation in less developed upstream areas when addressing water pollution in more developed downstream areas.

Next, we analyze another industrial policy — the subsidy policy for new-energy vehicles. We will see that policy spillover effects can even occur across different attribute dimensions of the same product. If policymakers ignore this, the industrial policy can be counterproductive.

New-energy vehicles are one of the seven strategic emerging industries identified by the State Council, which, in its Energy Saving and New-Energy Vehicle Industry Development Plan (2012–2020), noted that the development of new-energy vehicles is "a strategic measure to accelerate the transformation and upgrading of the automobile industry, and cultivate new economic growth pole and international competitive advantage." Since 2016, China has promoted new-energy vehicles nationwide, subsidizing the purchase of such vehicles and linking subsidies to driving range. For example, the 2016 policy states that pure electric passenger cars with a driving range of 100–150 km will receive a subsidy of 25,000 yuan per vehicle, while those with a range of 150–250 km will receive a subsidy of 45,000 yuan per vehicle. The policy links the subsidy to the driving range in hopes that firms will invest more R&D resources to produce more environment-friendly electric vehicles. Ideally, subsidies should cover the increased costs of innovation so that new technologies can be applied more quickly. In this process, China's automobile industry can establish an advantage in the field of new-energy vehicles, eventually achieving the purpose of government subsidies.

However, because of information asymmetry, firms are not necessarily motivated by such subsidies to extend the driving range of electric vehicles through R&D. In a recent study,[13] we found that the curb weight and motor power of pure electric vehicles were abnormally decreased to achieve the target driving range. Specifically, the average curb weight dropped by 18%, or 243.08 kg, and motor power decreased by more than 25 kW, or 36% of the average motor power of all models. The power performance and energy efficiency of those models also deteriorated. The maximum speed dropped by about 14.08 km/h, or more than 10% of the average maximum speed of all models, and the energy-to-weight ratio increased by more than 9% of the average.

The above findings suggest that industrial policies that use certain product dimensions as benchmarks will likely lead to an unexpected deterioration in the performance of other dimensions of the product. That is, a poorly designed industrial policy may struggle to accommodate multidimensional policy goals. Although we have only considered supportive policies for new-energy vehicles, the implications are applicable to the implementation of broader industrial policies.

Industrial Policies toward Long-Term, Overall, and Multidimensional Goals

Here, we combine theory and practice to summarize the experience of China's industrial policies from a more general perspective. The goal is for industrial policies to accommodate long-term, overall, and multidimensional development goals. For China, as a developing country with significant heterogeneity in regional development, achieving policy goals requires considering, first, the perspective of great-power governance and, second, the laws of industrial policies themselves.

Industrial policies in the context of great-power governance

The potential social benefits of industrial policy are accentuated by the economies of scale of great powers. The need for industrial policy is further increased by the lack of market coordination in developing countries. Thus, as we have seen, industrial policies have been widely implemented in China. In fact, we can still find industrial policies in developed countries such as the US, especially in frontier or emerging industries, where such policies stimulate innovation.

China has its own potential advantages in industrial policy practices, as demonstrated by its ability to form development concepts and formulate policy frameworks rapidly under central government guidance, which are then implemented by local governments. Properly applied, this system can reflect China's institutional advantages, especially regarding the role of the central government in coordinating the market mechanism. Nevertheless, we also need to be aware of potential problems that may arise under this system. If the efficiency principle is not adequately reflected, inefficiencies that impede competition can arise in the implementation of industrial policy. In particular, if impediments to market competition are linked to ownership preferences (e.g., policy bias in favor of state-owned enterprises), they are likely to raise international concerns as China's international power increases. In the integrated global economy, China should face up to such concerns in industrial policy formulation and make adjustments in conjunction with market system construction. China needs to adapt to changes in the international environment and make more use of market mechanisms and price signals when implementing policies, as opposed to government intervention and subsidies. China further needs to maintain ownership neutrality in policy implementation.

China needs to consider interregional coordination in industrial policy implementation because of significant regional disparities. For industrial policies to accommodate long-term, overall, and multidimensional development goals, local governments need to abandon the consideration of the strategic division of labor between countries. Especially for areas involved in innovation, the high spatial agglomeration of innovation activities requires rejecting the idea of different regions acting independently. Accordingly, the central government should compensate potentially affected regions with transfer payments and other means by taking advantage of policy's effect on making the pie bigger. The central government should also reconsider the need to adopt different assessment standards for different regions in the central–local governance relationship, and it should not emphasize GDP assessment for different regions using a one-size-fits-all approach. Regions differ in their stages of development, local resource endowments, and residents' interests. In this regard, the central government often does not possess the unique information that local governments possess. The central government should therefore introduce more evaluations from local people in the assessment of local governments. As General Secretary Xi noted during an inspection of Zhoushan in Zhejiang Province, "[i]t is not us, but the people, who have the final say on whether our cadres are good or not."

Several principles of industrial policies

We first propose several principles that industrial policies should follow and then explain the specific policy measures at different levels.

First, the implementation of inclusive industrial policies should be prioritized so that policies have a wider range of potential beneficiaries. The more high-end the policy goals for future industrial development, the greater the requirement that industrial policies not be targeted or selective but inclusive. This can help avoid the government's information disadvantage in industrial development, and judgments about industrial development can be delegated to entrepreneurs for implementation. This requires industrial policies to be oriented toward long-term regional development. It is also necessary to formulate talent policies and industrial financing policies that adapt to the positioning of industrial development to provide a good environment for industrial development. In addition, inclusive industrial policies can better reflect the principle of ownership neutrality, and, except for areas involving national security, such an approach is more consistent with fair competition in the market economy.

An important example is the talent policy that benefits industries in general. For example, the government increases investment in public resources for education to create a favorable environment for talent development. This can promote industry development as a whole since the concentration of talent benefits the development of both existing and potential industries.

Second, reasonable policy coverage needs to be determined for targeted industrial policies. Sometimes, certain industrial policies must be targeted or selective to highlight their role in promoting specific industries. Then, reasonable policy coverage should be determined for such industrial policies based on the following principles: (1) The coverage of the industrial area should be wide rather than narrow. For example, the industrial policy for new energy should not be limited to solar energy or wind energy but should give the same policy space to the development of related industries such as bioenergy and geothermal energy. Even though the government clearly knows that the new energy industry is a strategic industry with various options to choose from, the specific subsectors for development should be chosen with the help of entrepreneurs, not government designation. (2) The coverage of specific activities should be narrow rather than wide. Taking the integrated circuit industry as an example, compared with silicon wafer manufacturing, this highly technology-intensive design link requires more support from strategic industrial policies. In this case, policy coverage needs to be subdivided into different activities within the industry.

Third, the narrower the policy coverage, the more necessary it is to introduce a competitive mechanism. Industrial policies with narrow coverage should ensure a low threshold, high competition, and the ability to enter and exit. Here, a low threshold means there can be a technical threshold, but there should be no corporate identity-related barriers to enjoying support policies. That is, industrial policies should abandon discriminatory conditions related to firm characteristics, such as size, history, ownership, and place of registration. The ability to enter and exit means the enjoyment of supportive industrial policies is not permanent, and a corresponding exit mechanism should be developed in advance. For example, firms that have enjoyed policy support but exhibited poor market performance should be withdrawn in a timely manner, leaving the policy opportunities to other firms that compete with them.

Finally, industrial policies also need to be coordinated with other policies. For example, economic activities in an inclusive policy environment are likely to form spatial agglomerations according to the laws of the market. This means that, eventually, there will be differences in aggregate development between regions. This is particularly true for innovation activities.[14] This does not mean, however, that less developed regions cannot share the benefits derived from the agglomeration areas. As long as factors can flow freely, talent from less developed regions can flow into the centers of innovation activities to share the benefits of innovation. Since this is conducive to making the pie bigger, the central government can also provide the necessary support to less developed regions through transfer payments. Put differently, it is often the large metropolitan areas with a few large cities at their core that represent China in international competition; hence, industrial policies likewise impose similar requirements on regional development policies. Specifically, the development of frontier industries necessitates adequate mobility and competition among talent, which requires megacities to reduce the cost of factor mobility, particularly by easing access to household registration for immigrant populations and reducing commuting costs for economically active populations. Megacities should become the core hubs of intercity transportation networks. The establishment of a rapid urban agglomeration transportation network can facilitate the rational allocation of resources among regions and strengthen the agglomeration effect of megacities while reducing the negative effect of rising land prices on megacities.

Acknowledgments

This work was supported by the National Social Science Foundation of China (21ZDA009).

Endnotes

1. A recent work by Jiang *et al.* analyzes China's industrial policies from multiple perspectives. For details, see Jiang *et al.* (2021).
2. Justin Yifu Lin and Weiying Zhang publicly debated the pros and cons of industrial policy, as reported in *China Economic Weekly*, no. 44, 2016, under the title "Justin Yifu Lin vs. Weiying Zhang: A debate of the century on industrial policy." The sixth issue of *Comparative Studies* in 2016 also published a series of relevant articles, including J. Y. Lin, "Industrial policy and national development: A new structural economics perspective"; W. Zhang, "Why I oppose industrial policy: A debate with Justin Yifu Lin"; J. Y. Lin, "Several responses to Professor Weiying Zhang"; and Guoqiang Tian, "Right and wrong in the debate between Justin Yifu Lin and Weiying Zhang: With a discussion on thoughtful scholarship and academic thought." Subsequently, Yong Wang further elaborated on industrial policy from the perspective of New Structural Economics (Yong, 2017).
3. These two perspectives are not limited to specific types of industrial policies, and the present study does not simply discuss case-specific industrial policies. Therefore, this chapter does not cover the extensive literature on specific industrial policies.
4. China has become a global manufacturing base precisely because of its great-power advantage. The large concentration of production capacity has led to most chip application-related industries being located in China. These, in turn, are tied to the interests of other countries through the high integration of global industrial chains. Thus, the US' stranglehold on the chip field affects firms in other countries, including the US itself.
5. For a theoretical analysis of the strategic division of labor at the local government level and its consequences, see Lu *et al.* (2004). See also Lu *et al.* (2007).
6. This part is based on Zhao and Chen (2019).
7. Admittedly, there may be some exceptions, in which factors related to comparative advantage might nevertheless exist. For example, the

military industry in northeast China is related to the historical local development of heavy industry. Similarly, the construction of Tianyan ("Sky-eye") (Five-hundred-meter Aperture Spherical radio Telescope, or FAST) in Guizhou is related to the local natural environment (e.g., altitude and landform).

8. Empirical studies of China's development zones have not yielded entirely consistent findings. Some studies have emphasized the positive effects of development zones, such as the following: Wang (2013), Alder *et al.* (2016), and Lu *et al.* (2019). Others have focused on the misallocation of resources or loss of efficiency in the construction of development zones: Zeng *et al.* (2017) and Chen *et al.* (2019). Also, there are studies noting that the effects of industrial policies depend on whether local comparative advantages are utilized, including Chen *et al.* (2017).
9. For example, a recent study found that the spatial concentration of R&D personnel can significantly enhance local innovation generation: Moretti (2021).
10. The aforementioned study by Moretti (2021) is a good example.
11. Regarding the effects of innovation incentive policies on Chinese high-tech firms, see Chen *et al.* (2021).
12. A more detailed analysis can be found in Chen *et al.* (2018).
13. For details, see Zhou *et al.* (2021).
14. For example, the aforementioned study by Moretti (2021) found that the top 10 industrial clusters in the US attracted 69%, 77%, and 59% of patent inventors in the areas of computer science, semiconductors, and biology, respectively.

References

Alder, S., Shao, L., and Zilibotti, F. 2016. Economic reforms and industrial policy in a panel of Chinese cities. *Journal of Economic Growth*, 21(4): 305–49.

Chen, B., Lu, M., Timmins, C., and Xiang, K. 2019. Spatial misallocation: Evaluating place-based policies using a natural experiment in China. NBER Working Paper 26148.

Chen, Z., Poncet, S., and Xiong, R. 2017. Inter-industry relatedness and industrial-policy efficiency: Evidence from China's export-processing zones. *Journal of Comparative Economics*, 45(4): 809–826.

Chen, Z., Kahn, M., Liu, Y., and Wang, Z. 2018. The consequences of spatially differentiated water pollution regulation in China. *Journal of Environmental Economics and Management*, 88: 468–485.

Chen, Z., Liu, Z., Suárez Serrato, J.C., and Xu, D.Y. 2021. Notching R&D investment with corporate income tax cut in China. *American Economic Review*, 111(7): 2065–2111.

Jiang *et al.* 2021. *Understanding China's Industrial Policies.* Beijing: CITIC Press Group.

Lu, M., Chen, Z., and Yan, J. 2004. Increasing return, development strategy and regional economic segmentation. *Economic Research Journal*, 1: 54–63.

Lu, M., Chen, Z., and Yang, Z. 2007. Equality and growth hand in hand: Increasing returns, strategic behavior and efficiency loss in the division of labor. *China Economic Quarterly*, 2: 92–117.

Lu, Y., Wang, J., and Zhu, L. 2019. Place-based policies, creation, and agglomeration economies: Evidence from China's economic zone program. *American Economic Journal: Economic Policy*, 11(3): 325–360.

Moretti, E. 2021. The effect of high-tech clusters on the productivity of top inventors. *American Economic Review*, 111(10): 3328–3375.

Wang, J. 2013. The economic effect of special economic zones: Evidence from Chinese municipalities. *Journal of Development Economics*, 101: 133–147.

Yong, Y. 2017. On efficient market and facilitating state: Industrial policies from new structural economics perspective. *Study & Exploration*, 4: 100–104.

Zeng, S., Sun, W., Wu, J., and Kahn, M.E. 2017. The birth of edge cities in China: Measuring the effects of industrial parks policy. *Journal of Urban Economics*, 100: 80–103.

Zhao, T. and Chen, Z. 2019. Comparative advantage and central, local industrial policies in China. *The Journal of World Economy*, 10: 98–119.

Zhou, C., Zhao, C., and Shiyi, C. 2021. Stepwise subsidies and companies' strategic responses: Analysis based on new-energy vehicle manufacturers. *Economic Perspectives*, 2: 32–49.

https://doi.org/10.1142/9789819815241_0012

Chapter 12

FIVE PERSPECTIVES ON CHINA'S INDUSTRIAL POLICIES

Xiaohuan Lan

School of Economics, Fudan University
Shanghai, China
xhlan@fudan.edu.cn

Introduction

In the past two years, both the United States and the European Union have increased government investment in the semiconductor industry to provide support for research, development, and production. For instance, in 2022, the United States passed the CHIPS (Creating Helpful Incentives to Produce Semiconductors) for America Act, whereas the European Union is currently reviewing the European Chips Act. These are typical examples of industrial policies. In fact, both in the past and present, developed countries have widely employed industrial policies. Take the well-known company Apple as an example. Back in the 1970s and 1980s, it received investments from the government-backed "Small Business Investment Company" program. Nearly all the crucial technologies integrated into Apple's smartphones, such as lithium batteries, liquid crystal displays, multi-touch screens, and GPS, stem from various technology research and development (R&D) projects supported by the government. Moreover, Apple also enjoys various tax subsidies and benefits, including the common R&D expense tax refunds and tax exemptions for its specific products categorized as "educational devices." In addition, on the international stage, whether it's entering foreign markets or engaging in international intellectual property disputes, Apple has the backing of the United States government (Mazzucato, 2015).

During China's rapid industrial development, various industrial policies from both the central and local governments have been commonplace. However, the effects of these policies have been a subject of significant academic debate (Lin *et al.*, 2018). Supporters argue that industrial policies not only promote the development of specific industries but also serve as a crucial part of the national development strategy, guiding industrial upgrades and overall economic growth. On the other hand, opponents contend that industrial policies lead to distortions and wastefulness, reducing market competition efficiency and hindering long-term economic development. They believe that the government should minimize its intervention in the market.

This chapter attempts to clarify the debate surrounding industrial policies. In the second and third sections, the chapter analyzes two core theoretical perspectives related to industrial policies: externalities and comparative advantage. It also examines why theoretical deductions based on these perspectives often lead to controversies. In the fourth section, the chapter discusses a significant difference frequently overlooked in theoretical models: the distinction between large and small countries. In large countries, the impact of the domestic market size on the effectiveness of industrial policies is substantial. In a large domestic market, fierce competition is more likely to occur. The fifth section delves into the question of how to maintain competitiveness through industrial policies. This includes not only the competition between market entities (i.e., enterprises) that is emphasized in the literature but also the competitive clauses inherent in policy tools and the implementation details. Moreover, it includes competition among the actors involved in policy-implementing entities, such as local governments or central departments. The sixth section explains why it is difficult to achieve conclusive scientific evidence regarding the actual effects of industrial policies. This also accounts for the enduring academic disputes surrounding industrial policies. Finally, the conclusion briefly elucidates the value and significance of theoretical research in the highly practical domain of industrial policies.

Externalities and Industrial Policies

The economic analysis supporting industrial policies generally starts with three types of externalities (Rodrik, 2004): technological externalities, informational externalities, and coordination externalities. Technological externalities refer to industries where the technologies employed have strong spillover effects. These industries cannot capture all the benefits of industrial growth and development, leading to suboptimal outcomes in terms of scale and investment from a societal perspective. Therefore, policy interventions, such as subsidies and support, are needed to bridge the gap between private and social benefits. Based on this theory, policies should prioritize supporting industries involving general-purpose technologies and equipment, such as chips, artificial intelligence, and basic industrial equipment. In practice, countries around the world have indeed provided substantial policy support to similar industries, as seen in the previous mention of the European Union and the United States supporting the chip industry.

The logic of technological externalities also applies to the government's investment in R&D. Compared to R&D investments by enterprises that often focus on practical technologies, government R&D investments tend to emphasize general-purpose technologies or basic scientific research. For example, in the 1970s, the United States National Science Foundation made significant investments in computer technology, and in the early 21st century, it directed substantial funding toward life sciences (Bloom *et al.*, 2019; Mowery and Rosenberg, 1999). Therefore, from an "industrial" perspective, government R&D investments should be directed more to universities and research institutions rather than specific companies. Although the primary beneficiaries of investments in specific academic disciplines may still be related industries and enterprises, such policy-oriented R&D investments are often not considered "industrial policies."

Informational externalities pertain to the uncertainty in industry investment and learning processes. When enterprises enter an unfamiliar industry, they face significant information barriers and uncertainties. If they succeed, the information and experience will inevitably spread to more players, making it challenging for the enterprise to exclusively enjoy the benefits. However, if they fail, most of the costs are borne by the company alone. This asymmetry between the benefits and costs often deters many enterprises from entering unknown industries. The traditional calculation of expected marginal benefit equaling marginal cost is insufficient to stimulate enterprises to venture into new industries. Based on this theory, certain high-tech industries and emerging sectors may require support from industrial policies, especially when these industries involve substantial upfront investments and high entry barriers. Examples include the semiconductor, optoelectronic display, and large aircraft industries. Conversely, for some emerging industries with low entry barriers and costs, even though uncertainties are high, government intervention may not be necessary. This applies to some emerging service industries based on the internet.

Coordination externalities involve collaboration within and between industries. No individual enterprise can succeed on its own; it requires the coordination and cooperation of upstream and downstream enterprises, as well as infrastructure support. For some emerging industries or regions, the necessary external conditions for business development may be inadequate, and individual enterprises cannot independently coordinate and improve these conditions. In such cases, comprehensive planning and promotion by the government are required. Therefore, this helps us understand the emergence of various industrial parks and economic development zones throughout China. The government not only invests in building essential infrastructure ("seven connections and one leveling," referring to access to water, electricity, roads, telecommunications, etc.) but also strategically attracts investments focused on specific leading enterprises, aiming to foster industrial clusters.

In recent years, with in-depth research on network effects, the discussion of network externalities has been integrated into the study of industrial policies. Between different stages of an industry's supply chain, there are not only complex technological linkages but also interrelated pricing mechanisms. Favorable policies targeted at a specific industry will inevitably distort prices and impact other related industries. However, such distortions and impacts are not always negative. In developing countries, where the market is not fully mature, many distortions caused by imperfect markets may propagate through the industrial chain, ultimately accumulating in upstream industries. This can result in insufficient development of upstream industries, which, in turn, becomes a bottleneck that restricts the development of downstream industries — the so-called "bottleneck problem." In such cases, policies that prioritize supporting upstream industries may reduce distortions and enhance overall economic efficiency (Liu, 2019). Numerous examples exist in this regard, such as South Korea's priority development strategy for the steel and chemical industries during President Park Chung-hee's tenure (Lane, 2019). Similarly, in today's China, there is a focus on targeted investments in bottleneck industries.

Different concepts of externalities are merely used to clarify theoretical research perspectives. However, in practical situations, certain industries often exhibit multiple types of externalities simultaneously, and policies targeting these industries need to address multiple externalities at once. For example, the semiconductor industry faces both informational externalities for new entrants and strong technological externalities due to the spillover effects of its technologies. In addition, it serves as a common upstream supplier for many other industries, leading to strong network externalities. Therefore, policies targeting the semiconductor industry would need to consider and address these various externalities together. Similarly, the high-speed rail industry faced significant uncertainty and informational externalities during its early stages while involving numerous sectors and regional governments, leading to substantial coordination externalities. Successfully promoting such an industry requires collaboration and cooperation among different government entities (including state-owned enterprises and research and design institutions).

Of course, any theoretical support for industrial policies remains theoretical. The effectiveness of industrial policies ultimately depends on their implementation. Due to significant externalities, the effects of industrial policies go beyond the targeted industries. If policies fail, they may affect many related industries, causing substantial distortions and wastage. In reality, industrial policies cannot be a sufficient condition for industrial success. Policies can only help enterprises overcome policy uncertainties and financial difficulties but cannot directly change their management capabilities, learning abilities, entrepreneurial spirit, etc. (Lu, 2016; Beaudry and Francois, 2010). These specific and micro-level human factors, although crucial, fall under the randomness or heterogeneity that general macroeconomic theories find difficult to grasp. Therefore, whether industrial policies can succeed or "pick winners" is difficult to judge solely based on theoretical grounds. The reality is complex enough to provide numerous examples for various theories, contributing to the ongoing controversies surrounding industrial policies. Just as there are no guaranteed successful enterprises in a market economy, these specific micro-level factors are insufficient to counter macroeconomic policies aimed at creating a better environment for industrial development. Industrial policies may directly distort the behavior of microeconomic agents through preferential policies that not only fail to promote enterprise efforts but also incentivize beneficiary enterprises to form interest groups and seek rent, and this may cause even greater waste and distortions (Krueger, 1990). The fifth part of this chapter further discusses this viewpoint when discussing the competitiveness of industrial policies.

Comparative Advantage and Industrial Policies

Another important theoretical perspective in analyzing industrial policies is comparative advantage. Using this concept to analyze the division of labor and specialization is a significant tradition in economics. New Structural Economics, a theory by Justin Yifu Lin, takes the following comparative advantage as the foundation for a successful economic development strategy. When analyzing industrial policies, it suggests that the government should actively play a role in identifying and promoting industries that align with comparative advantage, known as "growth identification and facilitation" (Lin, 2014). This highly enlightening theoretical perspective has also sparked considerable controversy. Particularly within a continuous and incremental theoretical framework, explaining the dynamic changes in industrial comparative advantage and even the extraordinary growth with significant distortions in China and some East Asian economies poses a theoretical challenge (Zhang, 2013).

Taking South Korea as an example, starting in 1973, the South Korean government invested a considerable amount of funds into six major strategic industries through the National Investment Fund and the Industrial Bank of Korea. These industries were steel, non-ferrous metals, shipbuilding, machinery, electronics, and petrochemicals. This industrial development strategy faced many doubts at that time. In 1974, the World Bank explicitly expressed reservations about whether South Korea's industrial goals could be achieved, stating that these industries did not align with South Korea's comparative advantage. The World Bank recommended focusing on the textile industry, a sector with lower financial and technological barriers, as a breakthrough for industrialization (Studwell, 2013). However, South Korea did not heed this advice and continued to vigorously develop these strategic industries. As a result, it achieved tremendous success. Not only did it nurture world-class shipbuilding and top-tier enterprises, such as Pohang Iron and Steel Company (POSCO) and Samsung Electronics, but it also significantly reduced the prices of downstream industrial inputs, driving the development of downstream industries such as the automotive sector and cultivating leading automakers such as Hyundai Motor Group. By 1990, South Korea's top 10 exported goods with the most "comparative advantage," such as ships and electronic products, did not even exist in 1970 (Cherif and Hasanov, 2019).

Similar situations also exist in China. Many industries that traditionally did not have a comparative advantage in China have developed over the years and now possess a comparative advantage in the international market. Liu and Yang (2019) compiled data on 1,240 export commodities from China and identified their "revealed comparative advantage" for the year 2016. Among them, 196 commodities did not have a comparative advantage or did not even exist in 1995. Most of these newly added products came from industries with higher complexity, such as machinery, electronics, and chemicals. This empirical result corroborates the New Structural Economics theory, as the comparative advantage of the majority of export commodities was sustained from 1995 to 2016. However, these examples also raise challenging questions: What is the true source of comparative advantage in the development of complex modern industrial sectors and industrial networks? Can potential comparative advantages be easily identified in agriculture? To what extent is the process of industrial development discontinuous and uncertain? And why does this happen?

One crucial reason for this lies in the learning effects of complex industries. One of the significant drivers of dynamic comparative advantage changes is "learning by doing." In complex industries, there is substantial space for learning, technological innovations, and cost improvements (Stiglitz and Greenwald, 2015). However, complex industries are almost always capital- and technology-intensive, which are the very industries that developing countries may appear to lack comparative advantage in. Moreover, "learning by doing" is merely a theoretical concept, and in reality, it is difficult to determine the actual learning ability and learning effect. Simple statistics on the education level of the labor force are insufficient to predict learning abilities and outcomes. Furthermore, the foundation of the concept of comparative advantage lies in opportunity cost, which is not directly observable but rather a counterfactual concept. Researchers must infer changes in opportunity costs by observing the marginal behavioral shifts resulting from external competition. However, "learning competition" is not the same as market competition, and learning ability is not a tradable ability in the market (Lu Feng, 2016). As a result, it is not possible to provide observable price signals to researchers to infer either explicit or implicit comparative advantages. The inability to measure and predict learning abilities makes it challenging to theorize, and it has become one of the most critical uncertainties in industrial policy theory.

Learning ability, though difficult to directly assess, is inevitably accompanied by exploration and trial-and-error processes. It is not difficult to imagine that in countries with strong learning capabilities, the distribution of industries may exhibit a dynamic process of "divergence first, and then convergence" — initially trying out various industries and subsequently focusing on the advantageous ones. In fact, this pattern is evident in macroeconomic data. Imbs and Wacziarg (2003) constructed the Gini coefficient for the industrial distribution of manufacturing sectors in multiple countries and found that this coefficient showed a U-shaped pattern with a decline followed by an increase over time. In other words, the industrial distribution presented a process of "divergence first, then concentration" rather than the simple static prediction of comparative advantage theory, which suggests an immediate focus on industries with comparative advantage. Furthermore, with time, a country's industrial structure tends to become increasingly complex, with finer specialization and longer upstream–downstream chains. The Economic Complexity (the Atlas of Economic Complexity) Index, developed by Harvard University's Center for International Development, measures the complexity level of each country's export products. China's complexity level rose from 39th in the world in 2000 to 16th in 2019.

Another major source of uncertainty and comparative advantage is the government itself. The Chinese government possesses massive resources, and when it decides to promote a certain industry, it directly alters the endowment and external conditions of that industry's development. This proactive distortion is a necessary condition for achieving extraordinary growth (Zhang, 2013). In the efforts of China's local governments to attract investment, they place significant emphasis on the assets and investment scale of enterprises, showing a willingness to support large projects by providing cheap land, subsidized loans, and tax incentives. This directly distorts the relative prices of the production factors and encourages enterprises to increase capital investment while relatively reducing the demand for labor. Although China's industry is still relatively labor-intensive compared to developed countries, it exhibits an excessive capital investment phenomenon relative to its vast labor force, and this capital investment is not highly sensitive to returns and economic growth rates (Zhang, 2002; Lu, 2016). After joining the WTO, the reduction of import tariffs on capital goods in China has increased enterprise capital investment, and the concentration of industries in the southeastern coastal regions has triggered large-scale population migration. Policies related to household registration and land have raised housing prices and labor costs, leading to the phenomenon of labor shortages, prompting enterprises to further lean toward capital investment (Yu and Liang, 2014). For example, China is the world's largest user of industrial robots, accounting for 30% of the global industrial robot market in 2016, and one important reason is the rise in labor costs (Cheng *et al.*, 2019).

It can be seen that, starting from the concept of comparative advantage, understanding the macro-industrial layout and gradual development in the process of economic development is a highly enlightening theoretical perspective. However, a country's production factors and resources are ultimately limited, and if the overall industrial structure deviates significantly from comparative advantage for an extended period, it is difficult to achieve sustained economic growth (Lin *et al.*, 2014). This macro perspective does not contradict the development of some seemingly non-comparative advantage industries at the micro level. Although the government cannot change the overall resource endowment of a country, it can indeed directly distort resource input prices for a specific industry through industrial policies. By leveraging learning effects and the economies of scale discussed later, it can "create something out of nothing" and establish a comparative advantage. Especially for large countries, while following the development path based on comparative advantage, there is still room to invest a significant amount of resources into complex and high-tech industries without comparative advantage and achieve success. One crucial reason for this is the significant economies of scale brought about by the huge domestic market.

Domestic Market Size and Industrial Policy

After the classical theory of comparative advantage, economists began to introduce economies of scale and monopolistic competition to understand specialization and trade. For small countries, the main source of economies of scale is the international market; therefore, opening up the market and focusing on niche industries are appropriate strategies. However, for large countries, supporting domestic enterprises in certain industries can better leverage the scale effect of the domestic market, reduce costs, and enhance welfare compared to relying on foreign investment.

Consider an industry with economies of scale and perfect competition (Figure 1), where the industry's supply curve is represented by the average cost curve AC_{foreign} that slopes downward. The international market for this product is dominated by foreign companies, with the supply curve being AC_{foreign} and the demand curve being D_{world}. The equilibrium price in the world market is P_0. If domestic companies can develop technology with lower costs, the domestic equilibrium price (P_1) will be lower than P_0. If domestic companies also supply the international market, the price will further drop below P_1. However, if domestic companies are latecomers in this

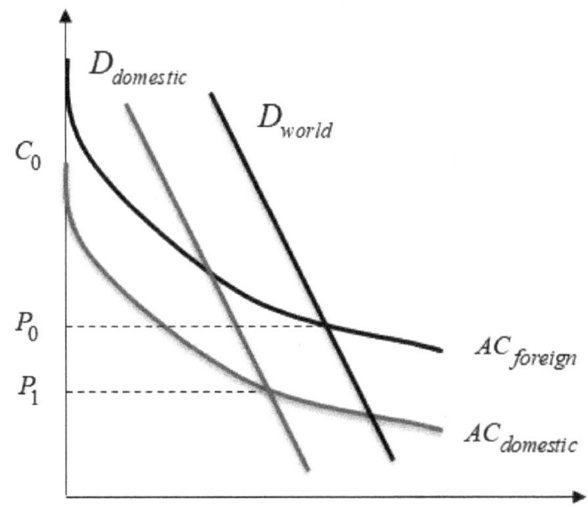

Figure 1. Domestic market size and trade losses.

industry and the market is open to foreign competition, they may not be able to enter the industry in practice. This is because their initial average cost C_0 upon entry is much higher than the market price P_0. In other words, the market may not provide opportunities for domestic companies to continuously reduce costs, even if their potential efficiency is higher. However, if the domestic industrial policy provides subsidies for entry, reducing the entry costs for domestic companies may increase the overall welfare of the country in the long run.

In the above model, the domestic market size is a crucial variable. If the domestic market is small and the demand curve D_{domestic} shifts to the left, far from the world market demand, then, even if domestic manufacturers have the potential for higher efficiency, the equilibrium price in the domestic market will still be higher than P_0. Importing instead of producing domestically would result in lower costs. In other words, for small countries, subsidizing domestic manufacturers to enter industries with high entry thresholds may not be cost-effective, as most of the benefits would be taken by consumers in the international market. However, for large countries, the pros and cons of subsidies need to be reconsidered and calculated. Of course, this model is highly simplified and does not consider the possibility of technology spillovers in some high-threshold industries that could enhance a country's overall industrial base and capabilities. In such cases, even relatively smaller countries (such as South Korea) may benefit from subsidizing domestic manufacturers' entry into those industries.

The rise of China's liquid crystal display panel industry is a typical example of the above phenomenon (Lu, 2016). China has the world's largest market for products such as computers, televisions, and smartphones, with nearly 80% of the hardware cost of computer displays and TVs coming from display panels. In 2008, the panel industry was dominated by enterprises from Japan, South Korea, and Taiwan, with negligible market share for mainland Chinese enterprises. However, by 2012, China's total imports of panels reached as high as US$50 billion, second only to integrated circuits, petroleum, and iron ore. Many local governments in China provided substantial subsidies and investments in this industry, ultimately fostering a group of domestic leading enterprises, such as BOE Technology Group, CSOT, Tianma Microelectronics, and Visionox Technology. These enterprises significantly reduced the panel prices, benefiting downstream industries and consumers alike. The industry also developed a strong export capacity and nurtured numerous domestic upstream enterprises. With the formation of a local industrial cluster, the combined economies of scale of individual enterprises and the entire industry improved efficiency, further reducing transportation and communication costs. This promoted independent and collaborative innovation across the entire value chain, accelerated technological progress and cost reduction, and further expanded China's competitive advantage and global market share. Taking BOE as an example, not only has it held the top spot in shipment volume for four consecutive years since 2018, but from 2016 to 2019, BOE was also among the top 10 companies globally with the highest number of international patent applications each year.

Certainly, although the Chinese domestic market is large, not all industries should receive government subsidies. The industries targeted by policies should still possess various characteristics of externalities. However, even when the market size and external conditions are present, industrial policies may not necessarily lead to success. The effectiveness of industrial policies is closely related to whether they encourage competition.

Competitiveness of Industrial Policies

The competitiveness of industrial policies has three aspects: whether the design of policy tools promotes competition, whether there is competition among the implementing entities of the industrial policies, and whether there is competition among the enterprises involved in the policies.

The implementation effect of industrial policies is inseparable from the design of specific policy tools. Although policies may be biased toward a certain target industry, within that industry, the policies should benefit all enterprises and encourage new entrants, promoting competition rather than targeting specific enterprises. Empirical research has found (Aghion *et al.*, 2015) that inclusive industrial policies, such as low-interest loans, tax incentives, and universal subsidies, do indeed promote competition, enhance industrial efficiency, and foster innovation capabilities.

In some aspects of policy design, industrial policies can also play a role in encouraging competition and innovation. For example, in China's subsidy policy for the photovoltaic (PV) industry, the feed-in tariff model introduced by Germany was adopted. Under this subsidy policy, the subsidy amount will continuously decrease over time, and all enterprises are well aware that the subsidies will gradually reduce until they are eventually phased out. As a result, there is motivation for companies to continuously improve efficiency and reduce costs. In fact, the progress in technology and cost reduction of PV enterprises has been faster than the pace of subsidy reduction (Lan, 2021).

The effectiveness of policy tools also relies on the supervision and evaluation mechanisms of the policies. Some policies' preferential treatment is directly linked to the level of competition, such as export subsidies or tax refunds, which are evaluated based on the market share in overseas markets. Encouraging enterprises to participate in fiercely competitive foreign markets not only improves their efficiency but also allows these enterprises to attract more industry resources, expand their share in the domestic market, and gradually squeeze out the survival space of backward enterprises, thereby enhancing the overall efficiency of the industry (Melitz, 2003; Brandt *et al.*, 2017). At the same time, export volume is easy to observe and measure, making it possible to evaluate the performance of subsidized enterprises and restrain them from continuously seeking rent and trade protection. Therefore, in East Asia, including China, industrial policies generally include export-oriented mechanisms.

In practice, the central government's industrial policies generally aim to benefit the entire industry, encourage competition, and are not specifically targeted at individual enterprises. However, implementing these policies ultimately comes down to specific local enterprises. What may be a universally beneficial policy at the national level becomes a special policy at the local level. Therefore, the competitiveness of industrial policies is also dependent on the competition between the implementing entities, which are the local governments.

The competition among various local governments in China for investment attraction is intense. The preferential policies offered by different regions are highly convergent in terms of content, but the extent of incentives is constrained by their local financial resources. Moreover, the specific industries strongly supported by local governments align with the industrial directions advocated by the central government, further intensifying the competition among local governments (Zhao and Chen, 2019). This "follow the trend" phenomenon has led to a lower threshold for industry entry, resulting in large-scale redundant construction and intensified industry competition. In this situation, enterprises must continuously engage in cost innovation and cost reduction to survive the fierce price wars at the lower end. Simultaneously, they must upgrade their technology and quality to escape the low-end price competition and gain greater development opportunities. Taking household appliances as an example, major Chinese enterprises, such as Haier, Midea, and Gree, have experienced this harsh competitive process, which has enabled them to grow into global giants within a short span of 20 years.

The level of competition between local governments is, of course, influenced by the specific policy tools they adopt. Broadly, preferential tools in industrial policies can be categorized into three types: non-repayable (such as subsidies and tax incentives), creditor-oriented (such as low-interest loans), and equity-oriented (through local industrial funds or direct equity investment by local state-owned enterprises). From the perspective of promoting healthy competition among governments, equity-oriented policy tools are superior to others. Implementing equity-oriented policies requires local governments to share risks with enterprises over a relatively long period; therefore, this approach tends to be more cautious. Unless investing in wholly state-owned enterprises, the interests of local governments are tied to the other shareholders of the enterprises. Unlike debt capital, equity capital is more standardized, has greater liquidity, and demands a higher return on investment, enabling stakeholders to "vote with their feet." As a result, before making investments, the government needs to carefully assess the return on investment and risks, thus indirectly optimizing the resource allocation required for implementing industrial policies.

The competitiveness of industrial policies ultimately needs to be implemented by encouraging competition among enterprises. First, the industries targeted by the policies should be competitive rather than monopolistic (Aghion *et al.*, 2015). Second, competition among enterprises should be based on the principle of "survival of the fittest," and policies should not become tools and shelters for inefficient enterprises seeking rent. If local governments protect local enterprises, even inefficient "zombie enterprises" need continuous financial support and rescue, which prevents the process of "elimination of the weak," thus undermining the effectiveness of competition and leading to misallocation and waste of resources. This is a primary reason why many economists oppose industrial policies. Especially in China, local governments have a strong preference for mega-projects, which stimulate enterprise expansion and investment. Once enterprises become large, they involve various interests related to employment, stability, and others. Local governments are reluctant to see these companies go bankrupt, as it would expose a series of contradictions. Therefore, the difficulty of allowing enterprises to go bankrupt has long been a persistent problem in China's economy. Whether it is enterprise restructuring or liquidation, there is still a long way to go in terms of institutional reform and construction to address the challenge of enterprise exit.

In general, the core of industrial policy should not be about picking winners among specific enterprises but rather about implementing inclusive policies targeting specific industries, reducing the impact of various externalities, lowering the entry threshold for enterprises, and promoting competition. However, neither market competition nor policy guidance can overcome the uncertainty of the future and guarantee the success of enterprises. Fundamentally, the advantage of a free-market economy lies not in decision-making superiority but in the ability to continuously experiment, learn from mistakes, and allow the survival of the fittest in competition. Therefore, effective industrial policy does not lie in pre-selecting winners but in maintaining competition and letting the strong emerge through it.

Causal Identification of Industrial Policy

The implementation effect of industrial policies has always been a subject of great controversy, mainly because it is challenging to provide convincing causal estimates in this field. Real-world industries and policies are diverse, and proponents of industrial policies can always find numerous successful examples, whereas opponents can also find many failed cases, making it difficult for either side to persuade the other. The difficulty in achieving a definitive conclusion through empirical study arises from the following reasons.

The first challenge lies in the endogeneity of policies. In reality, there are no randomly occurring industrial policies. Behind the formulation of policies, there is usually a lengthy process of negotiations and interest bargaining. Before policies are finally implemented, they undergo several rounds of discussions, solicitation of opinions and feedback, revisions, and further discussions. During this prolonged process, relevant enterprises are likely to participate, and some specific details of the policy are designed to address the specific issues faced by these enterprises. Therefore, enterprises may anticipate the general direction of the final policy and adjust their behavior and strategies in advance, whereas researchers can only rely on post-implementation data to make before-and-after comparisons, making it difficult to identify causal relationships.

The second difficulty lies in distinguishing policy combinations from individual policies. Most empirical studies attempt to isolate the effects of specific industrial policies. However, in reality, supporting a particular industry usually involves a combination of policies at different stages of industrial and enterprise development. This presents a challenge for researchers studying industrial policies, as many observable industry and enterprise performances already embody the effects of industrial policies, making it difficult to separate the causal effects of the policies. This challenge is particularly significant in China's data. The majority of investments and subsidies from local governments to support industrial development in China occur during the project initiation phase. As a result, many enterprises are influenced by industrial policies right from their inception. In other words, a large portion of observable enterprise data already include the effects of industrial policies from the beginning, and even their establishment is a result of the promotion of industrial policies. Therefore, there is a lack of "clean" data unaffected by policies for researchers to make comparisons.

For the implementers of industrial policies, the most important aspect is the overall outcome of industrial development, which is the combined effect of all policies rather than the marginal effect of a specific policy. The government can flexibly adjust all available policies according to needs without being constrained by a single policy. Moreover, the marginal effect of a single policy also depends on the environment created by all other related policies. Therefore, even if the effect of a single policy can be identified, it is difficult to replicate these effects in a completely different policy environment, which poses a challenge to the external validity of such empirical studies on policy effects.

The third challenge is that the data used by researchers often correspond to a specific period, which may coincide with the industrial cycle. Therefore, the policy effects estimated by studies may simply be the result of fluctuations in the industry cycle during that time. An industrial policy that appears successful during a certain period may later prove to be a failure, whereas an industrial policy that seems unsuccessful at a particular time might become highly successful later. In the 1980s, the Japanese economy was thriving, and the industrial policies led by the Ministry of International Trade and Industry were highly praised (Johnson, 1986). However, in the 1990s, as the Japanese economy fell into recession, the same industrial policies were viewed as hindering fair competition in industries and were considered one of the root causes of economic decline

(Porter and Sakakibara, 2004). Another contrasting example is China's PV industry. Around 2012, many Chinese PV companies collapsed under the dual impact of the global financial crisis and anti-dumping and countervailing measures investigations initiated by Western countries. This led the entire PV industry into a harsh winter. Consequently, the PV industry became a striking lesson on the challenges of industrial policies and government subsidies. However, after the industry reshuffling during that period, China's PV industry has now become a global leader, with domestic enterprises (including their overseas factories) accounting for 80% of the global production capacity. Chinese enterprises dominate nearly all critical aspects of the industry, such as polysilicon, wafers, cells, and modules (Gong and Lin, 2020). Driven by economies of scale and technological advancements, the price of PV modules decreased by 85% over the course of a decade (2010–2019), while the global installed capacity increased 16-fold during the same period (Yergin, 2020; REN21, 2020). PV has become another impressive emblem of "Made in China," alongside high-speed rail.

The fourth challenge lies in the distinction between partial equilibrium and general equilibrium. Industries are not only intricately interconnected in terms of upstream and downstream relations, but they also involve unpredictable technology and talent spillover effects. Hence, even if researchers can reasonably assess the impact of industrial policies on the target industries, it becomes difficult to evaluate the numerous spillover effects. For instance, the strong support from the government in Hefei for BOE Technology Group not only turned Hefei into a major base for China's optoelectronic display industry but also led to the development of technologies closely related to the chip and semiconductor industries. This allowed the Hefei government to leverage the collaboration with BOE Technology Group and attract leading semiconductor enterprises, such as GigaDevice, resulting in the establishment of Hefei Changxin, one of the key centers for China's dynamic random-access memory manufacturing industry. Similarly, the substantial support for emerging enterprises, such as NIO, in the new energy vehicle industry indirectly stimulated investments and layouts of the entire new energy vehicle industry chain in Anhui. For example, Midea Group transformed into a production base for new energy vehicle components, located in Anqing. Due to the complex connections between industries and technologies, industrial policies often have a ripple effect, making it challenging for researchers to evaluate their overall impact. Similarly, unsuccessful industrial policies could also have magnified negative effects, leading to complex and far-reaching impacts on the development trajectory of the entire economy. For instance, China's commercial aircraft industry has gone through a tortuous path, from halting the independent development of the Yun-10 project in 1986 to establishing the Commercial Aircraft Corporation of China in 2008. This loss of 20 years of development opportunities has had an immeasurable impact (Lu, 2019).

As counterfactuals are unknowable hypothetical scenarios, all their causal relationships are theoretical relationships, and empirical testing does not represent their objective facts — it is merely an interpretation of the available data based on theoretical assumptions. However, due to the complexity of industrial changes being much greater than individual behaviors, we need to be cautious in interpreting the far-from-perfect available data. Especially when research extends to guiding or influencing policy decisions, extra caution is essential.

Conclusion

Theoretical research and policy recommendations regarding industrial policies must be constrained by real-world conditions. Almost all market-based division of labor theories (including comparative advantage) assume that products not produced domestically can be obtained through trade. However, what if trade channels are obstructed? In recent years, the suppression and sanctions imposed by the United States on Chinese high-tech companies, such as Huawei, have become widely known, bringing to light the political and uncontrollable factors in international trade. The COVID-19 pandemic and the Russo–Ukrainian War have highlighted the fragility of global supply chains. In fact, even before the Huawei episode and the trade war, developed countries had long imposed embargoes and technology restrictions on certain Chinese industries (such as the nuclear and aerospace industries). Although these factors are generally not included in economic models, they are the everyday realities faced by decision-makers involved in industrial policies and by entrepreneurs and technology elites driving domestic industry development.

Due to the ever-changing nature of industries, markets, and international politics, industrial development and industrial policies are fundamentally practical issues rather than purely theoretical questions of "what should be done" or even "what can be done." The main task of theoretical research is not to confine reality with highly simplified theories and concepts but rather to utilize the rich experience of policies and industry practices to enrich our knowledge and deepen our understanding of the trends of industrial development and even the overall economic development of a country. It also helps us gain a deeper understanding of the interactions between the government and the market. Through this process of gaining an understanding of reality, researchers may gradually outline broader theoretical frameworks and possibilities and truly grasp the multiple contingencies that ignite these possibilities.

References

Aghion, P., Cai, J., Dewatripont, M., Du, L., Harrison, A., and Legros, P. 2015. Industrial policy and competition. *American Economic Journal: Macroeconomics*, 7(4): 1–32.

Beaudry, P. and Francois, P. 2010. Managerial skills acquisition and the theory of economic development. *Review of Economic Studies*, 77(1): 90–126.

Bloom, N., Van Reenen, J., and Williams, H. 2019. A toolkit of policies to promote innovation. *Journal of Economic Perspectives*, 33(3): 163–184.

Brandt, L., Van Biesebroeck, J., Wang, L., and Zhang, Y. 2017. WTO accession and performance of Chinese manufacturing firms. *American Economic Review*, 107(9): 2784–2820.

Cheng, H., Jia, R., Li, D., and Li, H. 2019. The rise of robots in China. *Journal of Economic Perspectives*, 33(2): 71–88.

Cherif, R. and Hasanov, F. 2019. The return of the policy that shall not be named: Principles of industrial policy. IMF Working Paper.

Gong, Y. and Lin, J. 2020. Difficult to shake China's photovoltaic industry chain dominant position in 'deglobalization'. CITIC Securities Research Report.

Imbs, J. and Wacziarg, R. 2003. Stages of diversification. *American Economic Review*, 93(1): 63–86.

Johnson, C. 1986. *MITI and the Japanese Miracle: The Growth of Industrial Policy, 1925–1975*. Redwood: Stanford University Press.

Krueger, A.O. 1990. Government failures in development. *Journal of Economic Perspectives*, 4(3): 9–23.

Lan, X. 2021. *Immersed in Affairs: Chinese Government and Economic Development*. Shanghai: Shanghai People's Publishing House.

Lane, N. 2019. Manufacturing revolutions: Industrial policy and industrialization in South Korea. Working Paper.

Lin, Y. 2014. *New Structural Economics: Reflections on the Theoretical Framework of Economic Development and Policy*. Beijing: Peking University Press.

Lin, Y., Cai, F., and Li, Z. 2014. *China's Miracle: Development Strategy and Economic Reform*. Shanghai: Gezhi Publishing House.

Lin, Y., Zhang, J., Wang, Y., and Kou, Z. 2018. *Industrial Policy: Summary, Reflection, and Prospects*. Beijing: Peking University Press.

Liu, E. 2019. Industrial policies in production networks. *Quarterly Journal of Economics*, 134(4): 1883–1948.

Liu, S. and Yang, J. 2019. The evolution and policy choices of China's industrial upgrading: Based on the perspective of product space. *Journal of Management World*, 6: 81–94, 194–195.

Lu, F. 2016. *Variable: A Business and Its Industrial History*. Beijing: Contemporary China Publishing House.

Lu, F. 2019. *Towards Independent Innovation: Seeking the Source of China's Strength*. Beijing: Renmin University of China Press.

Lu, M. 2016. *Big Country, Big City: Unity, Development, and Balance of Contemporary China*. Shanghai: Shanghai People's Publishing House.

Mazzucato, M. 2015. *The Entrepreneurial State: Debunking Public vs. Private Sector Myths*. Public Affairs Press.

Melitz, M.J. 2003. The impact of trade on intra-industry reallocations and aggregate industry productivity. *Econometrica*, 71(6): 1695–1725.

Mowery, D.C. and Rosenberg, N. 1999. *Paths of Innovation: Technological Change in 20th-century America*. Cambridge: Cambridge University Press.

Porter, M.E. and Sakakibara, M. 2004. Competition in Japan. *Journal of Economic Perspectives*, 18(1): 27–50.

REN21. 2020. Renewables 2020 Global Status Report. Renewable Energy Policy Network for the 21st Century.

Rodrik, D. 2004. Industrial policy for the twenty-first century. Working Paper, Harvard University.

Stiglitz, J. and Greenwald, B. 2015. *Creating a Learning Society: A New Approach to Growth, Development, and Social Progress.* New York: Columbia University Press.

Studwell, J. 2013. *How Asia Works: Success and Failure in the World's Most Dynamic Region.* New York: Open Road + Grove/Atlantic.

Yergin, D. 2020. *The New Map: Energy, Climate, and the Clash of Nations.* London: Penguin Press.

Yu, M. and Liang, Z. 2014. Trade liberalization and Chinese labor income share: An empirical analysis based on manufacturing trade enterprise data. *Journal of Management World*, 7: 22–31.

Zhang, J. 2002. Growth, capital formation, and technology choice: Explanation of long-term factors of China's economic growth slowdown. *China Economic Quarterly*, 1: 301–338.

Zhang, J. 2013. Expansion and limitations of 'comparative advantage theory': Reading Lin Yifu's new work 'new structural economics'. *China Economic Quarterly*, 3: 1087–1094.

Zhao, T. and Chen, Z. 2019. Comparative advantage and central and local industrial policies. *The Journal of World Economy*, 10: 98–119.

https://doi.org/10.1142/9789819815241_0013

Chapter 13

MULTIPLE POLICY OBJECTIVES AND LOCAL GOVERNMENT BEHAVIOR

Ying Fang[*,‡] and Qiang Wen[†,§]

[*] *WISE and School of Economics, Xiamen University, China*
[†] *Business School, Sichuan University, China*
[‡] *yifst1@xmu.edu.cn*
[§] *durianwen@scu.edu.cn*

Introduction

The report of the 19th National Congress of the Communist Party of China (CPC) noted that China's economy has shifted from high-speed growth to high-quality development. High-quality development necessarily requires all levels of government to abandon the single policy objective of solely pursuing gross domestic product (GDP) growth as the measure of success. Instead, they should shift toward multiple policy objectives based on new development concepts such as innovation, coordination, green, openness, and shared prosperity. China is a country characterized by regionally decentralized authoritarianism (Xu, 2011), where local governments have control over a significant portion of economic resources. The central government relies on local governments to implement its policy objectives effectively. Therefore, the central government is continuously improving and refining the assessment system for local officials, incorporating multiple objectives, such as economic, political, cultural, social, and ecological civilization construction and party building, into the assessment system and moving away from using regional GDP and growth rate as the primary assessment metrics.[1] Since the central government shifted its assessment of local governments from a single policy objective to multiple policy objectives, it has become more important to explore the changes that will occur in the behavior of local governments under the existing pattern of central–local relationships.

Local governments have played a key role in China's rapid economic growth since the beginning of the reform and opening up. The central government controls the assessment of local officials for promotion, sets a single policy objective for regional economic growth, and selects officials through the so-called "promotion tournament" mechanism, motivating local officials to promote economic development to pursue their career advancement (Li and Zhou, 2005; Zhou, 2007b; Zhang and Gao, 2007). Moreover, Chinese-style fiscal federalism can provide local governments with sufficient financial incentives (Jin *et al.*, 2005; Zhang *et al.*, 2007; Fang and Zhang, 2013). It achieves growth in local fiscal revenue through regional economic growth, meeting the inherent requirement of local officials to maximize regional fiscal revenue. Furthermore, the ample local fiscal revenue further supports regional economic growth, allowing local officials to gain advantages in political promotion. The series of institutional arrangements aimed at competition for growth has undoubtedly been a tremendous success, but it is clearly unsustainable under the new economic normal. Promotion incentives may lead local officials to prioritize GDP metrics over the preferences of residents in their jurisdictions and to focus on short-term economic growth during their tenure while ignoring long-term consequences. This approach can cause major socioeconomic problems, such as local protectionism, redundant construction, and environmental pollution, preventing the attainment of the inherent requirements for high-quality development.

Although using regional economic growth as the sole policy objective may seem oversimplified, it has considerable incentive-compatible advantages in the existing series of institutional arrangements for central–local relationships. When the single policy objective is replaced by multiple ones, the original incentive-compatible pattern may be disrupted, leading to deviations in the behavior of local governments from the prescribed policy track and resulting in implementation challenges under the multiple policy objectives. First, multiple policy objectives may contradict the intrinsic incentives of local governments to maximize their local fiscal revenue, reducing their internal drive to implement central policies. Second, although the promotion incentives for local officials remain strong, there may be some inherent conflicts between the multiple policy objectives, making it more difficult for the central government to conduct assessments for promotion. The lack of a simple, clear, and uniform benchmark assessment metric, such as the regional GDP growth rate, can weaken the efforts of local officials to implement central policies amid information asymmetry. Dewatripont *et al.* (1999) demonstrate in their multitask career concern model that policy implementation efforts decrease as the number of tasks increases. Finally, when there are multiple policy objectives, local governments may selectively determine the implementation efforts for different policies based on factors such as the intensity of policy assessments, compatibility of incentives, difficulty of policy implementation, clarity of assessment objectives, and period of assessment, increasing the uncertainty and complexity of achieving policy objectives. Zhang *et al.* (2020) use a dynamic general equilibrium model to quantitatively simulate the impact of different assessment metrics on changes in the real economy.

This study investigates the measures taken by local governments when facing multiple policy objectives, as well as the effectiveness of policy implementation, using the examples of "resolutely curbing the rise in housing prices" and the *Three-Year Action Plan for Winning the Blue Sky Defense War*. Both controlling housing prices and combating pollution are major livelihood issues of great social concern and important policy objectives of the central government. China faces numerous challenges caused by high housing prices. To suppress housing prices, the Political Bureau of the CPC Central Committee held a meeting on July 31, 2018, which called for "resolutely curbing the rise in housing prices," reflecting the central government's determination to control housing prices. Furthermore, environmental pollution has had severe negative impacts on the economy and society. The 19th National Congress of the CPC identified "pollution prevention and control" as one of the three major battles in the decisive period of building a moderately prosperous society. In response, the State Council issued the *Three-Year Action Plan for Winning the Blue Sky Defense War* on June 27, 2018. Housing price control and environmental protection both have a deterrent "veto power" in the assessment of local officials. However, these two major policy objectives are contradictory to the inherent incentives of local governments to maximize their fiscal revenue. The development of the real estate market can bring local governments land-related tax revenue, such as land concessions, forming a huge "land finance" (Zhou, 2007a). The inhibiting effect of controlling the rise of housing prices on the real estate market will compress the space for land finance, which will, in turn, reduce the fiscal revenue of local governments. In terms of pollution control, the strict implementation of environmental regulations by local governments requires the closure or restriction of polluting industries, which will significantly lower the economic growth rate (Chen *et al.*, 2018) and thus may similarly put pressure on local fiscal revenue. Both of the above policies were implemented around July 2018 and are characterized by a veto power, thus providing an ideal scenario for us to examine how local governments implement central policies when faced with multiple policy objectives.

Using pollution monitoring data from 1,496 air quality monitoring stations across the country, we employ the difference-in-differences (DID) method to discover that implementing the policy of "resolutely curbing the rise in housing prices" led to a decline in air quality. Specifically, when the local governments' land finance dependence increased by 1% after the policy implementation, with all other conditions remaining unchanged, the air quality index (AQI) at the city's monitoring stations increased by 0.039%. The result implies that the

AQI increased by an average of 2.5 units, a rise comparable to the improvement in China's air quality from 2016 to 2017, which is significant in an economic sense. Further analysis reveals that the higher the fiscal revenue growth target set by the local government before the implementation of the policy, the greater the impact of the housing price control policy on the city's air quality. Moreover, the decline in air quality after the implementation of the policy of controlling the rise in housing prices mainly stemmed from an increase in the concentration of sulfur dioxide (SO_2), an industrial pollutant. Therefore, when facing the financial pressure brought about by controlling housing price increases and protecting the environment, local governments tend to choose to control housing prices while sacrificing environmental objectives, resulting in a decline in environmental quality.

There is little existing literature that investigates the implementation dilemmas faced by local governments from the perspective of multiple policy objectives. We focus on the dual policy objectives of housing price control and environmental protection faced by local governments, and we utilize the policy shock of "resolutely curbing the rise in housing prices" to conduct novel research on the specific policy choices and implementation effectiveness of local governments facing multiple policy objectives. This study enriches the existing literature on central–local relationships and is important for achieving high-quality development in the presence of multiple policy objectives.

The rest of this chapter is organized as follows. Section "Central–Local Relationships under Multiple Policy Objectives: Theory of Local Government Behavior" discusses the implementation dilemmas and behavioral hypotheses of local governments when confronted with multiple policy objectives from the perspective of central–local relationships under multiple policy objectives. Section "Data and Benchmark Model Analysis" presents the data and identifies the impacts of the policy of controlling house price increases on air quality using the DID method. In section "Further Analysis", the mechanisms by which the curbing of house price increases affects air quality are further analyzed, followed by concluding remarks in section "Conclusion".

Central–Local Relationships under Multiple Policy Objectives: Theory of Local Government Behavior

Theoretical foundations

Before China's economy reached its new normal, the institutional arrangements of the central–local relationships could be summarized in three main points. First, the central government held the power to select and appoint local officials (i.e., a politically centralized system). Second, the fiscal federalism-style institutional arrangement resulted in a large degree of local economic decentralization, where local governments could share in the growth of local revenues due to regional economic growth. Last, the single policy objective centering around regional economic growth led to competition among local governments for growth, contributing to over four decades of rapid national economic growth. The three fulcrums of the Chinese-style central–local relationships (i.e., political incentives for the promotion of local officials, economic incentives for local governments to maximize fiscal revenue, and benchmark assessment by the central government with a single policy objective), while not sustainable under the new economic normal, have considerable incentive compatibility and inherent stability within the existing framework of central–local relationships. Changing any of these arrangements tends to disrupt their inherent incentive-compatible structure and stability. Blanchard and Shleifer (2001) argued that the difference in economic performance between Russia and China is due to the former's lack of an effective centralized political system. Zhang (2012) emphasized the role of tax-sharing system reform in preserving the advantages of fiscal federalism and constraining localist behavior.

In the current pattern of central–local relationships, after fiscal decentralization reform represented by the tax-sharing system, local governments can share fiscal revenues with the central government. The higher the fiscal revenue, the more funds local governments can retain, giving them sufficient motivation to develop the local economy and seek growth in local fiscal revenues. Local governments have been found to adjust their behavior based on economic incentives. For example, in terms of the distribution of tax revenue, the sharing of value-added tax (VAT) mainly corresponds to industrial land use, while business tax mainly corresponds to commercial and residential land use. Xie *et al.* (2019) find that an increase in the local share of VAT encourages local governments to allocate more industrial land, while an increase in the local share of business tax reduces the allocation of industrial land by local governments. Land revenue is an important component of local government fiscal revenues, so local governments also have economic incentives to vigorously pursue land-related revenues. For example, Sun and Zhou (2013) show that local governments have gradually adopted a development model that focuses on land requisition, development, and transfer, leading to the formation of an enormous amount of land finance.

In the case of multiple policy objectives, we first consider that the central government requires that local governments accomplish another specific policy objective, in addition to the original policy objective of regional economic growth rate. Since the central government still holds the power to promote local officials, it can help them fulfill the central government's policy objectives by providing both positive and negative political incentives. For example, the degree of completion of a specific policy objective is included in the assessment system as a veto. When a specific policy aligns with their economic incentive to maximize local fiscal revenue, local governments are sufficiently motivated to enact that specific policy. In this case, the political incentives for local officials are consistent with the economic incentives. However, when the implementation of a particular policy is not conducive to maximizing local fiscal revenue, the policy implementation depends on the relative levels of political and economic incentives associated with the particular policy. Chen *et al.* (2018) find that only after the State Council introduced a veto system in environmental assessment did local governments in the "two control zones" begin to lower their economic growth targets and take measures such as shutting down coal-fired power plants and increasing desulfurization facilities. Xi *et al.* (2017) reveal that from 2003 to 2011, when local governments' share of tax revenue decreased, they increased the number of industrial enterprises and relaxed environmental regulations to attract more pollution-intensive enterprises, leading to worse industrial pollution. Despite the existence of a veto system for environmental protection since 2006, local governments still have the motivation to relax environmental regulations, indicating that local governments may adjust their response to political incentives when faced with strong economic incentives. Thus, when a policy's political incentives conflict with its economic incentives, local governments do not simply comply with the political incentives but adjust their compliance based on the relative levels of political and economic incentives.

Further, we consider the more complex arrangement of multiple policy objectives, that is, the existence of two or more specific policies, the implementation of which imposes negative economic incentives on local governments, adversely affecting the growth of regional fiscal revenue. When the central government has multiple policy objectives, local governments are forced to simultaneously implement multiple central policies with negative economic incentives. In this situation, how would local governments choose the intensity of implementation for different policies? To simplify the analysis, we assume that these policies all have veto power in the assessment for promotion. Local governments lack sufficient economic motivation to implement these policies, but they need to do so under negative political incentives. Consequently, we explore the behavioral choices of local governments in this scenario and the combinations of different levels of policy implementation.

First, does the number of policies affect the level of compliance by local officials? Dewatripont *et al.* (1999) explore the policy implementation of local officials under multiple policy objectives and establish a multitask career concern (MCC) model, which assumes that local officials need to implement multiple central policies, that they are motivated for promotion, and that their promotion depends on the performance achieved in policy implementation. The performance, in turn, relies on two factors: local endowments and officials' efforts. However, the central government cannot directly assess local officials' efforts. Local officials who seek promotion are motivated to invest effort to achieve good performance. The higher their effort, the greater their compliance with central policies. Theoretical analysis reveals that when there are an increasing number of central policies to be implemented, the level of effort of local officials in implementing a particular policy is less likely to be differentiated from the endowment. As a result, their motivation to carry out that policy decreases, ultimately leading to a decline in overall effort. Consistent with the observations by Wilson (1989), local governments comply more strongly with the central government when it abandons some important policy objectives and focuses on specific ones. Therefore, while local governments may adhere to the veto system owing to political incentives for promotion, they may reduce the intensity of implementation of some policy objectives in the presence of a large number of policies with veto power.

Second, do policy characteristics lead to variations in the level of compliance of local officials with different policies? The MCC model assumes that the central government has clear criteria for the policy objectives that local officials must implement. However, in reality, some policy objectives have clear criteria for implementation, such as workplace safety, where local officials are held accountable in the event of major safety accidents and thus disqualified from promotion, so local officials have sufficient motivation to prevent safety accidents from occurring. However, some policy objectives are either not well defined or their criteria are not easily quantifiable. For example, in environmental protection, although the central government has set emission reduction targets for a certain period of time, the specific targets to be fulfilled for each phase are not fully specified. As a result, local officials may lack the necessary motivation to put maximum effort into environmental protection in each phase. When policy objectives are unclear, the implementation efforts of local governments may vary. Dewatripont *et al.* (1999) find that when policy objectives are unclear, the assessment criteria for officials become ambiguous, making it more difficult to differentiate their endowments from their efforts, lowering the level of their effort.

Therefore, it can be inferred that, in the context of multiple policy objectives, policies with clearer objectives for assessment tend to elicit stronger implementation efforts from local officials.

Finally, the MCC model assumes that performance is a necessary condition for the promotion of local officials, which implies that local officials must achieve a certain performance level before obtaining a promotion. As a result, the assessment of local officials only has a real incentive effect during their term in office. It has been found that the term of office influences officials' decision-making behavior. Wu and Zhou (2018) show that the term of office of municipal party secretaries and mayors has a significant inverted U-shaped relationship with expenditures on visible public goods. However, this significant relationship does not exist for invisible public goods. This is because, under promotion incentives and given limited financial resources, local officials tend to allocate more resources to highly visible public goods to maximize their performance during their term in office. Therefore, in the context of multiple policy objectives, the shorter the time span for policy assessment, the more likely it is to achieve performance assessment of local officials during their term in office, and the greater the effort for implementation of the corresponding policies by local officials.

In summary, when local governments need to implement multiple central policies, particularly those that directly impact local fiscal revenue, they have the motivation to reduce the effort for policy implementation to minimize financial losses while maximizing local fiscal revenue. Local governments may make a greater effort to implement central policies with clear assessment targets and short assessment periods, whereas they may exhibit weaker commitment when dealing with policies that have vague assessment targets and longer assessment periods.

Research hypothesis: The trade-off between housing price control and pollution protection

Controlling housing prices and protecting the environment are currently two major objectives of the central government. Both policies have negative economic incentives for local governments because of the restraining effect of controlling house prices on land finance and the disincentive effect of protecting the environment on economic growth, reducing the fiscal revenue of local governments. In terms of form, housing price control and environmental protection have the same level of negative incentives in the assessment system, and both have veto power. However, their differences in the clarity of assessment targets and period of assessment may affect the relative amount of effort made in their implementation. In terms of the assessment period, China's National Bureau of Statistics releases monthly housing price indices for 70 large and medium cities, and third-party organizations also compile monthly housing price indices for other major cities, indicating that the policy of "resolutely curbing the rise in housing prices" constitutes a *de facto* "monthly assessment." In comparison, the aforementioned three-year air pollution action plan sets pollution reduction targets for priority regions by 2020 and proposes to "assess the completion of annual targets and tasks," indicating that pollution control assessment is conducted on an "annual basis," which is longer than the period of monthly assessment of housing price control. Regarding the clarity of assessment targets, "resolutely curbing the rise in housing prices" means that the growth rate of housing prices should be less than or equal to zero. In other words, whether the housing price growth rate is greater than zero becomes a clear criterion for the monthly assessment of the housing price control policy. In comparison, the three-year air pollution action plan only defines annual and three-year assessment targets, and most cities and provinces have not publicly released specific targets for the annual assessment, indicating that the clarity of the monthly assessment metrics for pollution control is lower than that of the policy on curbing housing prices. In particular, the three-year air pollution action plan designates 80 cities as priority regions, but the policy of "resolutely curbing the rise in housing prices" does not specify implementation areas, indicating that all cities in the country have clear objectives for controlling housing prices, but in reality, only some cities have relatively clear objectives for the environmental protection policy.

Therefore, the policy of "resolutely curbing the rise in housing prices" not only has a shorter assessment period but also has clearer assessment objectives than the three-year air pollution action plan. Based on the aforementioned theory of local government behavior under multiple policy objectives, it is speculated that, when faced with negative economic incentives to control housing prices and protect the environment at the same time, local governments have a motivation to implement the housing price control policy more strictly but may sacrifice the environmental protection objective, leading to environmental pollution issues.

On this basis, the key hypothesis of this study is that after the implementation of the policy of "resolutely curbing the rise in housing prices," local governments may reduce their effort to implement the environmental protection policy in the trade-off between curbing housing prices and protecting the environment, leading to a decline in air quality.

Data and Benchmark Model Analysis

Data description

The air quality data used in this study are sourced from the National City Air Quality Real-time Publishing Platform, operated by the China National Environmental Monitoring Centre. This platform has collected hourly air quality data from various monitoring stations since May 13, 2014, including the AQI and its subindices. This study focuses on the impact of the policy of "resolutely curbing the rise in housing prices" in 2018 on air quality. Since local governments set new work targets every year (Xu *et al.*, 2018), we limit the time window after policy implementation to 2018 to avoid the possible impacts of work targets in different years on the development of the local real estate market and air quality. Since there is a five-month interval (August to December) after policy implementation in 2018, we select a five-month interval (March to July) before policy implementation as well. The hourly data from the monitoring stations are averaged at the monthly level, resulting in air quality monitoring data from March 2018 to December 2018, which comprise 14,881 observations from 1,496 sites in 339 cities.

The metric for local government's land finance dependence is calculated using the data from statistical yearbooks. In the literature, land finance dependence is generally measured by the proportion of land transfer revenue in the total fiscal revenue budget (Shao *et al.*, 2016). The China Land and Resources Statistical Yearbook provides the total land transfer revenues in various cities before 2017, and the China City Statistical Yearbook provides the fiscal revenue data for various cities before 2017. The land finance dependence for 289 cities from 2015 to 2017 can be calculated based on these two sets of data. To reduce the interference of annual data fluctuations on empirical conclusions, we use three-year average data to measure the cities' land finance dependence and use the data from 2017 for the robustness test.

Table 1 presents the descriptive statistics of the key variables in this study. The mean AQI is 63.9, considering all observations, indicating an overall level-2 (good) air quality in China, according to the Technical Regulations on Ambient Air Quality Index issued by the Ministry of Environmental Protection. However, the AQI varies considerably across monitoring stations, with a minimum of 15.5, indicating level-1 (excellent) air quality, and a maximum of 350.8, indicating level-6 (severely polluted) air quality. Since not all cities with AQI data have a land finance dependence metric, the two sets

Table 1. Descriptive statistics.

	(1)	(2)	(3)	(4)	(5)
Variables	Observations	Mean	Standard deviation	Minimum	Maximum
Part A: AQI					
All observations	14,881	63.886	26.968	15.509	350.780
Sample used for analysis	13,750	64.060	24.188	26.538	141.977
Part B: landfis (Land transfer revenue/Fiscal revenue * 100)					
Average from 2015 to 2017	289	47.716	30.454	4.115	199.797
2017	289	59.973	45.137	3.291	314.117
Part C: blue (observations affected by the three-year air pollution action plan)					
Blue	13,750	0.191	0.393	0	1

of data are combined to produce an AQI analysis sample of 13,750 observations, which are similar in descriptive statistics to the overall observations, and there are 6,875 observations both before and after policy implementation.

The 289 cities exhibit an average land finance dependence of 47.7% from 2015 to 2017. However, the land finance dependency varies greatly across cities, with a minimum of 4.1% and a maximum of 199.8%. Using 2017 data to measure the land finance dependence of cities, we find that the average is 60.0%, which is higher than the average from 2015 to 2017, indicating an upward trend for land finance dependence in China. The minimum land finance dependence in 2017 is lower than the minimum of the average from 2015 to 2017, while the maximum in 2017 is higher than the maximum of the average from 2015 to 2017, suggesting the possibility of a "dispersion" phenomenon of land finance dependence among cities (i.e., a possible increase in the differentiation of land finance dependence among cities).

Among all samples, 80 cities have been affected by the three-year air pollution action plan since July 2018, and the AQI at the monitoring stations in these cities has been impacted by this policy accordingly. We construct a variable "blue," which takes the value 1 if a station was affected by this policy and 0 otherwise. Table 1 shows that the proportion of samples affected is 19%.

Empirical model

This study examines the impact of the policy of "resolutely curbing the rise in housing prices" on air quality. Before and after the policy implementation, there could be significant changes in air quality in various regions. However, these changes could be attributed to the policy's treatment effect or other macro-socioeconomic environmental changes. In other words, the differences in air quality among different types of cities before and after the implementation of the housing price control policy were due to a mixture of the policy effect and the macro-environmental effect. Although the air quality of all cities was influenced by macro-environmental changes, the extent of the impact of the policy of "resolutely curbing the rise in housing prices" varied across cities, and cities with a higher land finance dependence were more affected. By comparing the differences in air quality among cities with different levels of land finance dependence (first difference) before and after policy implementation (second difference), we can isolate the policy treatment effect of the impact of controlling housing prices on air quality from the mixed effects; that is, the continuous DID model can be used to identify the causal impact of the policy of "resolutely curbing the rise in housing prices" on air quality. On this basis, the empirical model in this study is developed as follows:

$$\log(\mathrm{AQI}_{ijt}) = \beta \cdot \log(\mathrm{landfis}_j) \cdot \mathrm{post}_t + \gamma \cdot \mathrm{blue}_{jt} + \mathrm{city}_j \cdot f(t) + \delta_i + \theta_t + e_{ijt}, \tag{1}$$

where AQI_{ijt} is the monthly average AQI from the ith air quality monitoring station in the jth city during the tth period, with higher values indicating poorer air quality and higher pollution levels. The main policy variable is $\mathrm{Policy}_{jt} = \log(\mathrm{landfis}_j) \cdot \mathrm{post}_t$, in which $\mathrm{landfis}_j$ is the land finance dependence of the jth city, and post_t indicates whether the housing price control policy is implemented during the tth period, taking a value of 1 when $t >$ July 2018 and 0 otherwise. A higher value of Policy_{jt} indicates a more pronounced impact of the housing price control policy on the city. The parameter β captures the influence of the housing price control policy on air quality, with $\beta > 0$ meaning that the housing price control policy leads to a decline in air quality. blue_{jt} represents the implementation status of the three-year air pollution action plan in the jth city during the tth period, with a value of 1 indicating that the air quality monitoring station is located in a priority city participating in the three-year air pollution action plan and 0 otherwise. Besides, the regression equation controls for the interaction variable $\mathrm{city}_j \cdot f(t)$, which reflects the jth city-specific time trend. Here, $f(t)$ is a polynomial function of time t and takes a quadratic form in this study. The socioeconomic environmental changes at the city level may affect both the AQI and the real estate market's development, and ignoring these unobservable factors may lead to an omitted variable bias. Controlling for city-specific time trends helps reduce the impact of omitting these unobservable factors on the empirical findings. Additionally, δ_i represents the fixed effects of the ith air quality monitoring station, which is used to control for the impact of station-level time-invariant unobservable factors on air quality. θ_t represents the monthly fixed effects, which removes the influence of seasonal factors and macro-socioeconomic environmental changes on air quality. e_{ijt} represents the unobservable heterogeneity. Because of the possible serial correlation of the pollution data from different monitoring stations, the standard errors are adjusted by clustering at the station level during statistical inference.

Empirical results of DID analysis

First, the changes in the AQI of different types of cities before and after the implementation of the housing price control policy are visually examined. Based on the average land finance dependence data from 2015 to 2017, we divide all cities into five equal groups and define the cities in the first group (with the lowest land finance dependence) as the "low land finance dependence" group and the cities in the fifth group (with the highest land finance dependence) as the "high land finance dependence" group. The average values of AQI at the group-month level are shown in Figure 1. As can be observed from the figure, before the implementation of the policy of "resolutely curbing the rise in housing prices," the monthly average AQI values for the high and low land finance dependence groups are roughly the same, suggesting that there was no systematic difference in air quality between the two types of cities before the policy was implemented. However, starting from August 2018, the monthly average AQI for the high land finance dependence group becomes significantly higher than that of the low land finance dependence group, and this phenomenon continues until the end of the sample period. Therefore, it can be inferred that the housing price control policy may have led to a decline in air quality. Besides, the trends of AQI for different types of cities before August 2018 are

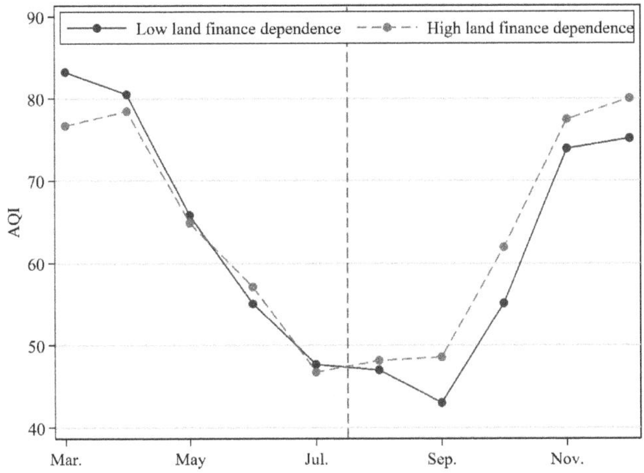

Figure 1. Changes in the AQI before and after August in different types of cities in 2018.

Source: Authors' calculations based on analysis of samples.

consistent, which is in line with the results of the "parallel trend" hypothesis test discussed later.

Table 2 reports the results obtained based on empirical model (1). In column (1), the analysis is conducted using the full sample while controlling for the influences of station fixed effects, month fixed effects, the "battle to defend the blue sky" campaign, and the city's second-order time trend. It is found that, all else being equal, a 1% increase in a city's land finance dependence correlates with a 0.039% increase in AQI at the city's monitoring stations after the implementation of the policy of "resolutely curbing the rise in housing prices," and this effect is statistically significant at the 1% level. According to the AQI sample average provided in Table 1, a 1% increase in land finance dependence correlates with a 2.5-unit increase in AQI on average. The calculation using the AQI data released by the National Urban Air Quality Real-Time Publishing Platform shows that the annual average AQI was 83.3, 77.8, and 75.6 in 2015, 2016, and 2017, respectively, indicating that the increase in AQI caused by the implementation of the policy of "resolutely curbing the rise in housing prices" was close to the degree of improvement

Table 2. Policy implementation and air quality.

	Dependent variable: log(AQI)		
Variables	(1) Full sample	(2) blue = 1	(3) blue = 0
log(landfis)*post	0.039***	0.025***	0.077***
	(0.007)	(0.008)	(0.010)
Blue	-0.167***		
	(0.009)		
Observations	13,750	4,370	9,380
Adjusted *R*-squared	0.905	0.923	0.883
City-specific time trend	2	2	2

Notes: Statistics in parentheses are the robust standard errors adjusted by clustering at the station level. Station fixed effects and month fixed effects are controlled for in all regressions. *** $p<0.01$, ** $p<0.05$, * $p<0.1$.

in China's air quality from 2016 to 2017. The air pollution caused by the housing price control policy was economically significant, thereby supporting the research hypothesis.

Note that the dummy variable *blue*, reported in column (1) of Table 2, has a regression coefficient of –16.7%, which shows that the policy of "resolutely curbing the rise in housing prices" had a greater impact on the air quality of non-priority cities in the "battle to defend the blue sky." Compared to that of the priority cities in the "battle to defend the blue sky," the AQI of non-priority cities reflects an increase of 16.7%, indicating a decline in air quality. This result is due to environmental protection policies in non-priority cities being weaker than those in priority cities. As a result, when faced with the shock of the policy of "resolutely curbing the rise in housing prices," non-priority cities are more likely to reduce their effort to implement environmental protection policies. Columns (2) and (3) of Table 2 show regressions on the sub-samples of priority cities and non-priority cities, respectively. The results show that after the implementation of the housing price control policy, the AQI of priority cities in the "battle to defend the blue sky" shows an increase of 0.025%, which is significantly lower than the increase in the AQI of non-priority cities.

Robustness checks of DID analysis

Parallel trend test

An important identifying assumption of the DID model is the "parallel trend"; that is, in the absence of policy intervention, the trend of AQI is consistent across cities with varying degrees of land finance dependence. The data presented in Figure 1 suggest that the "parallel trend" may be satisfied. Following the approach of Jacobson *et al.* (1993), we use the event study method to further test this assumption rigorously. The empirical model is set as follows:

$$\log(\text{AQI}_{ijt}) = \Sigma\beta^s\cdot\log(\text{landfis}_k)\cdot D_s + \gamma\cdot\text{blue}_{jt} + \text{city}_j\cdot f(t) + \delta_i + \theta_t + e_{ijt}, \quad (2)$$

where $s \neq 7$ denotes the month and D_s is a binary dummy variable for each month. For example, D_6 takes the value 1 for June and 0 otherwise.[2] The definitions of other variables in empirical model (2) are the same as those in empirical model (1). When $s < 7$, a failure to reject $\beta^s = 0$ statistically means that there was no systematic difference in the air quality among different types of cities before policy implementation, which aligns with the assumption of the "parallel trend."

Figure 2(a) reports the coefficients β^s and 95% confidence intervals based on empirical model (2). As can be seen from the figure, the extent of the impact of land finance dependence on the AQI is close to zero and not statistically significant before policy implementation. However, starting from the month of policy implementation,

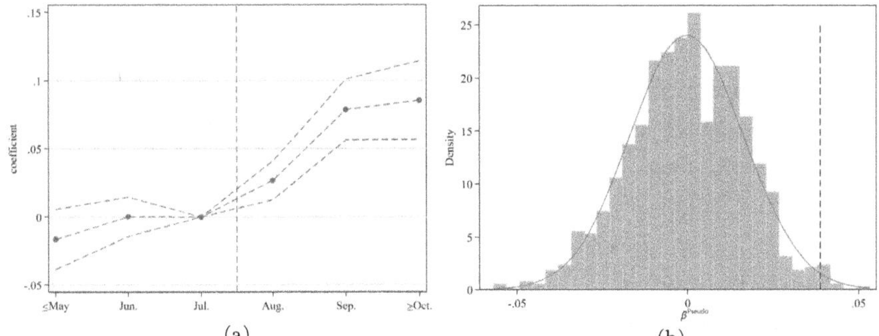

Figure 2. DID related test: (a) Parallel trend test and (b) placebo test.

the estimated value of β^s shows a significant increase and continues to rise at an increasing rate over time, indicating that there was no systematic difference in the AQI among different types of cities before the implementation of the policy of "resolutely curbing the rise in housing prices" and that the implementation of this policy led to a decline in air quality. Thus, the DID regression analysis in this study satisfies the "parallel trend" assumption.

Placebo test

Empirical model (1) assumes that, all else being equal, the change in AQI results from the policy of "resolutely curbing the rise in housing prices" rather than changes in other unobservable factors. If this assumption holds, the new pseudo policy will not significantly affect air quality if land finance dependence is randomly assigned to the cities (La Ferrara *et al.*, 2012). Specifically, we randomly draw a value for each city without replacement from the original data on land finance dependence. This process yields a pseudo land finance dependence variable, $\text{landfis}^{\text{Pseudo}}$, which is then used in empirical model (1) to re-estimate the parameter β^{Pseudo}. Figure 2(b) presents the distribution of β^{Pseudo} estimates obtained from 1,000 simulations. It is observed that β^{Pseudo} exhibits a normal distribution with a mean of 0 (specifically, a value of −0.001 and a standard deviation of 0.017), which is in line with the expected results of a placebo experiment.

Robustness test

In the previous section, we examined the impact of the housing price control policy on air quality based on the average land financial dependence in 2015 and 2017. In the robustness test, we also use the land financial dependence data from 2017 to construct a metric for measuring the intensity of the housing price control policy. As shown in column (1) of Table 3, the policy of "resolutely curbing the rise in housing prices" correlates with a significant improvement in the AQI. In addition, we calculate land finance dependence using the proportion of land transfer revenue in fiscal

Table 3. Policy implementation and urban air quality (DID robustness test).

Variables	Dependent variable: log(AQI)					
	(1) Land finance dependence in 2017	(2) Land finance dependence of fiscal expenditure	(3) Land finance dependence level	(4) The same period of 2017 as used for the reference group	(5) Two-period panel data	(6) City-level adjustment by clustering
log(landfis2017)*post	0.042***					
	(0.006)					
log(landfis_exp)*post		0.032***				
		(0.006)				
landfis*post			0.001***			
			(0.000)			
log(landfis)*year2018				0.020***		
				(0.005)		
log(landfis)*post					0.051***	0.039**
					(0.006)	(0.016)
Observations	13,750	13,750	13,750	13,500	2,750	13,750
Adjusted *R*-squared	0.905	0.905	0.905	0.881	0.875	0.905
City-specific time trend	2	2	2	2		2
Battle to defend the blue sky	X	X	X			X

Notes: Statistics in parentheses are the robust standard errors adjusted by clustering at the station level. Station fixed effects and month fixed effects are controlled for in all regressions. Data from August to December 2017 versus August to December 2018 are analyzed in column (4), where 2018 indicates that it takes the value of 1 for 2018 data and 0 otherwise. *** $p < 0.01$, ** $p < 0.05$, * $p < 0.1$.

expenditure and investigate the relationship between the AQI and the housing price control policy using a semi-elastic model, as shown in columns (2) and (3) of Table 3. The findings of this study remain robust.[3]

Figure 1 shows that the AQI exhibits certain seasonal characteristics. In the previous analysis, we controlled for month fixed effects to eliminate the interference of seasonal factors on the AQI to some extent. To conduct a robustness test, we use the data of the same period of the previous year for the analysis; that is, we compare the difference between the AQI of cities with different levels of land finance dependence from August to December 2018 with the same period in 2017. Column (4) of Table 3 shows that when a city's land finance dependence increases by 1%, the AQI from that city's station in 2018 reflects an increase of 0.02% over that in the same period of 2017, suggesting that the findings remain robust despite seasonal factors.

When we use multi-period panel data for the DID empirical analysis, the standard error of the coefficient β in empirical model (1) is biased owing to serial correlation, which can lead to over-rejection of the null hypothesis, mistakenly identifying policy effectiveness that is not statistically significant as a policy treatment effect. Bertrand *et al.* (2004) suggest that two-period panel data be constructed by separately averaging the multiple-period data before and after policy implementation for each observation unit to effectively reduce the bias in subsequent DID analysis. Following this approach, we average the AQI from each station before and after policy implementation separately and conduct a robustness test. As shown in column (5) of Table 3, the analysis using two-period data still shows that the policy of "resolutely curbing the rise in housing prices" correlates with a significant increase in the AQI at the 1% level, consistent with the earlier findings.

In the first five columns of Table 3, the standard errors are adjusted by clustering at the station level to control for within-station air quality correlations. For the robustness test, we similarly allow for within-city air pollution correlations and adjust the standard errors by clustering at the city level. Column (6) of Table 3 shows that the earlier findings of this study are robust.

Further Analysis

Using the policy shock of "resolutely curbing the rise in housing prices," we construct a continuous DID model using the land finance dependence of local governments and find that this policy shock led to a decline in air quality, a finding that remains valid after a series of robustness tests. On this basis, we conduct further analysis based on the theoretical logic of the behavioral choices of local governments under multiple policy objectives. Under multiple policy objectives, local governments need to weigh political incentives, economic incentives, and the relative strengths of different policy objectives, thereby leading to the implementation dilemmas of local governments under multiple policy objectives. The pursuit of local fiscal revenue is the most crucial economic incentive for local governments. When local governments face greater fiscal pressure, the pollution effect of the policy to curb housing prices may be further amplified, which is known as the "fiscal pressure hypothesis." However, local governments may develop industries at the cost of relaxing environmental regulations to increase their fiscal revenue. Then, after the implementation of the policy of "resolutely curbing the rise in housing prices," the primary reason for the decline in air quality should be the increase in industrial emissions. We can test the so-called "industrial development hypothesis" accordingly.

Fiscal pressure hypothesis test

The fiscal pressure hypothesis posits that the reduction in local governments' effort to implement environmental protection policies is related to their fiscal pressure. This hypothesis can be tested from the perspective of the moderating role of the fiscal revenue growth target. Accordingly, we establish an empirical model as follows:

$$\log(\mathrm{AQI}_{ijt}) = \beta \cdot \log(\mathrm{landfis}_j) \cdot \mathrm{post}_t + \alpha \cdot \log(\mathrm{landfis}_j) \cdot \mathrm{post}_t \cdot \mathrm{M}_j + \gamma \cdot \mathrm{blue}_{jt} + \mathrm{city}_j \cdot f(t) + \delta_i + \theta_t + e_{ijt}, \tag{3}$$

where M is a moderating variable, which focuses on the fiscal revenue growth target of the city; α captures the role of the moderating variable in moderating the pollution effect of "resolutely curbing the rise in housing prices"; and $\alpha > 0$ means that the moderating variable strengthens the environmental pollution caused by the housing price control. The definitions of other variables in empirical model (3) are the same as those in empirical model (1).

We manually collect the fiscal revenue growth target (fiscal) set by each city at the beginning of the year. The Chinese government has a strong sense of target management. At the annual sessions of the People's Congress, held at the beginning of each year, local governments announce their fiscal revenue growth targets for the year. While collecting the data, we compile a specific list of 337 cities based on the 2018 Administrative Division Codes of the People's Republic of China provided by the Ministry of Civil Affairs, then collect the 2018 government work reports of these cities, and finally obtain the data on the fiscal revenue growth targets of 307 cities. The fiscal revenue growth targets of the sample cities are averaged at 7.4%, with a minimum of 1.6% and a maximum of 15%, indicating large differences in the fiscal revenue growth pressures faced by different cities. Since the fiscal revenue growth target was set at the beginning of the year while the policy of "resolutely curbing the rise in housing prices" was implemented in the middle of the year, controlling housing prices could have a greater shock on fiscal revenue in cities with higher fiscal revenue growth targets. As shown in column (1) of Table 4, all else being equal, the implementation of the housing price control policy correlates with a significant increase in the AQI, consistent with the earlier finding. Moreover, the interaction term between policy implementation and fiscal revenue growth target is statistically significant at the 1% level, indicating that if cities with higher land finance dependence set higher annual fiscal revenue growth targets at the beginning of the year, the decline in air quality in those cities would become more severe after the implementation of the policy of "resolutely curbing the rise in housing prices," in line with the prediction of the fiscal pressure hypothesis.

Economic growth is an essential source of the increase in fiscal revenue. Since the fiscal revenue growth targets strengthen the pollution effects of housing price control policies, economic growth targets should, logically, amplify the impact of housing price

Table 4. Policy implementation, fiscal growth pressure, and urban air quality.

	Dependent variable: log(AQI)	
Variables	(1)	(2)
log(landfis)*post	0.068***	0.274***
	(0.014)	(0.023)
log(landfis)*post*log(fiscal)	0.014***	
	(0.005)	
log(landfis)*post*log(gdp)		0.100***
		(0.010)
Observations	13,100	13,650
Adjusted *R*-squared	0.906	0.906

Notes: Statistics in parentheses are the robust standard errors adjusted by clustering at the station level. Station fixed effects, month fixed effects, battle to defend the blue sky, and second-order city-specific time trend are controlled for in all regressions. *** $p < 0.01$, ** $p < 0.05$, * $p < 0.1$.

control policies on air quality. We also collect the GDP growth targets (GDP) of 323 cities, with a larger value indicating greater pressure on the government to achieve stable economic growth. According to column (2) of Table 4, the policy of "resolutely curbing the rise in housing prices" correlates with a significant rise in the AQI, consistent with the finding mentioned earlier. Moreover, the interaction term between policy implementation and the economic growth target has a significant positive impact on AQI at the 1% level. This finding similarly suggests that the pursuit of fiscal revenue is an important reason for the decline in air quality after the implementation of the policy of "resolutely curbing the rise in housing prices."

Industrial development hypothesis test

The key research hypothesis of this study states that controlling the rise in housing prices leads local governments to sacrifice the environmental objective, ultimately resulting in a decline in air quality. The "industrial development hypothesis" offers a concrete way to verify how local governments sacrifice the environmental objective. To examine the differential impact of the housing price control policy on the concentration of different types of pollutants, we establish an empirical model as follows:

$$\log(\text{poll}^k_{ijt}) = \beta^k . \log(\text{landfis}_j) . \text{post}_t + \gamma . \text{blue}_{jt} + \text{city}_j . f(t) + \delta_i + \theta_t + e_{ijt}, \tag{4}$$

where poll^k is the concentration of the pollutant of the kth type (or in the kth time period) and β^k captures the impact of the housing price control policy on pollutant concentration. The definitions of other variables in empirical model (4) are the same as those in empirical model (1).

Table 5 examines the influence of the housing price control policy on the concentration of different pollutants. As shown in Table 5, a 1% increase in the land finance dependence of a city correlates with a significant increase of 0.028% in the SO_2 concentration at the city station after policy implementation, but there is no significant increase in the concentration of other pollutants such as NO_2 and CO. Since industrial pollution is primarily reflected in the increase of SO_2 emissions, this result indicates that the decline in air quality caused by the policy of "resolutely curbing the rise in housing prices" mainly originated from the emission of pollutant gases

Table 5. Policy implementation and urban air quality (by pollutant).

Variables	(1) log(SO_2)	(2) log(NO_2)	(3) log(CO)
log(landfis)*post	0.028**	0.006	−0.000
	(0.012)	(0.009)	(0.007)
Observations	13,748	13,750	13,748
Adjusted R-squared	0.841	0.913	0.852

Notes: Statistics in parentheses are the robust standard errors adjusted by clustering at the station level. Station fixed effects, month fixed effects, battle to defend the blue sky, and second-order city-specific time trend are controlled for in all regressions. *** $p < 0.01$, ** $p < 0.05$, * $p < 0.1$.

from industrial production, aligning with the prediction of the "industrial development hypothesis."

Moreover, we examine the changes in pollutant concentrations during different time periods after the implementation of the housing price control policy. Enterprises are motivated to discharge pollutants during nighttime owing to the lower probability of regulatory enforcement at night. Agarwal *et al.* (2019) find a significant increase in the concentration of the industrial pollutant SO_2 after nightfall. When local governments prioritize industrial development because of financial pressures, they are likely to relax their environmental regulatory efforts, leading to an increase in pollutant emissions during the daytime and a corresponding decline in air quality during the daytime. Agarwal *et al.* (2019) report that industrial pollutant concentrations in China show a significant increase four hours after sunset. We collect daily sunset times for each city and calculate the AQI four hours before sunset (AQI_day) and four hours after sunset (AQI_night) for each monitoring station. As shown in Table 6, the policy of "resolutely curbing the rise in housing prices" mainly results in a decline in air quality before sunset. For every 1% increase in a city's land finance dependence, the implementation of the housing price control policy correlates with a significant increase of 0.061% in the average AQI at the city station four hours before sunset, while there is no significant impact on the AQI after sunset.

Table 6. Policy implementation and industrial pollution (daytime versus nighttime).

Variables	(1) log(AQI_day)	(2) log(AQI_night)	(3) AQI_day/AQI_night
log(landfis)*post	0.061^{***} (0.010)	0.008 (0.007)	0.014^{***} (0.002)
Observations	13,548	13,547	13,547
Adjusted *R*-squared	0.863	0.890	0.674

Notes: Statistics in parentheses are the robust standard errors adjusted by clustering at the station level. Station fixed effects, month fixed effects, battle to defend the blue sky, and second-order city-specific time trend are controlled for in all regressions. *** $p < 0.01$, ** $p < 0.05$, * $p < 0.1$.

Conclusion

High-quality development inevitably requires a shift from the previous mode of single policy objectives that overemphasize local economic growth. Under the current pattern of central–local relationships, the implementation of multiple policy objectives by local governments is not conducive to the maximization of local fiscal revenue. Consequently, the pursuit of multiple policy objectives may disrupt the original incentive-compatible structure. Although the central government still holds the power to promote local officials and can incorporate multiple policy objectives into their assessment metrics system, local officials may reduce their efforts to implement central policies under information asymmetry because of the increased difficulty of assessment in the presence of multiple policy objectives. The implementation dilemma faced by local governments under multiple policy objectives likely leads them to selectively prioritize their implementation efforts according to the different attributes of particular policies, increasing the complexity and uncertainty of policy implementation effectiveness under multiple policy objectives. Taking the implementation of the policies of "resolutely curbing the rise in housing prices" and the three-year air pollution action plan in 2018 as examples, we find that the housing price control policy has led local governments to relax their environmental protection efforts.

Based on the above theoretical discussion and empirical analysis, we posit that reshaping central–local relationships under multiple policy objectives is necessary for achieving high-quality development. The existing series of institutional arrangements for central–local relationships had inherent incentive compatibility in the era of solely emphasizing GDP as the measure of success, but they have been unsustainable since the economy entered the new normal, and the multiple policy objectives embedded in high-quality development have further disrupted the inherent incentive compatibility of the original system. Reshaping central–local relationships should focus on the comprehensive transformation of the relationship between the central and local governments in the new era. The key is to reform the incentive mechanism for local governments, strengthen their self-restraint through various institutional arrangements, increase the transparency of policy implementation by local governments through reforms, better leverage public supervision, and reduce the assessment costs for the central government.

Endnotes

1. Notice on Improving the Performance Assessment of Local Party and Government Leadership Teams and Leading Cadres, issued by the Organization Department of the Central Committee of the Communist Party of China on December 6, 2013.
2. In regression analysis, we group the data from May and earlier into one group and the data from October and later into another.
3. We also obtain results (not reported here) by using land finance dependence in 2016 and the average land finance dependence from 2014 to 2016, and the findings remain robust.

References

Agarwal, S., Qin, Y., and Zhu, H. 2019. Disguised pollution: Industrial activities in the dark. SSRN Working Paper.

Bertrand, M., Duflo, E., and Mullainathan, S. 2004. How much should we trust differences-in-differences estimates? *Quarterly Journal of Economics*, 119(1): 249–275.

Blanchard, O. and Shleifer, A. 2001. Federalism with and without political centralization: China versus Russia. *IMF Staff Papers*, 48(1): 171–179.

Chen, Y., Li, P., and Lu, Y. 2018. Career concerns and multitasking local bureaucrats: Evidence of a target-based performance evaluation system in China. *Journal of Development Economics*, 133: 84–101.

Dewatripont, M., Jewitt, I., and Tirole, J. 1999. The economics of career concerns. Part II: Application to missions and accountability of government agencies. *Review of Economic Studies*, 66(1): 199–217.

Fang, H. and Zhang, J. 2013. Grabbing hand, helping hand and tax-exceeding-GDP growth. *Economic Research Journal*, 3: 108–121.

Jacobson, L., LaLonde, R., and Sullivan, D. 1993. Earnings losses of displaced workers. *American Economic Review*, 83(4): 685–709.

Jin, H., Qian, Y., and Weingast, B. 2005. Regional decentralization and fiscal incentives: Federalism, Chinese style. *Journal of Public Economics*, 89(9): 1719–1742.

La Ferrara, E., Chong, A., and Duryea, S. 2012. Soap operas and fertility: Evidence from Brazil. *American Economic Journal: Applied Economics*, 4(4): 1–31.

Li, H. and Zhou, L. 2005. Political turnover and economic performance: The incentive role of personnel control in China. *Journal of Public Economics*, 89(9): 1743–1762.

Shao, C., Su, D., and Deng, H. 2016. House prices, land finance and city agglomeration characteristics: The road of China's city development. *Management World*, 2: 19–31, 187.

Sun, X. and Zhou, F. 2013. Land finance and tax-sharing system: An empirical explanation. *Social Sciences in China*, 4: 40–59, 205.

Wilson, J. 1989. *Bureaucracy: What Government Agencies Do and Why They Do It*. New York: Basic Books.

Wu, M. and Zhou, L. 2018. Political incentives and city construction: The visibility of public projects. *Economic Research Journal*, 12: 97–111.

Xi, P., Liang, R., and Xie, Z. 2017. Tax sharing adjustment, fiscal pressure and industrial pollution. *The Journal of World Economy*, 10: 170–192.

Xie, Z., Zhu, K., and Li, P. 2019. Tax sharing, fiscal incentives and urban land allocation. *Economic Research Journal*, 10: 57–73.

Xu, C. 2011. The fundamental institutions of China's reforms and development. *Journal of Economic Literature*, 49(4): 1076–1151.

Xu, X., Li, S., Wang, X., and Bi, Q. 2018. Growth target choices: Ending Chinese collapse fallacy with high-quality development. *The Journal of World Economy*, 10: 3–25.

Zhang, J. 2012. Understanding the mechanism of China's rapid economic development: Zhu Rongji may be right. *Comparative Studies*, 6. In Zhang, J., Fan, Z., and Fang, H. 2016. *The Race to the Top: Understanding the Mechanism of China's Economic Development*. Beijing: Peking University Press.

Zhang, J. and Gao, Y. 2007. Term limits and rotation of Chinese governors: Do they matter to economic growth? *Economic Research Journal*, 11: 91–103.

Zhang, J., Gao, Y., Fu, Y., and Zhang, H. 2007. Why does China enjoy so much better physical infrastructure? *Economic Research Journal*, 3: 4–19.

Zhang, J., Fan, H., Xu, Z., and Zhou, L. 2020. Structural decline in the GDP growth rate: The impact of the official assessment mechanism. *Economic Research Journal*, 5: 31–48.

Zhou, F. 2007a. The role of government and farmers in land development and transfer. *Sociological Studies*, 1: 49–82, 243–244.

Zhou, L. 2007b. Governing China's local officials: An analysis of promotion tournament model. *Economic Research Journal*, 7: 36–50.

https://doi.org/10.1142/9789819815241_0014

Chapter 14

FROM AN ENTREPRENEURIAL STATE TO AN INVESTOR STATE: CHINA'S SEMICONDUCTOR INDUSTRIAL POLICIES

Tomoo Marukawa

University of Tokyo, Tokyo, Japan
marukawa@iss.u-tokyo.ac.jp

Introduction

The most advanced countries in the world are currently fiercely competing to innovate processes of semiconductor production. In February 2022, the United States (US) House of Representatives passed the America COMPETES Act of 2022. This bill, together with the US Innovation and Competition Act of 2021, which was passed by the Senate in June 2021, enables the US government to subsidize US$52 billion to spur the production of semiconductors in the US. In December 2021, the Japanese Diet enacted bills to allow the government to support the domestic production of semiconductors. As the first step of this initiative, the Japanese government allotted JPY 617 billion from its 2021 budget to the semiconductor investment fund created under a government-affiliated agency. In February

2022, the European Commission proposed the European Chips Act, which aimed to mobilize more than €43 billion of public and private investments to bolster Europe's semiconductor industry and raise its global market share to 20% in 2030 from 10% in 2020.[1] It was China's ambitious semiconductor industrial policy that stimulated these initiatives by the US, Japan, and the European Union (EU). In 2014, China's State Council promulgated the "Outlines of Promoting the Development of National Integrated Circuit (IC) Industry." In the same year, the National IC Investment Fund was established, which was reported to invest RMB 138.7 billion for the development of the domestic IC industry.

The strong responses by developed countries against China's goals regarding the production of semiconductors suggest that they believe that it is possible for China to achieve its goals of enhancing its competitiveness and expanding its market share in the global semiconductor industry. More than seven years have passed since the implementation of China's ambitious semiconductor policy. Therefore, it has currently become possible to examine whether the developed nations' fear regarding China's advancement in semiconductor production is valid. The current study reveals that so far, China is still far from achieving its goal of localizing IC production, casting doubts on the validity of these countries' fears. It appears that the developed countries have overrated China's capability to increase domestically produced ICs' share in the global semiconductor market and launched aggressive industrial policies that risk triggering global overcapacity and trade wars. The overreaction by Western countries and other developed countries stems from their vision of China as a competent and entrepreneurial "developmental state." The study aims to adjust this vision, which the author believes is somewhat misleading, through a detailed study of China's industrial policies, with a special focus on its semiconductor industrial policy.

This chapter is structured as follows. The second section reviews the discussions on China's industrial policy in the existing literature and examines the validity of the discussions through a brief review of China's Five-Year Plans, which represent its industrial policies in the most comprehensive form. The third section describes China's semiconductor industrial policies from the 1990s until today, which is followed by a detailed analysis of the National IC Investment Fund's investments. The fourth section evaluates the achievements of China's semiconductor industrial policies, which is followed by the conclusion.

Is China a "Developmental State"?

Before questioning China's characterization as a developmental state, we first need to have a clear definition of "a developmental state." According to Knight (2014), a country that accords the highest policy priority to economic growth and adopts institutional arrangements and incentive structures that will promote that objective can be called a developmental state. If so, is not China, under central planning, a developmental state? The Chinese leadership placed the highest priority on heavy industrialization and made institutional arrangements such as the establishment of the State Planning Commission and numerous industrial ministries. However, the existing literature has tended to exclude planned economies from developmental states. Johnson (1982) argues that the means of the planned economy, which are state ownership of the means of production, state planning, and bureaucratic goal-setting, proved inefficient in achieving developmental goals. Countries which insist on using these means are selecting them not on the basis of a rational calculation but from an ideological adherence to these means; therefore, they cannot be regarded as developmental states. Knight (2014) argues that during the planned economy period, politics dictated economic policies; therefore, China was not a developmental state at that point in time.

In my view, the fundamental difference between a non-developmental planned economy and a developmental state is that in the latter, the improvement of people's living standards is regarded as one of the central purposes of economic growth, whereas in the former, it is not so. China, from the 1950s to the 1970s, suppressed grain prices and wages so that the state could amass investment funds at the sacrifice of people's living standards. In contrast, the Japanese government launched the "Income-Doubling Plan" in 1960. However, in 1982, the Chinese Communist Party launched a plan to quadruple its industrial and agricultural output by the end of the century and raise people's living standards to a "modest level(*xiaokang*)." Since that point in time, China has become a developmental state, according to my definition, even though the planned economic system remained dominant in the Chinese economy during the 1980s.

An important feature of a developmental state is the use of industrial policy — policies that aim to influence the structure of domestic industry and enhance its international competitiveness — in achieving the goal of economic growth. East Asian countries which experienced rapid industrialization during the latter half of the 20th century, such as Japan, South Korea, and Taiwan, implemented industrial policies that targeted some specific industries (Johnson, 1982; Amsden, 1989; Sato, 2007). However, when we apply this East Asian development model to China, we face the problem of defining industrial policy. Can industrial plans in China's planned economy be regarded as a variety of industrial policy? China, during the planned economy period, implemented industrial plans that prioritized specific industries, such as iron and steel during the 1950s and petrochemicals during the 1970s. If we define industrial policy as the government's attempt to remedy market failures, however, these plans do not fall into the category of industrial policy because the market mechanism did not exist in the first place at that point in time. Based on such a definition, Fischer *et al.* (2021) argue that industrial policies were formally deployed in China in 1994, only after China announced its intention to transform into a market economy. In this chapter, however, I will regard industrial plans during the planned economy period as a variety of industrial policy, owing to a practical reason: it is difficult to draw a line between industrial plans and industrial policies in the case of China, which shifted gradually from a planned economy to a market economy. The main tools of a planned economy, that is, five-year plans and state-owned enterprises, have been used as the means to achieve the goals of industrial policies even after China transformed itself into a market economy. In fact, five-year plans represent the most comprehensive design of China's industrial policy, even at the time of writing this, which is the second year of the 14th Five-Year Plan. Therefore, it is difficult to say when industrial plans ended and when industrial policies (in a narrow sense) began.

Besides the legacy of the planned economy, there are two other aspects of China's industrial policy that make it different from the East Asian model. First, due to the country's enormous scale, China's industrial policy has to be implemented through several layers of local governments, which may have goals not necessarily aligned with the central government's direction (Chu, 2017). This fact often attenuates the effectiveness of industrial policies. Chu (2017) points out that the policy of eliminating excess capacity in steel failed because local governments had different goals from those of the central government. Marukawa (2020) showed that five consecutive policies regarding the iron and steel industry issued during 2001–2016 had targets of consolidating the industry, which were expressed in the share of the top 10 enterprises in total crude steel production, but none of the targets have been met.[2] The difficulty in implementing industrial policy, which stems from the complexity of government bureaucracy, is one of the reasons for the ineffectiveness of industrial policies in guiding the direction of investment. Holz (2018) found that sector-wise investment patterns could largely be explained by profitability and private entrepreneurship but hardly by industrial policies.

Another aspect that differentiates China from the East Asian model is the extensive use of state-owned enterprises and state investment in pursuing industrial policy goals. It is true that other East Asian states also invested directly in their priority industries. The Japanese government established Yawata Steel in 1901, which has expanded to become one of the most competitive steel manufacturers in the world currently. The Korean government established Pohang Steel (POSCO) in 1968 despite opposition from the World Bank (Amsden, 1989). Taiwan's Ministry of Economic Affairs planned and created United Microelectronics Corporation (UMC), which subsequently became the leading semiconductor manufacturer in

Taiwan, by mobilizing state and private investments (Sato, 2007). China's state investment by far exceeds its East Asian counterparts in breadth and depth. As of 2019, the central and local governments of all layers in China owned 217,000 state-owned enterprises. The Chinese government often resorts to the merger or reorganization of state-owned enterprises to pursue its industrial policy goals.[3] The active investments by central and local governments in China prompted the model of an "entrepreneurial state," in which government bureaus embark on profit-seeking and risk-taking businesses to adapt and contribute to marketization (Duckett, 1996). Mazzucato (2018) went on to argue further that even successful advanced countries, including the US, could be called entrepreneurial states, in which the government targets promising industries and takes the risk of investing in their research and development.

However, the characterization of the Chinese government as "risk-taking" is questionable. It is true that the state's direct investment in business enterprises entails the risk of losing state assets by bankruptcy. However, if state investments are divided into hundreds of thousands of enterprises which belong to many industrial sectors ranging from high-tech to low-tech,[4] can we still regard the state as risk-taking? Policies such as the "Outline of the National Industrial Policy in the 1990s" (1994), which advocated for making machinery and electronics, petrochemicals, automobile manufacturing, and construction industries the "pillars" of the national economy, the "Decision on Accelerating Cultivation and Development of Strategic Emerging Industries" (2010), and "Made in China 2025" (2015) give us the impression that the government gave high priority to developing the leading industries or high-tech industries. However, we must consider that all of these policies were incorporated in the ensuing five-year plans, in which the focus on the leading or high-tech industries was attenuated because the plans had several other priorities. The 13th Five-Year Plan, which was issued in 2016, for example, incorporated the main contents of "Made in China 2025" but used even more words for describing tasks to promote the modernization of agriculture. The plan also gave importance to the development of services, transportation, and energy. The promotion of high-tech industries constitutes only a part of the numerous priorities listed in the 13th Five-Year Plan. Along with the development of new industries in China, the number of industrial sectors mentioned in the five-year plans tends to increase. In the Ninth Five-Year Plan (1996–2000), there were 20 industries mentioned, including the "pillar industries" in the "Outline of the National Industrial Policy in the 1990s." The number of industries mentioned increased to 32 in the 11th Five-Year Plan (2006–2010), mainly due to the development of high-tech industries. The 13th Five-Year Plan (2016–2020) mentioned 34 industries, and the recent 14th Five-Year Plan (2021–2025) mentions 41 industries. The five-year plans tend to be all-encompassing, rather than taking the risk of investing in a small number of industries.

The following sections argue that even with an industrial policy targeting a single industry — which is the semiconductor industry — a shift from a concentration on a limited number of projects to encompassing more and more enterprises and subsectors has taken place.

Review of China's Semiconductor Industrial Policies

China's efforts to localize the production of ICs began in the 1980s. The first mass-production factory of ICs in China was built by the state-run Jiangnan Radio Equipment Works (or the "742 Factory") in Wuxi in 1984 by importing the production lines and technology from Toshiba, a Japanese company. This project was part of the government's policy to localize the production of color television sets and their core components. The factory encompassed the full range of IC production, from the production of silicon ingots to the fabrication of three-inch wafers, photolithography, assembly, and testing. The factory produced linear ICs for amplifying analog signals, which was one of the core components of color television sets. The factory had an annual production capacity of 30 million chips, and the ICs produced at the plant were installed in approximately 40% of color television sets assembled in China (Chen and Dong, 2018; Zhu, 2018). At the end of the 1980s, the factory introduced technology and equipment from Toshiba and Siemens and upgraded its process technology from 5 μm to 2–3 μm. It started to produce CMOS digital ICs using four- and five-inch wafers. The factory was renamed China Huajing Electronics Corporation and became the center of China's semiconductor industry.

In August 1990, the government launched the "908 Project," which aimed to upgrade Huajing's IC manufacturing capability by introducing 1 μm process technology. However, the government spent five years on the project's approval process and the procurement of investment funds. When the factory was completed in 1997, it was equipped with a 0.9 μm process for six-inch wafers introduced from AT&T; however, this technology was already outdated by that time. Because of the lack of competitiveness, the factory began incurring losses as soon as it started operation (Chen and Dong, 2018: 150–151). In the same year, a delegation of Taiwanese semiconductor specialists visited Huajing. They decided to establish a company in Hong Kong, which borrowed the production lines of Huajing and used them for consignment manufacturing of ICs, receiving orders from foreign and domestic IC design houses. Hence, Huajing became the first "pure foundry" in China, a factory that specializes in IC fabrication based on orders from design houses outside (Zhu, 2018).

During the 1990s, foreign semiconductor manufacturers made a greater contribution to the advancement of Chinese semiconductor technology than the state-led "908 Project." Japan's NEC Corporation, for example, signed a contract with Capital Steel (Shougang) in 1990 to establish a joint venture for IC production. The joint venture Shougang NEC Corporation (SGNEC) began production in 1994 using the 1.2 μm process for six-inch wafers. SGNEC upgraded its process technology to 0.5 μm in 1997, which was more advanced than the 908 Project. SGNEC produced four-megabyte dynamic random-access memories (DRAMs) and microcontroller units (MCUs). As of 1999, 80% of its products were exported to Japan's NEC, and the latter sold them through its global distribution channel. NEC decided to establish the semiconductor joint venture because it was required by the Chinese government to help the development of China's semiconductor industry in exchange for the approval of establishing a factory for the production and sale of telephone switches.[5] During the 1990s, Alcatel and Philips also established semiconductor joint ventures in China, most likely based on motives similar to that of NEC.

The failure of the 908 Project and the success of foreign-invested semiconductor joint ventures did not deter the Chinese government from launching another project aimed at the localization of semiconductor production. In December 1995, the government decided to start the "909 Project," which aimed to upgrade the semiconductor process technology to 0.5 μm for eight-inch wafers. The speech delivered by Hu Qili, the Electronics Industry Minister, at the Central Economic Policy Meeting held in December 1995 suggests that Chinese leaders were stimulated by the rapid development of the semiconductor industry in Taiwan and South Korea. Apparently, Hu was not so happy with the success of foreign-invested semiconductor ventures in China. He suggested that the competition with the foreign-invested ventures would lead to the collapse of domestic semiconductor manufacturers. The Ministry of Electronics Industry envisaged a Taiwanese-style division of labor between a foundry and IC design houses. Therefore, the 909 Project consisted of three sub-projects, namely, an eight-inch semiconductor foundry equipped with 0.5 μm process technology, three or four world-class chip design centers, and an eight-inch monocrystalline silicon ingot factory (Hu, 2001).

However, the ministry realized that China could acquire state-of-the-art technology only through collaboration with the leading semiconductor manufacturers. NEC was the only one among the leading manufacturers in the world that agreed to provide its latest technology to the 909 Project. NEC insisted on making DRAMs at the new factory, because the company had strong competitiveness in DRAMs while lacking experience in running a foundry (Yuan, 2000; Hu, 2001). The new factory created by the 909 Project, which was named Huahong NEC, was a joint venture between NEC, the Shanghai City government, and the Ministry of Electronics Industry. Huahong NEC began semiconductor production in 1999, using 0.35 μm process technology on eight-inch wafers. More than 80% of Huahong NEC's production was 64-megabyte DRAMs, which were distributed through NEC's global sales network. The 909 Project ended up becoming one of the production sites of NEC's global IC production network. The collapse of the "dot-com bubble" in 2001, however, prompted Huahong NEC to stop producing DRAMs. The joint venture recorded a huge loss that year, and it consequently began to shift its production capacity from DRAM production to consignment manufacturing. To facilitate the shift to a foundry, in 2003, a new partner, Jazz Semiconductor, was called in, while NEC decreased its share of ownership at Huahong NEC.[6]

After the failure of two major projects ("908" and "909"), the Chinese government refrained from direct involvement in semiconductor production. Instead, the government launched an incentive policy named "Policies for Promoting the Development of Software and IC Industries" in 2000 (See Table 1). It stipulated that domestic IC manufacturers would be refunded 11 percentage points of their

Table 1. List of semiconductor industrial policies.

Year	Title	Main content
1990	908 Project	To acquire 1 μm process technology
1996	909 Project	To acquire 0.35–0.5 μm process technology
2000	Policies on Promoting the Development of Software and IC Industries	To refund 11 percentage point of 17% value added tax to IC manufacturers
2011	Renewed Policies on Promoting the Development of Software and IC Industries	To exempt corporate income tax on IC manufacturers using the process rule of 0.8 μm or less
2014	Outlines of Promoting the Development of National IC Industry	To establish the National IC Industry Investment Fund
2015	"Made in China 2025" and its Technology Roadmap	To raise localization ratio of semiconductors to 49% by 2020 and 75% by 2030
2020	Policies for Promoting High-Quality Development of the IC and Software Industries in the New Period	To exempt corporate income tax on IC manufacturers using the process rule of 28 nm, 65 nm, and 130nm or less

17% value-added tax. This policy encouraged the establishment of several new entrants. In 2000, Semiconductor Manufacturing International Corporation (SMIC), a foundry specialized in consignment manufacturing, was established in Shanghai by Richard Chang, a Taiwanese engineer who had worked for Texas Instruments for 20 years. Grace Semiconductors, another foundry, was also founded in the same year. Several Taiwanese and foreign manufacturers were also attracted by the incentive policy and constructed semiconductor factories in China; these included Hejian, TSMC, SK Hynix and ST Microelectronics, Intel, and Samsung. However, in 2004, the US appealed to the World Trade Organization (WTO) that the policy subjected imported ICs to higher taxes than applied to domestically produced ICs and therefore infringed upon the General Agreement on Tariffs and Trade (GATT). In the same year, China agreed to revoke the tax rebate policy.[7]

After the two big projects and the tax rebate policy, which the Chinese government was forced to retract later, the government did not take any further measures for the development of semiconductors until 2013, with the exception of an additional tax exemption policy in 2011. In 2014, China's semiconductor industrial policy suddenly gained steam with the issuance of the "Outlines of Promoting the Development of National IC Industry" by the Ministry of Industry and Information Technology. This policy aimed to alter the current situation of China's semiconductor market, which depended heavily on imports, and ensure China's entry into the most advanced levels in the global semiconductor industry in several fields, with several first-tier manufacturers by 2030. It stated that the state would soon establish the National IC Industry Investment Fund while expanding the income tax exemption to packaging, testing, materials, and equipment manufacturers of ICs.

In September 2014, the National IC Industry Investment Fund Corporation was established. Its main investors were the Ministry of Finance, China Tobacco Corporation, China Development Bank Capital, and Beijing E-Town International Investment and Development Company. It was reported that the fund planned to raise RMB 138.7 billion and invest in all components of the semiconductor supply chain, ranging from foundries, design houses, packaging, and testing to materials and manufacturing equipment. In 2019, the Second-Round National IC Industry Investment Fund Corporation was established. It planned to raise RMB 200 billion from investors, similar to the first-round fund. The details of the funds' investments are discussed in the following section.

In 2015, the State Council announced the "Made in China 2025 (MIC2025)" policy, which was the most important industrial policy implemented under Xi Jinping's rule (Marukawa, 2020). The policy identified 10 industries as its focus, including the "next-generation information technology industry," which includes semiconductors. The policy also prioritized strengthening the "basic and core component" industry, and this also included semiconductors. MIC2025's goal is to raise the ratio of "indigenous" components of "basic core components and important basic materials" to 40% by 2020 and 70% by 2025. Since semiconductors were regarded as the most important target of MIC2025, these figures are often mistaken in Western media as the goals of semiconductor localization (for example, Tabeta, 2021; IC Insights, 2020). But a report in *21st Century Economic Herald* (September 23, 2020) stated that "there is a widespread rumor that the Chinese government has a target to increase its localization rate of semiconductors to 70 percent in 2025. However, 'several authoritative people' denied the existence of such target and it is far from the reality."

However, the "Technology Roadmap of Key Industries" of 2015, which was one of the sub-policies of MIC2025, compiled by the Strategic Consultation Committee for Building a Strong Manufacturing Nation, had an even more aggressive target. The roadmap specified detailed targets of the semiconductor industry, such as "mass production using 16/14 nm process," and set the goals of the domestic production ratio of ICs at 49% by 2020 and 75% by 2030. The roadmap was revised in 2017, and in this version, the targets were raised to 58% in 2020 and 80% in 2030. The fact that MIC2025 was not mentioned in the 14th Five-Year Plan promulgated in March 2021 and the Technology Roadmap — which used to be the most detailed plan in the whole series of policy documents on MIC2025 — has not been revised since 2017 suggests that MIC2025 and the localization targets in the technology roadmap are no longer effective.

However, the Chinese government's drive to promote the development of the semiconductor industry has not weakened. That fact was revealed in the State Council's "Policies for Promoting High-Quality Development of the IC and Software Industries in the New Period," which was promulgated in August 2020 as a renewal of the tax exemption policies of 2000 and 2011. This policy announced that semiconductor manufacturers using 28 nm or more advanced process technology would enjoy 10 years of full exemption from corporate income tax. Manufacturers using less advanced process technology would enjoy a full or half tax exemption for a shorter period. Firms engaging in IC packaging, testing, materials, software, and equipment manufacturing would also enjoy tax exemption for a certain period. The policy also called for the creation of a "nationwide system" for developing the core technologies of semiconductors, such as high-end chips, equipment and manufacturing technologies, basic materials, IC design tools, and software.

The above review suggests that the 40 years of semiconductor industrial policy can be divided into two periods. During the first two decades, the Chinese government focused on a single project. During the next two decades, the government used generalized policies, such as tax incentives and investment funds. Although the government's strong inclination toward semiconductor development has remained unchanged, its method of promoting it has changed from a high risk-taking, entrepreneurial one to a less risk-taking one. Whether the activities of the National IC Industry Investment Fund since 2014 can be regarded as entrepreneurial or not will be discussed in the subsequent section.

Investments by the National IC Industry Investment Funds

As mentioned in the previous section, the National IC Industry Investment Fund Corporation was established in 2014, and the Second-Round National IC Industry Investment Fund Corporation was established in 2019. In the following, these will be called National

IC Fund 1 and 2, respectively. As of January 2022, the total amount of investments made by the two funds were RMB 96.7 billion and RM B56.0 billion, which falls far short of the original plans to invest RMB 138.7 billion and RMB 200 billion, respectively. However, National IC Fund 2 is still increasing the amount of outward investments at the time of this study (May 2022). The contents of the investments made by the two funds are summarized in Table 2.

Table 2. Investments made by the national IC industry development funds.

Investor	National IC Fund 1		National IC Fund 2		Investment companies receiving Investment from National IC Fund 1	
Sector	Number of firms	Amount (RMB million)	Number of firms	Amount (RMB million)	Number of firms	Amount (RMB million)
Investment company	25	27,741	0	0	26	5,202
Foundry	5	31,369	5	26,622	6	20,458
Packaging and testing	6	2,083	1	950	4	99
Design house	18	1,333	6	723	98	1,885
Integrated device manufacturer	8	28,749	3	24,410	7	940
Materials	8	3,746	4	24	16	447
Equipment	6	255	2	305	23	521
Discrete semiconductors	1	335	0	0	15	176
Software	1	48	1	1	5	1,024
Electric and electronic products	0	0	0	0	14	136
Others	3	1,004	1	5	53	9,101
Total	81	96,661	23	53,041	267	39,990

Note: Several firms received investments from two or more funds. Four firms received investments from both Fund 1 and 2. Thirty-one firms received investments from Fund 1 and/or 2 and from investment companies invested by Fund 1.

Source: Qichacha (retrieved during January 20–26th, 2022). Information from each company's website.

The National IC Fund 1 has invested in 81 firms, ranging from upstream to downstream of the semiconductor supply chain. There are 25 local investment companies among the firms invested by the fund. These local investment companies gather funds from the National IC Fund 1, local governments, and other investors, and they in turn invest in local semiconductor industrial firms. The direction of their investments is also shown in Table 2. If we add the recipient firms of investments from local investment companies, the two funds directly and indirectly invested RMB 190 billion in 313 firms.[8]

Two major semiconductor manufacturers received a big chunk of the National IC Funds' investment. One of these manufacturers is Unigroup, which was originally a subsidiary of Tsinghua University but became a half-privatized company in 2009 when Weiguo Zhao, a Tsinghua graduate who succeeded in the real estate business in Xinjiang, started to control 49% of its capital. Unigroup entered the IC industry in 2013 by acquiring Spreadtrum, a company that designs mobile baseband ICs, and RDA, a company that designs radio frequency ICs. The two were merged to become Unisoc, which received an investment of RMB 895 million from the National IC Fund 1. Unigroup heavily relied on bank loans to pursue its acquisition of Wuhan Xinxin, which is a NAND flash memory manufacturer created by investment from Hubei Province and Wuhan City in collaboration with Spansion (Xie and Chen, 2018). In 2016, Unigroup took over Wuhan Xinxin with help from National IC Fund 1 and renamed it Yangtze Memory. National IC Fund 1 invested RMB 27.7 billion in two projects of Yangtze Memory. In total, Unigroup extracted RMB 28.6 billion from the two funds, which accounted for 19.1% of their total investment. Unigroup has defaulted several times on its corporate bonds since October 2020, and finally, in July 2021, Huishang Bank, one of its creditors, appealed to the court for its bankruptcy (*21st Century Economic Herald*, July 15, 2021). The largest shareholder of Yangtze Memory shifted from Unigroup to an investment company under Hubei Province and Wuhan City, and National IC Fund 2 invested RMB 18 billion in the company to facilitate the expansion of its NAND flash memory capacity even after the bankruptcy of its former parent company.

Another major recipient of the funds' investment is SMIC — the largest IC foundry in China. In total, the two funds invested RMB 43.1 billion in SMIC's six subsidiaries, accounting for 28.8% of their total investment. The two funds control 14–38% shares of each subsidiary. Apparently, the funds are heavily involved in SMIC, which indicates the government's will to foster SMIC as the main driver of becoming one of the forerunners in the global semiconductor industry. SMIC is chasing Taiwan's TSMC, the leading foundry in the world, but there is always a gap of 4–5 years in processing technology between the two firms. The year of beginning mass production using the 28 nm process was 2011 in the case of TSMC and 2015 in the case of SMIC. TSMC began using the 14/16 nm process in 2014, while SMIC began using it in 2019. It was reported that the Dutch government did not allow ASML to export its most advanced extra ultraviolet (EUV) lithography machine to China due to US pressure (*Nihon keizai shinbun*, July 7, 2020). Without EUV lithography machines, it will be very difficult for SMIC to advance into the 7 nm process, while TSMC has already started the mass production of ICs using the 7 nm process in 2018. In December 2020, the US Department of Commerce added SMIC and its subsidiaries to its "Entity List," which is a list of foreign companies that are denied access to US technology and equipment without a specific license issued by the Department.

It is obvious from Table 2 that National Funds 1 and 2 invested heavily in foundries like SMIC and integrated device manufacturers (IDMs) like Unigroup. As both types of factories involve wafer processing, which is highly capital intensive, the amount of investment in these factories tend to be large. To gauge the extent of the National IC Funds' contribution to the development of China's IC manufacturing, the author of this chapter compiled Table 3, which is a full list of foundries and IDMs that have erected or plan to erect 12-inch wafer processing factories. Among the 33 manufacturers, 14 received investments from the funds, and two received investments from Shanghai IC Fund, of which National IC Fund 1 controls a 10% share.

If we convert US dollars to Renminbi using the average exchange rate in 2021 (US$1 = RMB 6.45), the total amount of registered

Table 3. Semiconductor manufacturers in China that have or plan to have 12-inch wafer processing factory.

Name of the firm	Registered capital	Investor (%)	Capital share of the funds			Business/Product
			National IC Fund 1 (%)	National IC Fund 2 (%)	Investment companies receiving investment from National IC Fund 1	
SMIC	US$31.6mil	HKSCC Nominees 57		1.61		Foundry
SMIC North	US$4800mil	SMIC Group 51%	32			Foundry
SMIC South	US$6500mil	SMIC International 38.5	14.6	23		Foundry
SMIC Ningbo	RMB4429mil	SMIC International 15.8	13.5			Foundry
SMIC Jingcheng	US$5000mil	SMIC International 51		24.49		Foundry
SMIC International Shenzhen	US$2415mil	SMIC International 49.7		22		Foundry
SMIC Dongfang	US$5500mil	SMIC International 66.5		16.80		Foundry
Unigroup						
Yangtze Memory	RMB56275mil	Hubei Unigroup 51	24.1			NAND flash
Hubei Zixin	RMB28721mil	Hubei Unigroup 50.8	49.2			NAND flash
Chengdu Unisplendour Guoxin	RMB1000mil	Chengdu Ziguang 100				NAND flash
Nanjing Unigroup Memory	RMB1000mil	Unigroup 100				NAND flash, DRAM

(*Continued*)

Table 3. (*Continued*)

Name of the firm	Registered capital	Investor (%)	Capital share of the funds			Business/Product
			National IC Fund 1 (%)	National IC Fund 2 (%)	Investment companies receiving investment from National IC Fund 1 (%)	
Wuhan Xinxin	RMB5557mil	Yangtze Memory 100				Flash memory, NOR flash, Foundry
Huali Microelectronics	RMB22072mil	Huahong Group 53.8			Shanghai IC Fund 39.8	Foundry
Huali Integrated Circuits	RMB29600mil	Huali Microelectronics 54	39.19		Shanghai IC Fund 6.8	Foundry
Yangtze Memory 2nd Phase	RMB60000mil	Hubei Changsheng 70		30.0		
Nexchip	RMB1504mil	Hefei City 31, Powerchip 27				Foundry, display driver
Hefei Changxin	RMB2005mil	Hefei City 100				Memory chips
TSMC Nanjing	US$1000mil	TSMC 100				Foundry
Intel Dalian	US$2220mil	Intel 100				PC chipsets, NAND flash
United Semiconductor Xiamen	RMB16198mil	UMC 40，Hejian 33				Foundry

Table 3. (*Continued*)

			Capital share of the funds			
Name of the firm	Registered capital	Investor (%)	National IC Fund 1 (%)	National IC Fund 2 (%)	Investment companies receiving investment from National IC Fund 1 (%)	Business/Product
SK Hynix China	US$5196mil	SK Hynix 100				DRAM, NAND flash
Cansemi	RMB1667mil	Guangzhou Yuxin 24.0				Foundry
Wuxi Huahong Grace	US$1800mil	Huahong Grace 29, Huahong Semiconductor 22	29			Flash memory
Samsung China Semiconductor	US$8623mil	Samsung 100				NAND flash
GTA Semiconductor	RMB9321mil	Huada Semiconductor 32.9			Shanghai IC Fund 19.3	Power IC, power management
Chongqing Alpha and Omega Semiconductor	US$395mil	Chongqing Yujiangxin 46.8, Alpha and Omega Semiconductor 30.1				Power IC, IGBT, MOSFET
JHICC	RMB17888mil	Jinjiang City, Fujian Electronic Group				DRAM

(*Continued*)

Table 3. (*Continued*)

Name of the firm	Registered capital	Investor (%)	Capital share of the funds: National IC Fund 1 (%)	National IC Fund 2 (%)	Investment companies receiving investment from National IC Fund 1 (%)	Business/Product
Xiamen Silan Microchip	RMB3828mil	Xiamen Semiconductor Investment 66.6, Hangzhou Silan 18.7		14.7		MEMS, Power IC
Huaian Imaging Device	RMB6043mil	Dekema, Huaian City				CMOS Image Sensor
Jiangsu Advanced Memory	RMB1000mil	Beijing Advanced Memory				Phase change memory
Wuhan Hongxin Semiconductor						Foundry
SiEn (Qingdao) Semiconductor	RMB5000mil	Aucma 57				Commune IDM
Runxi Microelectronics	RMB5000mil	Chongqing Xiyong, China Resources		33		Power IC

Source: Zhongtou chanye yanjiuyuan (2021), Fang (2021), Qichacha, Firms' website.

capital of the 33 manufacturers is calculated as RMB 558.6 billion. The National IC Funds directly or indirectly (through the Shanghai IC Fund) contributed RMB 107.7 billion, or 19% of the total capital. It is noteworthy that foreign and Taiwanese semiconductor manufacturers made a greater contribution. The total amount of capital invested by them is calculated as RMB 122.9 billion, or 22% of the total capital. Therefore, we can conclude that the National IC Funds made a considerable contribution to the development of foundries and IDMs, but market forces, including the inflow of foreign direct investment, made a greater contribution.

Investments made by the National Funds in other components of the semiconductor supply chain are relatively small. However, the distribution of investments reveals the government's strategy to enhance localization in all components of the supply chain. In the case of silicon wafers, Chinese manufacturers supply less than 10% of the domestic demand (Zhongtou chanye yanjiuyuan, 2021). Domestic wafer manufacturers were unable to produce 12-inch wafers until 2017. After National IC Fund 1 invested RMB 56.7 million in Shanghai National Semiconductor Industry Group, the latter began producing 12-inch wafers in 2018.

Semiconductor manufacturing equipment is another weak point for China. In 2019, China's domestic production of such equipment, including those for making discrete semiconductors, was RMB 16.2 billion, which accounted for 17% of the whole Chinese market. Chinese equipment manufacturers' global and domestic market shares are low, and they can produce only low-end equipment. The funds made investments in domestic equipment manufacturers, such as NAURA Technology Group Co., Ltd. (NAURA), Advanced Micro-Fabrication Equipment Inc. China (AMEC), Piotech, ACM Research, and Changchuan Manufacturing. Although their competitiveness is still weak, they cover almost all of the major equipment necessary for producing semiconductors, including lithography, physical and chemical vapor disposition, atomic layer disposition, etching, and testing.

Table 2 reveals that, among the sectors which received investments from the funds, "design house" is the largest group in terms of number of recipients. This is a reflection of the highly dispersed structure of China's semiconductor design industry. There were 2,218 semiconductor design houses in 2020, responsible for the trade of ICs worth RMB 382 billion in total. None of them could enter the rank of globally competitive IC design houses except HiSilicon, a subsidiary of Huawei, which was ranked No. 10 in 2019. However, HiSilicon's business was disrupted in 2020 because the US government forbade transactions with TSMC. The National IC Funds distributed investments of small amounts to many design houses because China's semiconductor design industry lacks leading firms. There are 97 design houses that directly or indirectly received investments from the two funds, receiving RMB 40.6 million on average. It is noteworthy that the funds are investing in several competing firms that design similar ICs, such as power management ICs, finger print sensors, mobile basebands, and memories. It seems that the funds are hedging risk by investing in several competitors.

The above review of the National IC Funds' investments offers a mixed picture. The concentration of investment in two major groups — SMIC and Unigroup — which accounted for 47.9% of total investment by the two funds appears to be a high risk-taking behavior. However, investment in the other sectors of the semiconductor supply chain seems rather risk-aversive, distributing small amounts of investment to many firms, including several mutually competing firms. Even in the sectors in which the two funds concentrated their investments — foundry and IDM, the contribution of the funds was 19% of the total capital of major foundries and IDMs. In total, the funds' contribution to the development of the Chinese semiconductor industry can be evaluated as significant but not indispensable.

Measurement of the Semiconductor Localization Ratio

The Chinese government has been pursuing the localization of semiconductor production since the 1980s. The pursuit of semiconductor industrial policy has gained steam since the launch of the

National IC Fund in 2014. As reviewed in the previous section, the funds are investing in all components of the semiconductor supply chain, including the manufacture of equipment and materials. The performance of the policy can be measured in terms of the localization ratio of semiconductor production.

However, the calculation of the semiconductor localization ratio is not straightforward. There are widely different views on the current status of the ratio. The 2017 version of the "Technology Roadmap of Key Industries" of MIC2025, which represents the official view of Chinese authorities, points out that domestically produced semiconductors satisfied 33% of the domestic demand in 2016 (Consultation Committee, 2018: 2). However, IC Insights (2020) regards that the localization ratios in 2014, 2016, and 2019 were 15.1%, 13.8%, and 15.7%, respectively.[9] Even the estimate provided by them regarding the size of China's IC market differs significantly. The former writes that China's semiconductor market in 2019 was US$180.5 billion, but the latter writes that it was US$124.6 billion in 2019. There is a wide gap between the estimates of the production value of the domestic IC industry in the two reports. While the "Technology Roadmap" estimates it at US$60 billion, IC Insights (2020) estimates it at US$19.5 billion.

China's IC trade data available from reports by China Customs are also puzzling. According to the customs statistics, China imported ICs worth US$306 billion and exported ICs worth US$102 billion in 2019, and it imported ICs worth US$351 billion and exported ICs worth US$117 billion in 2020. The export values of ICs are far greater than the value of domestic semiconductor production estimated in the reports mentioned above. The import values are also extraordinarily large. According to World Semiconductor Trade Statistics (WSTS), the global sales of ICs in these years were US$412 billion and US$440 billion, respectively. China's customs statistics suggest that it imported 74% and 80% of all ICs sold globally in 2019 and 2020, but that is simply impossible.

One of the reasons for the wide gap between trade statistics and the estimated domestic production value may lie in the fact that the former include parts of ICs. Half-finished ICs, which are silicon wafers etched with circuits, are traded widely. If the wafer-processing process is done in Taiwan, packaging is done on the mainland, and the end product is exported, China will have imports and exports of ICs, but packaging may not be counted as domestic IC production. Besides this, domestically produced ICs are often exported and reimported for domestic sales. Such trade is executed for the purpose of receiving tax refunds on exports (Wang, 2012). Therefore, considering these complexities, trade statistics become invalid for estimating the semiconductor localization rate.

Sales value statistics of the Chinese IC industry, reported by the China Semiconductor Industry Association (CSIA), seem to offer clues for estimating the localization ratio. CSIA reports that the sales value of China's IC industry in 2019 was RMB 756.2 billion, which was equivalent to US$109.6 billion. CSIA decomposes the sales values into three parts: IC design, which is RMB 306.4 billion; IC manufacturing, which is RMB 214.9 billion; and IC packaging and testing, which is RMB 235.0 billion. Since all ICs must go through all three stages, it is not correct to simply add their sales values to get the total sales of domestically produced ICs. Rather, it is proper to select one from the three stages. "IC design" may include ICs designed in China by design houses like HiSilicon and then sent to Taiwan for fabrication. Therefore, it cannot represent China's semiconductor industry's size. "IC packaging and testing" may include ICs which are assembled as half-finished ICs imported from abroad; therefore, it is not appropriate to measure the industry's size. As "IC manufacturing" measures the value of processed wafers, it is the most representative of the size of the semiconductor industry. Therefore, in Table 4, the author compared "IC manufacturing" data from CSIA and the size of China's IC market estimated by WSTS and calculated the localization ratio.

The estimated localization ratios in 2016 and 2019 are 15.8% and 21.5%, respectively, which are higher than the figures from IC Insights (2020) but lower than those reported by the Consultation Committee (2018). The change in localization ratio is consistent with what we have learned about China's semiconductor industrial policy since 2014 in the previous section. Investments by the

Table 4. Estimated IC localization ratio.

Year	2013	2014	2015	2016	2017	2018	2019	2020
China IC Manufacturing (Bil. RMB)	60.1	71.2	90.1	112.7	144.8	181.8	214.9	256.0
China IC Market (Bil. US$)	88.3	91.5	98.6	107.6	131.5	158.4	144.6	151.5
Localization Ratio	11.0%	12.7%	14.7%	15.8%	16.3%	17.4%	21.5%	24.5%

Source: IC Manufacturing: CSIA, IC Market: WSTS.

National IC Funds can be considered to be the main driving force that contributed to the doubling of IC localization ratio between 2014 and 2020. Large investments made in foundries and IDMs should have contributed to the rapid growth of IC manufacturing. However, the localization ratio in 2020 fell short of the target set in the "Technology Roadmap" of MIC2025, which, as mentioned above, was 49% in 2020.

Conclusion

This chapter began with the question of whether China is a "developmental state." The answer is a definite "Yes." China has accorded the highest policy priority to economic growth during the past 40 years and adopted institutional arrangements and incentive structures to promote that objective. The extensive use of state-owned enterprises, state investment, and industrial policies are characteristic of China's developmental state. The state's direct involvement in industrial development prompted the model of an "entrepreneurial state." However, this study does not support that model because China has many priority industries and many direct investments, which makes it possible to diversify risk. Individual industrial policy and individual state-owned enterprises have the risk of failure, but the Chinese state is mitigating the risk by having many other priority industries and hundreds of thousands of state-owned enterprises. Even the policy on an individual industry — the semiconductor industry — has shifted from an entrepreneurial one focusing on a single project to a generalized tax incentive. The establishment of the National IC Fund in 2014 was a major move toward more risk-taking state involvement. Indeed, the National IC Funds took the risk of investing 47.9% of their total investments in two major semiconductor manufacturers. However, the funds diversified the risk by investing in many other firms, even those that were mutually competitive. In total, the National IC Funds cannot be regarded as risk-taking entrepreneurs. Instead, they are more like investors, who take risks in some fields but mitigate risks by investing in other fields.

The misunderstanding of China as an entrepreneurial state seems to be driving developed countries into risk-taking endeavors. The Japanese government is planning to invest JPY 500 billion, which accounts for 81% of its semiconductor industry fund, into a single project — a 22/28 nm wafer processing factory, which TSMC is planning to erect in Kumamoto, Japan (*Nihon keizai shinbun*, November 8, 2021). Thus, Japan's semiconductor fund can be considered to be far more risk-taking than the Chinese National IC Fund.

Endnotes

1. European Commission Press Release, February 8, 2022. https://ec.europa.eu/commission/presscorner/detail/en/ip_22_729.
2. The Adjustment and Upgrading Plan of the Iron and Steel Industry (2016–2020) set the target of the top 10 enterprises' share in 2020 as 60% or more, but the actual share was 39% in 2020.
3. For example, to achieve the above-mentioned goal of raising the share of the top 10 enterprises in the iron and steel industry, the central government merged four major state-owned steelmakers (Baosteel, Wuhan, Taiyuan, and Maanshan) and created Baowu Steel in 2016, which is currently the largest steelmaker in the world. Even with this audacious move, the top 10 enterprises' share increased only modestly — from 34% in 2015 to 39% in 2020.
4. According to the 2018 Economic Survey, there existed at least some state-owned enterprises in all of the 90 industrial sectors, ranging from

furniture manufacturing, in which the state-owned enterprises had the lowest employment share (0.4%), to oil and gas extraction, in which state-owned enterprises had the highest employment share (97.6%).

5. Based on an interview conducted by the author at SGNEC on March 17, 1999.
6. Based on an interview conducted by the author at Huahong NEC on December 12, 2003.
7. World Trade Organization, DS309: China-Value Added Tax on Integrated Circuits. https://www.wto.org/english/tratop_e/dispu_e/cases_e/ds309_e.htm.
8. The number of firms receiving investment in Table 2 adds up to 371. However, since several firms received investments from two or more funds, the net number of recipient firms is 313.
9. The localization ratio includes ICs that are produced by foreign and Taiwanese semiconductor manufacturers in China. If only the China-headquartered manufacturers are counted, the report says, the localization ratio in 2019 was 6.1%.

References

Amsden, A.H. 1989. *Asia's Next Giant: South Korea and Late Industrialization.* New York, NY: Oxford University Press.

Chen, F. [陳芳] and Dong, R. [董瑞丰] (eds.). 2018. *Xinxiang shicheng: Zhongguo xinpian chanye de boyi yu tuwei.* ["芯"想事成: 中國芯片產業的博弈與突圍, *All Wishes Come True: Deciphering China's Chips Industry*]. Beijing, China: Renmin youdian chubanshe.

Chu, W. 2017. Industrial policy with Chinese characteristics: A multi-layered model. *China Economic Journal*, 10(3): 305–318.

Consultation Committee. [咨詢委員會]. 2018. *Zhongguo zhizao 2025 zhongdian lingyu jishu chuangxin lupishu: jishu luxian tu.* [中國製造 2025 重點領域技術創新綠皮書：技術路綫圖]. Beijing, China: Dianzi gongye chubanshe.

Duckett, J. 1996. The emergence of the entrepreneurial state in contemporary China. *The Pacific Review*, 9(2): 180–198.

Fang, Z. [方竹紫]. 2021. *The Deployment of Semiconductor Industrial Policy in China: A Case Study of the National Integrated Circuit Industry Investment Fund.* Tokyo: Mimeo.

Fischer, D., Gohli, H., and Habich-Sobiegalla, S. 2021. Industrial policies under Xi Jinping: A steering theory perspective. *Issues & Studies: A*

Social Science Quarterly on China, Taiwan, and East Asian Affairs, 57(4): 1–27.

Holz, C.A. 2018. Industrial policies and the changing patterns of investment in the Chinese economy. *The China Journal*, 81: 23–57.

Hu, Q. [胡啓立]. 2001. *Zhongguo xinxihua de tansuo he shijian* [中國信息化的探索和實踐, *The Quest and Implementation for China's Informatization*]. Beijing: Dianzi gongye chubanshe.

IC Insights. 2020. China to fall far short of its "Made-in-China 2025" goal for IC devices. *Research Bulletin* (May 21).

Johnson, C. 1982. *MITI and the Japanese Miracle: The Growth of Industrial Policy, 1925–1975*. Stanford, CA: Stanford University Press.

Knight, J.B. 2014. China as a developmental state. *The World Economy*, 37(10): 1335–1347.

Marukawa, T. 2020. The evolution of China's industrial policy and "Made in China 2025." In Ding, A. and Panda, J. (eds.). *Chinese Politics and Foreign Policy under Xi Jinping: The Future of Political Trajectory*. London: Routledge, pp. 131–149.

Mazzucato, M. 2018. *The Entrepreneurial State: Debunking Public vs Private Sector Myths*. London: Penguin Books.

Sato, Y. [佐藤幸人]. 2007. *Taiwan haiteku sangyō no seisei to hatten* [*The Emergence and Development of Taiwanese High-Tech Industries*]. Tokyo, Japan: Iwanami Shoten.

Su, J. [蘇建南]and Feng, H. [馮華]. 2019. "Zhongguo guojia he difang jicheng dianlu chanye jijin gaikuang" [中國國家和地方集成電路產業基金概況, Outline of China's national and local IC industry funds]. In Yin, L. [尹麗波] (ed.) *Jicheng dianlu chanye fazhan baogao 2018-2019* [集成電路產業發展報告 2018–2019]. Beijing, China: Social Science Academic Press.

Tabeta, S. [多部田俊輔]. 2021. Chugoku handotai, toi "jikyu 70 pasento" [China's semiconductors, far from reaching the target of 70-percent localization]. *Nihon keizai shinbun* (October 13).

Wang, D. [王東]. 2012. Sangyo seisaku to sangyo hatten: Chugoku ni okeru IC sangyo no jirei [Industrial policy and industrial development: The case of China's IC industry]. *Keizaigaku kenkyu ronshu*, 37: 23–36.

Xie, Z. [謝志軍] and Chen, D. [陳大明]. 2018. *Xinshi: Yiben shu dudong xinpian chanye* [芯事：一本書讀懂芯片產業, *Chip Affairs: A Guide to the Chip Industry*]. Shanghai, China: Shanghai Science and Technology Press.

Yuan, Z. [苑志佳]. 2000. Handotai sangyo. [The semiconductor industry]. In Marukawa, T. [丸川知雄] (ed.). *Ikoki chugoku no sangyo seisaku* [*Industrial Policy in China during the Transition Period*]. Tokyo: Nihon boeki shinko kai ajia keizai kenkyujo.

Zhongtou chanye yanjiuyuan. [中投產業研究院]. 2021. *Investigation & Investment Forecast Report on China Semiconductor Industrial Chain, 2021–2025*. Shenzhen: Zhongtou chanye yanjiuyuan.

Zhu, Y. [朱貽瑋]. 2018. Zhongguo jicheng dianlu chanye fazhan jiannan licheng huigu. [中國集成電路產業發展艱難歷程回顧. Retrospection on the difficult development path of the Chinese IC industry]. *Xin Sixiang Semi-News*. http://news.eeworld.com.cn/manufacture/article_2018060826306.html.

https://doi.org/10.1142/9789819815241_0015

Chapter 15

ENERGY TRANSFORMATION IN THE CONTEXT OF CARBON NEUTRALITY: FROM THE PERSPECTIVE OF TECHNOLOGICAL CHANGE AND GREEN FINANCE

Shiyi Chen

School of Economics (SOE), Fudan University, Shanghai, China
shiyichen@fudan.edu.cn

Introduction

Since the industrial revolution, with fossil fuels as the main energy source, countries all over the world have completed the industrialization process, however, at the expense of severe environmental damage. Among others, climate change is one of the most prominent threats originating from a high-level concentration of carbon dioxide in the atmosphere, mainly due to the combustion of fossil fuels. According to the report of the second working group in the Sixth Assessment Report of the IPCC (2022),[1] climate change, which is predominantly attributable to human activities, causes wide negative effects. A 1.5°C increase in temperature when compared to that before industrialization would inevitably bring about more disastrous climate events and pose significant risks to the ecosystem and human beings.

Countries all over the world have realized that cooperation toward climate change mitigation is urgent to protect the Earth and guarantee the sustainable development of human society. In 1992, the United Nations Conference on Environment and Development adopted "the Framework Convention on Climate Change" (hereinafter "the Convention") and set up goals and principles for dealing with climate change. The Convention aims to restrict the concentration of greenhouse gases in the atmosphere to an appropriate level so that the climate system will not be disturbed by human activities while guaranteeing food security and the sustainability of economic development. In addition, the Convention, the first framework and legal basis for international cooperation on climate issues, proposes to reduce global greenhouse gas emissions by 50% before 2050. In 1997, the Kyoto Protocol, adopted by the state parties of the Convention in Kyoto, Japan, elaborated the meaning of "common but differentiated responsibilities" and set quantitative carbon dioxide reduction obligations for developed countries. Meanwhile, the Kyoto Protocol also aimed to motivate developed countries to exchange capital and technologies for carbon emissions reduction by designing three flexible compliance mechanisms, namely International Emissions Trading (IET), Joint Implementation (JI), and Clean Development Mechanism (CDM). In 2015, the Paris Agreement, passed at the Paris Climate Conference, marked a milestone in history. The Paris Agreement proposes, for the first time, to realize the goal of "carbon neutrality" in the second half of the 21st century and to control the temperature increase under 2°C (or 1.5°C if possible) when compared to that in the pre-industrialization period.

Although climate change has exerted great challenges for China's realization of socialist modernization, it also provides great opportunities for green industrialization, urbanization, and agricultural and rural modernization. Over these years, China has been regularly raising its emission-reduction target. In November 2015, at the opening ceremony of the 21st United Nations Climate Change Conference (COP21), General Secretary Xi Jinping proposed that

China's carbon dioxide emissions would peak around 2030. On September 22, 2020, at the general debate of the 75th UN General Assembly, Xi Jinping announced that China would adopt more powerful measures to contribute to climate change mitigation and achieve the carbon peak by 2030 and carbon neutrality by 2060. On December 12, 2020, at the Climate Ambition Summit, Xi Jinping further announced that China's carbon dioxide emissions per capita GDP would reduce by more than 65% by contrast to 2005 emissions, the proportion of non-fossil fuels in China's primary energy consumption would reach 25%, forest stock volume would increase by 6 billion cubic meters by contrast to 2005 volume, and the total installed capacity of wind power and solar power would reach 1.2 billion kW. On September 21, 2021, the anniversary of China's "Dual-Carbon" strategy, General Secretary Xi Jinping again emphasized, at the general debate of the 76th UN General Assembly, that China would accelerate its low-carbon transformation and green development process and achieve carbon peaking before 2030 and carbon neutrality before 2060.

As for specific actions, China also incorporated "Carbon Peaking and Carbon Neutrality" in the plan of ecological civilization. The guidance for realizing "Carbon Peaking and Carbon Neutrality" is posted in many government documents, led by the Opinions of the CPC Central Committee and the State Council on Complete, Accurate and Comprehensive Implementation of the New Development Concept and how to better achieve "Carbon Peaking and Carbon Neutrality". Besides, the Chinese government has also made considerable efforts in adjusting its industry structure, raising energy efficiency, optimizing energy structure, increasing carbon sinks, controlling the emissions of greenhouse gases from non-energy activities and pollutants, and stimulating low-carbon actions of local governments. In general, China has made remarkable achievements in carbon reduction during the past few decades. As shown by the data from the National Bureau of Statistics, energy consumption and carbon dioxide emissions per capita GDP have reduced, respectively, by 35% from 2012 to 2021 and 50.3% from 2005 to 2021, basically reversing the situation of rapid carbon emissions increase.

Despite all these reduction achievements, China's carbon dioxide emissions are still large. In 2021, it exceeded 10 billion tons (BP, 2022),[2] of which the combustion of fossil fuels accounted for the major part. Therefore, the energy transformation from traditional to low- and zero-carbon is vital for China's realization of carbon neutrality by 2060. In the future, the dominant energy in China's energy structure is expected to be renewable energy.

The direction of China's energy transformation will be influential around the world. In 2014, at the 6th meeting of the Central Leading Group for Finance and Economics, Xi Jinping came up with the strategic concept of "four revolutions and one cooperation" for-secure energy development under open conditions, namely revolution in energy consumption, energy supply, energy technology, energy systems, and cooperation across countries. In April 2022, the "14th Five-Year Plan for Modern Energy System," issued by the National Development and Reform Commission and the National Energy Administration, further extended China's energy transformation target in the 14th Five-Year Plan period to "build modern energy system which is more secure, powerful, effective and with a stronger innovation ability and a continuously improved service level."

By detecting the temporal and spatial patterns of China's carbon dioxide emissions and energy consumption, we construct a medium- and long-term model incorporating energy transformation to predict energy consumption and carbon dioxide emissions under different scenarios in the future. Based on our predictions, we attempt to provide implications for energy transformation and energy structure optimization not only for carbon-intensive sectors but also for government policymakers.

The Historical Trends of Energy Consumption and Carbon Dioxide Emissions

History and current state

With the progress of the reform and opening up, China has experienced over 40 years' worth of rapid economic growth. However, this extensive growth pattern, driven by enormous production factor inputs, also results in continuously increasing energy consumption demand. Figure 1 shows the trend of China's total energy consumption from 1978 to 2021. With an average annual growth rate of 5.4%, China's total energy consumption in 2021 reached 5.24 billion tons of standard coal, nine times that in 1978. Based on the evolving trend, we divide China's energy consumption development into four stages.

The first stage is from 1978 to 1995. At this stage, although China's energy consumption fluctuated at the beginning, it stayed relatively stable in general, with an average growth rate of 5.2%.

The second stage is from 1996 to 2002. At this stage, energy consumption demand was restrained due to the negative economic effects produced by the Asian financial crisis and China's state-owned enterprise reform. The average annual growth rate was 3.8% during these years, and that in 1997 and 1998 was even below 1%.

The third stage is from 2003 to 2011. At this stage, with the progress of urbanization and industrialization, the augmenting output share of carbon-intensive heavy industries in total industrial output featured a new round of economic growth and also boosted energy consumption demand. In this period, the average annual growth

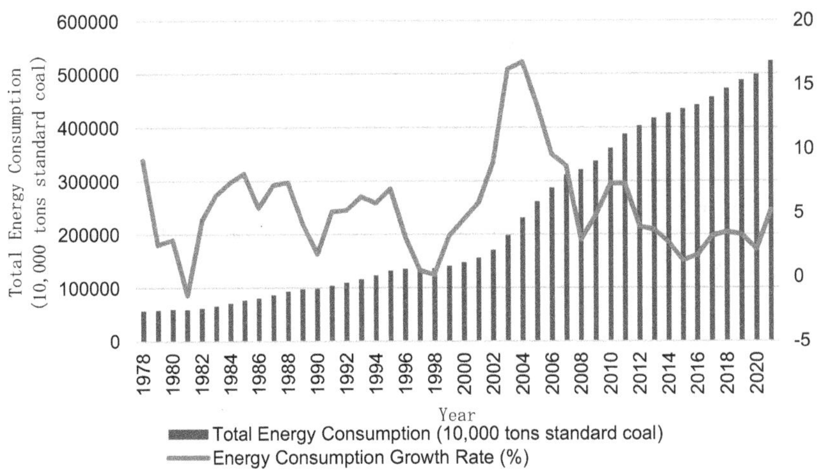

Figure 1. Total energy consumption and growth rate in China (1978–2021).
Source: China Statistical Yearbook and the National Bureau of Statistics of China.

rate of energy consumption exceeded 9.7%, and the growth rate from 2003 to 2005 even exceeded 13%.

The fourth stage is from 2012 to the present. At this stage, China's energy consumption demand is greatly restrained by various factors, such as economic structure transformation, low international oil prices, and the reduction of excessive capacity in the coal industry. The average annual growth rate of energy consumption had dropped to 2.5%.

As energy consumption grows, its structure is also changing. At the early stages of the reform and opening up, coal was dominant in China's energy consumption structure due to its underdeveloped industrial sector and the late discovery of China's own oil and gas resources. Fortunately, with the development of China's economy, the improvement in people's living standards, and the construction of ecological civilization, China's energy consumption structure is being continuously optimized.

Figure 2 shows the evolving trend of China's energy consumption structure. We find that coal consumption proportion shows an M-shaped trend, with two peaks in 1990 (76.2%) and 2007 (72.5%). After 2007, the proportion of coal consumption dropped rapidly,

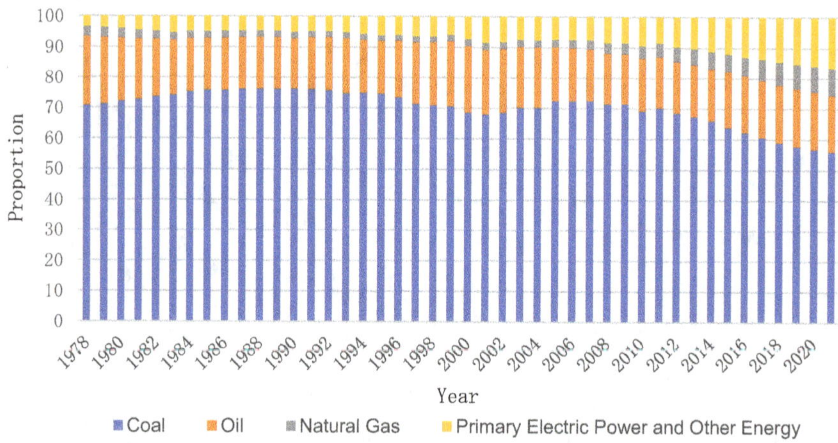

Figure 2. Changing trend of different types of energy consumption in China (1978–2021).

Source: China Statistical Yearbook and the National Bureau of Statistics of China.

reaching its lowest point, 56.0%, in 2021. In comparison to coal consumption, oil consumption proportion shows a W-shaped trend, with two valleys in 1990 (16.6%) and 2009 (16.4%). After 2009, the oil consumption proportion started to rebound and returned to a relatively high level, 18.5%, in 2021, but was still less than 22.7% in 1978. Natural gas consumption proportion shows a U-shaped trend, constantly increasing after 1999 and reaching its historical highest point, 8.9%, in 2021. The proportion of primary electric power and other energy consumption increases in a zigzag way, reaching its highest point, 16.6%, in 2021 as well. In general, although China still utilizes coal as the main energy source all these years after the reform and opening up with its abundant endowment of coal resources, the cleanness of China's energy consumption structure has significantly improved. One major observation is the obviously increasing trend in natural gas consumption.

With the continuous expansion of the economy and energy consumption, China's fossil-fuel-related carbon dioxide emissions have increased rapidly during the past 30 years (Figure 3). In 2021, energy-related carbon dioxide emissions reached 10.52 billion tons,

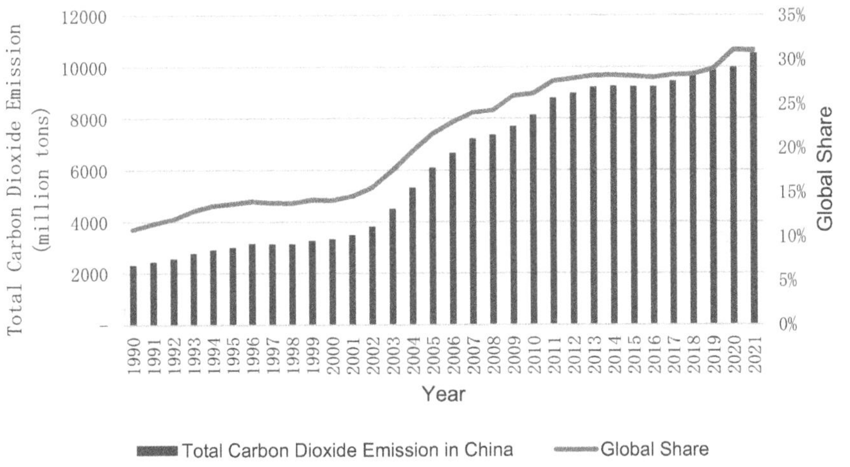

Figure 3. Total carbon dioxide emissions in China and its global share (1990–2021).

Source: BP (2022).

4.6 times that in 1990 and 3.1 times that in 2000. Based on the evolving trend, we divide China's fossil-fuel-related carbon dioxide emissions change after 1990 into three stages.

The first stage is from 1990 to 2000. At this stage, China's energy-related carbon dioxide emissions generally stayed constant, around 3 billion tons.

The second stage is from 2001 to 2013. At this stage, as China's economy entered a new round of rapid growth, the output proportion of carbon-intensive heavy industries kept increasing, thus leading to energy consumption growth and fossil-fuel-related carbon dioxide emissions growth. During this period, China's energy-related carbon dioxide emissions nearly tripled, increasing from 3.52 billion tons to 9.24 billion tons.

The third stage is from 2014 to the present. At this stage, under the comprehensive influence of economic structure transformation, the reduction of excessive capacity in the coal industry, and the tightening of dual-control requirements on energy consumption, China's energy consumption demand has been greatly restrained, and fossil-fuel-related carbon dioxide emissions have increased very slowly.

As shown in Figure 3, China's share in global carbon dioxide emissions rose from 10.9% in 1990 to 31.1% in 2021, making it the largest carbon dioxide emitter in the world at present. However, it is worth noting that the increasing speed of China's global emission share obviously slows down after 2011, which also indicates that China's climate governance has entered a new stage.

Relevant research points out that the relationship between economic growth and environmental damage differs at different economic development stages. As the economy becomes more and more advanced, economic growth would decouple from environmental damage. The "decoupling" of economic growth and environmental damage has several states: "strong decoupling," which is the most desirable state, means that the economy grows and environmental pressure reduces simultaneously; "weak decoupling" means that the economy grows faster than energy consumption or pollutants emissions grow; "connection" means that the economy and environmental pressure change in the same direction and at the same speed; "negative decoupling," which is the least desirable one, means that the economy's growing speed is slower than the environment's deteriorating speed, or an economic recession and pollution happen simultaneously. As shown in Figure 4, China's GDP increases while carbon dioxide emissions stay relatively constant. That's to say, the decoupling trend has started to appear in China.

Scenario analysis

We choose four carbon-intensive sectors on the energy supply and demand sides as our major research objects: the industrial sector, the construction sector, the transportation sector, and the electric power sector, as shown in Figure 5. By using the "bottom-up" modeling method, we utilize their energy-related activities, energy consumption, and energy structure data to construct a medium- and long-term model incorporating energy transformation to predict

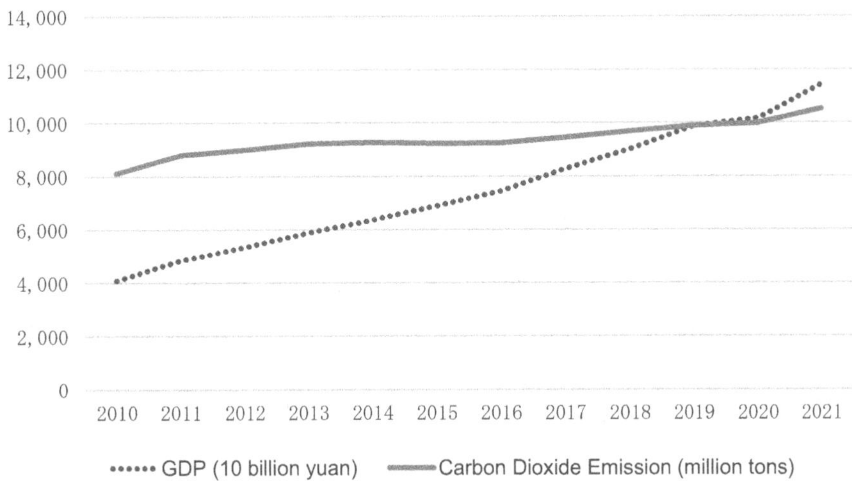

Figure 4. Trend of China's GDP growth and carbon dioxide emissions (2010–2021).

Source: BP (2022) and the National Bureau of Statistics of China.

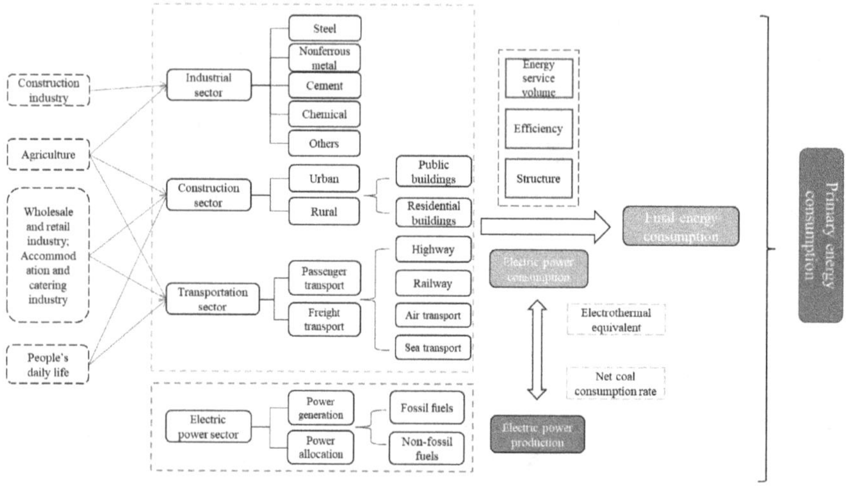

Figure 5. Model framework for China's medium- and long-term energy transformation and carbon emissions quantitative analysis.

energy consumption and carbon dioxide emissions in the four sectors under different scenarios from 2020 to 2060.

Since China has clearly put forward the goal of "Carbon Peaking and Carbon Neutrality," we build two scenarios in our model: the Business-As-Usual (BAU) Scenario and the Carbon Neutrality Scenario. Under the BAU Scenario, China would maintain its original policies on low-carbon development before the "Dual-Carbon" strategy is proposed, and thus the medium- and long-term energy-related technological progress would follow the historical trends. Under the Carbon Neutrality Scenario, China would spend more efforts to promote the green and low-carbon transformation of its economy and society, accelerate low-carbon technology innovation and penetration, and extend the share of non-fossil fuels in the energy consumption structure.

As shown in Figure 6, total energy consumption increases and then decreases under both scenarios, but the difference between them gradually enlarges after 2030 due to the impact of technological progress, energy efficiency improvements, demand-side industrial structure transformation and upgrading, and the growing popularity of a green and low-carbon lifestyle. Under the BAU Scenario,

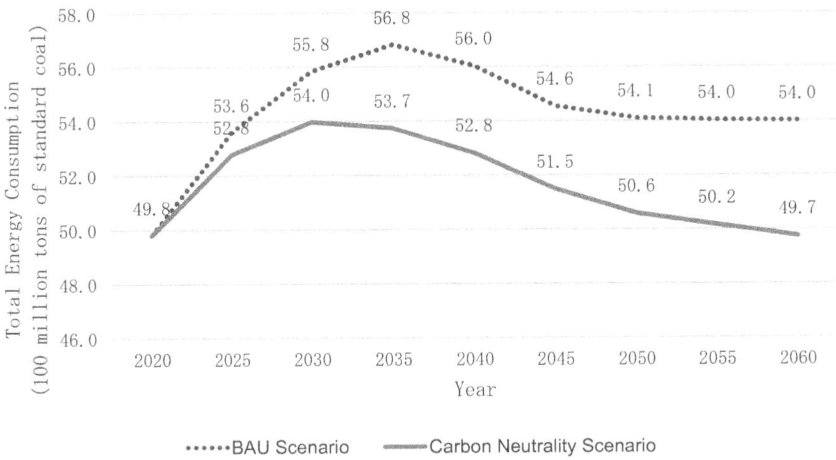

Figure 6. Forecast of the primary energy consumption under the two scenarios.

China's total primary energy consumption would peak in 2035, with a peak value of 5.68 billion tons of standard coal, and would stabilize at 5.4 billion tons of standard coal by 2060. Under the Carbon Neutrality Scenario, China's total primary energy consumption would peak around 2030, with a peak value of about 5.4 billion tons of standard coal. From 2030 to 2050, with China's comprehensive construction of a great modern socialist country and the basic realization of urbanization, the total primary energy consumption would drop rapidly to about 5.06 billion tons of standard coal in 2050. Then, the decreasing speed of energy consumption during the following 10 years would gradually slow down, and the total primary energy consumption would decrease to 4.97 billion tons of standard coal in 2060.

Under the BAU Scenario, as shown in Figure 7, the share of coal in energy consumption would decrease from 57% to 14%, the share of oil would decrease from 18% to 11%, the share of natural gas would increase from 9% to 15%, and the share of non-fossil fuels would increase from 16% to 60% from 2020 to 2060. For the Carbon Neutrality Scenario, as shown in Figure 8, the share of coal would decrease from 57% to 9%, the share of oil would decrease from 18% to 4%, the share of natural gas would increase from 9% to 12% in

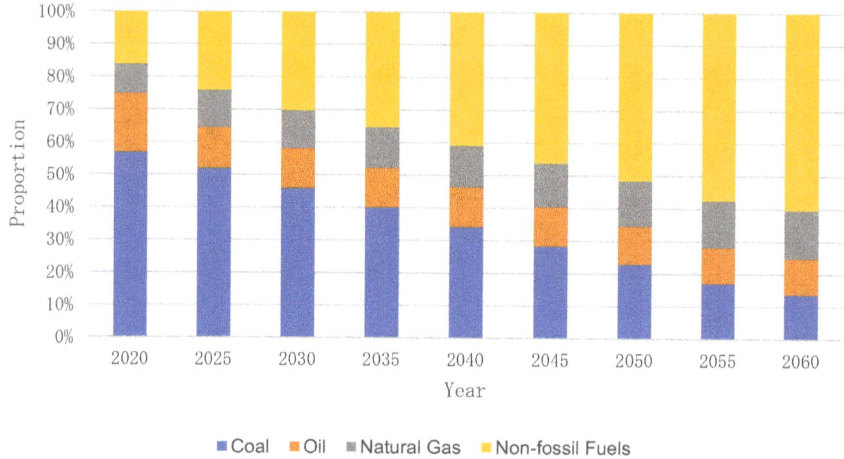

Figure 7. Forecast of primary energy consumption structure under the BAU Scenario.

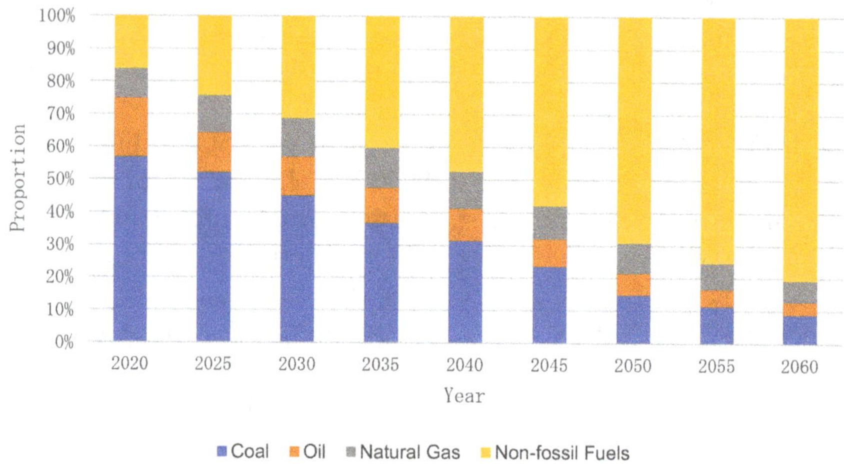

Figure 8. Forecast of primary energy consumption structure under the Carbon Neutrality Scenario.

2035 and decrease to 7% in 2060, and the share of non-fossil fuels would increase from 16% to 81% from 2020 to 2060.

The non-fossil fuel consumption under the Carbon Neutrality Scenario successfully meets the requirements set by the Chinese government. The "Action Plan for Carbon Dioxide Peaking Before 2030" issued by the State Council requires that the share of non-fossil fuels in total energy consumption should reach 20% in 2025 and 25% in 2030. The guiding document on the country's work to achieve carbon peaking and carbon neutrality goals under the new development philosophy requires that the proportion of non-fossil fuel consumption be above 80% by 2060. As we see under the Carbon Neutrality Scenario, the proportion of non-fossil fuel consumption would be 24% in 2025, 31% in 2030, and 81% in 2060, consistent with all the requirements.

As for China's carbon dioxide emissions, the BAU Scenario basically follows the same trend as the Carbon Neutrality Scenario (Figure 9). We expect carbon dioxide emissions to peak in 2025, with a peak value of around 10.31 billion tons under the BAU Scenario and of around 10.19 billion tons under the Carbon Neutrality Scenario. By 2060, carbon dioxide emissions under the BAU Scenario would drop to about 4.05 billion tons, while those under the Carbon Neutrality Scenario would drop to about 2.22 billion tons, resulting in a difference of 1.83 billion tons.[3]

Under the Carbon Neutrality Scenario, China's economic growth would decouple from energy consumption and carbon

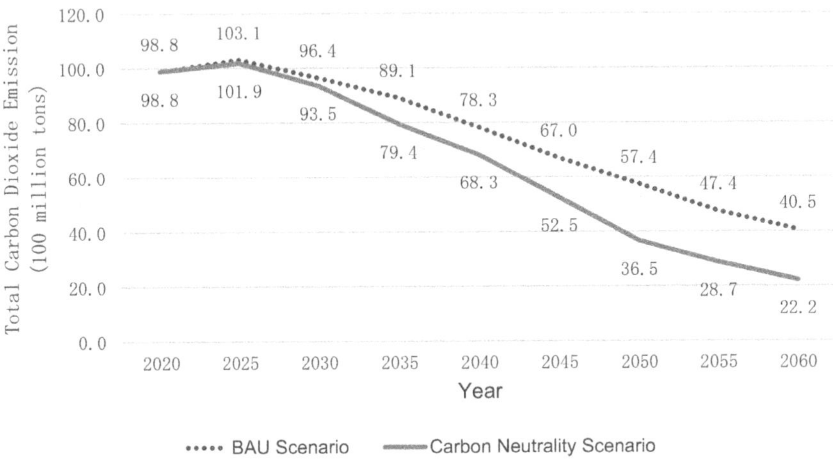

Figure 9. Forecast of China's total carbon dioxide emissions under the two scenarios.

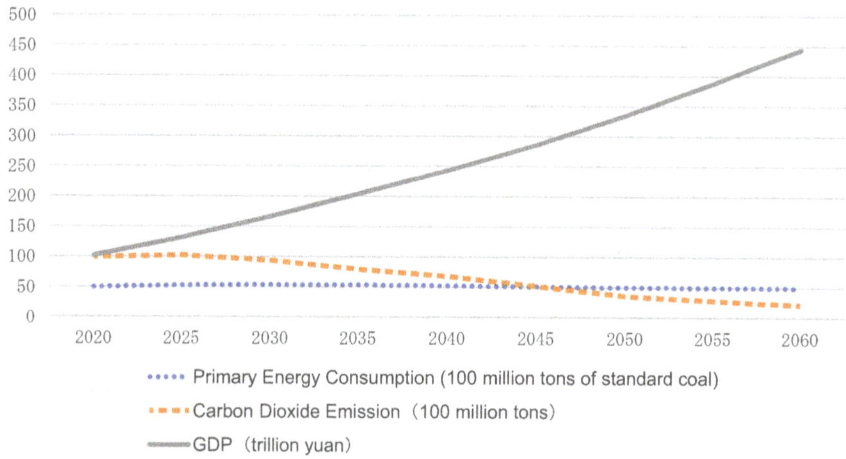

Figure 10. Trends of China's GDP, energy consumption, and carbon dioxide emissions under the Carbon Neutrality Scenario.

dioxide emissions. As shown in Figure 10, the decoupling trend of China's economic growth from carbon dioxide emissions would be significantly enhanced after 2025; meanwhile, the decoupling trend of carbon dioxide emissions from energy consumption would also appear after 2025. China's economy is developing toward the state of "strong decoupling," the most desirable state, with the gradual optimization of China's energy structure.

Technological Energy Transformation in Carbon-Intensive Sectors under the Carbon Neutrality Scenario

This section analyzes technological energy transformation in China's major four carbon-intensive sectors under the Carbon Neutrality Scenario. On the demand side, we discuss the industrial sector, the construction sector, and the transportation sector, while on the supply side, we discuss the electric power sector.

Industrial sector

After the reform and opening up, with the accelerated industrialization process, China's industrial sector developed rapidly, driven by foreign and domestic demand. In 2021, the added value of industrial enterprises above the designated size increased by 9.6%, and its average annual growth rate was 5.4% during the "13th Five-Year Plan" period.

Specifically, for the carbon-intensive industries in the industrial sector: the carbon dioxide emissions in the steel industry accounted for about 15% of China's total, the highest among all the domestic manufacturing industries (China Energy Conservation Association, 2020).[4] The cement industry is the third-largest energy-consuming and second-largest carbon dioxide-emitting industry in the world, on average accounting for 7% of total industrial energy consumption and 8.3% of total industrial carbon dioxide emissions (IEA, 2018).[5] China's cement industry emitted 1.48 billion tons of carbon dioxide in 2021, about 14% of the country's total (China Construction Material Association, 2022).[6] China's nonferrous metal industry emitted 660 million tons of carbon dioxide in 2020, according to the statistics of the China Nonferrous Metal Industry Association. The chemical industry, an important downstream industry of coal, is estimated to have emitted 1.378 billion tons of carbon dioxide in 2020 (Yan Gao and Lianfei Li, 2021).[7]

"The Plan for Carbon Peaking in Industrial Field," issued by the Ministry of Industry and Information Technology, the National Development and Reform Commission, and the Ministry of Ecology and Environment on August 1, 2022, emphasizes building a solid foundation for carbon peaking in the industrial sector during the 14th Five-Year Plan period. By 2025, energy consumption per unit added value in the industrial sector should decrease by 13.5%, in contrast to that in 2020; carbon dioxide emissions per unit added value in the industrial sector should decrease more than that of the whole society; and especially for those carbon-intensive industries, greater efforts should be made to control their carbon dioxide emissions. During the 15th Five-Year Plan period, China should build a modern industrial system featuring "effective," "green," "renewable," and "low-carbon" and make sure carbon dioxide emissions in the industrial sector peak before 2030.

From the perspective of the energy structure, as shown in Figure 11, under the Carbon Neutrality Scenario, the final energy

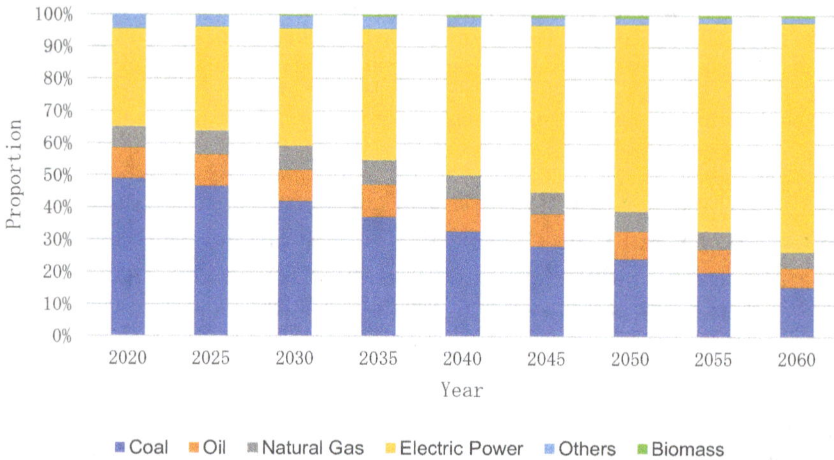

Figure 11. Forecast of final energy consumption structure in the industrial sector under the Carbon Neutrality Scenario.

consumption in China's industrial sector is developing toward "deeply electrified" and "low-carbon." With the share of fossil fuels in the final energy consumption decreasing and the share of electric power increasing, we expect that, in 2060, the share of fossil fuel consumption would drop to 26.4% and the electrification rate in China's industrial sector would reach 71.3%.

From the perspective of industrial segmentation, under the Carbon Neutrality Scenario, the final energy consumption in China's steel and chemical industries is expected to peak around 2025, with a peak value of 610 million tons of standard coal and 890 million tons of standard coal, respectively. At present, the cement industry has almost reached its peak, with a peak value of 220 million tons of standard coal. Energy consumption in the nonferrous metal industry would peak around 2035, slightly later than others mentioned above, with a peak value of about 280 million tons of standard coal.

From the perspective of energy consumption (Figure 12), under the Carbon Neutrality Scenario, the final energy consumption in China's industrial sector would keep growing in the 14th Five-Year Plan period but with a decreasing growth rate, and the peak, about 2.33 billion tons of standard coal, is expected to come in 2025. By

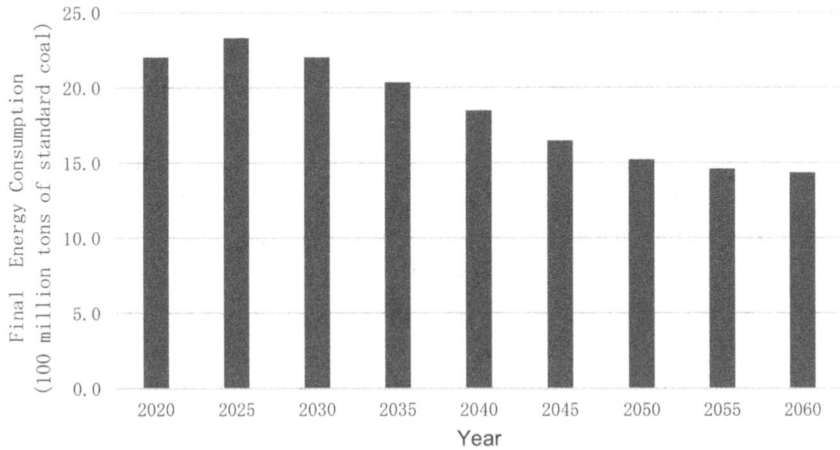

Figure 12. Forecast of total final energy consumption in the industrial sector under the Carbon Neutrality Scenario.

Table 1. Carbon dioxide emissions in the industrial sector (100 million tons).

	2020	2025	2030	2035	2040	2045	2050	2055	2060
BAU Scenario	68.5	70.3	62.6	56.6	48.3	40.0	33.6	28.1	24.5
Carbon Neutrality Scenario	68.5	69.6	61.3	50.6	42.4	31.6	22.3	17.8	14.3

2060, the final energy consumption in China's industrial sector would shrink to about 1.43 billion tons of standard coal.

Under the Carbon Neutrality Scenario, we expect the carbon dioxide emissions in the industrial sector to peak in 2025, with a peak value of 6.96 billion tons, and to drop to 1.43 billion tons by 2060 (Table 1).

To accelerate energy structure optimization and low-carbon transformation in the industrial sector, we suggest the following:

1. Make the production of energy-intensive goods peak as soon as possible. Producing less energy-intensive goods would definitely slow down energy consumption growth. Moreover, as

energy-intensive industries depend more on coal and oil, their production reduction would also shrink the demand for fossil fuels and promote energy structure optimization. Therefore, we should strictly control new additions to the capacities of energy-intensive industries and promote green transformation in the steel, cement, nonferrous metal, and chemical industries. Meanwhile, with the global prevalence of low-carbon transformation and the implementation of carbon tariffs, domestic energy-intensive goods will become less and less competitive. Thus, strictly controlling the export of energy-intensive products and vigorously developing high-value-added green products and high-end international trade are of great significance.

2. Improve energy-saving measures and reduce the energy consumption of products per unit. We should incorporate energy-saving principles into every aspect of industrial development, raise the informatization level of energy-saving management, modify online systems to monitor energy consumption in energy-intensive industries, establish a service platform to promote energy-saving technologies, and encourage energy-intensive enterprises to build energy management centers. It is also necessary to aim at an international advanced level, carry out energy-saving and carbon-reducing projects, promote energy-saving and carbon-reducing transformation in the steel, nonferrous metal, cement, chemical, and other carbon-intensive industries, raise energy utilization efficiency, and cultivate energy-saving and carbon-reducing "leaders" in the industrial sector. Moreover, to further raise energy utilization efficiency, we should focus on the development of efficient industrial equipment, set higher standards for energy efficiency, and motivate industrial enterprises to replace backward and inefficient industrial equipment with advanced efficient equipment by designing incentive and regulating mechanisms.
3. Optimize the industrial structure. We should promote a low-carbon revolution and digital transformation in the industrial sector, accelerate the development of information technology,

biotechnology, new energy, new materials, high-end equipment, new energy vehicles, aerospace and marine equipment, and other emerging strategically important industries, build green manufacturing systems, and apply the internet, big data, artificial intelligence, and other new technologies to green and low-carbon industries.

4. Develop clean energy and promote the application of green and low-carbon technologies. We should vigorously develop solar power, wind power, hydrogen power, biomass, and other renewable energy sources. By optimizing the final energy consumption structure in the industrial sector, hopefully by 2060, the electrification rate of China's industrial sector would exceed 71%. Meanwhile, with energy efficiency improvements and low-carbon technology innovations, we should also make breakthroughs in carbon capture and energy storage technologies and accelerate their application, such as CCUS, in the industrial sector on a large scale.

Construction sector

China's rapid GDP growth has also stimulated the rapid development of China's construction industry. According to the "China Census Yearbook 2020" issued by the National Bureau of Statistics, China's average living area per household reached 41.76 square meters in 2020, seven times that in 1990. The increase in average living area would, unsurprisingly, lead to an increase in the construction area and total energy consumption in construction sector. During the past 10 years, energy consumption in China's construction sector has increased rapidly. As stated by Zhou *et al.* (2020), energy consumption in the construction sector nearly tripled after 2000, constantly occupying about 20% of China's total primary energy consumption all the way through the past 20 years.[8]

For urban residential and public buildings, energy consumption mainly comes from electric power usage, the operation of heating systems, and natural gas directly consumed by the building itself. With ongoing energy saving policies, energy consumption intensity per unit building heating area is expected to decrease, offsetting the energy consumption growth brought about by the increasing heating area in north China. Meanwhile, with decreasing consumption of coal-fired power, the building electrification rate in China would also naturally increase. As electric power consumption accounts for the largest part of global building energy consumption, with the popularity of electrical appliances and the growth of the electrification rate, energy consumption structure in China's construction sector would also change.

Under the Carbon Neutrality Scenario, we expect the electrification rate in China's construction sector to reach 80% in 2060, with the consumption of coal, oil, and gas declining. Moreover, driven by the wider use of biogas and other biomass energy, the share of biomass in the energy consumption structure also presents a small increase after 2040 (Figure 13).

Under the Carbon Neutrality Scenario, the final energy consumption in China's construction sector would peak around 2030, with a peak value of about 890 million tons of standard coal, and then slowly drop to 790 million tons of standard coal by 2060 (Figure 14).

Under the Carbon Neutrality Scenario, the carbon dioxide emissions in the construction sector would reach a peak of 2.15 billion

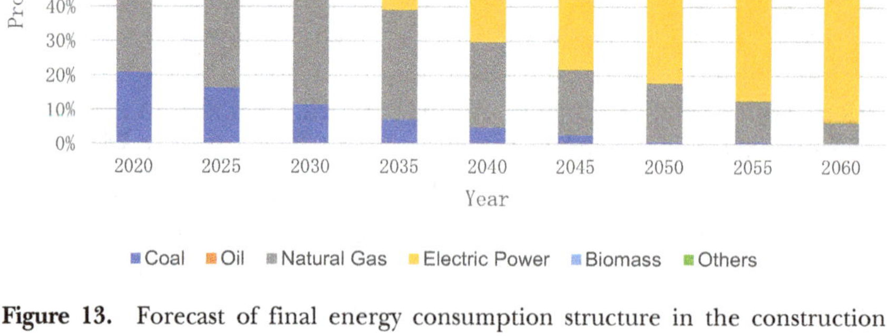

Figure 13. Forecast of final energy consumption structure in the construction sector under the Carbon Neutrality Scenario.

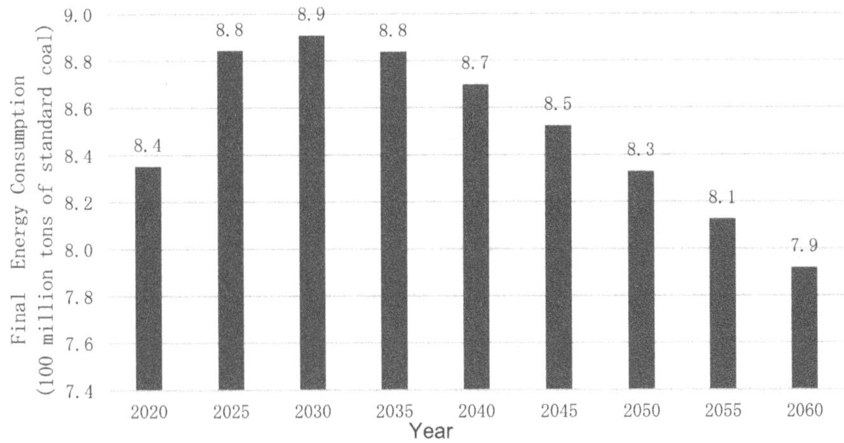

Figure 14. Forecast of final energy consumption in the construction sector under Carbon Neutrality Scenario.

Table 2. Carbon dioxide emissions in the construction sector (100 million tons).

	2020	2025	2030	2035	2040	2045	2050	2055	2060
BAU Scenario	21.2	21.4	20.3	18.6	16.2	13.9	11.8	9.0	7.2
Carbon Neutrality Scenario	21.2	21.5	19.9	17.0	14.8	11.5	7.4	5.6	4.0

tons in 2025 and then rapidly decrease to 400 million tons in 2060 (Table 2).

To achieve energy structure optimization and low-carbon transformation, the construction sector should focus on promoting energy-saving transformation, raising energy efficiency standards, developing zero-carbon buildings, and raising the electrification rate:

1. Vigorously promote the energy-saving transformation of existing urban buildings and municipal infrastructures.
2. Gradually tighten building energy-saving requirements and raise energy utilization efficiency. We should keep raising energy-saving standards for newly constructed buildings, accelerate the development of low-carbon buildings, construct a

building energy consumption quota system and an energy efficiency evaluation system, and implement regular evaluations of buildings' energy-saving performance.

3. Build clean and electrified heating systems and raise the building electrification level. We should actively adjust the energy consumption structure of heating systems, especially in cold areas, reduce the use of coal-fired boilers, and increase the use of cogeneration from waste heat and renewable energy. We should also improve the building electrification level and construct modern buildings equipped with photovoltaic power generation, energy storage, DC power distribution, and flexible power consumption technologies.
4. Invent specific energy-saving and low-carbon technologies for different climatic regions and building types, promote technology application, and support the development of zero-carbon buildings.

Transportation sector

The transportation sector ensures the connection between China's economic activities and social activities. In the past 40 years, China has made large-scale investments in transportation infrastructures. According to the 2021 statistical bulletin of Transportation Industry Development, the national mileage of highways reached 5,280,700 kilometers, and the highway density reached 55.01 kilometers per 100 square kilometers by the end of 2021. The national mileage of railways reached 150,000 kilometers, of which high-speed railways account for 40,000 kilometers, more than twice the 19,800 kilometers at the end of 2015.

With the rapid economic and social development and continuous improvement in people's living standards, demand for goods and passenger transportation is expected to rise, which would lead to constant energy consumption and carbon dioxide emissions increase in the transportation sector. According to data provided by the IEA (2019),[9] the compound growth rate of carbon dioxide emissions in China's transportation sector between 2010 and 2018 reached 7.63%, higher than 2.54% in the global transportation sector, which indicates that the carbon dioxide emissions in China's transportation sector would continue to grow at a relatively high rate. According to research by the Ministry of Ecology and Environment (2021), the current carbon dioxide emissions in China's transportation sector account for about 10% of the national total, while carbon dioxide emissions from road transportation account for about 80% of the transportation sector's total.[10]

From the perspective of the energy structure, road transportation should develop toward "completely electrified." According to the "Action Plan for Carbon Dioxide Peaking Before 2030" issued by the State Council, the proportion of vehicles utilizing new and clean energy power should reach 40% in 2030. As pointed out by the statistical bulletin of the Ministry of Transport, China's railway electrification rate has already reached 73.3% in 2021,[11] and with the expansion of high-speed railways' operating mileage, electrified high-speed railways would also become an important part of electrified road transportation.

Under the Carbon Neutrality Scenario, with a decreasing share of fossil fuel consumption and an increasing share of electric power consumption, the final energy consumption structure in China's transportation sector would evolve toward "low-carbon" and "deeply electrified" in the future. With the proportion of fossil fuels decreasing and electric power increasing in the final energy consumption, we expect that, by 2060, the electrification rate in China's transportation sector would increase to 52% and the share of fossil fuel consumption would decrease to 28% (Figure 15).

From the perspective of energy consumption (Figure 16), under the Carbon Neutrality Scenario, the final energy consumption in China's transportation sector is expected to peak around 2040, with a peak value of about 550 million tons of standard coal. By 2060, the total final energy consumption in the transportation sector would stabilize at around 470 million tons of standard coal.

Under the Carbon Neutrality Scenario, we expect the carbon dioxide emissions in the transportation sector to peak in 2030, with a peak value of 1.24 billion tons, and to drop to 400 million tons by 2060 (Table 3).

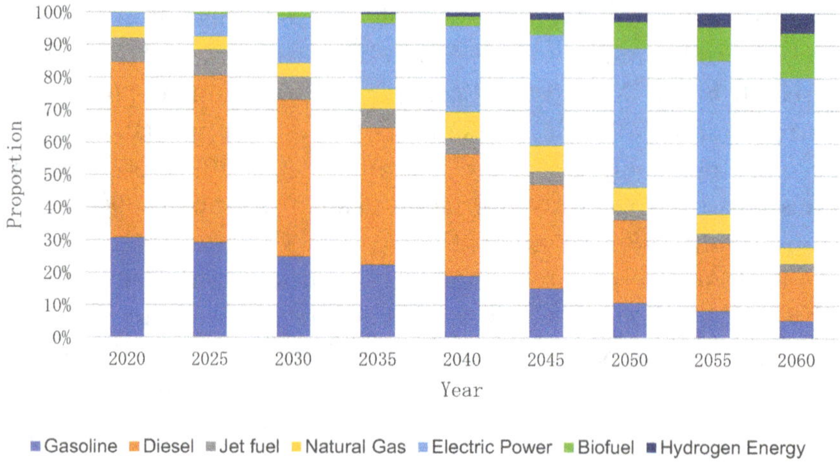

Figure 15. Forecast of energy structure in the transportation sector by different types of energy source under the Carbon Neutrality Scenario.

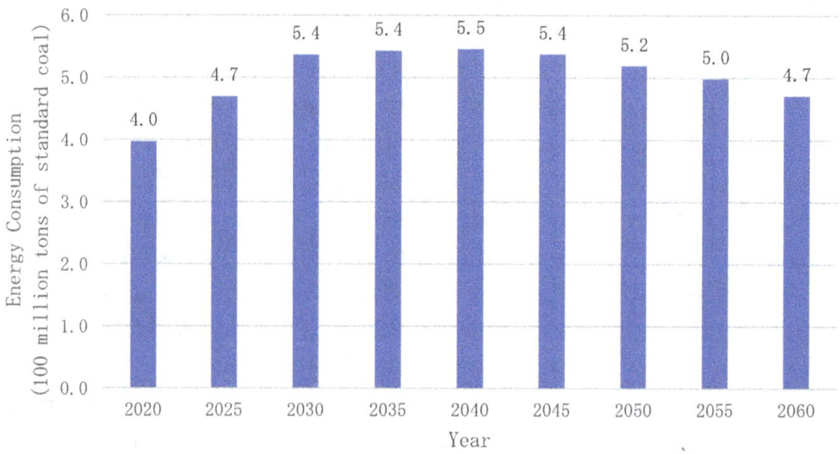

Figure 16. Energy consumption in the transportation sector under the Carbon Neutrality Scenario.

To realize energy structure optimization and low-carbon transformation, the transportation sector should work on promoting travel mode reforms, transportation structure optimization, new-energy traffic tool innovation, and intelligent transportation development:

Table 3. Carbon dioxide emissions in the transportation sector (100 million tons).

	2020	2025	2030	2035	2040	2045	2050	2055	2060
BAU Scenario	9.4	11.4	13.5	13.8	13.8	13.1	12.0	10.3	8.8
Carbon Neutrality Scenario	9.0	10.7	12.4	11.8	11.2	9.5	7.0	5.5	4.0

1. Guide the public to adopt green and low-carbon travel modes. We should accelerate the construction of mass public transport infrastructure, such as urban rail transit, bus lanes, and bus rapid transit systems, and the construction of bicycle lanes and pedestrian trails. We should also build an efficient, well-connected, and comfortable public transport service system supported by information technology and alleviate the urban traffic congestion problem by employing comprehensive methods. Meanwhile, we should investigate and establish carbon accounts to record residents' green commuting distances and integrate urban transportation into the carbon trade system.
2. Optimize transportation structure. To reduce energy consumption and carbon dioxide emissions intensity in goods transportation, we should encourage railways and waterways instead of highways and vigorously develop multimodal transportation with railways and waterways as the backbone. As for passenger transportation, we should optimize passenger transportation organization and encourage enterprises to function and operate on a large scale. Moreover, we should accelerate the development of green logistics by integrating and utilizing transportation resources more efficiently.
3. Accelerate the development of traffic tools utilizing new energy and clean energy. We should actively promote new energy and clean energy applications in the transportation sector, for example, to encourage new-energy vehicle utilization and the electric replacement of traditional public traffic tools. Besides,

we should also raise the electrification level in railway systems and develop new-energy-powered ships and aircrafts.

4. Develop intelligent transportation system and promote reform in the transportation service system. Based on traffic big data and intelligent technology, we could construct an intelligent urban traffic management system to organize optimal trips. Besides, for the application of autonomous driving and other intelligent technologies, we should prepare detailed plans for urban traffic construction, design related operation management systems, and deploy related traffic infrastructures in advance.

Electric power sector

With a long-term deep decarbonization strategy, the industrial, construction, and transportation sectors can speed up electrification development and raise electric power proportion in the final energy consumption and the energy consumption proportion of electric power supply in primary energy consumption. Therefore, we expect that electric power consumption would grow faster than total energy consumption, and electric power demand and supply would also continue to rise.

During the 13th Five-Year Plan period, the average annual growth rate of installed capacity of all-caliber power generation was 7.6%, and that of non-fossil fuel installed capacity and coal installed capacity was, respectively, 13.1% and 3.7%. The proportion of non-fossil fuel installed capacity in the total installed capacity increased from 34.8% by the end of 2015 to 44.8% by the end of 2020, an increase of 10 percentage points, while the proportion of coal installed capacity decreased from 59.0% by the end of 2015 to 49.1% by the end of 2020.

As the scale of international trade in the electric power sector is small, we assume electric power supply is completely determined by demand. Thus, when calculating electric power generation, we start by calculating the electric power demand. We first sum up the predicted electric power demand in terminal sectors, including the industrial, construction, and transportation sectors, and add the power transmission loss, and finally we get the predicted electric power supply.

Figure 17 shows the predicted electric power supply under the Carbon Neutrality Scenario. China's electric power supply would gradually increase from 7.6 trillion kWh in 2020 to about 15.4 trillion kWh in 2060. In this period, China's electric power supply is expected to be about 9.9 trillion kWh in 2030 and 13.6 trillion kWh in 2050.

After years of effort, China has made great achievements in the electric power generation structure. According to data provided by the National Energy Administration, in the first half of 2022, the newly installed capacity of renewable energy accounts for 80% of the total newly installed capacity in China. By the end of June 2022, the total installed capacity of renewable energy in China had reached 1.118 billion kilowatts, accounting for about 46% of the national total. In the future, China would replace coal with renewable energy in the electric power generation process and accelerate the decarbonization of the electric power sector. As renewable energy, such as wind power and solar power, in the short term cannot fill the vacancy in electric power demand, natural gas would serve as a transitional electric power generation measure. Therefore, in the

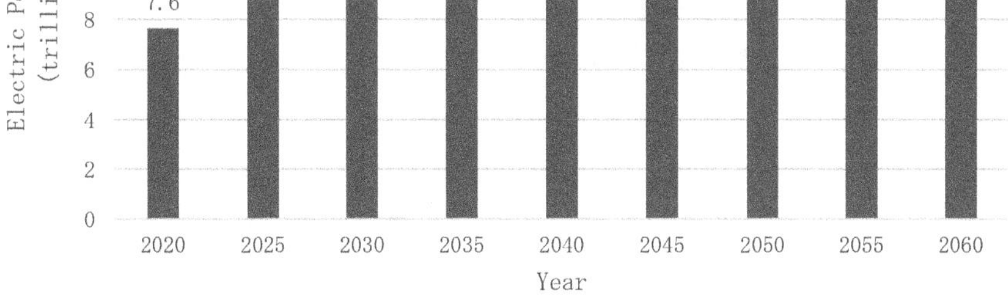

Figure 17. Forecast of electric power supply under the Carbon Neutrality Scenario.

following 10 years, the proportion of electric power generated from natural gas would increase slightly.

From the perspective of the electric power generation structure, under the Carbon Neutrality Scenario, most newly added electric power demand in China would be satisfied by non-fossil fuels (Figure 18). Compared with 2020, we expect that the proportion of electric power generated from non-fossil fuels in China would increase from 32.4% to about 90.5% in 2060, while the proportion of coal-fired power would drop from 64% to about 5.5%.

To achieve the low-carbon transformation and optimization of the electric power generation structure, the electric power sector should concentrate on structural optimization, technological innovation, power grid upgrading, and market reform:

1. Accelerate the replacement of coal-fired power and raise the proportion of power generated from renewable energy. We should strictly control the newly installed capacity of coal-fired power and eliminate other backward power-producing capacity. We should also optimize coal-fired power systems by building large, efficient coal-fired power stations and transform

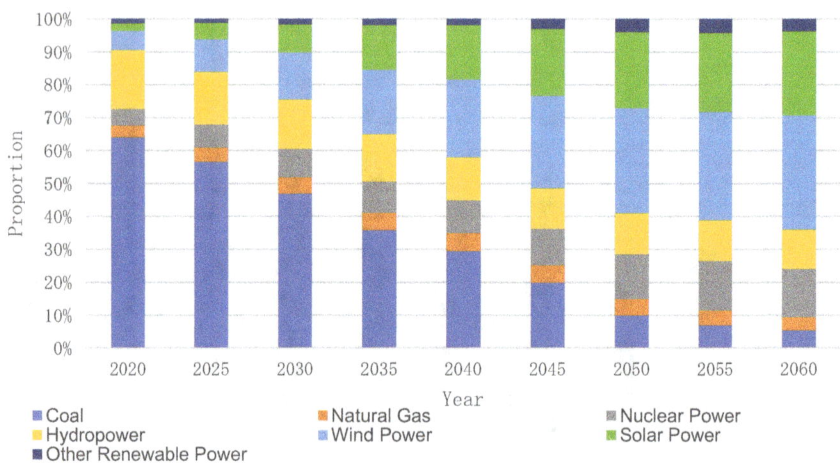

Figure 18. Forecast of power generation structure under the Carbon Neutrality Scenario.

coal-fired power's role from base load power to auxiliary power. Moreover, we should set more active goals for new energy and renewable energy development, accelerate the construction of wind power and solar power stations, encourage hydropower based on local conditions, and develop nuclear power in an orderly manner.

2. Support low-carbon transformation in the electric power sector through technological innovation. We should accelerate innovation and upgrading in the intelligent photovoltaic industry and promote its application. We should also actively develop the solar photothermal power generation technology and promote the construction of comprehensive renewable energy power stations with photothermal, photovoltaic, and wind power generation complementing and moderating each other. Besides, it is also vital to explore and make use of geothermal energy, wave energy, tidal current energy, ocean thermal energy, and other marine new energy and actively develop hydrogen energy, CCUS, energy storage, and other related technologies.
3. Improve the construction of power grid facilities. To ensure that the power supply matches the power demand well, we should optimize the electric power transmission and allocation mechanisms. To enhance power supply stability, we should accelerate the construction of synchronous power grids in the east and west, strengthen the interconnection among power grids across regions, and promote their cooperation in shifting peak load and building a mutual emergency protection system. To promote the optimal allocation of resources among regions, first, we should plan energy delivery patterns in advance, rely on power grids to allocate resources, make full use of power transmission channels, and raise the share of clean power transmitted; second, we should design smart power systems encompassing power supply and power demand in advance, and ensure the fair access of distributed energy; third, we should build a smart platform integrating advanced technologies, such as energy storage, big data, the Internet of Things, and 5G, and speed up the construction of power storage systems to flexibly convert and store different energy forms.

4. Build a modernized electric power market system. We should build a well-matched market system to absorb any extra electric power generated from new energy and renewable energy; improve the inter-provincial trading system, which mainly focuses on medium- and long-term transactions with spot transactions as supplements; expand the new energy and renewable energy trade scale across regions and provinces; and perfect the price formulating and cost distributing mechanisms. To make the market system adaptive to high proportions of new energy and renewable energy, we should also actively investigate green certification and carbon trading mechanisms and find possible ways to couple them with the electric power market.

Figure 19 summarizes the technological transformation paths required for energy transformation in China's carbon-intensive sectors under the Carbon Neutrality Scenario. Technological innovation is vital for transforming economic growth patterns from factor-driven to innovation-driven. As energy transformation also requires low-carbon technological innovations, we should vigorously modify and upgrade technologies in traditional carbon-intensive industries, combine technological innovations with industrial structure upgrading, accelerate market-oriented technological development, and further promote the collaborative innovation of developing low-carbon technologies while dealing with climate change. The industrial, construction, transportation, and electric power sectors, as important components of China's economy and society and the major sources of carbon dioxide emissions, need to explore individualized paths to technological energy transformation in combination with their own industrial structure and development needs and jointly contribute to realizing the "Dual Carbon" strategy.

Financial Support for Technological Energy Transformation

Under the "Dual Carbon" strategy, accelerating China's energy transformation process requires technological transformation and industrial development toward "energy-saving," "low-carbon," and "zero-carbon." This process would generate a huge demand for

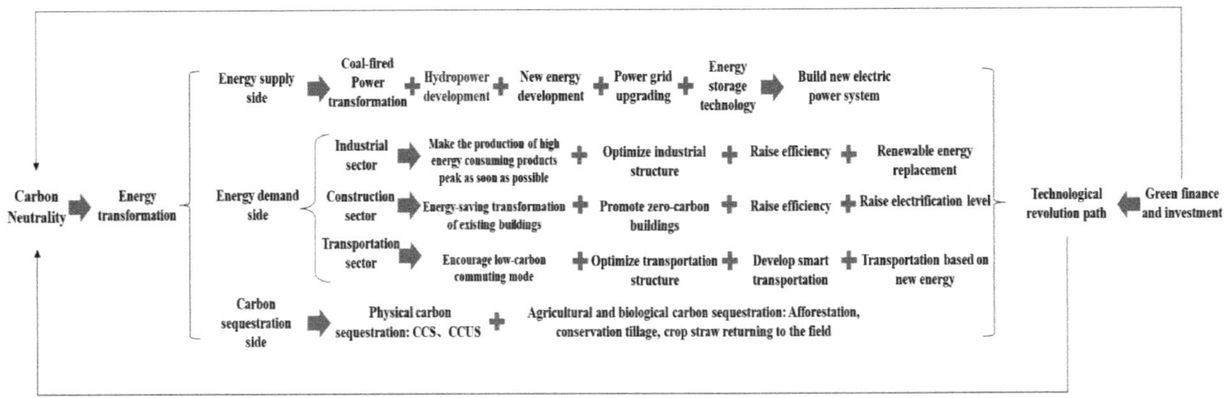

Figure 19. Schematic diagram of the technological transformation paths of energy transformation under the goal of carbon neutrality.

high-quality human capital and investment in various fields. For example, Goldman Sachs Research Department (2021) points out that, energy transformation would create a huge amount of new employment opportunities and that emerging low-carbon industries would create more than 40 million job opportunities, concentrated in the sustainable energy ecosystem, mainly in the fields of renewable energy power generation, power grids, and electrified infrastructure industries.[12]

According to our predictions, the achievement of carbon neutrality in China's carbon-intensive sectors requires about 314.97 trillion yuan in investment, including 246.76 trillion yuan for carbon emissions reduction and 68.21 trillion yuan for carbon capture. Estimating using different carbon-reducing technological transformation paths, new-energy and renewable-energy industries require 155.60 trillion yuan in investment, low-carbon technology transformation in traditional energy-intensive industries requires 63.01 trillion yuan, the clean transformation of fossil fuels requires 4.79 trillion yuan, and replacing coal with oil and gas requires about 23.34 trillion yuan. Among the carbon-intensive sectors (Table 4), the nonmetallic products industry and chemical raw materials industry require the most investment. In order to test the robustness

Table 4. Investment forecast of carbon-intensive sectors under the Carbon Neutrality Scenario.

	Investment required for carbon neutrality (unit: trillion yuan)	Green premium ratio (unit: %)
Petrochemical industry	7.54	8
Chemical raw material	127.45	61
Steel	14.79	21
Nonferrous metal	24.09	4
Nonmetallic products	128.70	151
General industry	9.46	NA
Power generation	2.94	17
Add up to	314.97	NA

Note: The green premium rate comes from the CICC (2021).

of our predictions, in the third column, we present the green premium ratio of each sector estimated by the China International Capital Corporation (CICC) based on suggestions from relevant government departments, relevant scholars at home and abroad, and leading enterprises in the industry (CICC, 2021).[13] By comparison, we could discover that our rank of industry's predicted investment to achieve carbon neutrality is similar to the rank of CICC's green premium ratio, which indicates that our predictions can accurately reflect the relative demand for investments in different sectors. It is worth mentioning that our prediction for the investment required to achieve carbon neutrality is larger than that given by current mainstream investment consulting organizations. For example, the prediction by CICC is 139 trillion yuan, while that by Standard Chartered's global research team is 127–192 trillion yuan. This is because investment consulting organizations calculate the required investment mainly by aggregating microprojects' investments, while we use shadow pricing to estimate the hidden price of carbon emission reduction. That is to say, we consider not only the investment required by setting up new low-carbon projects but also the economic system adjustment costs brought by quitting old projects and providing supporting measures for the new ones.

Green finance and carbon finance work as powerful levers to incite social capital for supporting low-carbon transformations. In order to better satisfy the huge investment demands from China's energy transformation under the "Dual-Carbon" strategy, we need to further optimize the development of green finance and carbon finance, make full use of their resource allocating, risk managing, and market pricing functions, improve the "five pillars," and make green finance and carbon finance better contribute to energy transformation:

1. Build a green financial support system to support green development. As the "lubricant" and "booster" of green development, green finance greatly influences industrial structure optimization and energy structure transformation and provides strong

support for the economy's green and high-quality development. As for concrete measures, we should formulate evaluation standards for green projects, construct a certification system for green finance, increase investment in green transformation and clean energy development in the industrial, construction, transportation, and electric power sectors, establish fiscal income and tax support mechanisms, and enhance the interaction between fiscal income and green finance.

2. Encourage financial institutions to enhance green financial product and service innovation. To give full play to the guiding role of financial institutions, we should encourage financial institutions to innovate green financial products and vigorously promote the development of green finance through product innovation. We should also extend financial services, actively develop green credit, encourage green bond financing and green insurance, support green enterprises' listing and refinancing, and vigorously promote national carbon market construction and carbon finance development.
3. Create a favorable atmosphere for green finance development. We should encourage qualified areas to actively apply and construct pilot zones for green finance reform and innovation, attract more capital into green investment, and promote green transformation and upgrading of local industries. Based on the national carbon market, we should promote the construction of an environmental rights trading market to allocate production factors more efficiently. We should also build a statistical monitoring system for green finance to provide reliable data for decision-making. We should accelerate the formation of green information-sharing mechanisms and build a comprehensive green financial service platform based on big data, integrating functions such as green policy announcements, green evaluations and ratings, green investment and green finance matching, ESG information publishing, green information sharing, green industry promotion, green equity trading, carbon asset management, and carbon credit evaluations.

Concluding Remarks

To achieve the goal of carbon neutrality, China needs to accelerate the energy transformation process and build a green, low-carbon, and sustainable modern energy system. Among others, security and green low-carbon sustainability would become the key directions for future energy transformation.

From the perspective of energy supply and demand, China's energy supply would be more accessible and stable, and energy demand would keep increasing for a period of time. From the perspective of energy structure, China's energy structure would restructure toward "clean" and "low carbon" in the future, with cleaner energy supply, decreasing coal consumption proportion, and raising electrification level in terminal sectors.

The energy transformation would pull carbon dioxide emissions to a plateau stage and make it peak as soon as possible. At present, the decoupling trend of China's economic growth from carbon dioxide emissions has already begun. With continuous progress in energy transformation, we expect that the decoupling trend of economic growth and carbon dioxide emissions would further enhance after 2025, and the decoupling trend of energy consumption and carbon dioxide emissions would also start to appear at that time. And with continuous progress in energy structure optimization, the two decoupling trends would gradually evolve toward the "strong decoupling" state.

Energy transformation requires strong support, not only from technological innovation but also from green finance. Key sectors, such as the industrial sector, the construction sector, the transportation sector, and the electric power sector, should focus on the needs of green and low-carbon development, scientifically design a technological energy transformation path, give priority to the development of core technologies, innovate incentive mechanisms to encourage technological breakthroughs, give full play to the strategic supporting role of technology in the energy transformation process, and efficiently lead related industries to realize carbon peaking as soon as possible. At the same time, to meet the huge demand for investment under the "Dual Carbon" strategy, we should fully employ the three functions of green finance and carbon finance (i.e., resource allocation, risk management, and market pricing), strengthen the construction of the "five pillars" (i.e., standards, products, market systems, etc.), attract more social capital inflows to green development and low-carbon transformation fields, and better promote technological innovation to support the energy transformation.

Acknowledgement

The author gratefully acknowledges the financial support of the Innovative Research Groups Project of the National Natural Science Foundation of China (72121002) and the MOE Project of Key Research Institute of Humanities and Social Sciences at Universities (22JJD790058). The author also thanks the members of his research team, Zhiqing LI and Shilin HU, for their contribution.

Endnotes

1. IPCC (2022).
2. BP (2022).
3. It should be noted that the study's scenario forecast for total carbon dioxide emissions does not take into account the negative emissions benefits of carbon sinks, carbon capture, utilization, and storage (CCUS), and other technologies, so there would still be some residual emissions by 2060.
4. Energy Conservation Committee of Metallurgical Industry of China Energy Conservation Association, Metallurgical Industry Planning and Research Institute (2020).
5. IEA (2018).
6. China Building Materials Federation (2022).
7. Gao Yan and Li Lianfei (2021).
8. Zhou *et al.* (2020).
9. IEA (2019).
10. Publicity and Education Center, Ministry of Ecology, School of Applied Economics, Renmin University of China, Didi Development Research Institute (2021).
11. Ministry of Transport (2022).
12. Goldman Sachs Research Department (2021).
13. CICC (2021).

References

BP. 2022. Statistical Review of World Energy 2022. https://www.bp.com/content/dam/bp/business-sites/en/global/corporate/pdfs/energy-economics/statistical-review/bp-stats-review-2022-full-report.pdf.

China Building Materials Federation. 2022. China Building Materials Industry Carbon Emission Report (2021).

China International Capital Corporation (CICC). 2021. Carbon Neutral Economics: Macro and Industry Analysis under New Constraints. CITIC Publishing Group.

Energy Conservation Committee of Metallurgical Industry of China Energy Conservation Association, Metallurgical Industry Planning and Research Institute. 2020. Energy Conservation and Low Carbon Development Report of China's Iron and Steel Industry (2020).

Gao Yan and Li Lianfei. 2021. Make the "double carbon" work in chemical industry park rule-based interview with Yang Ting, Secretary-General of the Park Committee of Petrochemical Federation on the occasion of the establishment of the "implementation guide of carbon neutralization in chemical industry park". *China Chemical Industry News* (August 17). http://www.ccin.com.cn/detail/1616882eae2be7c2f7e4755d00108c5e.

Goldman Sachs Research Department. 2021. Carbon Economics: China's Road to Net Zero Carbon Emissions.

IEA. 2018. Roadmap-Low-Carbon Transition in the Cement Industry. https://www.iea.org/publications/freepublications/publication/Technology RoadmapLowCarbonTransitionintheCementIndustry.pdf.

IEA. 2019. World Energy Outlook 2019. France.

IPCC. 2022. Climate Change 2022: Impacts, Adaptation, and Vulnerability. https://report.ipcc.ch/ar6wg2/pdf/IPCC_AR6_WGII_SummaryForPolicymakers.pdf.

Ministry of Transport. 2022. Statistical Bulletin on the Development of Transportation Industry in 2021. http://www.gov.cn/shuju/2022-05/25/content_5692174.htm.

Publicity and Education Center, Ministry of Ecology, School of Applied Economics, Renmin University of China, Didi Development Research Institute. 2021. Digital Travel Helps Carbon Neutralization-Practice Green Transportation to Lead Low-Carbon Travel.

Zhou, N., Lu, H., Khanna, N., Liu, X., Fridley, D., Price, L., Shen, B., Feng, W., Lin, J., Szum, C., and Ding, C. 2020. China Energy Outlook: Understanding China's Energy and Emissions Trends. Berkeley, CA: Lawrence Berkeley National Laboratory.

https://doi.org/10.1142/9789819815241_0016

Chapter 16

FISCAL INCENTIVE FOR MARKET INTEGRATION: EVIDENCE FROM THE REFORM OF INCOME TAX SHARING

Ziying Fan[*,‡] and Xiaochang Zhou[†,§]

[*]*Shanghai University of Finance and Economics, Shanghai, China*
[†]*Zhongnan University of Economics and Law, Wuhan, China*
[‡]*fan.ziying@sufe.edu.cn*
[§]*sddzzxc@126.com*

Introduction

According to Smith's classical economics theory, labor division is the endogenous driver of a country's growth, but its evolution depends on the size of the country's economy. Since the reform and opening up for more than 40 years, China has gained an extraordinary advantage from its market size as the economy keeps growing. However, due to long-term market segmentation and regional barriers, the market advantage has not been put to full use in stimulating growth. In order to unleash the driving force of economic development and respond to the challenges of "anti-globalization," the central government proposed a new growth pattern in 2020: the domestic market will be the mainstay while the domestic and foreign markets can boost each other. The key to "dual circulation" is "circulation." To achieve smooth domestic circulation, "industrial monopoly and local protection need to be brought down ... together with the institutional barriers that hinder the market allocation of production factors and the circulation of goods and services."[1] Therefore, actively maintaining domestic market integration, promoting the integration of the commodity and factor markets, and breaking down market fragmentation and local protectionism remain important tasks that we face today.

If we look back at history, market segmentation has been a prominent problem for China's economic growth. Young's QJE paper in Young (2000), which sparked researchers' interest in China's market segmentation, finds that provinces have very similar industrial structures, which is abnormal for a giant economy. Young's conclusion is that "China is a segmented domestic market." Poncet (2002) even believed that the degree of market fragmentation between provinces in China was even more serious than that between countries within the EU, resulting in an efficiency loss amounting to 20% of a region's total output (Zheng and Li, 2003), seriously restricting China's long-term sustainable economic growth. Market integration has been improved in China, especially in the product market (Liu and Li, 2008; He and Lv, 2019). However, in recent years, the degree of capital factor market segmentation has not shown a significant decrease, and even a "staggered tail" phenomenon has emerged (Liu and Kong, 2021). The microfoundation for market integration is cross-regional investment. But high transaction costs in domestic cross-regional operations caused by capital factor market segmentation (Boisot and Meyer, 2008) severely restrict enterprises' development in different regions of China (Song and Huang, 2014; Cao *et al.*, 2015), especially making it less likely for local state-owned enterprises (SOEs) to conduct M&A in other places (Fang, 2008). Therefore, the segmentation of the capital factor market is the main reason for uneven development across different regions (Guo and Wang, 2003).

Existing literature regarding the institutional arrangements causing market fragmentation primarily has two explanations. One is economic development motives. Driven by the desire for political promotion, the local officials have sufficient incentive to protect the local markets (Qian and Weingast, 1997; Zhou, 2007), and restricting the flow of resources can effectively maintain local economic interests (Yin and Cai, 2001). The second is fiscal incentive motivation. In the 1980s, there were different fiscal levels, and fiscal revenue was distributed according to the ownership structure of enterprises. As fiscal growth equaled "enterprise management," the local governments resorted to market segmentation to achieve more fiscal revenue, prioritizing local enterprises' demand for the local market and factor resources. More or less the same policy was adopted across the country, leading to a very similar industrial structure across the regions and economic segmentation (Shen and Dai, 1990). With the fiscal incentive, the local governments tend to protect industries that have high factor marginal productivity (Ping, 2004), high profit and tax rates, and high state-owned stake (Bai, 2004). Conversely, if the central fiscal system weakens the dependence of local fiscal systems on the local economy through transfer payments, the local government will relax the market segmentation (Fan and Zhang, 2010). While a vast amount of literature has focused on local protectionism caused by economic growth incentives, the fiscal incentives have not received enough attention. Under the new growth pattern, which emphasizes the promotion of factor market integration, it is important to examine the fiscal incentive for a unified market, which will lead to a benign circulation of the factor markets and an inclusive, coordinated fiscal system.

However, research on the fiscal incentive for factor market integration faces two problems. First, the fiscal incentive is usually endogenous in the market integration process. For example, a well-developed local industry means a higher share of the tax revenue for the local government, while making it impossible to link the fiscal incentive directly to market integration. Second, as previous research focuses on the product market, there is no appropriate way to measure the integration level of the factor markets. The 2002 income tax sharing reform, before which the distribution of corporate income tax directed the local enterprises' income tax to the local government, offers a good solution to this problem: after the reform, the central and local governments share the enterprises' income tax, with the local government getting only 40%. On the one hand, the reform, by scrapping the distribution of revenue based on the enterprises' ownership, has externally reduced the local government's fiscal revenue from the local tax base and thereby weakened their incentive to restrict cross-regional capital mobility. According to the official document on the income tax sharing reform, because the corporate income tax took an increasingly prominent role in the local fiscal revenue, with the local government fighting for the tax base, the old system "prevented ... the formation of a unified market across the country."[2] On the other hand, the local government that is in charge of the local SOEs can easily restrict their investment in other places. As a result, the integration level of the capital factor market can be measured by comparing the number of local SOEs' other-place subsidiaries before and after the reform.

To measure enterprises' investment in other provinces, the only appropriate public data are those of listed companies' subsidiaries, which provide registration locations and the investment relationship among enterprises. We manually collected the financial statement notes of listed companies from 1999 to 2007, collected the names of companies directly controlled by the parent company, and searched for the registered places of subsidiaries using platforms to define parent companies and domestic subsidiaries with registered places not in the same city as "cross-region investment." During the sample period, 19,901 subsidiaries of 1,500 parent companies are covered, 8,635 of which are located in a different place than their parent companies. Figure 1 illustrates that the number of subsidiaries of China's listed companies increased year by year in 1999–2007, and the number of subsidiaries located in places different from their parent companies increased faster, with the percentage rising from 22.57% in 1999 to 48.54% in 2007, which fully demonstrates the improved integration of China's capital factor market.

Using difference-in-differences identification, we have the following findings: First, the income tax sharing reform has effectively

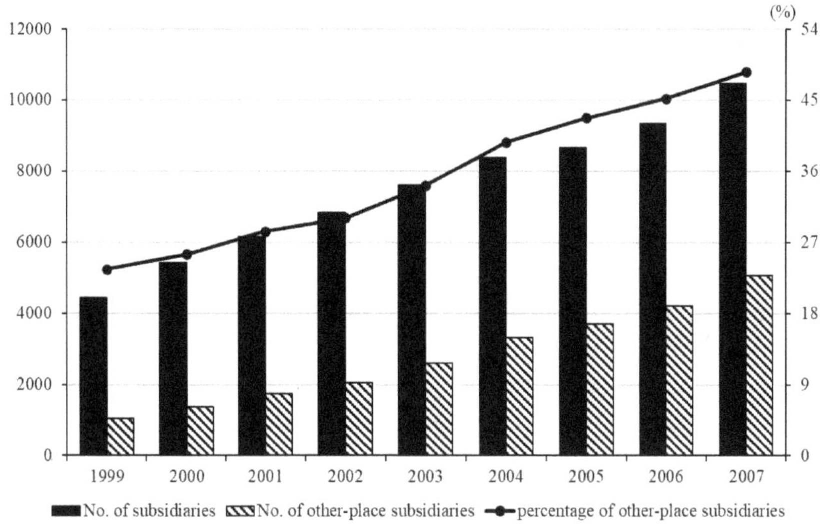

Figure 1. Number of subsidiaries, other-place subsidiaries, and percentage of other-place subsidiaries.

promoted the integration of the capital factor market, which is reflected in an apparent increase in the number of other-place subsidiaries of local SOEs compared with enterprises of different corporate ownership structures. Second, the promotion of policy on the off-site investment behavior of local SOEs is closely related to the local government's stake ratio, and only those enterprises where the local government's stake ratio exceeds the tax-sharing ratio (40%) will significantly increase off-site subsidiary companies. Third, the policy has promoted the integration of the provincial capital factor market, and the stimulating effect has been concentrated in manufacturers and regions whose fiscal revenue highly depends on SOEs. This shows that the effects of the policy are subject to the local fiscal conditions and regional competition. Fourth, enterprises' expansion into other places raises the return on capital and significantly increases the cash dividends of the local SOEsin which the local government's share-holding ratio exceeds its share of the tax revenue. The local government has strategically adjusted the way it obtains the returns.

Compared with the existing literature, this study may contribute in the following three aspects: First, it expands and enriches the existing research on market segmentation in China. This chapter discusses the causes and solutions of market segmentation in China from the perspective of fiscal incentives and uses the number of subsidiary companies located in different regions as a measure of capital mobility. This not only intuitively reflects the behavior of micro-individuals but also expands the research on market segmentation from product market to factor market.[3] Second, it adds to and expands the current research on the income tax sharing reform. This study expands the influence of the income tax sharing reform on the market integration effect, while the existing literature mainly focuses on the shock of the policy to tax revenue collection and management (Fan and Tian, 2013; Tian and Fan, 2016), the effect of the resulting different real tax rates on enterprises (Liu *et al.*, 2017; Li *et al.*, 2018), or the fiscal pressure the policy exerts on the local government (Chen *et al.*, 2017). Third, it has direct policy implications for the new growth pattern. Although this chapter discusses the income tax sharing reform of 2002, it reveals the fiscal incentive behind the local government's behavior, which is still the main impediment to market integration today. Finding that the distribution of fiscal revenue according to enterprise ownership is the cause of market segmentation, this chapter examines market integration from the new perspective of fiscal incentive, providing policy guidance for the formation of a unified national market with orderly competition as well as a reference for a better fiscal governance system.

The chapter is arranged as follows: section "Institutional Background and Theoretical Hypothesis" gives an analysis based on a review of the institutional background of the policy and proposes a hypothesis; section "Data and Regression Model" explains the sources of the data, the way they are handled, and the setup of the model; section "Basic Outcome and Robustness Test" presents the basic outcome and the robustness tests; section "Further Discussion" presents further analysis and section "Conclusion and Policy Suggestions" the conclusion and policy suggestions.

Institutional Background and Theoretical Hypothesis

Institutional background

After the reform and opening up, before the tax reform in 1994, in order to fully mobilize the enthusiasm of local governments for economic development, China implemented a "comprehensive responsibility" fiscal system, clearly defining the scope of the central and local governments' revenue and expenditure and ensuring the balance of local government fiscal on the premise of guaranteeing central government revenue. The comprehensive responsibility system replaced the traditional centralized control over revenues and expenditures, leading to more efficient fiscal management at all levels of government and more enthusiasm on the part of the local government for higher revenues, lower expenditures, and more growth. However, the comprehensive responsibility fiscal system has caused local governments to pay too much attention to their own interests and neglect the overall interests. This, combined with the lack of central government fiscal constraints on local government fiscal, has led local governments to reduce the proportion of revenue transferred to the central government through opportunistic behavior, resulting in the erosion of central government fiscal and a tendency for the state's fiscal to become dispersed, leading to the serious phenomenon of "feudal economy" (Shen and Dai, 1990). Under this system, fiscal revenues are based on enterprises' ownership, closely connecting the local fiscal revenue with the interests of the local enterprises. The development of businesses is equivalent to the development of fiscal, and the enhancement of fiscal can provide resources for further development of local businesses, forming a virtuous cycle. In order to grow local enterprises, the local government played the role of "a helping hand" (Liu, 2012), providing support in production factors and actively developing the product markets for the enterprises. Considering the fiscal revenue, different regions all preferred industries with high profit and tax and low technology. The similar industrial structure then encouraged the local government to protect the local markets and build a big tax base by restricting the mobility of products and factors. Hence the market segmentation.

China started to reform the tax sharing system in 1994 to adjust the relationship between the central and local fiscal management and to strengthen the role of the central fiscal. The tax-based fiscal system, based on the clarification of the jurisdiction of governments at all levels, divides budget revenues by tax categories, breaking down the original "block by block" management system to some extent and promoting the integration of the national market (Song and Fan, 2015). However, the reform adjusted the more mature circulation tax without changing the income tax. It retained the practice of distributing the enterprises' income tax by linking the local fiscal revenue with the productive tax base that belonged to the local government, because the information system and the system of collecting and managing tax were inadequate for any changes in the way of distributing income tax. As the corporate income tax scaled up, the local government paid more attention to the local enterprises and started to protect the corporate income tax base in order to protect its fiscal revenue. For example, the local government would use its power to keep the corporate income tax by holding back central enterprises' acquisition of local enterprises or preventing local enterprises from investing in other places. Under the trend of conglomerate diversification, scale economy, and regional division of labor, such obstructions to the mobility of capital factor did no good to the overall competitiveness of enterprises or the balance of fiscal resources among different regions.

Over time, the tax authorities have also gradually realized the serious problems with the income tax system. In the "Income Tax Revenue Sharing Reform Plan" issued by the State Council at the end of 2001, it was explicitly pointed out that the practice of dividing corporate income tax according to the affiliation of enterprises "restricted the gradual deepening of SOE reform and the establishment of modern enterprise systems, objectively helped to create repeated construction and regional blockades, hindered fair market competition and the formation of a national unified market, was not conducive to promoting regional economic coordination and development and realizing common prosperity, and also hindered strengthening tax collection and supervision." Hence, it was decided to adopt the new practice of central and local governments sharing the corporate income tax equally starting in 2002 (but after 2003, the central government took 60% and the local government 40%). For all levels of government, this reform means a decrease in the proportion of corporate income tax revenue allocated, with the tax authority centralized to higher-level governments. Figure 2 shows the calculated percentage of the corporate income tax in the fiscal revenues of the central and local governments in 1998–2007 based on the "Fiscal Year Book of China."[4] We can see that before the income tax sharing reform, the share of the corporate income tax in the local government's fiscal revenue increased year by year, rising from 10.6% in 1998 to 21.6% in 2001. In contrast, the share of the corporate income tax in the central government's fiscal revenue was smaller than that of the local government, and it increased very slowly, reaching only 11.01% in 2001. The income tax sharing reform has reversed this situation, lifting the share of the corporate income tax in the central fiscal revenue to as much as 18.12% in

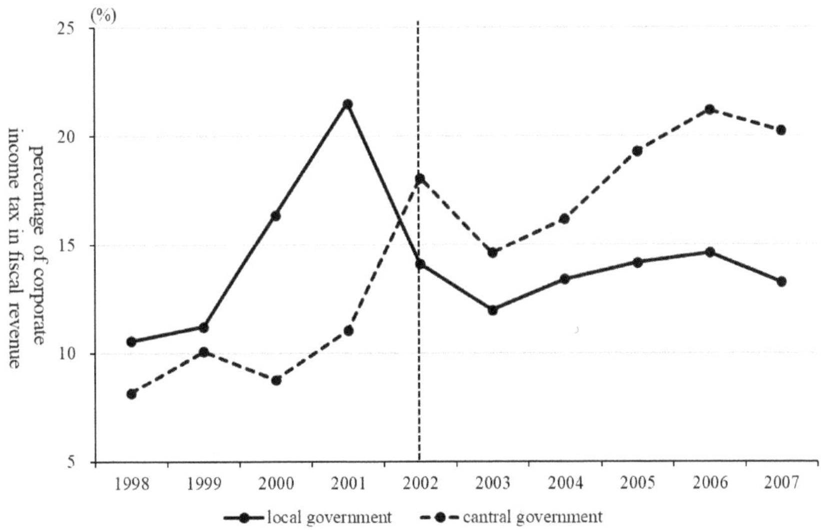

Figure 2. Percentage of corporate income tax in fiscal revenue.

2002, plus a gradual increase after 2003. For the local government, the share dropped sharply to 14.1% in 2002, and further to 11.97% in 2003, followed by a widening gap with the share for the central government in the subsequent years. Figure 2 shows a diversion of the corporate income tax revenue to the central government and a sharp drop in the local government's revenue from the corporate income tax after the reform. The big shock from the reform to the local fiscal has significantly weakened the direct link between the local government's fiscal revenue and the local enterprises' profits and marginally encouraged the local government to ease the fight for the productive tax base because it does not benefit as much from the growth of local enterprises. It can be expected, therefore, that the income tax sharing reform has weakened the local government's fiscal incentive to protect local enterprises' growth, reducing the obstacles to cross-regional allocation of capital factor and promoting the integration of the capital factor market.

Theoretical analysis

Most research on the causes of China's market segmentation focuses on institutional ones, such as regional development strategy (Lu *et al.*, 2004), promotion incentive (Zhou, 2004), institutional distance (Song and Huang, 2014), share of SOEs (Liu, 2012), and judicial independence (Chen and Li, 2013). Behind these factors, local governments' market segmentation is driven by a common goal: protecting their own economic interests (Yin and Cai, 2001). Shen and Dai (1990) argue that the tilt of the identity of local governments toward economic interests is a deeper cause of the formation of "prince economics." The strengthening of interest group ideology encourages local governments to interfere with market actors' decisions for the purpose of increasing fiscal revenue. In order to increase the tax base, local governments restrict local businesses from investing in other regions, which distorts the process of market-based allocation of production factors and creates a segmentation of the capital factor market.

The rules governing the tax revenue distribution between the central and local governments are important factors affecting the domestic market segmentation.The higher the proportion of local fiscal revenue retained, the higher the degree of market segmentation between regions (Lv and He, 2019). At this point, the central government can adjust the distribution of interests among local governments while ensuring the local governments' economic development and reducing the incentive for fiscal and tax competition. For example, according to Fanand Zhang (2010), transfer payments can reduce regional market segmentation as they weaken the connection between the local fiscal revenue and the local economic resources, making it more beneficial for the region to participate in the market division of labor than to seal off the local market. In addition to direct revenue transfers, the central government can affect the tax competition among the regions by adjusting the extent of administrative decentralization. Xie and Fan (2015) find through theoretical models and empirical analysis that centralized tax collection and management can reduce the horizontal tax revenue competition among the local governments. It follows that regional market segmentation is negatively correlated with the degree of fiscal decentralization. This is further proven by the empirical study of He and Lv (2019), who, based on the shock of the policies to transform counties into districts or to put counties into the direct charge of the provincial government, focus on the connection between vertical administrative decentralization and the integration of regional markets. They have the following finding: Transforming counties into districts worsens market segmentation among the cities, while putting cities under the direct charge of the provincial government reduces such segmentation, showing that market segmentation becomes worse, as the local government has more administrative power. With the above reasoning, we can find that the income tax reform reduces the local government's direct gains from the local capital factor and reduces the local government's fiscal power. The expectation is that the local government will have less incentive to impede the outflow of capital factor for the purpose of increasing fiscal revenue, which promotes capital market integration.

Enterprises' investment in other places, a process of capital allocation across regions and part of market integration, is also held back by administrative barriers and market segmentation (Wang and Dong, 2013). Against the background of decentralization, the local government intervenes in cross-regional capital flows and tends to concentrate quality resources in local enterprises to increase their scale. The local government spares no effort to obstruct the free mobility of resources, and the capital factor market segmentation has significantly inhibited Chinese enterprises' cross-regional operations (Song and Huang, 2014). The empirical work of Cao *et al.* (2015) looks at the relationship between market segmentation, the nature of ownership, and the distribution of other-place subsidiaries. The finding is that market segmentation has dramatically reduced the percentage of local SOEs' other-place subsidiaries compared with private enterprises. Therefore, based on the above analysis, if the income tax sharing reform reduces the government's control over the cross-regional flows of capital and strengthens the integration of the capital factor market, then after the reform, enterprises would be more enthusiastic about investing in other places, thereby increasing the other-place subsidiaries.

Local enterprises face more restrictions from the local government on cross-regional investment. On the one hand, due to "a helping hand" and "patriarchal love" (Kornai *et al.*, 2003; Lin and Li, 2004), the local government gives priority to SOEs when it comes to the allocation of scarce resources (Garnaut *et al.*, 2001). Liu (2012) finds that the higher the share of the state-owned economy in a region, the more segmented its markets. Market segmentation has become the "implicit subsidy" the local government gives to SOEs, which means that local SOEs have access to more resources in a sealed-off market. But this, in turn, reduces their incentive to invest in other places. On the other hand, the theory of "a predatory hand" suggests that the local SOEs, which assume the function of promoting regional investment, employment, and social welfare (Lin and Li, 2004; Zeng and Chen, 2006), are given plenty of policy burden. Therefore, in order to protect local economic interests, the local government will prevent outflows of local state capital via market segmentation. Whichever factor takes the lead, for local SOEs, their investment in other places is more sensitive to the degree of market segmentation compared with enterprises of other ownership structures. Fang (2008) finds that local SOEs prefer local acquisitions and inefficient multiple acquisitions, while central enterprises conduct acquisitions in different places as they can easily break the administrative barriers across the regions. As a result, if the income tax sharing reform promotes the integration of the capital factor market, it would have a more significant effect on local SOEs' behavior. Here is our hypothesis H1 that needs testing:

H1: After the income tax sharing reform, local SOEs have had significantly more other-place subsidiaries compared with enterprises of different ownership structures.

The local government plays dual roles for local SOEs. As a tax collector, the local government aims to collect as much tax from local SOEs as possible to increase fiscal revenue. As a shareholder, the local government has the right to a claim on local SOEs' profits. The local government's gains from local SOEs are made up of tax revenue and profit distribution. After the income tax sharing reform, the local government receives 40% of the corporate income tax, down from 100%, whereas its shareholding in local SOEs does not change much. The result is a principal–agent relationship between the central and local governments regarding the collection and management of local SOEs' tax revenue. Such a conflict in interest makes the local government weigh its gains from different ways of distribution. Before the reform, as long as the local government's shareholding was below 100%, it received more fiscal revenue from tax than from profits; after the reform, if the local government's shareholding in the enterprises is bigger than 40%, then its share of the dividends is bigger than the share of the tax revenue retained, which means the local government finds it more advantageous to gain from profit distribution and thus has the incentive to increase the enterprises' net profits. Conversely, for enterprises in which the local government owns less than 40% of shares, it has preferred the tax revenue for gains, prior to or following the reform. In other words, tax revenue is the best strategy with or without the reform. In fact, Tang *et al.* (2017) study the effect of the local government's changing share of profits on the magnitude of its effort to collect and manage tax from local SOEs in which it holds different percentages of shares. The finding is that, after the income tax sharing reform, for enterprises in which it owns more than 40% of shares, the local government has obviously reduced the effort to collect and manage their tax, which is reflected in these enterprises' lowered real corporate tax rate, increased net profit, and more distributed cash dividends. It shows that the local government maximizes its interest after rationally weighing the gains brought about by different economic policies.

On the other hand, although local SOEs' investment in other places is not beneficial to local tax revenue, the local government, as the major shareholder of the enterprise group, has the final right to claim the net profits of the various subsidiaries within the group. Therefore, after the income tax sharing reform, for enterprises in which it holds a higher ratio of shares, the local government can still gain a bigger share of the net profit from the other-place subsidiaries, which may even exceed the amount it receives from the tax revenue. However, if its shareholding ratio is low, then it would lose its claim on the enterprises' tax after they set up other-place subsidiaries. In general, the local government would prefer to relax the control over the cross-regional investment of enterprises in which it owns more than 40% of shares. Based on the above analysis, this study proposes the following hypothesis H2:

H2: The income tax sharing reform has a more promoting effect on local SOEs of which the local government owns more than 40% of shares when it comes to cross-regional investment.

Data and Regression Model

Data sources and processing

This study takes the listed A-share companies in 1999–2007 as the samples for primary analysis. For information on the listed companies' shareholding, the notes to "long-term equity investment" in the financial reports of the listed companies' parents during the sample period are collected, and the names of the companies of which these parent companies hold shares, their registration places, and their shareholding ratios are sorted out. If the registration places are not disclosed, the names or tools, such as "Tian Yan Cha" and "Baidu Map," are used to judge where they are registered. Finally, the records of control subsidiary companies that could not be determined were deleted. We organized a total of 109,176 records of control subsidiary companies and deleted 906 records, which accounted for 0.83% of the total, due to an inability to determine the registered place. This study defines a "subsidiary company" as a company with a direct holding ratio of more than 50% by the parent company, and a "remote subsidiary company" refers to those subsidiary companies not located in the same city as the parent company.

The variables other than the number of subsidiaries come from the CSMAR database. We use the corporate annual reports to complete some of the pre-2003 indicators that are missing in the database. The following are deleted from the samples in order to avoid interference from such changes to the empirical outcome: (1) companies that went public after 2002; (2) financial firms; (3) companies with incomplete disclosure of their controlling interests; (4) companies that were delisted during the sample period; (5) companies that went through major asset restructuring during the sample period; (6) companies that changed their ownership structure during the sample period.

Model setting

This study focuses on the policy impact of the 2002 income tax sharing reform, which changed the proportion of local government revenue from local enterprises' corporate income tax and thus affected the mobility of capital across regions. According to the analysis in the preceding text, after the income tax sharing reform, the local government's control over the mobility of local SOEs' capital was the strongest. Figure 3 shows the trends of changing

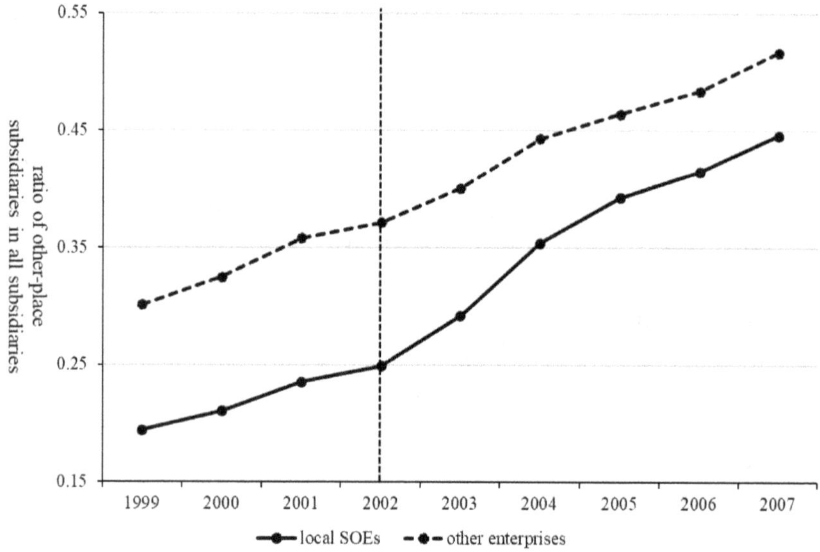

Figure 3. Nature of equity and percentage of other-place subsidiaries.

percentages of other-place subsidiaries set up by local SOEs and other enterprises, which proves the findings of our theoretical analysis. In Figure 3, the time trend tells us that all enterprises have increased investment in other places, which speaks volumes about the improved integration of China's capital factor market, and the fact that other enterprises have a higher percentage of other-place subsidiaries than local SOEs shows the former's flexibility. The two kinds of enterprises had similar trends before 2002, but after 2002, local SOEs have seen an apparent increase in the percentage of their other-place subsidiaries, while the other enterprises kept the previous trend, which means the reform has mainly affected local SOEs. This is direct empirical proof.

This study uses a double difference model to empirically test the effect of the income tax sharing reform on the cross-regional mobility of capital, with local SOEs as the processing group and enterprises of the other ownership structures as the control group. The regression model to be tested is

$$\text{diffsub}_{it} = \alpha + \beta_1 \text{treat}_i \times \text{post}_t + \boldsymbol{\beta_2 X'_{it}} + \gamma_i + \delta_t + \varepsilon_{it}$$

i and t represent company and year, respectively. Referring to the existing literature on the cross-regional mobility of capital (Giroud and Rauh, 2019; Ma *et al.*, 2020), we use the number of other-place subsidiaries of company i in year t as the explained variable. In the following robustness test, we replace the explained variable with whether there are other-place subsidiaries, and the number of new other-place subsidiaries. $treat_i$ is an indicator variable representing the nature of equity. If company i is a local SOE, then $treat_i$ is 1; otherwise, it is 0. To exclude the effect of SOE reforms, we set company i's nature of equity as the biggest shareholder's nature of equity in 2001; $post_t$ is an indicator variable representing time. If $t \geq 2002$, then it is 1; otherwise, it is 0; X_{it} is a control variable set including the logarithm of the number of subsidiaries, company size, asset–liability ratio, company age, profitability, the biggest shareholder's shareholding ratio, the percentage of independent directors, political connections, and the GDP per capita of the city the company is located in. The financial feature variable applies to the parent company; γ_i and δ_t represent year fixed effect and company fixed effect, respectively; ε_{it} represents a random perturbation term. OLS is used for the regression of the model, and the standard misclustering is at the company's level. This study winsorizes at the 1% and 99% tails of the financial feature variable to exclude the influence of extreme values. The explanation and descriptive statistics of the main variables are listed in Table 1.

Table 1. Explanation of key variables and descriptive statistics.

Variable	Explanation	Average value	Standard deviation	Minimum	Maximum
diffsub	No. of other-place subsidiaries	2.705	3.840	0	53
treat	1 for local SOEs, otherwise 0	0.600	0.489	0	1
post	1 for after 2002, otherwise 0	0.674	0.468	0	1
lnsub	ln(No. of subsidiaries +1)	1.638	0.856	0	4.094
size	Company size, take the logarithm of total assets (yuan)	20.952	1.005	12.314	27.117

(*Continued*)

Table 1. (*Continued*)

Variable	Explanation	Average value	Standard deviation	Minimum	Maximum
lev	Asset-liability ratio, total assets/total liabilities	0.449	0.318	0.027	2.538
age	Company's age, current year minus the founding year	8.808	4.178	0	27
roa	Return on assets, net profits/total assets	0.017	0.112	–0.700	0.209
first	Shareholding ratio of the biggest shareholder	0.423	0.174	0.010	0.992
outrat	No. of independent directors/No. of directors	0.227	0.157	0	0.727
pc	Political connections, 1 for any director, supervisor, executive acting as NPC member or CPPCC member, otherwise 0	0.390	0.487	0	1
lnagdp	Logarithm of the city's GDP per capital (10,000 yuan)	10.058	0.948	7.674	12.676

Basic Outcome and Robustness Test

Impact of the income tax sharing reform on cross-regional investment

The changing ratios of tax revenue between the central and local governments affect the local government's gains from the local productive tax base, reducing its incentive to control the cross-regional mobility of the capital factor. Table 2 shows the effect of the income tax sharing reform on enterprises' investment in other places. Column (1) indicates that without controlling variables, the number of cross-regional subsidiaries of local SOEs significantly increased by 0.506 compared to other enterprises after the reform. Columns (2) and (3) introduce controlling variables at the company level and regional level, respectively. Column (3) shows that after the income tax sharing reform, the increase in the number of local SOEs'

Table 2. Effect of the income tax sharing reform on investment in other places.

	(1)	(2)	(3)
treat × *post*	0.506**	0.485***	0.504***
	(0.213)	(0.187)	(0.192)
lnsub		2.502***	2.522***
		(0.164)	(0.169)
size		0.398***	0.405***
		(0.109)	(0.110)
lev		0.433***	0.422**
		(0.163)	(0.166)
age		0.181	0.215
		(0.751)	(0.751)
roa		−0.161	−0.191
		(0.210)	(0.217)
first		−0.285	−0.265
		(0.608)	(0.623)
outrat		−0.065	−0.012
		(0.331)	(0.338)
pc		0.056	0.067
		(0.095)	(0.097)
langdp			−0.191
			(0.346)
Firm fixed effect	Y	Y	Y
Year fixed effect	Y	Y	Y
Observed value	8,758	8,757	8,560
Adj-R^2	0.199	0.398	0.395

Notes: ***, **, * represent significance at the 1%, 5% and 10% levels, respectively and the numbers in parentheses are robust standard errors after clustering adjustment at the company level.

cross-regional subsidiaries is 0.504 more than that of other enterprises, accounting for 18.63% of the average number of other-place subsidiaries. The effect is significant at the 1% level, confirming hypothesis H1. The result of the control variables shows that for a company, the more subsidiaries, the bigger the total assets, and the higher the debt ratio, the more other-place subsidiaries it has. Table 2 shows that the income tax sharing reform has promoted cross-regional capital mobility. The local government would relax its control over capital mobility when its share of the corporate income tax lowers. Therefore, SOEs directly under the control of the local government are encouraged to expand their operations, as they are more affected by the reduced restrictions on cross-regional investment. The tax sharing reform helps to break the market lockout of capital factors, promotes the rational flow of funds, and helps to optimize the efficiency of resource allocation, effectively promoting the construction of a unified market for capital factors.

Local government ownership ratio and cross-regional investment

If the local government applies market segmentation with the intention of gaining from the local economic resources, then it would strategically adjust the controls over resource mobility depending on a comparison of gains obtained through different ways. As far as local SOEs are concerned, the local government can gain from both corporate income tax and direct profit distribution. According to the theoretical analysis in the preceding paragraphs, after the tax sharing reform, enterprises with a local government ownership ratio greater than 40% can obtain more profits through profit distribution. So, will the local government's restriction on cross-regional investment of local SOEs be affected by the government's ownership ratio? To answer the question, this study divides the local listed SOEs in the samples into two groups according to whether the government's shareholding ratio was above 40% in 2001. Regression is done with each group as the experimental group and enterprises of other ownership structures as the control group. The outcomes are listed in Table 3. Columns (1) and (2) show the regression outcomes for the experimental group of enterprises in which the government holds more than 40% of shares. Column (2) shows that after control variables are added, these local listed SOEs show a large increase of 0.644 in the number of other-place subsidiaries after the income tax sharing reform. The increase is significant at the 1% level, and the coefficient is apparently bigger than the benchmark regression result. In comparison, Columns (3) and (4) illustrate that for local

Table 3. Local government's shareholding ratio and investment in other places (1).

	Local government's shareholding ratio > 40%		Local government's shareholding ratio < 40%	
	(1)	(2)	(3)	(4)
treat × *post*	0.821***	0.644***	−0.026	0.289
	(0.219)	(0.199)	(0.262)	(0.238)
lnsub		2.673***		2.737***
		(0.200)		(0.263)
size		0.293***		0.456***
		(0.111)		(0.160)
lev		0.310*		0.408*
		(0.187)		(0.216)
age		0.268		−0.508
		(0.746)		(0.380)
roa		−0.285		−0.182
		(0.248)		(0.255)
outrat		0.109		0.008
		(0.353)		(0.425)
pc		0.074		0.084
		(0.105)		(0.129)
lnagdp		−0.336		−0.259
		(0.376)		(0.449)
Firm fixed effect	Y	Y	Y	Y
Year fixed effect	Y	Y	Y	Y
Observed value	6,810	6,658	5,447	5,340
Adj-R^2	0.207	0.416	0.138	0.364

Notes: ***, **, * represent significance at the 1%, 5%, and 10% levels, respectively, and the numbers in parentheses are robust standard errors after clustering adjustment at the company level.

listed SOEs in which the government holds less than 40% stake, there is not much change in their cross-regional investment after the reform, showing that the reform has not affected such local SOEs. From this, we see that the income tax sharing reform has only significantly promoted the cross-regional investment of those local SOEs in which the local government holds more than 40% stake, confirming hypothesis H1.

Furthermore, in order to study in more detail the effect of the reform on enterprises with different government shareholding ratios, this study divides the local SOEs into eight groups based on the government's shareholding ratios in 2001 (10%, 20%]...(80%, 90%], represented by *treat*2...*treat*9.) Regression is done for every group as the experimental group and other enterprises with different ownership structures as the control group. The outcomes are listed in Table 4. There are no groups with a government

Table 4. Local government's shareholding ratio and cross-regional capital mobility(2).

	(10%, 20%]	(20%, 30%]	(30%, 40%]	(40%, 50%]	(50%, 60%]	(60%, 70%]	(70%, 80%]	(80%, 90%]	Full sample
	(1)	(2)	(3)	(4)	(5)	(6)	(7)	(8)	(9)
treat2 × *post*	0.221								0.219
	(0.447)								(0.432)
treat3 × *post*		0.322							0.274
		(0.340)							(0.333)
treat4 × *post*			0.291						0.274
			(0.279)						(0.275)
treat5 × *post*				0.573**					0.597**
				(0.270)					(0.263)
treat6 × *post*					0.692***				0.702***
					(0.236)				(0.230)
treat7 × *post*						0.640**			0.684**
						(0.275)			(0.269)
treat8 × *post*							0.534		0.620*
							(0.362)		(0.355)
treat9 × *post*								0.145	0.176
								(0.726)	(0.651)
Control variables	Y	Y	Y	Y	Y	Y	Y	Y	Y
Firm fixed effect	Y	Y	Y	Y	Y	Y	Y	Y	Y
Year fixed effect	Y	Y	Y	Y	Y	Y	Y	Y	Y
Observed value	3,691	4,245	4,280	4,203	4,475	4,426	3,823	3,483	8,560
Adj-R^2	0.386	0.374	0.377	0.394	0.404	0.395	0.404	0.391	0.396

Notes: ***, **, * represent significance at the 1%, 5% and 10% levels, respectively, and the numbers in parentheses are robust standard errors after clustering adjustment at the company level.

shareholding ratio below 10% or bigger than 90% because the experimental group has no such samples. We can see that when the government's shareholding ratio is below 50%, the interaction coefficient is not significant, meaning the policy does not have a remarkable effect on such local SOEs' cross-regional investment. On the other hand, when the government's shareholding ratio is above 50%, the interaction coefficient becomes significant, indicating more cross-regional investment. The insignificant interaction coefficient of Group 9 may be attributed to the fact that the sample size is small for this group.

The outcomes of Tables 3 and 4 suggest that the local government weighs its gains from local SOEs via different methods of distribution when local governments relax the restrictions on cross-regional investment of local SOEs, they will weigh the size of the benefits they can obtain through different distribution methods within the local SOEs. Conversely, it gains more from the tax revenue distribution. Therefore, if the local government's shareholding ratio is bigger than its share of an enterprise's corporate income tax, the promotion effect of the income tax sharing reform on the enterprise's capital mobility is bigger.

Robustness test

Parallel trend test

A basic premise for causal inference using a difference-in-differences model is that there is no difference in the trend between the treatment and control groups, meaning that the two groups should have had parallel trends prior to the implementation of the policy. In other words, before the policy was implemented, the two groups should have parallel trends. Therefore, this study uses the event research method to test the hypothesis of parallel trends between the experimental and control groups, in order to prove this study's benchmark regression results are caused by differences in enterprise ownership structures rather than a pure time effect. To be specific, the independent variable, which is the interaction term of $treat_i$ and each independent year during the sample period excluding the year before the policy, replaces the interaction term in the benchmark regression model for regression, and we compare the effect in each year before and after the policy, with the year before the policy as the benchmark. The regression model is as follows:

$$\text{diffsub}_{it} = \alpha + \sum_{k=1999,\, k\neq 2001}^{2007} \beta_k D_k \text{treat}_i + \beta_2 X'_{it} + \gamma_i + \delta_t + \varepsilon_{it}$$

D_k represents the dummy variable in year k after the income tax sharing reform. The base period of the model is 2001. The value of coefficient β_k on each year's interaction term and its 90% confidence interval boundaries can be seen in Figure 4.

As shown in Figure 4, before the implementation of the policy, there was no significant difference in the number of out-of-province subsidiaries between the experimental group and the control group. However, starting from the first year after the reform, the number of out-of-province subsidiaries in the experimental group significantly exceeded that of the control group, indicating that the difference in ownership caused the changes between the two groups after the

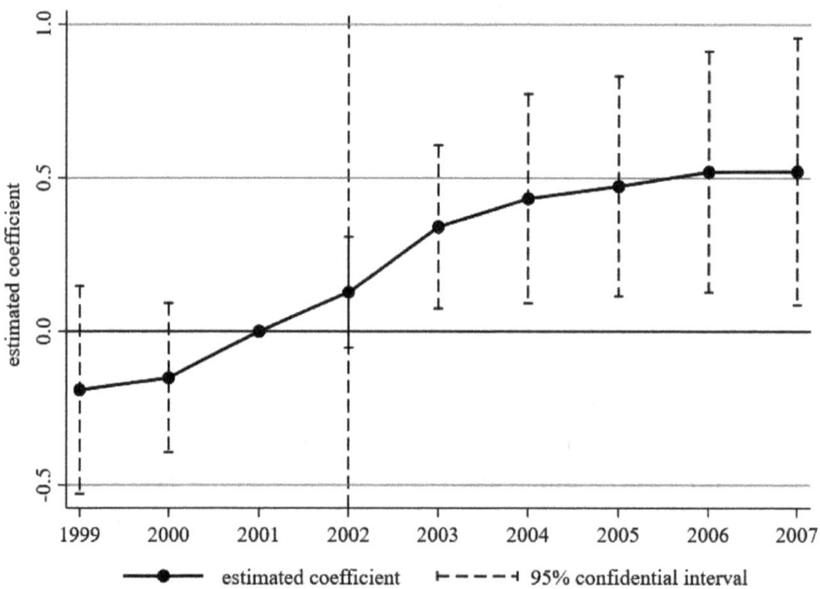

Figure 4. Test of parallel trends.

implementation of the policy, thus verifying the parallel trend assumption.

Virtual processing effect

The income tax sharing reform took place in 2002, and shocks from other policies of that year may also affect the cross-regional mobility of capital, such as joining the WTO. In order to further test whether the benchmark regression outcome of this study is caused by differences in enterprise ownership structures rather than other policy factors or noise effects of 2002, we randomly allocate $treat_i$ among the enterprises, and use the benchmark model for regression. The frequency distribution of the interaction term's *t*-value from repeated regressions is shown in Table 5 and Figure 5, where the coefficients of the interaction term mostly distribute around 0, with a small proportion of coefficients being significantly positive or negative, indicating that the virtual treatment effect constructed in this study does not exist and further eliminating the impact of noise on the empirical results.

Excluding samples from Beijing, Shanghai, and Guangdong

As a high share of Chinese listed companies have registered in Beijing, Shanghai, and Guangdong, where the capital factor market may be much more open, 29.94% of the observed values in our samples coming from these three areas suggest the possibility of a big effect on the benchmark regression results and therefore spurious regression. To eliminate this interfering factor, this study excludes

Table 5. Statistical distribution of the results from regression for virtual processing effect.

Sample size	Variable	Average value	Standard deviation	5% quantile	25% quantile	Median	75% quantile	95% quantile
500	coefficient	−0.0008	0.0333	−0.0582	−0.0242	0.0002	0.0226	0.0518
500	*t*-value	−0.0192	0.9695	−1.6681	−0.7151	0.0081	0.6455	1.5558

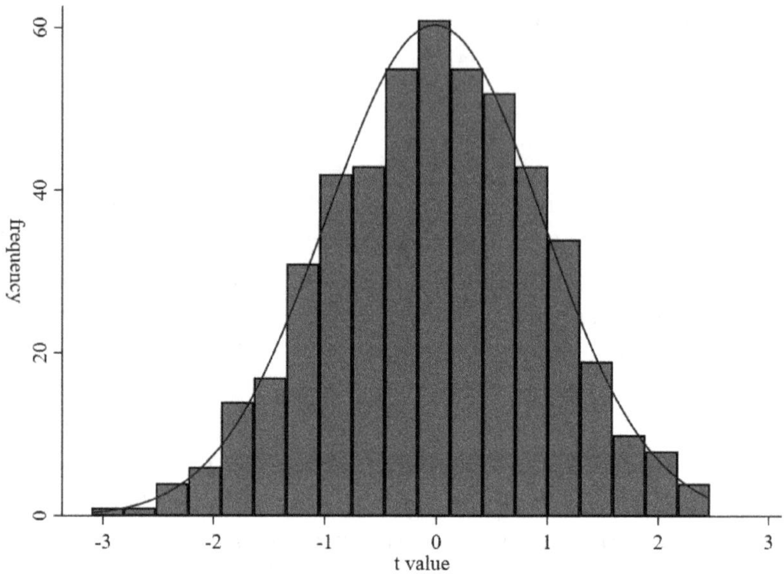

Figure 5. Distribution of the *t*-value from the 500 placebo tests.

the observed values from Beijing, Shanghai, and Guangdong and examines the policy effects in the remaining areas only. The regression results are shown in Column (1) of Table 6. A coefficient on the core explanatory variable of 0.441, which still has a 5% level significance, shows that this study's regression results are not caused by a biased error in sample selection.

Placebo test of central enterprises

The previously mentioned increase in cross-regional investment made by local SOEs may be caused by a relaxation of local capital controls, as this study suggests, or may be caused by the features of state-owned capital itself. Next, we exclude this cause by comparing central enterprises with local SOEs. For central enterprises in which the central government holds shares and controls the investment decisions, their operational outcomes have nothing to do with the local government other than some distribution of the corporate income tax. Therefore, the local government has neither the ability

Table 6. Robustness test (1).

	Excluding samples from Beijing, Shanghai and Guangdong	Placebo test of central enterprises	Extensive margin effect	Replacing the explained variable	Clustering at the city level
	(1)	(2)	(3)	(4)	(5)
treat × *post*	0.441**	0.365	0.743***	0.297***	0.504**
	(0.191)	(0.308)	(0.202)	(0.102)	(0.201)
Control variables	Y	Y	Y	Y	Y
Firm fixed effect	Y	Y	N	Y	Y
Year fixed effect	Y	Y	Y	Y	Y
Observed value	5,997	3,435	8,560	8,551	8,554
adj. R^2/ pseudo R^2	0.431	0.807	0.017	0.041	0.780

Notes: ***, **, * represent significance at the 1%, 5% and 10% levels , respectively. OLS regression model is used for all columns except Column (3). Columns (1), (2) and (4) cluster standard errors at the corporate level; Column (5) at the city level; Column (3) uses Logit regression.

nor the incentive to affect the central enterprises' investment in other places, but the common state ownership of central and local SOEs means they both are affected by policies concerning the state-owned capital. Regression is carried out on samples of non-local SOEs, with the central enterprises as the experimental group and the non-SOEs as the control group. The regression results can be found in Column (2) of Table 6. The number of cross-regional subsidiaries of SOEs did not change significantly before and after 2002, which indicates that the impact of the tax sharing reform on the off-site investment behavior of local SOEs is due to changes in the fiscal incentives of local governments, not the characteristics of SOEs themselves.

Extensive margin effect

The benchmark regression results in this study reflect the increase in the number of locally listed state-owned company's subsidiaries in different locations, which is due to the sharing reform of income tax and is known as the intensive margin effect. The study further validates the extensive margin effect generated by the policy and examines the policy's effect of promoting enterprises to "go global." To be specific, the explained variable of the benchmark regression model is replaced by the virtual variable 0–1: if the number of other-place subsidiaries is bigger than 0 for company i in year t, then we have 1 and otherwise 0. The model uses logit regression. The regression results are listed in Column (3) of Table 6. The coefficient on the interaction term is significantly positive at the 1% level, suggesting the policy's extensive margin effect because local listed SOEs are significantly more likely to expand into other places after the reform.

Replacement of the explained variable

Considering the difference between stocks and flows, this study, referring to the method used by Cao and Jia (2020), uses the number of new other-place subsidiaries for company i in year t to replace the explained variable in Column (4) of Table 6. The regression results show that after the income tax sharing reform, local listed SOEs' new other-place subsidiaries have a significant increase of 0.297, and the effect is significant under the 1% level, further verifying this study's benchmark regression results.

Clustering at the city level

In the previous regression, to eliminate the autocorrelation problem caused by random disturbance items at the company level in different periods, the standard error was aggregated to the company level. In addition, considering that companies located in the same city may also have autocorrelation due to geographical or policy factors, the standard error is further aggregated to the city level and re-estimated. The regression results are listed in Column (5) of Table 6. The regression coefficients are consistent with the results from clustering standard errors at the corporate level done previously.

Excluding the effect of SOEs' restructuring

With the progress of marketization reform, SOEs began to see large-scale losses and operational difficulties after the mid-1990s. To make SOEs more competitive and adjust their ownership structure, the government started the administration-led adjustment of the layout of the state economy. To be more specific, on the one hand, small- and medium-sized SOEs that were in the general competitive industries but did not have a competitive advantage had to go through bankruptcy and mergers; on the other hand, large-scale restructuring was conducted for medium- and big-sized SOEs in the industries that the state economy needed to enter. After the Fourth Plenary Session of the 15th CPC Central Committee, the industrial adjustment of the state-owned economy intensified, with the restructuring focused on monopoly industries and those with low efficiency, such as the coal, non-ferrous, and textile industries (Shao, 2014). The structural reform of the state-owned economy, which might affect the distribution of SOEs' subsidiaries across the regions, happened at about the same time as the income tax sharing reform and therefore may interfere with this study's basic conclusion. In order to exclude the effect of SOEs' restructuring, we first add the industry-year fixed effect to the benchmark regression model to control the shocks at the industry level. The regression results are listed in Column (1) of Table 7. The coefficient on the core explanatory variable remains significant at the 5% level. We further exclude from the samples industries that went through intense restructuring (coal selection, textiles, black metal smelting and pressure rolling processing, black metal mining and dressing, clothing and other fiber products manufacturing, non-ferrous metal mining and dressing, non-ferrous metal smelting, and pressure rolling processing). As shown in Column (2) of Table 7, the basic conclusion remains the same.

Table 7. Robustness test (1).

	Excluding the effect of SOEs' restructuring		Excluding the effect of WTO accession	
	Industry-time fixed effect	Excluding industries that went through restructuring	Province-time fixed effect	Controlling export proceeds
	(1)	(2)	(3)	(4)
treat × *post*	0.513**	0.480**	0.587***	0.464***
	(0.201)	(0.204)	(0.194)	(0.170)
Average export proceeds × *post*				0.020***
				(0.007)
Control variables	Y	Y	Y	Y
Firm fixed effect	Y	Y	Y	Y
Year fixed effect	N	Y	N	Y
Industry-year fixed effect	Y	N	N	N
Province-year fixed effect	N	N	Y	N
Observed value	8,361	7,737	8,757	7,728
adj. R^2	0.785	0.807	0.782	0.817

Notes: ***, **, * represent significance at the 1%, 5% and 10% levels, respectively, and the numbers in parentheses are robust standard errors after clustering adjustment at the company level.

Removing the effect of China's WTO accession

China's entry into the WTO provided new opportunities to Chinese enterprises by improving export circumstances and helping Chinese products enter the international market. Enterprises with closer international ties benefit the most from open international trade, which might go on to seek expansion in the domestic market after strengthening their international competitiveness. As a result, although the benchmark results of this study pass the placebo test of the virtual processing effect, they do not account for the heterogeneity in enterprises' international trade, which may pose a threat to the basic conclusion. To exclude the effect of China's accession to the WTO, the first consideration is that enterprises in different regions suffered different levels of shock from the accession, with those in the coastal provinces affected more strongly by the opening up compared with the inland provinces, due to the former's higher dependence on international trade. Therefore, we add the province-year fixed effect in Column (2) of Table 7 to control the shock at the regional level. It is easy to see that the basic conclusion remains the same. This study further examines the effect of opening up from the perspective of enterprise exports. The bigger an enterprise's export proceeds, the bigger the shock it receives from the WTO accession. However, it is hard to get from the disclosed information data about the listed companies' domestic and international revenue distribution before 2003. We use the customs enterprise database for 2000–2001, match them according to the names of the subsidiaries and the year, and calculate the average export proceeds of listed companies in the two years preceding China's WTO accession. Taking the logarithm of the average export proceeds multiplied by the virtual variable after 2002, we measure the shocks from the WTO accession for enterprises with different levels of dependence on international trade. The regression results are listed in Column (4) of Table 7. We can see that the bigger its export proceeds before the WTO accession, the more an enterprise has expanded in the domestic market after 2002. But the coefficient on the core explanatory variable is still significant at the 1% level, suggesting that the basic conclusion is not affected by China's accession to the WTO.

Further Discussion

Heterogeneity analysis

Industrial heterogeneity

The heterogeneity of enterprises' industries leads to the fact that they mainly pay different taxes, and there are significant differences in the proportion of local revenues from different taxes, which affects the local government's motivation to maintain different tax bases. If the goal of local governments restricting the flow of capital across regions is to maintain local fiscal and tax revenue, then during the market integration process, local governments not only need to consider the loss of corporate income tax due to the outflow of capital but also need to consider the changes in other tax revenue. The income tax sharing reform does not change the proportions the local government has from VAT, sales tax, and other kinds of tax. Before the "business tax to value-added tax" pilot reform in 2012, VAT was shared between the central and local governments: VAT from the import segment collected by the customs belonged to the central government, while the local government only had 25% of the VAT revenue. The sales tax, which however has always been a local tax, is the biggest source of local fiscal, accounting for one-third of the local government's entire tax revenue. Therefore, because enterprises paying VAT cause smaller losses to the local government's tax revenue when their capital flows out compared with enterprises paying sales tax, the local government tends to relax the control over the cross-regional investment of the former. The dual tax system of circulation tax in place before 2012 differentiated VAT and sales tax based on the industries: manufacturers mainly paid VAT, while non-manufacturers mainly paid sales tax. We divide the samples of the experimental group into manufacturing and non-manufacturing groups according to industries. Regression is done, respectively, with the control group. The results are listed in Columns (1) and (2) in Table 8. Column (1) shows that after the income tax sharing reform, for the local SOEs in the manufacturing industry, the number of their other-place subsidiaries has increased by 0.600, and this effect is significant at the 1% level. Column (2) suggests no obvious change in the number of other-place subsidiaries for local SOEs in the non-manufacturing industry before and after the reform. We can see that the local government considers gains and losses from other kinds of tax as well when relaxing market segmentation, which shows that the income tax sharing reform has significantly promoted local listed state-owned manufacturers' investment in other places.

Regional heterogeneity

Tax is the main source of local fiscal revenue, and local SOEs are the key contributors to the local tax revenue. According to the measure

Table 8. Heterogeneity analysis.

	Industrial heterogeneity		Dependence on local SOEs		Destinations of investment	
	Manufacturing	Non-manufacturing	High dependence	Low dependence	Investment in other provinces	Investment in other cities of the same province
	(1)	(2)	(3)	(4)	(5)	(6)
treat × *post*	0.600***	0.200	0.540**	0.039	0.351***	0.153
	(0.207)	(0.202)	(0.223)	(0.209)	(0.133)	(0.095)
lnsub	2.645***	2.706***	2.653***	2.826***	1.676***	1.030***
	(0.195)	(0.261)	(0.231)	(0.244)	(0.117)	(0.079)
size	0.332***	0.393***	0.316**	0.374***	0.268***	0.160***
	(0.122)	(0.139)	(0.125)	(0.141)	(0.075)	(0.054)
lev	0.290	0.356*	0.204	0.468**	0.214*	0.210**
	(0.186)	(0.213)	(0.219)	(0.199)	(0.110)	(0.087)
age	0.301	–0.621*	0.105	–0.504	–0.627	0.470***
	(0.748)	(0.369)	(0.613)	(0.356)	(1.115)	(0.065)
roa	–0.384*	–0.117	–0.472*	–0.074	–0.176	0.008
	(0.224)	(0.287)	(0.251)	(0.259)	(0.151)	(0.114)
first	0.307	0.424	1.089	0.256	–0.060	–0.053
	(0.673)	(0.964)	(0.775)	(0.861)	(0.411)	(0.304)
outrat	0.020	0.057	0.028	0.125	0.112	–0.000
	(0.361)	(0.393)	(0.371)	(0.416)	(0.239)	(0.177)
pc	0.061	0.053	0.046	0.126	0.063	0.002
	(0.103)	(0.115)	(0.117)	(0.128)	(0.072)	(0.049)
lnagdp	–0.274	–0.296	–0.344	–0.488	0.121	–0.063
	(0.404)	(0.415)	(0.384)	(0.468)	(0.220)	(0.168)
Firm fixed effect	Y	Y	Y	Y	Y	Y
Year fixed effect	Y	Y	Y	Y	Y	Y
Observed value	6,909	5,089	5,388	5,553	8,560	6,650
Adj-R^2	0.403	0.374	0.397	0.395	0.357	0.356

Notes: ***, **, * represent significance at the 1%, 5% and 10% levels, respectively, and the numbers in parentheses are robust standard errors after clustering adjustment at the company level.

and calculation of the "Chinese Database for Industrial Enterprises," on average, the tax paid by local SOEs accounted for 65.4% of all corporate tax in prefecture-level cities in 2001. At the same time, every local government's dependence on local SOEs for fiscal revenue varies greatly, and local SOEs' growth has different levels of effect on the local fiscal, thereby affecting the local government's incentive to restrict local SOEs' investment in other places. Before the income tax sharing reform, those areas which depended less on local SOEs for fiscal revenue had less incentive to restrict local SOEs' investment in other places, and their fiscal revenue received a smaller shock from the income tax sharing reform. As a result, it can be expected that in these areas, the reform has brought about no obvious change to the restrictions on local SOEs' investment in other places. Conversely, in areas which depended heavily on local SOEs for fiscal revenue, restrictions were more severe before the reform on the mobility of state-owned capital, meaning the income tax sharing reform has brought them bigger shocks and significantly reduced their fiscal incentive for controlling capital outflows. To examine the regional heterogeneity of the income tax sharing reform, we use the share of corporate tax revenue that came from local SOEs in the prefecture-level cities in 2001 ("Chinese Database for Industrial Enterprises") to measure the dependence of each city's tax revenue on local SOEs. In our calculation, we also include the local government's 25% share of VAT, as follows:

$$\text{ratio}_i = \frac{\text{local SOEs' tax contribution in city}_i + \text{corporate income tax} + \text{VAT} \times 0.25}{\text{the entire corporate tax in city}_i + \text{corporate income tax} + \text{VAT} \times 0.25}$$

Then, the samples in the experimental group are divided into two groups along the median of $ratio_i$. Regression is done, respectively, with the samples of the control group. The regression results are listed in Columns (3) and (4) of Table 8. For regions where the local fiscal depended heavily on local SOEs, the number of local SOEs' other-place subsidiaries on average has increased by 0.540

after the reform and the effect is significant at the 5% level. Conversely, in regions where there was low dependence on local SOEs, the number of local SOEs' other-place subsidiaries has not changed much after the reform. We can see that the income tax sharing reform has played a bigger role in promoting the integration of the capital factor market in regions where there was a heavy dependence on SOEs.

Direction of investment

Local SOEs' cross-regional investment benefits local fiscal revenue, but the local government's consideration of the accompanying potential cost will directly affect where local SOEs invest. From the previous analysis, we know that the capital integration effect of the income tax sharing reform is achieved mainly through local SOEs' investment in other places. The reason for the local government's practice to segment markets, be it the fiscal incentive or the promotion incentive, is after all within the framework of government competition. The local government, which depends on investment for economic growth, resorts to "beggar-thy-neighbor" policies in order to prevent products and factors from flowing into rival regions. For two prefecture-level cities within one province with about the same level of development, the competition for factors is even fiercer because, although investment in another city of the same province brings certain gains to the city where capital flows out, it will also result in an extra cost by changing the rankings of the two cities in the province. Pi (2008) finds that the level of market integration is limited when the return from it is low. In comparison, when factors flow to another province, the source city's competitive ranking in the province will not be changed, thereby reducing the local government's control over such outflows. This study divides the explained variable "number of other-place subsidiaries" into "number of subsidiaries in different provinces" and "number of subsidiaries in other cities of the same province." Regression is done, with the explained variable "number of subsidiaries in other cities of the same province" excluding the samples whose parent companies are located in the municipalities directly under the central government. We can see from Columns (5) and (6) of Table 8 that after the income tax sharing reform, local listed SOEs' subsidiaries in other provinces have increased significantly by 0.351, and the effect is significant at the 1% level, while the number of subsidiaries in different cities of the same province has not increased significantly. The results suggest that the extent of market segmentation is worse among the cities of the same province than among cities of different provinces. Regional competition has inhibited capital mobility within a province and weakened the promoting effect of the income tax sharing reform on market integration.

The effect of cross-regional investment on return on capital and cash dividends

The results of the regression in the previous section have led to the main conclusion of this study that the reform of the sharing of the income tax has reduced the proportion of the enterprise income tax shared by local governments, thus weakening the motivation of local governments to restrict the flow of state-owned capital across regions. As a result, the number of off-site subsidiaries of local SOEs has significantly increased after the reform, and this effect is more pronounced in companies with government stakes of more than 40%. One question that arises from this is whether the expansion of local SOEs in different locations is beneficial to improving their profitability. According to Cao *et al.* (2015), as the local government's "predatory" effect on local SOEs decreases with the increase in the share of other-place subsidiaries, local SOEs' expansion in other places can reduce overinvestment and raise their corporate value. Therefore, local SOEs' expansion in other places improves their return on capital better than enterprises of other ownership structures. This study uses the rate of return on common shareholder's equity (net profit/shareholder's equity) to represent enterprises' return on capital, the core explanatory variable being the interaction term between $treat_i$ and $diffsub_{it}$, and the control variables including the number of other-place subsidiaries, scale of enterprises, asset-liability ratio, outstanding funds of major shareholders, stake of the biggest shareholder, and percentage of independent directors. The regression results are listed in Columns (1) and (2) of Table 9. As Column (2) shows, an increase of one in the number of corss-regional subsidiary companies brings 0.005 local SOEs'profitability.

According to the logic of this study, the reason why local governments mainly relax restrictions on out-of-province investments by SOEs with a stake of more than 40% is because they can get more benefits through profit distribution. This study has proven that local SOEs' investment in other places raises the return on capital, but closed-loop logic requires an examination of whether enterprises' expansion in other places increases shareholders' dividends. We use the logarithm of the total cash dividends as the explained variable, the core explanatory variable remaining the interaction term between $treat_i$ and $diffsub_{it}$. The logarithm of the total share capital and the rate on assets are added to the control variables. We divide the samples into two groups based on whether the local government's shareholding ratio exceeds 40%. The regression results are

Table 9. The effect of investment in other places on the return on capital and cash dividends.

	Rate of return on common stockholders' equity		Logarithm of cash dividends			
			Local government's shareholding ratio >40%		Local government's shareholding ratio >40%	
	(1)	(2)	(3)	(4)	(5)	(6)
treat × *diffsub*	0.005*	0.005**	0.180**	0.139**	0.112	0.050
	(0.003)	(0.003)	(0.070)	(0.071)	(0.097)	(0.089)
Control variables	N	Y	N	Y	N	Y
Firm fixed effect	Y	Y	Y	Y	Y	Y
Year fixed effect	Y	Y	Y	Y	Y	Y
Observed value	8,757	8,757	6,810	6,733	5,447	5,396
Adj-R^2	0.006	0.026	0.057	0.103	0.061	0.111

Notes: ***, **, * represent significance at the 1%, 5% and 10% levels, respectively, and the numbers in parentheses are robust standard errors after clustering adjustment at the company level.

listed in Columns (3)–(6) of Table 9. It can be seen that for local listed SOEs in which the local government holds more than 40% stake, every one extra subsidiary in another place increases the average corporate cash dividends by 13.9%, and the effect is significant at the 5% level, while for listed companies in which the local government holds less than 40% stake, there is no significant increase in cash dividends. The regression results verify the logic of this study: local SOEs' expansion in other places helps increase the local government's gains, and when the local government's shareholding ratio is higher than its share of the corporate income tax distribution, the enterprises pay more cash dividends.

Conclusion and Policy Suggestions

The construction of a unified market is an important issue in the new stage of development. The cross-regional free mobility of factors is fundamental to the process of promoting market integration (Xia *et al.*, 2011). Despite the continuous improvement of market integration in China with the advancement of reform, local protectionist behaviors by local governments, who limit the flow of resources due to fiscal revenue constraints, have not been eradicated. Especially in the current context of building a unified national market and simultaneous reforms in the fiscal system, the inter-governmental fiscal relationship is undergoing a new round of restructuring. Using the external shock from the 2002 income tax sharing reform targeting the local fiscal incentive and the data about the distribution of A-share companies' other-place subsidiaries in 1999–2007, we empirically examine the reform's effect on local SOEs' investment in other places for an evaluation of its market integration effect. The research finds that after the income tax sharing reform, the number of local SOEs' other-place subsidiaries has significantly increased compared with enterprises of other ownership structures. This conclusion still holds after a series of robustness tests, suggesting that the income tax sharing reform has promoted the mobility of local state-owned capital. Furthermore, the effect of increasing local SOEs' cross-regional investment only exists in enterprises in which the local government's shareholding ratio is bigger than its share of their corporate income tax, meaning the local government weighs the gains from different sources when relaxing the factor market segmentation. Heterogeneity analysis shows that the results of the benchmark regression are more significant in regions where manufacturing enterprises and local SOEs with higher dependence on local tax revenue before the reform are located, and the reform significantly promotes the flow of capital factors across provinces but does not have a significant effect on the integration of intra-provincial capital factor markets. Further analysis of the consequences of the expansion of local SOEs in different locations finds that such investment is beneficial in improving the return on capital, and the more subsidiaries a local SOE has, the more dividends it will receive. Similarly, this conclusion is significant for local government-held enterprises with a stake of more than 40%, indicating that the local government has adjusted its methods of obtaining fiscal revenue.

This study suggests that fiscal incentives are the key to understanding the local government's behavior. Focusing on the construction of a unified market in the new development stage, we offer the following policy suggestions from the perspective of fiscal and tax reform:

(1) We should accelerate the construction of a national unified market and end the government's unreasonable intervention in resource allocation. This chapter's conclusion suggests that free mobility and reasonable allocation of production factors are essential to raising productivity and the return on investment, while the local government's administrative monopoly is an important reason why the market is segmented. Therefore, under the important background of the new development pattern, government departments need to pay attention to the issue of local protectionism and market segmentation, eliminate unreasonable government intervention in resource allocation, break down barriers to the free flow of factors between regions, and give full play to the decisive role of the market in resource allocation. In the current stage, when the global economy is facing great uncertainty, it is even more

necessary to shape a large-scale unified market with a regional coordination and integration strategy.

(2) The construction of market integration should be advanced in coordination with the reform of the fiscal system. This study finds that the right fiscal incentive helps promote market integration, as fiscal gains are one key reason why the local government segments the market. Therefore, in the process of building a nationwide unified market, it is important to fully utilize the basic and important support role of finance in national governance. On the one hand, fiscal and administrative powers in the vertical fiscal relationship should be balanced. Especially the administrative powers of the government below the provincial level need clarifying, with a smaller expenditure duty for the lowest-level government to relieve their excessive fiscal pressure. On the other hand, a coordinated horizontal fiscal relationship is desirable, and cross-regional division of labor and collaboration can be prompted by improving the horizontal distribution of fiscal revenue.

(3) Enhancing the centralization of the tax base with high mobility: Under the fiscal decentralization system, local governments have the incentive to compete horizontally for tax revenues in order to attract the tax base with high mobility. Therefore, only by enhancing the centralization of the tax base with high mobility and weakening the direct relationship between local government revenue and the tax base with high mobility can local protectionism be broken. It follows that in the fiscal reform, a higher distribution ratio for the central government from the mobile tax base can weaken the local government's incentive to segment markets. Meanwhile, a better fiscal revenue sharing scheme can reduce disorderly competition resulting from the local government's fight for fiscal revenue by guaranteeing, through transfer payments. a fair distribution of tax revenue among all regions.

(4) Promoting internal and external openness in coordination: In the face of great opportunities emerging with the Belt and Road initiative, the government sectors can increase the appeal of the business environment to foreign companies by removing

barriers to domestic product and factor mobility and providing an equal footing to various market participants. At the same time, the government should promote communication and cooperation between regions and market participants by expanding external openness, drive market integration domestically, and achieve high-quality economic growth.

Endnotes

1. See "CPC Central Committee's Proposals on the Formulation of the 14th Five-Year Plan for National Economic and Social Development and Vision 2035 of the People's Republic of China."
2. "State Council's Notice on Income Tax Sharing Reform", 2001.
3. The document on the tax sharing reform also mentions that the previous system "affected the formation of a unified market and the optimization of industrial structure." See "State Council's Decision on the Implementation of Fiscal Management System of Tax Sharing" in 1993.
4. "Fiscal revenue" refers to the sum of the tax revenue and the non-tax revenue at this level.

References

Bai, C., Du, Y., Tao, Z., and Tong, Y. 2004. Determinants and trend of local protection and local industrial concentration. *Economic Research*, 2004(04): 29–40.

Boisot, M. and Meyer, M.W. 2008. Which way through the open door? Reflections on the internationalization of Chinese firms. *Management and Organization Review*, 4(3): 349–365.

Cao, C. and Jia, F. 2020. Chamber of commerce in other places and cross-regional development of enterprises. *Economic Research*, 2020(04): 150–166.

Cao, C., Zhou, D., Wu, C., and Zhang, T. 2015. Market segmentation and distribution of other-place subsidiaries. *Management World*, 2015(09): 92–103.

Chen, G. and Li, S. 2013. Judicial independence and market segmentation — a study on the experiment of judges transferred to courts of other places. *Economic Research*, 2013(09): 30–42.

Chen, S., Xu, W., and Zhang, L. 2017. Fiscal pressure and local economic growth — policy experiment from China's income tax sharing reform. *Finance and Trade Economics*, 2017(04): 37–53.

Fan, Z. and Tian, B. 2013. Tax revenue competition, law enforcement, and corporate tax avoidance. *Economic Research*, 2013(09): 99–111.

Fan, Z. and Zhang, J. 2010. Fiscal decentralization, transfer payments and domestic market integration. *Economic Research*, 2010(03): 53–64.

Fang, J. 2008. Government intervention, nature of ownership and corporate M&A. *Management World*, 2008(09): 119–123.

Garnaut, R., Song, L., Yao, Y., and Wang, X. 2001. *The Emerging Private Enterprise in China*. Canberra: The National University of Australia Press.

Giroud, X. and Rauh, J. 2019. State taxation and the reallocation of business activity: Evidence from establishment-level data. *Journal of Political Economy*, 127(3): 1262–1316.

Guo, J. and Wang, H. 2003. A study on China's cross-regional capital mobility and regional growth gap. *Management World*, 2003(07): 45–58.

He, Y. and Lv, B. 2019. Administrative decentralization and regional market segmentation — a study based on prefecture-level cities. *Economic Research*, 2019(04): 127–157.

Kornai, J., Maskin, E., and Roland, G. 2003. Understanding the soft budget constraint. *Journal of Economic Literature*, 41(4): 1095–1136.

Li, M., Li, D., and Feng, Q. 2018. An evaluation of the economic effects of China's tax relief — a quasi-natural experiment based on the income tax sharing reform. *Economic Research*, 2018(07): 121–135.

Lin, Y. and Li, Z. 2004. Policy burden, moral hazard and soft budget constraints. *Economic Research*, 2004(02): 17–27.

Liu, R. 2012. State-owned enterprises, implicit subsidies and market segmentation: Theory and empirical evidence. *Management World*, 2012(04): 21–32.

Liu, Z. and Kong, L. 2021. From segmentation to integration: Impediments to a national unified market and solutions. *China Industrial Economics*, 2021(08): 20–36.

Liu, X. and Li, Z. 2008. An empirical study on fiscal decentralization and local market segmentation. *Journal of Finance and Economics*, 2008(02): 88–98.

Liu, X., Zhao, J., and Ye, K. 2017. Corporate tax avoidance, debt financing and sources of debt financing — a regression discontinuity analysis based on the reform of income tax collection and management. *Management World*, 2017(10): 113–129.

Lu, M., Chen, Z., and Yan, J. 2004. Incremental increases in return, development strategy and regional economic segmentation. *Economic Research*, 2004(01): 54–63.

Lv, B. and He, Y. 2019. Decentralization, tax sharing & market segmentation. *Journal of Peking University Philosophy and Social Sciences*, 2019(03): 54–66.

Ma, G., Cheng, X., and Yang, E. 2020. How has transport infrastructure facilitated capital mobility — a study based on availability of high-speed rail services and listed companies' investment in other places. *China Industrial Economics*, 2020(06): 5–23.

Pi, J. 2008. Regional market integration under competition among local governments of China. *Economic Research*, 2008(03): 115–124.

Ping, X. 2004. Motive behind the government's protection and its effect — an empirical study. *Finance and Trade Economics*, 2004(05): 3–10.

Poncet, S. 2002. Is Chinese market heading towards non-integration? — A comparative analysis of the level of integration in Chinese domestic market and the international market. *World Economic Papers*, 2002(02): 3–17.

Qian, Y. and Weingast, B.R. 1997. Federalism as a commitment to preserving market incentives. *Journal of Economic Perspectives*, 11(4): 83–92.

Shao, N. 2014. *Record of State-Owned Enterprises' Reform (1998-2008)*. Beijing: Economic Science Press.

Shen, L. and Dai, L. 1990. Local government's protection of its own economic interests, its causes and disadvantages. *Economic Research*, 1990(03): 12–19.

Song, D. and Fan, X. 2015. Has tax sharing reform promoted market integration? *Study and Exploration*, 2015(04): 87–93.

Song, Y. and Huang, L. 2014. Why is it hard for Chinese companies to operate across regions in China? *Management World*, 2014(12): 115–133.

Tang, T., Mo, P.L.L. and Chan, K.H. 2017. Tax collector or tax avoider? An investigation of intergovernmental agency conflicts. *The Accounting Review*, 92(2): 247–270.

Tian, B. and Fan, Z. 2016. Tax revenue sharing, tax collection effort and corporate tax evasion — evidence from the income tax sharing reform. *Management World*, 2016(12): 36–46.

Wang, F. and Dong, F. 2013. Competition among local governments and integration mechanism of China's regional markets — a study on regional specialization under Chinese decentralization. *Journal of Shandong University Philosophy and Social Sciences*, 2013(03): 11–25.

Xia, L., Lu, M., and Yu, W. 2011. Government-company connections and cross-provincial investment — empirical evidence from Chinese listed companies. *Management World*, 2011(07): 128–140.

Xie, Z. and Fan, Z. 2015. Chinese tax sharing system, centralized tax collection and management, and tax revenue competition. *Economic Research*, 2015(04): 92–106.

Yin, W. and Cai, W. 2001. Causes of and solutions for China's local market segmentation. *Economic Research*, 2001(06): 3–12.

Young, A. 2000. The razor's edge: Distortions and incremental reform in the People's Republic of China. *Quarterly Journal of Economics*, 115(4): 1091–1135.

Zeng, Q. and Chen, X. 2006. State shareholding, redundant employees and labor cost. *Economic Research*, 2006(05): 74–86.

Zheng, Y. and Li, C. 2003. Efficiency loss from China's local segmentation. *Social Sciences in China*, 2003(01): 64–72.

Zhou, L. 2004. Incentive and cooperation of government officials in promotion games — also on the reasons why China's local protection and duplicated construction have persisted. *Economic Research*, 2004(06): 33–40.

Zhou, L. 2007. A study on the pattern of Chinese local officials' promotion tournament. *Economic Research*, 2007(07): 36–50.

https://doi.org/10.1142/9789819815241_0017

Chapter 17

THE CHINESE-STYLE MACROECONOMIC CONTROL: THE ROLE OF STATE-OWNED ENTERPRISES

Hongsheng Fang[*,‡,**], Wen-Quan Hu[†], Ruhua Shi[§], and Xufei Zhang[¶]

[*]*School of Economics, Zhejiang University, Hangzhou, China*
[†]*School of Economics, Zhejiang University of Finance and Economics, Hangzhou, China*
[‡]*Institute for Fiscal Big-Data & Policy of Zhejiang University, Hangzhou, China*
[§]*HwaBao Securities Co. Ltd., Shanghai, China*
[¶]*School of Public Finance and Taxation, Zhejiang University of Finance and Economics, Hangzhou, China*
[**]*fhs@zju.edu.cn*

Introduction

In the past 10 years, many scholars have found that whether in response to the Great Depression in the 1930s or the global financial crisis in 2008, a great deal of countries tend to adopt nationalization methods and take state-owned enterprises (SOEs) as a useful temporary emergency tool for macroeconomic control (Millward, 2005,

2011; Florio and Fecher, 2011; Thynne, 2011; Brei and Schclarek, 2013; Florio, 2013, 2014; Bernier, 2014; Bertay *et al.*, 2015; Coleman and Feler, 2015; Szarzec and Nowara, 2017; Bernier and Reeves, 2018). It is generally believed that 1940–1980 was the heyday of SOEs (Bernier and Reeves, 2018). Historically, the Great Depression in the 1930s was the reason why some countries set up SOEs (Guo and Ma, 2019). Research by Millward (2005, 2011) shows that SOEs in most European countries accounted for 10% of GDP, 20% of annual capital formation, and 10% of employment by the 1940s, whereas the scale of European SOEs has not changed much in the following 30 years. After 80 years, governments faced a similar situation (Florio, 2014). As Bernier (2014) pointed out, since the 2008 economic crisis, governments and scholars have "rediscovered" SOEs as useful policy instruments. During the 2007–2009 financial crisis, governments in high-income economies were forced to provide financial support to bankrupt companies to avoid further financial instability and contagion effects, which were particularly evident in the US and the UK (Szarzec and Nowara, 2017). Several countries were forced to nationalize failing private banks (Bertay *et al.*, 2015). Abn Amro in the Netherlands, for instance, was fully owned by the Dutch government after the crisis. As a result, the average share of government ownership of banks by bank assets has increased in high-income countries from 7.3% in 2007 to 10.8% in 2009. In addition, many countries have strengthened the dominance of SOEs in the oil, gas, aviation, and railway industries (Putniņš, 2015).

It is well known that SOEs play an important role in China's economic system (Lin and Milhaupt, 2013). Then, does the Chinese government also use SOEs as a tool for macroeconomic control in the face of economic recessions? This is an important question worth studying. Reviewing the existing literature, we find that the following issues have been extensively studied: the efficiency of SOE investments and whether or not they are excessive (Bertero and Rondi, 2002; Alesina *et al.*, 2005; Chen *et al.*, 2011; He and Kyaw, 2018; Wei and Liu, 2007; Cheng *et al.*, 2008; Tang *et al.*, 2010; Zhang *et al.*, 2010; Zhong *et al.*, 2010); the influence of SOE investment on private enterprise investment (Wang *et al.*, 2013; Tan *et al.*, 2016;

Wang *et al.*, 2018); and whether SOEs can act as "stabilizers of macroeconomic economy" in the transition period (Liu, 2001; Zhang, 2009; Liu and Wang, 2010; Wang, 2011; Gong, 2019; Guo and Ma, 2019). However, there are few studies on whether the Chinese government actually uses SOEs as a useful tool for macroeconomic control and whether such a tool is effective.

As far as we know, studies by Wang (2011) and Guo and Ma (2019) are the only representative works to have confirmed the important role of SOEs in macroeconomic stability through rigorous measurement methods. However, Wang (2011) does not empirically study whether or not the Chinese government would use SOEs as a tool for macroeconomic control. Although Guo and Ma (2019) have done this work, they only observed whether the investment of SOEs presents countercyclical characteristics through graphing and did not conduct in-depth empirical research. We believe that the empirical research by Wang (2011) and Guo and Ma (2019) will have a solid foundation only when it is confirmed that the Chinese government indeed uses SOEs as a tool for macroeconomic control. Under the same condition, the proposition that SOEs can play an important role in the macroeconomic control system with Chinese characteristics (Liu, 2001; Zhang, 2009; Liu and Wang, 2010; Wang, 2011; Gong, 2019; Guo and Ma, 2019) will have a practical basis.

This study makes the following contributions to the literature. First, it theoretically explains in depth the internal logic mechanism of the expansion-biased investment behaviors of Chinese SOEs, revealing that during an economic recession, their countercyclical investment behaviors result from the local government intervening to achieve local growth goals.[1] Second, this study is the first to provide systematic evidence for the countercyclical investment behaviors of Chinese SOEs during economic recessions. Using data from Chinese listed companies and applying the system GMM method to deal with the endogeneity problem, we obtain three main conclusions: (1) both central and local SOEs exhibit expansion-biased investment behaviors; (2) the expansion-biased investment of central SOEs mainly goes to the tertiary industry and the western regions of

China, while the expansion-biased investment of local SOEs mainly occurs in the tertiary industry and the middle and western regions of China; (3) during an economic recession, the higher the local growth targets, the more bank credit central and local SOEs can obtain, and the more pronounced the expansion-biased investment.

Third, our work extends the existing studies of cyclical fiscal policy behavior. Currently, the research on cyclical fiscal policy behavior can be divided into the following two branches: cyclical spending policy (Riascos and Vegh, 2003; Hercowitz and Strawczynski, 2004; Jaimovich and Panizza, 2007; Kaminsky *et al.*, 2004; Talvi and Vegh, 2005; Alesina *et al.*, 2008; Ilzetzki and Vegh, 2008; Cuadra *et al.*, 2010; Frankel *et al.*, 2013) and cyclical tax policy (Sorensen *et al.*, 2001; Kaminsky *et al.*, 2004; Sturzenegger and Werneck, 2006; Cuadra *et al.*, 2010; Furceri and Karras, 2011; Strawczynski, 2014; Vegh and Vuletin, 2015; Srebrnik and Strawczynski, 2016; Abdellatif and Tran-Nam, 2016). Our research focuses on the quasi-fiscal policy of SOE investments, which greatly extends the existing research on cyclical fiscal policy behavior. We show that, apart from the countercyclical fiscal policy implemented by the central and local governments (Fang and Zhang, 2009), the quasi-fiscal function of central and local SOE investments is also key to China recovering quickly from a recession. It can also become an essential component of the Chinese-style macro-control system.

The rest of this chapter is organized as follows: section "Hypothesis Development" develops our hypotheses; section "Empirical Strategy and Data" introduces empirical strategy and data; section "Empirical Results" discusses empirical findings; and section "Conclusions and Policy Implications" concludes the chapter by offering important policy implications.

Hypothesis Development

The cyclical investment behaviors of enterprises with different ownerships

During economic downturns, companies suffer from decreased external demand, which leads to reduced corporate investment

(Bernanke and Gertler, 1989; Bernanke *et al.*, 1996; Wang and Song, 2014). Wang and Song (2014) argue that negative shocks can increase macroeconomic uncertainty, which in turn strengthens the negative impact of reduced external demand on investment through the channel of expectation. On the contrary, companies face rising external demand during economic booms, which will result in more investments. However, as the existing literature points out, positive shocks can lead to higher prices for real options through increased macroeconomic uncertainties (Ghosal, 1991; Peeters, 2001; Bontempi *et al.*, 2010; Dangl and Wu, 2016). Such an effect would make companies more cautious in their investment decisions and suppress their responses to positive external demand shocks. Therefore, we expect that during a recession, enterprise investment will significantly fall, whereas during a boom period, investment may not greatly increase. As investment decisions by non-SOEs are usually market-oriented, the above expectation applies to non-SOEs.

However, the logic of SOEs in making investment decisions is more complicated. While following commercial principles, they must also bear in mind the purpose of the state capital; therefore, SOEs are a major channel for governments to conduct macroeconomic control. Since the 1980s, the major criteria for assessing local government officials have shifted from political performance to a combination of local economic growth and leadership qualities (Zhou *et al.*, 2005). Using Chinese provincial data, Li and Zhou (2005) find that the promotion of local officials is closely linked with the relative growth rate. As investment is a direct and strong stimulus to economic growth (Guo and Zhao, 2012), local government officials have great incentives to intervene in SOE investment with the aim of personal political promotion to promote local economic growth. Tang *et al.* (2010) reveal that with local governments intervening in SOEs to improve local economies, SOEs tend to overinvest. This suggests that local governments are motivated to intervene in SOE investments in order to gain relative economic performance and obtain greater opportunities for promotion, whether during economic booms or recessions.

Nevertheless, the degree of intervention varies during different periods. In a recession, local economic growth will slow down. Local officials will be more likely to get promotion opportunities if the downturn can be mitigated or even reversed (Li and Zhou, 2005). As a result, local governments have a particularly strong incentive to intervene in SOEs, such as speeding up the administrative approval of SOE investment projects or strengthening bank credit support (Guo and Ma, 2019), which will lead to a remarkable increase in SOE investments during recessions. Conversely, during economic booms, non-SOEs may have more enthusiasm to make an investment. Meanwhile, banks are willing to give greater support to SOE investments (Fang, 2010; Yu *et al.*, 2012), encouraging SOEs to make more investments as well. At this moment, local economic growth goals could be easily realized by relying on the autonomous investments of both SOEs and non-SOEs. In this way, local governments will not have strong incentives to intervene in SOE investments (Zhao *et al.*, 2016). Based on this, the first hypothesis is proposed:

Hypothesis 1. In the macro-control system with Chinese characteristics, the investment behaviors of SOEs are highly expansion-biased, whereas the investment behaviors of non-SOEs are procyclical during recessions.

The periodical investment behaviors of SOEs may be different between central and local SOEs. As the biggest shareholder of local SOEs, local governments have the power to appoint SOE executives (Zhao *et al.*, 2016). Therefore, the local governments can directly intervene in the investment of local SOEs (namely provincial or municipal SOEs). The central SOEs are directly controlled by the central government rather than local governments. However, from a practical viewpoint, local governments also have a certain ability to intervene in the decision-making of central SOEs (Chen, 2016; Lv *et al.*, 2016). As central SOEs rely on the support of local governments in terms of children's enrollment, medical welfare, office building land approval, and so on, central SOEs may be restricted and influenced by local governments and may even collude with local governments. As Lv *et al.* (2016) found, the tax collection and administration intensity of the branches of the State Taxation Administration in regions will be affected by the local governments. When the local government's income tax share increases, the tax collection and administration intensity of the branches of the State Taxation Administration will also strengthen. Moreover, most central SOEs are in monopolistic industries with strong pricing and profitability and low volatility in earnings (Chen *et al.*, 2016). Compared with local SOEs, central SOEs can obtain more abundant capital, technology, human, and other resources. Consequently, the ability of central SOEs to resist risk is relatively stronger than that of local SOEs. This means that during economic recessions, the intervention of local governments in central SOEs may be higher than that in local SOEs.

In addition to the reasons for local government intervention, there are also two possibilities for the increase in investment by central SOEs during economic recessions: (1) the central government directly intervenes in central SOEs for macroeconomic stability during the recession; (2) for business opportunities embedded in industrial characteristics due to their dominant positions in specific industries. For the above reasons, the central SOEs' investment will be larger than that of local SOEs during economic recessions. Therefore, we put forward the second hypothesis:

Hypothesis 2. In the macro-control system with Chinese characteristics, both central and local SOEs have clearly expansion-biased investment behaviors, but the expansion bias of central SOEs may be stronger than that of local SOEs during economic recessions.

The role of local growth targets in the expansion-biased investment behaviors of SOEs

The economic growth targets set by local governments play an important role in promoting economic development (Zhou *et al.*, 2015). The People's Congress at the provincial level is often held in late January. At the meeting, the provincial governor (mayor or district chairman) produces the year's government work report for the Congress on behalf of the provincial government. On the one hand, the report reviews the previous year's work. On the other hand, it sets the current year's development goals, including the economic growth rate. This growth target is an *ex ante* number issued by the local government at the beginning of each year. It is a public commitment to the People's Congress at the local level (Xu and Liang, 2014). In this context, the higher the growth target, the more pressure is placed on local economic growth, and the more likely it is that the local government will intervene in SOE investment. According to the above analysis, during economic booms, local governments have little incentive to intervene in SOE investments because the pressure to realize development goals is relatively low. On the contrary, local governments face high pressure to maintain economic growth during recessions and therefore will intervene aggressively. In view of this, the third hypothesis is as follows:

Hypothesis 3. In the macro-control system with Chinese characteristics, local growth targets have a stronger influence on the expansion-biased investment behaviors of SOEs during recessions than booms.

We further discuss the possible measures local governments may take to intervene in SOEs. China's financial system is dominated by state-owned banks (Walter and Howie, 2012). Although China has developed many financial institutions, the financial system is still mainly controlled by the governments (including the central and local governments), and the proportion of financial institutions controlled by private capital is extremely low (Hong *et al.*, 2021). Existing studies have already noted that bank credit is a possibly important channel of intervention by local governments in China (Brandt and Li, 2003; Fang, 2010; Lu *et al.*, 2009; Fan *et al.*, 2012; Allen *et al.*, 2017; Guo and Ma, 2019; Tan and Zhang, 2021). Fan *et al.* (2012) analyze government intervention in enterprise debt. On the one hand, by subsidizing enterprises, the government reduces the possibility of corporate debt default, making it easier for enterprises to obtain long-term loans from banks. On the other hand, the government helps enterprises obtain bank credit, usually in the form of long-term loans, by directly intervening in a bank's decision-making. The support of bank credit has a substantial impact on the expansion of SOE investment. Sun *et al.* (2005) and Fang (2010) conclude that compared to listed private companies, SOEs get more bank loans and a longer debt maturity structure, which helps to alleviate the financing constraints of SOEs and expand their investments. Consequently, in order to achieve the goal of local economic growth, it is an effective means for local governments to intervene in the investment of SOEs through bank credit, which is particularly important during economic recessions. Therefore, we put forward the fourth hypothesis:

Hypothesis 4. In the macro-control system with Chinese characteristics, SOEs in regions with higher economic growth targets will receive more bank credit during recessions than booms.

Empirical Strategy and Data

Empirical strategy

In order to identify the cyclical investment behaviors of enterprises with different ownership, this study follows the standard empirical framework on the cyclical behavior of fiscal policy research (Alesina *et al.*, 2008; Jaimovich and Panizza, 2007; Hercowitz and Strawczynski, 2004; Fang and Zhang, 2009; Andersen and Holbøll Westh Nielsen, 2010). We construct the following dynamic panel data model of investment:

$$\begin{aligned} lnInvest_{it} = \alpha lnInvest_{i,t-1} + \beta_1 Gap_{jt} \times Boom_{jt} + \beta_2 Gap_{jt} \\ \times Recession_{jt} + \gamma X_{it} + Ind + \omega_t + \mu_i + \varepsilon_{it} \end{aligned} \quad (1)$$

where the dependent variable, $lnInvest_{it}$, is company i's investment in year t. Following Zwick and James (2017), we take the log of fixed asset investment, which is measured as the change in the sum of the original value of fixed assets and the value of projects under construction and engineering materials (Wang and Song, 2014). The variable of interest, Gap_{jt}, is province j's output gap in year t. Using the method proposed by Fang and Zhang (2009), and nominal gross domestic product (GDP) and GDP index data from the website of the National Bureau of Statistics of China, we first calculate the real GDP of each province and then obtain the provincial output gap using the Hodrick–Prescott (HP) filter (Ravn and Uhlig, 2002).[2] $Boom_{jt}$ represents economic prosperity. If $Gap_{jt} > 0$, $Boom_{jt}$ is 1; otherwise, it is 0. $Recession_{jt}$ represents an economic recession. If $Gap_{jt} < 0$, $Recession_{jt}$ is 1; otherwise, it is 0.[3] Ind represents the industry fixed effect of the company. ω_t is the time effect, which controls the shock of the national economic cycle. And, μ_i is the individual fixed effect.

For the dynamic panel data model, this study uses the popular system GMM method for estimation. According to representative literature such as Roodman (2009), Fang and Zhang (2009), Li and Shen (2010), Guo and Lv (2011), and Dai and Jin (2014), the system GMM method, which uses the lags as instruments, can not only cope with the endogenous problem of lagged dependence in the dynamic panel data model but also deal with the endogeneity of other variables. The key explanatory variables, $Gap_{jt} \times Boom_{jt}$ and $Gap_{jt} \times Recession_{jt}$, have obvious reverse causality with the explained variable of investment and have endogeneity, or they are endogenous due to correlation with the omitted official characteristics and political cycle variables. Subsequently, this study treats them as endogenous variables and uses their lag periods as instrumental variables. As this method is widely used and the principle has already been detailed in the above-mentioned literature, it is unnecessary for us to discuss it further here.

In order to explore the influence of local growth goals on the cyclical investment behaviors of enterprises, we add the variable $Goal_{jt}$ to the model above to account for the impact of local growth targets:

$$lnInvest_{it} = \alpha lnInvest_{i,t-1} + \beta_1 Gap_{jt} \times Boom_{jt} \times Goal_{jt} + \beta_2 Gap_{jt} \times Recession_{jt} \times Goal_{jt} + \delta Goal_{jt} + \gamma X_{it} + Ind + \omega_t + \mu_i + \varepsilon_{it} \quad (2)$$

Following Xu and Liang (2014), this study collects the economic growth targets from provincial government work reports. In total, we obtain the economic growth targets of 30 provinces and cities (excluding Tibet) between 2003–2016. However, in the first year of a five-year plan period, some provinces and cities do not report the target for the year. Instead, they set a five-year average growth rate. When this happens, we use the five-year average as the growth target for the first year. Besides, Henan Province and the city of Shanghai did not report their growth targets for 2011 and 2015, respectively. For the two missing numbers, we use the average of the growth rates of the previous and later years.

X_{it} is a series of control variables. Following the studies by Wang *et al.* (2014) and Cheng *et al.* (2008), it includes the following:

(1) Size, measured as the log of total assets. The bigger the company, the larger the investment size;
(2) Cash flow, the ratio of net cash flow from operating to beginning balances of fixed assets. Enterprises are more likely to make investments when cash flow is abundant;
(3) Leverage (with one lag), measured as the ratio of total debt to total assets, is expected to have a negative impact on investment;
(4) Cash (with one lag), the ratio of the end balance of cash to total assets. It has a positive impact on investment;
(5) Management fee rate, which reflects the corporate governance situation of a company. Good corporate governance will lead to expansion through investment;
(6) Asset turnover, which measures the agency cost of a company and negatively correlates with investment;
(7) Return on assets (ROA), which is an indicator of a company's profitability relative to its total assets. A higher ROA means a higher expected return on investment;
(8) Tobin's Q ratio (with one lag), the total market value of a company divided by the replacement value of the assets. We use market value A/(total assets – net intangible assets) to measure

company growth opportunities. The higher the index, the larger a company's investment;

(9) Internal financing: the ratio of (net profit + depreciation) to total assets at the beginning. When abundant internal financing can be acquired, a company is more likely to invest.

In order to distinguish between SOEs and non-SOEs, we calculate the equity control chain from the China Securities Market and Accounting Research (CSMAR) database to identify the actual controller each year. Table 1 provides a detailed classification.

To account for regional heterogeneity, we divide China into four regions: eastern, northeast, middle, and western, as detailed in Table 2.

Table 1. Classification of enterprises by ownership.

Type of enterprise	Type of actual controller
Central SOEs	Central institutions, central SOEs.
Local SOEs	Local SOEs, administrative agencies, public institutions, local institutions.
Non-SOEs	Collective ownership enterprises, private enterprises, joint ventures with funds from Hong Kong, Macau and Taiwan, foreign owned enterprises, social associations, natural person, domestic natural person, natural person from Hong Kong, Macau and Taiwan, foreign natural person, etc.

Table 2. Regional division.

Region	Provinces and cities
Eastern	Beijing, Tianjin, Hebei, Shanghai, Jiangsu, Zhejiang, Fujian, Shandong, Guangdong, Hainan.
Northeast	Liaoning, Jilin, Heilongjiang.
Middle	Shanxi, Anhui, Jiangxi, Henan, Hubei, Hunan.
Western	Inner Mongolia, Guangxi, Chongqing, Sichuan, Guizhou, Yunnan, Tibet, Shaanxi, Gansu, Qinghai, Ningxia and Xinjiang.

Data

This study uses data regarding Chinese listed companies from 2003 to 2016. Most data come from the Wind database, except for the actual controller data, which are obtained from the CSMAR database. As shown in Table 3, after excluding specially treated (ST) and financial companies, in addition to companies with missing key variables, such as investment, total assets, fixed assets, and Tobin's Q, we finally obtain a total of 18,873 observations of 2,702 companies. Then, we winsorize the company-level continuous variable data by replacing observations whose quantiles are outside (1%, 99%) with the 1% and 99% quantiles.

In the following, we provide descriptive evidence for our hypotheses. Conditional on other independent variables, Figures 1–4 show the correlations between enterprise investment (logarithm) grouped by ownership and economic cycle. Following the practice of Gallup

Table 3. Screening of enterprises.

Procedure	Number of enterprises	Observations
Non-ST and non-financial companies	3,007	26,543
Exclude companies with missing investment data	2,713	19,400
Exclude companies with missing key variables	2,703	18,877
Exclude companies with unknown provinces and cities	2,702	18,873

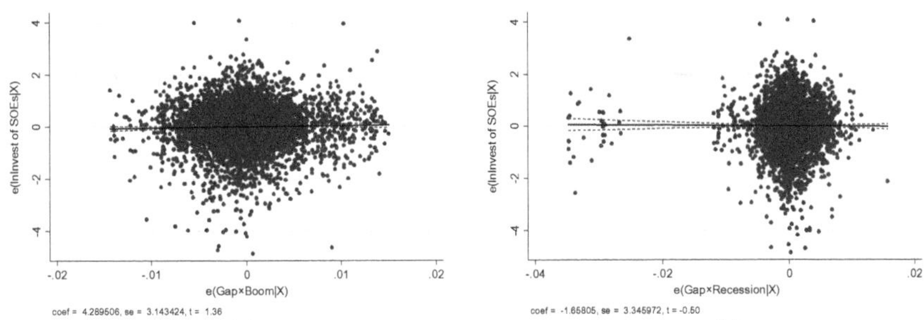

(a) (b)

Figure 1. The correlation between the SOE investment and economic cycle.

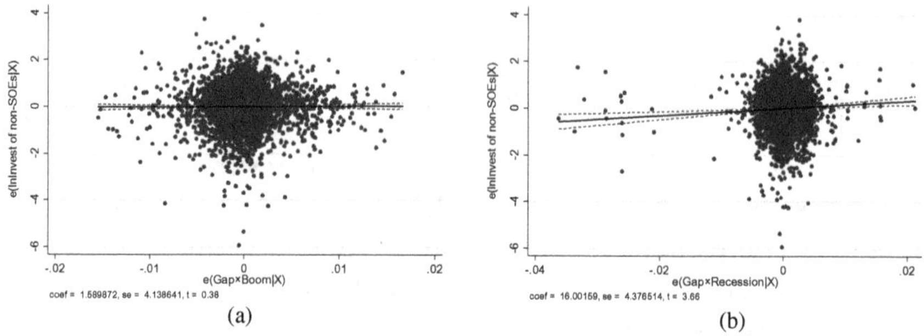

Figure 2. The correlation between the non-SOE investment and economic cycle.

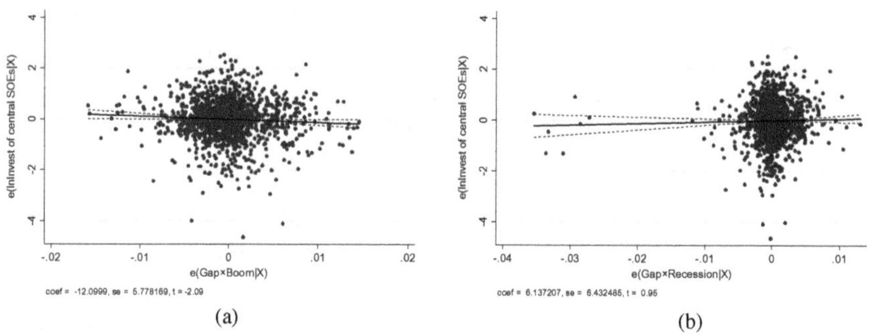

Figure 3. The correlation between the central SOE investment and economic cycle.

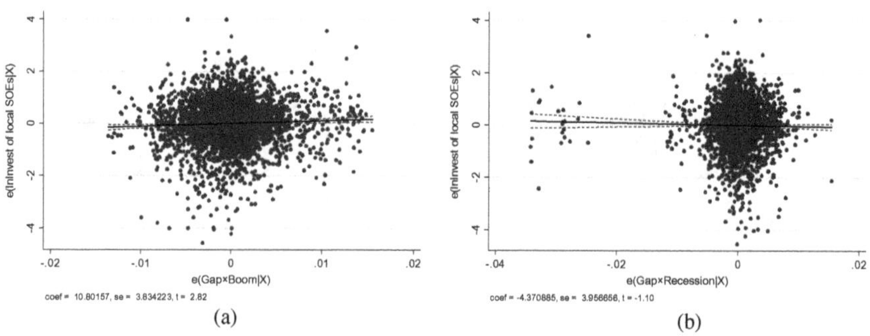

Figure 4. The correlation between the local SOE investment and economic cycle.

(2020), all panels plot the correlations after controlling for the fixed effects and control variables mentioned above. The left panel of Figure 1 presents the relationship between SOE investment and economic booms, while the right panel shows their relationship with economic recessions. Among them, the *x*-axis represents the Gap × Boom (or Gap × Recession) in the model (1), while the *y*-axis represents the investment of SOEs (non-SOEs, central SOEs, or local SOEs). We can clearly observe a positive relationship in booms and a negative relationship in recessions, which are in line with theoretical expectations. Similarly, except for central SOEs, the correlations between investment and economic cycle of other ownership enterprises all fit the expectations. Rigorous econometric analysis dealing with endogeneity by the system GMM method is described in the following section.

Table 4 presents descriptive statistics for the main variables. For the corporate investment (*lnInvest*), the average value is 9.272, with

Table 4. Descriptive statistics of main variables.

Variable	N	Mean	SD	Min	P50	Max
lnInvest	18,873	9.272	1.943	3.826	9.309	14.170
Gap	18,873	0	0.008	–0.050	–0.001	0.032
Boom	18,873	0.467	0.499	0	0	1
Recession	18,873	0.533	0.499	0	1	1
Gap × Boom	18,873	0.003	0.005	0	0	0.032
Gap × Recession	18,873	–0.003	0.005	–0.050	–0.001	0
Size	18,873	12.720	1.250	10.340	12.540	16.570
Cash flow	18,873	0.274	2.721	–15.590	0.206	15.280
Leverage	18,873	45.430	20.840	5.083	45.880	92.200
Cash	18,873	0.182	0.132	0.012	0.145	0.648
Managemeng fee rate	18,873	9.367	7.444	0.902	7.618	46.430
Asset turnover	18,873	0.707	0.493	0.087	0.586	2.758
ROA	18,873	6.404	5.933	–12.610	5.688	26.810
Tobin's Q ratio	18,873	2.227	2.069	0.224	1.585	11.710
Internal financing	18,873	0.080	0.070	–0.114	0.069	0.374
Goal	18,703	0.093	0.015	0.060	0.090	0.150

the minimum of 3.826 and the maximum of 14.170, indicating a large variation in *lnInvest*. During booms, the average value of *Gap* × *Boom* is 0.003 and the maximum value is 0.032, while in a recession period, the average value of *Gap* × *Recession* is −0.003 and the minimum value is −0.050, suggesting a uniform distribution of business cycle indicators. Table 4 also shows the relevant information of other variables, which will not be described here.

Empirical Results

Cyclical investment behaviors of enterprises with different ownerships

Results of basic regression

Table 5 shows the results of regression when corporate investment is the dependent variable. Columns (1)–(3) are the results for the whole sample. Among them, Column (1) is the result of OLS regression, Column (2) is the result of fixed effects (FE) regression, and Column (3) is the result of system GMM regression. The results in Column (3) can be regarded as robust and reliable for the following reasons: (1) the Hansen test cannot reject the null hypothesis that the instrumental variable is valid; (2) AR(2) cannot reject the null hypothesis that there is no second-order serial correlation in the first-difference function; (3) the estimated coefficient for the lagged dependent variable is between the results of the FE and OLS models. Due to space limitations, Columns (4)–(5) only report the system GMM results.

Column (3) shows that, in general, corporate investment is not highly cyclical. It is neither procyclical nor countercyclical. Possible reasons include the following: (1) during a recession, SOEs increase their investment under government intervention, then the increased amount evens out the drop in non-SOE investment and stabilizes total investment; and (2) during an economic boom, government intervention incentives are weakened, slowing down the pace of investment by SOEs. As a result, total corporate investment would not largely increase.

Table 5. Cyclical investment behaviors of enterprises with different ownership.

	$lnInvest_{i,t}$				
Dependent variable	(1)	(2)	(3)	(4)	(5)
$lnInvest_{i,t-1}$	0.43***	0.12***	0.27***	0.24***	0.16**
	(0.000)	(0.000)	(0.000)	(0.000)	(0.027)
$Gap_{jt} \times Recession_{jt}$	0.33	4.36*	−2.19	−7.40*	12.45*
	(0.893)	(0.098)	(0.542)	(0.059)	(0.092)
$Gap_{jt} \times Boom_{jt}$	3.08	2.59	4.38	6.78*	−2.16
	(0.177)	(0.295)	(0.180)	(0.078)	(0.792)
Year	Yes	Yes	Yes	Yes	Yes
Firm		Yes	Yes	Yes	Yes
Industry	Yes	Yes	Yes	Yes	Yes
Sample	Total	Total	Total	SOEs	Non-SOEs
N	14,068	14,068	14,068	7,007	7,061
AR(1)			0.000	0.000	0.000
AR(2)			0.103	0.128	0.196
Hansen Test			0.204	0.280	0.468

Notes: (1) p values are displayed in parentheses; (2) *, **, and *** indicate significance at 10%, 5%, and 1% levels, respectively; (3) $lnInvest_{i,t-1}$, $Gap_{jt} \times Recession_{jt}$ and $Gap_{jt} \times Boom_{jt}$ are endogenous variables, and the rest are exogenous variables. (4) all other variables are controlled.

Column (4) is the regression result of the SOEs sample. Compared with the overall sample, SOE investment is clearly countercyclical during recessions and pro-cyclical during booms. In other words, investment by SOEs is expansion-biased. Specifically, during a recession, when real GDP is one percentage point less than potential GDP, corporate investment will increase by 7.40%. During a boom, when real GDP is one percentage point greater than potential GDP, corporate investment will increase by 6.78%.

Column (5) is the result for non-SOEs. Unlike SOEs, the behaviors of non-SOEs are more market-oriented and are therefore procyclical during recessions; when real GDP is one percentage point lower than potential GDP, corporate investment will decrease by 12.45%. During economic booms, non-SOE investments do not increase significantly. A plausible explanation for such tepidness is that positive shocks usually come together with rising economic uncertainty, which pushes up the prices of real options and makes enterprises cautious about investment. Thus, corporate investment is less responsive to positive shocks arising from increased external demand (Ghosal, 1991; Peeters, 2001; Bontempi *et al.*, 2010; Dangl and Wu, 2016; Wang and Song, 2014).

Based on the results shown in Columns (3)–(5), Hypothesis 1 is supported: in the macro-control system with Chinese characteristics, the investment behaviors of SOEs are highly expansion-biased, whereas the investment behaviors of non-SOEs are procyclical during recessions.

Cyclical investment behaviors of central and local SOEs

We further investigate the cyclical investment behaviors of central and local SOEs, and the estimated results of system GMM are shown in Table 6. The first two columns indicate that both the central and local SOEs show expansion-biased investment behavior. Specifically, for central SOEs, during an economic recession, for every percentage point of real GDP lower than potential GDP, investment increases by 19.56%. During economic prosperity, for every percentage point of real GDP higher than potential GDP, investment increases by 16.07%. For local SOEs, during an economic recession, for every percentage point of real GDP lower than potential GDP, investment increases by 10.08%. During economic prosperity, for every percentage point of real GDP higher than potential GDP, investment increases by 10.19%. In order to test the statistical significance of the difference in coefficients, we constructed a dummy variable, *Central_SOE*: when the enterprise belongs to central SOEs, the value of *Central_SOE* takes 1, otherwise it takes 0. As shown in Column (3) of Table 6, we further introduced the interaction term of $Gap_{jt} \times Recession_{jt}$ and *Central_SOE* into the regression, as well as the interaction term of $Gap_{jt} \times Boom_{jt}$ and *Central_SOE*. It can be seen that the coefficient of the interaction term $Gap_{jt} \times Recession_{jt} \times$ *Central_SOE* is significantly negative, indicating that the expansion

Table 6. Cyclical investment behaviors of central and local SOEs.

Dependent variable	$lnInvest_{i,t}$		
	(1)	(2)	(3)
$lnInvest_{i,t-1}$	0.09*	0.30***	0.23***
	(0.097)	(0.000)	(0.000)
$Gap_{jt} \times Recession_{jt}$	−19.56**	−10.08**	−8.58*
	(0.044)	(0.049)	(0.075)
$Gap_{jt} \times Boom_{jt}$	16.07*	10.19**	9.74*
	(0.059)	(0.033)	(0.062)
$Gap_{jt} \times Recession_{jt} \times Central\_SOE$			−13.89*
			(0.097)
$Gap_{jt} \times Boom_{jt} \times Central\_SOE$			−2.02
			(0.800)
Year	Yes	Yes	Yes
Firm	Yes	Yes	Yes
Industry	Yes	Yes	Yes
Sample	Central SOEs	Local SOEs	SOEs
N	1,870	5,137	7,007
AR(1)	0.000	0.000	0.000
AR(2)	0.821	0.454	0.292
Hansen Test	0.115	0.153	0.733

Notes: (1) p values are displayed in parentheses; (2) *, **, and *** indicate significance at 10%, 5%, and 1% levels, respectively; (3) $lnInvest_{i,t-1}$, $Gap_{jt} \times Recession_{jt}$, $Gap_{jt} \times Boom_{jt}$, $Gap_{jt} \times Recession_{jt} \times Central\_SOE$ and $Gap_{jt} \times Boom_{jt} \times Central\_SOE$ are endogenous variables, and the rest are exogenous variables; (4) all other variables are controlled.

bias of central SOEs is indeed stronger than that of local SOEs during economic recessions. As a result, Hypothesis 2 is verified.

Cyclical investment behaviors of enterprises with different ownerships: Industry heterogeneity

As companies in different industries face varying degrees of competition and overcapacity, they may behave differently when making investment decisions. Based on the fact that stricter supervision means the tertiary industry experiences less competition and fewer overcapacity problems than other industries, we refer to the practice of Hansen (1999), Alesina *et al.* (2008), Fang and Zhang (2009, 2013), and Fang *et al.* (2017), which divides all industries into two categories: non-tertiary (the primary and second industries) and tertiary. Two dummy variables, *notertiary* and *tertiary*, are set up accordingly. If a company is in the primary or secondary industry, *notertiary* is assigned a value of 1; if a company is in the tertiary industry, then *tertiary* is 1. Table 7 shows the estimated results.

Table 7. Cyclical investment behaviors of enterprises with different ownership: Industry heterogeneity.

Dependent variable	$lnInvest_{i,t}$				
	(1)	(2)	(3)	(4)	(5)
$lnInvest_{i,t-1}$	0.24***	0.26***	0.25***	0.29***	0.32***
	(0.000)	(0.000)	(0.000)	(0.000)	(0.000)
$Gap_{jt} \times Recession_{jt} \times notertiary$	1.14	–2.25	1.37	–6.96	12.12*
	(0.841)	(0.576)	(0.849)	(0.153)	(0.063)
$Gap_{jt} \times Recession_{jt} \times tertiary$	–15.54*	–19.01**	–24.84*	–21.81**	2.75
	(0.099)	(0.021)	(0.081)	(0.024)	(0.765)
$Gap_{jt} \times Boom_{jt} \times notertiary$	5.32	–0.45	–4.80	4.93	1.99
	(0.319)	(0.915)	(0.516)	(0.309)	(0.719)
$Gap_{jt} \times Boom_{jt} \times tertiary$	25.68**	21.70***	20.68*	28.76***	10.03
	(0.011)	(0.005)	(0.088)	(0.001)	(0.360)
Year	Yes	Yes	Yes	Yes	Yes
Firm	Yes	Yes	Yes	Yes	Yes
Industry	Yes	Yes	Yes	Yes	Yes
Sample	Total	SOEs	Central SOEs	Local SOEs	Non-SOEs
N	14,068	7,007	1,870	5,137	7,061
AR(1)	0.000	0.000	0.000	0.000	0.000
AR(2)	0.293	0.289	0.354	0.444	0.172
Hansen Test	0.738	0.424	0.597	0.270	0.439

Notes: (1) p values are displayed in parentheses; (2) *, **, and *** indicate significance at 10%, 5%, and 1% levels, respectively; (3) $lnInvest_{i,t-1}$, $Gap_{jt} \times Recession_{jt} \times notertiary$, $Gap_{jt} \times Recession_{jt} \times tertiary$, $Gap_{jt} \times Boom_{jt} \times notertiary$ and $Gap_{jt} \times Boom_{jt} \times tertiary$ are endogenous variables, and the rest are exogenous variables; (4) all other variables are controlled.

By analyzing the results presented in Table 7, we draw the following main conclusions. First, only companies in the tertiary industry have a clear tendency to make an expansion-biased investment, whereas companies in other industries have no obvious tendency to make a procyclical investment. Second, the expansion-biased investment of SOEs only happens in the tertiary industry. In the other two industries, SOE investment is slightly countercyclical. Third, the expansion-biased investment behaviors of central and local SOEs only appear in the tertiary industry rather than in the primary and secondary industries.

As mentioned above, the tertiary industry has fewer problems with competition and overcapacity. Therefore, we argue that local governments are rational in making more intervention in central and local SOEs in the tertiary industry than in the non-tertiary industry. Fourth, in the highly competitive primary and secondary industries, non-SOE investment is highly procyclical during recessions but less so during economic booms. In contrast, in the less competitive tertiary industry, non-SOE investment is slightly procyclical. These phenomena could be explained by the market-oriented behaviors of non-SOEs.

Cyclical investment behaviors of enterprises with different ownerships: Regional heterogeneity

China is a vast country, and subsequently, there are regional differences in terms of economic development, possibly causing differences in the investment behaviors of companies in different regions. This study uses four dummy variables to account for such differences: *east*, *northeast*, *mid*, and *west*, which represent the eastern, northeastern, middle, and western regions, respectively. If a company is in one of the four regions, the corresponding dummy variable will be given the value of 1, and the other three dummies for the other three regions will be 0. Results are shown in Table A1, from which we draw the following main conclusions.

First, only enterprises in the middle region have expansion-biased investment behaviors. Second, only SOEs in the middle region exhibit a tendency for expansion-biased investment behaviors. Third, only central SOEs in the western region and local SOEs in the middle and western regions are expansion-biased in terms of investment. Although central SOEs in the middle region show an expansion bias during economic recessions, their expansion bias is not obvious during prosperity. Why do local governments in the middle and western regions intervene differently from those in the eastern and northeastern regions during recessions? One possible explanation is that in a recession, local governments generally have two choices: implement conventional countercyclical fiscal policies or implement unconventional countercyclical quasi-fiscal policies in order to expand investment by SOEs.

For the local governments in the eastern and northeastern regions, it may be concluded through research and judgment that the implementation of conventional countercyclical fiscal policies can maintain stability during economic recessions, and there is no need to start unconventional countercyclical quasi-fiscal policies. As for local governments in the middle and western regions, they may conclude from analysis that during economic recessions, the implementation of conventional countercyclical fiscal policies is not enough to maintain economic stability, and an unconventional countercyclical quasi-fiscal policy should be initiated. Finally, there is a clear difference between the investment behaviors of non-SOEs and SOEs. In any region, non-SOEs have not exhibited countercyclical investment behaviors during recessions.

Local growth targets and the expansion-biased investment behavior of SOEs

To explore the impact of local growth targets on corporate investment, especially that of SOE cyclical investment, we introduce a local growth targets variable into the equations. Please see Table 8 for the estimation. By analyzing the results in Table 8, we find that the investment behaviors of central and local SOEs are closely linked with local growth targets during recessions: the higher the local growth targets, the greater the countercyclical investment of

Table 8. Local growth targets and the expansion-bias investment behavior of SOEs.

Dependent variable	$lnInvest_{i,t}$		
	(1)	(2)	(3)
$lnInvest_{i,t-1}$	0.23^{***}	0.25^{**}	0.26^{***}
	(0.000)	(0.050)	(0.000)
$Goal_{jt}$	5.78^{*}	18.33	6.68^{*}
	(0.060)	(0.173)	(0.051)
$Gap_{jt} \times Recession_{jt} \times Goal_{jt}$	-146.41^{***}	-234.60^{*}	-177.13^{***}
	(0.005)	(0.056)	(0.004)
$Gap_{jt} \times Boom_{jt} \times Goal_{jt}$	13.89	−128.59	57.66
	(0.750)	(0.406)	(0.253)
Year	Yes	Yes	Yes
Firm	Yes	Yes	Yes
Industry	Yes	Yes	Yes
Sample	SOEs	Central SOEs	Local SOEs
N	6,951	1,867	5,084
AR(1)	0.000	0.000	0.000
AR(2)	0.155	0.419	0.423
Hansen Test	0.144	0.374	0.319

Notes: (1) p values are displayed in parentheses; (2) *, **, and *** indicate significance at 10%, 5%, and 1% levels, respectively; (3) $lnInvest_{i,t-1}$, $Gap_{jt} \times Recession_{jt} \times Goal_{jt}$, and $Gap_{jt} \times Boom_{jt} \times Goal_{jt}$ are endogenous variables, and the rest are exogenous variables; (4) all other variables are controlled.

central SOEs than that of local SOEs. This shows that the intervention intensity of local governments in central SOEs is higher than that in local SOEs during economic recessions.

However, such linkage is not obvious during economic booms. In other words, the influence of growth targets on central and local SOEs mainly occurs during recessions. A plausible explanation is that local governments refrain from intervention in central and local SOEs during economic booms because they believe that the increase in non-SOE investment is sufficient to achieve growth goals. Therefore, there is no need to intervene in the investment of central and local SOEs. In summary, Hypothesis 3, that local growth targets have a stronger influence on the expansion-biased investment behaviors of SOEs during economic recessions than boom periods in the macro-control system with Chinese characteristics, is supported.

Credit channels for government intervention in SOE investment

We have further expanded on the basis of Table 8 in order to test Hypothesis 4: SOEs in regions with higher economic growth targets will receive more bank credits during economic recession periods than in boom periods. Considering that the bank credit of the current year can match investment, we follow the approach of Lu *et al.* (2009) to use two variables to measure bank credit: (1) total loans ($Loan_{i,t}$): (long-term loans at the end of the period + short-term loans at the end of the period + long-term loans with less than one year to maturity at the end of the period – long-term loans at the beginning of the period – short-term loans at the beginning of the period – long-term loans with less than one year to maturity at the beginning of the period)/total assets at the beginning of the period; and (2) long-term loans ($LLoan_{i,t}$): (long-term loans at the end of current period – long-term loans at the beginning of current period)/total assets at the beginning of the period.

Table 9 results from using the first variable. Column (1) shows that during a period of economic recession, the higher the local growth targets, the more bank credit the SOEs in the region can obtain. However, this situation is not observed during economic booms. That is, the SOEs in the region with higher local economic growth goals do not get more bank credit during economic booms. All the above prove that bank credit is the means of intervention taken by local governments to achieve the economic growth target during economic recessions, which verifies Hypothesis 4.

Columns (2)–(3) of Table 9 show that Hypothesis 4 holds for both central and local SOEs. In particular, during a period of economic recession, the higher the local growth targets, the more loans the central SOEs can obtain than the local SOEs, which supports the conclusion in Table 8. As mentioned above, during an economic

Table 9. Credit channels for government intervention in SOEs investment: Total loans.

Dependent variable	$Loan_{i,t}$		
	(1)	(2)	(3)
$Loan_{i,t-1}$	0.07^{***}	0.01	0.07^{***}
	(0.000)	(0.690)	(0.001)
$Goal_{jt}$	0.27	1.02	0.23
	(0.157)	(0.135)	(0.266)
$Gap_{jt} \times Recession_{jt} \times Goal_{jt}$	-10.26^{*}	-27.91^{**}	-12.19^{*}
	(0.078)	(0.042)	(0.071)
$Gap_{jt} \times Boom_{jt} \times Goal_{jt}$	3.10	2.41	5.18
	(0.427)	(0.801)	(0.245)
Year	Yes	Yes	Yes
Firm	Yes	Yes	Yes
Industry	Yes	Yes	Yes
Sample	SOEs	Central SOEs	Local SOEs
N	6,951	1,867	5,084
AR(1)	0.000	0.000	0.000
AR(2)	0.355	0.694	0.322
Hansen Test	0.794	0.253	0.105

Notes: (1) p values are displayed in parentheses; (2) *, **, and *** indicate significance at 10%, 5%, and 1% levels, respectively; (3) $Loan_{i,t-1}$, $Gap_{jt} \times Recession_{jt} \times Goal_{jt}$, $Gap_{jt} \times Boom_{jt} \times Goal_{jt}$ are endogenous variables, and the rest are exogenous variables; (4) refer to Lu *et al.* (2009), control variables include size, ROA and capital intensity.

recession, the higher the local growth targets, the greater the countercyclical investment of central SOEs than the countercyclical investment of local SOEs.

Table 10 is the result of adopting the second indicator, and the conclusion is consistent with Table 9.

Conclusions and Policy Implications

This study initiates the theoretical and empirical studies of the cyclical investment behaviors of Chinese enterprises with different

Table 10. Credit channels for government intervention in SOEs Investment: Long-term loans.

	$LLoan_{i,t}$		
Dependent variable	(1)	(2)	(3)
$LLoan_{i,t-1}$	0.02	0.01	0.02
	(0.402)	(0.780)	(0.566)
$Goal_{jt}$	0.19*	0.75**	0.20
	(0.099)	(0.045)	(0.115)
$Gap_{jt} \times Recession_{jt} \times Goal_{jt}$	−6.55**	−15.86*	−7.54 **
	(0.045)	(0.051)	(0.042)
$Gap_{jt} \times Boom_{jt} \times Goal_{jt}$	−0.64	−2.67	0.89
	(0.766)	(0.588)	(0.724)
Year	Yes	Yes	Yes
Firm	Yes	Yes	Yes
Industry	Yes	Yes	Yes
Sample	SOEs	Central SOEs	Local SOEs
N	6,951	1,867	5,084
AR(1)	0.000	0.000	0.000
AR(2)	0.861	0.580	0.686
Hansen Test	0.473	0.441	0.380

Notes: (1) p values are displayed in parentheses; (2) *, **, and *** indicate significance at 10%, 5%, and 1% levels, respectively; (3) $LLoan_{i,t-1}$, $Gap_{jt} \times Recession_{jt} \times Goal_{jt}$, $Gap_{jt} \times Boom_{jt} \times Goal_{jt}$ are endogenous variables, and the rest are exogenous variables; (4) refer to Lu *et al.* (2009), control variables include size, ROA and capital intensity.

ownership and draws the following main conclusions. First, non-SOE investment has a procyclical tendency, indicating that decision-making is market-oriented. Second, the investment behaviors of SOEs are expansion-biased, which is mainly caused by the expansion-biased investment behaviors of central and local SOEs. Third, the expansion-biased investment of central and local SOEs mainly goes to the tertiary industry rather than to the primary and secondary industries. Considering that the tertiary industry has less competition and less severe overcapacity problems, we argue for the validity of the local government's rationale for greater intervention in tertiary industry SOEs than in non-tertiary industry SOEs.

Fourth, only central SOEs in the western region and local SOEs in the middle and western regions show expansion-biased investment behaviors. Although SOEs in the middle region show an expansion bias during economic recessions, such expansion bias is not obvious during prosperity. Why do local governments in the middle and western regions intervene differently from those in the eastern and northeastern regions during economic recessions? One possible explanation is as follows: local governments in the eastern and northeastern regions may judge through research that it is sufficient to maintain economic stability by implementing conventional countercyclical fiscal policies during economic recessions and that there is no need to start unconventional countercyclical quasi-fiscal policies; as for local governments in the middle and western regions, a necessary analysis may lead them to a different conclusion that during economic recessions, the implementation of conventional countercyclical fiscal policies is not enough to maintain economic stability and an unconventional countercyclical quasi-fiscal policy should be initiated. Finally, during economic recessions, the higher the local growth targets, the more bank credit central and local SOEs can obtain, and the more pronounced the expansion-biased investment.

The study shows that, apart from the countercyclical fiscal policy implemented by the central and local governments (Fang and Zhang, 2009), the quasi-fiscal effect of central and local SOE investment is also key to the Chinese economy quickly recovering from recessions. According to the report delivered at the 19th National Congress of the Communist Party, China will, "improve the systems for managing different types of state assets, and reform the system of authorized operation of state capital." In the state-owned sector, China will, "step up improved distribution, structural adjustment, and strategic reorganization." The country will work "to ensure state assets maintain and increase their value, and support state capital in becoming stronger, doing better, and growing bigger." This study provides an important justification for the central government's decision to make SOEs stronger, bigger, and better. This means that when central and local governments can no longer stabilize the economy by relying solely on fiscal policies during a recession, they could intervene in the investment of central and local SOEs to safeguard macroeconomic stability and growth, respectively. It suggests that both the countercyclical fiscal policies of the central and local governments and the quasi-fiscal policy functions of investment by central and local SOEs have become indispensable components of the Chinese-style macro-control system.

We believe that when the central and local governments are hit by a recession and fiscal policies prove too difficult to stabilize the economy, they can intervene in the investment of central and local SOEs to ensure macroeconomic stability and growth. Our proposal is highly consistent with the ideas of the "Thought on Socialism with Chinese Characteristics for a New Era of Xi Jinping" (Publicity Department of the CPC Central Committee, 2019).

"The Thought on Socialism with Chinese Characteristics for a New Era of Xi Jinping" (2019) clearly states the following points:

> Our country implements the socialist market economic system, and we must continue to give full play to the superiority of the socialist system and the active role of the party and government.
>
> To better play the role of the government is not to give more play to the role of the government, but to manage those matters that the market cannot control or cannot control well, while ensuring that the market plays a decisive role.
>
> The responsibilities and roles of the government are mainly to maintain macroeconomic stability, strengthen and optimize public services, ensure fair competition, strengthen market supervision, maintain market order, promote sustainable development, promote common prosperity, and make up for market failures.

Given that one of the main functions of the government is to maintain macroeconomic stability and make up for market failures if the fiscal policies of the central and local governments fail to stabilize the macroeconomy (for example, restricted by the deficit rate), it indicates that China has experienced a severe economic recession. In this case, it is essential that the central and local governments adopt some unconventional policy tools to maintain macroeconomic stability. This chapter reveals that central and local SOE investment can be used as a quasi-fiscal policy tool or an unconventional policy tool to play a role in stabilizing the macroeconomy. Therefore, incorporating such investment into the Chinese-style macro-control system importantly demonstrates the merits of adherence to the supreme socialist system, giving greater play to the role of the government.[4]

Acknowledgments

This research was supported by the Fundamental Research Funds for the Central Universities of China. In addition, we would like to thank the editor and the reviewers for their valuable suggestions.

Endnotes

1. We formally define the periodicity of enterprise investment. If the enterprise investment increases during economic recession, decreases during economic prosperity, and is conducive to smoothing the economic cycle, then enterprise investment is said to be countercyclical. On the contrary, if the investment of enterprises declines in the economic recession and rises during economic prosperity, then enterprise investment is not conducive to flattening the economic cycle, and the investment of enterprises is procyclical. If enterprise investment rises during both recessions and prosperity, then the enterprise investment is expansion-biased or is countercyclical during economic recessions (conducive to economic stability) and pro-cyclical during economic prosperity (not conducive to economic stability).
2. Following Ravn and Uhlig (2002), the parameter is set at 6.25.
3. The period when the output gap is greater than 0 is economic prosperity period, while the output gap is less than 0 is economic recession period.
4. With the spread of the global epidemic, in order to prevent a great economic recession, if conventional macro-control tools are not effective, the Chinese government can consider using unconventional quasi-fiscal policy tools.

References

Abdellatif, M. and Tran-Nam, B. 2016. Tax policy challenges in an era of political transition: The case of Egypt. *Ejournal of Tax Research*, 14(3): 683–706.

Alesina, A., Ardagna S., Nicoletti, G., and Schiantarelli, F. 2005. Regulation and investment. *Journal of the European Economic Association*, 3(4): 791–825.

Alesina, A., Campante, F.R., and Tabellini, G. 2008. Why is fiscal policy often procyclical? *Journal of the European Economic Association*, 6(5): 1006–1036.

Allen, F., Qian, J.Q., and Gu, X. 2017. An overview of China's financial system. *Annual Review of Financial Economics*, 9: 191–231.

Andersen, A.L. and Holbøll Westh Nielsen, L. 2010. Fiscal transparency and procyclical fiscal policy. EPRU Working Paper Series, No. 2010-01. Retrieved from: https://www.econstor.eu/handle/10419/82132.

Bernanke, B.S. and Gertler, M.L. 1989. Agency cost, net worth and business fluctuations. *American Economic Review*, 79: 14–31.

Bernanke, B.S., Gertler, M.L., and Gilchrist, S. 1996. The financial accelerator and the flight to quality. *Review of Economics and Statistics*, 78: 1–15.

Bernier, L. 2014. Public enterprises as policy instruments: The importance of public entrepreneurship. *Journal of Economic Policy Reform*, 17(3): 253–266.

Bernier, L. and Reeves, E. 2018. The continuing importance of state-owned enterprise in the twenty-first century: Challenges for public policy. *Annals of Public and Cooperative Economics*, 89(3): 453–458.

Bertay, A.C., Demirgüç-Kunt, A., and Huizinga, H. 2015. Bank ownership and credit over the business cycle: Is lending by state banks less procyclical? *Journal of Banking & Finance*, 50: 326–339.

Bertero, E. and Rondi, L. 2002. Does a switch of budget regimes affect investment and managerial discretion of state-owned enterprises? Evidence from Italian firms. *Journal of Comparative Economics*, 30(4): 836–863.

Bontempi, M.E., Golinelli, R., and Parigi, G. 2010. Why demand uncertainty curbs investment: Evidence from a panel of Italian manufacturing firms. *Journal of Macroeconomics*, 32: 218–238.

Brandt, L. and Li, H. 2003. Bank discrimination in transition economies: Ideology, information, or incentives? *Journal of Comparative Economics*, 31(3): 387–413.

Brei, M. and Schclarek, A. 2013. Public bank lending in times of crisis. *Journal of Financial Stability*, 9(4): 820–830.

Chen X.G. 2016. Fiscal pressure, tax administration and regional inequality. *Social Sciences in China (Zhong Guo She Hui Ke Xue)*, 4: 53–70, 206 (in Chinese).

Cheng, Z.M., Xia, X.P., and Yu, M.G. 2008. Government intervention, pyramid structure and investment of local state-owned listed companies. *Management World (Guan Li Shi Jie)*, 9: 37–47 (in Chinese).

Chen, S., Sun, Z., Tang, S., and Wu, D. 2011. Government intervention and investment efficiency: Evidence from China. *Journal of Corporate Finance*, 17(2): 259–271.

Chen, D., Kong, M.Q., and Wang, H.J. 2016. Give me a peach and repay it with a plum: Business cycle and tax avoidance of state-owned enterprises. *Management World (Guan Li Shi Jie)*, 5: 46–63 (in Chinese).

Coleman, N. and Feler, L. 2015. Bank ownership, lending and local economic performance during the 2008~2009 financial crisis. *Journal of Monetary Economics*, 71: 50–66.

Cuadra, G., Sanchez, J.M., and Sapriza, H. 2010. Fiscal policy and default risk in emerging markets. *Review of Economic Dynamics*, 13(2): 452–469.

Dai, X. and Jin, B. 2014. Intra-product specialization, institution quality and export sophistication. *Economic Research Journal (Jing Ji Yan Jiu)*, 49(7): 4–17, 43 (in Chinese).

Dangl, T. and Wu, Y. 2016. Corporate investment over the business cycle. *Review of Finance*, 20(1): 337–371.

Fan, J.P.H., Titman, S., and Twite, G. 2012. An international comparison of capital structure and debt maturity choices. *Journal of Financial and Quantitative Analysis*, 47(1): 23–56.

Fang, J.X. 2010. Are private listed companies really facing bank loan discrimination? *Management World (Guan Li Shi Jie)*, 11: 123–131 (in Chinese).

Fang, H.S. and Zhang, J. 2009. Chinese local government, soft budget constraint and expansion-biased fiscal behavior. *Economic Research Journal (Jing Ji Yan Jiu)*, 46(12): 4–16 (in Chinese).

Fang, H.S. and Zhang, J. 2013. Grabbing hand, helping hand and tax-exceeding-GDP growth. *Economic Research Journal (Jing Ji Yan Jiu)*, 48(03): 108–121 (in Chinese).

Fang, H.S., Bao, Y.X., and Zhang, J. 2017. Asymmetric reform bonus: The impact of VAT pilot expansion on China's corporate total tax burden. *China Economic Review*, 46: S17–S34.

Florio, M. 2013. Rethinking on public enterprise: Editorial introduction and some personal remarks on the research agenda. *International Review of Applied Economics*, 27(2): 135–149.

Florio, M. 2014. Contemporary public enterprises: Innovation, accountability, governance. *Journal of Economic Policy Reform*, 17(3): 201–208.

Florio, M. and Fecher, F. 2011. The future of public enterprises: Contributions to a new discourse. *Annals of Public and Cooperative Economics*, 82(4): 361–373.

Frankel, J.A., Vegh, C.A., and Vuletin, G. 2013. On graduation from fiscal procyclicality. *Journal of Development Economics*, 100: 32–47.

Furceri, D. and Karras, G. 2011. Average tax rate cyclicality in OECD countries: A test of three fiscal policy theories. *Southern Economic Journal*, 77(4): 958–972.

Gallup, J.L. 2020. Added-variable plots for panel-data estimation. *The Stata Journal*, 20(1): 30–50.

Ghosal, V. 1991. Demand uncertainty and the capital-labor ratio: Evidence from the U.S. manufacturing sector. *Review of Economics and Statistics*, 73: 157–161.

Gong, G. 2019. Understand the macro-control with Chinese characteristics. Observer network, 03-08. Retrieved from: https://www.guancha.cn/GongGang/2019_\03_08_492779.shtml.

Guo, Q. W. and Lv, B.Y. 2011. The influence of tax on factor income distribution. *Economic Research Journal (Jing Ji Yan Jiu)*, 46(6): 16–30 (in Chinese).

Guo, J. and Ma, G.R. 2019. Macroeconomic stability and state-owned economic investment: Mechanism and evidence. *Management World (Guan Li Shi Jie)*, 35(9): 49–64, 199 (in Chinese).

Guo, Q.W. and Zhao, X.J. 2012. Local government investment competition and economic fluctuation. *The Journal of World Economy (Shi Jie Jing Ji)*, 5: 3–21 (in Chinese).

Hansen, B.E. 1999. Threshold effects in non-dynamic panels: Estimation, testing, and inference. *Journal of Econometrics*, 93(2): 345–368.

He, W. and Kyaw, N.A. 2018. Ownership structure and investment decisions of Chinese SOEs. *Research in International Business and Finance*, 43: 48–57.

Hercowitz, Z. and Strawczynski, M. 2004. Cyclical ratcheting in government spending. *Review of Economics and Statistics*, 86(1): 353–361.

Hong, Z., Zhang, L., and Xiao, R. 2021. Industrial upgrading, financial structure, and China's economic growth. *Management World (Guan Li Shi Jie)*, 37(8): 58–88 (in Chinese).

Ilzetzki, E. and Vegh, C.A. 2008. Procyclical fiscal policy in developing countries: Truth or fiction? NBER Working Paper, No. 14191. Retrieved from: https://www.nber.org/papers/w14191.

Jaimovich, D. and Panizza, U. 2007. Procyclicality or reverse causality? IDB Working Paper, No. 501. Retrieved from: https://ssrn.com/abstract=1820869.

Kaminsky, G., Reinhart, C., and Vegh, C.A. 2004. When it rains, it pours: Procyclical capital flows and macroeconomic policies. *NBER Macroeconomics Annual*, 19: 11–82.

Li, H.B. and Zhou, L.A. 2005. Political turnover and economic performance: The incentive role of personnel control in China. *Journal of Public Economics*, 89(9–10): 1743–1762.

Li, Y.Y. and Shen, Y.P. 2010. Vertical distribution of fiscal revenue and its effect on balancing economic growth. *Social Sciences in China (Zhong Guo She Hui Ke Xue)*, 6: 108–124, 222–223 (in Chinese).

Lin, L.W. and Milhaupt, C.J. 2013. We are the (national) champions: Understanding the mechanisms of state capitalism in China. *Stanford Law Review*, 65: 697–761.

Liu, Y.C. 2001. On the macroscopic efficiency of state-owned enterprises — theory and its verification. *Social Sciences in China (Zhong Guo She Hui Ke Xue)*, 5: 69–81, 206 (in Chinese).

Liu, R. and Wang, Y. 2010. The role of state-owned enterprises in the macro-economic control and adjustment under the dissension of "the stated sector forward as the private sector backward". *China Review of Political Economy (Zheng Zhi Jing Ji Xue Ping Lun)*, 1(3): 37–50 (in Chinese).

Lu, Z.F., Zhu, J.G., and Fan, Z. 2009. Monetary contractions, bank discrimination and the wealth loss of non-state listed firms' investors. *Journal of Financial Research (Jin Rong Yan Jiu)*, 8: 124–136 (in Chinese).

Lv, B.Y., Ma, G.R., and Mao, J. 2016. Tax sharing and tax rate: From government to entrepreneurs. *Economic Research Journal (Jing Ji Yan Jiu)*, 51(7): 13–28 (in Chinese).

Millward, R. 2005. *Private and Public Enterprise in Europe: Energy, Telecommunications and Transport, 1830–1990.* UK: Cambridge University Press.

Millward, R. 2011. Public enterprise in the modern western world: An historical analysis. *Annals of Public and Cooperative Economics*, 82(4): 375–398.

Peeters, M. 2001. Do demand and price uncertainty affect Belgian and Spanish corporate investment? *Louvain Economic Review*, 67: 235–255.

Publicity Department of the CPC Central Committee. 2019. *The Thought on Socialism with Chinese Characteristics for a New Era of Xi Jinping*. China: Learning Press, People's Publishing House (in Chinese).

Putniņš, T.J. 2015. Economics of state-owned enterprises. *International Journal of Public Administration*, 38(11): 815–832.

Ravn, M.O. and Uhlig, H. 2002. On adjusting the Hodrick-Prescott filter for the frequency of observations. *The Review of Economics and Statistics*, 84: 371–375.

Riascos, A. and Vegh, C.A. 2003. Procyclical government spending in developing countries: The role of capital market imperfections. IMF Staff Papers. Retrieved from: http://citeseerx.ist.psu.edu/viewdoc/download?doi=10.1.1.586.5801&rep=rep1&type=pdf.

Roodman, D. 2009. How to do xtabond2: An introduction to difference and system GMM in Stata. *The Stata Journal*, 9(1): 86–136.

Sorensen, B.E., Lisa, W.U., and Yosha, O. 2001. Output fluctuations and fiscal policy: US state and local governments 1978–1994. *European Economic Review*, 45(7): 1271–1310.

Srebrnik, N. and Strawczynski, M. 2016. Cyclicality of taxes and external debt. *Applied Economics*, 48: 4622–4634.

Strawczynski, M. 2014. Cyclicality of statutory tax rates. *Israel Economic Review*, 11(1): 67–96.

Sturzenegger, F. and Werneck, R. 2006. Fiscal federalism and procyclical spending: The cases of Argentina and Brazil. *Económica*, 52: 151–194.

Sun, Z., Liu, F.W., and Li, Z.Q. 2005. Degree of marketization, government intervention and corporate debt maturity structure: Empirical evidence from listed companies in China. *Economic Research Journal (Jing Ji Yan Jiu)*, 5: 52–63 (in Chinese).

Szarzec, K. and Nowara, W. 2017. The economic performance of state-owned enterprises in Central and Eastern Europe. *Post-Communist Economies*, 29(3): 375–391.

Talvi, E. and Vegh, C.A. 2005. Tax base variability and procyclical fiscal policy in developing countries. *Journal of Development Economics*, 78(1): 156–190.

Tan, X.F. and Zhang, W.J. 2021. Fiscal decentralization, local government behavior and divergence of firm leverage ratio. *Economic Research Journal (Jing Ji Yan Jiu)*, 56(6): 76–92 (in Chinese).

Tan, Y.Y., Huang, Y.P., and Wo, W.T. 2016. Zombie firms and the crowding-out of private investment in China. *Asian Economic Papers*, 15(3): 32–55.

Tang, X.S., Zhou, X.S., and Ma, R.J. 2010. Government intervention, GDP growth and local SOE overinvestment. *Journal of Financial Research (Jin Rong Yan Jiu)*, 8: 33–48 (in Chinese).

Thynne, I. 2011. Ownership as an instrument of policy and understanding in the public sphere: Trends and research agenda. *Policy Studies*, 32(3): 183–197.

Vegh, C.A. and Vuletin, G. 2015. How is tax policy conducted over the business cycle? *American Economic Journal: Economic Policy*, 7(3): 327–370.

Walter, C. and Howie, F. 2012. *Red Capitalism: The Fragile Financial Foundation of China's Extraordinary Rise.* US: John Wiley & Sons.

Wang, W.C. 2011. The influence of different ownership on economic growth. *China Soft Science (Zhong Guo Ruan Ke Xue)*, 6: 178–185 (in Chinese).

Wang, Y.Z. and Song, M. 2014. Macroeconomic uncertainty, demand for financing and corporate investment. *Economic Research Journal (Jing Ji Yan Jiu)*, 49(02): 4–17 (in Chinese).

Wang, W.C., Shen, H.W., and Wang, Y.H. 2013. Study on the driving effect of investment by state-owned economy on investment by non-state-owned economy. *China Soft Science (Zhong Guo Ruan Ke Xue)*, 7: 132–144 (in Chinese).

Wang, Y.Z., Chen, C.R., and Huang, Y.S. 2014. Economic policy uncertainty and corporate investment: Evidence from China. *Pacific-Basin Finance Journal*, 26(3): 227–243.

Wang, Y.C., Zhang, L., and Zheng, X.Y. 2018. Is quasi-fiscal policy useful: An evaluation of the effect of central investment on local investment. *Management World (Guan Li Shi Jie)*, 34(8): 67–83, 191–192 (in Chinese).

Wei, M.H. and Liu, J.H. 2007. Dividends, governance factors and overinvestment in state-owned enterprises. *Management World (Guan Li Shi Jie)*, 4: 88–95 (in Chinese).

Xu, X.X. and Liang, J.X. 2014. Strategic adjustment of growth target. *Economic Research Journal (Jing Ji Yan Jiu)*, 49(1): 27–40 (in Chinese).

Yu, W., Wang, M.J., and Jin, X.R. 2012. Political connection and financing constraints: Information effect and resource effect. *Economic Research Journal (Jing Ji Yan Jiu)*, 47(9): 125–139 (in Chinese).

Zhang, M., Wu, L.S., and Wang, Y.P. 2010. State-owned equity, corporate performance and investment behavior. *Journal of Financial Research (Jin Rong Yan Jiu)*, 12: 115–130 (in Chinese).

Zhang, Y. 2009. On the leading role of the state-owned economy. *Economic Perspectives (Jing Ji Xue Dong Tai)*, 12: 46–49 (in Chinese).

Zhao, Y.Q., Zhang, Y., and Hu, W.J. 2016. State-ownership, economic cycle and corporate investment comovement. *Research on Economics and Management (Jing Ji Yu Guan Li Yan Jiu)*, 37(11): 11–21 (in Chinese).

Zhong, H.Y., Ran, M.S., and Wen, S. 2010. Government intervention, insider control and corporate investment. *Management World (Guan Li Shi Jie)*, 7: 98–108 (in Chinese).

Zhou, L.A., Li, H.B., and Chen, Y. 2005. Relative performance assessment: An empirical study on promotion of local officials in China. *China Journal of Economics (Jing Ji Xue Bao)*, 1(1): 83–96 (in Chinese).

Zhou, L.A., Liu, C., Li, X., and Weng, X. 2015. Layer by layer and official incentive. *World Economic Papers (Shi Jie Jing Ji Wen Hui)*, 1: 217–248 (in Chinese).

Zwick, E. and Mahon, J. 2017. Tax policy and heterogeneous investment behavior. *American Economic Review*, 107(1): 217–248.

Appendix

Table A1. Cyclical investment behaviors of enterprises with different ownership: Regional heterogeneity.

Dependent variable	$lnInvest_{i,t}$				
	(1)	(2)	(3)	(4)	(5)
$lnInvest_{i,t-1}$	0.21^{***}	0.17^{***}	0.20^{***}	0.28^{***}	0.28^{***}
	(0.000)	(0.000)	(0.000)	(0.000)	(0.000)
$Gap_{jt} \times Recession_{jt} \times east$	6.59	−6.81	−0.93	−6.60	13.09
	(0.280)	(0.461)	(0.960)	(0.460)	(0.125)
$Gap_{jt} \times Recession_{jt} \times northeast$	4.00	−7.48	4.35	−9.84	14.62^{**}
	(0.402)	(0.282)	(0.619)	(0.182)	(0.042)
$Gap_{jt} \times Recession_{jt} \times mid$	-11.14^{**}	-11.19^{**}	-25.16^{*}	-9.25^{*}	−4.75
	(0.022)	(0.046)	(0.063)	(0.063)	(0.610)
$Gap_{jt} \times Recession_{jt} \times west$	−3.57	−10.44	-24.95^{*}	-16.17^{**}	6.54
	(0.514)	(0.139)	(0.094)	(0.024)	(0.458)

Table A1. (*Continued*)

Dependent variable	$lnInvest_{i,t}$				
	(1)	(2)	(3)	(4)	(5)
$Gap_{jt} \times Boom_{jt} \times east$	−4.84	−0.77	−18.08	6.03	2.81
	(0.338)	(0.905)	(0.169)	(0.377)	(0.712)
$Gap_{jt} \times Boom_{jt} \times northeast$	3.87	3.05	5.26	3.83	−3.02
	(0.556)	(0.763)	(0.682)	(0.683)	(0.764)
$Gap_{jt} \times Boom_{jt} \times mid$	20.57***	14.33**	20.70	20.57***	8.91
	(0.000)	(0.018)	(0.223)	(0.001)	(0.267)
$Gap_{jt} \times Boom_{jt} \times west$	8.42	0.75	39.77**	11.69*	14.94**
	(0.100)	(0.918)	(0.024)	(0.076)	(0.040)
Year	Yes	Yes	Yes	Yes	Yes
Firm	Yes	Yes	Yes	Yes	Yes
Industry	Yes	Yes	Yes	Yes	Yes
Sample	Total	SOEs	Central SOEs	Local SOEs	Non-SOEs
N	14,068	7,007	1,870	5,137	7,061
AR(1)	0.000	0.000	0.000	0.000	0.000
AR(2)	0.106	0.568	0.327	0.128	0.295
Hansen Test	0.209	0.414	0.315	0.157	0.727

Notes: (1) *p* values are displayed in parentheses; (2) *, **, and *** indicate significance at 10%, 5%, and 1% levels, respectively; (3) $lnInvest_{i,t-1}$, $Gap_{jt} \times Recession_{jt} \times east$, $Gap_{jt} \times Recession_{jt} \times northeast$, $Gap_{jt} \times Recession_{jt} \times mid$, $Gap_{jt} \times Recession_{jt} \times west$, $Gap_{jt} \times Boom_{jt} \times east$, $Gap_{jt} \times Boom_{jt} \times northeast$, $Gap_{jt} \times Boom_{jt} \times mid$ and $Gap_{jt} \times Boom_{jt} \times west$ are endogenous variables, and the rest are exogenous variables; (4) all other variables are controlled.

https://doi.org/10.1142/9789819815241_0018

Chapter 18

WHAT MAKES CHINA'S INFLATION SO DIFFERENT?

Qu Feng*, Shihao Zhou†, and An Dong‡

Economics Division, Nanyang Technological University, Singapore
**qfeng@ntu.edu.sg*
†SHIHAO002@e.ntu.edu.sg
‡DONG0128@e.ntu.edu.sg

Abstract

In this chapter, we characterize China's inflation time series at different frequencies and compare the results with those of other advanced and emerging economies. This chapter first provides a comprehensive picture of inflation in China based on quarterly data from 1993Q1 to 2022Q2. Then, we examine the characteristics of China's inflation rate and compare them with those from OECD countries and additional developing nations. There are three major findings in this chapter. First, China has sustained a fast economic growth with low inflation rate, exhibiting a negative correlation, which is not observed in both advanced and emerging economies. Second, more volatile inflation does not lead to higher inflation rate in China. In contrast, we observe positive relationship in other countries. Lastly, while China's CPI inflation does not exhibit a strong correlation with that of others, its PPI is highly correlated with that of the US since 1996.

Introduction

Inflation has been an essential topic in the context of macroeconomic studies (Bernanke and Mishkin, 1997; Bryan and Cecchetti, 1993, 1994; Friedman, 1968; Reis and Watson, 2010). For instance, in addressing the price puzzle in a vector autoregressive (VAR) model setting, Sims (1992) and Bernanke *et al.* (2005) suggest improved measurement and factor-augmented models, respectively. Regarding the Phillips curve, Hazell *et al.* (2022) observe a flattening pattern in the US, while Stock and Watson (2020) argue it persists with filtered data. In examining the stationarity property of inflation rates, Lucas Jr (1972), Sargent (1971), and Culver and Papell (1997) found mixed results across countries, while Hendry (2001) notes UK's inflation is non-stationary. Finally, Cogley and Sargent (2001, 2015) and Cogley *et al.* (2010) explore inflation's mean, volatility, and persistence, with mixed findings across different measures and time periods.

As a conventional key macroeconomic indicator, it has been extensively explored in the literature. Nevertheless, most of the conclusions are drawn based on developed economies only. The existing literature only focuses on the inflation targeting (IT) regime in developing countries. Thus, there is lack of studies about the inflation and its dynamic with other macroeconomic variables in emerging economies. As the second largest economy in terms of economic size, China received more attention in the literature compared with its counterparts (Chen *et al.*, 2017; Gerlach and Peng, 2006; Mehrotra *et al.*, 2010; Narayan *et al.*, 2009; Scheibe and Vines, 2005; Zhang and Murasawa, 2012). Nonetheless, there is no complete investigation of the characteristics of China's inflation as well as its dynamic with other macroeconomic variables. Also, the comparison with other advanced and emerging economies is not well discussed.

Since 1978, China's open-door policy marks its modern economic history. From 1980 to 2020, China's average real GDP growth is almost 10%, while its inflation is maintained constantly low at 4.9%.[1] High GDP growth with low inflation rate seems to be the ideal economic situation to any economy. On the other hand, it is also common that many countries are practicing inflation targeting (IT) regime to address the overheating economy. Therefore, it seems that there is a tradeoff between economic development and inflation for most countries in world, including developing countries, such as Brazil, Mexico, and India. This triggers the question of what makes China's inflation so different from other countries? Interestingly, Nakamura *et al.* (2016) found that such unique relationship between economic growth and inflation in China in fact is attributed to the data quality issue. In particular, they show that inflation and output growth reported by the government are the smoothed version of actual statistics. In particular, inflation of China was overstated during the 1990s and understated in the 2000s, while the output growth was understated during the 1990s and overstated in the 2000s. This implies that the dynamics between inflation and output growth has been changing over time.

Furthermore, China's macroeconomic pattern has always been compared with countries like Japan. From 1950s to 1970s, Japan embraced substantial economic growth, while its economy stagnated in the next decades. In the context of China, it has consistently achieved a significantly strong economic growth rate over the past few decades. Nevertheless, economists have been pessimistic toward China's recent economic performance as it suffers from deflation and relatively low economic growth as a developing country. The inflation in Japan has been extensively discussed in the literature (Toyoda, 1997; Dees *et al.*, 2009; De Veirman, 2009; Smith, 2008). Therefore, we aim to characterize the macroeconomic patterns of China leveraging on the historical findings in Japan. In the context of emerging economies, IT proposed by Bernanke and Mishkin (1997) is one of the most important topics in the literature (Brito and Bystedt, 2010; Gonçalves and Salles, 2008). It has been further extended to the context of China by Lin and Ye (2019) and Xiong (2012).

To provide a more comprehensive picture of inflation in China, we first collect annual data from 1987 to 2021 at aggregate level. Then, we compare the essential properties of China's inflation data with those of OECD and other emerging economies. Furthermore, we conclude that the characteristics of China's inflation and its dynamic with key macroeconomic variables such as GDP growth are vastly different from the observations of both advanced and emerging economies. On one hand, China's inflation exhibits an I(1) process, which is consistent with the unit root hypothesis in the literature (Ball *et al.*, 1990; Nelson and Schwert, 1977). Also, it has sustained a fast economic growth with low inflation rate, which shows some similarities with that of other emerging economies. On the other hand, unlike both advanced and emerging economies, which have a positive relationship between inflation and economic growth, indicating a tradeoff between the two variables, China exhibits an inverse relationship. In particular, the tradeoff coefficient of –0.95 based on a time series regression suggests that an increase of GDP growth by 1% leads to almost the same amount of decrease in inflation rate, suggesting positive effect of economic growth on its domestic price level.

Overall, we find a negative and significant correlation between output growth and inflation in China at national level in this chapter. Nevertheless, the results are rather true instead of controversial in the context of China. First, China's economic growth leads to higher supply and hence, lower price level, within China and across the world. This is found to be the impact of China's growth on itself, as well as the world by Wang *et al.* (2021). Hence, this chapter contributes to the literature by exploring the underlying reasons about China's unique inflation patterns.

Next, our analysis shows no significant link between the volatility of inflation and the inflation rate itself within China, whereas a positive correlation exists between these two variables in other countries. This extends the findings of Narayan *et al.* (2009), who reported a negative correlation between inflation volatility and the inflation rate in China's earlier years. Our results suggest that this negative correlation has weakened over time.

Lastly, we discover that China's CPI inflation rate shares a weaker correlation with the global inflation landscape. Conversely, other major economies, such as the US, exhibit a robust correlation with countries that are either geographically proximate or economically connected. However, an interesting finding is that China's PPI inflation is highly correlated with that of the US since 1996.

The remainder of this chapter is structured as follows. In section "Data and Facts", we provide a comprehensive description of the data and facts, including an analysis of mean, volatility, persistence, unit root hypothesis, and a comparison of the inflation rate in China with those of other countries. In addition, we also discuss about the disaggregate level data in China. Section "Tradeoff between Economic Growth and Inflation" investigates tradeoff relationship between inflation and GDP growth and section "Correlation of Inflation Rates across Countries" explores the corss-country correlation of inflation rates. Lastly, section "Conclusion" concludes.

Data and Facts

Aggregate level

This chapter first aims to investigates China's inflation pattern at aggregate level. We first collect data of aggregate CPI, on a yearly basis (Previous Year = 100). The sample period is from 1987 to 2021. The dataset is collected from the World Bank database. We then split the full sample into three groups of subsamples, namely, 1987–1999, 2000–2010, and 2011–2021. Figure 1 presents the trend of aggregate CPI inflation over the sample period. Overall, China's inflation has been consistently low after joining the World Trade Organization (WTO) in 2001. We observe volatile fluctuations in 1980s and 1990s. Besides, we observe large dips in inflation around 2008 and 2021 from Figure 1. These are mainly due to the global financial crisis in 2008 and the outbreak of COVID-19 in 2019. On the other hand, the impact of the global financial crisis on China's inflation is significantly more substantial compared to that of the pandemic in 2019. However, the inflation bounced back quickly after the global financial crisis, while the negative impact of the pandemic is more persistent.

The results are corroborated by Table 1, where it displays the summary statistics for both inflation and GDP growth during both

Figure 1. China's CPI inflation from 1993 to 2022.

full sample and subsample periods. According to Batta *et al.* (2014), it is crucial to identify the fundamental characteristics of the inflation rate within a country, as it can differ from one country to another.

We observe that the average of inflation has been around 4.9% throughout the full sample period, implying a reasonably low domestic inflation rate. On the other hand, the GDP growth is around 9.1% on average from 1987 to 2021, a super high growth rate. During the subsample of 2000–2010, we observe an even lower average of inflation rate of 2.0%, associated with a larger mean of GDP growth rate of 10.4%, again showing a high GDP growth with a low inflation rate. Similarly, during 2011–2021, the mean inflation rate is still reasonably small (2.4%), while that of the GDP growth rate is 7.0%, showing a modest slowdown of the economy. On average, the inflation rate of China has been low over time, while the GDP growth has been consistently high. More specifically, China achieves a high economic growth even during the global financial crisis in 2008, while the pandemic since 2019 causes sizeable impact on its economic performance.

Table 1. Descriptive statistics in China and OECD countries.

		CPI Inflation				GDP Growth			
Country	Statistics	1987–2021	1987–1999	2000–2010	2011–2021	1987–2021	1987–1999	2000–2010	2011–2021
China	Mean	4.9	9.4	2.0	2.4	9.1	9.8	10.4	7.0
	SD	6.2	8.3	2.2	1.2	2.8	3.3	1.8	1.8
	Median	2.6	7.2	1.6	2.2	9.2	9.9	10.0	7.0
	AR(1) w/ constant	0.7	0.5	0.0	0.5	0.6	0.5	0.5	0.1
	AR(1) w/o constant	0.8	0.8	0.5	0.9	1.0	1.0	1.0	1.0
S Korea	Mean	3.6	5.6	3.1	1.6	5.4	8.1	5.1	2.7
	SD	2.3	2.3	0.8	1.1	3.8	4.5	2.3	1.3
	Median	2.9	5.7	2.8	1.3	5.2	9.3	5.2	2.9
US	Mean	2.6	3.3	2.5	2.0	2.5	3.4	2.0	2.1
	SD	1.2	1.1	1.2	1.2	1.8	1.3	1.9	2.0
	Median	2.7	3.0	2.8	1.8	2.7	3.7	2.7	2.3
India	Mean	7.3	9.3	6.1	6.2	6.0	5.9	6.5	5.4
	SD	3.0	2.7	3.0	2.4	2.9	2.3	2.1	4.2
	Median	6.7	9.0	4.3	5.1	6.5	5.9	7.9	6.5
Emerging	Mean	27.6	73.5	4.2	3.2	5.0	6.0	5.1	3.6
	SD	207.0	349.8	3.8	2.7	4.1	4.4	3.7	3.8

(*Continued*)

Table 1. *(Continued)*

Country	Statistics	CPI Inflation				GDP Growth			
		1987–2021	1987–1999	2000–2010	2011–2021	1987–2021	1987–1999	2000–2010	2011–2021
	SD excluding Brazil	4.9	6.3	3.8	2.6	4.1	4.4	3.8	3.7
	Median	3.8	6.4	3.5	2.8	5.2	6.2	5.3	4.1
OECD	Mean	10.1	23.1	3.6	2.0	2.7	3.2	2.7	2.1
	SD	60.5	99.6	5.0	2.2	3.3	2.8	3.6	3.4
	SD excluding outliers	4.4	6.3	2.1	1.3	3.0	2.5	2.8	3.4
	Median	2.5	4.5	2.6	1.7	2.8	3.4	2.9	2.2
		1960–1990	1961–1970	1971–1980	1981–1990	1960–1990	1961–1970	1971–1980	1981–1990
	Mean	5.5	5.4	9.1	2.1	6.2	9.6	4.5	4.5
	SD	4.4	1.3	5.7	1.4	3.5	3.3	2.7	1.0
	Median	4.9	5.3	8.0	2.1	5.0	10.9	4.5	4.5
Japan	AR(1) w/ constant	0.6	–0.2	0.4	0.7	0.5	–0.4	0.0	0.2
	AR(1) w/o constant	0.8	1.0	0.8	1.0	0.9	0.9	0.7	1.0

Note:

1. The statistics are computed based on annual data from 1987 to 2021.

Also, Table 1 presents the standard deviation of both inflation and GDP growth, indicating the changes of volatility over time. Before 2000, the inflation was extremely volatile, which is consistent with our findings in Figure 1. Also, the inflation volatility of 2.2 during 2000–2010 is almost doubled compared to that of 2011–2021, suggesting that the global financial crisis in 2008 led to higher volatility of price changes compared to the pandemic in 2019. In contrast, the GDP growth after 2000 was relatively stable as the standard deviations in 2000–2010 and 2011–2021 were 1.8 and 1.8, respectively. This indicates that the inflation in China is relatively more volatile compared to the GDP growth.

In addition, we observe that the AR(1) coefficient (with constant) is 0.7 for the full sample, which implies that the inflation is persistent in China. The persistence measure then declines from 0.5 before 2000 to 0 in the 2000s. Nevertheless, the persistence of 0.5 during 2011 and 2021 shows an increasing explaining power of the past inflation on the current values. Conversely, the past value of GDP growth from 1987 to 2021 explains about 62% of the current GDP growth. Furthermore, the persistence declines over time as it drops from 0.6 to 0.1 from 1987–1999 to 2011–2021.

Comparison with the OECD countries

Inflation in advanced economies or Western countries has been studied extensively. Hendry (2001) explores main determinants of inflation in the UK. He finds that factors such as excess demand for goods and services, world price inflation, and nominal money growth are essential to inflation, while excess money, debt, and labor demand are not important. Also, Bataa *et al.* (2014) found that France experiences significant changes in mean inflation, and the mean volatility of inflation in Italy, Japan, and the US varies over time. Furthermore, outliers in the inflation data seem to be severe in Canada, while those of Germany and the UK show seasonality.

The conventional Phillips curve theory implies that there must be a tradeoff between inflation and GDP growth. In other words, high economic growth must be accompanied with high inflation. In fact, Artis *et al.* (1995) found that there were a total of nine complete inflation cycles in the UK. Nevertheless, this relationship does not exist in China based on its historical data. Since the Phillips curve relationship is developed empirically based on advanced economies, here we first investigate the statistics in OECD countries.[2] In Table 1, we also display the descriptive statistics of CPI inflation and GDP growth in OECD countries.[3]

As shown in Table 1, we observe that the average inflation in OECD countries from 1987 to 2021 is 10.09%, which is more than two times greater than that of China. In contrast, the average GDP growth in those advanced economies is three times lower compared to the growth rate in China. Based on the subsamples after 2000, we also find that when the GDP growth is high during 2000–2010 (2.7%), its corresponding inflation rate is relatively higher (3.6%) compared to its counterpart. Similarly, lower GDP growth rate in 2011–2021 (2.1%) leads to lower inflation rate (2.0%).

Besides, we observe that the volatility of inflation in OECD countries is the highest in the 1980s and 1990s. Then, it substantially declined to 5.0 during 2000–2010. Furthermore, the volatility does not rise substantially during 2011–2021, suggesting that the pandemic in 2019 does not affect inflation volatility significant. These are consistent with the findings in China. However, the volatility of GDP growth is lower than inflation from 2000 to 2021, which shows different patterns compared to that of China.

Ciccarelli and Mojon (2010) show that OECD countries share a common factor that accounts for nearly 70% of their variance, using the data from 1960 to 2008. This clearly implies that global inflation is an important factor in determining national inflation. Conversely, we observe significantly different patterns of inflation in China, again indicating the unique features of China's inflation.

Comparison with other emerging countries

Unlike advanced economies, we have found that China does not have strong tradeoff relationship. Nevertheless, these unique characteristics of China may be due to its nature as an emerging economy.[4] Thus, we include the descriptive statistics for other emerging economies in Table 1 as well.[5]

Overall, we observe high inflation rate together with high GDP growth from 1987 to 2021. After 2000, we observe higher GDP growth (5.1% and 3.6%) among emerging economies compared to the average inflation rate (4.2% and 3.2%) in 2000–2010 and 2011–2021, respectively. Moreover, the impact of global financial crisis on inflation in 2008 is also greater than the effect of pandemic in 2019. This implies that China shares a common pattern with its counterparts. On the other hand, we still observe a weak tradeoff between economic growth and inflation among these developing countries. Particularly, when the GDP growth is 5.1% during 2000–2010, its corresponding inflation rate is 4.2%. Similarly, when the GDP growth is relatively lower during 2011–2021, we observe lower inflation rate of 3.2%. This does not align with China's tradeoff pattern. Instead, it is consistent with the findings in OECD countries.

This similarity with OECD countries could primarily stem from the IT policy that has been implemented in some of the developing countries. Among the 36 developing countries, 13 of them including Brazil, Mexico, and South Korea adopted the inflation targeting (IT) policy by the end of 2004, while the remaining 23 countries including Argentina, China, and Singapore are the non-targeters. Gonçalves and Salles (2008) question the effectiveness of the IT policy. They find that IT fails to control the inflation and inflation volatility in developed countries. Although it brings down the inflation in developing countries, the economic growth volatility in those countries declined at the same time. Similarly, Brito and Bystedt (2010) also show that IT does not lead to disinflation in developing countries. Furthermore, they find evidence of lower output growth after IT being implemented. Additionally, Xiong (2012) claims that the People's Bank of China adopts informal IT policy.

In addition, the volatility of inflation reaches its lowest level during 2000–2010, again suggesting sizeable positive impact of global financial crisis on inflation. Also, the volatility of inflation becomes lower during the pandemic, which is consistent with findings in both

China and OECD countries. Lastly, the GDP growth does not fluctuate drastically in different country groups.

Comparison with Japan

China's macroeconomic pattern has always been compared with countries like Japan. Japan achieved fast economic growth since the 1950s until the economic bubble burst in 1990. Afterwards, it struggled with deflation as well as low or negative economic growth. Recently, China's inflation dropped to zero in June 2023 and the producer prices also declined substantially. Since most countries in the world are suffering from high inflation, this indicates China's weak domestic demand. Hence, it is crucial to examine whether China's economy is following a similar path of recession as seen in Japan after the 1990. In Table 1, we also present the descriptive statistics of CPI inflation and GDP growth in Japan during 1960 and 1990. This is the period when Japan embraced fast economic growth.

Overall, we observe that the average GDP growth in Japan from 1960 to 1990 is 6.2% which is greater than the inflation of 5.5%. This reflects the common pattern shared among developing economies including China. Particularly, the economic growth rate is 9.6% in the 1960s, while the inflation rate is relatively lower (5.4%). Nonetheless, Japan encountered extremely high inflation rate of 9.1% in the 1970s, associated with low GDP growth of 4.5%. Interestingly, its inflation quickly declined to 2.1% while maintaining almost the same rate of economic growth (4.5%). This indicates that the tradeoff relationship does not exist in Japan during its early stage of the economy.

De Veirman (2009) found that Japan experienced recession in the past decades while it had low inflation. This questions the existence of Phillips curve in Japan in recent years. His findings indicate a gradual flattening of the Phillips curve. Similarly, the empirical results of the New Keynesian Phillips curve (NKPC) in Japan during 1980 and 2006 also show insignificant Phillips curve coefficient (Dees *et al.*, 2009). Additionally, we observe that Japan has slightly different macroeconomic pattern compared with of China. Unlike China, Japan encountered high inflation during its developing phase of the economy, while China sustains a consistently low inflation rate when its economy is booming.

Based on the statistics, we conclude that different country groups may exhibit different tradeoff pattern between inflation and economic growth. Specifically, both the GDP growth and inflation rate among advanced economies are generally low. In contrast, emerging economies always achieve higher economic growth with relatively low inflation rate. Moreover, Japan shares similar pattern with the emerging economies during 1960 and 1990, even though such pattern varies in the subsamples. Interestingly, China exhibits similar tradeoff pattern compared with other emerging economies. However, such pattern does not remain in the subsamples.

Unit root hypothesis

In Table 2, we present the outcomes of the unit root tests conducted for different inflation measures and their first-differenced counterparts, as well as the real GDP growth in China. The CPI, RPI, PPI, and growth data are specifically collected on a quarterly basis, from 1993Q1 to 2023Q2, whereas the two Core CPI data are from 2006Q1 to 2023Q2. We conduct both Augmented Dickey–Fuller (ADF) test and Phillips–Perron (PP) tests with different specifications to examine the unit root hypothesis.

We observe from Table 2 that all price indices including CPI, RPI, and PPI display strong unit root features as it does not pass both ADF and PP tests, clearly indicating its non-stationary nature in China. This is consistent with the unit root hypothesis in the literature as inflation is assumed to have unit root in the context of Western countries (Crowder and Hoffman, 1996; Crowder and Wohar, 1999; Evans and Lewis, 1995; King and Watson, 1994; Ng and Perron, 2001). Furthermore, the outcomes of the unit root tests for its first-differenced counterparts show that CPI inflation of China follows an I(1) process. On the other hand, the real GDP growth is a stationary process that passes all our unit root tests.

Table 2. Unit root tests.

Variables	Test	Test Statistic	1%	5%	10%
CPI Inflation	ADF	–1.59	–3.50	–2.89	–2.58
	PP	–2.18	–3.50	–2.89	–2.58
CPI Inflation (First Differenced)	ADF	–6.66	–3.50	–2.89	–2.58
	PP	–6.67	–3.50	–2.89	–2.58
Core CPI (excl. Food)	ADF	–2.32	–3.56	–2.92	–2.59
	PP	–1.54	–2.61	–1.95	–1.61
Core CPI (excl. Food) (FD)	ADF	–4.47	–3.56	–2.92	–2.59
	PP	–4.67	–2.61	–1.95	–1.61
Core CPI (excl. Energy & Food)	ADF	–1.90	–3.56	–2.92	–2.59
	PP	–1.14	–2.61	–1.95	–1.61
Core CPI (excl. Energy & Food) (FD)	ADF	–4.58	–3.56	–2.92	–2.59
	PP	–4.69	–2.61	–1.95	–1.61
RPI	ADF	–1.67	–3.50	–2.89	–2.58
	PP	–1.87	–2.60	–1.95	–1.61
RPI (FD)	ADF	–7.03	–3.50	–2.89	–2.58
	PP	–6.92	–2.60	–1.95	–1.61
PPI	ADF	–2.63	–3.50	–2.89	–2.58
	PP	–2.90	–2.60	–1.95	–1.61
PPI (FD)	ADF	–6.65	–3.50	–2.89	–2.58
	PP	–6.73	–2.60	–1.95	–1.61
Real GDP Growth	ADF	–16.85	–3.50	–2.89	–2.58
	PP	–17.17	–3.50	–2.89	–2.58

Notes:

1. The data are collected on a quarterly basis, from the CEIC database.
2. The sample period for CPI, RPI, and PPI inflation rates are from 1993Q1 to 2023Q2.
3. The sample period for the two Core CPI inflation rates are from 2006Q1 to 2023Q2.
4. The sample period for Real GDP Growth rate is from 1993Q1 to 2023Q2.
5. In addition, we also conduct unit root tests with different specifications for all the three variables. The results are consistent with our findings in the table.

Alternative aggregate measures

Besides CPI inflation, there are also other alternative inflation measures in the literature. Clark (2001) provides a comprehensive summary of alternative inflation measures. Particularly, core inflation is

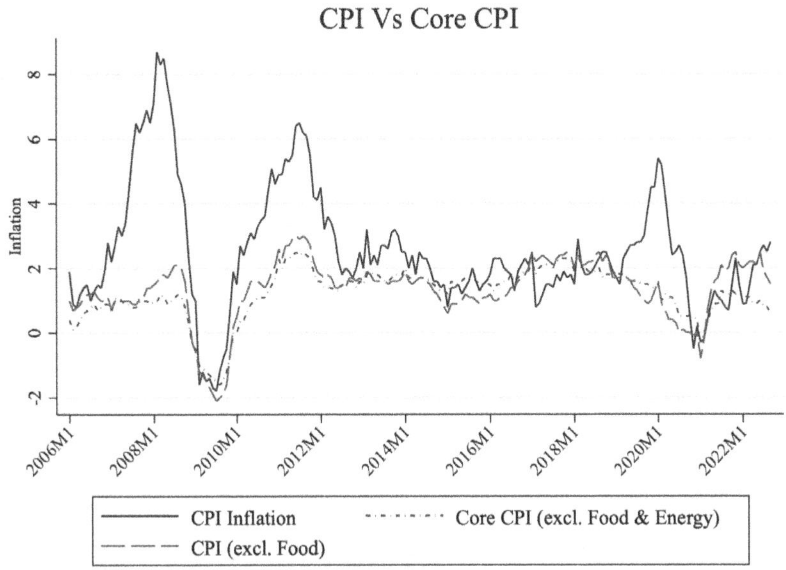

Figure 2. CPI and core CPI inflation rates in China from 2006 to 2022.

another common inflation measure which excludes food and energy as prices in those sectors have been highly volatile. Besides, other measures such as CPI excluding energy or the eight most volatile components of the overall index also have been discussed. In Figure 2, we illustrate the monthly CPI inflation together with Core CPI Inflation excluding Food and Energy Prices, as well as CPI inflation excluding Food prices only.

Obviously, CPI inflation is more volatile than the Core CPI inflation, suggesting that the big part of volatility in inflation comes from the shocks to food and energy prices. Given the fact that core CPI inflation follows a similar pattern to inflation figures that exclude only food, food prices could be the main contributing factor of China's CPI inflation and its volatility. Additionally, the CPI inflation is more sensitive to external shocks including the 2008 Global Financial Crisis, China's economic stimulus package in 2008 and 2009, and the pandemic outbreak in 2021.

Beside CPI inflation, there are also Retail Price Index (RPI) and Producer Price Index (PPI) which are also commonly used as a

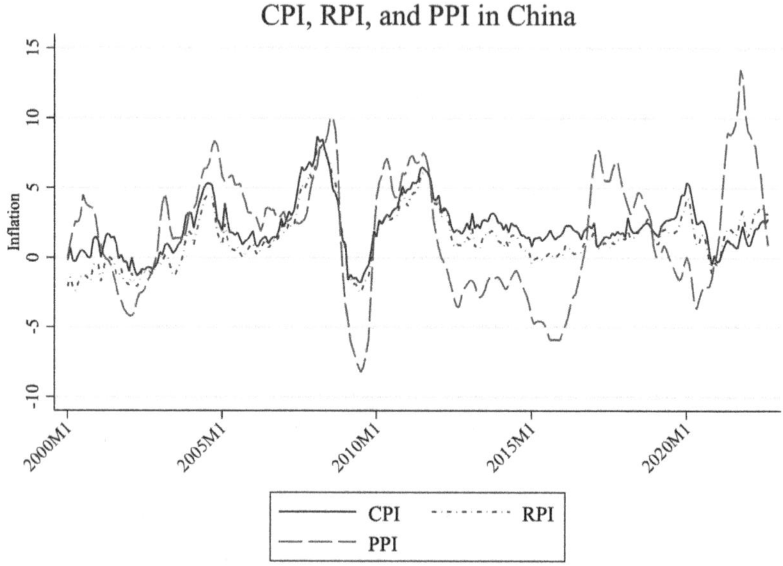

Figure 3. CPI, RPI, and PPI inflation rates in China from 2000 to 2022.

reference of price level. In Figure 3, we display the inflation rates induced by CPI, RPI, and PPI from 2000M1 to 2022M9.

The figure illustrates that CPI and RPI inflation rates closely track each other over time. For much of the period, RPI inflation tends to be slightly lower than CPI inflation. Meanwhile, although PPI inflation exhibits a similar trend to the other two inflation rates, it shows greater volatility.[6]

Besides, we also link China's PPI to other countries' PPI. As shown in Figure 4, a striking fact is that China's PPI is highly correlated with the PPI in the US starting from 1996 with a correlation coefficient of 0.88. Before 1996, the correlation between China's PPI and the US PPI is –0.31.

Disaggregate level data

Subsequently, we analyze the properties of China's inflation data, at both sector and city levels. To examine city-level inflation, we

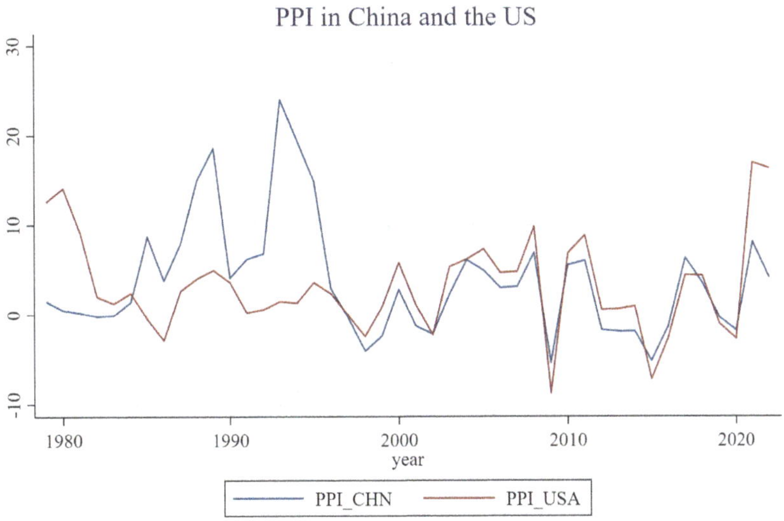

Figure 4. PPI in China and US from 1978 to 2022.

have collected monthly CPI data spanning from 1994M1 to 2022M10. For the sectoral analysis, we have compiled sectoral CPI data from 2000M1 to 2022M11. Both inflation rates are available at the CEIC database.

We first present the descriptive statistics for China's regional inflation data in Table 3.[7]

Based on the full sample result, it is evident that we observe more volatile inflation in Central and West regions of China. Furthermore, inflation rate in the East region is relatively lower compared to that of the other two regions.[8] Next, we divide the dataset into four subperiods, each spanning five years. Overall, inflation has shown fewer fluctuations over time. Specifically, it was most unstable between 2005 and 2010 and has been the least volatile in the last five years. Likewise, the average rate of inflation has also declined over time.

Given the diverse economic characteristics of cities across China, it is crucial to examine the correlation between city-level inflation rates to uncover potential spatial or economic interdependencies among different cities in China. In addition, we also present the cor-

Table 3. Descriptive statistics for China's regional inflation.

Region	Mean	SD	Period
Eastern	2.07	2.05	
Central	2.18	2.20	2000M1–2022M10
Western	2.19	2.36	
Eastern	0.77	2.20	
Central	1.07	2.44	2000M1–2005M10
Western	1.01	2.47	
Eastern	2.30	2.64	
Central	2.75	3.03	2005M2–2010M1
Western	2.79	3.34	
Eastern	3.19	1.50	
Central	3.11	1.50	2010M2–2015M1
Western	3.38	1.67	
Eastern	2.04	1.12	
Central	1.93	1.14	2015M2–2022M10
Western	1.82	1.12	

relation of CPI inflation across China's 36 major cities from 2000 to 2022 in Table A2 in Appendix.[9]

Besides, Stock and Watson (2016) investigate the sectoral inflation by a univariate/multivariate unobserved components/stochastic volatility outlier adjustment (UCSVO) model. In Table 4, we also explore the characteristics of sectoral inflation in China by presenting the summary statistics. Table 4 shows that the inflation rate is the highest in the Food sector, followed by the Residence sector. On the other hand, the price level in the Clothing and Household sectors are relatively small. In addition, we observe negative values for the inflation rate in the Transport and Communication sector, indicating deflation in the sector.

Additionally, prices within the Food sector show considerable variability over time. This is largely attributed to the perishable nature of food products, which tend to experience high inflation and volatility. This finding is consistent with our argument that the food prices are the main contributing factor of CPI inflation and its

Table 4. Descriptive statistics of sectoral inflation in China from 2000 to 2022.

Sectors	Mean	SD	Min	Max	Median
Food	4.13	5.59	–6.26	20.97	2.95
Clothing	0.16	1.78	–3.08	3.96	–0.04
Household	0.36	1.61	–2.80	3.38	0.79
Residence	2.46	2.40	–5.82	7.42	2.34
Transport and Communication	–0.72	2.51	–6.77	8.03	–0.75
Medicine	1.67	1.69	–1.57	7.03	1.52
Recreational, Educational, Cultural Article & Service	0.89	1.41	–4.73	3.78	1.12

volatility in the comparison between CPI inflation and Core inflation in Figure 2. Furthermore, despite the observed decrease in prices within the Transport and Communication sector, the inflation rates remain volatile. The deflation occurring in this sector can be interpreted as the declining prices in the communication industry. Lastly, the price level in the Recreational, Educational, Cultural Article and Service remains stable as the products in the sector are defined as luxury goods instead of necessities.[10]

Tradeoff between Economic Growth and Inflation

In this section, we investigate the tradeoff between economic growth and inflation among different country groups by leveraging on a simple panel regression of CPI inflation rate on GDP growth rate. The benchmark panel regression for our empirical study is as follows:

$$\pi_{it} = \beta + \alpha_{it} y_{it} + \varepsilon_{it} \qquad (1)$$

where π_{it} is the CPI inflation in country i at year t and y_{it} is the corresponding GDP growth. In addition, we also examine the cross-sectional regression for China using its quarterly data. The regression is expressed as

$$\pi_t = \alpha + \alpha_t y_t + \gamma_1 D_1 + \gamma_2 D_2 + \gamma_3 D_3 + \varepsilon_t \tag{2}$$

where D_1, D_2, and D_3 are quarter dummies from quarter 1 to quarter 3. The empirical results based on the regression models are presented in Table 5.

In column (1) of Table 5, the coefficient associated with China's GDP growth is significantly negative, indicating an inverse relationship between CPI inflation and GDP growth in China. In particular, when the real GDP growth rises by 1%, China's CPI inflation drops by 0.9%. To eliminate any potential issues caused by the I(1) process of CPI inflation, we also conduct the Dynamic OLS (DOLS) in column (2) of Table 5. Again, we obtain significantly negative coefficient associated with the GDP growth. In addition, the R^2 increases from 0.54 in column (1) to 0.83 in column (2), indicating stronger explaining power of our regression.

Using cross-country data, we do not find this significant negative correlation among real GDP growth and inflation in OECD countries, emerging economies and Japan (during 1960–1990) in columns (3)–(5) of Table 5. In the regressions using first-differenced (FD) data from columns (7)–(11), only Japan during the period of 1960–1990 exhibits a similar pattern to China.

In addition, we also examine the tradeoff within three sets of subsamples in Table 6. Overall, different from the negative correlation between inflation and GDP growth in China, we do not observe significant tradeoff relationship between inflation and GDP growth in OECD countries after 2000, while the tradeoff theory exists in emerging economies from 2000 to 2021. The result remains after including both OECD and emerging economies in the tradeoff regression. Interestingly, from 2011 onwards, we observe significant tradeoff between economic growth and inflation. While OECD countries still exhibit weak relationship between the two variables, we obtain substantially steeper slope coefficient for emerging

Table 5. Tradeoff regression.

Dependent variable	CPI Inflation						First-Differenced				
	China	DOLS	OECD	Emerging	Japan	All	China	OECD	Emerging	Japan	All
GDP Growth	–0.948***	–1.471***	–0.051	–2.025	–0.361	–0.569	–0.091***	–0.060	–1.708	–0.727***	–0.668
	(–11.727)	(–6.096)	(–0.444)	(–1.001)	(–1.564)	(–1.025)	(–3.217)	(–0.902)	(–1.030)	(–4.545)	(–1.143)
Quarter 1	–26.982***						–3.095***				
	(–10.809)						(–3.041)				
Quarter 2	1.007						2.078***				
	(1.016)						(2.733)				
Quarter 3	–5.066***						–0.941*				
	(–4.650)						(–1.947)				
Observations	121	118	1,210	467	30	1,677	120	1,173	453	29	1,626
R-squared	0.54	0.83	0.00	0.01	0.080	0.00	0.087	0.003	0.002	0.434	0.00

Notes:

1. For China, we use quarterly data from 1993Q1 to 2021Q4.
2. For the rest of the world, we use annual data from 1987 to 2021.
3. For Japan, we use annual data from 1960 to 1990.
4. The panel results are based on clustered robust standard error.
5. We present t-statistics in the parentheses below the coefficients.
6. We conduct the Dynamic OLS (DOLS) by including the first-differenced, lead, and lag terms of inflation in column (2) due to potential I (1) process of inflation.

Table 6. Tradeoff regression: Subsamples.

Dependent variable	CPI Inflation			First-Differenced		
	2000–2021			2000–2021		
	OECD	Emerging	All	OECD	Emerging	All
GDP Growth	0.038	0.092**	0.054*	0.088***	0.059**	0.078***
	(0.972)	(2.230)	(1.733)	(4.988)	(2.308)	(5.500)
no. of Obs.	814	307	1,121	777	293	1,070
R-squared	0.02	0.01	0.02	0.03	0.01	0.02

Note:
1. The results are based on clustered robust standard error.
2. We present t-statistics in the parentheses below the coefficients.

Table 7. The relationship between inflation and volatility.

	Average CPI Inflation			
Dependent variable	OECD	Emerging	All	China Provincial
Inflation Volatility	0.459***	0.991***	0.437***	–0.255
	(4.928)	(3.868)	(3.696)	(–0.646)
Observations	22	22	22	88
R-squared	0.548	0.428	0.406	0.006

Note:
1. The results are based on sample period from 2000 to 2021.
2. We present t-statistics in the parentheses below the coefficients.
3. The dependent is average CPI inflation across countries/China Provinces.
4. Volatility of inflation is defined as the standard deviation (SD) of CPI inflation across countries/provinces in China.
5. We control for quarter effect for China's provincial regression.
6. Average CPI inflation and inflation volatility are cointegrated.

economies. This indicates that developing countries have been facing more tradeoff between GDP growth and price level in recent years. Again, even though the tradeoff coefficient for the OECD countries becomes more significant, the small magnitude of it implies a relatively flat relationship between inflation and GDP growth in advanced countries.

Besides, we also aim to investigate the relationship between inflation and its volatility across various groups of countries in Table 7. It is evident that there exists a significant positive relationship between inflation and its volatility across OECD and emerging economies. The results remain for full sample regression in column (3). In order to investigate the relationship within China, we have to leverage on its provincial level data from 2000Q1 to 2021Q3. In column (4), we obtain insignificant coefficient associated with China's inflation volatility, indicating no relationship between inflation and its volatility measure.[11]

Correlation of Inflation Rates across Countries

While examining the relationship between CPI inflation and GDP growth in China shows unique patterns, we also explore how its inflation rates correlate with those of other countries or regions. In Table 8, we first present the correlation of CPI inflation across selected countries. Interestingly, China's CPI inflation does not show strong correlation with most of the countries or regions. It is intuitive that the correlation between China's CPI inflation rates and those of Hong Kong is fairly strong (0.68), yet it is surprising to find a weak correlation between China's CPI inflation and that of the US (0.37). Furthermore, we also observe weak correlation between the inflation rates of China and its neighboring countries include Japan (0.25) and Singapore (0.32). On the other hand, there is a noticeable strong relationship between the inflation rates of the US and other major economies, including Canada (0.79), France (0.84), and the UK (0.72). In summary, although geographical proximity and economic connections are key factors in establishing the correlation between inflation rates among major economies, China's CPI inflation exhibits a lower correlation with others.

Table 9 shows the correlation of PPI inflation across countries. We observe synchronization of the PPI across countries, that is, PPI is highly correlated in most countries. In addition to the US, China's

Table 8. Correlation of CPI inflation rates across countries/regions.

	CHN	AUS	AUT	BRA	CAN	DEU	FRA	GBR	SGP	HKG	IND	JPN	KOR	MEX	NOR	USA
CHN	1.00															
AUS	0.38	1.00														
AUT	0.40	0.24	1.00													
BRA	0.56	0.35	0.53	1.00												
CAN	0.16	0.76	0.38	0.29	1.00											
DEU	0.36	0.02	0.89	0.53	0.31	1.00										
FRA	0.45	0.71	0.66	0.46	0.78	0.55	1.00									
GBR	0.32	0.58	0.58	0.60	0.75	0.55	0.77	1.00								
SGP	0.32	0.23	0.71	0.30	0.27	0.57	0.54	0.53	1.00							
HKG	0.68	0.31	0.54	0.63	0.35	0.57	0.50	0.72	0.48	1.00						
IND	0.30	0.09	0.23	0.24	0.06	0.25	0.22	0.51	0.43	0.63	1.00					
JPN	0.25	0.17	0.41	0.54	0.44	0.51	0.39	0.65	0.32	0.71	0.29	1.00				
KOR	0.45	0.37	0.53	0.59	0.48	0.56	0.64	0.74	0.42	0.66	0.62	0.52	1.00			
MEX	0.40	0.66	–0.06	0.14	0.47	–0.14	0.46	0.37	–0.06	0.34	0.27	0.10	0.33	1.00		
NOR	0.25	0.75	–0.01	0.21	0.63	–0.06	0.47	0.44	–0.01	0.30	0.15	0.23	0.28	0.81	1.00	
USA	0.37	0.66	0.65	0.47	0.79	0.57	0.84	0.72	0.49	0.44	0.07	0.43	0.58	0.36	0.45	1.00

Note:

1. The correlation coefficients are computed based on annual data from 1987 to 2021.

Table 9. Correlation of PPI inflation rates across countries.

	CHN	AUS	CAN	DEU	FRA	GBR	SGP	JPN	KOR	NOR	USA	ARG	COL	POL	THA
CHN	1.00														
AUS	0.61	1.00													
CAN	0.66	0.74	1.00												
DEU	0.43	0.81	0.79	1.00											
FRA	0.51	0.83	0.84	0.98	1.00										
GBR	0.69	0.81	0.76	0.87	0.89	1.00									
SGP	0.81	0.85	0.85	0.77	0.84	0.82	1.00								
JPN	0.62	0.86	0.81	0.80	0.81	0.84	0.80	1.00							
KOR	0.82	0.63	0.78	0.68	0.72	0.86	0.77	0.69	1.00						
NOR	0.71	0.74	0.87	0.85	0.87	0.88	0.84	0.80	0.87	1.00					
USA	0.86	0.78	0.88	0.75	0.81	0.84	0.93	0.82	0.85	0.89	1.00				
ARG	–0.03	0.23	0.37	0.40	0.36	0.23	0.11	0.34	0.12	0.27	0.16	1.00			
COL	0.44	0.74	0.79	0.88	0.89	0.74	0.71	0.65	0.71	0.81	0.75	0.36	1.00		
POL	0.39	0.62	0.74	0.88	0.89	0.75	0.69	0.59	0.72	0.78	0.64	0.29	0.88	1.00	
THA	0.73	0.70	0.50	0.57	0.62	0.76	0.70	0.59	0.73	0.71	0.77	–0.10	0.56	0.44	1.00

Note:
1. The correlation coefficients are computed based on annual data from 2000 to 2022.

PPI also closely related to its neighboring countries, such as Singapore (0.81), South Korea (0.82), and Thailand (0.73). We then investigate the correlation of China's PPI with advanced countries and emerging and developing countries. Compared to emerging and developing countries, China's PPI shows higher correlation with advanced countries in general. It is obvious to find a remarkably close correlation between China's PPI and that of other major countries, including Australia (0.61), Canada (0.66), the UK (0.69), Japan (0.62), and Norway (0.71). However, the relationship between PPI inflation of China and that of Argentina (–0.03), Colombia (0.44), and Poland (0.39) is relatively weaker. Auer *et al.* (2019) support the PPI synchronization among countries by OECD country data. They argue that cross-country PPI synchronization is mainly driven by common sectoral shocks and amplified by input–output linkages.

Conclusion

Based on a time series regression, we observe that the relationship between inflation and GDP growth in China is different from that of OECD and other emerging economies. Specifically, the inflation and GDP growth exhibit statistically significant inverse relationship, which contradicts the conventional tradeoff theory between GDP growth and inflation. While the results are controversial, they are not surprising to us. Particularly, the lower price level associated with high economic growth in China reflects the "China price effect" as the price level declines due to increase of aggregate supply.

As a developing economy, China has been sustaining markedly high GDP growth while keeping the inflation low and stable. It is essential to investigate their tradeoff coefficient in recent years. Nakamura *et al.* (2016) leverage on micro-level data and found that in the 2000s, the inflation in China was understated while the GDP growth was overstated by the government. Thus, we suggest that future studies should examine the dynamics of inflation and its economic performance within China using more detailed disaggregate-level data.

Endnotes

1. The statistics are computed based on the dataset collected from the CEIC database.
2. OECD countries in this chapter include Australia, Austria, Belgium, Canada, Chile, Colombia, Costa Rica, Czech Republic, Denmark, Estonia, Finland, France, Germany, Greece, Hungary, Iceland, Ireland, Israel, Italy, Latvia, Lithuania, Luxembourg, Mexico, Netherlands, New Zealand, Norway, Poland, Portugal, Slovakia, Slovenia, Spain, Sweden, Switzerland, Turkey, the United States (US), and the United Kingdom (UK).
3. We also provide the average inflation and GDP growth among OECD countries in Figure A1 in the Appendix. In addition, we also divide the OECD countries into European countries and non-European countries and display the plots in Figures A2 and A3. Overall, there is no significant differences across the two subgroups.
4. Emerging economies in the paper include China, Botswana, Brazil, Hong Kong, Indonesia, India, South Korea, Malaysia, Malta, Oman, Singapore, Thailand, Vietnam, and South Africa.
5. We also provide the average inflation and GDP growth among emerging economies in Figure A4 in the Appendix. Overall, the average inflation rate is similar for both OECD and emerging economies. Thus, any differences in the patterns can be attributed to the heterogeneity across country groups.
6. In addition, we also illustrate alternative price indices based on online data in Figures A5 and A6 in the Appendix. Specifically, the iCPI inflation illustrated in Figure A5 exhibits less volatility compared to CPI inflation, as we do not observe the sharp decline in iCPI inflation during the 2019 pandemic. Additionally, changes in iCPI inflation occur one or two periods earlier than those in CPI inflation, indicating that online prices respond more quickly than the traditional prices captured in the CPI data. In Figure A6, we present the data collected by Cavallo *et al.* (2018). It is evident that both CPI and online inflation rates move at the same direction, even though the online inflation rate demonstrates higher volatility.
7. The data are collected from 36 major cities in China, which are subsequently divided into three regions based on their geographical locations. The regions are as follows:

East region: Beijing, Changchun, Dalian, Fuzhou, Guangzhou, Haikou, Hangzhou, Harbin, Jinan, Nanjing, Ningbo, Qingdao, Shanghai, Shenyang, Shijiazhuang, Shenzhen, Tianjin, and Xiamen.
Central region: Changsha, Hefei, Nanchang, Taiyuan, Wuhan, and Zhengzhou.
West region: Chengdu, Chongqing, Guiyang, Hohhot, Kunming, Lanzhou, Lhasa, Nanning, Urumqi, Xi'an, Xining, and Yinchuan.

8. This finding is supported by the regression results presented in Table A1 in the Appendix. In particular, the coefficients associated with Eastern Region dummy are significantly negative or the full sample and for most of the subsamples.
9. The table demonstrates that the correlation coefficients for each pair of cities are significantly high, with the notable exception of Lhasa, which displays negative values. This indicates that the inflation rates across different cities in China are rather homogeneous and hence, they can be summarized into one common factor.
10 Furthermore, we also examine the correlation among sectoral inflation rates in Table A3 in the Appendix. Interestingly, it is evident that the inflation rate in the Housing sector shows weak correlation with other sectors, suggesting that property prices in China are not the primary drivers of the overall price level. This finding contradicts to the prevailing assumption commonly held.
11. Narayan *et al.* (2009) found negative relationship between the two measures using China's provincial data from 1987M1 to 2006M1. We extend the sample period by using quarterly inflation data at provincial level. It turns out that the negative relationship no longer exists in recent years. However, it is still vastly different from the positive correlation that we observe from the rest of the world.

References

Artis, M.J., Bladen-Hovell, R.C., and Zhang, W. 1995. Turning points in the international business cycle: An analysis of the OECD leading indicators for the G-7 countries. *OECD Economic Studies,* (24): 125–166.

Auer, R.A., Levchenko, A.A., and Sauré, P. 2019. International inflation spillovers through input linkages. *Review of Economics and Statistics,* 101(3): 507–521.

Brito, R.D. and Bystedt, B. 2010. Inflation targeting in emerging economies: Panel evidence. *Journal of Development Economics*, 91(2): 198–210.

Ball, L., Cecchetti, S.G., and Gordon, R.J. 1990. Inflation and uncertainty at short and long horizons. *Brookings Papers on Economic Activity*, 1990(1): 215–254.

Bataa, E., Osborn, D.R., Sensier, M., and Dijk, D.V. 2014. Identifying changes in mean, seasonality, persistence and volatility for G7 and Euro Area inflation. *Oxford Bulletin of Economics and Statistics*, 76(3): 360–388.

Bernanke, B.S., Boivin, J., and Eliasz, P. 2005. Measuring the effects of monetary policy: A factor-augmented vector autoregressive (FAVAR) approach. *The Quarterly Journal of Economics*, 120(1): 387–422.

Bernanke, B.S. and Mishkin, F.S. 1997. Inflation targeting: A new framework for monetary policy? *Journal of Economic Perspectives*, 11(2): 97–116.

Bryan, M.F. and Cecchetti, S.G. 1993. Measuring core inflation. In *Monetary Policy*. Chicago, IL: The University of Chicago Press, pp. 195–219.

Bryan, M.F. and Cecchetti, S.G. 1994. Measuring core inflation. In *Monetary policy*. Chicago, IL: The University of Chicago Press, pp. 195–219.

Cavallo, A., Diewert, W.E., Feenstra, R.C., Inklaar, R., and Timmer, M.P. 2018. Using online prices for measuring real consumption across countries. *AEA Papers and Proceedings*, 108: 483–487.

Chen, H., Chow, K., and Tillmann, P. 2017. The effectiveness of monetary policy in China: Evidence from a Qual VAR. *China Economic Review*, 43: 216–231.

Clark, T. 2001. Comparing measures of core inflation. *Economic Review* 86(Q II): 5–31.

Cogley, T. and Sargent, T. J. 2001. Evolving post-world war II US inflation dynamics. *NBER macroeconomics annual*, 16: 331–373.

Cogley, T., Primiceri, G.E., and Sargent, T.J. 2010. Inflation-gap persistence in the US. *American Economic Journal: Macroeconomics*, 2(1): 43–69.

Cogley, T. and Sargent, T.J. 2015. Measuring price-level uncertainty and instability in the United States, 1850–2012. *Review of Economics and Statistics*, 97(4): 827–838.

Crowder, W.J. and Hoffman, D.L. 1996. The long-run relationship between nominal interest rates and inflation: The Fisher equation revisited. *Journal of Money, Credit and Banking*, 28(1): 102–118.

Crowder, W.J. and Wohar, M.E. 1999. Are tax effects important in the long-run fisher relationship? Evidence from the municipal bond market. *The Journal of Finance,* 54(1): 307–317.

Culver, S.E. and Papell, D.H. 1997. Is there a unit root in the inflation rate? Evidence from sequential break and panel data models. *Journal of Applied Econometrics,* 12(4): 435–444.

Dees, S., Pesaran, M.H., Smith, L.V., and Smith, R.P. 2009. Identification of new Keynesian Phillips curves from a global perspective. *Journal of Money, Credit and Banking,* 41(7): 1481–1502.

De Veirman, E. 2009. What makes the output-inflation trade-off change? The absence of accelerating deflation in Japan. *Journal of Money, Credit and Banking,* 41(6): 1117–1140.

Evans, M.D. and Lewis, K.K. 1995. Do expected shifts in inflation affect estimates of the long-run Fisher relation? *The Journal of Finance,* 50(1): 225–253.

Friedman, B. 1968. Introduction. In Solow, R.M. and Taylor, J.B. (eds.), *Inflation, Unemployment, and Monetary Policy.* Cambridge, MA: MIT Press.

Gerlach, S. and Peng, W. 2006. Output gaps and inflation in Mainland China. *China Economic Review,* 17(2): 210–225.

Gonçalves, C. E. S. and Salles, J. M. 2008. Inflation targeting in emerging economies: What do the data say?. *Journal of Development Economics,* 85(1–2): 312–318.

Hendry, D.F. 2001. Modelling UK inflation, 1875–1991. *Journal of Applied Econometrics,* 16(3): 255–275.

Hazell, J., Herreno, J., Nakamura, E., and Steinsson, J. 2022. The slope of the Phillips curve: Evidence from US states. *The Quarterly Journal of Economics,* 137(3): 1299–1344.

Kiley, M.T. 2015. Low inflation in the United States: A summary of recent research. *Feds Notes,* 23 November 2015.

King, R.G. and Watson, M.W. 1994. The post-war US Phillips curve: A revisionist econometric history. In *Carnegie-Rochester Conference Series on Public Policy,* Vol. 41. North-Holland, pp. 157–219.

Lucas Jr, R.E. 1972. Econometric testing of the natural rate hypothesis. In O. Eckstein (ed.), *The Econometrics of Price Determination.* Washington: Board of Governors of the Federal Reserve System.

Nakamura, E., Steinsson, J., and Liu, M. 2016. Are Chinese growth and inflation too smooth? Evidence from Engel curves. *American Economic Journal: Macroeconomics,* 8(3): 113–144.

Narayan, P.K., Narayan, S., and Smyth, R. 2009. Understanding the inflation–output nexus for China. *China Economic Review,* 20(1): 82–90.

Nelson, C.R. and Schwert, G.W. 1977. Short-term interest rates as predictors of inflation: On testing the hypothesis that the real rate of interest is constant. *The American Economic Review,* 67(3): 478–486.

Ng, S. and Perron, P. 2001. Lag length selection and the construction of unit root tests with good size and power. *Econometrica,* 69(6): 1519–1554.

Mehrotra, A., Peltonen, T., and Rivera, A.S. 2010. Modelling inflation in China–A regional perspective. *China Economic Review,* 21(2): 237–255.

Reis, R. and Watson, M.W. 2010. Relative goods' prices, pure inflation, and the Phillips correlation. *American Economic Journal: Macroeconomics,* 2(3): 128–157.

Sargent, T.J. 1971. A note on the "accelerationist" controversy. *Journal of Money, Credit and Banking,* 3(3): 721–725.

Scheibe, J. and Vines, D. 2005. A Phillips curve for China.

Stock, J.H. and Watson, M.W. 2016. Core inflation and trend inflation. *Review of Economics and Statistic,* 98(4): 770–784.

Stock, J.H. and Watson, M.W. 2020. Slack and cyclically sensitive inflation. *Journal of Money, Credit and Banking,* 52(S2): 393–428.

Wang, Z., Wei, S.J., Yu, X., and Zhu, K. 2021. *Re-examining the Effects of Trading with China on Local Labor Markets: A Supply Chain Perspective* (No. w24886). Cambridge, MA: National Bureau of Economic Research.

Xiong, W. 2012. Measuring the monetary policy stance of the People's Bank of China: An ordered probit analysis. *China Economic Review,* 23(3): 512–533.

Zhang, C. and Murasawa, Y. 2012. Multivariate model-based gap measures and a new Phillips curve for China. *China Economic Review,* 23(1): 60–70.

Appendix

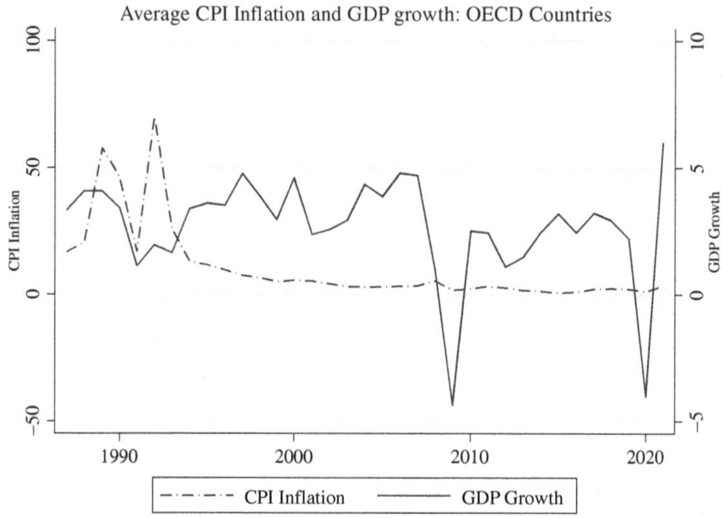

Figure A1. Average inflation and GDP growth in OECD countries from 1987 to 2022.

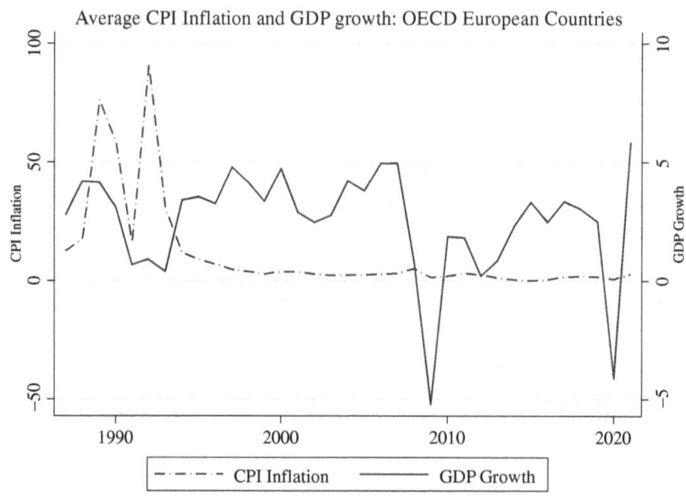

Figure A2. Average inflation and GDP growth in OECD EU countries from 1987 to 2022.

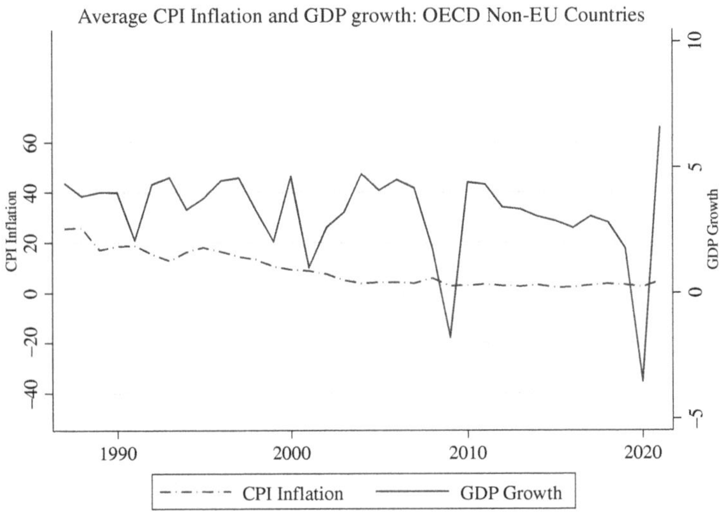

Figure A3. Average inflation and GDP growth in OECD non-EU countries from 1987 to 2022.

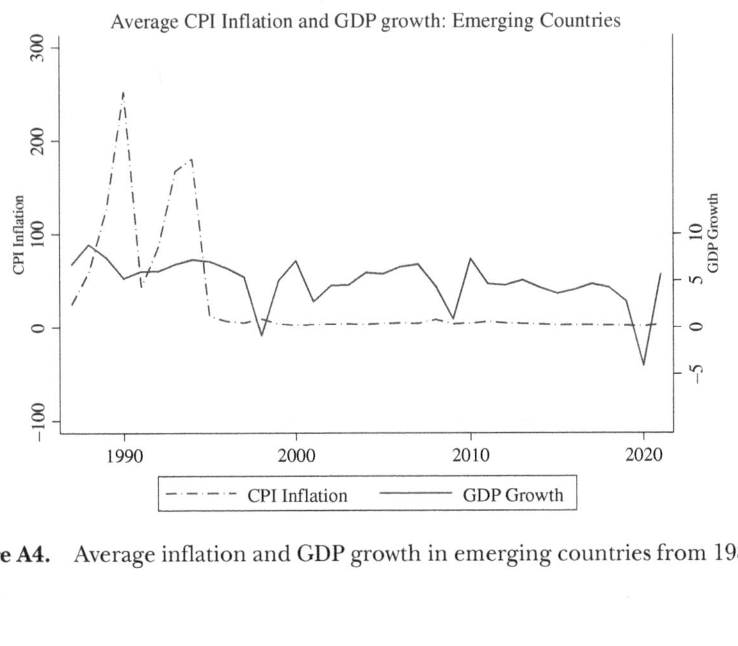

Figure A4. Average inflation and GDP growth in emerging countries from 1987 to 2022.

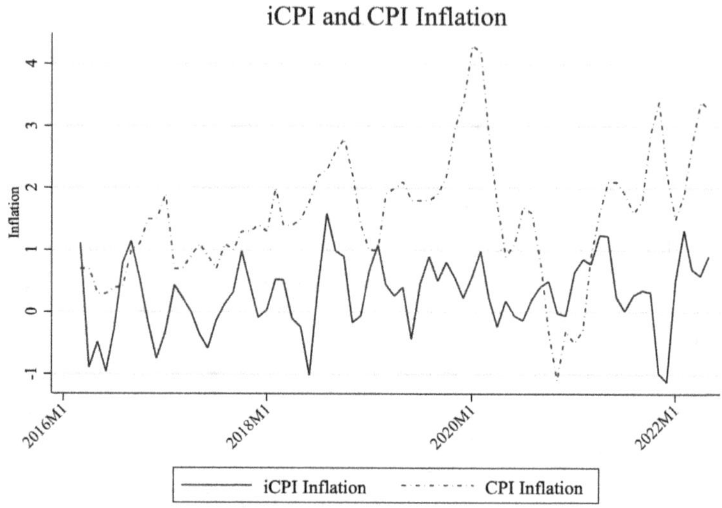

Figure A5. iCPI inflation in China from 2016 to 2022.

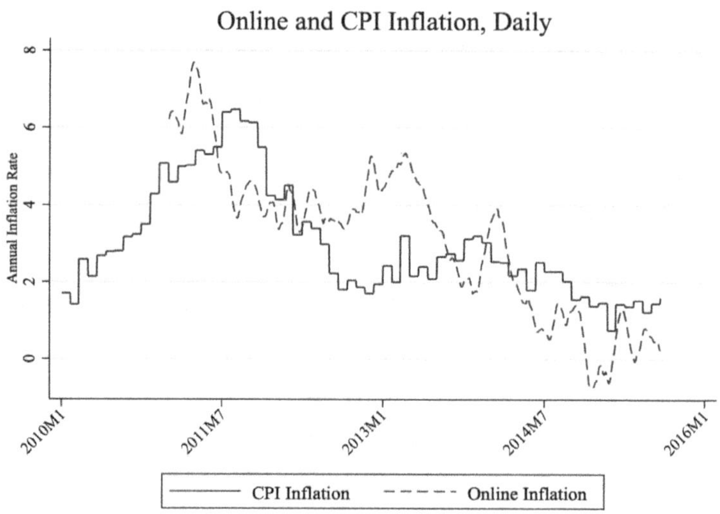

Figure A6. Online and CPI inflation in China from 2010 to 2015.

Table A1. Inflation and regions.

Dep Var	CPI Inflation				
Period	2000M1–2022M10	2000M1–2005M10	2005M2–2010M1	2010M2–2015M1	2015M2–2022M10
Eastern Region	–0.114**	–0.092	–0.484***	–0.189**	0.240***
	(–2.332)	(–0.956)	(–3.433)	(–2.534)	(5.537)
Central Region	–0.003	0.195	–0.036	–0.266***	0.126**
	(–0.051)	(1.518)	(–0.191)	(–2.656)	(2.174)
Observations	9,828	2,592	2,160	2,160	3,312
R-squared	0.001	0.002	0.006	0.004	0.009

Table A2. Correlation of inflation across China's cities from 2000M1 to 2022M10.

	Beijing	Tianjin	Shijiazhuan	Taiyuan	Hohhot	Shenyang	Dalian	Changchu	Harbin	Shangha	Nanjing	Hangzhou	Ningbo	Hefei	Fuzhou	Xiamen	Nanchang	Jinan	Qingdao	Zhengzho	Wuhan	Changsh	Guangzhou	Shenzhen	Nanning	Haikou	Chongqing	Chengdu	Guiyan	Kunming	Lhasa	Xi'an	Lanzhou	Xining	Yinchuan	Urumqi
Beijing	1.00																																			
Tianjin	0.95	1.00																																		
Shijiazhuan	0.94	0.95	1.00																																	
Taiyuan	0.91	0.91	0.95	1.00																																
Hohhot	0.93	0.91	0.94	0.95	1.00																															
Shenyang	0.92	0.94	0.95	0.92	0.92	1.00																														
Dalian	0.94	0.96	0.96	0.92	0.92	0.95	1.00																													
Changchun	0.93	0.95	0.94	0.92	0.92	0.94	0.95	1.00																												
Harbin	0.93	0.95	0.93	0.92	0.91	0.96	0.95	0.95	1.00																											
Shanghai	0.93	0.91	0.93	0.94	0.95	0.90	0.92	0.92	0.91	1.00																										
Nanjing	0.93	0.96	0.95	0.93	0.90	0.93	0.96	0.94	0.93	0.92	1.00																									
Hangzhou	0.94	0.94	0.93	0.92	0.92	0.92	0.95	0.95	0.93	0.94	0.93	1.00																								
Ningbo	0.94	0.95	0.94	0.93	0.93	0.92	0.96	0.95	0.93	0.95	0.95	0.96	1.00																							
Hefei	0.91	0.92	0.93	0.93	0.91	0.91	0.93	0.92	0.89	0.93	0.94	0.92	0.94	1.00																						
Fuzhou	0.91	0.92	0.93	0.94	0.94	0.93	0.92	0.93	0.93	0.94	0.93	0.92	0.94	0.90	1.00																					
Xiamen	0.85	0.85	0.89	0.91	0.89	0.87	0.87	0.86	0.86	0.89	0.87	0.87	0.89	0.87	0.94	1.00																				
Nanchang	0.93	0.93	0.95	0.95	0.95	0.94	0.94	0.93	0.95	0.95	0.94	0.94	0.94	0.92	0.96	0.92	1.00																			
Jinan	0.96	0.96	0.96	0.94	0.93	0.96	0.96	0.94	0.96	0.93	0.96	0.94	0.95	0.92	0.94	0.87	0.95	1.00																		
Qingdao	0.94	0.95	0.93	0.92	0.91	0.93	0.95	0.93	0.94	0.92	0.94	0.92	0.94	0.90	0.94	0.88	0.94	0.95	1.00																	
Zhengzhou	0.90	0.94	0.94	0.93	0.91	0.96	0.93	0.93	0.94	0.89	0.94	0.90	0.90	0.90	0.92	0.84	0.93	0.95	0.92	1.00																
Wuhan	0.93	0.96	0.95	0.94	0.93	0.94	0.95	0.95	0.94	0.94	0.97	0.94	0.96	0.96	0.94	0.87	0.95	0.96	0.94	0.94	1.00															
Changsha	0.91	0.93	0.95	0.94	0.94	0.93	0.93	0.93	0.94	0.94	0.93	0.93	0.94	0.89	0.97	0.91	0.96	0.95	0.92	0.92	0.93	1.00														
Guangzhou	0.91	0.93	0.93	0.92	0.89	0.90	0.93	0.91	0.91	0.92	0.93	0.92	0.94	0.91	0.93	0.92	0.93	0.93	0.92	0.89	0.94	0.92	1.00													
Shenzhen	0.90	0.93	0.93	0.91	0.91	0.92	0.92	0.90	0.93	0.91	0.92	0.92	0.92	0.88	0.94	0.90	0.94	0.94	0.92	0.91	0.93	0.94	0.96	1.00												
Nanning	0.85	0.90	0.90	0.88	0.87	0.90	0.88	0.88	0.91	0.86	0.89	0.85	0.87	0.83	0.90	0.84	0.91	0.91	0.86	0.91	0.89	0.90	0.90	0.90	1.00											
Haikou	0.84	0.90	0.91	0.89	0.87	0.90	0.91	0.88	0.88	0.88	0.92	0.87	0.89	0.88	0.90	0.91	0.91	0.88	0.89	0.88	0.90	0.89	0.92	0.90	0.86	1.00										
Chongqing	0.90	0.95	0.93	0.91	0.91	0.94	0.94	0.95	0.95	0.91	0.93	0.92	0.92	0.87	0.93	0.83	0.93	0.94	0.91	0.95	0.94	0.94	0.91	0.92	0.94	0.88	1.00									
Chengdu	0.92	0.94	0.94	0.93	0.94	0.95	0.94	0.95	0.95	0.92	0.94	0.93	0.93	0.90	0.95	0.88	0.95	0.95	0.93	0.95	0.94	0.95	0.90	0.92	0.90	0.90	0.95	1.00								
Guiyang	0.91	0.91	0.88	0.87	0.85	0.88	0.89	0.91	0.93	0.87	0.90	0.90	0.89	0.84	0.88	0.79	0.89	0.92	0.89	0.90	0.90	0.89	0.88	0.89	0.90	0.79	0.94	0.90	1.00							
Kunming	0.84	0.87	0.85	0.84	0.85	0.83	0.87	0.90	0.87	0.86	0.85	0.88	0.88	0.83	0.86	0.77	0.84	0.88	0.82	0.86	0.87	0.87	0.83	0.83	0.83	0.75	0.89	0.86	0.89	1.00						
Lhasa	-0.11	-0.02	-0.01	-0.01	-0.05	0.00	-0.01	-0.01	0.02	-0.05	-0.01	-0.01	-0.04	0.02	-0.05	0.02	-0.02	-0.03	-0.09	0.01	-0.01	-0.02	0.06	0.06	0.09	0.07	0.01	-0.03	0.03	0.07	1.00					
Xi'an	0.94	0.96	0.95	0.94	0.93	0.95	0.95	0.94	0.95	0.91	0.95	0.94	0.94	0.93	0.93	0.86	0.95	0.96	0.94	0.96	0.96	0.93	0.93	0.94	0.91	0.89	0.94	0.95	0.91	0.87	0.02	1.00				
Lanzhou	0.92	0.94	0.93	0.92	0.92	0.93	0.93	0.94	0.95	0.92	0.93	0.93	0.93	0.90	0.94	0.85	0.94	0.95	0.92	0.93	0.95	0.94	0.92	0.93	0.93	0.85	0.96	0.94	0.95	0.90	0.04	0.95	1.00			
Xining	0.91	0.92	0.93	0.91	0.91	0.91	0.92	0.93	0.92	0.92	0.91	0.92	0.92	0.91	0.90	0.81	0.92	0.93	0.89	0.92	0.93	0.91	0.88	0.89	0.89	0.83	0.94	0.93	0.92	0.89	0.02	0.94	0.96	1.00		
Yinchuan	0.91	0.93	0.93	0.92	0.92	0.93	0.92	0.92	0.94	0.91	0.92	0.91	0.91	0.86	0.94	0.85	0.93	0.94	0.91	0.94	0.91	0.94	0.90	0.92	0.94	0.86	0.96	0.95	0.93	0.88	0.03	0.94	0.96	0.93	1.00	
Urumqi	0.93	0.93	0.94	0.91	0.90	0.90	0.93	0.93	0.92	0.91	0.93	0.91	0.92	0.91	0.90	0.85	0.93	0.93	0.92	0.91	0.93	0.90	0.91	0.88	0.88	0.88	0.92	0.92	0.90	0.84	0.00	0.94	0.94	0.94	0.91	1.00

Table A3. Correlation coefficient of sectoral inflation in China from 2000 to 2022.

Sectors	Food	Clothing	Household	Residence	Transport and Communication	Medicine	Recreational, Educational, Cultural Article
Food	1.00						
Clothing	0.07	1.00					
Household	0.40	0.62	1.00				
Residence	0.29	–0.03	0.11	1.00			
Transport and Communication	0.01	0.35	0.49	–0.03	1.00		
Medicine	0.25	0.47	0.59	0.11	0.20	1.00	
Recreational, Educational, Cultural Article & Service	–0.06	0.30	0.07	–0.11	0.48	0.13	1.00

https://doi.org/10.1142/9789819815241_0019

Chapter 19

INNOVATION IN CHINA: CHALLENGES AND OPPORTUNITIES

Yanrui Wu

The University of Western Australia, Perth, Australia
yanrui.wu@uwa.edu.au

Introduction

After continuous high growth at an average rate of 9.4% per annum during 1980–2019, China's economic development has slowed down. The slow growth is expected as the country reaches middle-income status with a GDP per capita of approximately US$12,000 in 2021, and the so-called population dividends are exhausted. Future growth will largely rely on productivity improvement through innovation, particularly indigenous innovation. However, does the country have the innovation capacity to propel economic growth in the coming decades? A thorough understanding of this question can help gain insights into China's future growth potential and hence has important implications for economic policy.

The objective of this chapter is to present a brief overview of the current status of innovation in China. The rest of the chapter begins with a description of the progress in innovation, including major achievements in science and technology. This is followed by a discussion of the challenges that China's innovation sector faces. Subsequently, opportunities for further improvement and advancement in innovation are explored. The final section presents the concluding remarks.

Progress in Innovation

Innovation is the key to technological progress in a society. The latter can be achieved in two ways, namely by the acquisition and absorption of external technology and knowledge creation through indigenous innovation. The roles of the two can change over time. External technology is particularly critical to developing and emerging economies during their earlier stages of development. Even in some developed economies, imported technology could be more important than domestic technology (Papaconstantinou *et al.*, 1996). For several decades, China has been very successful in acquiring and absorbing external technology through international trade, foreign capital inflow, and offshore investment. The country is now a leading player in these areas. China's success is well documented in the literature (Li, 2011; Liang *et al.*, 2022). For example, Fu (2008) demonstrated that foreign direct investment has a significant positive effect on the overall innovation capacities of China's regional economies. Fisch *et al.* (2019) also showed that acquisitions by Chinese firms have a positive effect on their post-acquisition innovation output. Kowalski (2021) argued that the core to China's development success lies in reducing the technological gap through importing existing technology.

The successful acquisition of external technology over the decades has enabled the Chinese economy to catch up with advanced economies. However, the role of external technology is now diminishing as China closes its technology gap with advanced economies. This is well illustrated by Shi and Wu (2019), who analyzed China's input–output tables to consider product-embodied research and development (R&D) expenditure. They further decomposed the total R&D content in a sector into five components, namely the

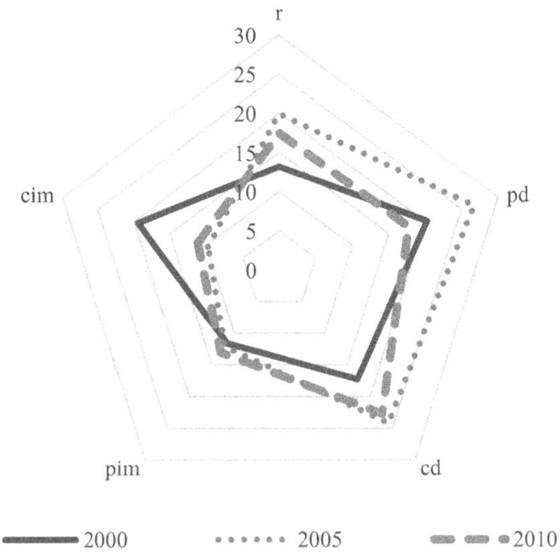

Figure 1. Five components of embodied R&D intensity in selected years.
Source: Shi and Wu (2019).

direct R&D expenditure® of the industry, R&D incorporated in domestic intermediate inputs (*pd*), domestic investment goods and services (*cd*), imported intermediate inputs (*cim*), and imported investment goods and services (*pim*). Their decomposition results demonstrate the evolution of the five components of product-embodied R&D intensity, as shown in Figure 1.

The important role of the intensity of R&D embodiment in imported capital goods is reflected by the sharp corner in the pentagon of year 2000 in Figure 1. Thus, there is clear evidence that China's innovation heavily relies on knowledge spillover from imported capital goods. But this sharp point vanished in 2005 and 2010. It has probably shrunk further in the recent decade. R&D embodied in domestic investment goods and services and direct R&D of the industry instead took the dominant positions. This change implies the switching roles of external technologies and indigenous knowledge. China's innovation is becoming less dependent on external knowledge transfer and increasingly independent and self-enforced in the 21st century (Shi and Wu 2019).

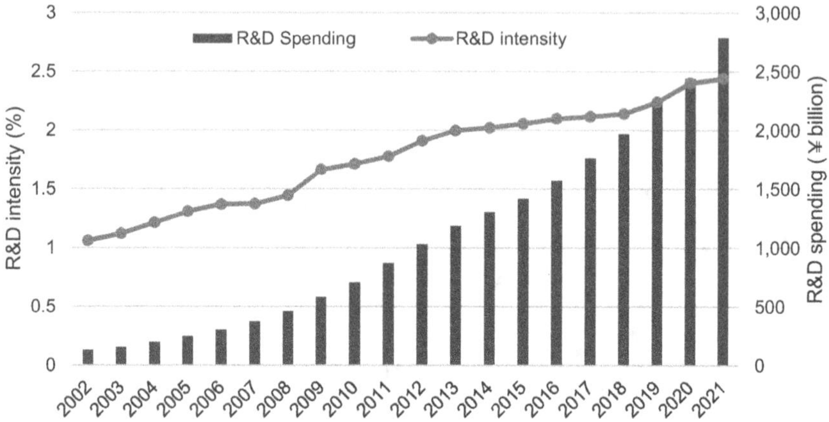

Figure 2. China's R&D spending and intensity, 2002–2021.
Source: Raw data are drawn from NBSC (2022).

As indigenous innovation becomes more important, Chinese government is responding by increasing R&D spending. During the decades of 2002–2021, China's R&D spending maintained an average growth rate of 18.01% per annum. This growth was sustained even during the COVID-19 outbreak (Figure 2). By 2021, R&D spending as a proportion of the country's GDP (or R&D intensity) reached 2.44%. This is about the average level of OECD countries in 2018, though China's income per capita was much lower than the average income in OECD countries. In aggregate terms, China is now the second-largest R&D investor, just behind the United States (US). In 2021, China spent a total of about US$551 billion in R&D, which is close to the combined investment of Japan, Germany, South Korea, France, and India in the same year. The consequence of such a spending spree is the rapid growth in innovation outcomes, such as invention patents. In 2009, China, for the first time, overtook the US in terms of the number of invention patent applications. In 2010, China's invention patent applications exceeded those of Japan, which was then the country with the largest number of patent applications (Figure 3). Since then, China has maintained the top position, with more than 1.2 million patent applications annually in recent years.

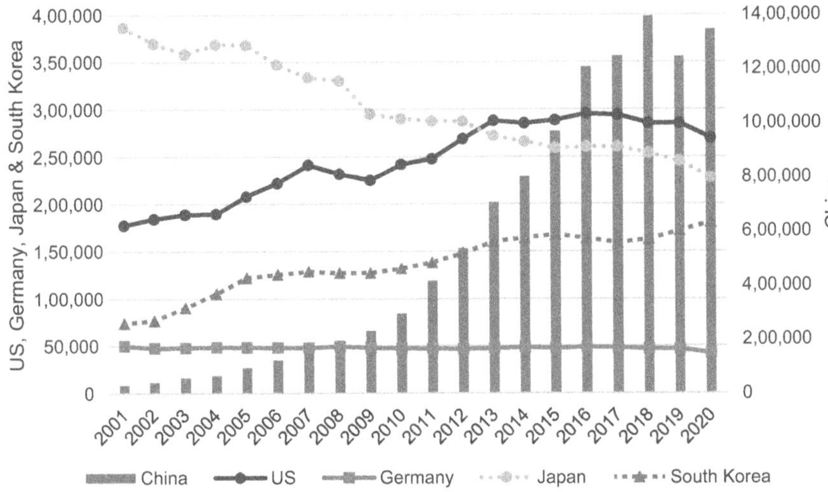

Figure 3. Number of invention patent applications in selected countries, 2001–2020.

Source: Raw data are drawn from OECD (2022a).

China's progress in innovation is also captured by the number of research articles published in academic journals, which is tracked by *InCites*, the metadata of publications collected by the Web of Science (2022). According to the *InCites* database, China has narrowed the gap with the US, the world's research leader. In 2021, American researchers published a total of 786,258 papers, while their Chinese counterparts recorded a total of 714,472 articles. The number of articles published by American researchers declined modestly for two consecutive years during the pandemic (2020 and 2021). This decline may be related to COVID-19 interruptions or the anti-migration policies during the Trump administration. Whether this is a long-term trend or a temporary diversion is to be assessed in the coming years. In contrast, China's research productivity maintained its trend of steady growth during the pandemic. If the current trend continues, China is likely to overtake the US to have the largest number of research papers published in 2022 (so far, 422,224 vs. 282,918 articles, according to the *InCites* database, accessed on October 7).

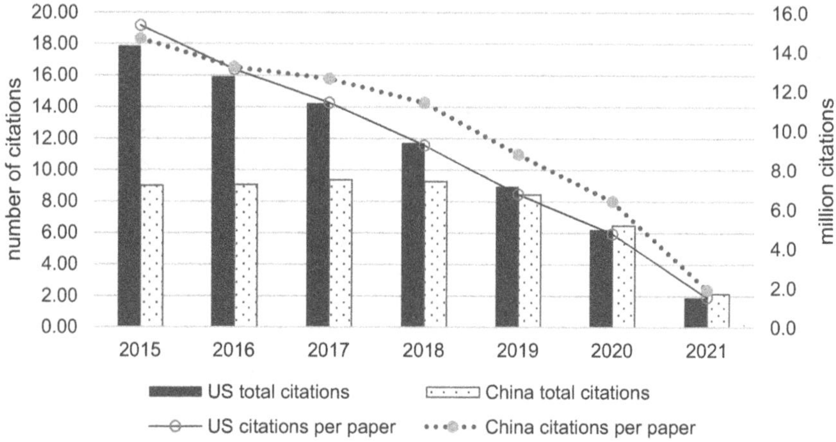

Figure 4. Total citations and citations per paper in China and the US, 2015–2021.
Source: Raw data are drawn from the Web of Science (2022).

Furthermore, there is evidence of improvement in the quality of research outcomes by Chinese researchers. Though controversial, citation counts of research papers are often used as an important indicator of research impact or quality (Aksnes *et al.*, 2019). According to the *InCites* database, the total number of citations of China's research papers for the first time exceeded that of America's in 2020 (5.2 million vs. 5.0 million citations), and this trend resumed in 2021 (1.7 million vs. 1.5 million citations). In addition, the US has been ahead of China in terms of the average number of citations per paper until 2016, when China overtook the US (Figure 4). Since then, China has maintained the lead.

Challenges

Though there has been significant progress in innovation in China, the country is still facing tremendous challenges. In several areas, there is considerable room for further improvement. The weakness of China's innovation capacity in developing key technologies is exposed through the current tech war between the US and China. Overcoming this technology weakness is a huge challenge in the coming years. The US and its major allies regard China as a national security threat and hence deny it access to core technologies, such as cutting-edge semiconductors and related state-of-the-art manufacturing technologies and software for building them. This situation is likely to continue and even get worse in the coming decade (Jiang and Murmann, 2022; Kenney and Lewin, 2022). Without removing potential technology bottlenecks, China's innovation progress would be affected, and hence economic growth may slow down further.

Apart from the need to catch up with advanced economies in key technology areas, there are other challenges associated with more fundamental issues and policies in innovation. While R&D intensity has increased steadily in recent decades, China still lags behind major players in the world (Figure 5). Despite being the world's second-largest R&D spender, China's gap with the global leader, the US, is still huge. For example, in 2021, R&D spending by the US was US$128 billion more than China's. In the coming years, China has to accelerate its investment in R&D. Especially, investment in basic research is its weakest area. China's investment in

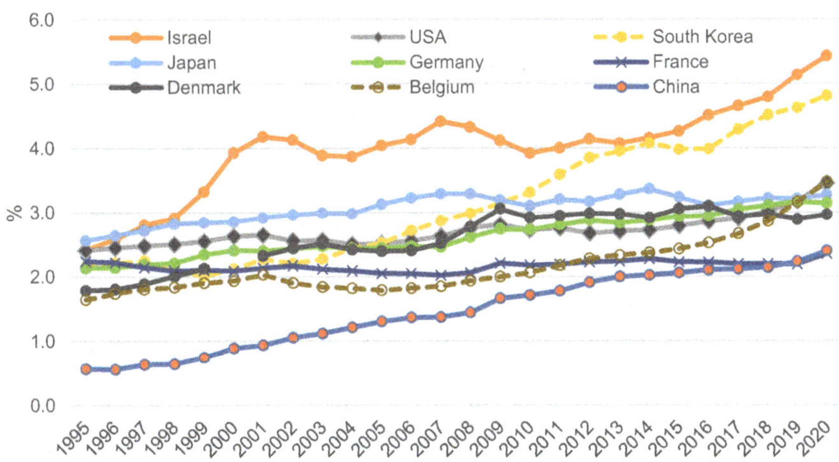

Figure 5. R&D intensity in selected economies, 1995–2020.

Source: Raw data are drawn from the World Bank (2022).

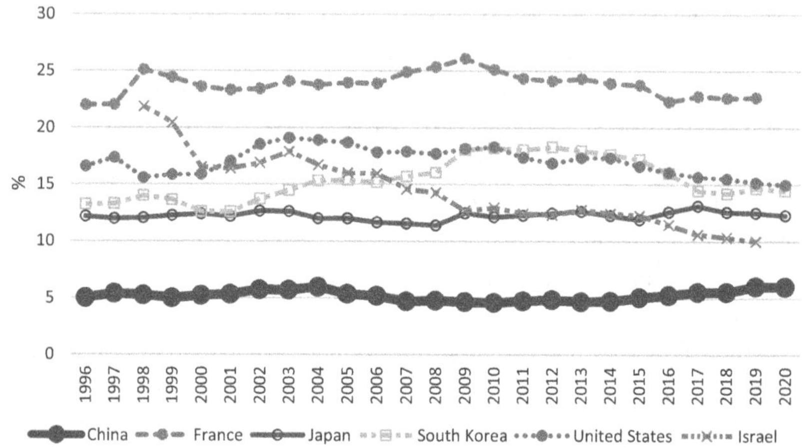

Figure 6. Basic research spending over total R&D investment (%), 1996–2020.
Source: Raw data are drawn OECD (2022b).

basic research as a share of total R&D spending is far below the trend of innovation leaders in the world (Figure 6). Further investigation shows that basic research spending by business enterprises is particularly small. In 2019, for example, China's business sector only accounts for 6.5% of total spending on basic research, while the same share is 47.1% in Japan, 32.1% in the US, and 57.5% in South Korea, according to the OECD (2022b) database.

Another interesting observation is that non-resident applicants have a relatively small share of total invention patent applicants in China (Figure 7). The pattern of changes in this share in China is similar to that in South Korea. As the number of patent applications increased, non-resident applicants as a share initially declined and then remained about 10% in recent years. This ratio is very low in China relative to other countries, such as Japan (19%) and South Korea (22%), not to mention the US (52%). One may argue that the low share in China is due to the extraordinary growth in invention patent applications (the denominator) in recent years. However, an alternative explanation could be that non-residents may be concerned with intellectual property rights (IPR) protection in the Chinese market and hence have no incentive to lodge patent applications in China. A recent survey confirms that foreign-funded

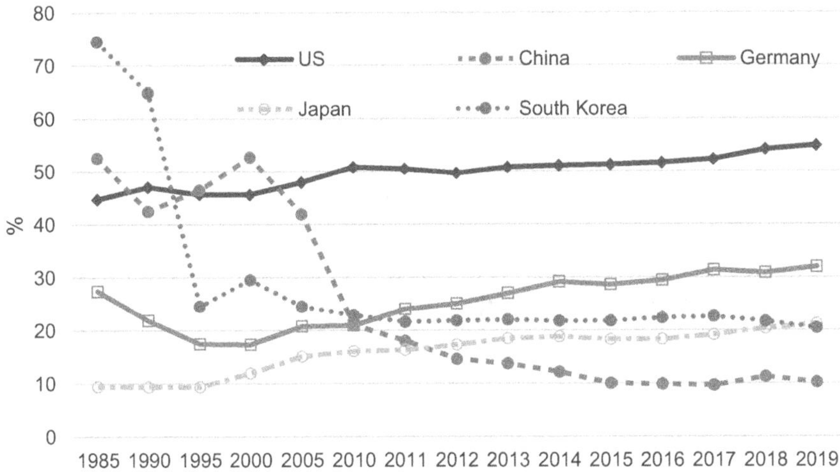

Figure 7. Shares (%) of patent applications by non-residents.

Source: Raw data are drawn from the World Bank (2022).

firms, particularly those from OECD countries, are more likely to confront patent infringements in China than domestic firms (CNIPA, 2022). The same survey also shows that high-tech firms are more likely to be victims of patent infringements than other firms. Therefore, policymakers in the country must confront the issue of IPR protection and further strengthen the enforcement of IPR laws and regulations. An improvement in the IPR environment can become an incentive for investment in innovation.

As a large country with a diverse culture, regional disparity is always a concern for China's policymakers. The sources of disparity are controversial. There is evidence of substantial disparity in the regional distribution of innovation resources and capacities, which may contribute to imbalanced development (Xiao *et al.*, 2019). In terms of R&D intensity, only six regions (Beijing, Shanghai, Tianjin, Guangdong, Jiangsu, and Zhejiang) exceeded the national average of 2.4% in 2020, and not surprisingly, these regions turn out to be the most developed regions in the country. All other regions fall behind the national R&D intensity, and in particular, there are 13 regions with less than 1.5% of their regional GDP invested in innovation (NBSC, 2022). The picture is similar in terms of R&D

personnel. The above-mentioned six regions recorded the highest R&D personnel/total employment ratio (from 12‰ in Guangdong to 29‰ in Beijing) in 2020. This ratio is less than 10‰ for the rest of the country (25 regions), among which 16 regions recorded less than 5‰. As innovation is becoming the main driver of economic growth, regional differences in innovation capacities and resources will lead to further regional imbalances in economic development. Thus, reducing regional inequality in innovation resources and capacities will be a major challenge for both the central and local governments.

Opportunities

Challenges go hand in hand with opportunities. Dealing with the challenges may also bring about opportunities for innovation breakthroughs. The current technological war between the US and China, initiated by the Trump administration, not only reveals the existence of technology bottlenecks in China but also identifies areas of focus for future innovation policies and resources. It is anticipated that there will be, if not already, major policy adjustments toward self-sufficiency in critical technology fields, such as cutting-edge semiconductors. To achieve this goal, a massive injection of innovation resources, such as funds and human capital, into these fields is needed. For human capital, the technological war and resultant restrictions may represent opportunities for China to benefit from the reverse brain drain between the US and China (Marini and Yang, 2021). Therefore, appropriate policies are needed to attract talents from world markets, especially the US market. For example, China's relatively low compensation costs imply that competitive salaries could be offered to recruit researchers from international markets.

China's high growth of four decades benefited tremendously from population dividends. The country's innovation can exploit a different type of population dividend which is associated with the world's largest research team (Figure 8). Apart from the large size, the research team also has a relatively low compensation cost, which,

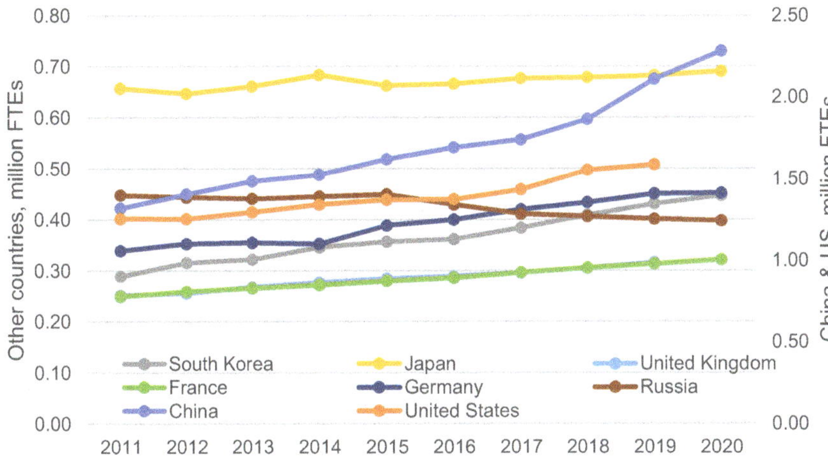

Figure 8. Total number of FTE researchers.

Source: Raw data are drawn from the World Bank (2022).

on average, only amounts to 36.4% of total costs during 2018–2020 (OECD, 2022b). This share is lower than 43.6% in Japan, 46.9% in South Korea, 50.3% in the United Kingdom, 65.4% in Germany, and 71.1% in France during the same period (OECD, 2022b). Furthermore, there is room for further reforms. In China, full-time equivalent (FTE) researchers, on average, amount to just 43.2% of total personnel in R&D entities in the recent decade. At the regional level, this share is even lower in Guangdong (33.9%), Zhejiang (29.5%), and Jiangsu (39.2%), which are three leading R&D players. These shares are much lower than those of Russia (53.4%), Germany (60.3%), France (65.5%), and the United Kingdom (68.9%), not to mention Japan (75.9%) and South Korea (80.0%).[1] Thus, in comparison with other countries, there is large scope for improvement in efficiency in research management. This can only be achieved through deepening reforms in the R&D sector so that resources can be distributed more efficiently.

International collaboration plays an important role in global knowledge creation and exchange. There is evidence that international collaboration generally leads to research outcomes of better quality. Statistics from the Web of Science (2022) show that research papers with international collaborators attract much higher citation counts than those without international collaboration. For example, research papers published by Chinese institutions or researchers without international collaboration in 2020, on average, recorded 6.9 citation counts per paper, while those involving international collaboration had 11.1 counts per paper. Therefore, even though there are voices calling for technology and science decoupling between the US and China in the midst of the technological war, China should continue to adopt policies encouraging the country's researchers and institutions for international engagement in scientific research and exchange. According to the Web of Science (2022) database, in 2021, China's research papers involving international collaboration account for 24.1% of the total number of papers. This number is 32.8% in Japan and 36.1% in the US, not to mention 59.2% in Australia in the same year. Therefore, there is considerable room for improvement in international collaboration.

Climate change actions have created a new frontier of innovation: the emergence of green innovation. Green innovation involves creating or adopting new or modified technologies, processes, practices, and products to protect the environment (Yang *et al.*, 2020; Takalo *et al.*, 2021). Businesses can adopt cleaner technologies through green innovation to reduce pollution emissions, avoid environmental penalties, and reduce compliance costs. Businesses can also improve resource utilization to reduce production costs via green innovation. Scholars call these the "double externalities," or positive externalities, in knowledge spillovers and environmental effects (Qi *et al.*, 2021; Shi *et al.*, 2022). However, green innovation is risky and requires massive investment with a long payback period. Therefore, further reforms are needed to provide incentives for companies to invest in green innovation.

In order to promote the construction of a green financial system and hence green innovation, the State Council in 2017 decided to select eight regions in Guangdong, Guizhou, Jiangxi, Xinjiang, and Zhejiang provinces for the first batch of green finance reform and innovation pilot zones (or simply "pilot zones"). These pilot zones are beneficial complements to building a comprehensive green finance system. To achieve the two goals of carbon emission peak by 2030 and carbon neutrality by 2060, the government should further support the construction of these pilot zones and expand the pilot zones to other regions so that these pilot zones become an effective vehicle for promoting innovation, especially green innovation. Furthermore, local governments should utilize local advantages to make the best use of these pilot zones and encourage enterprises to participate in green innovation.

It is argued that the pilot zones can promote enterprise green innovation by alleviating firm financing constraints and reinforcing environmental regulations. Incentive measures for the pilot zones to promote the green innovation of enterprises should be further strengthened. For example, a green financial risk prevention mechanism and a green project investment risk compensation mechanism could be established to encourage financial institutions to carry out green financial product innovation and thereby provide more financial support for enterprise green innovation (Shi *et al.*, 2022). Besides, the construction of trading markets for environmental rights and interests and an information-sharing platform for enterprises' environmental violations and pollution emissions should be further promoted. These measures could force enterprises to carry out green innovation and hence improve their production processes.

Finally, Shi *et al.* (2022) argued that the promotion effect of the pilot zones is heterogeneous across different types of enterprises. Therefore, governments should adopt differentiated policies and adjust the relevant policies accordingly. For example, for SOEs, the government should encourage these firms to participate in green innovation by fully exploiting their resource advantages. In addition, enterprises should take the initiative to engage in or expand their green innovation activities, which will reduce their pollutant emissions, meet the environmental regulation requirements, and hence improve enterprises' performance and market competitiveness.

Digital technology is the new engine of economic growth in China, creating numerous new opportunities, such as jobs and efficient crisis management during the COVID-19 pandemic

(Huang *et al.*, 2021). On this front, China is catching up rapidly. In some sectors, China is not a latecomer and instead enjoys first-mover advantages. For example, China distinguishes itself from most advanced markets by focusing on the development of mobile-first, fiber-intensive, and inclusive digital technologies (Jiang and Murmann, 2022). The digital economy in China will likely grow more rapidly in the coming years, bringing about more fundamental changes. However, authorities will also need to address a wide range of policy issues to ensure the smooth development of the digital economy, including the easing of the data inequality problem, protection of individual rights, and regulation of platform behavior.

While China is leading the world in consumer-internet technologies, or soft technologies, there are gaps in hard technologies, such as quantum computing, robotics, and semiconductors, with globally leading players, and more R&D efforts should be directed toward these fields (Kenney and Lewin, 2022). The 14th Five-Year Plan rightly highlighted the importance of these cutting-edge technologies. Given today's geopolitics and competition, self-sufficiency may be the long-term reality which the country has to face. With the world's largest cohort of science, technology, engineering, and mathematics (STEM) graduates, including PhD students, trained at home and abroad every year, China clearly has the potential to maintain an edge in some technology fields and catch up with the leading players in other areas. The realization of this potential requires government policy support to maintain and attract talents in the arena of digital technologies. In addition, Liu *et al.* (2022) argued that digital technology development can not only reduce local carbon emissions but also promote carbon abatement in neighboring cities. Thus, digital technology breakthroughs and applications will also contribute to the cause of climate change control.

Concluding Remarks

In summary, this chapter presented a brief review of the progress, challenges, and opportunities of China's innovation. Through four decades of reforms and high economic growth, China has astonishingly closed its gap with advanced economies in some technology areas. The achievement is observable by any casual visitor to the country. Bullet trains, space stations, and supercomputers are tangible examples of technological advancement, for instance. However, significant innovation challenges lie ahead. These include external access to cutting-edge technologies, underinvestment in basic research, weak IPR protection, and regional disparities. These challenges, together with current geopolitics, may hinder China's ambition of becoming a technology superpower in the coming decades.

However, every challenge is an opportunity. The current technological war between the US and China could be an opportunity to strengthen self-sufficiency in major technologies through more investment in R&D, particularly in basic research, the development of domestic supply chains to remove technology bottlenecks, and increased openness to international engagement and exchanges. Furthermore, the Chinese government's commitments of peaking carbon emissions by 2030 and reaching carbon neutrality by 2060 create a great opportunity for green innovation. In the fields of both green innovation and digital technologies, China is not a latecomer. Policymakers should exploit the country's first-mover advantage in these fields to accelerate technological development. If so, the country's technology superpower dream may perhaps come true in these areas first.

Endnote

1. These statistics are calculated by using data from the OECD (2022b).

References

Aksnes, D.W., Langfeldt, L., and Wouters, P. 2019. Citations, citation indicators, and research quality: An overview of basic concepts and theories. *SAGE Open* (January-March): 1–17.

CNIPA. 2022. Report of 2021 Patent Survey of China. Beijing: Development Research Centre of China National Intellectual Property Administration (in Chinese).

Fisch, C., Block, J., and Sandner, P. 2019. The impact of acquisitions on Chinese acquirers' innovation performance: An empirical investigation of 1545 Chinese acquisitions. *Journal of Business Economics*, 89: 125–153.

Fu, X. 2008. Foreign direct investment, absorptive capacity and regional innovation capabilities: Evidence from China. *Oxford Development Studies*, 36(1): 89–110.

Huang, Y., Qiu, H., and Wang, J. 2021. Digital technology and economic impacts of Covid-19: Experiences of the People's Republic of China. ADBI Working Papers No. 1276.

Jiang, H. and Murmann, J.P. 2022. The rise of China's digital economy: An overview. *Management and Organization Review*, 18(4): 790–802.

Kenney, M. and Lewin, A.Y. 2022. Semiconductor catch-up is not enough: Twigging the context of China's ambitions. *Management and Organization Review*, 18(4): 816–826.

Kowalski, A.M. 2021. Dynamics and factors of innovation gap between the European Union and China. *Journal of the Knowledge Economy*, 12: 1966–1981.

Li, X. 2011. Sources of external technology, absorptive capacity, and innovation capability in Chinese state-owned high-tech enterprises. *World Development*, 39(7): 1240–1248.

Liang, Y., Giroud, A., and Rygh, A. 2022. Strategic asset-seeking acquisitions, technological gaps, and innovation performance of Chinese multinationals. *Journal of World Business*, 57(4): 101325.

Liu, J., Yu, Q., Chen, Y., and Liu, J. 2022. The impact of digital technology development on carbon emissions: A spatial effect analysis for China. *Resources, Conservation and Recycling*, 185: 106445.

Marini, G. and Yang, L. 2021. Globally bred Chinese talents returning home: An analysis of a reverse brain-drain flagship policy. *Science and Public Policy*, 48(4): 541–552.

NBSC. 2022. National Bureau of Statistics of China Online Database. http://www.stats.gov.cn/english/Statisticaldata/AnnualData/.

OECD. 2022a. Intellectual Property (IP) Statistics and Analysis. https://www.oecd.org/sti/inno/intellectual-property-statistics-and-analysis.htm.

OECD. 2022b. Research and Development Statistics (RDS). https:/www.oecd.org/science/inno/researchanddevelopmentstatisticsrds.htm.

Papaconstantinou, G., Sakurai, N., and Wyckoff, A. 1996. Embodied technology diffusion: An empirical analysis for 10 OECD countries. OECD STI Working Papers, 1996/1.

Qi, G., Jia, Y., and Zou, H. 2021. Is institutional pressure the mother of green innovation? Examining the moderating effect of absorptive capacity. *Journal of Cleaner Production*, 278: 123957.

Shi, X. and Wu, Y. 2019. Evolution of product-embodied R&D in China. *Structural Change and Economic Dynamics*, 49: 324–333.

Shi, X., Zeng, Y., Wu, Y., and Wang, S. 2022. Outward foreign direct investment and green innovation in Chinese multinational companies. Economics Discussion Papers, UWA.

Takalo, S.K., Tooranloo, H.S., and Parizi, Z.S. 2021. Green innovation: A systematic literature review. *Journal of Cleaner Production*, 279: 122474.

Web of Science. 2022. InCites Benchmarking and Analytics. https://clarivate.com/webofsciencegroup/solutions/incites/.

World Bank. 2022. World Development Indictor Online Database. https://databank.worldbank.org/source/world-development-indicators.

Xiao, Z.-L., Fan, R.-G., and Du, X.-Y. 2019. Measurement and convergence of China's regional innovation capability. *Science, Technology and Society*, 24(1): 1–28.

Yang, Z., Ali, S.T., Ali, F., Sarwar, Z., and Khan, M.A. 2020. Outward foreign direct investment and corporate green innovation: An institutional pressure perspective. *South African Journal of Business Management*, 51(1): 12.

https://doi.org/10.1142/9789819815241_0020

Chapter 20

MASS ENTREPRENEURSHIP AND INTELLECTUAL PROPERTY PROTECTION IN CHINA*

Naoki Murakami

Nihon University, Chiyoda, Tokyo, Japan
murakami.naoki@nihon-u.ac.jp

Introduction

Entrepreneurship is an important driving force for economic development. In China, its role is becoming increasingly important as the period of high economic growth is over and the country is seeking a transition to a new normal. With this in mind, China has been promoting the popularization of entrepreneurial and innovative activities in recent years under the "Mass Entrepreneurship and Innovation" initiative.

The first official public use of the concepts of mass entrepreneurship and mass innovation appeared in Premier Li Keqiang's

*I would like to express my sincere thanks to Professor Y. Y. Kueh and Professor Jun Zhang for inviting me to attend the International Symposium on "the Origin and Model of China's Economic Emergence" on September 17, 2022, and for including the paper, on which this chapter is based, in the conference. I would also like to thank Professor Qu Feng for his valuable comments and suggestions at the symposium.

speech at the opening ceremony of the Eighth Annual Meeting of the New Champions in 2014 (September 10, 2014, Tianjin). Subsequently, at the Third Session of the 12th National People's Congress held from March 5 to 15, 2015, the *Government Work Report 2015* put forward the concept of "mass entrepreneurship and innovation." On June 16, 2015, the State Council issued the *Opinions on Several Policy Measures to Vigorously Promote Mass Entrepreneurship and Innovation* (hereafter referred to as the *Opinions*), officially launching the policy to promote the popularization of entrepreneurship and innovation.[1] Based on what is written in the first section of the *Opinions*, the background to these policies and their objectives can be summarized as follows. First, as the Chinese economy has entered a new normal and the high-speed growth based on expanding the input of production factors has come to an end, innovation-led growth is needed. Democratizing entrepreneurship and innovation holds the promise for new growth.

Second, a major objective of the policy is to secure and expand employment opportunities through entrepreneurship. Ensuring enough job opportunities has always been a top priority for the Chinese government: with the rapid development of technologies such as information technology and artificial intelligence, the employment absorption capacity of traditional industrial sectors is weakening, but the number of new college graduates alone is more than 10 million each year in China. For these new entrants to the labor market, expanding employment opportunities through entrepreneurship is crucial. Third, by promoting entrepreneurship and innovation in a popular way, people's ideas will change, and entrepreneurship and innovation will become common societal values.

The *Opinions* set out specific policies to promote entrepreneurship and innovation, with the protection of intellectual property rights (IPR) and the promotion of their use receiving special attention. In particular, in Section 3 of the *Opinions*, "innovating the system and mechanism to achieve entrepreneurship facilitation," although with a focus on improving the market environment for fair competition, deepening the reform of the business system, and improving the training and flow mechanism of entrepreneurial talents, it also mentions strengthening the protection of entrepreneurial IPR. Specific measures include intellectual property (IP) protection for new forms of innovation, such as research and business models, and vigorous promotion of IP trade; a national IP public service platform was quickly established.

This chapter examines whether such policies to protect and exploit IP have an impact on the development of entrepreneurship through an econometric analysis using regional data from China. The chapter thus follows the view that entrepreneurship is embodied in the establishment of "individual industrial and commercial businesses" (hereafter, "self-employed"). Accordingly, the key variables we use are the number of newly registered self-employed households in China's provinces (municipalities directly under the central government, provinces, and autonomous regions, all hereafter referred to as "provinces") and the indicators developed by the Intellectual Property Development Research Center of the State Intellectual Property Administration to assess the state of IP protection and utilization in each province. Inter-provincial interdependence is likely to emerge in the protection and use of IPR. That is, the protection and utilization of IPR in one province will affect the establishment of new self-employed businesses in other provinces. This chapter investigates this possibility by estimating a spatial Durbin model (SDM) that takes into account inter-regional interdependence.

The rest of this chapter is organized as follows. Section "Mass Entrepreneurship and IP protection" examines how self-employed businesses are set up in China and then summarizes China's IPR policy. Section "SDM Estimation" describes the SDM used in this analysis. Basic estimates are presented in section "Estimation Results", which also briefly discusses the use of Moran scatter plots. Section "Impact of Individual Indices" examines the relationship between individual indicators and the establishment of the self-employed. Section "Conclusion" gives the conclusion.

Mass Entrepreneurship and IP Protection

Status of the establishment of self-employed households

Based on previous studies (Pietrobelli *et al.*, 2004; Liu and Huang, 2016; Burke *et al.*, 2021), this study measures entrepreneurship in terms of the establishment of self-employed households because entrepreneurship, by its very nature, can be understood as a risk-taking activity (Parker, 2018). In recent years, China has usually measured the effectiveness of its policies to promote entrepreneurship by the increase in the number of market players. The term "market entity" is stipulated in Article 2 of Chapter I of the *Regulations of the People's Republic of China on the Administration of Registration of Market Entities*:[2] (1) companies, non-company enterprise legal persons, and their branches; (2) sole proprietorship enterprises, partnership enterprises, and their branches; (3) specialized farmers cooperatives (associations) and their branches; (4) individual industrial and commercial enterprises; (5) branches of foreign companies; and (6) other market entities as stipulated by laws and administrative regulations. Sections (1), (2), and (5) refer to enterprises (companies). Because enterprises vary in size and include those established by other enterprises, especially by foreign capital, we believe that to describe the popularization of entrepreneurship, we should focus on the creation of new self-employed households. As Li (2018) has pointed out, for individuals, the original intention to become self-employed is still to start a business. After all, being self-employed is one way to start a business with a low threshold.[3] In addition to data on the self-employed, microdata from the Global Entrepreneurship Monitor (GEM) questionnaire can also be used as indicators to measure entrepreneurship. This index is often used in international comparative analysis.[4]

In China, Article 2 of the *Regulations on Individual Industrial and Commercial Enterprises*[5] defines the self-employed as "individual industrial and commercial enterprises engaged in industrial and commercial operations of citizens capable of business operation registered by the administrative department for industry and commerce in accordance with the provisions of these Regulations." This clearly requires registration in accordance with the *Measures for the Administration of Registration of Individual Industrial and Commercial Enterprises*.[6] On March 1, 2022, the *Regulations of the People's Republic of China on the Administration of the Registration of Market Entities* and the *Implementation Rules of the Regulations of the People's Republic of China on the Administration of the Registration of Market Entities* came into effect, and the *Measures on the Administration of the Registration of Individual Industrial and Commercial Households* were abolished.

In the field of labor economics, many studies in the existing literature have used microdata when examining the self-employed and regard the generation of self-employment as an individual's choice of employment mode (Yueh, 2009; Liu and Huang, 2016; Ma, 2018, Chapter 6; Murakami, 2019). A key question is whether the self-employed are motivated to choose out of necessity or to actively seek new opportunities. The latter means that the self-employed are exerting their entrepreneurial spirit, whereas the former does not. The incentives for individuals to choose to become self-employed (the nature of being self-employed) change over time throughout the economy. By using data on the number of new registrations (flow) rather than the actual number of self-employed (stock), this study analyzes the self-employed of a new nature, especially entrepreneurship.

According to the World Bank Group and the Development Research Center of the State Council (2019), there have been three waves of entrepreneurship in China since the reform and opening up. The first wave occurred in the 1980s, when rural reforms and an increase in the rural labor force allowed farmers to develop production in collective ownership, giving rise to a number of township and village enterprises.[7] The second wave began in the 1990s, when the reform goal of the socialist market economic system stimulated the enthusiasm of broad masses of people for entrepreneurship, and the emergence of domestic private enterprises fundamentally reshaped China's economic structure. The third is the current wave of entrepreneurship initiated by the 2015 Mass Entrepreneurship and Innovation Initiative.[8]

Figure 1 illustrates the evolution of the actual number of self-employed households in China from 1992 to 2019 based on data from the *China Statistical Yearbook* of the National Bureau of Statistics; the data for 2020 come from the Department of Comprehensive Planning of the State Administration for Market Regulation.[9] This time frame does not include the first wave, but it does include the second wave. The number of self-employed households increased from 15.34 million in 1992 to 31.60 million in 1999. By 2000, however, that number had fallen to 25.71 million and remained in

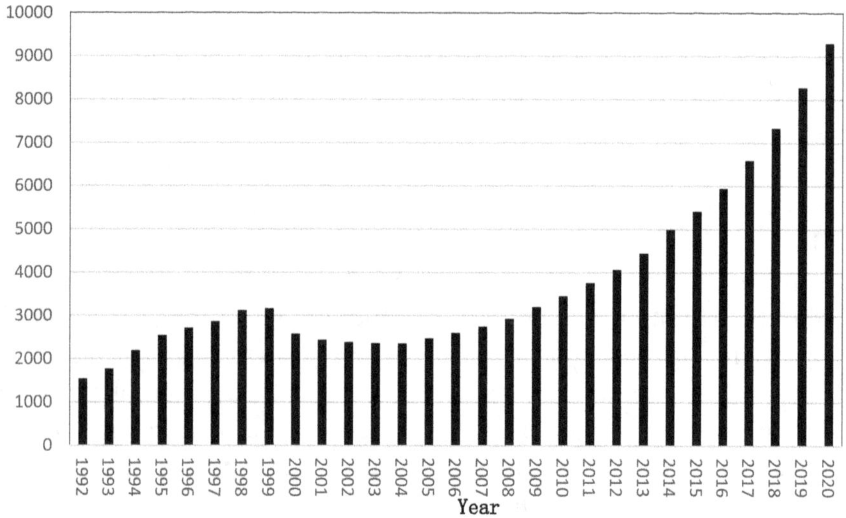

Figure 1. Growth in the number of self-employed households (10,000 households, 1992–2020).

Source: China Statistical Yearbook. Among them, the data for 2020 came from the Department of Comprehensive Planning of the State Administration for Market Regulation (June 11, 2021).

decline or flat for some time after that, perhaps because of too many start-up procedures, a heavy tax burden, and high entry threshold problems.[10] The introduction of a large number of industry management laws around 1995 is also considered to be a factor (Lin, 2012). However, the number of self-employed began to rise again in 2005 and was expected to reach 92.87 million by 2020. The rapid growth from 2015 was reflected in the third wave of entrepreneurship, which saw the number of self-employed households increase after the introduction of the mass entrepreneurship and innovation policy. In recent years, with changes in the market, WeChat businesses, e-commerce, Internet celebrities, and other new forms of business have developed rapidly, which has also promoted the increasing number of self-employed households.

In which industries are the self-employed more prevalent? The distribution of actual self-employed individuals by industry sector at the end of 2015 and 2020 is shown in Table 1. The data come from

Table 1. Distribution of actual self-employed households (at the end of 2015 and 2020).

	End of 2015 actual number	Proportion (%)	End of 2020 actual number	Proportion (%)	2020/2015 (times)
Total	54,079,372	100.0	92,871,987	100.0	1.72
Agriculture, forestry, animal husbandry and fishery	1,455,442	2.7	3,287,345	3.5	2.26
Mining industry	34,099	0.1	26,023	0.0	0.76
Manufacturing industry	3,562,297	6.6	5,236,575	5.6	1.47
Electricity, heat, gas and water production and supply industries	16,597	0.0	30,772	0.0	1.85
Construction industry	148,010	0.3	575,267	0.6	3.89
Wholesale and retail	35,026,803	64.8	52,943,361	57.0	1.51
Transportation, warehousing and postal services	1,480,798	2.7	3,552,988	3.8	2.40
Accommodation and catering	5,235,128	9.7	12,584,766	13.6	2.40
Information transmission, software and information technology services	294,809	0.5	693,910	0.7	2.35
Finance industry	3,624	0.0	7,831	0.0	2.16
Real estate industry	67,987	0.1	159,988	0.2	2.35
Leasing and business services	759,007	1.4	2,805,836	3.0	3.70
Scientific research and technical services	171,869	0.3	188,317	0.2	1.10
Water conservancy, environment and public facilities management industry	14,217	0.0	253,399	0.3	17.82
Residential services, repairs and other services	5,250,022	9.7	9,182,120	9.9	1.75
Education	28,710	0.1	91,853	0.1	3.20
Health and social work	126,680	0.2	223,693	0.2	1.77
Culture, sports and entertainment	270,911	0.5	550,123	0.6	2.03
Other	132,362	0.2	477,820	0.5	3.61

Source: Report on the Development of China's Mass Entrepreneurship and Innovation (2015, 2020).

the 2015 and 2020 editions of the *Report on the Development of China's Mass Entrepreneurship and Innovation,* published by the National Development and Reform Commission. First, at the end of 2015, the total number of self-employed households was 54.08 million. Divided by industry type, wholesale and retail had the largest number (35.03 million households; 64.8% of the total); this was followed by residential services, repair, and other services, with 5.25 million households (9.7%), followed by accommodation and catering, with 5.24 million households (9.7%). These three industries together accounted for 84.2% of the total number of self-employed households.

By the end of 2020, the share of wholesale and retail trade in the above three industries dropped to 57.0%, while the share of residential services, repair, and other services and accommodation and catering rose to 9.9% and 13.6%, respectively, with the combined share of the three industries remaining high, at 80.4%. It can be seen that even under the policy of mass entrepreneurship and innovation, the changes in the industry structure of the self-employed are not obvious. However, from the quantity change (multiple) from 2015 to 2020, divided by industry — except for the water conservancy, environment, and public facilities management industries, which increased by 17.82 times — the construction industry, leasing and business service industry, and education all increased more than threefold (3.89 times, 3.70 times, and 3.20 times, respectively). This suggests that the self-employed are expanding into new areas.[11]

In addition, the latest data released by the State Administration for Market Regulation showed that "by the end of 2021, there were 103 million registered individual industrial and commercial households in China, up 11.1 percent year on year, accounting for about two-thirds of the total number of market entities (154 million). ... (The self-employed) have become a positive force for transformation and upgrading. In 2021, new self-employed businesses in emerging services will grow strongly, with 'culture, sports and entertainment', 'scientific research and technology services' and 'information transmission, software and information technology services' leading the growth."[12]

China's IP policy

At the same time, China has emphasized the protection and utilization of IPR as a national strategy in recent years. On June 11, 2008, the State Council issued the *Outline of the National Strategy on Intellectual Property Rights,* putting forward the 16-character policy of "encouraging creation, effective utilization, legal protection and scientific management," which divides IP work into four aspects: creation, utilization, protection, and management. In addition, on December 22, 2015, the State Council issued *Several Opinions on Accelerating the Building of a Strong Country with Intellectual Property Rights under the New Situation,* which set the goal of "significantly improving China's ability to create, utilize, protect, manage and service intellectual property rights" by 2020.

Last year, on September 23, 2021, the CPC Central Committee and the State Council issued the *Outline for Building an Intellectual Property Power (2021–2035*), and on October 11, the State Council issued the *Circular on the 14th Five-Year Plan for the Protection and Application of National Intellectual Property Rights.* In addition, in response to these new policies, the Office of the National Leading Group on Combating Infringement of Intellectual Property Rights and Production and Sale of Fake and Inferior Commodities released the *New Progress Report on China's Intellectual Property Protection and Business Environment* (2021) in April 2022: "IPR protection is an important indicator to measure the business environment, and optimizing the business environment is an important guarantee for IPR protection," the report said. Further, "[t]he Chinese government will coordinate efforts to protect IPR and improve the business environment." These measures aim to obtain more IP in greater quantity and of higher quality by strengthening the protection of IP and implementing various research and development (R&D) promotion policies.

This study thus seeks to empirically investigate whether such IP policies can effectively increase the establishment of the self-employed. The possible effects of IP protection on the establishment of the self-employed include the following. First, the protection of

IPR is supposed to facilitate the establishment of the self-employed by guaranteeing their rights and ensuring fair market competition. Second, the self-employed themselves often infringe IPR (Wang and Jiang 2014); in this case, strengthening the protection of IPR can improve the credibility of self-employed businesses by reducing such infringements, which is beneficial to the establishment of self-employed businesses. Moreover, if the self-employed are established in a way that takes advantage of new ideas (innovation in a broad sense), stronger protection of IPR may generate more such innovation and increase the establishment of the self-employed. Generally, stronger protection of IPR is also likely to stimulate innovative activity throughout the economy and enable the self-employed to enjoy and take advantage of the spillover effects of new knowledge and technologies.

All of these are positive effects of IP protection. However, it may also have negative effects. Even if the development of an IP protection regime is generally desirable, it may lead to increased costs for the self-employed, which may discourage the establishment of new self-employed businesses. The spillover effects of new knowledge discussed above may also be mitigated by the strengthening of IPR, which may make it more difficult for the self-employed to take advantage of new knowledge. In order to evaluate a series of IP strategies, the Intellectual Property Development Research Center of the State Intellectual Property Administration has, since 2012, compiled an annual "Evaluation Index on the Status of Intellectual Property Development" and released it in the form of an *Evaluation Report on the Status of Intellectual Property Development in China*. In this study, these indicators are used as the data for the empirical analysis.

The evaluation index for IP development follows the logical framework put forward in the *Outline of National Intellectual Property Strategy* and *Some Opinions on Accelerating the Construction of a Powerful Country with Intellectual Property under New Situation*. The first-level index of the evaluation system is divided into four aspects: creation, utilization, protection, and environment. The corresponding secondary indicators are quantity, quality, and efficiency (creation); scale and benefit (utilization); judicial protection, administrative protection, and protection effect (protection); system, service, and awareness (environment). Under the secondary indicators, there are 45 third-level indicators (see Table A1 in Appendix for details; see the *Report* for how these indicators are defined and constructed).

The relevant literature can be found in international comparative analysis. Burke *et al.* (2021) conducted a regression analysis using micro data from 35 EU countries (sample size: 5,141, covering the years 2010 and 2015), showing that the more active the R&D activities in the countries concerned, the more self-employed people there were (considered by the authors to be high-quality self-employed people). LêKhang and Thành (2018) used data from 13 emerging economies in the period 2002–2013 for regression analysis and found that using the number of patents as an indicator of innovation could not significantly explain the proportion of nascent entrepreneurs in related countries (the number of nascent entrepreneurs as a percentage of the population aged 18–64) in related countries.[13] Sanandaji and Leeson (2012) and Chowdhury *et al.* (2015) found that IPR protection, in a broad sense, is negatively correlated with the scale of self-employment in relevant countries.

Similar to this paper, Li and Zhao (2011) used panel data for each province and year of China (1999–2008) to conduct regression analysis with the ratio of self-employment to non-agricultural employment (self-employed employment ratio) as the explained variable. However, variables related to IPR were not included in the analysis. In the current study, regional (provincial) data are used for regression analysis to study the possibility of spillover effects from strengthening IPR protection and exploitation. Spillover effects are considered in two categories: within the region (province), implementing enhanced IPR protection and utilization (provincial spillover effect), and a broader spillover effect to other regions or counties (cross-provincial spillovers).

SDM Estimation

Estimation model

Using regional (provincial) and annual panel data, we estimated the following SDM, which considers the spatial dependence of explained and explanatory variables:

$$y_t = \rho W y_t + X_t \beta + W X_t \theta + \mu + \varepsilon_t \qquad t = 1 \ldots T, \tag{1}$$

where t is time. In this analysis, $T = 6$. y_t is the $n \times 1$ column vector of the explained variable, and X_t is the $n \times k$ matrix of the explanatory variable; n is the number of sample areas ($n = 31$ in this study), and k is the number of explanatory variables. W is the $n \times n$ adjacency matrix as the space weight matrix. An adjacency matrix is a matrix with normalized rows (where the sum of the elements in each row is 1), and in the original matrix from which the normalized matrix was calculated, the element is 1 if the two provinces share a common border, and 0 otherwise (the diagonal element is 0). ρ, β, and θ are the coefficients to be estimated, and ρ represents the spatial autoregressive coefficient. Because fixed effects are assumed in this analysis, μ is also a coefficient to be estimated. For the error term, making the standard assumption that $\varepsilon_{it} \sim N(0, \sigma_\varepsilon^2)$ and for $i \neq j$ or $t \neq s$, $\mathrm{E}(\varepsilon_{it}\varepsilon_{js}) = 0$ are established.

The SDM accounts for the possibility that sample values in one region depend on those in other regions (Elhorst, 2014, pp. 7–8). First, the first term on the right in Equation (1) represents the endogenous interaction effects between the explained variables. This captures the possibility that the explained variable in one region is related to the explained variable in another region. Second, the third term in Equation (1) represents the exogenous interaction effects. As for exogenous interdependence effects, SDM can estimate both direct and indirect effects. Here, a direct effect refers to the influence of the change in the explanatory variable in one region on the explained variable in this region, while an indirect effect refers to the influence of the change in the explanatory variable in another region on the explained variable in this region.

In this study, a direct effect includes intra-provincial spillover effects, while an indirect effect captures inter-provincial spillover effects (generally, an indirect effect is also a spatial spillover effect).

Variables and data

This study estimated that the explained variable in the equation is the number of new registrations of self-employed households per year. The panel data from 31 provinces for the six years from 2015 to 2020 came from the *Report on the Development of China's Mass Entrepreneurship and Innovation* (various years) issued by the National Development and Reform Commission. The core explanatory variable is the comprehensive IP development index in the *Evaluation Report on the Status of Intellectual Property Development in China* by the Intellectual Property Development Research Center of the State Intellectual Property Administration. The index ranges from 0 to 100, with higher numbers indicating more advanced IP development.

The model in this analysis takes the nominal gross regional product (GRP), per capita real GRP (2012 baseline), real GRP growth rate, and population urbanization rate as explanatory variables to control exogenous factors. The nominal GRP represents the market size, while the real GRP per capita is an indicator measuring the level of economic development in the province. The real GRP growth rate represents the state of the business cycle. The population urbanization rate refers to the percentage of permanent urban residents in the total permanent population at the end of the year. Different provinces may have different procedures for registering self-employed households. In this paper, this is adjusted for fixed effects at the provincial level.

Basic statistics for each variable are shown in Table 2 (rows 1, 2, and 7–9). Figure 2 shows the number of new self-employed registrations by region in 2020. Jiangsu Province had the largest number of newly established self-employed households, with 2.003 million, followed by Shandong Province (1.379 million) and Guangdong Province (1.214 million). It should be noted that, in this graph,

Table 2. Data sources and descriptive statistics.[a]

	Source	Mean	Standard deviation	Minimum	Maximum
Newly registered self-employed (households)	Report on the Development of China's Mass Entrepreneurship and Innovation	437,073	346,209	16,050	2,003,002
Comprehensive IP development index	Evaluation Report on the Status of Intellectual Property Development in China	64.8	11.8	43.5	89.1
IP creation index	Evaluation Report on the Status of Intellectual Property Development in China	67.6	14.2	41.6	99.2
IP utilization index	Evaluation Report on the Status of Intellectual Property Development in China	61.0	10.2	43.4	83.2
IP judicial protection index	Evaluation Report on the Status of Intellectual Property Development in China	59.8	15.1	38.4	100.0
IP institutional-environment index	Evaluation Report on the Status of Intellectual Property Development in China	68.7	21.2	14.7	100.0
Nominal GRP (100 million yuan)	China Statistical Yearbook	28,293	22,973	1,026	110,761
Per capita real GRP (2012 basis) (10,000 yuan)	China Statistical Yearbook	6.312	2.750	2.550	15.662
Real GRP growth rate (%)	China Statistical Yearbook	6.5	2.4	–5.0	11.0
Population urbanization rate (%)[b]	China Statistical Yearbook	60.7	11.9	28.9	89.3

Notes: [a]Sample size is 186 (= 31 provinces × 6 years), [b]Urban population/total population (year-end, permanent residents).

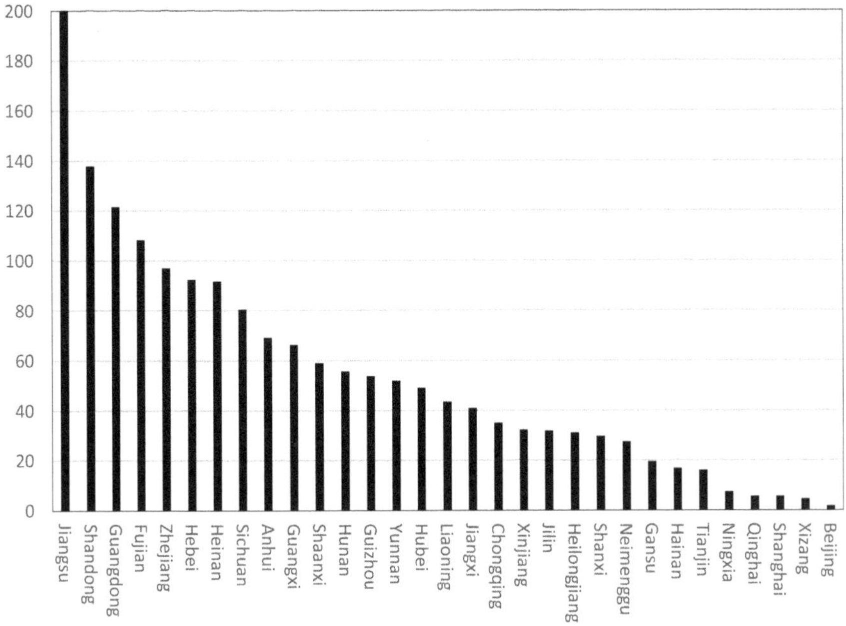

Figure 2. Number of newly registered self-employed households by region (10,000 households in 2020).

Source: Report on the Development of China's Mass Entrepreneurship and Innovation 2020.

Beijing and Shanghai are very small, coming in first and third from the bottom. Both cities are low on the scale of mass entrepreneurship. In terms of the comprehensive IP development index by region, Guangdong province had the highest value at 86.7, followed by Jiangsu Province (82.6) and then Beijing (80.8). Conversely, the three regions with the lowest index values are Ningxia (43.8), Qinghai (44.5), and Tibet (44.9) (the relevant figure is omitted).

Estimation Results

Moran scatter plot

Before discussing the estimates, we examine whether there is spatial autocorrelation in the number of new self-employed registrations by drawing a Moran scatter plot. Figure 3 shows the Moran scatter plot using 2020 data, with the number of new self-employed registrations

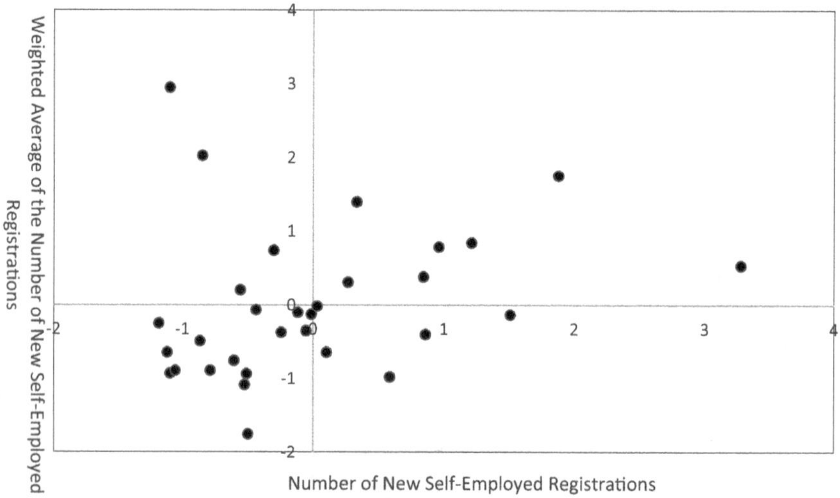

Figure 3. Moran scatter chart (2020).[a]

Notes: [a]mean = 0, standard deviation = 1 normalized values.

in the province on the horizontal axis and a weighted average of the number of new self-employed registrations in neighboring provinces on the vertical axis. They are normalized to a mean of 0 and a standard deviation of 1. In the first quadrant at the top right, new registrations in the province and neighboring provinces are above average, including Shandong and Fujian. In the third quadrant at the bottom left, new registrations in this province and those in neighboring provinces, including Inner Mongolia and Xinjiang, are below average.

The situation in both quadrants is that the number of new registrations in the province exhibits the same large/small relationship as the number of new registrations in the neighboring provinces, while the second quadrant in the upper left indicates that the number of new registrations in the province is below average and the number of new registrations in the neighboring provinces is above average. The fourth quadrant, in the lower right corner, represents an above-average number of new registrations in that province and a below-average number in neighboring provinces. Specifically, Shanghai, Hainan, and four other provinces belong to the second quadrant. The fourth quadrant includes Hebei, Sichuan, and other provinces. Because there are a certain number of points in each of the four quadrants, it is difficult to see a clear overall trend. When fitting a line, the slope (equivalent to Moran's I) is 0.25, the *t*-value is small, 1.40, and no spatial autocorrelation is observed.

Estimated results

First, the usual fixed effects model is estimated, which does not consider the possibility of spatial interdependence. The results are shown in the first column of Table 3. Note that the estimates for year dummy variables and constant terms are omitted. The coefficient

Table 3. Estimated results (effect of comprehensive IP development index).[a]

		spatial Durbin model (SDM)[c]		
	Fixed effect model[b]	Total effect	Direct effect	Indirect effect
Comprehensive IP development index	17612.3*** 3.90	23047.5*** 4.41	13160.9*** 3.00	9886.6* 1.84
Nominal GRP (100 million yuan)	14.93*** 7.00	17.36*** 8.69	14.42*** 7.60	2.94 1.50
Per capita actual GRP (10,000 yuan)	104490.2** 2.35	92530.2 1.47	90410.0** 2.04	2120.3 0.03
Real GRP growth rate (%)	14291.2** 2.20	29754.7** 2.26	13974.8** 2.47	15779.9 1.32
Population urbanization rate (%)	39638.8*** 3.03	11398.4 0.57	53546.1*** 4.55	-42147.8** 2.06
ρ			−0.205* 1.95	
R^2	0.595		0.330	

Notes: [a]The explained variable is the number of newly registered self-employed (households). The upper number in each cell is the parameter estimate.
[b]The lower number in each cell is the absolute value of *t*-value. The estimated results of the constant terms and year dummy variables are omitted.
[c]The lower number in each cell is the absolute value of *z*-value.
***, **, and * represent significance at the 1%, 5%, and 10% levels, respectively. The sample size is 186 (=31 provinces × 6 years).

estimates for the comprehensive IP development index are positive and highly significant (1% level). If other conditions remain unchanged, an increase of one unit in the IP index will increase the number of newly registered self-employed households in the province by about 17,600. While increased protection and use of IPR have both positive and negative effects on newly established self-employed households, the results of this paper show that the positive side dominates.

For other exogenous variables, the coefficient estimates for nominal GRP are positive and significant at the 1% level. The larger the market, the greater the number of new self-employed businesses. The coefficient estimates of real GRP per capita are also positive and significant (5% level), which means that the more developed an area's economy relative to its neighbors, the more self-employment will be established.[14] The coefficient estimates for the real GRP growth rate are also positive and significant (5% level). The faster the economy grows, the greater the number of newly registered self-employed households. The coefficient estimates of the population urbanization rate are also positive and significant (1% level). As expected, the more urbanized a region is, the greater the number of new self-employed businesses.

With 2015 as the base year, the coefficient estimates for each year of the dummy variables are negative and, with the exception of the coefficient estimates for 2020, are significant at levels above 5% (omitted in Table 3). Moreover, the size of its absolute value increases year by year until 2019. This means that, after adjusting for exogenous factors, the overall number of new registrations of self-employed households can be seen to be declining in recent years (in the raw data before the adjustment, the number of new registrations of self-employed households per year continued to increase, though at a slower rate).

It is now worth looking at the estimated results of the SDM, which takes into account the interdependence effects between regions. It also adjusts for fixed effects in terms of region and year (see rows 2–4 of Table 3). First, the estimate for ρ is negative and significant (at the 10% level), indicating spatial autocorrelation.

If a province has a larger (smaller) number of newly registered self-employed households, the neighboring provinces tend to have a smaller (larger) number of newly registered self-employed households. Generally, self-employed businesses are scattered rather than concentrated. The estimated results of the comprehensive IP development index, the core explanatory variable in this study, show that the total effect is positive and significant at the 1% level. Again, the direct effect is positive and significant at the 1% level.

An increase in the comprehensive IP development index has the effect of increasing the number of newly registered self-employed households in the province. Note that the coefficient of the comprehensive IP development index estimated in the fixed-effects model is greater than this direct effect because the fixed-effects model does not consider spatial interdependence. It is also worth noting that the estimates suggest an indirect effect of increasing the number of new self-employed registrations in other provinces (i.e., cross-provincial spillovers).

Because SDM considers endogenous interdependence effects (*Wy* in Equation (1)), direct effects include feedback effects. Here, the feedback effect means that a change in the number of newly registered self-employed households in one province (such as Beijing) will change the number of newly registered self-employed households in another province (such as Tianjin), which will then feed back to the original province (Beijing) to further change the number of newly registered self-employed households in that province (see Elhorst, 2014, p. 31).

For the explanatory variables included to adjust for exogenous factors, namely nominal GRP, real GRP per capita, and real GRP growth, indirect effects were not significant at the usual level, and the existence of these factors on the new establishment of self-employment in neighboring provinces was not statistically proven. In contrast, the urbanization rate had a negative and significant (5% level) indirect effect. This negative cross-provincial effect may be seen as a result of urbanization in one province, which attracts rural residents from neighboring provinces into the labor force and thus discourages the establishment of new self-employed businesses in their home provinces.

Impact of Individual Indices

As described in section "China's IP policy", the comprehensive IP development index, which is an explanatory variable in the estimation model in the previous section, consists of four component indexes (indicators): the creation index, the utilization index, the protection index, and the environment index. As seen in the previous section, when the composite index (comprehensive index) is used as an explanatory variable, the registration of new self-employed individuals has significant positive effects in terms of total, direct, and indirect effects. This section considers the effects of the four individual indices.

The protection index is composed of three secondary indices: judicial protection, political protection, and protection effect indices. For the purposes of this study, the judicial protection index is used as an explanatory variable. Similarly, the environmental index is composed of three secondary indices: the institutional environment, service environment, and awareness environment indices. The institutional environment index is used as an explanatory variable in the estimation. Other explanatory variables and samples are the same as the estimates in the previous section. The basic statistics for the four types of protection index are shown in rows 3–6 of Table 2.

The estimated results are shown in Table 4. First, for ρ indicating whether there is spatial autoregression, all models with the four individual indices as explanatory variables are negative. The sign is the same as when the comprehensive index is used as the explanatory variable, but the level of significance is not high (i.e., not significant at the usual level). When the effects of the four individual indices are examined, the total effect is positive and significant (at the 5% or 1% level). In terms of the total combined direct and indirect effects, this suggests that strengthening the protection and use of IPR can promote the establishment of self-employment.

Table 4. Estimated spatial Durbin model results (effects of individual IP indices).[a]

	Total effect	Direct effect	Indirect effect	Total effect	Direct effect	Indirect effect	Total effect	Direct effect	Indirect effect	Total effect	Direct effect	Indirect effect
IP creation index	11,532.7**	3,910.1	7,622.6	—	—	—	—	—	—	—	—	—
	2.10	1.45	1.59									
IP utilization index	—	—	—	17,375.1***	3,361.1	14,014.0**	—	—	—	—	—	—
				2.86	0.92	2.43						
IP judicial protection index	—	—	—	—	—	—	65,37.5**	3,285.8**	3,251.7	—	—	—
							2.48	1.96	1.31			
IP institutional environment index	—	—	—	—	—	—	—	—	—	7,766.2***	4,615.2***	3,150.9
										3.26	3.73	1.49
Nominal GRP (100 million yuan)	17.71***	14.01***	3.70*	16.07***	13.43***	2.65	19.55***	14.95***	4.61**	16.51***	12.74***	3.77*
	7.76	7.21	1.75	7.05	6.92	1.26	8.21	7.60	2.13	7.57	6.65	1.84
Per capita actual GRP (10,000 yuan)	47,568.7	97,276.2**	−49,707.5	60,085.2	95,307.6**	−35,222.3	108,399.0	94,637.4**	13,761.6	128,529.3*	113,682.6***	14,846.7
	0.66	2.17	0.60	0.87	2.13	0.44	1.49	2.10	0.17	1.86	2.57	0.19
Real GRP growth rate (%)	27,437.9*	14,236.0**	13,201.9	44,713.2***	18,135.1***	26,578.1**	39,681.5***	17,052.5***	22,629.0*	39,228.9***	15,464.1***	23,764.9*
	1.69	2.32	0.94	3.15	3.17	2.07	2.75	2.95	1.75	2.84	2.72	1.91
Population urbanization rate (%)	−4,497.4	50,297.2***	−54,794.6**	−4,591.6	51,486.2***	−56,077.8**	17,928.2	55,927.4***	−37,999.2*	30,289.3	70,030.2***	−39,740.9*
	0.19	4.21	2.41	0.21	4.35	2.54	0.77	4.54	1.71	1.35	5.49	1.88
ρ		−0.106			−0.135			−0.126			−0.137	
		1.02			1.28			1.20			1.31	
R^2		0.277			0.147			0.533			0.478	

Notes: [a]The explained variable is the number of newly registered self-employed (households). The upper number in each cell is the parameter estimate, and the lower number is the absolute value of z-value.

However, looking at direct and indirect effects separately, there are differences. For the judicial protection and institutional environment indices, the direct influence is significant, while the indirect influence is not significant at the usual level. Although strengthening the judicial protection or institutional environment for IPR will increase the number of new self-employed households in the province, the cross-provincial spillover effect on the number of new self-employed households in other provinces is not obvious. In contrast, estimates using the creation index and the utilization index as explanatory variables showed no significant direct effect. The effect of strengthening the creation or use of IPR in a province on the number of new self-employed households in the province is not obvious, indicating that the positive effects described in section "China's IP policy" that self-employed households in the province should be able to enjoy are not fully in play.

When the utilization index is used as an explanatory variable, indirect effects show positive signs and significant estimates. Strengthening the utilization of IPR in one province has positive cross-provincial spillover effects on the establishment of self-employed businesses in other provinces. When the creation index was used as an explanatory variable, the indirect effect was not significant at the usual level (*t*-value = 1.59), but the value was much larger than the direct effect, suggesting some cross-provincial spillover effect. With regard to the coefficient estimates of the explanatory variables included to adjust for exogenous factors, the results are essentially the same as those using the comprehensive index as the explanatory variable (Table 3), regardless of the explanatory variables related to IP. In particular, for he population urbanization rate, the indirect (cross-provincial spillover) effect is limited, and there is a negative inter-provincial spillover effect for the population urbanization ratio.

Conclusion

As China's breakneck economic growth comes to an end, people are looking for structural changes in the economy. Popularizing entrepreneurship under the policy of mass entrepreneurship and innovation is part of that quest and aims to promote entrepreneurship and translate it into business creation, which will become a new driving force for quality economic growth. A particularly important policy is to strengthen IPR. This chapter attempts to clarify whether this strengthening of IPR helps to promote entrepreneurship (i.e., setting up new self-employment) using data on the number of new registrations of self-employed households in each province and the "Indicators of the State of Intellectual Property Development" compiled by the State Intellectual Property Office of China. Using regional and annual panel data, an SDM, which takes into account spatial interdependence among regions, was estimated, showing overall that enhanced protection and use of IPR have a positive effect on the creation of new self-employed households, and a negative spatial autocorrelation is found in the number of new self-employed registrations by region. Analysis using each of the four component indexes that make up the composite index as explanatory variables shows that there is an indirect (cross-provincial spillover) effect in the creation and utilization of IP. In contrast, for judicial protection and institutional environment, no impact on other provinces could be found. Moreover, contrary to previous expectations, the direct effects were not significant in terms of creation and utilization. One possible reason for this result is that strengthening the creation and use of IPR has both positive and negative effects on the self-employed, and these effects may have cancelled each other out, leaving no clear effect.

The econometric analysis in this study has some limitations. In particular, given that spillovers are a time-related phenomenon, it is a significant problem that the model in this study does not include dynamic structures. Further establishing the robustness of the results of this study is a task for the future. There may be a downside to strengthening IP protection, which suggests the need for new thinking. We would like to conclude by pointing out that the concept of open source has recently become more important in China. In the *14th Five-Year Plan for National Economic and Social Development of the People's Republic of China* and *the Outline of the 2035 Vision Goals* released on March 12, 2021, "Open source" was explicitly listed in the Five-Year Plan Outline for the first time. As mentioned in the outline, "Support the development of innovation consortium such as open-source community of digital technology, improve open-source IP and legal system, and encourage enterprises to open software source code, hardware design and application services." We can thus see the country's recognition and support for open source at the strategic level,[15] which can be seen as a policy approach to promote IP sharing while strengthening IP protection.

Endnotes

1. Policy documents related to the "mass entrepreneurship and innovation" policy issued by the State Council are included in the Policy Database of Mass Entrepreneurship and Innovation: http://www.gov.cn/zhengce/shuangchuangzck/index.htm.
2. The document was issued by the State Council on August 24, 2021, and took effect on March 1, 2022.
3. Kambayashi (2017) agrees that choosing to be self-employed is a sign of entrepreneurship and, in this regard, points to the need to analyze the factors behind the recent decline in the number of self-employed households in Japan.
4. Li and DaCosta (2016) used GEM data in their analysis of China.
5. The document was released by the State Council on April 16, 2011; the first revision was made on February 19, 2014, and the second revision was made on February 6, 2016.
6. This document was issued by the State Administration for Industry and Commerce (now the State Factory Supervision Administration) on September 30, 2011, and came into force on March 1, 2014.
7. See Otsuka *et al.* (1998) for more details.
8. See World Bank Group and the Development Research Center of The State Council (2019, p. 38).
9. The statistics are reported as of June 11, 2021.
10. See page 1 of *Government Law*, September 2006 (II).
11. However, the following update on the education industry should be noted. In 2021, China's Ministry of Education launched a "double reduction" campaign to effectively reduce the heavy homework burden and off-campus training burden of students in compulsory

education. The "double reduction" action is derived from the *Opinions on Further Reducing the Homework Burden and Off-campus Training Burden of Students Receiving Compulsory Education* issued by the General Offices of the CPC Central Committee and the State Council on July 24, 2021. Under the "double reduction" action, a large number of education and guidance institutions had to shrink. Given this background, the number of self-employed households in education is likely to decline sharply after 2021.

12. See *People's Daily* (Overseas Edition) February 24.
13. In the GEM survey, a "nascent entrepreneur" is defined as someone actively involved in setting up a business they will own or co-own: the business has yet to pay wages, salaries, and benefits, or any other payment made to the owner over a period of three months.
14. Li and Zhao (2011) found that, contrary to this study, the higher the per capita actual GRP, the lower the self-employed employment ratio. Pietrobelli *et al.* (2004) made a regression analysis using data from different countries from the 1960s to the 1990s and found that there was basically a negative correlation between the degree of economic development and the scale of self-employment.
15. *OSCHINA*, 17 March 2021. See also, Takasu (2022).

References

Burke, A., Lyalkov, S., Millán, A., Millán, J.M., and van Stel, A. 2021. How do country R&D change the allocation of self-employment across different types? *Small Business Economics*, 56: 695–721.

Chowdhury, F., Terjesen, S., and Audretsch, D. 2015. Varieties of entrepreneurship: Institutional drivers across entrepreneurial activity and country. *European Journal of Law & Economics*, 40: 121–148.

Elhorst, J.P. 2014. *Spatial Econometrics: From Cross-Sectional Data to Spatial Panels.* Heidelberg: Springer.

Intellectual Property Development Research Center, State Intellectual Property Administration. 2021. Evaluation Report on the Status of Intellectual Property Development in China 2020 (in Chinese).

Kambayashi, R. 2017. *The Formal World and the Non-formal World: Fundamental Issues in Contemporary Japanese Labor Economics.* Tokyo: Keio University Press (in Japanese).

LêKhang, T. and Thành, N.C. 2018. Economic growth, entrepreneurship, and institutions: Evidence in emerging countries. In *The 5th IBSM*

International Conference on Business, Management and Accounting, 19–21 April, Hanoi University of Industry, Vietnam, pp. 357–374.

Li, Z. 2018. The historical trajectory of the development of the self-employed since the reform and opening up: Based on the oral history of the self-employed in Hanzheng Street. *Seeker* (April): 88–95 (in Chinese).

Li, Y. and DaCosta, M.N. 2016. The enterprise reforms and entrepreneurial development in China. *Journal of the Asia Pacific Economy,* 21(2): 151–173.

Li, K. and Zhao, C. 2011. Determinants of self-employment in China: Evidence from cross-regional data. *China & World Economy,* 19(3): 49–67.

Lin, Y. 2012. The evolution of the self-employed over 30 years. *China Youth Daily* (April 25) (in Chinese).

Liu, C.Y. and Huang, X. 2016. The rise of urban entrepreneurs in China: Capital endowments and entry dynamics. *Growth and Change,* 47(1) (March): 32–52.

Ma, X. 2018. *Economic Transition and Labor Market Reform in China.* Singapore: Palgrave Macmillan.

Murakami, N. 2019. Self-employment as occupational choice in the Zhongyuan rural area. Working Paper Series. Research Institute of Economic Science, College of Economics, Nihon University, No. 18-03, March.

Office of the National Leading Group on Combating Infringement of Intellectual Property Rights and Production and Sale of Fake and Inferior Commodities. 2022. New Progress Report on China's Intellectual Property Protection and Business Environment 2021.

Otsuka, K., Liu, D., and Murakami, N. 1998. *Industrial Reform in China: Past Performance and Future Prospects.* Oxford: Oxford University Press.

Parker, S.C. 2018. *The Economics of Entrepreneurship* (2nd edn.). Cambridge: Cambridge University Press.

Pietrobelli, C., Rabellotti, R., and Aquilina, M. 2004. An empirical study of the determinants of self-employment in developing countries. *Journal of International Development,* 16: 803–820.

Sanandaji, T. and Leeson, P.T. 2012. Billionaires. Research Institute of Industrial Economics (IFN) Working Paper No. 893.

Takasu, M. 2022. Chinese government incorporates 'open source intellectual property strategy' into 14th five-year plan. *Science Portal China*

(Japan Science and Technology Promotion Agency), No. 22-06, May 20 (in Japanese).
Wang, H. and Jiang, Y. 2014. Industrial distribution, survival condition and contingent trend of the individual business. *Reform,* 242: 112–119 (in Chinese).
World Bank Group and the Development Research Center of the State Council. 2019. *Innovative China: New Drivers of Growth.* Washington, D.C.: World Bank.
Yueh, L. 2009. China's entrepreneurs. *World Development,* 37(4): 778–786.

Appendix

The index system for evaluating China's intellectual property development established by the Intellectual Property Development Research Center of the State Intellectual Property Administration consists of the 45 three-level indicators in the attached table (Table 1, pp. 3–4 of *Evaluation Report on the Status of Intellectual Property Development in China* 2020, excerpts). Please note that the series contained in the tertiary index changes slightly from year to year, but for the purposes of this study, such changes were not considered problematic when comparing the indices from year to year (for details of the changes, see the annual edition of "Evaluation Report").

Table A1. Evaluation Index System for IPR development in China 2020.

First-level indicators	Second-level indicators	Third-level indicators
Creation	Quantity	Number of invention patents granted (pieces)
		Number of trademark registrations (pieces)
		Copyright registrations (copies)
		Authorized quantity of new plant variety right (pieces)
		Composite index of the number of geographical Indications (score)
		Number of integrated circuit layout designs registered and issued (pieces)

(*Continued*)

Table A1. (*Continued*)

First-level indicators	Second-level indicators	Third-level indicators
	Quality	Average life of invention patent (years)
		Number of PCT international patent applications accepted (PCS)
		Number of Madrid trademark international registration applications (pieces)
	Efficiency	Number of invention patents per 10,000 population (pieces)
		Number of invention patents granted per 10 million yuan of R&D expenditure (pieces)
		Number of effective registered trademarks per 100 market entities (pieces)
		Software registrations per 10,000 population (pieces)
Utilization	Scale	Number of Patent Licensing Contracts filed (pieces)
		Number of patent application rights and transfer of patent rights (pieces)
		Number of trademark licensing records (pieces)
		Quantity of books exported (10,000 copies)
		Quantity of copyright exported (item)
		Number of contracts concluded in technology market (items)
	Benefit	Recorded amount of patent licensing contract (10,000 yuan)
		Ratio of value added of patent-intensive industries to GDP (%)
		Ratio of industrial value added of copyright industry to GDP (%)
		Software revenue (100 million yuan)
		Technical market contract amount (10,000 yuan)
Protection	Judicial protection	Intellectual property civil trial protection index (score)
		Intellectual property administrative trial protection index (score)
		Intellectual property criminal trial protection index (score)

Table A1. (*Continued*)

First-level indicators	Second-level indicators	Third-level indicators
		Intellectual property inspection and supervision index (score)
	Political protection	Patent administrative protection index (score)
		Trademark administrative protection index (score)
		Copyright administrative protection index (score)
		Effective quantity of intellectual property filed for customs protection (pieces)
	Protective effect	R&D investment intensity (%)
		Proportion of industrial enterprises above designated size applying for patents (%)
		Renewal rate of registered trademarks (%)
		Social satisfaction with intellectual property protection (score)
		Import and export of intellectual property royalties (US $100 million)
Environment	Institutional	Quantity of intellectual property laws and regulations (part)
		Amount of intellectual property strategic planning (part)
		Number of intellectual property service institutions (PCS)
	Service	Number of personnel in intellectual property service industry (persons)
		Intellectual property mortgage financing service Index (score)
	Awareness	Patent applications per 10,000 population
		Number of trademark applications per 10,000 population (cases)
		Copyright registrations per 10,000 population (pieces)

Source: Intellectual Property Development Research Center, State Intellectual Property Administration (2021), pp. 3–4.

https://doi.org/10.1142/9789819815241_0021

Chapter 21

FINANCING DIFFICULTIES OF SMALL AND MEDIUM-SIZED ENTERPRISES (SMEs) IN CHINA: A THEORETICAL PERSPECTIVE*

Zhiwei Xu[†,§] and Haolin Bai[‡,¶]

[†]*China Center for Economic Studies, Fudan University, China*
[‡]*HSBC Business School of Peking University, Shenzhen, China*
[§]*xuzhiwei09@gmail.com*
[¶]*baihaolin@stu.pku.edu.cn*

Introduction

As one of the most important micro decision-makers in the market-oriented economy, enterprises are key to China's rapid growth. In the past decade, China's policy of encouraging entrepreneurship has spurred more Small and Medium-sized Enterprises (SMEs) into

*This research has been supported by the National Foundation for Natural Sciences of China: Excellent Youth Project (72022011). The authors have written for the Festschrift International Conference on "The Pattern of China's Economic Rise." The major theoretical discussions in the paper provide the micro-foundation for Prof. Zhang Jun's opinion on the financing difficulties of China's SMEs in his 2020 speech entitled "What should the SMEs do?"

the market, which has played a pivotal role in safeguarding employment and stabilizing the economy.

In 2014, the Ministry of Education issued "The 2014 New Policy on College Graduates' Entrepreneurship." That year saw a striking rise in the number of new business entities to over 2.4 million (Figure 1). With this policy support, the total number of China's SMEs has in the past decade reached 25 million (Figure 1). Compared with big enterprises, SMEs are more heterogeneous.

As a result, the policy has led to the entry of more low-quality enterprises as well as the stimulus effect, which has significantly increased the variance of enterprise productivity. The low-efficiency enterprises on the tail end of productivity distribution pose a higher default risk to commercial banks. Figure 1 shows that since 2014, there has been an apparent rising trend in banks' rates of non-performing loans, in tandem with the increases in enterprises and new enterprises.

The positive correlation between the number of new business entities and the rate of non-performing loans shows that as more enterprises enter the market, whereas employment and output can be promoted, non-performing loans can rise too due to the lower average quality of the enterprises, thus leading to more friction in the credit market. In order to theoretically examine the correlation between enterprise entry and credit market friction and to understand the core micro-mechanism of SMEs' financing difficulties, this study constructs a model of heterogeneous enterprises with the endogenous entry decision. In this model, micro-enterprises have heterogeneous productivity (which signifies quality), and it is private information that banks cannot directly observe. Therefore, there is an information asymmetry between banks and enterprises applying for credit. For a given enterprise that has entered the market and started production, the productive capital available comes from its own capital and bank loans. Unable to differentiate enterprises with different quality (productivity), banks use uniform lending standards for heterogeneous enterprises (reflected in the enterprises' loan-to-assets ratio or the leverage ratio). For a given level of leverage ratio, there is moral hazard between banks and enterprises

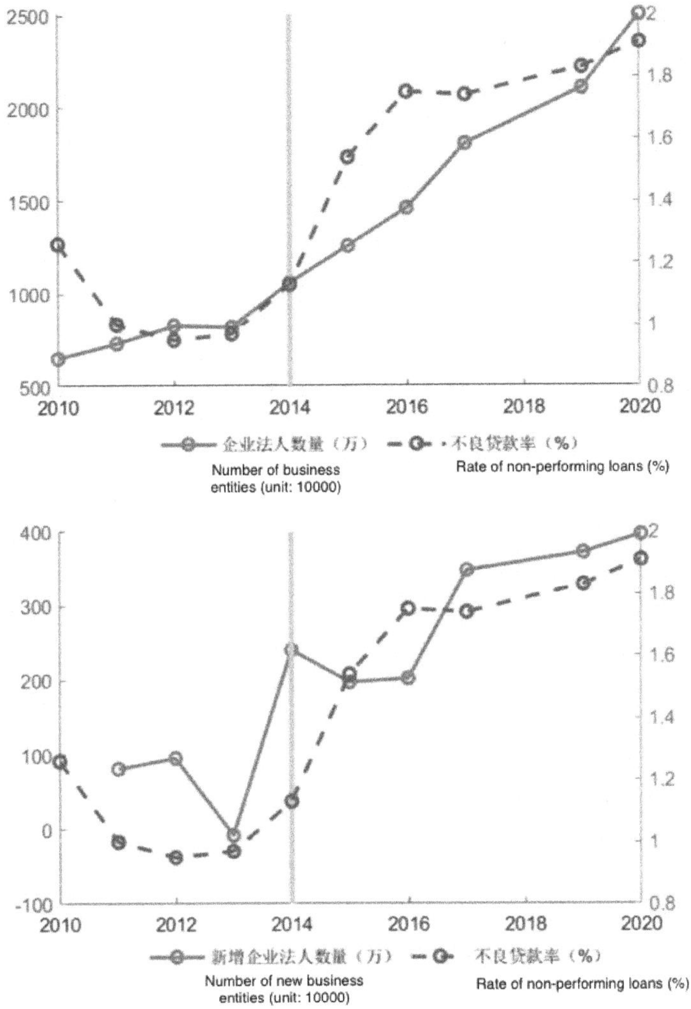

Figure 1. Number of enterprises and rate of non-performing loans.

Notes: The top figure shows the time series of the number of business entities (unit of 10,000, left axis) and the rate of non-performing loans (%, right axis); However, the number of business entities in 2018 is missing. The bottom figure shows the time series of the number of new business entities (unit of 10,000, left axis) and the rate of non-performing loans (%, right axis); the number for 2019 is replaced by the average of the 2017 and 2020 numbers.

Source: The websites of the State Statistical Bureau and the Banking and Insurance Regulatory Commission.

applying for credit, i.e., low-productivity enterprises have more incentive to default than high-productivity enterprises, and the probability of default is a strictly increasing function of the leverage ratio. Hence, when making credit decisions, banks have to consider the trade-off between the default losses from loans to low-efficiency enterprises and the returns from loans to high-efficiency enterprises. When low-efficiency enterprises increase as a percentage of the whole economy, banks will set stricter lending standards and reduce the leverage ratio in order to decrease the default losses from loans to low-efficiency enterprises. Conversely, banks will loosen the lending standards and increase the leverage ratio in order to earn more income from loans to high-efficiency enterprises. This theory suggests that an indiscriminate entrepreneurship-promoting policy (e.g., lower market entry costs) brings more low-quality SMEs into the market and exacerbates the moral hazard problem between banks and enterprises. Information asymmetry leads to stricter lending standards that banks apply to all enterprises, worsening SMEs' financing difficulties. High-efficiency SMEs face tighter financing constraints, and the misallocation of credit resources among enterprises becomes worse. Moreover, when banks face a tighter macro-prudential policy, an indiscriminate entrepreneurship-promoting policy will lead to tighter financing constraints for enterprises, thereby worsening credit misallocation and lowering the average productivity of the whole economy.

Information asymmetry has been extensively discussed in the literature as a key factor accounting for the difficulties of enterprises in obtaining credit resources (Stiglitz and Weiss, 1981). The analysis by Li Zhiyun (2002) suggests that the more heterogeneous SMEs are, the worse the information asymmetry is between banks and enterprises, and the less credit small enterprises can obtain. According to Lin Yifu and Sun Xifang (2005), SMEs find it harder to obtain financing as formal financial institutions have difficulty identifying SMEs' credit qualifications compared with big enterprises. In addition, some academics have provided empirical evidence based on Chinese data. Ping Xinqiao and Yang Muyun

(2009) perform an empirical analysis on the individual credit data of one state-owned bank in 1998–2006 and find moral hazard, instead of adverse selection, is the main information asymmetry problem in China's personal credit market. Yin Zhichao and Gan Li (2011) provide direct evidence for the coexistence of moral hazards and adverse selection in China's credit market based on one state-owned bank's enterprise credit data.

The existing literature also covers the effects of policy distortion and financial market frictions on the macro economy. Song *et al.* (2011) construct a two-sector model to explain why China has been able to maintain huge foreign currency surpluses in the long term while keeping a high growth rate: banks prefer SOEs rather than private enterprises when extending credit. The sharp drop in the weight of China's state-owned economy since 1992 means banks have much fewer enterprises to lend to, while at the same time, household savings, especially bank deposits, have seen a dramatic increase. The gap between deposits and loans has encouraged the central bank to allocate the surplus capital factor by holding foreign bonds. Brandt *et al.* (2013) find that the same discrimination based on ownership also exists in the implementation of the policy to develop the western regions, causing more capital factor to flow toward low-efficiency SOEs instead of high-efficiency private enterprises. Such policy distortion explains the yearly drop of 0.87% in the growth rate of the potential total factor productivity in the west of China. Chang *et al.* (2006) point out that the long-term plan made in the 1990s to prioritize the heavy industry in the 15 years to come resulted in banks' preference for capital-intensive enterprises whose better ability to provide collateral gave them priority in receiving credit resources. Against such an institutional background, the paper gives a better explanation for a higher share of investment and a lower share of labor income in China's GDP by constructing a two-sector model which introduces the collateral constraints of the heavy industry and the credit friction of banks. Bai *et al.* (2018) build a model of heterogeneous enterprises with endogenous credit constraints which uses default risk and the cost of loan extension to describe two financial frictions. Identifying and estimating based on data about Chinese enterprises, they find that the model can explain 12% of the loss in total factor productivity. Wu (2018) examines the Chinese enterprise data too and finds that frictions in financial markets account for up to 9.4% of the loss in total factor productivity. This is just 39% of the total loss in China, with the rest of the loss likely caused by some distortions in the economic policy of China. The two-sector model of Liu *et al.* (2021) describes the dynamic general equilibrium of heterogeneous enterprises, giving a theoretical and empirical analysis of how the marketization of Chinese interest rates has affected the efficiency of enterprise credit allocation against the background of policy distortions. The paper finds that, given the policy distortions, the interest rate marketization, which aims to remove price controls, has not effectively promoted the efficiency of bank credit allocation.

Another important measure this study focuses on is the relationship between enterprise entry and banks' credit decisions. The latter is affected by enterprise productivity (Cheng and Yang, 2022), while the entry threshold and entry decisions are relevant to the average productivity of the enterprises in the market. Ates and Saffie (2021) introduce interest rate shocks into their model and find that during a financial crisis, as banks tighten lending standards, fewer enterprises enter the market, which, however, have a higher average quality. Hu (2022) describes the two-way feedback mechanism between enterprises' incentive to enter and banks' lending standards via a dynamic adverse selection model. The lending standards are determined by the average quality of the enterprises applying for credit, and at the same time, the enterprises' decision to enter is also affected by the financing cost. Right now, there is little literature on policies directly stimulating micro-entities, and researchers seldom analyze the effect of a large number of SMEs' market entry on bank decisions and financial market frictions. The marginal contribution of this study lies in a model of heterogeneous enterprises with endogenous market entry against the background of large-scale entrepreneurship-promoting policies in China, which explains why such policies targeting micro-enterprises may exacerbate information asymmetry and moral hazard in the financial markets. This study adds to research about Chinese SMEs' financing difficulty and explains the credit resource misallocation in China from the perspectives of both policy and market.

The theoretical significance of this study is that, although from a historical perspective entrepreneurship-promoting policies have played a positive role in protecting employment and stabilizing the economy, these policies may also have worsened credit resource misallocation and negatively affected China's quality growth in the future, due to frictions in the financial markets. Therefore, at this stage, frictions of the market mechanism and micro-heterogeneity should be taken into account when formulating stimulus policies for micro-entities so that precise targeting can reduce the side effects of the policies on the real economy.

Theoretical Model

In this section, we present a theoretical analysis of enterprises' endogenous entry decisions and banks' credit extending decisions, along with a discussion of the core mechanism through which the entrepreneurship-promoting policies affect enterprises' credit constraints. For simplicity, a static partial equilibrium model is considered, which consists of a potential heterogeneous enterprise measuring 1 and a representative bank.

Every potential enterprise (entrepreneur) has its own funds of e and a heterogeneous productivity of z. Assume z in the cumulative distribution function $F(z)$ has a value range of $[z_{\min}, z_{\max}]$. The decision-making of a potential enterprise or entrepreneur goes through two stages. In stage 1, z is given, and the potential enterprise decides whether to enter the market for new business. Market entry generates a fixed cost. In stage 2, the enterprise finances its productive capital through bank credit and its own funds, with the loan amount (or the leverage ratio) set by the bank. Afterward, the enterprise decides whether to default or not. In the case of not defaulting, the enterprise conducts normal production and pays back the loan along with interest; in the case of default, the enterprise diverts the loan (together with its own funds) to other uses (e.g., investment in storage technology). As a result, moral hazard arises between the enterprise and the bank. The reason is productivity, z, is private information of the enterprise that the bank cannot directly observe. As the bank cannot differentiate the heterogeneity of enterprises, this study assumes it sets uniform lending standards (or leverage ratio) for enterprises in order to maximize the expected profit.

Enterprise decision

In stage 1, a potential enterprise decides whether to enter the market or not. The entry generates a fixed cost $\xi > 0$. $V(e, z)$ is the profit of the enterprise determined by its initial capital e and productivity z. The details will be determined in stage 2. The net value of the enterprise after entry is $V(e, z) - \xi$. For convenience, the potential enterprise's opportunity cost (or the value of the external choice) is further standardized as 0. Therefore, the enterprise will choose to enter the market when the following condition holds:

$$V(e, z) - \xi \geq 0 \tag{1}$$

We prove later that $V(e, z)$ is a monotonic increasing function of productivity z. Formula (1) determines the threshold productivity z, i.e., $V(e, z) = \xi$. The enterprise will choose to enter the market only when its productivity is higher than $\underline{z}$. Therefore, the conditional distribution of the new enterprise is $\mathbf{G}(z) = \frac{F(Z)}{1-F(z)}$. The policies encouraging entrepreneurship lower the enterprise's entry cost ξ and thereby the threshold productivity $\underline{z}$, bringing more low-efficiency enterprises into the market and shifting the conditional distribution curve $\mathbf{G}(z)$ leftward.

In stage 2, the enterprise obtains a bank loan amounting to b, and its total capital k is

$$k = e + b \tag{2}$$

The enterprise uses capital k to produce the final product y. For simplicity, we assume the production function is linear:

$$y = Azk \tag{3}$$

in which z is the heterogeneous productivity and A is the overall productivity of the whole economy. The assumption that the enterprise uses the capital and labor for production and follows a more general production function does not fundamentally change the general outcome of the model.

The leverage ratio λ is defined as the ratio of the loan to the enterprise's own funds, i.e., $\lambda = \frac{b}{e}$. The enterprise borrows the amount of $b = \lambda e$ from the bank at the interest rate of r^f. If the enterprise chooses to produce and pay back the loan (not to default), then the total profit will be $Az(1 + \lambda)e - r^f\lambda e$. Please note that the leverage ratio is set by the bank, and so given the enterprise's own funds e, the bank determines how much the enterprise can borrow.

There is moral hazard between the bank and the enterprise. The enterprise, as the borrower, can choose to default and divert θ of the loan to invest in storage technology, receiving the total return of $\psi z(1 + \theta\lambda)e$; $(1 + \theta\lambda)e$ is the maximum capital the enterprise can use in case of a default decision; ψ is the return rate of investing in storage technology. We assume that the return ratio from storage technology is low and $\psi < A$.

z^* represents the threshold productivity that causes no difference between default and non-default, and the variable is determined as follows:

$$Az^*(1 + \lambda) - r^f\lambda = z^*\psi(1 + \theta\lambda) \tag{4}$$

The left-hand side of the equation is the return of non-default, and the right-hand side is the return of default. From the equation, we can get the threshold value z^*:

$$z^*(\lambda) = \frac{r^f \lambda}{(A-\psi)+(A-\psi\theta)\lambda}. \tag{5}$$

For enterprises whose productivity is higher than z^*, they will pay back the loan on time instead of walking away from the debt because production generates a relatively higher value. In other words, there is no moral hazard problem for such enterprises. However, for enterprises whose productivity is lower than z^*, they have more incentive to divert part of the loan and invest it in storage technology, which brings the default risk to the bank.

Under the assumption of $\psi < A$, $z^*(\lambda)$ is an increasing function of λ, which suggests that an enterprise is more likely to walk away and default if the leverage ratio is relatively higher (which means a bigger bank loan). Therefore, owing to moral hazard, a higher leverage ratio or looser lending standards may cause more credit risk.

Given the decision of default or non-default, the value of the enterprise can be summarized by the following: function:

$$V(e,z;\lambda)=\begin{cases}\left[Az(1+\lambda)-r^f\lambda\right]e & \text{if} \quad z\geq z^*(\lambda)\\ \psi z(1+\theta\lambda)e & \text{if} \quad z\leq z^*(\lambda)\end{cases} \tag{6}$$

And the entry threshold $\underline{z}$ is determined by the following function:

$$V(e, \underline{z}; \lambda) = \xi \tag{7}$$

The assumption of a minimal entry cost of ξ leads to

$$\underline{z}=\frac{\xi}{\psi(1+\theta\lambda)e}< z^* \tag{8}$$

This means those enterprises whose productivity falls into the range of $(\underline{z}, z^*)$ will have an endogenous choice of default, thereby causing default risk to the bank. Figure 2 shows the function of enterprise value and the corresponding threshold productivity for different endogenous decisions (market entry and loan default).

The figure shows that enterprises which enter the market but have low productivity are more likely to default. To be more specific, there is moral hazard for enterprises whose productivity is $z \in (\underline{z}, z^*)$. They would divert the bank loan to invest in storage technology. Formula (8) shows that $\underline{z}$ is a decreasing function of the leverage ratio λ but an increasing function of the entry cost ξ. With the average productivity being $\frac{\underline{z}+z_{max}}{2}$, $\underline{z}$ reflects the average quality of

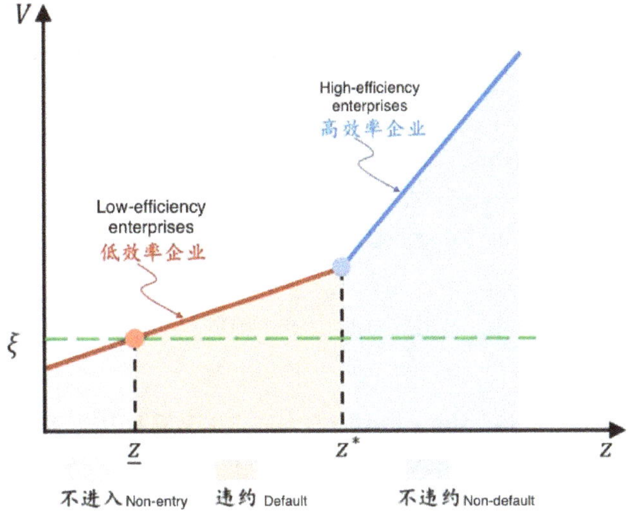

Figure 2. Function of enterprise value and the threshold productivity.

Notes: The vertical axis is the function of enterprise value (Formula (6)) and the horizontal axis is the heterogeneous productivity. The blue segment (with productivity higher than z^*) corresponds to high-efficiency enterprises with no incentive to default; the orange and grey segments below the red line are low-efficiency enterprises. The gray area to the left of $\underline{z}$ denotes low-efficiency enterprises that do not enter the market, while the orange area spanning ($\underline{z}$, z^*) denotes the low-efficiency enterprises which enter the market but choose to default. The green dotted line indicates the fixed cost required to enter the market. Enterprises choose to enter when the value of entry is higher than ξ (with the corresponding threshold productivity of $\underline{z}$).

borrowing enterprises in the market. If the lending standards are loose (which means a higher leverage ratio of λ) or the government encourages entrepreneurship (which means ξ is lower), then more low-efficiency enterprises will enter the market, leading to a lower average quality of producing enterprises. The following section focuses on banks' lending decisions for further analysis of the credit supply.

Banks' credit decisions

Let's consider a typical bank's decision-making. The bank attracts deposits at the interest rate of r^d and lends to enterprises at the rate of r^f. In the basic model, we assume there is perfect competition among banks and the lending rate of r^f is exogenously given. In the expanded model, the endogenous decision about the lending rate is made. The major results are valid. The bank achieves profit maximization by choosing the leverage ratio λ. If an enterprise defaults, the bank can retrieve ϖ of the loan. The bank's profit maximization can be expressed as follows:

$$\max_{\{\lambda\}} \int_{\underline{z}}^{z^*(\lambda)} \varpi\lambda e d\mathbf{F}(z) + \int_{z^*(\lambda)}^{z_{max}} r^f \lambda e d\mathbf{F}(z) - \int_{\underline{z}}^{z_{max}} r^d \lambda e d\mathbf{F}(z) \tag{9}$$

The first item of the above profit function is the portion of the loan the bank can retrieve after the default of an enterprise whose productivity satisfies $z \in (\underline{z}, z^*)$; the second item of the function is the interest income from a normal loan to an enterprise whose productivity satisfies $z \in (z^*, z_{max})$; and the third item is the financing cost of the bank (interest payout for deposits).

In stage 2, the number of enterprises the bank deals with is $1-\mathbf{F}(\underline{z})$. To the bank, the conditional distribution of enterprises is a given; therefore, when deciding to lend or not, it does not consider the strategic interaction between its credit supply and the enterprises' entry decision. The optimization of the bank can be further simplified as follows:

$$\max_{\{\lambda\}} \lambda\{(r^f - r^d)[1-\mathbf{F}(\underline{z})] - (r^f - \varpi)[\mathbf{F}(z^*(\lambda)) - \mathbf{F}(\underline{z})]\} \tag{10}$$

The first-order condition results in

$$(r^f - r^d)[1-\mathbf{F}(\underline{z})] - (r^f - \varpi)[\mathbf{F}(z^*(\lambda)) - \mathbf{F}(\underline{z})] = \lambda(r^f - \varpi)\mathbf{F}'(z^*(\lambda))\frac{dz^*(\lambda)}{d\lambda} \tag{11}$$

A higher leverage ratio will increase the return of the bank's lending business, and the left-hand side of the above formula describes the marginal return from a higher leverage ratio. Meanwhile, a higher leverage ratio worsens the moral hazard problem, resulting in more loan defaults that reduce the bank's profit. The right-hand side of Formula (11) represents the bank's marginal cost. It is worth mentioning that the moral hazard problem caused by a high leverage ratio comes from two extensive margin effects. The definitions of the threshold value $\underline{z}$ and $z^*(\lambda)$ mean that as the leverage ratio increases, more low-efficiency enterprises enter the market, which will receive credit from the bank; whereas, a higher leverage ratio increases the threshold value $z^*(\lambda)$, making enterprises more likely to default. The combination of the two extensive margin effects makes looser bank credit supply the cause of more corporate defaults.

For simplicity, we assume z follows the uniform distribution of $[0, z_{max}]$, i.e., $\mathbf{F}(z) = \frac{z}{z_{max}}$. From Formula (12), we know that the leverage ratio λ assumed for the bank's optimal decision strictly increases with the enterprises' entry threshold $\underline{z}$. As the borrowing enterprises' average productivity is $\frac{\underline{z}+z_{max}}{2}$, we derive the following theorem.

Theorem 1. *The bank's optimal leverage ratio λ strictly increases with the average quality of borrowing enterprises. The more low-efficiency enterprises enter the market, the more stringent the bank's credit constraints are.*

Proof. See Appendix.

Theorem 1 suggests that the more enterprises enter the market, or the higher percentage of low-quality enterprises there are among the total, the more serious the moral hazard problem facing banks and the bigger the default risk and loan losses. Banks that aim at maximum profits would tighten their lending standards and reduce premium loans, thus causing more stringent credit constraints for micro-enterprises. The core of this outcome is that, because information asymmetry makes banks unable to differentiate enterprises of different qualities, in order to mitigate the moral hazard problem and reduce default losses, banks will tighten the credit supply through an optimal decrease in business loans.

The endogenous loan interest rate

The main outcome of the above analysis does not depend on the assumption that the lending interest rate is exogenously given. In order to explain it, we further assume the bank sets the lending rate of r^f, and the bank's optimal decision about $\{\lambda, r^f\}$ can be expressed by Formulas (11) and (12):

$$1-\mathbf{F}(z^*)=(r^f-\varpi)\mathbf{F}'(z^*)\frac{dz^*}{dr^f} \tag{12}$$

According to Formula (12), the lending rate r^f can be expressed as a function of the leverage ratio λ, i.e., $r^f(\lambda)$. It is easily proven that r^f strictly decreases with λ. The intuitive economic explanation is that the default rate $\mathbf{F}(z^*)$ decreases as the bank sets a lower leverage ratio. Now, the marginal return from a higher loan rate increases while the marginal cost decreases, giving the bank more incentive to increase the lending rate. Use $r^f(\lambda)$ in the optimal condition of λ in a similar way as previously mentioned in this chapter, and we can prove that under certain conditions, the leverage ratio λ has a strict monotonic increasing relation with the entry threshold $\underline{z}$. Thus, the major outcome of Theorem 1 still holds. The detailed analysis can be found in Appendix.

Market equilibrium

When the equilibrium is reached, Formulas (8) and (11) jointly determine the leverage ratio λ and the average quality of enterprises $\underline{z}$. Formula (8) shows that $\underline{z}$ strictly increases with λ, while Formula (11) shows that λ strictly decreases with $\underline{z}$. Therefore, only one equilibrium outcome satisfies both (8) and (11). Further, the government's policies stimulating enterprises to enter the market (which means the entry cost ξ decreases) will shift the $z(\lambda)$ curve of Formula (8) downward, which means a lower leverage ratio λ. Due to information asymmetry, the bank sets the uniform leverage ratio for enterprises with different levels of efficiency, and as a result, a lower leverage ratio also causes more stringent financing conditions for enterprises with higher productivity. From this, we see that policies stimulating enterprises to enter the market will worsen the misallocation of credit resources among them due to frictions in the credit market.

Figure 3 explains the above mechanism, and the details are as follows: More low-efficiency entrepreneurs enter the market after the stimulus policies lower the entry cost ξ. In the credit market, the moral hazard problem becomes worse with the declining average quality of enterprises. Due to information asymmetry, the bank's optimal decision will be to tighten the lending standards with a lower leverage ratio in order to lower the losses from loan defaults, which further decreases the efficiency of credit resource allocation.

Total factor productivity

Due to frictions in the credit market, entrepreneurship-promoting policies may worsen the misallocation of credit resources, there

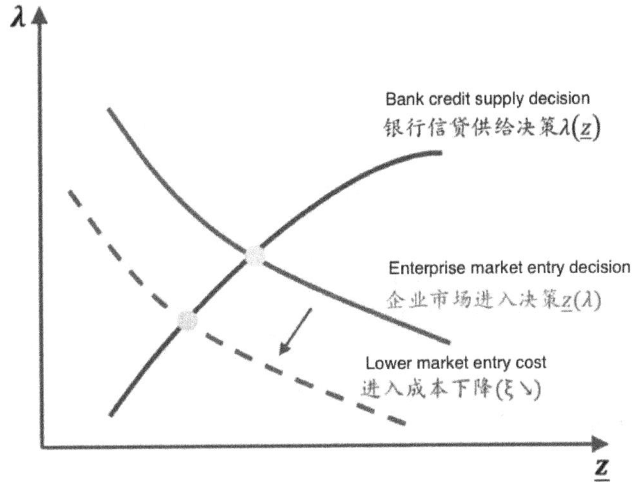

Figure 3. The effect of entrepreneurship-promoting policies on the equilibrium leverage ratio and average efficiency of enterprises.

Notes: This figure describes the equilibrium leverage ratio and the corresponding threshold productivity of enterprises entering the market. The vertical axis is the leverage ratio (the ratio of loan amount to the enterprise's self-owned funds), and the horizontal axis is the threshold productivity corresponding to market entry. The black line is the function of the leverage ratio from the bank's credit supply decision and the threshold productivity (which is determined by the bank's optimal decision (11)); the blue line describes the relationship between the threshold productivity from the enterprise's optimal entry decision and the leverage ratio the bank sets (determined by the enterprise's optimal entry decision (8)).

by lowering productivity. This section gives a theoretical analysis of the whole economy's productivity under credit market frictions. First, we define the total output Y and the total capital input K as follows:

$$Y = Y_1 + Y_2 = \int_{\underline{z}}^{z^*} \psi z(1+\theta\lambda)e d\mathbf{F}(z) + \int_{z^*}^{z_{\max}} [Az(1+\lambda)]e d\mathbf{F}(z) \tag{13}$$

$$K = K_1 + K_2 = \int_{\underline{z}}^{z^*} (1+\theta\lambda)e d\mathbf{F}(z) + \int_{z^*}^{z_{max}} (1+\lambda)e d\mathbf{F}(z) \tag{14}$$

Y_1 and K_1 represent the total output and capital input of low-productivity (defaulting) enterpwrises respectively; Y_2 and K_2 represent the total output and capital input of higher-productivity (non-defaulting) enterprises, respectively.

$$TFP = \frac{Y}{K} = \frac{Y_1}{K_1}\frac{K_1}{K} + \frac{Y_2}{K_2}\frac{K_2}{K} \tag{15}$$

We further define total factor productivity as follows:

$$TFP = \psi(z^* + \underline{z})\frac{K_1}{K} + A(z_{\max} + z^*)\frac{K_2}{K} \tag{16}$$

It can be further simplified, as shown in the following, based on the function of production.

Because ξ strictly increases with both $\underline{z}$ and z^*, the effect of the government policy on the whole economy's productivity is determined by how ξ affects the relative share of the two kinds of capital: $\frac{K_1}{K_2}$. If $\frac{\partial \frac{K_1}{K_2}}{\partial \xi} \leq 0$, that means with the entry cost decreasing, the share of low-productivity defaulting enterprises' capital input will not decrease, and the government policy will reduce total factor productivity, i.e., $\frac{\partial \text{TFP}}{\partial \xi} > 0$. The definition of the two kinds of enterprises' capital shows that

$$\frac{K_1}{K_2} = \frac{1+\theta\lambda}{1+\lambda} \cdot \left(1 - \frac{z_{\max} - z^*}{z_{\max} - \underline{z}}\right), \tag{17}$$

Theorem 2 proves that with the given parameters, $\frac{\partial \text{TFP}}{\partial \xi} > 0$ holds.

Theorem 2. *When the enterprise diverts loan proceeds to invest in storage technology and its productivity ψ is small enough, the indiscriminate entrepreneurship-promoting government policies will lead to a fall in the total factor productivity of the whole production sector, i.e.,* $\frac{\partial \text{TFP}}{\partial \xi} > 0$.

Proof. See Appendix.

Effects of the macro-prudential policy

For the mechanism of how enterprise entry affects bank credit, the core idea lies in the bank's trade-off between loan income and the default risk resulting from frictions in the credit market (information asymmetry and moral hazard). Therefore, the government's macro-prudential policy targeting banks' non-performing loans definitely affects their credit-extending behavior. That is why this section focuses on how the macro-prudential policy targeting non-performing loans affects enterprises' entry and credit allocation through bank credit decisions.

Let us assume that under the macro-prudential policy, the regulator targeting non-performing loans punishes the bank. To be specific, the ratio of non-performing loans in the model ρ satisfies

$$\rho = \frac{\mathbf{F}(z^*(\lambda)) - \mathbf{F}(\underline{z})}{1 - \mathbf{F}(\underline{z})} = \frac{z^*(\lambda) - \underline{z}}{z_{\max} - \underline{z}} \tag{18}$$

i.e., the share of default loans in the total. The penalty the bank receives from the regulator is a linear function of the ratio of non-performing loans, i.e., the cost of the penalty is $c = \delta\rho$ with $\delta > 0$.

$$\max_{\{\lambda\}} \lambda\{(r^f - r^d)[1 - \mathbf{F}(\underline{z})] - (r^f - \varpi + \delta)[\mathbf{F}(z^*(\lambda)) - \mathbf{F}(\underline{z})]\} \tag{19}$$

Given the penalty, the bank's optimal decision (Formula (10)) can be written as follows:

The first-order condition of the leverage ratio means

$$\begin{aligned}(r^f - r^d)[1 - \mathbf{F}(\underline{z})] - (r^f - \varpi + \delta)[\mathbf{F}(z^*(\lambda)) - \mathbf{F}(\underline{z})] \\ = \lambda(r^f - \varpi + \delta)\mathbf{F}'(z^*(\lambda))\frac{dz^*(\lambda)}{d\lambda}\end{aligned} \tag{20}$$

From Formula (20), we can get

$$\mathbf{F}_{\lambda}' = -(r^{f} - \varpi + \delta) \cdot \left(2 \cdot \frac{dz^{*}(\lambda)}{d\lambda} - \lambda \cdot \frac{d\left(\frac{dz^{*}(\lambda)}{d\lambda} \right)}{d\lambda} \right) < 0 \tag{21}$$

$$\mathbf{F}_{\underline{z}}' = r^{d} - \varpi + \delta > 0 \tag{22}$$

$$\mathbf{F}_{\delta}' = -(z^{*} - \underline{z}) - \lambda \cdot \frac{dz^{*}(\lambda)}{d\lambda} < 0 \tag{23}$$

As we know $\frac{dz^{*}(\lambda)}{d\lambda} > 0$, and $\frac{d\left(\frac{dz^{*}(\lambda)}{d\lambda}\right)}{d\lambda} < 0$ always holds, we can easily demonstrate that $\frac{d\lambda}{d\underline{z}} > 0$. That is, after we introduce the macro prudence, the leverage ratio λ set by the bank still strictly increases with the enterprise's entry threshold $\underline{z}$.

Now, $\frac{d\lambda}{d\delta} < 0$ and $\frac{d\underline{z}}{d\delta} > 0$, which suggests that intensified macro prudence will lead to a lower leverage ratio in the bank's optimal decision; and meanwhile higher average quality of entering enterprises. In addition, $\frac{d\left(\frac{d\lambda}{d\underline{z}}\right)}{d\delta} > 0$ suggests that as macro prudence intensifies, the bank's credit strategy (the leverage ratio) becomes more sensitive to enterprises' average quality (entry threshold).

If we look back at Formula (17), we know that the share of the two kinds of enterprises' capital, $\frac{K_1}{K_2}$, is a function of the leverage ratio λ and the average enterprise quality $\underline{z}$. When the intensity of macro prudence, δ, rises, λ will be lower and $\underline{z}$ higher, exerting a nonlinear effect on $\frac{K_1}{K_2}$. This suggests that the negative effects of the government's entrepreneurship-promoting policies on total factor productivity are subject to the intensity of macro prudence, and the direction of the influence is determined by the net effect of the following two factors: the direct effect of a lower leverage ratio, and the indirect effect of rising average enterprise quality. Theorem 3 sums up the above analysis.

Theorem 3. *When a stricter macro-prudential policy is adopted* (*higher* δ), *the bank will set a lower leverage ratio* ($\frac{d\lambda}{d\delta} < 0$), *and the average quality of enterprises entering the market will rise* ($\frac{d\underline{z}}{d\delta} > 0$). *Now, the tuning of the* *bank's leverage ratio will be more sensitive to the average quality of the enterprises in the market* ($\frac{d^2\lambda}{d\delta d\underline{z}} > 0$).

In addition, macro prudence will affect the effects of the government's entrepreneurship-promoting policies on total factor productivity. The direction of the influence will be determined by the net effect of the following two: the direct effect from a lower leverage ratio, and the indirect effect from the rising average quality of enterprises. Figure 4 explains the mechanism. Tighter macro prudence (rising cost of penalty for a high non-performing-loan ratio) causes the bank to tighten the credit supply (shifting the black line downward) and makes the bank credit supply more sensitive to the average quality of enterprises (with the $\lambda(\underline{z})$ curve becoming steeper). When equilibrium is finally reached, the leverage ratio

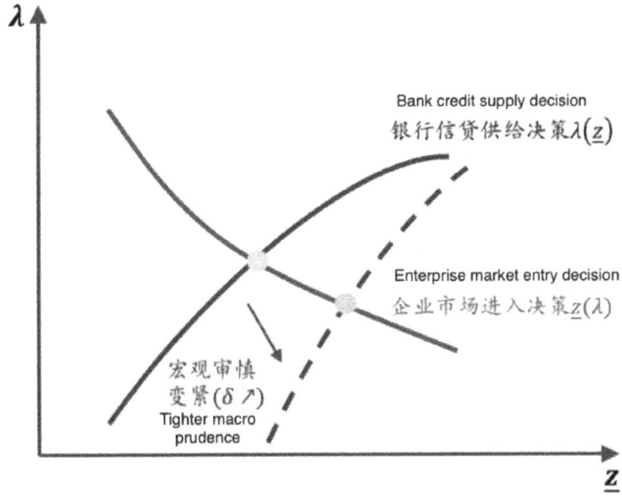

Figure 4. Effects of the macro-prudential policy on the equilibrium leverage ratio and average enterprise efficiency.

Notes: This figure describes the equilibrium leverage ratio and the corresponding threshold productivity of entering enterprises under the macro-prudential policy. The vertical axis is the leverage ratio (the ratio of the enterprise's loan to its own funds), and the horizontal axis is the corresponding threshold productivity of the entering enterprises. The black line is the function of the leverage ratio from the bank credit supply decision and the threshold productivity (determined by the bank's optimal decision (20)); the blue line is the relationship between the threshold productivity from the enterprise's optimal entry decision and the leverage ratio set by the bank (determined by the enterprise's optimal entry decision (8)).

decreases, fewer enterprises enter the market, and the average quality of enterprises is higher. The negative effect of the macro-prudential policy on the leverage ratio mainly results from the bank's practice to reduce the leverage ratio in order to decrease the default risk due to the penalty for a high non-performing-loan ratio (the default threshold $z^*(\lambda)$ is an increasing function of the leverage ratio). The positive effect of the macro-prudential policy on the average quality of producers is that only enterprises with higher productivity choose to enter because the lower leverage ratio weakens the enterprises' incentive to enter. Therefore, the macro-prudential policy affects bank credit and enterprises' entry decision through the leverage ratio. Its overall effect on the productivity of the whole economy is determined by the interaction of the negative effect from credit misallocation and the positive effect of enterprises' entry decision.

Conclusion

This chapter presents a theoretical frame for understanding the financing difficulties of China's huge numbers of micro- and small enterprises. The core mechanism is as follows. The entrepreneurship-promoting policies lower the market entry threshold, thereby causing more low-efficiency micro- and small enterprises to enter and lowering the overall efficiency of the economy. At the same time, an enterprise's productivity is private information. When the share of micro- and small enterprises with medium or low efficiency rises, banks face the trade-off between losses from defaults and interest income from loans due to information asymmetry and moral hazard. The final result is that banks tighten the credit supply, and thus the credit resource misallocation becomes worse.

The main conclusions of the study are as follows. First, the bank's optimal leverage ratio strictly increases with the average quality of credit-applying enterprises. The more low-efficiency enterprises enter the market, the tighter the banks' credit constraints. Second, under certain circumstances, the government's entrepreneurship-promoting policies will lead to a fall in the total factor productivity of the whole producing sector. Third, when the government adopts a more stringent macro-prudential policy, the leverage ratio set by banks will be lower, and the average quality of enterprises entering the market will be higher. Moreover, banks' tuning of the leverage ratio becomes more sensitive to the average quality of enterprises in the market. In addition, macro prudence influences the effect of entrepreneurship-promoting policies on total factor productivity. The direction of the influence is determined by the net effect of the following two: the direct effect from the lower leverage ratio, and the indirect effect from the rising average quality of enterprises.

This study's theoretical framework provides the economic micro-foundation for understanding the financing difficulties of SMEs. Meanwhile, the study shows that stimulus policies targeting micro-enterprises need to fully account for frictions in the financial markets in order to avoid the potential negative effects of resource misallocation.

References

Ates, S.T. and Saffie, F.E. 2021. Fewer but better: Sudden stops, firm entry, and financial selection. *American Economic Journal: Macroeconomics*, 13(3): 304–356.

Bai, Y., Lu, D., and Tian, X. 2018. Do financial frictions explain Chinese firms' saving and misallocation? (No. w24436). National Bureau of Economic Research.

Brandt, L., Tombe, T., and Zhu, X. 2013. Factor market distortions across time, space and sectors in China. *Review of Economic Dynamics*, 16(1): 39–58.

Chang, C., Chen, K., Waggoner, D.F., and Zha, T. 2016. Trends and cycles in China's macroeconomy. *NBER Macroeconomics Annual*, 30(1): 1–84.

Cheng, C. and Yang, L. 2022. What drives the credit constraints faced by Chinese small and micro enterprises? *Economic Modelling*, 113: 105898.

Hu, Y. 2022. A dynamic theory of bank lending, firm entry, and investment fluctuations. *Journal of Economic Theory*, 204: 105515.

Li, Z. 2002. Bank structure and SME financing. *Economic Research*, 2002(06): 38–45, 94.

Lin, Y. and Sun, X. 2005. Information, informal finance and SME financing. *Economic Research*, 2005(07): 35–44.

Liu, Z., Wang, P., and Xu, Z. 2021. Interest-rate liberalization and capital misallocations. *American Economic Journal: Macroeconomics*, 13(2): 373–419.

Ping, X. and Yang, M. 2009. An empirical study on the information asymmetry in the credit market — evidence from China's state-owned banks. *Financial Research*, 2009(03): 1–18.

Song, Z., Storesletten, K., and Zilibotti, F. 2011. Growing like china. *American Economic Review*, 101(1): 196–233.

Stiglitz, J.E. and Weiss, A. 1981. Credit rationing in markets with imperfect information. *American Economic Review*, 71(3): 393–410.

Wu, G.L. 2018. Capital misallocation in China: Financial frictions or policy distortions? *Journal of Development Economics*, 130: 203–223.

Yin, Z. and Gan, L. 2011. Information asymmetry, enterprise heterogeneity and credit risk. *Economic Research*, 46(09): 121–132.

Appendix

Proof of Theorem 1.

Formula (11) can be adjusted as follows:

$$\left(1-\frac{r^f-r^d}{r^f-w}\right)\underline{z}+\frac{r^f-r^d}{r^f-w}z_{\max}=z^*(\lambda)+\lambda\frac{dz^*(\lambda)}{d\lambda} \tag{A1}$$

As we know that $z^*(\lambda)=\frac{r^f\lambda}{(A-\psi)+(A-\psi\theta)}\lambda$, we can get

$$\frac{\partial \text{RHS}}{\partial\lambda}=r^f\frac{4(A-\psi)^2[(A-\psi)+(A-\psi\theta)\lambda]}{[(A-\psi)+(A-\psi\theta)\lambda]^4}>0 \tag{A2}$$

$$\frac{\partial \text{LHS}}{\partial\underline{z}}=\left(1-\frac{r^f-r^d}{r^f-w}\right)>0 \tag{A3}$$

Therefore, λ strictly increases with $\underline{z}$. Theorem 1 is proven.

Likewise, when the lending rate r^f endogenously becomes a function of λ, i.e., $r^f(\lambda)$, seek the partial derivative of the implicit function (A1), and we get

$$F'_\lambda=-\frac{1}{2}z_m\frac{A-\psi}{\lambda^2}\frac{r^d-\omega}{(r^f-\omega)^2}(z_m-\underline{z})+\frac{1}{2}z_m$$
$$\times\frac{A-\psi}{\lambda^2}\frac{2\lambda(A-\psi)+(A-\theta\psi)\lambda^2}{[A-\psi+(A-\theta\psi)\lambda]^2}-\frac{2r^f(A-\psi)^2}{[A-\psi+(A-\theta\psi)\lambda]^3}<0 \tag{A4}$$

$$F'_{\underline{z}}=\frac{r^d-\omega}{r^f-\omega}>0$$

Thus, under the condition above, $\frac{\partial \lambda}{\partial \underline{z}} > 0$. In other words, when the lending rate becomes endogenous, λ and $\underline{z}$ still maintain a strict monotonic increasing relationship.

Proof of Theorem 2.
From Formula (16),

$$\frac{K_1}{K_2} = \frac{1+\theta\lambda}{1+\lambda} \cdot \left(1 - \frac{z_{\max} - z^*}{z_{\max} - \underline{z}}\right) \tag{A5}$$

We can easily prove that $\frac{1+\theta\lambda}{1+\lambda}$ is a decreasing function of λ. Suppose $Q(\lambda) = \left(1 - \frac{z_{\max} - z^*}{z_{\max} - \underline{z}}\right)$, then

$$\frac{\partial Q}{\partial \lambda} = \frac{\partial Q}{\partial z^*}\frac{\partial z^*}{\partial \lambda} + \frac{\partial Q}{\partial \underline{z}}\frac{\partial \underline{z}}{\partial \lambda} \tag{A6}$$

We can get the following from Formulas (5) and (19):

$$\frac{\partial \underline{z}}{\partial \lambda} = \frac{r^f - \varpi}{r^d - \varpi} \cdot \frac{2r^f (A-\psi)^2}{[(A-\psi)+(A-\psi\theta)\lambda]^3}, \tag{A7}$$

$$\frac{\partial z^*}{\partial \lambda} = \frac{r^f (A-\psi)}{[(A-\psi)+(A-\psi\theta)\lambda]^2} \tag{A8}$$

As $\frac{\partial Q}{\partial z^*} = \frac{1}{z_{\max} - \underline{z}}$ and $\frac{\partial Q}{\partial \underline{z}} = \frac{z_{\max} - z^*}{(z_{\max} - \underline{z})^2}$, the simpler formula is

$$\frac{\partial Q}{\partial \lambda} = \frac{r^f (A-\psi)}{[(A-\psi)+(A-\psi\theta)\lambda]^2 (z_{\max} - \underline{z})} \times \left(1 - \frac{z_{\max} - z^*}{z_{\max} - \underline{z}} \cdot \frac{r^f - \varpi}{r^d - \varpi} \cdot \frac{2(A-\psi)}{(A-\psi)+(A-\psi\theta)\lambda}\right) \tag{A9}$$

When $\frac{\partial Q}{\partial \lambda} < 0$, we get

$$\xi > \psi(1+\theta\lambda)e\left\{ z_{\max} - \frac{r^f - \varpi}{r^d - \varpi} \cdot \frac{2(A-\psi)z_{\max} - r^f \lambda}{(A-\psi)+(A-\psi\theta)\lambda} \right\} \tag{A10}$$

When (A10) holds, Theorem 2 is proven.

https://doi.org/10.1142/9789819815241_0022

Chapter 22

ECONOMIC REFORM, TECHNOLOGICAL PROGRESS, AND DEVELOPMENT OF THE SELF-EMPLOYMENT SECTOR

Xinxin Ma

Faculty of Economics, Hosei University, Tokyo, Japan
xxma@hosei.ac.jp

Introduction

Nearly 40 years of economic reforms have led to rapid economic growth in China. In 2010, China's GDP surpassed that of Japan, making it the second-largest economic entity in the world. In the process of economic growth, there are unique Chinese experiences reflected in Chinese economic growth models. Although there are unique significances (e.g., institutional reform and innovation) in these models, the majority of them are also in line with neoclassical economic theories. Among them, the most distinctive one is that of "incremental reform (*Zengliang Gaige*)" (Lin *et al.*, 1994): while stabilizing the state-owned sector, the Chinese government has allowed the development of a non-state-owned sector, including foreign-invested enterprises, privately owned enterprises, and the self-employment sector.

The development of the informal sector,[1] dominated by self-employment, can promote economic growth in developing countries (International Labor Organization [ILO], 1972). Data from the National Bureau of Statistics (NBS) show that the number of self-employed workers[2] in China has increased significantly, and the number of registered laborers in the self-employment sector has increased from 0.15 million in 1978 to 74.765 million in 2000 and 228.332 million in 2019 (NBS, 2003, 2020). Therefore, the self-employment sector has become prominent.

Another phenomenon worthy of attention is that since the 2000s, with the development of business platforms and the expansion of internet use, more workers have voluntarily entered the self-employment sector. The Chinese government launched the "Internet Plus" policy to promote the development of the information industry represented by the internet in various fields. Simultaneously, to promote entrepreneurship, the Chinese government issued a series of policies, including mass entrepreneurship and innovation policies, after 2016. According to the new economic growth theory (Lucas, 1988; Romer, 1994), which is known as the representative of the Fourth Industrial Revolution (information industrial revolution), new technological progress (e.g., internet use) may promote economic growth. According to Schumpeter's "creative destruction" economic growth theory (Schumpeter, 1934, 1942), entrepreneurship as the core and the creative destruction caused by innovation are key factors in promoting economic growth.

Therefore, from the perspective of promoting employment and economic growth, investigating the impact of the internet on the choice of entering the self-employment sector is an important issue. This study conducts an empirical analysis to answer the following questions: First, does internet use affect the choice to enter the self-employment sector? Second, does the effect of internet use differ across the groups? Third, does the effect of internet use on self-employment differ by purpose of internet use? I attempt to provide empirical evidence to explain the features and challenges of the development of the self-employment sector in China.

Some studies focused on the issue for developed countries, such as Europe and the United States, and analyzed the impact of internet use on employment (Crandall *et al.*, 2007; Hair *et al.*, 2007; Shirazi, 2012; Czernich, 2014; Novo-Corti *et al.*, 2014; Alam and Mamun, 2017; Dettling, 2017). They found that internet use may increase employment. Mao *et al.* (2017), Zhou and Fan (2018), Ding and Yuan (2019), and Mao *et al.* (2019) investigated the impact of internet use on family entrepreneurship in China and reported that internet use may promote entrepreneurship.

This study contributes to the literature in three ways: First, most studies use cross-sectional data and the instrumental variable (IV) method to address endogeneity. However, they did not address the individual heterogeneity issues. This study uses national longitudinal survey data and panel data analysis methods (i.e., the lagged variable (LV), fixed effects (FE), and random effects (RE) models) to address endogeneity problems. I also use two new IVs to address endogeneity. Second, previous literature did not consider the differences in the effects of internet use among different groups (low education vs. high education, younger age generation vs. older age generation, rural residents vs. urban residents). Because internet access or internet use skills may differ among different groups and the situations of labor supply and demand in the labor market may differ by group, the effect of internet use may differ across different groups. This study compares the effects of internet use between groups. Third, most previous studies only analyzed internet use (whether using the internet) (extensive effect) and did not consider the volume of internet use (the frequency of using the internet) (intensive effect), whereas this study investigates both the extensive and intensive effects of internet use and also compares the effects of internet usage for different purposes. Therefore, this study provides new empirical findings, which are important additions to the literature.

The remainder of this chapter is organized as follows: section "Economic Reform, Technological Progress, and Development of Self-Employment Sector in China" reviews the process of economic reform and development of the self-employment sector in China and compares Japanese experiences. Section "Literature Review" summarizes economic theories and empirical studies on self-employment. Section "Methodology" introduces the methodology, including the econometric model and the data used in the empirical study. Section "Results of Descriptive Statistics" describes the results of the descriptive statistics. Section "Econometric Analysis Results" reports and discusses the results of the econometric analysis. The last section concludes the chapter with empirical results and policy implications.

Economic Reform, Technological Progress, and Development of Self-Employment Sector in China

Economic reform and development of self-employment in China

The non-agricultural self-employment sector has developed along with economic reforms.[3] During the period of the planned economy (1949–1977), the socialist transformation of handicraft industries changed private ownership in the self-employment sector into collective ownership. After 1956, self-employment was banned as a capitalist market activity. During the market-oriented reform period (after 1978), in the early 1980s, to solve the unemployment problem in urban areas caused by the return of educated youths (*Zhishi Qingnian*) from the rural areas to their hometowns (urban areas), the government began to allow the existence of the self-employment sector.

Figure 1 shows that the number of employees in state-owned enterprises (SOEs) increased from 74.51 million in 1978 to 162.61 million in 1995 and then declined after reaching a peak in 1995, falling to 54.73 million in 2019; a downward trend is also observed for collectively owned enterprises (COEs): from 20.48 million in

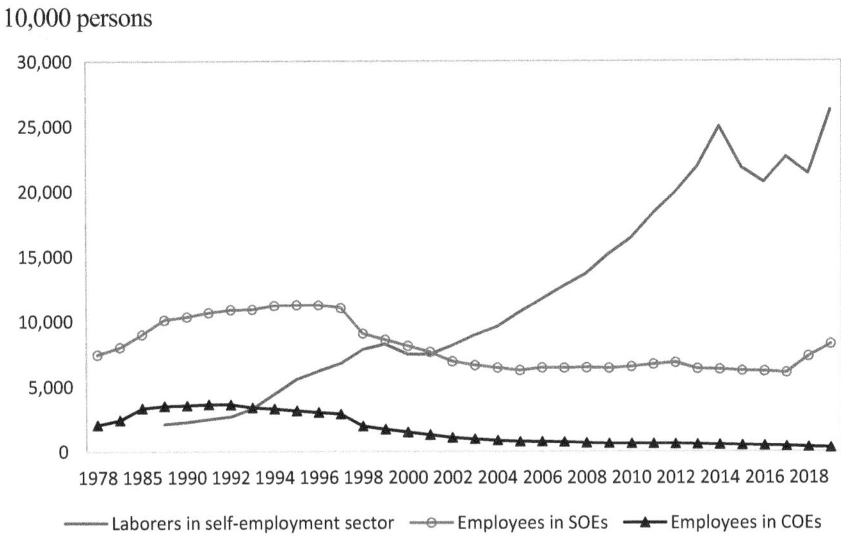

Figure 1. Trends in the number of laborers in self-employment sector, employees in SOEs and COEs in China (1978–2019).

Notes: The number of laborers in the self-employment sector is the sum of the number of self-employed individuals without employees (own-account workers), the number of employees in small and micro enterprises with fewer than eight employees, and the number of entrepreneurs in small and micro enterprises with fewer than eight employees, excluding the self-employed in the agricultural industry sector. SOEs and COEs are registered enterprises.
Source: Data from China Statistical Yearbook (annual edition).

1978 to 2.960 million in 2019. In contrast, the number of laborers in the self-employment sector increased significantly: from 41.42 million in 1989 to 228.333 million in 2019. It can be observed that after 2012, the number of laborers in the self-employment sector increased rapidly, while the number of employees in SOEs and COEs continued to decline significantly. In 2019, the number of laborers in the self-employment sector was 3.07 times the total number of employees in both SOEs and COEs.

The development of China's self-employment sector is mainly attributable to economic development and institutional reforms. First, according to Lewis' (1954) dual economy model, in the early stages of economic development, there are a large number of surplus laborers in traditional sectors (e.g., the agricultural sector), and modern sectors (e.g., the manufacturing industry sector) only need to pay wages equivalent to the subsistence level. Labor migration from rural to urban areas may occur. Todaro (1969, 1980) developed the Lewis model and stated that if the number of rural surplus laborers exceeds labor demand in the urban labor market, the urban unemployment rate will increase. The majority of rural–urban migrants enter the non-agricultural self-employment sector and wait for the opportunity to become employees of enterprises. Regarding labor migration in China, in 1978, the Chinese government initiated reforms in rural areas and implemented the household responsibility system, which brought about a substantial increase in rural labor productivity and highlighted the problem of surplus laborers (Minami and Ma, 2010, 2014; Ma and Minami, 2022). The reform of the household registration system (*hukou*) allowed surplus laborers in the agricultural industry sector to move from rural to urban areas for work. Along with an increase in the number of migrant workers, the number of laborers in the self-employment sector increased significantly. Figure 2 shows that during the period 2008–2019, as the number of migrant workers increased, self-employed individuals without employees (own-account workers) and the total number of laborers in the self-employment sector increased simultaneously.[4]

Rural–urban labor migration can promote economic growth by moving laborers from the low-productivity agriculture industry sector to the high-productivity manufacturing or service industry sectors. Taking the experience of Japan as a case study, Figure 3 shows the changes in the number of employees and laborers in the self-employment sector by Japanese economic development period.

(i) During the economic high-growth period (1957–1972), the total number of laborers in the self-employment sector (the sum of the number of agricultural and non-agricultural self-employed individuals) declined from 10.54 million in 1957 to 9.9 million in 1971, while the number of employees increased

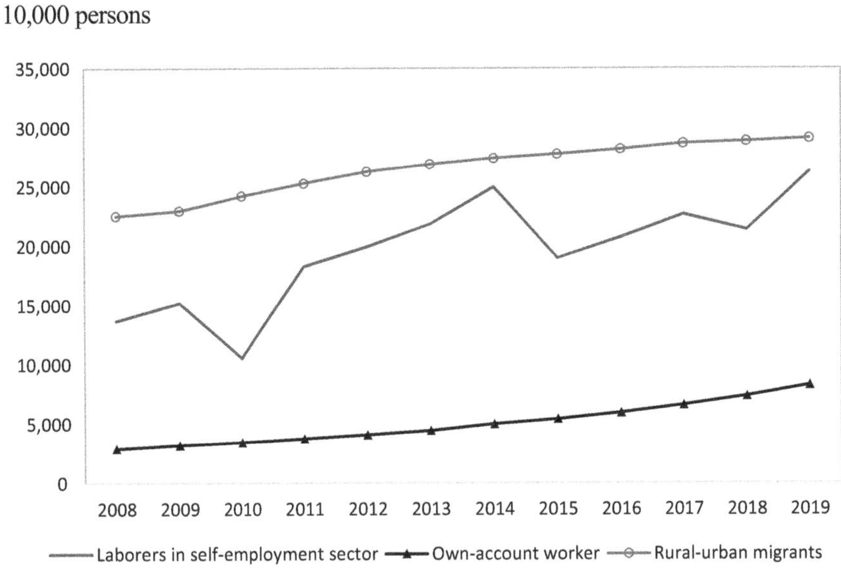

Figure 2. Trends in the number of migrant workers, own-account workers, and laborers in the self-employment sector in China (2008–2019).

Note: An own-account worker is a self-employed individual without employees; the laborers in the self-employment sector include the own-account workers, employees in small and micro enterprises with fewer than eight employees, and entrepreneurs of small and micro enterprises with fewer than eight employees, but exclude the self-employed individuals in agricultural industry sector.

Source: Data from China Statistical Yearbook (annual edition) and National Migrant Workers Monitoring Survey Report (annual edition).

from 17.7 million in 1957 to 33.65 million in 1971. Surplus laborers in the agricultural industry sector moved to the manufacturing industry sector, which promoted the rapid growth of the Japanese economy. This is in line with Lewis's dual economy model (Minami and Ma, 2010, 2014; Ma and Minami, 2022). Although it is observed that the total number of laborers in the self-employment sector declined during the rapid economic growth period, the number of non-agricultural self-employed individuals increased from 4.76 million in 1957 to 6.11 million in 1971, and the number of entrepreneurs in small and micro enterprises increased from 1.08 million people to 1.69 million,

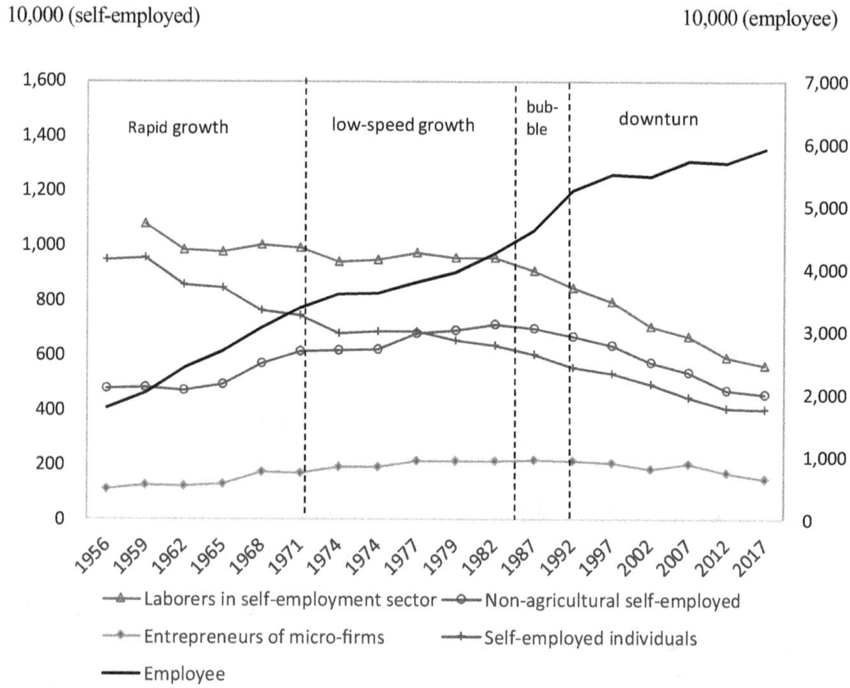

Figure 3. Trends in the number of laborers in the self-employment sector and employees in Japan (1956–2017).

Note: The number of laborers in the self-employment sector is the sum of the number of agricultural and non-agricultural self-employed individuals and entrepreneurs of small and micro enterprises; the number of self-employed individuals is the own-account worker.
Source: Ministry of Internal Affairs and Communications, Japan "Basic Statistics on Employment Structure" (annual edition).

suggesting that entrepreneurship was very active during the period. According to Schumpeter's theory, entrepreneurial activities promote rapid economic growth in Japan.

(ii) During the economic low-growth period (1972–1985), the changing trend of the total number of laborers, employees, non-agricultural self-employed individuals, and entrepreneurs of small and micro enterprises was similar to that of the rapid economic growth period, although the growth rate of these groups was lower than that during the rapid economic growth period.

(iii) However, during the bubble economy period (December 1986–February 1991) and the economic downturn period (after 1991), although the number of employees continued to increase, which was the same as the previous two periods, the number of non-agricultural self-employed individuals decreased from 6.67 million in 1992 to 4.55 million in 2017, and entrepreneurs of small and micro enterprises decreased from 2.11 million in 1992 to 1.46 million in 2017. The decrease in the number of non-agricultural self-employed individuals and entrepreneurs of small and micro enterprises suggests that during the bubble economy and economic downturn periods, individual entrepreneurial innovation decreased greatly. Even in the late 1990s, the development of information and communications technology (ICT) did not increase employment in Japan's self-employment sector. The decrease in individual entrepreneurial innovation is the main reason the Japanese economy has been in an economic downturn since 1990. Although the Japanese Ministry of International Trade and Industry has issued policies to promote entrepreneurship and innovation since the 2000s, Figure 3 shows that these policies have had little impact.

Compared with the Japanese experience, the development of the self-employment sector in China in the current period is similar to that during the Japanese economic high- and low-growth periods.

The development of the self-employment sector in China is closely related to SOEs' reform. In the late 1990s, the Chinese government implemented reforms of SOEs such as "*broke the iron rice bowl*" (change permanent employment to temporary employment) and gave SOEs more autonomy to determine their employees' employment and wages. To reduce surplus employment, SOEs implemented employment adjustments that led to an increase in the number of laid-off workers, highlighting the problem of urban unemployment. In response to the new situation in the urban labor market, the Chinese government introduced a series of policies to encourage laid-off workers to enter the self-employment sector, which promoted the development of self-employment in urban areas.

Figure 4 shows the changes in the number of registered urban unemployed (most of whom are laid-off SOE workers) and the number of laborers in the self-employment sector during 1990–2010. The trends for these two are similar. During this period (especially during the period of enforcing SOEs reform from 1990 to 2002), as the registered unemployment rate rose, the number of laborers in the non-agricultural self-employment sector also increased, indicating that the non-agricultural self-employment sector absorbed a part of the laid-off workers of SOEs, playing a role in promoting employment for the laid-off workers of SOEs.

Simultaneously, economic liberalization enabled the development of foreign investment enterprises and privately owned

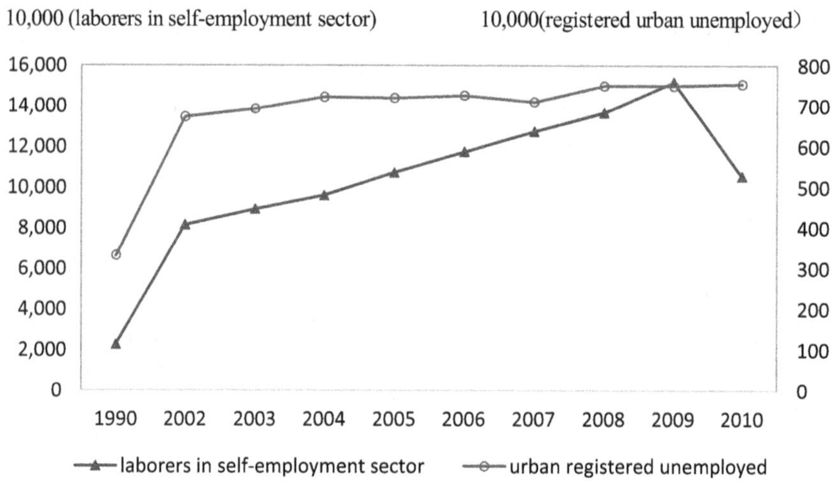

Figure 4. Trends in the number of urban registered unemployed and laborers in the self-employment sector (1990–2010).

Note: The number of laborers in the self-employment sector is the sum of the number of non-agricultural self-employed individuals, employees in small and micro enterprises with fewer than eight employees, and entrepreneurs in small and micro enterprises with fewer than eight employees, excluding agricultural self-employed individuals.

Source: National Bureau of Statistics "China Statistical Yearbook" (annual edition).

enterprises. Market mechanisms began playing an increasingly significant role in the commodity market. Market-oriented reforms promoted the development of the self-employment sector in China.

Technological progress and development of the self-employment sector in China

Looking back at the impact of previous industrial revolutions on industrial society, it can be assumed that internet technology, as a representative of the ICT industry revolution, may significantly affect the outcomes of the labor market. Some empirical studies have found that ICT (e.g., computers, internet) affects income levels (Krueger, 1993; Miller and Mulvey, 1997; Pabilonia and Zoghi, 2005), income inequality (Lloyd-Ellis, 1999; Hanley, 2000; Furuholt and Kristiansen, 2007; Dimaggio and Bonikowski, 2008; Pradhan *et al.*, 2016; Philip *et al.*, 2017; Ghosh, 2020), and employment (Atasoy, 2013; Alam and Mamun, 2017; Deyyling, 2017).

In China, since the 2000s, with the development of the digital economy, internet use has rapidly spread to urban and rural areas. Figure 5 shows the internet penetration rate in China. The national internet penetration rate increased from 4.6% in 2002 to 70.4% in 2020, the urban internet penetration rate increased from 26.0% in 2007 to 79.8% in 2020, and the rural internet penetration rate increased from 7.4% in 2007 to 55/9% in 2020. Since 2012, the internet penetration rate has risen rapidly in both urban and rural areas.

In 2012, the Chinese government emphasized that employment was the greatest sign of welfare for the nation. To promote national employment, the government promoted employment in the self-employment sector, which is known as "flexible employment."[5] For example, in 2016, the government issued a series of policies on mass entrepreneurship and innovation. In 2020, *Government Work Report* pointed out that "[t]here are currently hundreds of millions of flexible workers in China, and that new business forms such as e-commerce, online shopping, and online services have played an important role in the fight against

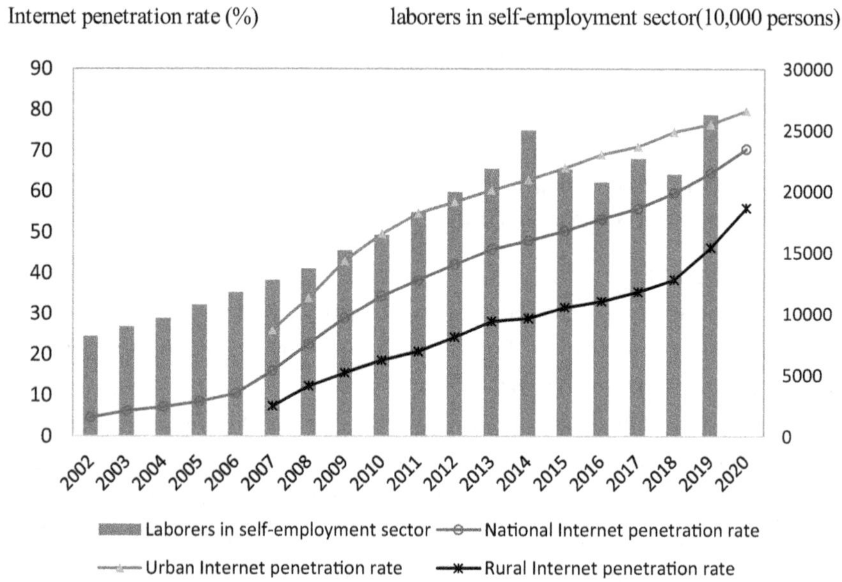

Figure 5. Trends of China's internet penetration rate and the number of laborers in self-employment sector (2002–2020).

Source: Annual data published by China Internet Network Information Center (annual edition) and China Statistical Yearbook (annual edition).

the epidemic. In the future, we must vigorously develop the platform and sharing economy, and create new advantages for the digital economy." In July 2020, Premier Li Keqiang emphasized in the *Opinions on Supporting Multi-channel Flexible Employment* that "[i]n the current period, the new business forms have significantly developed; we should remove the unreasonable restrictions on flexible employment, encourage self-employment and self-innovation, and stabilize the overall employment situation." In July 2020, with the support and encouragement of the National Development and Reform Commission, eight internet platform companies, including Alibaba, Baidu, Tencent, Didi Chuxing, Meituan, and Zhaopin, jointly released the *Proposal for Platform Enterprises to Support Flexible Employment* and aimed to promote entrepreneurship based on internet use. Figure 5 shows that, with the expansion of internet use, the number of laborers in the self-employment sector increased significantly.

To sum up, along with economic development and institutional reform, the Chinese government has promoted the development of the self-employment sector. Since the 2000s, the government has vigorously promoted entrepreneurship and mass innovation based on the internet and information platforms through the "Internet Plus" policies to promote Chinese economic growth. Since 2012, the internet penetration rate has increased rapidly, and the number of laborers in the self-employment sector has also increased significantly.

Does internet use affect the probability of an individual choosing to enter the self-employed sector? I conduct an empirical study to answer this question in the following section.

Literature Review

Empirical studies on the determinants of entering the self-employment sector

Regarding the determinants that govern entry into the self-employment sector, the results of the empirical studies, except for China,[6] can be summarized as follows.

First, Blau (1985), Borjas (1986), Evans and Leighton (1989), Amit *et al.* (1990), Bruce (1999), Dunn and Holtz-Eakin (2000), Chen and Hu (2018), and Molina (2020) pointed out that individual attributes (e.g., education, age, and sex), family factors (e.g., marital status, child, and parents' work) and income/wealth factors affect the choice of self-employment. For example, married women with more children are more likely to choose to become self-employed than men.

Second, Evans and Jovanovic (1989), Lentz and Laband (1990), Holtz-Eakin *et al.* (1994), Dunn and Holtz-Eakin (2000), Adelino *et al.* (2015), and Schmalz *et al.* (2017) found that family background (e.g., parents' work, education and occupation, household income, wealth, and home ownership) affects the likelihood of entering the self-employment sector.

Third, Poon *et al.* (2012) and Kwon *et al.* (2013) indicated that social capital and social networks affect the choice of self-employment. Finally, Brzozowski and Lasek (2019) and Wassink (2020) explored that immigrants are more likely to enter the self-employment sector than are local residents.

Regarding the empirical studies on determinants of self-employment in China, Wu (2006), Yueh (2009a, 2009b), Zhang and Pan (2012), Zhang and Zhao (2015), Ma (2018), Ma (2017), and Ma and Li (2022) indicated that individual attributes significantly affect the choice of self-employment. Chen and Hu (2019) pointed out that owning a house can increase the likelihood of becoming an entrepreneur. Yueh (2009a, 2009b) showed that having more social networks increases the probability of self-employment. Zhang and Zhao (2015) found that urban–rural migrants with more social and family networks are more likely to enter the self-employment sector. Wu (2006) examined self-employment in urban and rural areas during different reform periods in China, focusing on how public sector cadres responded to new market opportunities, and found that higher education and cadre status may increase the probability of urban residents entering the self-employment sector, but these factors had opposite effects on rural residents.

Empirical studies on the association between internet use and self-employment

Empirical studies on developing and developed countries, except China, have demonstrated that digital technologies, such as broadband and the internet, affect employment and entrepreneurship, but the analysis results are not consistent. For example, Crandall *et al.* (2007) demonstrated that in the United States, every additional three million lines (i.e., a 1% increase in broadband access) may create nearly 300,000 jobs. Czernich (2014) found a negative association between the availability of DSL broadband and the unemployment rate in Germany; however, the results of the IV method indicated that the causal relationship between the two was not significant. Atasoy (2013) indicated that broadband internet use may increase employment. Alam and Mamun (2017) analyzed the impact of internet use on employment using survey data from 391 households in rural Australia and the propensity score matching (PSM) method and showed that there was no significant causal relationship between internet use and employment. Hair *et al.* (2007), Shirazi (2012), and Novo-Corti *et al.* (2014) pointed out that the popularization of digital technologies, such as internet use, can promote entrepreneurship, which they called "digital entrepreneurship." Dettling (2017) used the US Current Population Survey data and the IV method to analyze the impact of high-speed internet use on female employment and found that internet use can increase the employment rate of married women by 4.1 percentage points.

Empirical studies in China indicate that internet use promotes entrepreneurship. For example, using the China General Social Survey (CGSS) data and a combination of the IV method and multivariate logit regression model, Mao *et al.* (2019) found that internet use may increase the probability of opportunity entrepreneurship. Using survey data from the China Family Panel Studies (CFPS) of 2010 and 2014 and the IV_Probit model, Zhou and Fan (2018) showed that internet use may increase the probability of family entrepreneurship by three percentage points compared with families that do not use the internet. Using the 2017 CGSS data and the logit regression model, Mao *et al.* (2017) indicated that the frequency of internet use may increase the probability of business start-ups among rural women. Using data from the CGSS for 2010, 2013, and 2015 and the IV_probit model, Ding and Yuan (2019) reported that internet use can increase the probability of female entrepreneurship.

Although these studies have investigated the relationship between internet use and self-employment, the following issues need to be resolved. First, most studies used cross-sectional data and IV methods to address endogeneity issues, whereas the individual heterogeneity issue was not addressed. Second, there is no detailed research on the differences in the effects of internet use among different groups. Third, studies comparing differences in the effects of internet use for different purposes are scarce. This study attempts to address these questions. These new empirical results enrich the empirical research on self-employment in China.

Methodology

Model

First, I used a logit model to analyze the effect of the internet on the probability of entering the self-employment sector, as shown in Equation (1):

$$\Pr(Y_i^* = 1) = \frac{\exp(a + \beta_I \text{Int}_i + \beta_H H_i + u_i)}{1 + \exp(a + \beta_I \text{Int}_i + \beta_H H_i + u_i)} \quad (1)$$

where i expresses an individual, $\Pr(Y_i^* = n)$ expresses the probability of entering the self-employment sector, Int is an indicator of internet use (e.g., whether they have used the internet in the past year, the frequency of using the internet), H expresses the other factor that affects the choice of entering the self-employment sector (e.g., education, age, gender), β is the coefficient, a is a constant term, and u is a random error term.

I used three methods to address endogeneity issues. First, two variables — (i) the number of optical cable circuits in 1999 and (ii) the number of digital circuits in provincial areas in 1999 — were used as IVs.[7] I matched the provincial internet penetration data with the individual survey data from the CFPS. Regional internet penetration has been based on regional communication facilities (e.g., optical cable circuits and digital circuits) in the past; thus, the two variables may affect the probability of using the internet in the present period. It can be imagined that a region with relatively developed communication facilities in the past will build internet facilities faster, and the probability of using the internet may be greater for individuals in the region than those in other regions. However, the situation of regional communication facilities in 1999 will not have a significant impact on an individual's choice to enter the self-employment sector 20 years later, which theoretically meets the conditions of an IV.

$$\Pr(\text{Int}_i = 1) = b_1 + \gamma_Z Z_i + \gamma_X \Sigma X_i + v_i \tag{2}$$

$$\Pr(Y_i^* = 1) = \frac{\exp(a + \beta_I \widehat{\text{Int}_i} + \beta_H H_i + u_i)}{1 + \exp(a + \beta_I \widehat{\text{Int}_i} + \beta_H H_i + u_i)} \tag{3}$$

$$\text{corr}(Z, u) = 0 \text{ and } \text{corr}(Z, v) \neq 0$$

In Equations (1)–(3), $\Pr(\text{Int}_i = 1)$ expresses the probability of using the internet, $\widehat{\text{Int}}$ is the endogenous variable of internet use, γ is the coefficient, v and δ are random error terms, and Z expresses the instrument variable. I use the endogeneity test (Durbin–Wu–Hausman test), exclusion test (overidentification test), and weak IV test to judge whether the IVs are valid.

Second, I used a one-period LV model (LV_{t-1}) to address the possible reverse causality problem. In Equation (4), t is the current period (e.g., 2018), $t - 1$ is the prior period (e.g., 2016), and Int_{t-1} expresses the internet use situation in the previous period:

$$\Pr(Y_i^* = 1) = \frac{\exp(a + \beta_I \text{Int}_{it-1} + \beta_H H_i + u_i)}{1 + \exp(a + \beta_I \text{Int}_{it-1} + \beta_H H_i + u_i)} \tag{4}$$

Third, because u includes the errors related to individual-specific and time-invariant factors (ρ_i, personality, unobserved individual abilities, etc.) and true random error term (ε), individual heterogeneity problems may arise. I used FE or RE models (see Equation (5)) to address this issue. I used the Breusch–Pagan Lagrange multiplier test and the Hausman test to judge the validity of the OLS, RE, and FE models:

$$\Pr(Y_i^* = 1) = \frac{\exp(a + \beta_I \text{Int}_{it-1} + \beta_H H_i + \rho_i + \varepsilon_{it})}{1 + \exp(a + \beta_I \text{Int}_{it-1} + \beta_H H_i + \rho_i + \varepsilon_{it})} \tag{5}$$

In the analyses of the heterogeneous group, I used the interaction terms of internet usage and different groups in the above models.[8]

Data

I used three-wave longitudinal survey data (2014, 2016, and 2018) from the China Family Panel Studies (CFPS). The CFPS is a national longitudinal survey project conducted by Beijing University since 2010. The CFPS collects data at individual, family, and community levels. The baseline national survey was officially launched in 25 provinces, municipalities, and autonomous regions, and it successfully interviewed members of 14,960 households, of which 33,600 adults and 8,990 youths were interviewed in the first wave (2010). We can obtain information from the CFPS on internet use, income, employment status, and other factors (e.g., education, age, and sex) for analysis. The CFPS survey samples were drawn through multi-stage probability stratification. I used recent three-wave longitudinal survey data (2014, 2016, and 2018) because only these three waves had questionnaire items on internet use. The samples of CFPS are 37,147 (2014), 36,892 (2016), and 37,354 (2018).

I used a sample of non-agricultural laborers in the self-employment sector, employees, and non-work individuals. Considering the mandatory retirement system[9] implemented by the public sector, I limited the sample to individuals aged 16–60 and excluded samples with missing values. The total number of longitudinal survey data points used in the analysis was 23,286.

According to the questionnaire items in the CFPS on "work status," "occupation," and "number of workers in workplace," the Chinese government's definitions of micro-enterprises in the self-employment sector and referring to ILO (1972) and Earle and Sakova (2000), I divided the labors into three groups: (i) laborers in the self-employment sector, including the entrepreneurs of small and micro enterprises with fewer than eight employees, and the self-employed individuals without employees (own-account workers); (ii) employees; and (iii) non-work individuals. For example, when the work status is "self-employment" and the number of laborers in the workplace is "0," I classify the individual as own-account workers. When the work status is "employer" and the number of laborers in the workplace is more than "1," and fewer than eight, the individual works as an employer in the self-employment sector and creates new jobs for others; thus, the individual is an entrepreneur of a small and micro enterprises. When the work status is "employed," the individual is classified as an employee. When the work status is "no job (no work)," the individual is non-work. I used a binary variable (1 = laborer in the self-employment sector, including own-account workers and entrepreneurs of small and micro enterprises, 0 = otherwise) as the independent variable in the probability function of self-employment.

The key independent variables are indicators of internet use. First, I used a binary variable to investigate the extensive effect of internet use (1 = have used the internet in the past year, 0 = have not used the internet) based on the question, "Have you used the internet in the past year?". Second, I also conducted three variables for the purpose of investigating the intensive effect of internet use: (i) the frequency of using the internet for e-commerce (e.g., online banking, online shopping), (ii) the frequency of using the internet for communication (e.g., chatting, online communication), and (iii) the frequency of using the internet for work or study. All three variables for internet use purposes are scale value variables ranging from 1 (almost never used) to 7 (almost every day).

I used the official data of the regional (provincial level) number of optical cable circuits in 1999 and digital circuits in 1999 as IVs.

Referring to the literature (e.g., Wu, 2006; Yueh, 2009a, 2009b; Zhang and Pan, 2012; Zhang and Zhao, 2015; Ma, 2016, 2017, 2018; Ma and Li, 2022), I used a set of variables as control variables (Appendix Table A1):

(i) Human capital variables include the year of education, age and its squared term, and health status (1 = very healthy or healthy, 0 = normal, unhealthy, or very unhealthy).
(ii) Other individual attributes included gender (1 = male, 0 = female), ethnicity (1 = Han majority, 0 = ethnic minority), and party member (1 = member of the Communist Party of China, 0 = non-party member).

(iii) Family factors include the logarithm of per capita household income and the number of family members.
(iv) Considering the influence of some special factors in China's labor market, such as the existence of labor market segmentation caused by the household registration system (*hukou*), I used a dummy variable for urban *hukou* (1 = urban *hukou*, 0 = rural *hukou*).
(v) Social insurance may increase unearned income and reduce the uncertainty that may affect the probability of entering the self-employment sector. I conducted two dummy variables: pension insurance participants (1 = participated in pension, 0 = otherwise) and medical insurance participants (1 = participated in medical insurance, 0 = otherwise).
(vi) Because there are large regional differences in China and the macroeconomic environment and business cycle may change over time, I used regional (western, central, or eastern regions) and year dummy variables to control the impact of these factors on the choice of self-employment.

Results of Descriptive Statistics

Distributions of non-agricultural work status in China

Figure 6 shows the distribution of non-agricultural work status in China. Here, I excluded laborers in the agricultural industry[10] and mainly discuss non-agricultural employment.

First, the proportion of employees is 60–70%, which is the main form of employment status. The proportion of laborers in the self-employment sector (including own-account workers and entrepreneurs in small and micro enterprises) is relatively small, at around 10%.

Second, from 2014 to 2018, the proportion of laborers in the self-employment sector increased from 10.91% to 13.92%, indicating that internet penetration might encourage business start-ups, resulting in an increase in this proportion. Simultaneously, the proportion of employees increased from 63.56% in 2014 to 74.08%

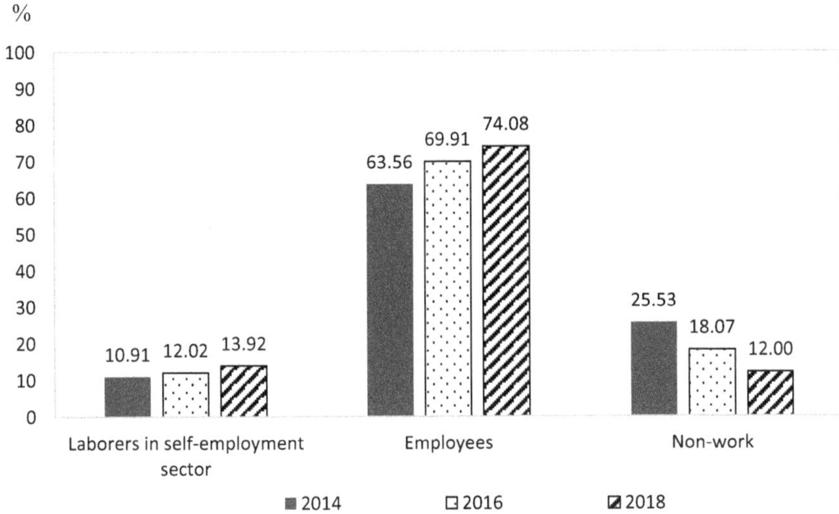

Figure 6. Distribution of non-agricultural employment in China.

Note: Laborers in the self-employment sector include the own-account workers and entrepreneurs of small and micro enterprises with fewer than eight employees. Employees are those employed in both small and micro enterprises in the self-employment sector and enterprises with eight employees and more.

Source: Calculated based on the data from CFPS of 2014, 2016, and 2018.

in 2018. The increase in the proportion of laborers in the self-employment sector and employees brought about a decrease in the proportion of non-workers, from 25.53% to 12.00%, indicating that the employment situation improved and more labor forces participated in work in this period.

Internet use status by employment group

Figure 7 shows the proportion of internet users in each employment group. First, in 2014, 2016, and 2018, the proportion of internet users was highest in the employee group and lowest in the non-work group.

Second, from 2014 to 2018, the proportion of internet users increased in each group. For example, the proportion of internet users in the self-employed group increased from 48.4% in 2014 to

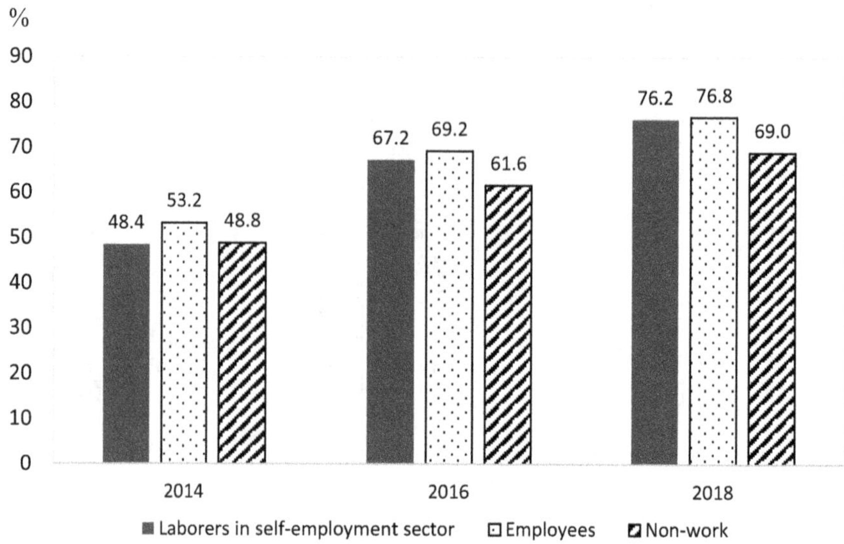

Figure 7. Internet use status by employment group.

Note: Laborers in the self-employment sector include the own-account workers and entrepreneurs of small and micro enterprises with fewer than eight employees. Employees are those employed in both small and micro enterprises in the self-employment sector and enterprises with eight employees and more.
Source: Calculated based on the data from CFPS of 2014, 2016, and 2018.

76.2% in 2018, and this increase was greater than that in the employee group (from 53.2% in 2014 to 76.8% in 2018), suggesting that the internet penetration rate is greater in the self-employed group than in the employee group.

Does internet use promote employment in the self-employed sector? In the following section, we conduct an empirical analysis to answer this question.

Econometric Analysis Results

Effects of internet use on the choice of self-employment

Table 1 presents the results on the influence of internet use on self-employment choices. I used a binary logit regression model to investigate the probability of entering the self-employment sector.

Table 1. Basic results: Internet use and probability of entering self-employment sector.

	(1) Logit	(2) IV_ Logit	(3) LV_ Logit	(4) RE_ Logit	(5) FE_ Logit
Internet use	0.216***	0.235*	0.156**	0.441***	0.275*
	(4.17)	(1.75)	(2.47)	(3.83)	(1.65)
Control variables	Yes	Yes	Yes	Yes	Yes
First-stage estimation					
Optical cable circuits in 1999		0.117***			
		(2.73)			
Digital circuits in 1999		–0.326***			
		(–8.63)			
Obs.	23,286	23,286	14,445	23,286	1,751
Group				10941	691
Hausman test		47.15			56.52
		($p = 0.000$)			($p = 0.000$)
BP test				7049.37	
				($p = 0.000$)	
Cragg–Donal Wald F statistic		17.772			
Sargan statistic		$p = 0.239$			
Adjusted R^2	0.056		0.055		
Log likelihood	–8,433.272	–8,473.032	–5,494.238	–602.908	–602.908
LR test Prob > chi^2				0.000	0.000

Notes:

1. *** $p < 0.01$; **$p < 0.05$; *$p < 0.1$. *t*-values or *z*-values are shown in parentheses.
2. IV: the instrument variable method; LV: the model using the lagged variable in $t - 1$ time; RE: the random effects model; FE: the fixed effects model; BP test: Breusch and Pagan Lagrangian multiplier test.
3. Control variables, including the year of education, age and its squared term, health, gender, Han majority, party member, household income, number of family, urban *hukou*, pension, medical insurance, region and year dummy variables, were estimated; they were not expressed in the table. The results of other variables are available upon request. The control variables were also used in the first-stage estimations.

Source: Calculated based on the data from CFPS of 2014, 2016, and 2018.

The benchmark group is a non-self-employed group that includes employees and non-work individuals. To address endogeneity issues, I used five models.

The results of the endogenous tests indicate that the internet use indicator is an endogenous variable. The result of the Cragg–Donal Wald F statistic is 17.772, which is greater than 10, indicating that there is no problem with the weak IVs. The Sargan statistic results show that the IV is not statistically correlated with the residuals of the second-stage equation and that the exogenous conditions are met. These results indicate that the two IVs are valid. In addition, the results of the Breusch and Pagan Lagrangian multiplier tests show that the RE model is much more appropriate than the logit regression model based on cross-sectional data analysis, and the results of the Hausman test show that the FE model is much more appropriate than the RE model.

The main findings can be summarized as follows: First, when endogeneity issues are not considered, the results of Model 1 (logit regression using cross-sectional data) show that internet use significantly increases the probability of entering the self-employment sector. When endogeneity issues are considered, the results from Models 2 (IV_Logit), 3 (LV_Logit), 4 (RE_Logit), and 5 (FE_Logit) also indicate that internet use may significantly improve the probability of entering the self-employment sector. These results suggest that internet use can increase the probability of choosing self-employment.

Second, the results using the FE model show that although internet use can increase the probability of entering the self-employment sector, the significance level is 10%, which is lower than that of other models, indicating that some unobserved individual heterogeneity (i.e., personality, intelligent ability, etc.) may significantly affect self-employment choice.

Results of heterogenous groups

Considering the differences between the groups, I used the interaction terms of internet use and each group (e.g., age, *hukou*, gender, and education group). Five models were used, as listed in Table 1. The results are summarized in Table 2 (age), Table 3 (*hukou*), Table 4 (gender), and Table 5 (education). If the result of the interaction term is statistically significant, it indicates a difference between heterogeneous groups.

Table 2 presents the results of the differences in the effects of internet use among age groups. The results of Model 2 and Model 3 show that the interaction terms of internet use and middle-aged (30–49 years old) and older groups (50–60 years old) are all positive and significant at the 1% level, suggesting that compared with the young generation, the effect of internet use on the likelihood of entering the self-employment sector is greater for the middle-aged and older generations. This may be because firms are more inclined to hire young laborers. Because the labor demand of middle-aged and older generations is lower than that of the younger generation (there is less chance for middle-aged and older generations to become employees), middle-aged and older people may have to choose to enter the self-employment sector.

Second, Table 3 presents the results of the differences in the effects of internet use between urban and rural *hukou* residents. In the results of Models 1–4, the interaction terms of internet use and urban *hukou* are all negative and significant at the 1% or 10% level, indicating that the impact of internet use on the probability of entering the self-employment sector is greater for rural residents than for urban residents.

These results may be caused by the existence of *hukou* discrimination in the Chinese labor market (Cai, 2016; Ma, 2018; Zhang and Wu, 2019), and the public sector is likely to hire urban *hukou* laborers. Because it is difficult for rural *hukou* laborers to enter formal employment sectors (e.g., public sector, large-size firms), most of them had to choose to enter the informal sector, such as becoming self-employed individuals. The results suggest that internet use can facilitate more rural *hukou* laborers to enter the non-agricultural self-employment sector, although this may be an involuntary choice. As there is no information on the data relating to the voluntary and involuntary choices of entering the self-employment sector, I could

Table 2. Differences in the effects of internet use by age group.

	(1) Logit	(2) IV_ Logit	(3) LV_ Logit	(4) RE_ Logit	(5) FE_ Logit
Internet use	1.235***	0.107	0.075	0.300	0.197
	(6.57)	(0.62)	(1.14)	(1.00)	(0.55)
Age (Ref. age 16–29)					
Age 30–49	0.396***	0.142	0.089	0.353	0.001
	(2.62)	(1.57)	(0.80)	(1.13)	(0.00)
Age 50 and above	0.162	–0.055	0.030	–0.106	–0.072
	(1.06)	(–0.46)	(0.26)	(–0.33)	(–0.14)
Internet use × Age 30–49	–0.127	0.206***	0.319***	0.075	–0.062
	(–0.79)	(3.18)	(3.72)	(0.23)	(–0.15)
Internet use × Age 50 and above	–0.114	0.242***	0.269***	0.386	0.294
	(–0.66)	(2.70)	(2.62)	(1.08)	(0.60)
Control variables	Yes	Yes	Yes	Yes	Yes
First stage estimation					
Optical cable circuits in 1999		0.117***			
		(2.73)			
Digital circuits in 1999		–0.326***			
		(–8.63)			
Obs.	23,286	23,286	14,445	23,286	1,757
Group				10,941	691
Hausman test		53.61			92.94
		(p = 0.000)			(p = 0.000)
BP test				7,042.84	
				(p = 0.000)	
Cragg–Donal Wald F statistic		11.853			
Sargan statistic		p = 0.051			
Adjusted R^2	0.064		0.053		
Log likelihood	–8,358.817	–8,472.551	–5,507.476	–6,528.737	–605.323
LR test Prob > chi^2				0.000	0.000

Notes:

1. *** $p < 0.01$; ** $p < 0.05$; * $p < 0.1$. t-values or z-values are shown in parentheses.
2. IV: the instrument variable method; LV: the model using the lagged variable in $t - 1$ time; RE: the random effects model; FE: the fixed effects model; BP test: Breusch and Pagan Lagrangian multiplier test.
3. Control variables, including the year of education, health, gender, Han majority, party member, household income, number of family, urban *hukou*, pension, medical insurance, region and year dummy variables, were estimated; they were not expressed in the table. The results of other variables are available upon request. The control variables were also used in the first-stage estimations.

Source: Calculated based on the data from CFPS of 2014, 2016, and 2018.

Table 3. Differences in the effects of internet use by urban and rural groups.

	(1) Logit	(2) IV_ Logit	(3) LV_ Logit	(4) RE_ Logit	(5) FE_ Logit
Internet use	1.199***	0.628**	0.449***	0.660***	0.150
	(10.24)	(2.54)	(4.79)	(3.96)	(0.62)
Urban	0.195***	0.426***	0.309***	0.272*	–0.306
	(2.85)	(4.82)	(3.85)	(1.64)	(–0.96)
Internet use × Urban	–0.247***	–0.743***	–0.450***	–0.359*	0.210
	(–2.82)	(–5.47)	(–4.25)	(–1.82)	(0.71)
Control variables	Yes	Yes	Yes	Yes	Yes
First stage estimation					
Optical cable circuits in 1999		0.117***			
		(2.73)			
Digital circuits in 1999		–0.326***			
		(–8.63)			
Obs.	23,286	23,286	14,445	23,286	1,751
Group				10,941	691
Hausman test		34.25 ($p = 0.000$)			67.08 ($p = 0.000$)
BP test				7,031.01 ($p = 0.000$)	
Cragg–Donal Wald F statistic		17.124			
Sargan statistic		0.241			
Adjusted R^2	0.061		0.056		
Log likelihood	–8,388.344	–8,426.459	–5,485.177	–6,487.573	–602.658
LR test Prob > chi^2				0.000	0.000

Notes:
1. *** $p < 0.01$; ** $p < 0.05$; * $p < 0.1$. t-values or z-values are shown in parentheses.
2. IV: the instrument variable method; LV: the model using the lagged variable in $t - 1$ time; RE: the random effects model; FE: the fixed effects model; BP test: Breusch and Pagan Lagrangian multiplier test.
3. Control variables, including the year of education, age and its squared term, gender, health, Han majority, party member, household income, number of family, pension, medical insurance, region and year dummy variables, were estimated; they were not expressed in the table. The results of other variables are available upon request. The control variables were also used in the first-stage estimations.
Source: Calculated based on the data from CFPS of 2014, 2016, and 2018.

Table 4. Differences in the effects of internet use by gender.

	(1) Logit	(2) IV_ Logit	(3) LV_ Logit	(4) RE_ Logit	(5) FE_ Logit
Internet use	1.331***	0.684***	0.211***	0.523***	0.301
	(10.61)	(2.72)	(2.71)	(3.58)	(1.37)
Females	–0.109*	–0.201**	–0.180**	–0.542***	14.023
	(–1.64)	(–2.72)	(–2.37)	(–3.18)	(0.01)
Internet use × Females	–0.248***	–0.151	–0.121	–0.179	–0.058
	(–2.96)	(–1.17)	(–1.21)	(–0.91)	(–0.19)
Control variables	Yes	Yes	Yes	Yes	Yes
First stage estimation					
Optical cable circuits in 1999		0.117***			
		(2.73)			
Digital circuits in 1999		–0.326***			
		(–8.63)			
Obs.	23,286	23,286	14,445	23,286	1,751
Group				10,941	691
Hausman test		43.89 ($p = 0.000$)			56.57 ($p = 0.000$)
BP test				7,046.08 ($p = 0.000$)	
Cragg–Donal Wald F statistic		14.562			
Sargan statistic		0.283			
Adjusted R^2	0.061		0.055		
Log likelihood	–8,383.949	–8,425.776	–5,493.508	–6,488.205	–602.891
LR test Prob > chi^2				0.000	0.000

Notes:
1. *** $p < 0.01$; ** $p < 0.05$; * $p < 0.1$. t-values or z-values are shown in parentheses.
2. IV: the instrument variable method; LV: the model using the lagged variable in $t - 1$ time; RE: the random effects model; FE: the fixed effects model; BP test: Breusch and Pagan Lagrangian multiplier test.
3. Control variables, including the year of education, age and its squared term, health, Han majority, party member, household income, number of family, urban *hukou*, pension, medical insurance, region and year dummy variables, were estimated; they were not expressed in the table. The results of other variables are available upon on request. The control variables were also used in the first-stage estimations.

Source: Calculated based on the data from CFPS of 2014, 2016, and 2018.

Table 5. Differences in the effects of internet use by education.

	(1) Logit	(2) IV_ Logit	(3) LV_ Logit	(4) RE_ Logit	(5) FE_ Logit
Internet use	–0.579***	–0.661	–0.773***	–0.421	0.525
	(–2.66)	(–1.15)	(–3.38)	(–0.82)	(0.53)
Senior high school and lower	0.304 (1.45)	0.499 (1.05)	0.262 (1.21)	1.239** (2.40)	0.146 (0.14)
Internet use × Senior high school and lower	0.786*** (3.56)	0.540 (1.04)	0.936*** (4.01)	0.861* (1.64)	–0.251 (–0.25)
Control variables	Yes	Yes	Yes	Yes	Yes
First stage estimations					
Optical cable circuits in 1999		0.117*** (2.73)			
Digital circuits in 1999		–0.326*** (–8.63)			
Obs.	23,286	23,286	14,445	23,286	1,751
Group				10,941	691
Hausman test		49.66 (p = 0.000)			89.97 (p = 0.000)
BP test				7,009.55 (p = 0.001)	
Cragg–Donal Wald F statistic		1.190			
Sargan statistic		0.561			
Adjusted R^2	0.065		0.006		
Log likelihood	–8,345.571	–8,357.240	–5,427.380	–6,448.013	–603.308
LR test Prob > chi^2				0.000	0.000

Notes:

1. *** $p < 0.01$; ** $p < 0.05$; * $p < 0.1$. t-values or z-values are shown in parentheses.
2. IV: the instrument variable method; LV: the model using the lagged variable in $t - 1$ time; RE: the random effects model; FE: the fixed effects model; BP test: Breusch and Pagan Lagrangian multiplier test.
3. Control variables, including age and its squared term, gender, health, Han majority, party member, household income, number of family, urban *hukou*, pension, medical insurance, region and year dummy variables, were estimated; they were not expressed in the table. The results of other variables are available upon request. The control variables were also used in the first-stage estimations.

Source: Calculated based on the data from CFPS of 2014, 2016, and 2018.

not conduct an analysis on this issue, which should be investigated in future research.

Third, the results in Table 4 indicate that the interaction terms of internet use and female dummies in Models 1–4 are not significant, suggesting that gender differences in the effect of internet use on the probability of entering the self-employment sector are not significant.

Fourth, the results of Models 1, 3, and 4 in Table 5 show that the interaction terms of internet usage and low- or middle-education dummies are all positive and significant at the 1% or 10% level, indicating that internet use has a significant impact on the probability of entering the self-employment sector. The positive effect of internet use on self-employment is greater for the low- and medium-education groups than for the high-education group.

These results can be explained by the dual labor market (or labor market segmentation) hypothesis (Piore, 1970; Doeringer and Piore, 1971). According to the dual labor market hypothesis, there exists a primary labor market (e.g., the formal sector) and a secondary labor market (e.g., the informal sector, such as the self-employment sector). Compared to self-employed individuals in the informal sector, employees in the formal sector can obtain higher earned income, more stable jobs, and higher levels of social security. Therefore, highly educated laborers are more likely to choose to become employees (not self-employed individuals). The results suggest that internet use may increase the probability of entering the self-employment sector in the low and middle education groups. Although this may be because low- and middle-education laborers have fewer opportunities to enter the formal sector and must enter the self-employment sector, internet use can be said to promote the employment of low-skilled laborers.

Results considering the purpose and volume of internet use

Considering that internet use effects may differ by the purpose and volume of internet use, I estimated the effect of internet use for three purposes: (i) using the internet for commerce, (ii) using the internet for communication, and (iii) using the internet for work and study. I used the frequency of internet use as the key independent variable in these estimations. The results are summarized in Table 6 (e-commerce), Table 7 (communication), and Table 8 (work and study).

First, considering the purpose of using the internet for e-commerce, the results of Models 1–4 in Table 6 are all positive and significant at the 1% level, indicating that the more frequently the internet is used for e-commerce (e.g., online banking and online shopping), the greater the probability of entering the self-employment sector.

Second, in terms of the purpose of using the internet for communication, the results of Model 3 in Table 7 are negative and significant at the 5% level, and the results of other models are not statistically significant, suggesting that using the internet for communication (such as chatting and online communication) has no significant effect on promoting self-employment.

Finally, regarding the purpose of using the internet for work and study, the results of Models 1 and 2 in Table 8 are all positive values for the primary term and negative values for the squared term, and they are all significant at the 1% level; the results of the other models are insignificant. The results suggest that using the internet to study and work in an appropriate volume can increase the possibility of entering the self-employment sector, whereas when frequently using the internet, the probability of entering self-employment may decline. These results may be due to the greater time constraints for self-employed individuals than for non-work individuals or employee groups. The results also suggest that individual heterogeneity has a significant effect on self-employment choices. For example, when the RE or FE model is used to address the individual heterogeneity issue, the effect of using the internet for work or study on the probability of entering the self-employment sector becomes insignificant. Therefore, the use of FE or RE models to address heterogeneity is necessary in empirical studies.

Table 6. Results of using the internet for e-commerce.

	(1) Logit	(2) IV_ Logit	(3) LV_ Logit	(4) RE_ Logit	(5) FE_ Logit
Frequency of using Internet for e-commerce	0.146*** (10.11)	1.313*** (4.92)	0.172*** (8.90)	0.165*** (5.37)	–0.026 (–0.58)
Control variables	Yes	Yes	Yes	Yes	Yes
First stage estimation					
Optical cable circuits in 1999		0.117*** (2.73)			
Digital circuits in 1999		–0.326*** (–8.63)			
Obs.	14,983	14,983	8,725	14,983	1,021
Group				7,749	417
Hausman test		38.59 ($p = 0.000$)			40.06 ($p = 0.000$)
BP test				2,999.62 ($p = 0.000$)	
Cragg–Donal Wald F statistic		15.000			
Sargan statistic		0.389			
Adjusted R^2	0.091		0.055		
Log likelihood	–5,135.154	–8,429.946	–3,025.459	–4,260.791	–602.908
LR test Prob > chi^2				0.000	0.000

Notes:
1. *** $p < 0.01$; ** $p < 0.05$; * $p < 0.1$. t-values or z-values are shown in parentheses.
2. IV: the instrument variable method; LV: the model using the lagged variable in $t-1$ time; RE: the random effects model; FE: the fixed effects model; BP test: Breusch and Pagan Lagrangian multiplier test.
3. Control variables, including the year of education, age and its squared term, health, gender, Han majority, party member, household income, number of family, urban *hukou*, pension, medical insurance, industry, region and year dummy variables, were estimated; they were not expressed in the table. The results of other variables are available upon request. The control variables were also used in the first-stage estimations.

Source: Calculated based on the data from CFPS of 2014, 2016, and 2018.

Table 7. Results of using the internet for social communication.

	(1) Logit	(2) IV_ Logit	(3) LV_ Logit	(4) RE_ Logit	(5) FE_ Logit
Frequency of using Internet for social communication	−0.005 (−0.40)	−0.040 (−0.17)	−0.033** (−2.09)	0.009 (0.31)	0.027 (0.65)
Control variables	Yes	Yes	Yes	Yes	Yes
First stage estimation					
Optical cable circuits in 1999		0.117*** (2.73)			
Digital circuits in 1999		−0.326*** (−8.63)			
Obs.	14,983	14,983	8,725	14,983	1,021
Group				7749	417
Hausman test		13.01 ($p = 0.000$)			37.87 ($p = 0.000$)
BP test				3,095.91 ($p = 0.001$)	
Cragg–Donal Wald F statistic		11.912			
Sargan statistic		0.001			
Adjusted R^2	0.091		0.055		
Log likelihood	−5,135.154	−8,441.985	−3,025.459	−4,270.221	−343.207
LR test Prob > chi^2				0.000	0.000

Notes:
1. *** $p < 0.01$; ** $p < 0.05$; * $p < 0.1$. *t*-values or *z*-values are shown in parentheses.
2. IV: the instrument variable method; LV: the model using the lagged variable in $t - 1$ time; RE: the random effects model; FE: the fixed effects model; BP test: Breusch and Pagan Lagrangian multiplier test.
3. Control variables, including the year of education, age and its squared term, health, gender, Han majority, party member, household income, number of family, urban *hukou*, pension, medical insurance, region and year dummy variables, were estimated; they were not expressed in the table. The results of other variables are available upon request. The control variables were also used in the first-stage estimations.

Source: Calculated based on the data from CFPS of 2014, 2016, and 2018.

Table 8. Results of using the internet for work or study.

	(1) Logit	(2) IV_ Logit	(3) LV_ Logit	(4) RE_ Logit	(5) FE_ Logit
Frequency of using Internet for work or study					
Frequency	0.080***	2.076***	0.023	0.069	0.027
	(2.56)	(9.04)	(0.57)	(1.02)	(0.65)
Squared term	–0.005	–0.046***	–0.001	–0.005	0.027
	(–2.60)***	(–10.07)	(–0.63)	(–1.42)	(0.65)
Control variables	Yes	Yes	Yes	Yes	Yes
First stage estimation					
Optical cable circuits in 1999		0.117***			
		(2.73)			
Digital circuits in 1999		–0.326***			
		(–8.63)			
Obs.	22,054	22,054	22,054	22,054	1,631
Group				10,786	645
Hausman test		21.58 (p = 0.000)			53.19 (p = 0.000)
BP test				6,889.45 (p = 0.000)	
Cragg–Donal Wald F statistic		19.920			
Sargan statistic		2.672			
Adjusted R^2	0.053		0.054		
Log likelihood	–8,166.832	–8,370.404	–5,495.377	–6,288.744	–556.033
LR test Prob > chi^2				0.000	0.000

Notes:
1. *** $p < 0.01$; ** $p < 0.05$; * $p < 0.1$. t-values or z-values are shown in parentheses.
2. IV: the instrument variable method; LV: the model using the lagged variable in $t - 1$ time; RE: the random effects model; FE: the fixed effects model; BP test: Breusch and Pagan Lagrangian multiplier test.
3. Control variables, including the year of education, age and its squared term, health, gender, Han majority, party member, household income, number of family, urban *hukou*, pension, medical insurance, region and year dummy variables, were estimated; they were not expressed in the table. The results of other variables are available upon request. The control variables were also used in the first-stage estimations.

Source: Calculated based on the data from CFPS of 2014, 2016, and 2018.

Conclusions

Along with economic reforms and the development of the digital economy, the self-employment sector has grown considerably in China. Does internet use promote employment in the self-employed sector? This study reviews the economic reform and development of the self-employment sector in China, compares the Japanese experience, and then uses the latest three-wave national longitudinal survey data from CFPS to address endogeneity issues. I conducted an empirical analysis to investigate the effect of internet use on the probability of entering the self-employment sector in China.

Several main conclusions were drawn. First, internet use may increase the possibility of entering the self-employment sector, and individual heterogeneity has a significant impact on the choice of self-employment. Second, the effects of internet use differ by group. The positive effect on self-employment choice is greater for middle-aged and older generations, low- and middle-educated groups, and rural *hukou* laborers than for their counterparts (young generation, high-educated group, and urban *hukou* laborers), suggesting that internet use may significantly increase the probability of entering the self-employment sector for the disadvantaged group. Third, the effects of internet use differ by the purpose of internet use. Using the internet for e-commerce (e.g., online banking, online shopping) or using the internet for study or work may increase the probability of entering the self-employment sector, but the effect of using the internet for communication (e.g., chatting, online communication) is not significant.

The enlightenment and policy implications of the empirical results are as follows. First, the results of the analysis show that internet use may increase the likelihood of entering the self-employment sector. Among the laborers in the self-employment sector, some, namely entrepreneurs of small and micro enterprises, start their own businesses on their own initiative. The results suggest that policies that promote the development of the digital economy can promote entrepreneurial innovation. New technological progress can bring new business opportunities and innovations in business models (e.g., online shopping, internet celebrities, electronic payments, etc.), which may drive rapid economic growth and make economic development jump to new and higher levels. Promoting the development of the digital economy is in line with Schumpeter's "creative destruction" economic growth theory (Schumpeter, 1934, 1942). The results of this study provide empirical evidence on the Chinese government's policies for promoting the development of the digital economy (i.e., "Internet Plus" policies) that were successively introduced after 2010. In the future, various forms of e-commerce activities through internet platforms should be encouraged to promote entrepreneurship and innovation in China.

Some studies have pointed out that liquidity constraints may remain in the initial stage of entrepreneurship (Haggard and Huang, 2008; Ma, 2017; Ma and Li, 2022). If entrepreneurs of small and micro enterprises cannot obtain sufficient financing through the formal financial market, the survival and development of small and micro enterprises will become difficult. In fact, in China, there remain liquidity constraints for small and micro-privately owned enterprises. For example, state-owned banks are unwilling to lend to small and micro-privately owned enterprises, these small and micro-privately owned enterprises must obtain high-priced loans through the informal financial markets, such as shadow banks, or through the intra-household risk-taking mechanism (Haggard and Huang, 2008). To promote entrepreneurs' business start-ups, which may create more business opportunities to drive new economic growth in the future, the government should attach importance to the development of the self-employment sector, provide financial subsidies for entrepreneurship through various means of financing, and actively implement financial support for small and micro-privately owned enterprises.

Second, the results suggest that the positive effect of internet use on self-employment is greater for the disadvantaged groups (middle-aged and older generations, rural *hukou* laborers, and low- and middle-educated people). Internet use can increase the probability of these disadvantaged groups' access to the self-employment sector, which may increase employment and promote economic growth.

The ILO (1972) pointed out that employment in the informal sector in developing countries can promote economic development. Therefore, promoting internet use among disadvantaged groups and improving internet use skills in these groups will promote employment nationwide. However, it should be noted that because there remains discrimination against disadvantaged groups (e.g., discrimination against rural *hukou* laborers), most of these groups are potentially unemployed, and they have to enter the self-employment sector because they have no opportunity to enter the formal sector. Therefore, policies that eliminate barriers to entering the formal sector due to the various institutions (e.g., the *hukou* system) will contribute to the rational distribution of labor force resources. Policies such as promoting vocational training are expected to increase the skills of self-employed individuals and improve the quality of employment. These measures will further promote the sustainable development of Chinese economy in the future.

Finally, this study had some limitations. Although this study used the IV method and the LV and FE models to attempt to deal with endogeneity issues, further analysis to investigate the causality between internet use and self-employment should also be challenged in the future. The evaluation of the policy impact on the development of the self-employment sector should be investigated (Ma and Li, 2022).[11] A dynamic analysis of the mechanism of entering the self-employment sector is also a critical issue (Le, 1999).[12] Furthermore, although internet use can promote self-employment, it can also affect income distribution (Lloyd-Ellis, 1999; Hanley, 2000; Furuholt and Kristiansen, 2007; Dimaggio and Bonikowski, 2008; Pradhan *et al.*, 2016; Philip *et al.*, 2017; Ghosh, 2020). Empirical studies on the impact of internet use on income inequality and digital divisions among groups have also become future research issues (Philip *et al.*, 2017; OECD, 2018; Ma, 2022a, 2022b).

Acknowledgement

This study was supported by the Japan Society for the Promotion of Science (Grant numbers 20H01512 and 20H01489). I acknowledge the helpful suggestions and comments provided by Professor Jun Zhang (Fudan University), Dr. Shuo Shi, Dr. Litian Yu, and other participants at the biweekly seminar of the School of Economics Fudan University on April 7, 2022. I also would like to express my gratitude to Professor Feng Qu (Nanyang Technological University, Singapore), and Professor Changyuan Luo (Fudan University) for their useful comments at the International Conference "Economic Growth in China: Rise and Pattern" at Fudan University on September 17, 2022.

Endnotes

1. There is no uniform definition of the informal sector. The definition of informal employment in most literature is based on ILO (1993, 2003, 2013), survey data and the situation of the labor market in each country. Informal employment includes informal employment in the formal sector, and informal employment in the informal sector (e.g., employees in small and micro enterprises in the self-employment sector, self-employed individuals, family helpers, etc.). Therefore, the majority of those engaged in the self-employment sector are laborers in the informal sector. In most Chinese literature, informal employment is also referred to as flexible employment.
2. The data on the self-employed include laborers in the self-employment sector registered in the industrial and commercial department, China, including (i) self-employed individuals without employees (own-account workers), (ii) employees of small and micro enterprises with fewer than eight employees, and (iii) entrepreneurs of small and micro enterprises with fewer than eight employees. Following the definition of self-employed by ILO (1972) and Earle and Sakova (2000), (i) and (iii) are self-employed, while (ii) are classified as employees. The empirical analysis of this study defines the self-employed and employee according to the international standard based on ILO (1972) and Earle and Sakova (2000).
3. Due to space constraints, I did not summarize the Chinese government's policies of promoting the development of self-employment sector and the process of the development of the self-employment sector in detail. For more detailed information on these issues, please refer to Hu (2003), Shi (2005), Ma (2012), and Zhu and Lei (2020).

4. After 2004, there occurred a phenomenon of shortage of migrant workers in the southern and eastern regions, which aroused academic controversy about whether the Chinese economy had passed the Lewis turning point. For details on the empirical studies on surplus laborers and Lewis turning point in China, please refer to Minami and Ma (2010, 2014), Cai (2010), Cai and Du (2011), Zhang *et al.* (2018), Wei and Kwan (2018), Ma and Minami (2022).
5. Employment in the self-employment sector is mostly referred to as "flexible employment" in Chinese government's documents.
6. For the literature review on the determinants of self-employment, please see Le (1999) and Yamada (1996).
7. I obtained the information on two instrument variables from the *China Statistical Yearbook 1999* (NBS, 1999). Although Cao and Jiang (2020) and Zhao and Li (2020) used the provincial internet penetration in the survey year as an IV, I found that this IV did not pass the exclusivity and weak IV tests, while the two new IVs used in this study have passed these tests (see Tables 1–8 for the test results).
8. This study also conducted the analyses using the subsamples of each group, and the results were like those using the interaction terms. Considering that the results using interaction terms assume that the other variables are held consistent, which is more rigorous, and because of the space constraints, I only show the results using the interaction terms here. The other results are available upon request.
9. According to the public pension regulations and mandatory retirement system in the public sector (e.g., government organizations, SOEs), the retirement age is 55 years for female cadres, 50 years for female workers, and 60 years for male cadres and workers. Considering that the laborers in the self-employment sector are mostly not affected by the mandatory retirement system, this study selects samples aged 16–60. I also used two samples of women aged 16–50 and 16–55 to analyze and found these results were approximately similar. Due to space limitations, I only show the results of women aged 16–60, and the other results are available upon request.
10. In the classification of laborers, the laborers in agricultural industry sector are usually considered agricultural self-employed individuals.
11. Using the data from the China Household Income Project Survey (CHIP) of 2013 and 2018 and the difference-in-differences method, Ma and Li (2022) first investigated the impact of the mass entrepreneurship and innovation policy implemented in 2016 on self-employment. They found that, overall, the policy has no significant

impact on self-employment, but in the high-educated and younger generation groups, the policy significantly promotes the probability of entering the self-employment sector. However, Ma and Li (2022) did not consider the effect of internet use.

12. For a dynamic analysis of self-employment using longitudinal survey data, please refer to Blau (1987), Evans and Jovanonic (1989), Blanchflower and Meyer (1992), and Xie (2012). Xie (2012) analyzed the transition from other forms of employment to self-employment in China, and Evans and Leighton (1989) and Bates (1990) analyzed the transition from self-employed individuals to employees in European countries and the United States.

References

Adelino, M., Schoar, A., and Severino, F. 2015. House prices, collateral, and self-employment. *Journal of Financial Economics*, 117(2): 288–306.

Alam, K. and Mamun, S.A.K. 2017. Access to broadband internet and labour force outcomes: A case study of the Western Downs Region, Queensland. *Telematics and Informatics*, 34(4): 73–84.

Amit, R., Glosten, L., and Muller, E. 1990. Entrepreneurial ability, venture investments, and risk sharing. *Management Science*, 36(10): 1232–1245.

Atasoy, H. 2013. The effects of broadband internet expansion on labour market outcomes. *Industrial and Labor Relations Review*, (6682): 315–345.

Blanchflower, D.G. and Meyer, B. 1992. A longitudinal analysis of young entrepreneurs in Australia and the United States. In Gregory, R.G. and Canberra, T.K. (eds.), *Youth in the Eighties Papers from the Australian Longitudinal Survey Research Project*. DEET and Centre for Economic Policy Research, Australian National University.

Blau, D.M. 1985. Self-employment and self-selection in developing country labor markets. *Southern Economic Journal*, 52(2): 351–363.

Blau, D.M. 1987. A times-series analysis of self-employment in the United States. *Journal of Political Economy*, 95(3): 445–467.

Borjas, J. 1986. The self-employment experience of immigrants. *Journal of Human Resources*, 21(4): 485–506.

Bruce, D. 1999. Do husbands matter? Married women entering self-employment. *Small Business Economics*, 13(4): 317–329.

Brzozowski, J. and Lasek, A. 2019. The impact of self-employment on the economic integration of immigrants: Evidence from Germany. *Journal of Entrepreneurship Management and Innovation*, 15(2): 11–28.

Cai, F. 2010. Demographic transition, demographic bonus and Lewis turning point. *Economic Research Journal*, 4: 4–13 (in Chinese).

Cai, F. 2016. *China's Economic Growth Prospects: From Demographic Divided to Reform Divides.* Beijing, China: Social Sciences Academic Press.

Cai, F. and Du, Y. 2011. Wage increase, wage convergence and Lewis turning point. *Economic Perspectives*, 9: 9–16 (in Chinese).

Cao, J. and Jiang, T. 2020. The impact of internet usage on women's income: An analysis based on CFPS data. *Modern Finance and Economics (Journal of Tianjin University of Finance and Economic)*, 12: 79–95 (in Chinese).

Chen, J. and Hu, M. 2018. What types of homeowners are more likely to be entrepreneurs? The evidence from China. *Small Business Economics*, 52(3): 633–649.

Crandall, R.W., Lehr, W., and Litan, R.E. 2007. The effects of broadband deployment on output and employment: A cross-sectional analysis of US data. *The Brookings Institution: Issue in Economic Policy*, 6: 1–34.

Czernich, N. 2014. Does broadband internet reduce the unemployment rate? Evidence for Germany. *Information Economics and Policy*, 29: 32–45.

Dettling, L.J. 2017. Broadband in the labor market: The impact of residential high-speed internet on married women's labor force participation. *Industrial & Labor Relations Review*, 70: 451–482.

Deyyling, L.J. 2017. Broadband in the labour market: The impact of residential high-speed internet on married women's labour force participation. *Industrial & Labor Relations*, 70(2): 451–482.

Dimaggio, P. and Bonikowski, B. 2008. Make money surfing the web? The impact of internet use on the earnings of U.S. workers. *American Sociological Review*, 2: 227–250.

Ding, D. and Yuan, W. 2019. Internet use and probability of female entrepreneurship: An empirical study based on micro data. *Journal of Technology Economics*, 38(5): 68–78 (in Chinese).

Doeringer, P. and Piore, M. 1971. *Internal Labor Markets and Manpower Analysis.* Lexington Mass: Health.

Dunn, T.A. and Holtz-Eakin, D. 2000. Financial capital, human capital, and transition to self-employment: Evidence from intergenerational links. *Journal of Labor Economics*, 18(2): 282–305.

Earle, J.S. and Sakova, Z. 2000. Business start-ups or disguised unemployment? Evidence on the character of self-employment from transition economics. *Labor Economics*, 7(5): 575–601.

Evans, D.S. and Jovanovic, B. 1989. An estimated model of entrepreneurial choice under liquidity constraints. *Journal of Political Economy*, 97(4): 808–827.

Evans, D.S. and Leighton, L. 1989. Some empirical aspects of entrepreneurship. *American Economic Review*, 79(3): 519–535.

Furuholt, B. and Kristiansen, S. 2007. A rural-urban digital divide? Regional aspects of internet use in Tanzania. *The Electronic Journal of Information Systems in Developing Countries*, 31(1): 1–15.

Ghosh, S. 2020. Impact of economic growth volatility on income inequality. *Quality & Quantity*, 54(3): 807–850.

Haggard, S. and Huang, Y. 2008. The political economics of private sector development in China. In Brandt, L. and Rawski, T.G. (eds.), *China's Great Economic Transformation*. Cambridge UK: Cambridge University Press.

Hair, N., Wetsch, L., Hull, C.E., Hung, Y.C., Perotti, V., and DeMartino, R. 2007. Taking advantage of digital opportunities: A typology of digital entrepreneurship. *International Journal of Networking and Virtual Organisations*, 4(3): 290–303.

Hanley, E. 2000. Self-employment in post-communist Eastern Europe: A refuge from poverty or road to riches. *Communist and Post-Communist Studies*, 33(3): 379–402.

Holtz-Eakin, D., Joulfaian, D. and Rosen, H.S. 1994. Sticking it out: Entrepreneurial survival and liquidity constraints. *Journal of Political Economy*, 102(1): 53–75.

Hu, J. 2003. Review and prospect of individual economy development in China. *Journal of Finance and Economics*, 4: 3–9, 72 (in Chinese).

International Labor Organization (ILO). 1972. *Employment, Incomes and Equality: A Strategy for Increasing Productive Employment in Kenya*. Geneva, CH: International Labor Organization.

International Labor Organization (ILO). 1993. Resolutions concerning international classification of status in employment. In *Proceedings of the 15th International Conference of Labour Statisticians*, January 1993.

International Labor Organization (ILO). 2003. Guidelines concerning a statistical definition of informal employment. In *Proceedings of the 17th International Conference of Labour Statisticians*, 17th ICLS Guidelines, 24 November–3 December.

International Labor Organization (ILO). 2013. *Measuring Informality: A Statistical Manual on the Informal Sector and Informal Employment*. Geneva, CH: International Labor Organization.

Krueger, A.B. 1993. How computers have changed the wage structure: Evidence from microdata, 1984–1989. *The Quarterly Journal of Economics*, 108(1): 33–60.

Kwon, S.W., Heflin, C., and Ruef, M. 2013. Community social capital and entrepreneurship. *American Sociological Review*, 78(6): 980–1008.

Le, A.T. 1999. Empirical studies of self-employment. *Journal of Economic Surveys*, 13(4): 381–461.

Lewis, W.A. 1954. Economic development with unlimited supplies of labor. *Manchester School of Economic and Social Studies*, 28(2): 139–151.

Lentz, B.F. and Laband, D.N. 1990. Entrepreneurial success and occupational inheritance among proprietors. *Canadian Journal of Economics*, 23(3): 563–579.

Lin, Y., Cai, F., and Li, Z. 1994. *China's Miracle Development Strategy and Economic Reform*. Shanghai: SDX Joint Publishing Company (in Chinese).

Lloyd-Ellis, H. 1999. Endogenous technological change and wage inequality. *American Economic Review*, 89(1): 47–77.

Lucas, R.E. 1988. On the mechanics of economic development. *Journal of Monetary Economics*, 22: 3–42.

Ma, F. 2012. Review and prospect of individual economy development in my country. *Market Regulation*, 19: 15–19 (in Chinese).

Ma, X. 2016. Economic transition and the determinants of self-employment in urban China: 2007–2013. *Journal of Chinese Economic and Business Studies*, 14(3): 279–307.

Ma, X. 2017. An empirical analysis on the employment mechanism of the self-employed in urban China: Disguised unemployment or business creation? *World Economic Papers*, 1: 205–233 (in Chinese).

Ma, X. 2018. *Economic Transition and Labor Market Reform in China*. Singapore: Palgrave Macmillan.

Ma, X. 2022a. Internet use and income gaps between urban and rural residents in China. *Journal of the Asia Pacific Economy*, 29(2): 789–809.

Ma, X. 2022b. Internet use and gender wage gap: Evidence from China. *Journal for Labor Market Research*, 56. Article 15.

Ma, X. and Li, S. 2022. Self-employment in urban China: Entrepreneurship or disguised unemployment? *China & World Economy*, 30(1): 166–195.

Ma, X. and Minami, R. 2022. Dual economic structure, surplus labor, and rural-urban migration. In Ma, C. and Tang, C. (eds.), *Growth Mechanism and Sustainable Development of Chinese Economy*. Singapore: Palgrave Macmillan.

Mao, Y., Zeng, X., and Zhu, H. 2017. Internet use, employment decision-making, and employment quality: Empirical evidence based on CGSS data. *Economic Theory and Business Management*, 1: 72–85 (in Chinese).

Mao, F.Y., Qian, Y., Zhao, Z., and Kong, X. 2019. The impact of internet use frequency on rural women's entrepreneurship: Based on the empirical analysis of CGSS (2017). *Rural Finance Research*, 4: 14–23 (in Chinese).

Miller, P. and Mulvey, C. 1997. Computer skills and wages. *Australian Economic Papers*, 36(68): 106–113.

Minami, R. and Ma, X. 2010. The Lewisian turning point of Chinese economy: Comparison with Japanese experience. *China Economic Journal*, 3(2): 165–181.

Minami, R. and Ma, X. 2014. Labor market and Lewisian turning point in China. In Minami, R., Makino, F., and Kim, K. (eds.), *Lewisian Turning Point in the Chinese Economy*. London: Palgrave Macmillan.

Molina, J.A. 2020. Family and entrepreneurship: New empirical theoretical results. *Journal of Family and Economics Issues*, 41: 1–3.

National Bureau of Statistics (NBS). 2003. *China Statistical Yearbook 2003*. Beijing: China Statistics Press (in Chinese).

National Bureau of Statistics (NBS). 2020. *China Statistical Yearbook 2020*. Beijing: China Statistics Press (in Chinese).

Novo-Corti, I., Varela-Candamio, L., and García-Álvarez, M. 2014. Breaking the walls of social exclusion of rural women by means of ICTs: The case of 'digital divides' in Galician. *Computers in Human Behavior*, 30: 497–507.

Organization for Economic Co-operation and Development (OECD). 2018. *Bridging the Digital Gender Divide: Include, Upskill, Innovate*. Paris: OECD.

Pabilonia, S.W. and Zoghi, C. 2005. Returning to the returns to computer use. *American Economic Review*, 95(2): 314–317.

Philip, L., Cottrill, C., Farrington, J., and Wiliams, F. 2017. The digital divide: Patterns-policy and scenarios for connecting the 'final few' in rural communities across Great Britain. *Journal of Rural Studies*, 54: 386–398.

Piore, M.J. 1970. The dual labor market: Theory and applications. In Barringer, R. and Beer, S.H. (eds.), *The State and the Poor*. Cambridge, MA: Winthrop.

Poon, J.P.H., Thai, D.T., and Naybor, D. 2012. Social capital and female entrepreneurship in rural regions: Evidence from Vietnam. *Applies Geography*, 35(1–2): 308–315.

Pradhan, R.P., Arvin, M.B., Norman, N.R., and Bennett, S.E. 2016. Financial depth, internet penetration rates and economic growth: Country-panel evidence. *Applied Economics*, 48(4): 331–343.

Romer, P.M. 1994. The origins of endogenous growth. *Journal of Economic Perspectives*, 8: 3–22.

Schmalz, M.C., Sraer, D.A., and Thesmar, D. 2017. Housing collateral and entrepreneurship. *The Journal of Finance*, 72(1): 99–132.

Schumpeter, J.M. 1934. *The Theory of Economic Development: An Inquiry into Profits, Capital, Credit, Interest, and the Business Cycle*. Cambridge, MA: Harvard University Press.

Schumpeter, J.M. 1942. *Capitalism, Socialism, and Democracy*. New York: Haper and Row.

Shi, B. 2005. The review of the development of China's private economy and the analysis of the present situation. *Jinan Journal (Philosophy & Social Sciences)*, 3: 6–14, 19 (in Chinese).

Shirazi, F. 2012. Information and communication technology and women empowerment in Iran. *Telematics and Informatics*, 29(1): 45–55.

Todaro, M.P. 1969. A model of migration and urban unemployment in less developed countries. *American Economic Review*, 59(1): 138–148.

Todaro, M.P. 1980. Internal migration in developing countries: A survey in population and economic change in developing countries. In Richard, A.E. (eds.), *Population and Economic Change in Developing Countries*. Chicago: University of Chicago Press.

Wassink, J. 2020. International migration experience and entrepreneurship: Evidence from Mexico. *World Development*, 136. Article 105077.

Wei, Z. and Kwan, F. 2018. Revisit China's Lewis turning point: An analysis from a regional perspective. *Asian Economic Journal*, 32(4): 333–357.

Wu, X.G. 2006. Communist cadres and market opportunities: Entry into self-employment in China, 1978–1996. *Social Forces*, 85: 389–411.

Xie, Y. 2012. Analysis of the transformation of non-agricultural self-employment in China. *Economic Research Journal*, 2: 54–66 (in Chinese).

Yamada, G. 1996. Urban informal employment and self-employment in developing countries: Theory and evidence. *Economic Development and Culture Change*, 44(2): 289–314.

Yueh, L. 2009a. Self-employment in urban China: Networking in a transition economy. *China Economic Review*, 20(3): 471–484.

Yueh, L. 2009b. China's entrepreneurs. *World Development*, 37(4): 778–786.

Zhang, Q. F. and Pan, Z. 2012. Women's entry into self-employment in urban China: The role of family in creating gendered mobility patterns. *World Development*, 40(6): 1201–1212.

Zhang, J.F. and Zhao, Z. 2015. Social-family network and self-employment: Evidence from temporary rural-urban migrants in China. *IZA Journal of Labor & Development*, 4. Article 1.

Zhang, Y., Shao, T., and Dong, Q. 2018. Reassessing the Lewis turning point in China: Evidence from 70,000 rural households. *China & World Economy*, 26(1): 4–17.

Zhao, Y. and Li, X. 2020. The impact of internet use on individual health: An empirical analysis based on the data of Chinese family tracking survey. *Jianghan Tribune*, 5: 139–144 (in Chinese).

Zhu, C. and Lei, J. 2020. 70 years of Chinese entrepreneurship research: Review and prospect. *China Soft Science*, 1: 11–20 (in Chinese).

Appendix

Table A1. Descriptive statistics of variables.

	Total a	User b	Non-user c	Gap b–c	*t*-test
Internet use	0.644				
Self-employed	0.128	0.125	0.134	–0.009	$p < 0.019$
Years of education	10.056	11.420	7.592	3.828	$p < 0.000$
Age	38.418	34.043	46.315	–12.272	$p < 0.000$
Females	0.495	0.490	0.504	–0.014	$p < 0.000$
Urban *hukou*	0.638	0.665	0.588	0.077	$p < 0.000$
Ethnicity (Han majority)	0.944	0.935	0.959	–0.024	$p < 0.000$
Married	0.807	0.731	0.946	–0.215	$p < 0.000$
Number of family member	4.267	4.267	4.267	0.000	$p < 0.000$
Party member	0.065	0.075	0.046	0.029	$p < 0.000$
Health	0.359	0.383	0.316	0.067	$p < 0.000$

(*Continued*)

Table A1. (*Continued*)

	Total a	User b	Non-user c	Gap b–c	*t*-test
Logarithm of per capita Household income	9.474	9.604	9.239	0.365	$p < 0.000$
Pension	0.503	0.491	0.523	–0.032	$p < 0.000$
Medical insurance	0.890	0.884	0.901	–0.017	$p < 0.000$
Region					
East	0.465	0.470	0.455	0.015	$p < 0.000$
Central	0.317	0.311	0.329	–0.018	$p < 0.000$
West	0.218	0.218	0.216	0.002	$p < 0.000$
Year					
2014	0.350	0.284	0.471	–0.187	$p < 0.000$
2016	0.322	0.336	0.295	0.041	$p < 0.000$
2018	0.328	0.380	0.234	0.146	$p < 0.000$
Obs.	23,286	14,985	8,301		

Notes: The number of samples varies depending on the model used.
Source: Calculated based on the data from CFPS of 2014, 2016, and 2018.

https://doi.org/10.1142/9789819815241_0023

Chapter 23

THE CHINA EFFECT: A FINANCIAL PERSPECTIVE

Changyuan Luo[*,§], Mei Tao[†,¶], and Xiang Shao[‡,**]

[*]*Institute of World Economy, Fudan University, Shanghai, China*
[†]*School of Economics, Fudan University, Shanghai, China*
[‡]*School of Management, Fudan University, Shanghai, China*
[§]*chyluo@fudan.edu.cn*
[¶]*18392885173@163.com*
[**]*xshao@fudan.edu.cn*

Introduction

China and the United States (US) are currently the world's largest trading entities and trading partners. According to the National Bureau of Statistics of China, the total value of imports and exports between China and the US was US$583.68 billion in 2017. In 2018, trade friction between China and the US intensified, but bilateral trade between the two still increased by 8.54%, reaching US$633.52 billion, and China's trade surplus with the US has increased by 17.2% year-on-year, reaching US$323.32 billion. In 2019, the bilateral trade between China and the US fell by 14.6% year-on-year to US$541.223 billion, and China's total imports from the US, China's total exports to the US, and the China–US trade surplus all declined.

In recent years, with the rapid development of China–US economic and trade relations, bilateral trade friction has been increasing. With the rapid growth of Chinese exports and the adjustment of the US industrial structure, the China–US trade surplus has been expanding annually. With the upgrading of China's industrial structure, however, the quality and technological content of Chinese exports have been greatly improved, and competition between Chinese and American products in the international market has intensified. The US has initiated "Section 301 investigations" against China six times in history, with the latest round of investigations in August 2017. On March 23, 2018, then-US President Trump officially signed a trade memorandum with China at the White House, announcing a 25% punitive tariff on Chinese goods based on the results of the "Section 301 investigation," involving US$3 billion in goods. On the same day, the Chinese Ministry of Commerce issued a list of suspended concessions against US steel and aluminum products under Section 232 and solicited public comments, planning to impose additional tariffs on some products imported from the US. Since then, trade friction has continued to escalate. After several rounds of mutual tariff increases and more than a dozen rounds of arduous negotiations, the two sides reached a first-phase agreement on December 13, 2019, which was formally signed on January 15, 2020.

The causes of trade frictions between China and the US are manifold, one of which involves the distribution of trade gains, with the US arguing that China has greatly benefited from the China–US trade surplus, whereas the US has gained little or even suffered losses. But has China–US trade really harmed US interests? To answer this question, it is necessary to examine comprehensively the impact of China–US trade on the welfare and development of both countries. In recent years, many scholars have focused on the impact of China's foreign trade on the rest of the world, forming a stream of literature known as the "China effect." This study examines the impact of China–US trade on the financing constraints of listed US firms from a financial perspective, which not only complements the "China effect" research but also provides a new perspective for assessing and understanding the trade relationship between China and the US.

This study first examines the impact of imports from China on the financing constraints of firms in the US by taking the listed US manufacturing firms from 1989 to 2007 as an empirical sample and using constraining word frequency, Kaplan–Zingales (KZ) index, size–age (SA) index, and Whited–Wu (WW) index to measure financing constraints and import penetration and import share to measure import competition from China. Furthermore, in this study, we also construct Tobin's Q model and the Euler model of investment based on the investment–cash flow sensitivity framework to test the impact of imports from China on the financing constraints of US firms. For the robustness test, this study introduces the instrumental variable of import penetration and constructs a difference-in-differences (DID) model to address the endogeneity problem. The results of the baseline estimation and the robustness test indicate that, overall, imports from China have an alleviating effect on the financing constraints of US firms. As we extend the sample to listed US manufacturing firms from 1989 to 2017 and perform the regression again, we find that the alleviating effect of imports from China on the financing constraints of US firms was mainly manifested before the 2008 financial crisis (the early stages) and has diminished as China's trade structure has been upgraded. Further analysis finds heterogeneity in the impact of imports from China on the financing constraints of US firms: firms with exports, high capital intensity, high market share, and high productivity have their financing constraints alleviated, whereas firms with no exports, low capital intensity, low market share, and low productivity have their financing constraints unaffected. According to these results, imports from China have shifted US financial resources to higher-quality, more efficient firms, thus improving the allocation efficiency of US financial resources.

Compared with previous studies, this study has three marginal contributions. First, this study provides a new perspective on the impact of China–US trade on the US, as most of the existing studies have focused on factors such as prices, innovation, and employment in the real sector and have provided little insight on the financial sector. In this study, we explore the role of China–US trade in US financial resource allocation from the perspective of firm financing constraints. Second, in terms of the relationship between trade and finance, most of the existing studies have used country-level data to explore the impact of trade or capital market openings on a country's financial market from a macro perspective. The trade patterns and financial systems of different countries differ greatly, however, and the impact of trade openings on financial development also varies across countries. Therefore, in this study, we use firm-level data for empirical research and conduct a heterogeneity analysis from multiple perspectives, which makes it easier to capture the micro mechanism of relevant effects. Finally, in this study, we use a variety of measures to capture firms' financing constraints as well as import competition from China. Furthermore, we employ the instrumental variable as well as the DID method based on baseline estimation to maximally ensure the robustness of the estimation results.

The rest of this chapter is organized as follows: section "Literature Review" presents a literature review. Section "Theoretical Thinking" provides a theoretical analysis of the research problem. Section "Variables, Data, and Identification Strategy" describes the variables and the sample, as well as the identification strategies in the study. Section "Baseline Estimation and Robustness Tests" focuses on the baseline estimation and robustness test; section "Extended Analysis" conducts an extended analysis on sample years and firm heterogeneity, and finally, section "Conclusions and Policy Recommendations" offers conclusions and policy implications.

Literature Review

The literature on the "China effect" has focused on the impact of Chinese exports on the US. Many scholars have discussed the impact of China–US trade on the US from the perspectives of price effects, employment and wage effects, innovation effects, and social effects.

In terms of price effects, Kamin *et al.* (2004) used the price and import data of 74 sectors in the US manufacturing industry from 1993 to 2002 and found that imports from China have almost no impact on US producer prices. Auer and Fischer (2008) selected nine low-income countries, including China, Brazil, Indonesia, and India, and analyzed the impact of imports from these countries on the producer price index of the US manufacturing industry from 1997 to 2006. The results show that for every 1% increase in imports from these low-income countries in the total sales of the sector, producer prices in the US manufacturing industry fall by 2.35%. In addition, imports from China have a stronger impact on US prices than imports from other low-income countries. Amiti *et al.* (2017) investigated the impact of China's accession to the World Trade Organization (WTO) on the US in terms of two dimensions, namely, lowering export prices and increasing export variety, showing that China's accession to the WTO led to a 7.6% decrease in the US manufacturing price index from 2000 to 2006.

In terms of employment and wage effects, Autor *et al.* (2013) examined the impact of imports from China on the US labor market, showing that imports from China have a significant negative impact on employment in the local manufacturing industry. Autor *et al.* (2014) conducted further research using individual-level worker data, demonstrating that industries that are more affected by imports from China have workers with lower earnings, a higher reliance on social security, and a higher likelihood of changing jobs. Pierce and Schott (2016) examined the impact of the US granting permanent normal trade relations to China in 2001 on US employment and found that industries with a greater reduction in policy uncertainty have a larger decline in employment. Acemoglu *et al.* (2016) conducted research from a general equilibrium perspective and concluded that imports from China have a significant negative impact on employment in the trade sector. The conclusion for the impact on related industries is that employment in downstream industries has not been significantly affected, but employment in upstream industries has declined significantly. Caliendo *et al.* (2015) showed that the import shock from China has reduced the share of the US manufacturing employment but increased the share of employment in nonmanufacturing sectors, such as services and retail. Imports from China have slightly lowered the overall US unemployment rate by providing cheaper intermediate goods to nonmanufacturing sectors. Shen and Silva (2018) examined the value-added perspective and showed that value-added trade from China has a smaller impact on the US labor market than gross value trade, with US value-added exports to China almost offsetting the shock of value-added imports from China. Wang *et al.* (2018) revealed that the import of cheap intermediate goods from China has a positive effect on the employment in US downstream industries and that exports to China also boost US employment. Although import competition from China has led to a decline in manufacturing employment, it has a positive impact on downstream industries and nonmanufacturing employment. Feenstra *et al.* (2017) showed that at the industry level, the import penetration from China and US export expansion has resulted in the unemployment of 300,000–400,000 US workers in general between 1991 and 2011, and that the increase in imports from China has boosted workers' overall wages. Feenstra and Sasahara (2018) conducted empirical research based on world input–output data, showing that from 1995 to 2011, the export expansion of the US commodity sector helped to boost the employment of 3.7 million workers, whereas imports from China in the commodity sector led to 2 million job losses, with a net effect of 1.7 million job gains.

In terms of innovation effects, Lu and Ng (2013) analyzed the impact of import competition on labor skill levels in US industries, showing that industries with higher import penetration employ more non-routine skill sets, a finding that holds true even after excluding imports from low-wage countries, such as China. Autor *et al.* (2016) studied the impact of imports from China on the innovation of US firms and showed that the increase in the penetration of imports from China reduced the number of patents obtained by US firms. Hombert and Matray (2018) examined the performance of firms with different levels of innovation in the face of import shocks and found that more innovative firms are less adversely affected when facing import shocks from China.

In terms of social effects, the study conducted by Che *et al.* (2016) on the US showed that the greater the impact of imports from China on a county, the more likely its citizens are to vote for the Democratic Party in the election. Autor *et al.* (2017) explored whether imports from China influenced the 2016 US presidential election and found that the increased penetration of imports from China boosted the Republican share of the vote. Ramirez and Rong (2012) examined the impact of trade imbalances on news reports about China, showing that the proportion of negative news about China in the US rose by about 0.045% in the three months following a trade deficit shock before slowly declining. Lu *et al.* (2018) similarly focused on whether imports from China affect the US newspapers' media bias against China, showing that newspapers whose readership faces greater exposure to Chinese imports report more negative news related to China and also tend to support the Democratic Party, which represents labor rights and criticizes globalization. Autor *et al.* (2018) examined the impact of import shocks from China on the US marriage market. Their results showed that an increase in import penetration from China is accompanied by an increased unemployment rate and premature mortality among US young males, a decline in the supply of economically secure young men, and a decline in marriage and fertility rates. McManus and Schaur (2016) investigated the impact of import competition from China on the health status of US workers, demonstrating that the growth of imports from China increases the rate of injuries and illnesses among US workers in both short and medium terms. Che *et al.* (2018) examined the impact of import competition from China on the crime rate in the US. They found that counties that are hit harder by import competition from China have higher crime rates, with property crimes being more significantly affected than violent crimes.

Theoretical Thinking

In this section, we theoretically analyze the impact of import competition from China on the financing constraints of US firms. Firm financing methods can be divided into external financing and internal financing. External financing means that firms raise funds through external channels, such as issuing stocks and bonds and borrowing from banks. Internal financing relies on firms' own earnings and cash flow accumulation to invest. If the cost of external financing is equal to the cost of internal financing, the firm does not have a financing constraint. If the cost of external financing is greater than the cost of internal financing, the firm is subject to financing constraints. This study focuses on the impact of imports from China on the financing constraints of US listed firms. We argue that this impact depends on the relationship between the products manufactured by US firms and Chinese exports, as well as on the strategies adopted by firms in the face of import competition from China.

We consider whether a complementary relationship exists between the products manufactured by US firms and those exported by China. For example, US firms import low-value-added intermediate inputs from China to produce high-value-added finished goods. Wang *et al.* (2018) noted that about 40% of US imports from China are intermediate inputs, and these imports save production costs for US firms downstream and improve their productivity and competitiveness. Therefore, the financing constraints of US firms could be alleviated if their products and Chinese exports are complementary.

If a substitution relationship, or a direct competition relationship, exists between the products manufactured by US firms and Chinese exports, then the underlying mechanisms of influence are more complex. Because of the low costs and prices of Chinese products, the competition of Chinese exports may reduce profit margins and increase business risk and default risk for US firms (Valta and Paris, 2012; Xu, 2012; Rahaman, 2016; Bustamante and Donangelo, 2017), making it more difficult to obtain external financing. Deterioration of firm performance because of intensified competition results in an increased risk of management turnover (DeFond and Park, 1999; Fee and Hadlock, 2000). Management may conceal bad business information to gain investors' trust and avoid being replaced (Kim, 1999; Kothari *et al.*, 2009; Rogers *et al.*, 2014; Li and Zhan, 2018), thus exacerbating the degree of information incompleteness and asymmetry, widening the difference between internal and external financing costs, and increasing the financing constraints faced by firms. Bernini and Montagnoli (2017) pointed out that intensified competition increases firms' demand for external financing. In the face of fierce external competition, firms need to invest and innovate substantially to avoid being eliminated. At the same time, more external financing is needed because firms' internal cash flow and retained earnings cannot meet investment needs because of the decline in profits caused by competition. Conversely, intensified competition leads to an increased risk of firm bankruptcy. To avoid personal losses from bankruptcy, management makes more efforts to increase the value of the firm (Holmström, 1982; Grossman and Hart, 1983; Nalebuff and Stiglitz, 1983; Schmidt, 1997). As a result, it has to increase research and development investment and innovation efforts and shift to the manufacturing of more technologically advanced products. In fact, many studies have shown that firms in competitive industries have lower agency costs and better corporate governance than those in less competitive industries (Giroud and Mueller, 2010; Balakrishnan and Cohen, 2014; Alimov, 2014). From this point of view, import competition leads to higher management incentives, more efficient business operations, and reduced financing constraints for firms.

The impact of imports from China on the financing constraints of US firms may manifest differently at different stages. In the early stages, China mainly exports primary products and labor-intensive industrial products, whereas US domestic products are mainly capital- and technology-intensive products. Therefore, the China–US trade is highly complementary during this stage. As China upgrades its industrial structure and trade structure, Chinese exports constantly shift to capital- and technology-intensive products, and the substitutability between Chinese exports and US domestic products is strengthened. Therefore, we expect that in the early stages, import competition from China is more likely to alleviate the financing constraints of US firms, although this alleviating effect may diminish in the later stages.

The impact of imports from China on the financing constraints of US firms may also manifest differently for different firms. First, compared with firms that focus only on the domestic market, global firms are able to spread their risks through diversified international markets when facing the shock of import competition and can also make better use of low-cost imported intermediate goods to increase productivity, and thus financing constraints may be alleviated. Second, based on China's trade structure, the products of US firms with high capital intensity are less homogeneous with and more complementary to Chinese exports, and hence the financing constraints of these firms may be alleviated. In contrast, the products of US firms with low capital intensity are highly homogeneous and highly substitutable with Chinese exports, and hence these firms are vulnerable to negative shocks from Chinese imports, and their financing constraints may increase. Finally, compared with firms that have small market shares and low productivity, firms with large market shares and high productivity have a higher industry position, more optimized cost structures, and stronger technological capabilities. Therefore, they are better able to maintain their competitive advantages through measures such as product differentiation and to continuously improve their productivity in the face of import competition from China, and thus their financing constraints may tend to be alleviated. Both Iacovone *et al.* (2013) and Bloom *et al.* (2016) found that import competition from China has a "creative destruction" and a "market selection effect," that is, it makes efficient firms grow and inefficient firms shrink in size.

Variables, Data, and Identification Strategy

In this section, we first introduce the construction of the measures, then describe the data and samples used in this study, and finally present the identification strategy of this study.

Measures of financing constraints

There is some controversy in the academic community about the measurement of financing constraints. To ensure the robustness of the empirical results, we measure financing constraints using five metrics: constraining word frequency, KZ index, SA index, WW index, and investment–cash flow sensitivity.

Constraining word frequency (frequency)

We draw on the work of Bodnaruk *et al.* (2015) to measure financing constraints using the frequency of constraining words in the financial reports of listed firms. They constructed a list of 184 constraining words, which were selected with the criteria that these words have the meaning of constraint in most cases in financial reports, such as *required, obligations, requirements, permitted, comply*, and *imposed.* The frequency is calculated as follows:

$$frequency = ln\left(\frac{number\ of\ constraining\ words}{number\ of\ total\ words}\right) \tag{1}$$

where *number of constraining words* and *number of total words* are the number of constraining words and the total number of words in a firm's financial report, respectively. When performing regression, we logarithmize the frequency of constraining words, and the larger the value, the more severe the financing constraints.

KZ index

We also follow Lamont *et al.*'s (2001) method to construct the KZ index to measure the severity of a firm's financing constraints. It is a linear combination of five financial variables:

$$\begin{aligned} KZ = -1.002 * \left(\frac{CF}{K}\right) + 0.283 * Q + 3.139 \\ * DAR - 39.368 * \left(\frac{DIV}{K}\right) - 1.315 * \left(\frac{Cash}{K}\right) \end{aligned} \tag{2}$$

where *CF, K, Q, DAR, DIV*, and *Cash* represent the firm's cash flow, capital stock, Tobin's Q, leverage, dividend payment, and cash holdings, respectively. The larger the KZ index, the more severe the financing constraints.

SA index

Hadlock and Pierce (2010) argued that a serious endogeneity problem exists when using the KZ index to measure financing constraints. For this reason, they constructed the SA index through two relatively exogenous variables, firm size and age, to measure financing constraints, as follows:

$$SA = -0.737 * size + 0.043 * size^2 - 0.04 * age \tag{3}$$

where *size* and *age* are the size and age of the firm, respectively. The larger the SA index, the more severe the financing constraints.

WW index

We also drawn on the work of Whited and Wu (2006) to measure financing constraints using the WW index, as follows:

$$\begin{aligned} WW = & -0.091 * CF - 0.062 * DIVPOS + 0.021 * TLTD \\ & - 0.044 * LNTA + 0.102 * ISG - 0.035 * SG, \end{aligned} \tag{4}$$

where *DIVPOS* is a dummy variable, which takes 1 if the firm pays cash dividends and 0 otherwise; *TLTD* is the ratio of the firm's long-term debt to total assets; *LNTA* is the logarithm of the firm's total assets; *ISG* is the industry's sales growth rate; and *SG* is the firm's sales growth rate. A larger value of the WW index indicates more severe financing constraints.

Investment–cash flow sensitivity

Fazzari *et al.* (1988) proposed for the first time the use of investment–cash flow sensitivity to capture financing constraints. If the external financing of a firm is constrained, then the investment will rely heavily on internal cash flows. The greater the external financing constraints, the more sensitive the investment is to cash flow. Therefore, we construct the following Tobin's Q investment model:

$$\left(\frac{I}{K}\right)_{ijt} = \beta_0 + \beta_1 Q_{it} + \beta_2 \left(\frac{CF}{K}\right)_{it-1} + \eta_j + \gamma_t + \varepsilon_{it} \tag{5}$$

where i is the firm, j is the industry, and t is the year; I, K, and CF represent the firm's investment spending, capital stock, and cash flow, respectively; Q is Tobin's Q; η_j represents the industry-level fixed effects; γ_t represents the year fixed effects; and ε_{it} represents the random disturbance item. Tobin's Q is the ratio of the market value of a firm to the replacement cost of its assets, reflecting the firm's performance and future growth. In this model, we focus on the size of the coefficient β_2. $\beta_2 > 0$ indicates that the firm is subject to financing constraints, and $\beta_2 < 0$ or β_2 being insignificant indicates that the firm is not subject to financing constraints.

In response to the issues of Tobin's Q model in actual application,[1] we further draw on the approach of Laeven (2003) by using the Euler model of investment to capture the financing constraints of a firm:

$$\left(\frac{I}{K}\right)_{ijt} = \beta_0 + \beta_1 \left(\frac{I}{K}\right)_{it-1} + \beta_2 \left(\frac{I}{K}\right)^2_{it-1} + \beta_3 \left(\frac{Y}{K}\right)_{it-1} + \beta_4 \left(\frac{CF}{K}\right)_{it-1} + \eta_j + \gamma_t + \varepsilon_{it} \tag{6}$$

where Y represents the total output or total revenue of the firm. The firm is subject to financing constraints if β_4 is significantly positive, and otherwise, it is not.

Measurement of import competition from China

The core explanatory variable in this study is import competition from China, which is measured by two metrics: import penetration and import share. We first draw on studies by Xu (2012) and

Rahaman (2016) to construct the industry-level import penetration to measure the degree of import competition from China to different US industries, as follows:

$$IP_{jt} = \frac{M_{jt}^{c}}{Y_{jt} + M_{jt} - X_{jt}} \tag{7}$$

where j represents the industry (three-digit North American Industry Classification Standard, or NAICS); t represents the year; IP_{jt} represents the import penetration of industry j from China in year t; M_{jt}^{c} represents the import value of industry j from China in year t; and Y_{jt}, M_{jt}, and X_{jt} represent the output, import value, and export value of industry j in year t, respectively.

We also draw on Bernard and Jensen's (2006) work to measure the import competition from China using the share of imports from China for each US industry in total industry imports, with the import share expressed by *share*:

$$share_{jt} = \frac{M_{jt}^{c}}{M_{jt}} \tag{8}$$

Control variables

We introduce variables that have been proven in the previous literature to affect firm financing constraints as control variables, including firm size, age, market power, and the ratio of tangible assets to total assets. Additionally, we control for the year fixed effects and industry fixed effects in the model.[2]

Berger and Udell (1998) pointed out that the opacity of financial information most importantly characterizes the financing of small to medium firms. In addition, small to medium firms face serious adverse selection and moral hazard (Hyytinen and Vaananen, 2006), making banks less willing to provide loans to firms. For this reason, this study introduces firm size as a control variable and measures it by the logarithm of the firm's total assets:

$$size = \ln K. \tag{9}$$

Short-established firms have little public information and exhibit serious information asymmetry, making it difficult to obtain external financing. In this study, firm age is included as a control variable. Because of the lack of information on the establishment time of listed firms, this study refers to Atawnah *et al.* (2017) and uses the logarithm of the year when the firm appeared in the Compustat database to represent the firm age.

The Lerner index measures a firm's ability to price above marginal cost (Lerner, 1934; Lindenberg and Ross, 1981). The higher the Lerner index, the stronger the market power of the firm, and the easier it is to obtain external financing. In this study, we calculate the Lerner index using Atawnah *et al.*'s (2017) method, as follows:

$$lerner = \frac{Sale - COGS - XSGA}{Sale}, \tag{10}$$

where *Sale* is the revenue from sales, *COGS* is the cost of goods sold, and *XSGA* is the selling, general, and administrative expenses.

Compared with intangible assets, the return on tangible assets tends to be more certain. The higher the proportion of a firm's tangible assets to total assets, the more symmetrical the information (Atawnah *et al.*, 2017). In addition, more tangible assets mean that firms have more collateral assets and thus have easier access to external financing (Rahaman, 2016). Referring to Atawnah *et al.* (2017), we introduce the ratio of a firm's tangible assets to its total assets as a control variable, which is calculated as follows:

$$tangibility = \frac{0.715 * rect + 0.547 * invt + 0.535 * ppent + che}{at}, \tag{11}$$

where *rect* is the receivable, *invt* is the inventory, *ppent* is net property, plant, and equipment, and *che* is cash and short-term investments.

Sample selection and data sources

The full sample for the empirical analysis in this study consists of the listed manufacturing firms in the US from 1989 to 2017. To avoid the additional interference from the 2008 financial crisis that affects the accuracy of the empirical results, we use the data from 1989 to 2007 as the sample to obtain the baseline results of this study. We then extend the sample to data from 1989 to 2017 in the extended analysis section to analyze the changes after the financial crisis. For each listed firm, we obtain the year-end market value for each year from the Center for Research in Security Prices (CRSP) database; next, we obtain the financial data of each listed firm from Compustat and match the data from both databases according to the Committee on Uniform Securities Identification Procedures (CUSIP) codes, followed by removing data with negative total assets, revenue, cash flow, and market value. Bodnaruk *et al.* (2015) posted their calculations of the number of constraining words and the number of all words in the annual reports of listed US firms on McDonald's personal homepage.[3] We match this data with data from CRSP and Compustat based on firms' Central Index Key (CIK) codes. Because the available data of Bodnaruk *et al.* (2015) are from 1993 to 2018, we use the frequency of constraining words to measure the regression of financing constraints, with all data years starting from 1993. The latest available data for the WW index are those from 2011, and we use the WW index to measure the regression of financing constraints, with the data year ending in 2011. Industry-level import and export data are obtained from Schott's International Economics Resource Page,[4] and industry-level GDP data are from the US Bureau of Economic Analysis database. We match the data from the two databases according to three-digit NAICS codes. Table 1 presents the definitions of relevant variables and data sources.

Descriptive statistics

Table 2 gives the descriptive statistics of the variables. Table 3 shows the import penetration and import share of the US manufacturing industry from China in 1989 and 2017. The import penetration and import share of various US manufacturing sectors from China in 2017 increased significantly compared with those in 1989.

Table 1. Variables and data sources.

Variable	Variable symbol	Data source
Constraining word frequency	*frequency*	McDonald's sentiment word lists: ln (number of constraining words/total number of words)
KZ index	*KZ*	Calculated
SA index	*SA*	Calculated
WW index	*WW*	Calculated
Value of imports	*M*	Schott's International Economics Resource Page
Value of exports	*X*	Schott's International Economics Resource Page
Output	*Y*	US Bureau of Economic Analysis
Import penetration	*IP*	Calculated
Firm investment	*I*	COMPUSTAT: capx (capital expenditure)
Capital stock	*K*	COMPUSTAT: at (total assets)
Market value	*me*	CRSP: prc*shrout
Tobin's Q	*Q*	COMPUSTAT & CRSP: (lse + me – ceq – txdb)/lse
Cash low	*CF*	COMPUSTAT: ib + dp
Leverage	*DAR*	COMPUSTAT: (dlc + dltt)/lse
Dividends	*DIV*	COMPUSTAT: dvp + dvc
Cash	*Cash*	COMPUSTAT: che (cash and short-term investment)
Firm size	*size*	COMPUSTAT: ln(at)
Firm age	*age*	Calculated
Lerner index	*lerner*	COMPUSTAT: (sale – cogs – xsga)/sale
Tangible assets	*tangibility*	COMPUSTAT: (0.715*rect + 0.547*invt + 0.535*ppent + che)/at

Table 2. Descriptive statistics of variables.

	Number of observations	Mean	Standard deviation	Minimum	Maximum
Explained variables:					
frequency	53,957	-4.988	0.273	-7.253	-3.856
KZ	32,571	0.235	2.215	-111.726	21.872
SA	32,657	-3.542	0.924	-5.878	-.282
WW	11,482	-0.207	0.151	-0.642	0.521
I/K	32,657	0.060	0.066	0.000	1.978
CF/K	32,657	0.119	0.078	0.001	4.850
Y/K	32,657	0.078	0.075	0.000	4.826
Q	32,657	2.008	1.826	0.114	80.964
Explanatory variables:					
IP	32,657	0.053	0.086	0.000	0.444
share	32,657	0.127	0.137	0.000	0.591
Control variables:					
size	32,657	5.804	2.016	0.278	12.836
age	32,657	2.791	0.845	0.000	4.22
lerner	31,950	0.164	0.211	-19.876	0.900
tangibility	32,488	0.522	0.14	0.002	0.996

Notes: Because of data availability, the data years of *frequency* are 1993–2017, the data years of WW index are 1989–2011, and the data years of other metrics are 1989–2017; I/K, CF/K, Y/K, and Q correspond to the investment–cash flow sensitivity framework.

Table 3. US import penetration and import share from China by industry in 1989 and 2017 (unit:%).

Industry	Import penetration 1989	Import penetration 2017	Import share 1989	Import share 2017
Food, beverage, and tobacco manufacturing	0.05	0.39	1.32	4.55
Textile mills and textile product mills	0.84	19.59	10.58	46.80
Apparel, leather, and related products	4.13	35.78	11.57	40.40
Wood products	0.22	3.19	2.25	19.71
Paper products	0.03	1.82	0.33	16.48

Table 3. (*Continued*)

Industry	Import penetration		Import share	
	1989	2017	1989	2017
Printing and related support activities	0.16	3.50	4.32	50.65
Petroleum and coal products	0.02	0.13	0.28	1.32
Chemical products	0.09	2.16	1.21	8.35
Plastic and rubber products	0.12	6.79	2.00	32.32
Nonmetallic mineral products	0.27	5.62	3.01	34.17
Primary metals	0.73	1.67	0.73	4.84
Metal products	0.23	5.84	3.48	32.50
Machinery manufacturing	0.13	8.44	0.61	20.73
Computer and electronic products	0.46	33.30	1.67	46.01
Electrical equipment, appliances, and components	0.78	24.23	5.07	38.47
Transportation equipment	0.01	1.64	0.07	4.94
Furniture and related products	0.18	20.94	2.08	56.02
Other manufacturing products	2.70	19.50	9.91	34.01

Note: The industry classification in the table is that in the Gross Output by Industry database of the US Bureau of Economic Analysis; only manufacturing is included in the table.

Identification strategies

Ordinary least squares model

To investigate the impact of imports from China on the financing constraints of US firms, in this study, we first take firm-level financing constraints as the explained variable and industry-level import penetration as the explanatory variable. Then, we introduce firm size, age, Lerner index, and tangible asset ratio as control variables and control for industry- and year-level fixed effects. We use ordinary least squares (OLS) as the baseline estimation, as follows:

$$FC_{ijt} = \alpha_0 + \alpha_1 IP_{jt} + \alpha_2 Ctrl_{it} + \eta_j + \gamma_t + \varepsilon_{it} \tag{12}$$

where i is the firm, j is the industry, and t is the year; FC is the financing constraint, which is proxied by the constraining word frequency

(*frequency*), KZ index, SA index, and WW index; *IP* is the core explanatory variable, representing import penetration; *Ctrl* denotes the control variables; η and γ denote industry and year fixed effects, respectively; and ε represents the residual.

Investment–cash flow sensitivity

To further test the impact of imports from China on the financing constraints of US firms, we add the cross-product term of import penetration and cash flow to Tobin's Q model based on the investment–cash flow sensitivity framework. According to Laeven (2003), a significantly negative coefficient β_3 of the cross-product item indicates that imports from China weaken the sensitivity of firms' investment to internal cash flow and alleviate their financing constraints:

$$\left(\frac{I}{K}\right)_{ijt} = \beta_0 + \beta_1 Q_{it} + \beta_2 \left(\frac{CF}{K}\right)_{it-1} + \beta_3 \left(\frac{CF}{K}\right)_{it-1} * IP_{jt-1} + \eta_j + \gamma_t + \varepsilon_{it} \quad (13)$$

Similarly, we add the cross-product term of import penetration and cash flow to the Euler model of investment. A significantly negative coefficient of the cross-product term means that imports from China make firms' investment less sensitive to internal cash flow and alleviate their financing constraints:

$$\left(\frac{I}{K}\right)_{ijt} = \beta_0 + \beta_1 \left(\frac{I}{K}\right)_{it-1} + \beta_2 \left(\frac{I}{K}\right)^2_{it-1} + \beta_3 \left(\frac{Y}{K}\right)_{it-1} + \beta_4 \left(\frac{CF}{K}\right)_{it-1} + \beta_5 \left(\frac{CF}{K}\right)_{it-1} * IP_{jt-1} + \eta_j + \gamma_t + \varepsilon_{it}. \quad (14)$$

Instrumental variable method

Using import penetration to measure import competition has certain endogeneity problems. For example, some shocks to US domestic industries may affect both China–US trade and the financing constraints of firms. Therefore, referring to the practice of

Autor *et al.* (2013), we construct a new variable by using imports from China in corresponding industries to eight other high-income countries as an instrumental variable for import penetration in each US industry, and then estimate the baseline model using the least squares method:

$$IP_{jt}^{o} = \frac{\sum_{k} M_{jktc}}{Y_{jt} + M_{jt} - X_{jt}} \tag{15}$$

where IP_{jt}^{o} is the instrumental variable for IP_{jt}, which is the import penetration from China in US industry j; k denotes country; and M_{jktc} represents the import value of industry j in country k from country c (i.e., China) in year t. Here, the eight high-income countries are Australia, Denmark, Finland, Germany, Japan, New Zealand, Switzerland, and Spain.

DID model

To further demonstrate the robustness of the results, we draw on the work of Pierce and Schott (2016) by treating the granting of permanent normal trading partner status to China by the US in 2001 as an exogenous shock from Chinese import competition. On January 1, 2002, the US Permanent Normal Trade Relations with China Act went into effect, exempting China's trade status from annual review by the US Congress and guaranteeing Chinese goods the same low-tariff treatment as those of other countries when entering the US market. The enactment of the US Permanent Normal Trade Relations with China Act removes the uncertainty of a sharp increase in tariffs (from low Normal Trade Relations [NTR] tariffs to high non-NTR tariffs) on imported goods from China, allowing the US to import more goods from China and causing more intense import competition from China for various industries in the US. In this study, we use the gap between NTR tariffs and non-NTR tariffs (NTR gap) to measure the policy uncertainty faced by various industries before 2001 and use the DID method to analyze whether there was a difference in changes in financing constraints between firms in industries with different NTR gaps (first difference) before and after 2001 (second difference). We obtain the NTR gap data from Schott's International Economics Resource Page. According to the analysis by Pierce and Schott (2016), there were large differences in the NTR gaps of different industries, with the mean and standard deviation of the NTR gaps of various industries in 1999 being 33% and 14%, respectively. The difference in NTR gaps between different industries was mainly due to the difference in non-NTR tariffs, which were enacted in 1931 — that is, NTR gaps were exogenous, thereby avoiding the impact of reverse causality on model estimation:

$$FC_{ijt} = \alpha_0 + \alpha_1 Post_t * NTRGap_j + \alpha_2 Ctrl_{it} + \eta_j + \gamma_t + \varepsilon_{it} \tag{16}$$

where $NTRGap_j$ represents the gap between NTR tariffs and non-NTR tariffs for industry *j*. In this study, we use the NTR gaps of various industries in 1999; and $Post_t$ is an indicator variable:

$$Post_t = \begin{cases} 1 & t \geq 2001 \\ 0 & t < 2001 \end{cases} \tag{17}$$

Baseline Estimation and Robustness Tests

In this section, we first carry out baseline estimation using OLS and then conduct a series of robustness tests: we replace measures of import competition; we estimate Tobin's Q model and the Euler model of investment based on the investment–cash flow sensitivity framework; and we perform instrumental variable estimation and DID estimation separately to solve the endogeneity problem.

Baseline estimation: OLS model

Bodnaruk *et al.* (2015) compared the predictive power of the KZ, SA, and WW indices and constraining word frequency on firm liquidity using a sample of listed US firms from 1996 to 2011.[5] They demonstrated that the frequency of constraining words better reflects the severity of firm financing constraints than the KZ, SA, and WW indices. Farre-Mensa and Ljungqvist (2016) also found that the KZ, SA, and WW indices fail to accurately identify firms that really face financing constraints. In view of this concern, we first use the frequency of constraining words and then use the KZ, SA, and WW indices to proxy for financing constraints.

We carried out the OLS estimation of Equation (12), and the results are shown in Table 4. With the introduction of all control variables as well as industry and year fixed effects, the estimated coefficients of import penetration are −0.191, −1.475, and −0.080, all of which are significant at the 5% level when using the constraining word frequency, KZ, and WW indices to measure financing constraints, respectively. The coefficient of import penetration is −0.884, which is significant at the 1% level when the SA index is used to measure financing constraints. This result indicates that import competition from China can alleviate the financing constraints of listed US firms.

Table 4. Baseline estimation results: OLS.

	Frequency	*KZ*	*SA*	*WW*
IP	−0.191**	−1.475**	−0.884***	−0.080**
	(0.068)	(0.661)	(0.292)	(0.032)
age	−0.065***	−0.217***		0.009***
	(0.005)	(0.038)		(0.002)
size	0.008***	−0.028		−0.055***
	(0.002)	(0.026)		(0.001)
lerner	0.000***	−0.155	−0.162	0.000**
	(0.000)	(0.179)	(0.147)	(0.000)
tangibility	−0.101***	−2.826***	2.035***	0.003
	(0.025)	(0.323)	(0.213)	(0.007)
Fixed effects	*j, t*	*j, t*	*j, t*	*j, t*
Observations	28,177	23,314	23,360	5,710
Adj. R^2	0.146	0.051	0.223	0.930

Notes: The data years in this table are 1993–2007 for the constraining word frequency, 1989–2007 for the KZ and SA indices, and 1989–2007 for the WW index; the regression standard errors for all models are clustered to the industry level; numbers in parentheses are robust standard errors; *, **, and *** indicate significance at the 10%, 5%, and 1% levels, respectively.

Robustness test

Replacement of metrics for measuring import competition

To ensure that our results are not affected by the import competition metrics, we instead use the share of imports from China in different industries to capture the import competition from China; adopt the constraining word frequency, KZ, SA, and WW indices to measure the financing constraints of firms; control for firms' size, age, proportion of tangible assets, and market power as well as year fixed effects and industry fixed effects; and repeat the OLS estimation. As shown in the results in Table 5, the coefficient of the import share is significantly negative at the level of 5%, regardless of which metric is used to measure financing constraints. Therefore, this finding preliminarily suggests that import competition from China can alleviate the financing constraints of US firms.

Table 5. Estimation results after the replacement of the import competition measure: OLS.

	Frequency	*KZ*	*SA*	*WW*
share	−0.111**	−1.161**	−0.484**	−0.066**
	(0.047)	(0.437)	(0.186)	(0.021)
age	−0.065***	−0.217***		0.009***
	(0.005)	(0.038)		(0.002)
size	0.008***	−0.028		−0.055***
	(0.002)	(0.026)		(0.001)
lerner	0.000***	−0.155	−0.162	0.000**
	(0.000)	(0.179)	(0.147)	(0.000)
tangibility	−0.101***	−2.839***	2.031***	0.003
	(0.025)	(0.327)	(0.211)	(0.007)
Fixed effects	*j*, *t*	*j*, *t*	*j*, *t*	*j*, *t*
Observations	28,177	23,314	23,360	5,710
Adj. R^2	0.146	0.051	0.223	0.930

Notes: The data years in this table are 1993–2007 for the constraining word frequency, 1989–2007 for the KZ and SA indices, and 1989–2007 for the WW index; the regression standard errors for all models are clustered to the industry level; numbers in parentheses are robust standard errors; *, **, and *** indicate significance at the 10%, 5%, and 1% levels, respectively.

Investment–cash flow sensitivity analysis

Table 6 presents the OLS estimation results of Tobin's Q model and the Euler model of investment based on the investment–cash flow sensitivity framework. First, we do not control for year fixed effects and industry fixed effects and conduct the OLS estimation on the two investment models without introducing cross-terms. As shown in the results in columns (1) and (4) of Table 6, the coefficients of the cash flow variable are 0.191 and 0.470, respectively, and both are significant at the 1% level. This result indicates that the investment of listed US firms is highly sensitive to cash flow — that is, financing constraints do exist for listed US firms. We then control for industry and year fixed effects and cluster the standard errors at the industry level. As shown in the corresponding estimation results in columns

Table 6. Estimation results using the Tobin's Q model and Euler model of investment: OLS.

Explanatory variable	Tobin's Q model			Euler model of investment		
	(1)	(2)	(3)	(4)	(5)	(6)
Q	-0.001 (0.002)	0.002** (0.001)	0.002* (0.001)			
$(I/K)_{i,t-1}$				0.741*** (0.072)	0.667*** (0.019)	0.667*** (0.019)
$(I/K)^2_{i,t-1}$				-0.275*** (0.065)	-0.382*** (0.075)	-0.383*** (0.075)
$(Y/K)_{i,t-1}$				-0.443*** (0.084)	-0.322*** (0.021)	-0.322*** (0.020)
$(CF/K)_{i,t-1}$	0.191*** (0.076)	0.128*** (0.040)	0.141*** (0.048)	0.470*** (0.077)	0.358*** (0.022)	0.363*** (0.024)
$(CF/K)_{i,t-1}*IP_{i,t-1}$			-0.330 (0.280)			-0.158* (0.091)
Fixed effects	None	*j*, *t*	*j*, *t*	None	*j*, *t*	*j*, *t*
Observations	17,802	17,802	17,802	17,802	17,802	17,802
Adj. R^2	0.048	0.367	0.367	0.560	0.601	0.601

Notes: The data years in this table are 1989–2007; numbers in parentheses are robust standard errors; *, **, and *** indicate significance at the 10%, 5%, and 1% levels, respectively.

(2) and (5) of Table 6, the cash flow coefficients are 0.128 and 0.358, respectively, and both are significant at the 1% level. Again, this result indicates that listed US firms are indeed limited by financing constraints.

We next introduce the cross-term of import penetration and cash flow into the models and control for the industry and year fixed effects. The estimation results are shown in columns (3) and (6) of Table 6. The coefficient of cash flow is still positive and statistically significant, and the coefficient of the cross-term of cash flow and import penetration in Tobin's Q model is –0.330, which is not significant, but the coefficient of the cross-term of cash flow and import penetration in the Euler model of investment is significantly negative. This result indicates that the import competition from China reduces the dependence of listed US firms' investment on cash flow — that is, the import competition from China alleviates the financing constraints of US firms.

In the Euler model of investment, the estimated coefficients of $(I/K)_{i,t-1}$ are all significantly positive, and the estimated coefficients of $(I/K)^2_{i,t-1}$ are all significantly negative. This finding is consistent with Laeven's (2003) estimation results and indirectly indicates that our model setting is correct.

Estimation results using the instrumental variable

To avoid the bias of OLS estimation results caused by the endogeneity problem, we adopt Autor *et al.*'s (2016) approach by constructing an instrumental variable of import penetration using the imports from China in the corresponding industries of eight other high-income countries and then performing the two-stage least squares (2SLS) estimation on Equation (12). As shown in the results in Table 7, when financing constraints are measured by constraining word frequency and SA index, the 2SLS estimated coefficients of import penetration are –0.239 and –0.861, respectively, and both are significant at the 1% level. When the KZ index is used to measure financing constraints, the 2SLS estimated coefficient of import penetration is –1.215, which is significant at the 10% level. When financing constraints are measured using the WW index, the 2SLS

Table 7. Estimation results using instrumental variables: 2SLS.

	Frequency	*KZ*	*SA*	*WW*
IP	-0.239***	-1.215*	-0.861***	-0.066**
	(0.078)	(0.661)	(0.309)	(0.034)
age	-0.065***	-0.218***		0.009***
	(0.005)	(0.037)		(0.002)
size	0.008***	-0.028		-0.055***
	(0.002)	(0.025)		(0.001)
lerner	0.000***	-0.155	-0.162	0.000***
	(0.000)	(0.174)	(0.144)	(0.000)
tangibility	-0.101***	-2.826***	2.035***	0.003
	(0.024)	(0.315)	(0.208)	(0.006)
Fixed effects	*j, t*	*j, t*	*j, t*	*j, t*
Observations	28,177	23,314	23,360	5,710
Adj. R^2	0.146	0.051	0.223	0.930

Notes: The data years in this table are 1993–2007 for the constraining word frequency, 1989–2007 for the KZ and SA indices, and 1989–2007 for the WW index; the regression standard errors for all models are clustered to the industry level; numbers in parentheses are robust standard errors; *, **, and *** indicate significance at the 10%, 5%, and 1% levels, respectively.

estimated coefficient of import penetration is –0.066, which is significant at the 5% level. These findings demonstrate that our results are robust, and hence the import competition from China can alleviate the financing constraints of US firms.

Estimation results using the DID model

We also draw on the practice of Pierce and Schott (2016) to construct a DID model to determine whether there are differences in the changes in financing constraints after 2001 for firms in industries with different NTR gaps. The DID model in Equation (16) is estimated, and the results are presented in Table 8. The coefficients of the DID variable are –0.083, –1.038, and –0.313, all of which are significant at the 5% level when financing constraints are measured using the constraining word frequency, KZ, and SA indices, respectively. When the WW index is used to measure financing constraints,

Table 8. Estimation results using DID model.

	Frequency	*KZ*	*SA*	*WW*
*Post*NTRGap*	−0.083**	−1.038**	−0.313**	−0.024
	(0.036)	(0.404)	(0.129)	(0.017)
age	−0.065***	−0.218***		0.009***
	(0.005)	(0.038)		(0.002)
size	0.008***	−0.028		−0.055***
	(0.002)	(0.026)		(0.001)
lerner	0.000***	−0.154	−0.164	0.000**
	(0.000)	(0.178)	(0.148)	(0.000)
tangibility	−0.106**	−2.833**	2.046***	0.003
	(0.025)	(0.324)	(0.216)	(0.007)
Fixed effects	No	No	No	No
Observations	28,077	23,227	23,273	5,676
Adj. R^2	0.146	0.051	0.224	0.930

Notes: The data years in this table are 1993–2007 for the constraining word frequency, 1989–2007 for the KZ and SA indices, and 1989–2007 for the WW index; the regression standard errors for all models are clustered to the industry level; numbers in parentheses are robust standard errors; *, **, and *** indicate significance at the 10%, 5%, and 1% levels, respectively.

the coefficient of the DID variable is −0.024 but is statistically insignificant. Overall, firms in industries with larger NTR gaps do experience greater reductions in financing constraints after 2001, which provides further evidence that import competition from China has an alleviating effect on the financing constraints of US firms.

Extended Analysis

In this section, we carry out a series of extended analysis. First, we extend the sample year to 2017 and again perform regression on the baseline model; then, we group listed US firms according to five metrics — namely, whether firms export, capital intensity, market share, revenue per worker, and total factor productivity (TFP) — to investigate whether the impact of import competition from China is heterogeneous on the financing constraints of US firms.

Extension of sample years

We extend the time span of the sample of US manufacturing listed firms to 1989–2017 and repeat the regression. The results are shown in Tables 9(a) and 9(b). With the sample years of 1989–2017, we first use import penetration to capture import competition. The OLS estimated coefficient of import penetration is negative but insignificant when financing constraints are measured using the constraining word frequency. Nevertheless, beyond that, the OLS estimated coefficients of import penetration are significantly negative for the results in all columns. Second, we use import shares to capture import competition. The OLS estimated coefficient of import shares is statistically insignificant when financing constraints are measured using the constraining word frequency. Nevertheless, beyond that, the OLS estimated coefficients of import share are significantly negative for the results in all columns. Third, we introduce the instrumental variable of import penetration. The 2SLS estimated coefficient of import penetration is negative but not significant when financing constraints are measured using the constraining word frequency and the KZ index, and significantly negative when financing constraints are measured using the SA and WW indices. Fourth, using the DID model, the estimated coefficient of the DID variable is significantly negative regardless of which metric is used to measure firms' financing constraints. This result provides further evidence that import competition from China can alleviate the financing constraints of US firms.

We compare the regression results in Tables 9(a) and 9(b) with those in Tables 4–8. When we extend the end of sample year from 2007 to 2017, the estimated coefficients of the import penetration, import share, and DID variables remain essentially unchanged when the SA index is used as the explained variable; however, the absolute values of the estimated coefficients of the import penetration, import share, and DID variables all become smaller in the rest of the model settings. In addition, when the constraining word frequency is used as the explained variable, the estimated coefficients of import penetration, import share, and DID variables are all significantly negative with the end of the sample year in 2007,

Table 9(a). Estimation results after changing sample years: 1989–2017.

Explanatory variable	*Frequency*				*KZ*			
	OLS	OLS	2SLS	DID	OLS	OLS	2SLS	DID
IP	−0.024		−0.065		−1.019***		−0.552	
	(0.036)		(0.052)		(0.331)		(0.477)	
share		−0.023				−0.777**		
		(0.028)				(0.279)		
*Post*NTRGap*				−0.047*				−0.896*
				(0.023)				(0.459)
age	−0.056***	−0.056***	−0.056	0.019***	−0.228***	−0.229***	−0.230***	0.005
	(0.005)	(0.005)	(0.005)	(0.001)	(0.051)	(0.051)	(0.050)	(0.022)
size	0.019***	0.019***	0.019***	−0.057***	0.005	0.005	0.005	−0.231***
	(0.001)	(0.001)	(0.001)	(0.005)	(0.022)	(0.022)	(0.021)	(0.052)
lerner	0.000*	0.000*	0.000**	−0.044	−0.441	−0.441	−0.440	−2.847***
	(0.000)	(0.000)	(0.000)	(0.026)	(0.371)	(0.371)	(0.362)	(0.340)
tangibility	−0.040	−0.040	−0.040	0.000*	−2.849***	−2.857***	−2.843***	−0.440
	(0.026)	(0.026)	(0.025)	(0.000)	(0.337)	(0.339)	(0.329)	(0.370)
IV	No	No	Yes	No	No	No	Yes	No
Fixed effects	*j, t*	*j, t*	*j, t*	*j, t*	*j, t*	*j, t*	*j, t*	*j, t*
Observations	45,847	45,847	45,847	45,597	31,713	31,713	31,713	31,585
Adj. R^2	0.215	0.215	0.215	0.216	0.052	0.052	0.052	0.052

Notes: The data years in this table are 1993–2017 for the constraining word frequency; the regression standard errors for all models are clustered to the industry level; numbers in parentheses are robust standard errors; *, **, and *** indicate significance at the 10%, 5%, and 1% levels, respectively.

Table 9(b). Estimation results after changing sample years: 1989–2017.

Explanatory variable	*SA*				*WW*			
	OLS	OLS	2SLS	DID	OLS	OLS	2SLS	DID
IP	–0.911***		–0.967***		–0.056***		–0.057***	
	(0.213)		(0.272)		(0.017)		(0.022)	
share		–0.656***				–0.051***		
		(0.178)				(0.015)		
*Post*NTRGap*				–0.661***				–0.034*
				(0.187)				(0.017)
age					0.008***	0.008***	0.008***	–0.055***
					(0.003)	(0.003)	(0.002)	(0.001)
size					–0.055***	–0.055***	–0.055***	0.008***
					(0.001)	(0.001)	(0.001)	(0.003)
lerner	–0.160	–0.161	–0.160	1.928***	–0.000***	–0.000***	–0.000***	0.002
	(0.134)	(0.135)	(0.131)	(0.179)	(0.000)	(0.000)	(0.000)	(0.004)
tangibility	1.914***	1.911***	1.913***	–0.162	0.002	0.001	0.002	0.000***
	(0.177)	(0.175)	(0.173)	(0.136)	(0.004)	(0.004)	(0.004)	(0.000)
IV	No	No	Yes	No	No	No	Yes	No
Fixed effects	*j, t*	*j, t*	*j, t*	*j, t*	*j, t*	*j, t*	*j, t*	*j, t*
Observations	31,791	31,791	31,791	31,663	9,672	9,672	9,672	9,608
Adj. R^2	0.271	0.271	0.271	0.271	0.931	0.931	0.931	0.931

Notes: 1989–2011 for the WW index; the regression standard errors for all models are clustered to the industry level; numbers in parentheses are robust standard errors; *, **, and *** indicate significance at the 10%, 5%, and 1% levels, respectively.

but they are all insignificant with the end of the sample year in 2017. This result suggests that import competition from China had a stronger alleviating effect on the financing constraints of US firms before 2008 than after 2008. In the early stages, Chinese exports were mostly primary products and labor-intensive industrial products, whereas US domestic products were mainly capital- and technology-intensive ones. As a result, the complementarity between Chinese exports and US domestic products was strong, and imports from China had a greater alleviating effect on the financing constraints of US firms. In the later stages, as China upgraded its industrial structure and trade structure, China's export structure shifted to capital- and technology-intensive products, and the substitutability between Chinese exports and US domestic products increased, which led to more intense competition. Therefore, the alleviating effect of imports from China on the financing constraints of US firms diminishes.

Analysis of firm heterogeneity

Faced with import competition from China, different types of firms may respond differently and also be affected differently, that is, there is firm heterogeneity. On this basis, we select five metrics — whether firms export, capital intensity, market share, revenue per worker, and TFP — to examine the heterogeneity of import competition affecting firms' financing constraints. Capital intensity is the ratio of a firm's capital stock to its employed population. A firm's market share is the ratio of the firm's sales to industry sales. The revenue per worker is the ratio of a firm's sales revenue to its employed labor force, and the TFP is calculated according to Olley and Pakes' (1996) method. The last two metrics measure the efficiency of a firm's production and operation. The identification of firms' exports is based on whether firms have positive foreign sales. A firm is assigned to the global group if it had positive foreign sales in 1999 and assigned to the domestic group otherwise. We divide firms into a low group and a high group according to the level of the other four metrics in 1999. For example, a firm is assigned to the low group if its TFP in 1999 was in the lower 25% of all firms' TFPs in 1999, and a firm is assigned to the high group if its TFP in 1999 was in the upper 25% of all firms' TFPs in 1999. Then, we carry out 2SLS regression on different groups of samples. Table 10 shows the results of heterogeneity analysis of samples from 1993 to 2007, and Table 11 shows the results of heterogeneity analysis of samples from 1993 to 2017.

According to the estimation results in Table 10, in terms of whether or not firms export, the import competition from China has no significant impact on firms focusing on the domestic market but can alleviate the financing constraints of exporting firms. As pointed out by Campa and Shaver (2002) and Bridges and Guarigli (2008), the sales revenue of exporting firms is more dispersed and thus can cushion local demand shocks. Therefore, the impact of import competition from China has a smaller shock on these firms. In terms of capital intensity, import competition from China has no significant impact on the financing constraints of low-capital-intensive firms but can alleviate the financing constraints of high-capital-intensive firms. Because Chinese exports are mainly low-capital-intensive and high-labor-intensive goods, US firms with low capital intensity face more serious import competition shocks. In terms of market share, import competition from China has no significant impact on the financing constraints of firms with low market shares but can alleviate the financing constraints of firms with high market shares. In terms of production and operation efficiency, import competition from China has no significant impact on the financing constraints of firms with low revenue per worker but can alleviate the financing constraints of firms with high revenue per worker. In terms of TFP, although the coefficients of import penetration are insignificant for both groups, the absolute value of the coefficient of the high TFP group is larger than that of the low TFP group. This may be because firms with high productivity have a more optimized cost structure and greater technological strength and are therefore better at coping with import shocks from China.

Based on the results of this analysis of firm heterogeneity, we find that import competition from China alleviates the financing

Table 10. Estimation results of firm heterogeneity (1993–2007): 2SLS.

	Frequency									
	Export		Capital intensity		Market share		Sales per employee		Productivity	
	Domestic	Global	Low	High	Low	High	Low	High	Low	High
IP	−0.042	−0.466***	0.167	−0.449***	−0.200	−0.334***	0.218	−0.472***	−0.031	−0.215
	(0.227)	(0.141)	(0.11)	(0.060)	(0.149)	(0.178)	(0.190)	(0.118)	(0.132)	(0.210)
age	−0.052***	−0.057***	−0.071***	−0.088***	−0.055***	−0.086***	−0.083***	−0.076***	−0.084***	−0.056***
	(0.015)	(0.011)	(0.010)	(0.011)	(0.010)	(0.008)	(0.014)	(0.014)	(0.022)	(0.010)
size	−0.009*	−0.005	−0.014**	−0.005	−0.031*	−0.009	−0.013***	0.005	0.003	−0.012***
	(0.005)	(0.004)	(0.005)	(0.004)	(0.004)	(0.008)	(0.004)	(0.004)	(0.005)	(0.004)
lerner	0.000	−0.064**	0.000	0.000***	0.000	−0.282***	0.000	0.000***	−0.000	−0.000
	(0.000)	(0.032)	(0.000)	(0.000)	(0.000)	(0.068)	(0.000)	(0.000)	(0.000)	(0.000)
tangibility	−0.172**	−0.206***	−0.178**	−0.097**	−0.053**	−0.248***	−0.097*	−0.146***	−0.157	−0.105**
	(0.075)	(0.055)	(0.089)	(0.042)	(0.040)	(0.073)	(0.055)	(0.049)	(0.044)	(0.044)
IV	Yes	Yes	Yes	Yes	Yes	Yes	Yes	Yes	Yes	Yes
Fixed effects	*j, t*	*j, t*	*j, t*	*j, t*	*j, t*	*j, t*	*j, t*	*j, t*	*j, t*	*j, t*
Observations	1,460	7,050	5,777	4,830	4,576	5,668	4,714	5,577	4,953	5,367
Adj. R^2	0.220	0.180	0.139	0.173	0.153	0.210	0.160	0.151	0.157	0.122

Notes: The data years in this table are 1993–2007; the regression standard errors for all models are clustered to the industry level; numbers in parentheses are robust standard errors; *, **, and *** indicate significance at the 10%, 5%, and 1% levels, respectively.

Table 11. Estimation results of firm heterogeneity (1993–2017): 2SLS.

Explanatory variable	*Frequency*									
	Export		Capital intensity		Market share		Sales per employee		Productivity	
	Domestic	Global	Low	High	Low	High	Low	High	Low	High
IP	0.051	−0.193**	0.010	−0.089***	0.100	−0.081***	0.086	−0.190**	−0.033	−0.093
	(0.140)	(0.082)	(0.122)	(0.080)	(0.139)	(0.094)	(0.117)	(0.091)	(0.094)	(0.139)
age	−0.053***	−0.058***	−0.068***	−0.085***	−0.055***	−0.087***	−0.083***	−0.078***	−0.088***	−0.053***
	(0.012)	(0.010)	(0.009)	(0.011)	(0.011)	(0.008)	(0.013)	(0.015)	(0.021)	(0.012)
size	0.010***	−0.004	0.014***	0.005**	0.031***	−0.010	0.017***	0.006*	0.010***	0.011
	(0.003)	(0.005)	(0.004)	(0.003)	(0.005)	(0.007)	(0.003)	(0.004)	(0.004)	(0.003)
lerner	0.000	−0.024***	0.000	0.000**	0.000	−0.264***	0.000	0.000***	0.000	0.000
	(0.000)	(0.004)	(0.000)	(0.000)	(0.000)	(0.070)	(0.000)	(0.000)	(0.000)	(0.000)
tangibility	−0.175***	−0.130**	−0.153**	−0.078*	−0.052	−0.200***	−0.120***	−0.106**	−0.120***	−0.104*
	(0.056)	(0.051)	(0.074)	(0.047)	(0.040)	(0.070)	(0.038)	(0.042)	(0.040)	(0.048)
IV	Yes	Yes	Yes	Yes	Yes	Yes	Yes	Yes	Yes	Yes
Fixed effects	j,t	j,t	j,t	j,t	j,t	j,t	j,t	j,t	j,t	j,t
Observations	1,994	10,202	7,896	6,997	6,286	8,232	6,542	7,869	7,095	7,653
Adj. R^2	0.236	0.239	0.181	0.237	0.211	0.256	0.204	0.210	0.213	0.175

Notes: The data years in this table are 1993–2017; the regression standard errors for all models are clustered to the industry level; numbers in parentheses are robust standard errors; *, **, and *** indicate significance at the 10%, 5%, and 1% levels, respectively.

constraints of firms with exports, high capital intensity, high market share, and high productivity, but it does not affect the financing constraints of firms with no exports, low capital intensity, low market share, and low productivity. Therefore, imports from China actually divert US financial resources to higher-quality and more efficient firms.

As shown in the results in Table 11, we can still draw these conclusions when using the sample from 1993 to 2017 for heterogeneity analysis. Comparing the estimation result in Table 11 with the results in Table 10, we find that the absolute value of the estimated coefficient of import penetration of the global and high groups in Table 11 is smaller than that in Table 10. In other words, imports from China had a greater alleviating effect on the financing constraints of US firms with exports, high capital intensity, high market share, and high productivity before 2008 than after 2008. These results are consistent with our findings from the previous analysis.

Conclusions and Policy Recommendations

This study measures import competition from China for different industries by import penetration and import share using an empirical sample of listed US manufacturing firms from 1989 to 2007. We first examine the impact of imports from China on the financing constraints of US firms by using the constraining word frequency, KZ, SA, and WW indices to measure financing constraints. We then construct Tobin's Q model and the Euler model of investment based on the investment–cash flow sensitivity framework to further test whether US firms are subject to financing constraints and the impact of imports from China on the financing constraints of US firms. We also introduce an instrumental variable of import penetration and employ a DID model to address the endogeneity issue. Through baseline estimation and robustness analysis, we find that, in general, US firms do suffer from financing constraints and that import competition from China alleviates the financing constraints of US firms.

By changing the end of sample year from 2007 to 2017 and performing regression again, we find that imports from China alleviated the financing constraints of US firms mainly in the early stages (before the 2008 financial crisis). This is because of the strong complementarity between Chinese exports and domestic US products in the early stages. The alleviating effect of import competition on the financing constraints of US firms, however, diminishes as the substitutability between Chinese exports and domestic US products increases as China upgrades its trade structure.

The firms are grouped according to five metrics — namely, whether firms export, capital intensity, market share, revenue per worker, and TFP — for each of which the regression is conducted. We find that the impact of import competition from China on the financing constraints of US firms is heterogeneous, as evidenced by the fact that firms with exports, high capital intensity, high market share, and high productivity have their financing constraints alleviated and that firms with no exports, low capital intensity, low market share, and low productivity have their financing constraints unaffected. To some extent, imports from China have shifted US financial resources to higher-quality and more efficient firms, improving the allocation efficiency of US financial resources.

This study examines the impact of China–US trade on the US from a new perspective of financing constraints. In addition, it further demonstrates the positive impact of globalization and trade liberalization, that is, import competition from China can improve the allocation efficiency of US financial resources. On the basis of the conclusions of this study, we propose the following policy recommendations. First, at the country level, globalization and trade liberalization are the general trend of world economic development, and countries should participate in the process of globalization and trade liberalization with a comprehensively open, mutually beneficial, and win–win attitude. In the face of the impact of import competition on domestic firms, the key lies in improving the technological level and efficiency of domestic firms, rather than defending against import competition through trade protection and restrictive measures. Second, from the perspective of firms, although import competition has increased business risks to a certain extent, it has also stimulated firms to improve efficiency, while firms can optimize their cost structures by importing intermediate goods. Firms must continuously improve their efficiency and actively participate in globalization if they intend to gain the most benefits from trade liberalization. Third, from the perspective of China–US economic and trade interaction, the two countries should shift from trade relations to investment relations and encourage Chinese exporters with competitive advantages to go global. Chinese investment in the US has created a direct link between the Chinese and US markets, which are becoming increasingly connected. In addition, Chinese firms' greenfield investment in the US brings production lines to the US, thus circumventing potential trade barriers as well as increasing US jobs and reducing China–US trade frictions.

Endnotes

1. When capital markets are not fully efficient, Tobin's Q value cannot represent the investment opportunity of a firm. In addition, it is the marginal Q that determines the firm's investment, but in reality, we can only calculate the average Q and use it to approximate the marginal Q, which leads to some measurement errors.
2. Because the SA index is a linear combination of firm size and age, firm age and firm size are not used as control variables when financing constraints are measured by the SA index to avoid the endogeneity problem.
3. "Loughran-McDonald Master Dictionary w/Sentiment Word Lists," Software Repository for Accounting and Finance, University of Notre Dame, January 2022, https://sraf.nd.edu/loughranmcdonald-master-dictionary/.
4. Peter K. Schott. "Data," https://sompks4.github.io/sub_data.html.
5. BLM (2015) argues that a firm's liquidity events can reflect the improvement or deterioration of the firm's external financing conditions, and these liquidity events include nonpayment of dividends, dividend increases, share repurchases, and pension shortfalls.

References

Acemoglu, D., Autor, D., and Dorn, D. 2016. Import competition and the Great US employment sag of the 2000s. *Journal of Labor Economics*, 34(S1): S141–S198.

Alimov, A. 2014. Product market competition and the value of corporate cash: Evidence from trade liberalization. *Journal of Corporate Finance*, 25: 122–139.

Amiti, M., Dai, M., and Feenstra, R.C. 2017. How did China's WTO entry benefit US consumers? NBER Working Paper, No. 23487.

Atawnah, N., Balachandran, B., and Duong, H.N. 2018. Does exposure to foreign competition affect stock liquidity? Evidence from industry-level import data. *Journal of Financial Markets*, 39: 44–67.

Auer, R. and Fischer, A.M. 2008. The effect of trade with low-income countries on US industry. Federal Reserve Bank of Dallas, No. 14.

Autor, D., Dorn, D., and Hanson, G.H. 2013. The China syndrome: Local labor market effects of import competition in the United States. *American Economic Review*, 103(6): 2121–2168.

Autor, D., Dorn, D., Hanson, G.H., and Song, J. 2014. Trade adjustment: worker-level evidence. *The Quarterly Journal of Economics*, 129.

Autor, D., Dorn, D., and Hanson, G.H. 2016. Foreign competition and domestic innovation: Evidence from US patents. NBER Working Paper, No. 22879.

Autor, D., Dorn, D., Hanson, G., and Majlesi, K. 2017. A Note on the Effect of Rising Trade Exposure on the 2016 Presidential Election. Mimeo.

Autor, D., Dorn, D., and Hanson, G. 2018. When work disappears: Manufacturing decline and the falling marriage market value of young men. IZA Discussion Papers, No. 11465.

Balakrishnan, K. and Cohen, D.A. 2014. Competition and financial accounting misreporting. *SSRN Electronic Journal*, 115(Pt11): 2433–2442.

Berger, A.N. and Udell, G.F. 1998. The economics of small business finance: The roles of private equity and debt markets in the financial growth cycle. *Journal of Banking and Finance*, 22(6): 613–673.

Bernard, A.B. and Jensen, J.B. 2006. Survival of the best fit: Exposure to low-wage countries and the (uneven) growth of US manufacturing plants. *Journal of International Economics*, 68(1): 219–237.

Bernini, M. and Montagnoli, A. 2017. Competition and financial constraints: A two-sided story. *Journal of International Money and Finance*, 70: 88–109.

Bloom, N., Draca, M., and Reenen, J.V. 2016. Trade induced technical change? The impact of Chinese imports on innovation, IT and productivity. *Review of Economic Studies*, 83(1): 87–117.

Bodnaruk, A., Loughran, T., and McDonald, B. 2015. Using 10-K text to gauge financial constraints. *Journal of Financial and Quantitative Analysis*, 50(4): 623–646.

Bridges, S. and Guariglia, A. 2008. Financial constraints, global engagement, and firm survival in the United Kingdom: Evidence from micro data. *Scottish Journal of Political Economy*, 55(4): 444–464.

Bustamante, M.C. and Donangelo, A. 2017. Product market competition and industry returns. *Review of Financial Studies*, 30(12): 4216–4266.

Caliendo, L., Dvorkin, M.A., and Parro, F. 2015. The impact of trade on labor market dynamics. NBER Working Paper, No. 21149.

Campa, J.M. and Shaver, J.M. 2002. Exporting and capital investment: On the strategic behavior of exporters. IESE Research Papers D/469, IESE Business School.

Che, Y., Lu, Y., Pierce, J.R., Schott, P.K., and Tao, Z. 2016. Does trade liberalization with China influence US elections? NBER Working Paper, No. 22178.

Che, Y., Xu, X., and Zhang, Y. 2018. Chinese import competition, crime, and government transfers in US. *Journal of Comparative Economics*, 46(2): 544–567.

Defond, M. and Park, C. 1999. The effect of competition on CEO turnover. *Journal of Accounting & Economics*, 27(1): 35–56.

Farre-Mensa, J. and Ljungqvist, A. 2016. Do measures of financial constraints measure financial constraints? *Review of Financial Studies*, 29(2): 271–308.

Fazzari, S., Hubbard, G., and Petersen, B. 1988. Financing constraints and corporate investment. *Brookings Papers on Economic Activity*, 1: 141–195.

Fee, C.E. and Hadlock, C.J. 2000. Management turnover and product market competition: Empirical evidence from the U.S. newspaper industry. *Journal of Business*, 73(2): 205–243.

Feenstra, R.C., Ma, H., and Xu, Y. 2017. US exports and employment. NBER Working Paper, No. 24056.

Feenstra, R.C. and Sasahara, A. 2018. The 'China shock', exports and US employment: A global input-output analysis. *Review of International Economics*, 26(5): 1053–1083.

Giroud, X. and Mueller, H.M. 2010. Does corporate governance matter in competitive industries? *Journal of Financial Economics*, 95(3): 312–331.

Grossman, S.J. and Hart, O.D. 1983. An analysis of the principal-agent problem. *Econometrica*, 51(1): 7–45.

Hadlock, C.J. and Pierce, J.R. 2010. New evidence on measuring financial: Moving beyond KZ index. *Review of Financial Studies*, 23(5): 1909–1940.

Holmström, B. 1982. Moral hazard in teams. *Bell Journal of Economics*, 13(2): 324–340.

Hombert, J. and Matray, A. 2018. Can innovation help U.S. manufacturing firms escape import competition from China? *Journal of Finance*, 73(5): 2003–2039.

Hyytinen, A. and Vaananen, L. 2006. Where do financial constraints originate from? An empirical analysis of adverse selection and moral hazard in capital market. *Small Business Economics*, 27(4): 323–348.

Iacovone, L., Rauch, F., and Winters, L.A. 2013. Trade as an engine of creative destruction: Mexican experience with Chinese competition. *Journal of International Economics*, 89(2): 379–392.

Kamin, S.B., Marazzi, M., and Schindler, J.W. 2004. Is China 'exporting deflation'? International Finance Discussion Papers, No. 791.

Kim, O. 1999. Discussion of the role of the manager's human capital in discretionary disclosure. *Journal of Accounting Research*, 37: 183–185.

Kothari, S.P., Xu, L., and Short, J.E. 2009. The effect of disclosures by management, analysts, and business press on cost of capital, return volatility, and analyst forecasts: A study using content analysis. *Accounting Review*, 84(5): 1639–1670.

Laeven, L. 2003. Does financial liberalization reduce financing constraints? *Financial Management*, 32(1): 5–34.

Lamont, O., Polk, C., and Saa-Requejo, J. 2001. Financial constraints and stock returns. *Review of Financial Studies*, 14(2): 529–554.

Lerner, A.P. 1934. The concept of monopoly and the measurement of monopoly power. *Review of Economic Studies*, 1(3): 157–175.

Li, S. and Zhan, X. 2018. Product market threats and stock crash risk. *Management Science*, 65(9): 4011–4031.

Lindenberg, E.B. and Ross, S.A. 1981. Tobin's Q ratio and industrial organization. *Journal of Business*, 54(1): 1–32.

Lu, Y. and Ng, T. 2013. Import competition and skill content in U.S. manufacturing industries. *Review of Economics and Statistics*, 95(4): 1404–1417.

Lu, Y., Shao, X., and Tao, Z. 2018. Exposure to Chinese imports and media slant: Evidence from 147 US local newspapers over 1998–2012. *Journal of International Economics*, 114: 316–330.

McManus, T.C. and Schaur, G. 2016. The effects of import competition on worker health. *Journal of International Economics*, 102: 160–172.

Nalebuff, B.J. and Stiglitz, J.E. 1983. Prizes and incentives: Towards a general theory of compensation and competition. *Bell Journal of Economics*, 14(1): 21–43.

Olley, S. and Pakes, A. 1996. The dynamics of productivity in the telecommunications equipment industry. *Econometrica*, 64: 1263–1298.

Pierce, J.R. and Schott, P.K. 2016. The surprisingly swift decline of US manufacturing employment. *American Economic Review*, 106(7): 1632–1662.

Rahaman, M.M. 2016. Chinese import competition and the provisions for external debt financing in the US. *Journal of International Business Studies*, 47(8): 898–928.

Ramirez, C.D. and Rong, R. 2012. China bashing: Does trade drive the "bad" news about China in the USA? *Review of International Economics*, 20(2): 350–363.

Rogers, J.L., Schrand, C.M., and Zechman, S.L.C. 2014. Do managers tacitly collude to withhold industry-wide bad news? Chicago Booth Research Paper, No.13-12.

Schmidt, K. 1997. Managerial incentives and product market competition. *Review of Economic Studies*, 64(2): 191–213.

Shen, L. and Silva, P. 2018. Value-added exports and US local labor markets: Does China really matter? *European Economic Review*, 101: 479–504.

Valta, P. and Paris, H. 2012. Competition and the cost of debt. *Journal of Financial Economics*, 105(3): 661–682.

Wang, Z., Wei, S.-J., Yu, X., and Zhu, K. 2018. Re-examining the effects of trading with China on local labor markets: A supply chain perspective. NBER Working Paper, No. 24886.

Whited, T.M. and Wu, G. 2006. Financial constraints risk. *Review of Financial Studies*, 19(2): 531–559.

Xu, J. 2012. Profitability and capital structure: Evidence from import penetration. *Journal of Financial Economics*, 106(2): 427–446.

https://doi.org/10.1142/9789819815241_0024

Chapter 24

MARKETIZING CHINA'S FUSION SECTOR: BASED ON THE US LESSONS OF EXPERIENCE

Shuo Shi

Fudan Development Institute (FDDI), Fudan University, Shanghai, China
shishuo@fudan.edu.cn

Introduction

In 2022, a great leap took place in human energy technology history. That December, the US Department of Energy announced the "success" of nuclear fusion ignition.[1] In plain words, the energy produced by America's fusion reaction exceeded the input energy used by its National Ignition Facility, achieving net energy gains. In a high-profile media launch, the Department of Energy considered this ignition "success" a milestone breakthrough toward commercial fusion power generation. Is it easy for the US to commercialize its fusion technology? Moreover, against the background of escalating Sino–US rivalry, what is the impact of the US ignition "success" on China's thinking over energy strategy?

Indeed, the US "success" of the nuclear fusion reaction did ignite in China a broad debate on how to interpret the technological advances and commercial patterns of America's nuclear fusion sector, leading to three main viewpoints. First, proponents of "technological exploration" claim that, although the ignition experiment was "successful" in enhancing proficiency in energy conversion, such "success" is still far from initiating the full commercialization of nuclear fusion energy. Therefore, the significance of ignition "success" is much greater in technological terms than in commercial terms, mainly serving as a technological exploration for the US. Second, advocates of "nuclear deterrence" believe that US nuclear fusion ignition experiments have always been a camouflage for nuclear weapons experiments. The "success" of this fusion ignition experiment is nothing else but a dangerous move to surpass the sensitive moral boundaries of advancing nuclear weapon technology, mainly serving the US in maintaining nuclear deterrence against other nuclear powers, namely Russia and China. Third, supporters of "competition against China" state that the US' strategic purpose of holding such a high-profile announcement for ignition "success" is to compete with China for the global leadership of nuclear fusion technology development, mainly serving the US in securing technological advantages over China.

Although these three viewpoints above make intriguing sense from a pragmatic perspective, they have not yet paid sufficient attention to the impact of the US political dispute on its nuclear fusion policy, thus leaving an analytical gap in a political-economic perspective. Therefore, this chapter focuses on the conflicts of bipartisan interests in the US Congress and Senate. Our analysis shows that the ignition "success" played a much more critical role, as a Democratic political accomplishment, in the Congressional arena than in technological and commercial fields. Currently, US nuclear fusion ignition technology is far from reaching the level of commercial power generation, with great difficulties in dispelling the suspicion of serving nuclear weapon experiments. Nevertheless, the US government insisted on promoting the ignition "success" to Congress, indicating that the Biden administration's primary purpose was to use the ignition "success" as a political achievement to persuade Congress to increase funding for developing green technologies and new-energy value chains. However, there are still significant differences between the Republican and Democratic parties on nuclear fusion policy, which has added uncertainty to the policy focus of US support for nuclear fusion.

Moreover, the financial funding approved by Congress has yet to reach the investment target envisioned by the industry for the commercialization of nuclear fusion. Moreover, in industrializing new energy, the US has always faced the problem of information asymmetry between government and enterprises, leading to collusion between politics and business. Overall, the US' industrialization of nuclear fusion needs to overcome a series of vital technological bottlenecks and potential significant trust crises, amounting to insuperable difficulties in the short term. Nevertheless, nuclear fusion ignition's "success" has dramatically inspired the US science–technology–capital complex to actively expand its role in core segments of supply–industry–value chains in the fusion energy sector. The US is gradually ratcheting up its long-term fusion energy development by steadily marketizing its fusion sector.

The technological advances in ignition and commercial development in the US high-energy sector have significant strategic implications for China's energy industry. Compared with America, China is confronting three urgent challenges in the industrialization of nuclear fusion. First, it should be wary of the instigative effect that the US ignition "success" may have on both global and China's domestic capital markets. Second, the objective trend of continuous technological progress will gradually and then suddenly lower thresholds for private enterprises, especially equipment producers, to enter the nuclear fusion industry, resulting in higher economic costs for China to isolating its fusion sector from private entities. Third, it should pay more attention to three latent risks in the process of China's nuclear fusion industrialization: overinvestment or overcapacity in the fusion sector, instability in the capital market brought about by startup fusion tech firms being more competitive than non-fusion incumbents, and loss of market power of state-owned enterprises (SOEs) to fusion private entities.

These significant challenges will likely undermine the long-term stability of China's nuclear fusion industrialization. Therefore, China should start designing a comprehensive, coordinated, and sustainable strategy for the national energy sector by emphasizing the marketization of its nuclear fusion sector to tilt its technological competition against the US in favor of Chinese enterprises.

Therefore, this chapter proposes that China plans a national-level strategy to form an energy powerhouse by combining a national system with market forces. We name such a national plan the "Energy Powerhouse Strategy." While this strategy should undoubtedly promote the industrialization of nuclear fusion, it is equally important to focus on the overall energy security of the country, encourage inclusive progress that balances gradual and disruptive scientific and technological advances, and promote the stable development of the energy–capital–ownership relationship. China should base the Energy Powerhouse Strategy on the carbon peaking and neutrality goals and establish a multi-energy complementary energy development pattern to achieve those goals. With safety and stability as basic concepts, China should promote the development of nuclear power by leveraging both the role of state-owned capital as a central pillar and the role of private capital as innovative potential.

This chapter contributes to the extant literature in the following three threads. First, based on bipartisan policy behavior over the marketization of the fusion sector, we provide a fresh case study in which the US follows interventionism to ratchet up the marketization of a high-tech infant industry, such as the nuclear fusion sector. Since the work of David Ricardo and Frederic Bastiat, industrial organization theory in mainstream economics has been advocating a private initiative approach which sees the government's core role as an "invisible hand" to set the table for private innovation and entrepreneurship (Ketels, 2007; Romer, 1990; Sakoh, 1984). As the Heritage Foundation, the flagship of a conservative US think tank, constantly argues, "the federal government should fund only fundamental scientific research and get out of the business of helping companies commercialize new energy technologies" (Plumer and

Davenport, 2017). However, the US industrial policy on nuclear fusion provides ammunition for controversy. By reviewing bipartisan conflicts over the federal government's role in the industrialization of the US fusion sector, this chapter sheds new light on the political behavior of US interventionism, thus supporting the opposite argument that the US has been relying on and still requires the implementation of effective industrial policies (Buigues and Sekkat, 2009; Reich, 1982; Schrank and Whitford, 2009).

Second, this chapter adds China's policy behavior regarding the marketization of its fusion sector, a high-tech infant industry in a transformative economy with a high to medium growth rate, to the perennial debate around industrial policy's role in the East Asian miracle. Extant literature has been emphasizing that state intervention helps to fund startup firms by mitigating financial constraints, protecting nascent industries from ruinous competition, and facilitating the learning-by-doing paradigm for industrial upgrading, in particular, among other interventional policy tools (Johnson, 1982; Kim, 1997; Wade, 2004; World Bank, 1993). In contrast, this chapter highlights the increasing importance of lowering barriers for Chinese private enterprises to enter the fusion sector after the intensifying Sino–US technological competition. As advocated by Brandt and Rawski (2019), when designing industrial policy for the energy and electricity sectors, China should focus on leveling the playing field for both SOEs and reliable private entities to jointly enhance the efficiency of financing, innovation, and entrepreneurship.

Third, this chapter offers novel rethinks over China's "Three-Step" strategy for nuclear energy development since 1983, which follows a mechanical sequence of technological upgrading from pressurized water reactors to fast reactors and eventually to fusion reactors (Andrews-Speed, 2023; Hibbs, 2018; Ping, 1987). Given significant, and even disruptive, technological advances in supercomputers, 3D printing, and artificial intelligence, among others, plus technological diffusion from US and European fusion firms, China's fusion sector is very likely to expedite its industrial upgrading earlier and faster than expected, leading to a possible momentum paralleling the development of fast reactor technology. Therefore,

China should adapt its nuclear sector to the increasingly dynamic era of technological advances by coordinating fusion and fast reactors in a comprehensive national energy strategy.

This chapter proceeds as follows. Section "Fusion Ignition: An Overestimated Success" reviews the three main viewpoints on the "success" of the US fusion ignition, namely "technological-exploration theory," "nuclear-deterrence theory," and "competition-with-China theory," to show significant doubts about the commercial prospects of the US fusion sector. Then, by considering congressional political conflicts, nuclear fusion technology development, and relevant industry support policies in the US, section "Industrial Policy: A Never-Ending Political Turmoil" discusses the underlying political logic of the US government's high-profile announcement for the "success" of nuclear fusion ignition. Section "Industrialization Challenges: China's Fusion Sector" analyzes the three urgent challenges faced by China's nuclear fusion sector, including external shocks, disruptive technological advances, and latent risks in terms of over-investment and overcapacity in the fusion sector, instability in the capital market brought by startup fusion tech firms' greater competitiveness over non-fusion incumbents, and SOEs losing market power to fusion private entities. Section "Energy Powerhouse Strategy: Marketization Matters" proposes a brief policy approach of the "three pillars" to promote the planning of China's Energy Powerhouse Strategy by emphasizing the necessity of marketing the nuclear fusion sector. Section "Conclusion" concludes.

Fusion Ignition: An Overestimated Success

To launch the "success" of the fusion ignition, the US Department of Energy held a high-profile press conference which was more like a political who's who in supporting new-energy development. A key objective behind the US push for nuclear fusion ignition experiments is to attract the science–technology–capital complex to invest more in the nuclear fusion market, thus spurring the marketization of the nuclear fusion industry. However, it was still a stretch to consider this ignition experiment a legit "success," either in terms of technology or commercialization. Moreover, this ignition experiment utilized equipment from US national laboratories aimed at advancing nuclear weapons, which inevitably increased broad concerns in the international community that the US might be teasing the Comprehensive Nuclear-Experiment-Ban Treaty by conducting physical experiments with hydrogen bombs. Besides, the US still faces engineering and technological constraints in nuclear fusion equipment manufacturing and challenges from China's rapid technological progress. These issues raise doubts as to whether the "success" of the ignition could effectively enhance the US' technological advantage over China.

Therefore, this historic ignition experiment is, at best, an overestimated "success." Although the accomplishment of net energy gain in a single ignition experiment is genuine evidence of solid technological advancement, overstating the implication of this experiment should bear serious caveats. Specifically, asserting the experiment a "success" has raised doubts in at least three aspects: extremely high economic costs, nuclear ethics violation risks, and feeble technological advantage over China.

Commercial frustrations

Does the "success" of the ignition genuinely imply that this technology is now profitable? Far from it. Unsolved concerns remain about whether this laboratory technology can be successfully commercialized.

The critical evidence supporting the "success" of the ignition is net energy gain, which means that the energy generated by the nuclear fusion reaction exceeds the input energy for triggering the ignition. In this experiment, the US research team used pulsed lasers to input 2.05 megajoules of energy into the deuterium-tritium target, producing 3.15 megajoules of fusion energy, resulting in a net energy gain of 1.5 times.[2] Net energy gain was indeed achieved. However, this net energy gain only considers the input energy, not the total energy consumption required to generate this input energy.

The ignition device consumed over 300 megajoules of regular energy to generate the input pulsed lasers, resulting in only 3.15 megajoules of fusion energy. The total energy conversion ratio, surprisingly, is less than 1%. In comparison, the energy gain ratio for civilian power plants generally reaches an output energy of 30–100 times the input energy. In other words, the energy gain level of civilian power plants is not only much higher than that of ignition, but also the total energy conversion ratio of ignition is far less than the standard of civilian power plants. Therefore, based on the energy gain ratio or the total energy conversion ratio, the energy conversion efficiency of this ignition still has a long way to go before reaching the standard of civilian power plants.

Moreover, the economic costs of a single ignition remain incredibly high. Currently, it costs over US$100,000 per ignition. The problem is that, according to the US Department of Energy's estimation, maintaining commercial power generation capacity requires at least 10 ignitions per second.[3] At current costs, such a fusion power plant would spend at least US$1 million per second on ignition alone, let alone enormous expenses for operating the whole facility. Therefore, from the perspective of total operating costs, ignition technology would still result in substantial economic losses.

Even if the US can afford such high ignition costs, the engineering efficiency of ignition cannot meet the requirements for commercialization. The US research team typically needs hundreds of hours to construct, debug, and operate the National Ignition Facility for just one ignition. The charging of the ignition laser alone takes a long time. After ignition, analyzing data and summarizing engineering experience takes even longer. Although this engineering efficiency reflects the rigorous scientific professionalism of the US research team, it still cannot meet the engineering efficiency requirements of maintaining at least 10 ignitions per second and, therefore, cannot support sustainable power generation capacity on a commercial power plant scale.

So, can such high economic costs and laggard engineering efficiency produce vast amounts of energy on a scale required for a commercial power plant? The answer is still negative. The ignition device, which occupies an area equivalent to three standard football fields, has only produced 3.15 megajoules of energy in this "successful" experiment, less than 0.9 kilowatt-hours, which is only enough to power a 60-watt light bulb for less than 15 hours. Such a meager amount of electricity can hardly meet the power generation level required for a commercial power plant.

Based on the information available publicly, the US ignition technology still needs to overcome significant technical obstacles, such as high total energy consumption, insufficient energy gain efficiency, extremely high costs for a single ignition, unsustainable ignition, and weak power productivity. Sure, the progress of US ignition technology deserves excellent credit. In 2014, the power produced by the National Ignition Facility was only enough to power a 60-watt light bulb for 5 minutes. Nearly 10 years later, the output energy is enough to power the same light bulb for over 10 hours. Even so, the speed of such technological progress still needs to be increased to support US fusion ignition technology to meet civilian power plants' commercial power generation standards, which should be profitable and sustainable. Such loss-making ignition technology still requires massive investment from the US government and industry, as well as the hard work of scientific research teams in basic science research and engineering technology breakthroughs, which also require long-term inputs of time.

Risking violating nuclear ethics

In the face of criticism of the low efficiency of ignition technology, some analyses have pointed out that the laser engineering devices used in ignition experiments were from the 1980s to the 1990s (Behr, 2022a). Once modern laser devices are in effect, the conversion efficiency of the National Ignition Facility will be significantly improved (Seife, 2000). Such an excuse would likely be misleading, implying that the US fusion experiments using the "laser ignition" technology route are purely for engineering considerations. However, the US cannot avoid serious questions of nuclear ethics regarding the underlying relationship between "laser ignition" and nuclear experimenting.

Why does "laser ignition" raise nuclear ethical questions? The reason is related to the technical origin of "laser ignition." The more rigorous terminology for "laser ignition" is inertial confinement fusion (ICF). In simple terms, this complex ICF is similar to the ignition of a car engine cylinder. In other words, achieving "laser ignition" requires a set of "engine cylinders" as an experimental facility. In the case of this "successful" experiment at the end of 2022, the set of "engine cylinders" is called the National Ignition Facility, which belongs to Lawrence Livermore National Laboratory (LLNL) in California, US.

The problem first arises from the background of the laboratory. In 1952, during the peak of the Cold War, America decided to establish the Laboratory in response to the nuclear threat from the Soviet Union. Since then, the laboratory has contributed significantly to developing advanced nuclear weapon technology. Since the 1950s, the principal scientific research achievements of the laboratory included the Arctic Star sea-based ballistic missile strategic nuclear warhead, the Peacekeeper silo-based ballistic missile strategic nuclear warhead, closed underground nuclear explosions, and low-altitude nuclear bombs. The laboratory also cooperated with US intelligence agencies, such as the Central Intelligence Agency (CIA), to analyze the Soviet Union's nuclear experimentation projects.

Based on long-term progress in physics and nuclear technology, the laboratory initially established the "laser project" in 1972 to explore the "laser ignition" technology for achieving energy gain in nuclear fusion.[4] In 1974, the "laser project" built the first single-beam laser facility, named Janus. That same year, Janus was upgraded and could emit dual-beam lasers, but the maximum power was only 0.5 terawatts. Even so, Janus still paved the way for a US nuclear fusion ignition facility. After nearly 50 years of scientific research and technological development, the US National Ignition Facility can now launch 192 pulse lasers, and the single-shot launch power reaches 500 terawatts, which is 1,000 times the power of Janus in 1974.

Sure, the laboratory has also promoted the transformation of nuclear technology for civilian use and continuously generated significant derivative technologies in nuclear technology research and development. For example, supercomputers, parallel processors, global climate analysis models, radiation detectors, biocompatible material, and medical microelectronics all came from the laboratory. However, developing these civilian technologies can produce new resources such as funding, application scenarios, and partnerships, benefiting the laboratory's research and development of nuclear weapon technology. "Laser ignition" technology and the National Ignition Facility have also become the laboratory's key projects serving the US nuclear deterrence strategy.

Another issue worth noting is that the emergence of "laser ignition" technology is closely related to hydrogen bombs. After the US succeeded in hydrogen bomb experiments in the 1950s, it focused on exploring the transformation of hydrogen bomb technology into civil energy technology, using the colossal energy generated by hydrogen bomb nuclear fusion reactions for power generation. The initial idea was to use nuclear fusion explosions directly for power generation, which required continuously detonating small hydrogen bombs to generate energy. Although this conceptual idea is feasible in engineering, significant safety and operational risks remain. Achieving small-scale nuclear fusion under low-temperature, controllable conditions thus became a key technological challenge. To address the challenge, inertial confinement fusion provided a new idea. The idea is to use lasers to shoot hydrogen isotope solid target pellets to trigger nuclear fusion, that is, "laser ignition."

Unlike hydrogen bombs, the fusion material used in "laser ignition" is extremely small. The so-called fusion material is the carrier of nuclear fusion. In the ignition experiment, the fusion material used by the US research team is the hydrogen isotope solid target capsule mentioned above. Although the specific composition and quality of the target capsule have not been publicly disclosed by the laboratory, based on other publicly available information, the target capsule is only the size of a peppercorn. Even so, "laser ignition" can still be regarded as a miniature-scale physical experiment with some hydrogen bombs, which contradicts the purpose of energy technology research initially proposed by the laboratory. Direct evidence comes from a 2014 report from the Livermore Laboratory titled "Support for the National Ignition Facility Experiments in the Nuclear Stockpile Management Program" (Wan and Scott, 2014). The report pointed out that the National Ignition Facility experiments contributed to maintaining US nuclear deterrence during the suspension of nuclear experiments. The report also revealed that the National Ignition Facility experiments helped to demonstrate the performances of nuclear weapons, improve physics models for simulated design and experimentation of nuclear stockpiles, and train teams for nuclear weapon projects.

The US is a signatory to the Comprehensive Nuclear-Experiment-Ban Treaty of the United Nations and should legally abide by its moral obligation to "suspend nuclear experimenting." However, the situation has changed in recent years. In 2020, the Comprehensive Nuclear-Test-Ban Treaty Organization (CTBTO) issued a statement expressing deep concern over media reports of the possibility of the US discussing the resumption of nuclear experimentation (Borger, 2022). Russia expressed support for the CTBTO statement, and China also expressed grave concern about the issue of the US discussing the resumption of nuclear experiments.[5] These signals indicate that the US is beginning to loosen its commitment to "suspend nuclear experimenting" and is constantly seeking opportunities for nuclear weapon experimenting. Currently, "laser ignition" provides the US with a technological opportunity to wander on the edge of nuclear ethics.

Although "laser ignition" has not reached the energy level of a hydrogen bomb explosion, it reflects the strategic motivation of the US to persist in researching hydrogen bomb physical experiments to maintain nuclear deterrence. The US behavior of probing the nuclear ethics boundary through "laser ignition" deserves high vigilance from the international community.

A feeble technological advantage over China

Despite developing energy technology and maintaining nuclear deterrence, another purpose of the US' promotion of nuclear fusion ignition technology is to maintain its technological advantage over China. Since the 1990s, China has been catching up with the international frontier in nuclear fusion. In 2003, China joined the International Thermonuclear Experimental Reactor (ITER) program led by the European Union, Japan, Russia, and the US. Three years later, China, the European Union, the US, and four other countries partnered to fund the ITER program. China has significantly improved in fusion technology and international primary scientific project management by participating in the ITER program. Since 2020, China's HL-2M tokamak and "artificial sun" EAST tokamak devices have made significant technological advancements, enabling China's nuclear fusion research to leap from following and running in parallel to the international frontier.[6] Based on existing medium and large tokamak devices, China has set short-, medium-, and long-term technical goals in the field of magnetic confinement fusion and is expected to develop fusion power plants and explore the engineering, safety, and economic feasibility of commercial fusion power plants by 2060 (Zheng *et al.*, 2022).

China and the US are currently neck-by-neck in the nuclear fusion field, which has shocked and threatened the US. In order to accelerate the US development of nuclear fusion technology and industry, Congress has continuously increased its budget appropriations for the Department of Energy in recent years and emphasized its investment in nuclear fusion research funds. According to the Fusion Industry Association (2023), in the 2019 fiscal year, the Department of Energy's budget was US$35.69 billion, with an average annual growth rate of 6.7%, reaching US$49.35 billion by the 2023 fiscal year, an increase of 38.3% from 2019. The Fusion Industry Association (2023) also shows that in 2019, the Department of Energy's budget for fusion energy research reached US$430 million, more than other advanced nuclear technology budgets. Moreover, the Department of Energy recently received two additional budget appropriations from the Biden administration. The first is US$35.07 billion, added from 2022 to 2027 as part of the "Inflation Reduction Act." The second is US$13.1 billion added in 2023 as part of the "Infrastructure Investment and Jobs Act." These massive appropriations have made the Department of Energy a super executive department with an annual budget of nearly US$70 billion, enhancing its leadership in nuclear fusion research and industrialization.

The US has always considered China a hypothetical strategic opponent in nuclear fusion. In 2020, the Fusion Energy Sciences Advisory Committee (FESAC) of the US released a report entitled "Powering the Future Fusion & Plasmas," which pointed out that China has invested hundreds of millions of dollars in government and social capital cooperation projects in the field of nuclear fusion, so the US urgently needs to strengthen its public–private partnerships to consolidate its leadership position in this emerging industry.[7] In 2021, the National Academy of Sciences, Engineering, and Medicine of the US released a report entitled "Bringing Fusion to the US Grid," which proposed that considering China's Fusion Engineering Experiment Reactor (CFETR) project is expected to achieve operation in 2041, the US should achieve experimental power plant operation around 2035 to 2040.[8] In nuclear fusion, the US urgently hopes to maintain its advantage over China in technology and industry.

However, it is only wishful thinking for the US to take an absolute technological advantage over China. The US can continue to increase its investment in nuclear fusion research and industrialization. However, it cannot contain China's independent progress in nuclear fusion, nor can it prevent China from forming an indigenous supply chain for nuclear fusion. China has some advantages over the US, especially in magnetic confinement fusion, such as high-flux reactors, neutron sources, and accelerators. Therefore, the US has proposed using China's nuclear facilities for material irradiation experiments and fusion-reactor blanket technology research in ITER.

Moreover, China is also the most important manufacturer of ITER, undertaking many primary scientific research and engineering construction projects for the procurement package and experimental blanket project. Through participation in ITER projects, China has enhanced its capability to design, develop, and experiment with independent intellectual property module systems, established a comprehensive and coordinated nuclear fusion supply chain, and trained a group of high-level talents. These technological capabilities, supply chain foundation, and talent teams ensure China can independently advance nuclear fusion research and industrial system construction. Therefore, in nuclear fusion, the US has less technological reserves and industrial strength to hold China back than expected, making it greatly difficult to achieve an absolute technological advantage over China.

Industrial Policy: A Never-Ending Political Turmoil

Hosted by Jennifer M. Granholm, head of the US Department of Energy, the press conference on the "success" of ignition has evidently shown significant political intentions. At the conference, the Department of Energy invited six heavyweight Democratic senators and House representatives who chaired committees responsible for army services, intelligence, appropriations, and energy research.[9] The participation of these senators and representatives made the conference more like a political vanity fair for the Democratic Party rather than merely a press conference about technological progress. If the "success" of the ignition was just a technological event, why did the US Department of Energy purposely politicize the launch?

Tribute to Congress

Nuclear fusion has always been a political bargaining chip for Democrats and the Biden administration. In 2021, as soon as the Biden administration took office, it changed the nuclear fusion policy of the Trump administration and emphasized that the federal government's role should not only be reflected in the basic scientific research of nuclear fusion but also participate in the industrialization of nuclear fusion. This policy shift is because the Biden administration regards nuclear fusion as a critical technology for the US to achieve zero emissions in 2050, thereby enhancing its global leadership in climate change.

Moreover, the outbreak of the Russia–Ukraine conflict has made the US urgently need to reduce its dependence on oil energy, which requires the US to establish an independent and controllable nuclear fusion energy system. Therefore, in 2022, the Biden administration signed the "Inflation Reduction Act" and, based on the congressional budget, added billions of dollars in funding and subsidies to support the research and industrialization of nuclear fusion.

Against this background, the US Department of Energy has implemented the Biden administration's nuclear fusion strategic policy. The question is whether Congress will keep on approving such substantial federal funding for nuclear fusion. The US Department of Energy must speak for itself.

What is the attitude of Congress? Of course, most Democratic representatives support the Biden administration's nuclear fusion policy. However, Republican representatives are not likely to accept it easily. Making the situation more complicated are the US midterm elections that began in November 2022. As a result, Democrats lost nine congressional seats, and Republicans became the majority in Congress, thereby gaining the power to approve the Biden administration's budget. Therefore, whether the Republican-led Congress would approve the budget for the Biden administration to increase funding for nuclear fusion research and industrialization in the 2023 fiscal year was a tricky issue that the US Department of Energy had to address.

The "successful" ignition thus became a fruitful answer that the US Department of Energy submitted to Congress. Although the ignition experiment took place on December 5, the Department of Energy did not immediately release the news. On the one hand, this was due to cautious considerations. Researchers needed time to analyze the data to confirm the robustness of the experimental results. On the other hand, the Department of Energy needed to schedule an appropriate release opportunity, which should not only make the press conference a wonderful political tribute before

Congress reviewed the budget bill but also give Democrats enough time to reconcile with the policy viewpoints of Republicans and blend political interests.

To this end, the Department of Energy waited until December 11 to release the news and officially announced the "successful" ignition on the 13th. Just 10 days after the press conference, on December 23, Congress passed a US$1.7 trillion budget bill for the 2023 fiscal year.[10] In the new budget bill, the "Fusion Energy Science" project, which the US Department of Energy leads, received US$760 million, not only a 7% increase compared to the previous year but also US$40 million more than the budget applied for by the Biden administration. Moreover, the "Inertial Confinement Fusion" research project, which the US National Nuclear Security Administration leads, received US$630 million, a nearly 9% increase compared to the previous year. Among them, the "National Ignition Facility" project received US$380 million, and the project team is mainly responsible for the "laser ignition" experiment, which can be said to be the most significant contributor to the "successful" ignition. Overall, the US' federal budget for nuclear fusion reached a record US$1.4 billion in the 2023 fiscal year. With the support of substantial financial resources, the US Department of Energy has strengthened its leadership in nuclear fusion research and industrialization.

In sum, the "successful" ignition is not only a technological advancement event but also a key political achievement for the Biden administration to persuade Congress to increase the budget for nuclear fusion under the careful planning of the Department of Energy. However, a problem still exists: Republicans are not genuinely supportive of the Democrats' nuclear fusion policy. The bipartisan dispute on nuclear fusion will likely jeopardize the industrialization of the US fusion sector.

Political rift on fusion policy

Although Congress has approved a massive budget for nuclear fusion, there are still significant disagreements between Democrats and Republicans on fusion policy. The focus of controversy is what role the federal government and the market should play in the development of nuclear fusion. Ideally, the government and the market should cooperate, bearing the cost of scientific research, and enterprises should use the technology from government research projects to promote the industrialization and commercialization of nuclear fusion technology and achieve profitability. However, Democrats and Republicans have different views on the extent of federal government involvement.

The Trump administration's nuclear fusion policy reflected the Republican stance that the federal government should focus on basic research on nuclear fusion. Basic research is expensive, risky, and unprofitable, making it difficult for firms to undertake research and development. Moreover, the Trump administration believed enterprises should complete technology commercialization and industrialization to stimulate entrepreneurial spirit, strengthen market competition, and stimulate industrial vitality.

In contrast, since taking office, the Biden administration has emphasized that the federal government should actively participate in the scientific research, technology development, and marketization of nuclear fusion. Furthermore, Democrats emphasize that the government should participate in the whole process, not only supporting the startup phase of research and industrial projects and managing the mid-term operation phase of the project but also playing a role in safeguarding the industrialization and commercialization phases in the later stages. The reason is that emerging technology industries, such as, nuclear fusion require massive investment at every stage of industrialization, and only massive financial investment at the federal government level can solidify the foundation of nuclear fusion development. Additionally, firms can be attracted to invest more in nuclear fusion only with sustained and massive financial resources from the federal government.

However, the more pressing problem is that the considerable investment by the US government so far still needs to be more to promote the industrialization and commercialization of nuclear fusion, leaving the US project of a nuclear fusion experimental power plant in a difficult situation. In 2022, Congress approved the "Chip and Science Act," which plans to invest US$1 billion in the

"Fusion Energy Science" project in 2023. However, the actual funding for the project is only 74% of this budget target. Moreover, the Biden administration held a summit on "Developing a Bold Decadal Vision for Commercial Fusion Energy" in 2022.[11] The summit was to promote active investment by the industry in nuclear fusion development. The industry believed that at least US$1 billion in government investment is needed for nuclear fusion commercialization. However, the budget approved by Congress fails to meet the industry's expectations.

Even if the government budget is entirely in place, more funds are needed to achieve nuclear fusion industrialization and launch the experimental power plant the US Department of Energy envisioned. At this writing, more than 15 US companies have applied to participate in the experimental power plant project, with a total application funding of US$2.6 billion. However, the US Energy Department's budget for the experimental power plant is only US$500 million. These funds will be quickly used up in the 18-month startup phase of the project, and then the US Department of Energy will have to apply for extra budgets from the Republican-led Congress. By then, whether there will be a dazzling political achievement like this "successful" ignition and whether Republican representatives can be persuaded are big questions.

In sum, the government-funded fusion industrial policy promoted by the Biden administration has always been challenging to obtain Republican support. Whether the Republican-led Congress will continue to increase its budget for the fusion industry in the next four years is still unpredictable. Democrats' attempts to increase the budget for nuclear fusion development still faces the political risk of being "blocked" by the Republican-controlled Congress. The conflicts between the two parties make providing a stable policy foundation for the US fusion industry highly difficult.

Trust crisis

The political turmoil occurs in the decision-making stage of US fusion policy and industrialization. Currently, the primary mode of nuclear fusion industrialization in the US is a public–private partnership (PPP).[12] Specifically, private enterprises and the government establish cooperative projects to pool research and development resources, reduce duplication and waste, and share R&D results. However, in a PPP, the information controlled by the government and private enterprises could be more symmetrical. Enterprises may falsify R&D and financial data to obtain government subsidies and R&D funds, which can generate severe moral risks and lead to a trust crisis.

The new-energy industry in the US is not a la-la land, as incidents of corporate fraud, information manipulation, and interest groups' obstruction frequently emerging are an innate part of the game. In fact, there have been cases of US new-energy companies using PPP projects to obtain government funds. In 2009, Solyndra, a US solar system manufacturer, received a US$535 million federal loan guarantee approved by the US Department of Energy.[13] The then-US President Obama once promoted the company as a pioneer in new-energy manufacturing.[14] However, after receiving the loan, Solyndra suddenly applied for bankruptcy, turning the loan that the US government had just issued into lousy debt for the Federal balance sheet. This case triggered an independent investigation by the US Department of Justice and Congress in 2011, and the "Solyndra scandal" broke out.

Solyndra's loan fraud was successful because of the support of entrenched political interests in the US, which reflects the deep-rooted collusion between government and business in the country. It bears noting that Solyndra had intricate connections with then-US President Obama. After Obama took office, he appointed his confidant Steve Spinner to supervise loans at the US Department of Energy.[15] As a bundler, Spinner urged the Department of Energy to expedite the approval process for Solyndra's loan and constantly sought personal gain.[16] As the Solyndra scandal continued to ferment, the White House repeatedly denied Spinner's participation in supervising Solyndra's loan, but this "deny everything" response could not escape congressional scrutiny. Ironically, the Solyndra investigation resulted in the US political and solar industry turning its attention to China. One year after the bankruptcy, Solyndra accused Chinese government agencies, solar companies, and financial sectors of forming a "monopoly organization" that allowed solar components produced in China to be "dumped" in the US market. Accordingly, China's "unfair competition" caused Solyndra to go bankrupt in the US and caused the US government's loan to become bad debt. Ultimately, the Chinese government and companies became the "scapegoats" for the US to evade this political–business collusion scandal.

As shown by the Solyndra case, the commercialization of the US nuclear fusion industry still confronts the trust crisis caused by political–business collusion. After the Democratic Party suffered a midterm election defeat, the Biden administration urgently needed to create star companies in the nuclear fusion industry as a political achievement to maintain its legitimacy in power. Moreover, as Biden is very likely to seek re-election in 2024, Democrats need to seek campaign funds through the new-energy industry and offer "reassurance" to voters who are concerned about climate change and support the green economy to retain their support. Therefore, the nuclear fusion industry will always be a critical political force for the Biden administration and Democrats to maintain their political power. However, Biden and Democrats have always been unable to solve the problem of information asymmetry between the government and enterprises. Therefore, scandals like Solyndra's loan fraud are only a matter of time before they happen again.

The analysis above demonstrates that the political significance of the US fusion ignition "success" is far greater than its technological and commercial significance. The US fusion ignition technology needs to be more comprehensive to support the commercial application of civil power generation on a large scale. Moreover, the frequent laser ignition experiments in the US are suspected of nuclear weapon experimentation and should be highly alert to the international community. Furthermore, in nuclear fusion, the US still lacks enough strength to maintain its advantage over China, at least for now.

Even so, the US government is still loudly promoting the "success" of fusion ignition to Congress, indicating that the primary goal of the Biden administration is to use the success of nuclear fusion ignition as a political achievement to persuade Congress to increase financial appropriations. However, there are still significant disputes between Republicans and Democrats on nuclear fusion policy. Republicans believe the federal government should only support basic research, while Democrats believe the federal government should provide strong support at all stages, from scientific research to industrialization. The bipartisan disagreements always make the policy focus of US support for nuclear fusion uncertain.

Moreover, the financial funds approved by Congress are still far from the investment targets envisioned by the industry for the commercialization of nuclear fusion. Even more serious is that in the process of new-energy industrialization, the US always faces the problem of information asymmetry between government and enterprises, which leads to companies cheating to obtain government support. Overall, the commercialization of the US nuclear fusion industry faces not only a series of critical technological bottlenecks but also potential major trust crises, making success in the short term highly difficult.

Industrialization Challenges: China's Fusion Sector

The deep-rooted problems facing the industrialization of nuclear fusion in the US are worth pondering for China. Unlike America's myopic approach, which focuses on grabbing political benefits from the ignition's "success," China has always adhered to a steady and long-term strategy for nuclear energy development. In 1983, China proposed the "Three-Step" strategy for nuclear energy development, which follows a mechanical sequence from thermal reactors to fast reactors and fusion reactors.[17] China is still in the first stage of the "Three-Step" strategy, and the construction of nuclear power will continue to be dominated by thermal reactors for some time. Moreover, China's research on fast reactors has made significant progress, and the prototype fast reactor project was completed and put into operation in 2023. An integrated fast reactor project has been started and will constitute a new-generation prototype by 2035. Nevertheless, although China has made continuous technological breakthroughs in nuclear fusion, China's fusion reactors are still in the early stages of research, and there is still a long way to go to achieve commercial power generation.

While following the "Three-Step" strategy, China is currently facing three urgent challenges in the industrialization of nuclear fusion. First, China should be cautious about the instigative effect of the US' ignition "success" on global and domestic capital markets. Currently, the world and China are facing the conundrum of secular stagnation, which leads to a need for more investment themes and business model narratives with commercial value in the industry. Given that, the ignition "success" of nuclear fusion could excite the capital market, likely leading to the emergence of investment narrative themes swirling around nuclear fusion. Overseas capital has already started to lay out investment tracks for nuclear fusion power generation.[18] Moreover, domestic venture capital's investment interest in nuclear fusion development is increasing considerably.[19] Of course, the stable development of venture capital will contribute to the industrialization of nuclear fusion in China. However, suppose China does not strengthen the guidance of private investment in nuclear fusion. In that case, a wave of overinvestment will also create significant investment risks, ultimately dragging down the development of China's nuclear fusion industrialization.

Second, China should recognize objective trends of continuous technological progress in which the threshold for private enterprises to enter the nuclear fusion industry is dramatically being lowered. So far, significant technological progress has emerged in supercomputers in recent years. Increasing computing power has dramatically reduced the cost of large-scale computing, which helps promote the development of small-scale nuclear fusion reactors. Rapid prototyping technologies such as 3D printing have allowed companies like Shapeways to manufacture compact fusion reactors and accelerate the speed of design iteration. Moreover, PPP projects in the US and the United Kingdom have made it easier for enterprises to obtain the latest achievements of government nuclear fusion research projects, significantly reducing unknown research and development risks and accelerating enterprises' progress in landing nuclear fusion reactors. In this sense, China should recognize that technological upgrading features iterative and disruptive progress characteristics. These two characteristics will become the objective forces driving the industrialization of nuclear fusion.

Third, China should consider the three hurdles hidden in China's nuclear fusion industrialization. The industrialization of fusion reactors could aim to develop in parallel with fast reactors. Currently, more private capital bets on the vast commercial potential of nuclear fusion for commercial power generation, making fusion reactors have more efficient business development models than fast reactors. Meanwhile, after miniaturization, fusion reactors can adapt to civil energy demands differently from fast reactors, making the commercialization of fusion reactors competitive. It means that fast and fusion reactors may not be two separate stages, as the "Three-Step" strategy expected, but a parallel development process. Without a comprehensive and coordinated energy industry development plan, the investment mania of private capital in fusion reactors will not only increase risk exposure but also crowd out credit resources, research and development inputs, and strategic talents for commercializing fast reactors, thereby perhaps undermining the security of China's energy sector.

Moreover, startups might enjoy a first-mover advantage over those listed companies in China's nuclear fusion industry chain. More than 10 A-share listed companies have entered the nuclear fusion business.[20] However, nuclear fusion has never been their primary business, and the contribution of the nuclear fusion business to their profit growth is minimal. Moreover, their nuclear fusion business has yet to form a complete industry chain. Instead, it focuses on specific nodes of the ITER, the CFETR, and other scientific research projects, requiring coordination at the project level and cooperation with the industrial chains of developed countries. In contrast, Chinese startup companies and venture capital projects focus more on the complete industry chain, its relevant R&D projects, and overall landing solutions for power plant engineering projects. As a result, a bizarre but understandable scene in China's future nuclear fusion industry may emerge: startup companies enjoy high value-added benefits from the complete value chain, while listed companies can only share low value-added profits from the partial value chain. The difference in value chain status will lead to the rapid rise of startups and emerging listed companies, while listed companies face weak profit growth. Although this results from market competition, this first-mover advantage of startup firms over incumbents may seriously disturb the order of China's capital market, thereby denting the market's confidence in China's financial stability.

More noteworthy is the imbalance in private and state-owned capital's narrative ability to finance the nuclear fusion industry. Only a few state-owned nuclear power enterprises have launched commercial nuclear fusion (artificial sun) power generation projects.[21] These SOEs often have a background in China's nuclear military industry and have long been engaged in highly classified nuclear industry research and construction, making these state-owned entities naturally reject the narrative and roadshow techniques for wooing the capital market. In contrast, private capital, although inferior to state-owned capital in investment amount and technological level, could be better at coining new concepts and narratives to attract venture capital and equity investors. This imbalance in financing narrative ability may lead to the market financing efficiency of state-owned capital lagging behind that of private capital, thereby imperiling the cornerstone status of the state-owned economy in the nuclear fusion industry.

In sum, external shocks from the US, disruptive technological progress, and emerging industrialization hurdles are likely to jeopardize the current thriving momentum of China's nuclear fusion development. To address those challenges, China should start to design a comprehensive, coordinated, and sustainable energy development strategy and actively and steadily promote the marketization of its nuclear fusion sector. Such a strategy should secure the resistance of the domestic nuclear fusion industry chain to external shocks, accommodate both gradual and disruptive technological progresses, and balance the energy structure, capital structure, and ownership structure.

Energy Powerhouse Strategy: Marketization Matters

Given the above-mentioned challenges confronting the development of the fusion sector, China should design a national-level development blueprint called the Energy Powerhouse Strategy. The 2021 Central Economic Work Conference, attended by the top Chinese political leaders, has already proposed "to deeply promote energy revolution and accelerate the construction of an energy powerhouse."[22] To establish an energy-resistant economy for China, the Energy Powerhouse Strategy could incorporate a feasible plan for marketizing the nuclear fusion sector. Specifically, the Energy Powerhouse Strategy should focus on national energy security, encourage inclusive progress that accommodates gradual and disruptive technological advancements, and promote balanced and stable energy development, capital, and ownership structures. Implementing the Energy Powerhouse Strategy will involve enormous and substantial interdisciplinary, cross-industry, cross-level, and cross-departmental conundrums, which go beyond the scope of this chapter. However, to outline the design work of the Energy Powerhouse Strategy, we propose a concise approach based on "three pillars."

The first pillar of the Energy Powerhouse Strategy is the carbon peaking and carbon neutrality strategy. It means that China should construct a multi-energy complementary energy development pattern. China is rich in coal but scarce in oil and gas. Such energy resource endowment of China adds critical challenges to the already daunting task of transitioning to a green and low-carbon energy structure. To deal with the challenge, China should transition from the current coal-based energy system to a diversified one of fossil and renewable energy and explore a strategy to rely more on green energy. However, green energy development is still under multiple constraints: unstable supply, equipment industry chain bottlenecks, and an immature electricity market. Tackling these problems needs time. Therefore, China still needs fossil energy to provide a stable, reliable, and robust energy supply system. Meanwhile, China should establish and strengthen a multi-energy complementary energy development pattern.

The second pillar is to follow safe, steady development and coordinated innovation to promote nuclear power. It means that China should ensure the stability and reliability of its full nuclear power industrial chain, especially the independent and controllable reserves of nuclear raw materials, complete project construction, and technological iteration. Moreover, China should actively build third-generation thermal neutron power stations, support nuclear power technology development for energy base load systems, enhance inherent safety capabilities, steadily promote controllable nuclear fusion technology, and attach particular importance to the coordinated innovation and development of fast and fusion reactors.

The third pillar is to build a market economy system balanced between the leading role of state-owned capital and the innovation potential of private capital. It means that China should promote the marketization reform of industry access rules, energy trading mechanisms, and innovation management mechanisms in the energy sector, improve the resource allocation capabilities of the market, and fully stimulate the vitality of the energy market. While giving full play to the leading role of state-owned capital in energy transformation, China should also strengthen the assessment of new-energy technology research and development investment by SOEs. Last but not least, China should encourage the market-oriented development of new-energy industries and nuclear fusion power generation and strengthen the supervision and regulation of private capital.

Conclusion

Industrial upgrading and innovation should count on the market rather than the political game. China should avoid the US lessons of politicalizing the ignition's "success," a technologically advancing event in the fusion sector. To build such an emerging high-tech strategic sector as nuclear fusion, we should recall the wisdom of Joseph Schumpeter (1942), who famously wrote that a system:

> that at *every* given point in time fully utilizes its possibilities to the best advantage may yet in the long run be inferior to a system that does so at *no* given point in time, because the latter's failure to do so may be a condition for the level or speed of long-run performance (with emphasis in the original).

The Schumpeterian disconnect between efficiency and growth shows that innovation is an inherently wasteful process. That is why industrial policy is always needed to balance short-term losses with long-term economic gains. One of the most worrying US lessons regarding the fusion sector is to use a myopic strategy that focuses on maximizing the political value of the advancing ignition technology. However, the US might miss its original goal by adding too much political pressure on a single immature technology in an infant high-tech sector such as the fusion industry.

While insisting on the "Three Step" strategy for almost 40 years, China might consider transforming from rigid industrial planning to a more flexible and market-oriented strategy to promote the development of its fusion sector. Above all, China's success in building modern and widely accessible infrastructure, including expressways, high-speed rail networks, civil aviation, ports, and the fusion and energy industries analyzed in this chapter, demonstrate the economic values of industrial policy. In 1959, China decided to develop nuclear technology on its own. Since then, China's nuclear sector has followed a policy of isolation from the market. With the escalation of Sino–US strategic competition in an era of disruptive technological advancements, China should design a comprehensive Energy Powerhouse Strategy to lower the entrance barrier for private capital to enter the once-closed fusion sector and expedite the opening up of the general energy industry earlier than expected. It does not mean that the energy sector should be completely privatized. On the contrary, it means marketizing China's energy sector by building a productive production network where SOEs and private enterprises can coexist and work together to enhance China's strategic competitiveness over the US. On this front, China will keep surprising economists, for sure.

Acknowledgements

The author thanks Jun Zhang, Weiqi Tang, Yi Shen, Xu Yao, Tianjiao Jiang, Zhiwei Gu, Henning Kristoffersen, Tomas Casas-Klett, Hanzhen Ouyang, Passant Mamdouh Ridwan, Yi Zhang, and Hao Huang for helpful comments and discussion. Sincere thanks also go to the FDDI 2025 Project on National Developmental Forces, the "Super Post-doc" project of Shanghai Municipal People's Government, and the Fudan-Pingan Research Institute for Macroeconomy.

Endnotes

1. Eastern Time (2022). See DOE National Lab (2023).
2. See Behr (2022b).
3. See Behr (2022a).
4. See Lawrence Livermore National Laboratory (1974).
5. See the regular press conference of the Chinese Foreign Ministry (2020) on June 8, 2020.
6. In December 2020, China's new generation "artificial sun" device, HL-2M, was officially completed and achieved its first discharge at the Southwest Institute of Physics in Chengdu, Sichuan. In December 2021, China's "artificial sun" EAST achieved a long-pulse, high-parameter plasma operation of 1,056 seconds, becoming the world's most prolonged high-temperature plasma operation achieved by a tokamak device and breaking the world record. In October 2022, China announced that the plasma current of the HL-2M device had exceeded 1 million amperes (1 tera-ampere), setting a new record for the operation of controllable fusion devices.
7. See the Fusion Energy Sciences Advisory Committee (2020).
8. See the National Academies of Sciences, Engineering, and Medicine (2021).

9. Among them, Senator Jack Reed chairs the Senate Committee on Armed Services. Congressman Eric Swalwell is a member of the House Committee on Homeland Security. Congressman Chuck Fleischmann is a member of the House Appropriations Committee, chairing the Energy and Water Development Subcommittee. By the end of 2022, Congressman Jerry McNerney chaired the House Committee on Energy and Commerce and the Energy Subcommittee of the House Science, Space, and Technology Committee. Jerry McNerney did not seek re-election after his term as a representative expired on January 3, 2023. Congressmen Conor Lamb and Jamaal Bowman were also invited to attend the press conference. In addition, Senator Zoe Lofgren, a senior member of the House Science, Space, and Technology Committee, was invited but could not attend the press conference due to a temporary matter.
10. See Fusion Industry Association (2022a).
11. See Fusion Industry Association (2022b).
12. The US Fusion Industry Association (FIA) is the leading lobbying group that promotes public–private partnerships (PPPs) for nuclear fusion. At least one PPP project has been participated by the FIA's 22 US private enterprise members. For this purpose, these private entities have raised nearly US$2 billion in private equity to develop fusion energy technology routes, and some companies accordingly expect to achieve fusion energy commercialization before 2040.
13. See Mosk and Greene (2011).
14. On May 26, 2010, the then-US President Obama visited Solyndra's solar panel factory in Fremont, California.
15. Stephen Spinner raised at least US$500,000 for Obama's presidential campaign, making him a fundraising hero. As a result, Spinner received a reciprocal appointment from Obama and became a key figure in driving the implementation of the Obama administration's new-energy loan policy at the US Department of Energy.
16. Spinner recommended billionaire George Kaiser, a major investor in Solyndra, to then-Vice President Biden's assistant. In addition, the law firm of Spinner's wife charged the US government $2.4 million in service fees for handling legal matters related to Solyndra's loan guarantee.
17. In 1983, the Chinese State Council's Science and Technology Leading Group chaired an expert consultation meeting. It proposed the strategic roadmap for China's nuclear energy development, known as the

"Three-Step Plan (pressurized water reactors — fast reactors — fusion reactors)," as well as the policy of "adhering to a closed fuel cycle for nuclear fuel."

18. Among other international investors, Amazon, Lockheed Martin, Google, Goldman Sachs, and the Gates Foundation have long been investing in fusion energy. In 2011, Amazon invested in General Fusion, a Canadian producer of fusion power devices that aimed to build the world's first nuclear fusion power plant. In 2014, Lockheed Martin began developing compact fusion reactors. In 2017, Google supported Tri Alpha Energy in developing plasma experimental computer algorithms and researching new commercial fusion energy devices.
19. So far, Chinese and foreign institutional investors such as Sequoia China, BlueRun Ventures, CASSTAR, Shunwei Capital, MSA Capital, K2VC, Legendstar, and others have already established a presence in fusion energy. In February 2022, Energy Singularity, an enterprise exploring the commercialization of fusion energy technology, announced the completion of its Series A financing round worth nearly RMB 400 million. NIO Capital and miHoYo led the financing round, with participation from Sequoia China Seed Fund and BlueRun Ventures. In June 2022, Startorus Fusion, a commercial fusion energy device developer established just one year prior, announced the completion of a multi-hundred-million RMB angel round financing, with participation from CASSTAR and ten other well-known venture capitals.
20. According to incomplete information, the A-share companies involved in the nuclear fusion business are as follows: China National Nuclear Power Co., Ltd., Advanced Technology & Materials Co., Ltd., Guoguang Electric Co., Ltd., Western Superconducting Technologies Co., Ltd., China Nuclear Engineering & Construction Co., Ltd., Orient Tantalum Industry Co., Ltd., Neway Valve (Suzhou) Co., Ltd., Aerosun Corporation, Tianjin Benefo Tejing Electric Co., Ltd., Baoding Tianwei Baobian Electric Co., Ltd., LBT Group, and Baiyin Nonferrous Group Co., Ltd.
21. For example, the research institute under the China National Nuclear Corporation has already commenced research projects, and the China Nuclear Engineering Corporation has initiated engineering design, technological research, and project planning.
22. See The People's Daily (2021).

References

Andrews-Speed, P. 2023. *Nuclear Power in China: Its Role in National Energy Policy.* Oxford: Oxford Institute for Energy Studies.

Behr, P. 2022a. After 'breakthrough,' DOE eyes fusion power plant. *Politico.* Retrieved July 14, 2023 from https://www.politico.com/news/2022/12/13/fusion-breakthrough-doe-energy-00073631.

Behr, P. 2022b. What to know about DOE's fusion milestone. *Politico.* Retrieved July 14, 2023 from https://www.politico.com/news/2022/12/13/fusion-breakthrough-doe-energy-00073631.

Borger, J. 2022. Nuclear Watchdog Says Any Us Experiment Would Be 'Grave Challenge to Peace' (2023).

Brandt, L. and Rawski, T.G. 2019. Policy, regulation, and innovation in China's electricity and telecom industries. In Brandt, L. and Rawski, T.G. (eds.), pp. 1–51. Cambridge: Cambridge University Press. http://doi.org/DOI: undefined.

Buigues, P. and Sekkat, K. 2009. *Industrial Policy in Europe, Japan and the USA: Amounts, Mechanisms and Effectiveness.* London: Palgrave Macmillan.

Chinese Foreign Ministry. 2020. Foreign Ministry Spokesperson Hua Chunying presided over the regular press conference on June 8, 2020. https://www.mfa.gov.cn/web/wjdt_674879/fyrbt_674889/202006/t20200608_7816276.shtm.

DOE National Lab. 2023. Press conference: Secretary Granholm & DOE leaders announced fusion breakthrough. https://www.youtube.com/watch?v=K2ktAL4rGuY&t=2s (Accessed July 14, 2023).

Eastern Time. 2022. The US Department of Energy addressed the first-ever "success" of nuclear fusion ignition. December 13, 2022.

Fusion Energy Sciences Advisory Committee. 2020. Powering the future: Fusion & plasmas. In Vol. 2023. Retrieved from https://usfusionandplasmas.org/wp-content/themes/FESAC/FESAC_Report_2020_Powering_the_Future.pdf.

Fusion Industry Association. 2022a. Congress provides record funding for fusion energy. https://www.fusionindustryassociation.org/congress-provides-record-funding-for-fusion-energy/.

Fusion Industry Association. 2022b. A bold decadal vision for fusion energy: FIA participates in White House fusion summit. Retrieved July 14 from https://www.fusionindustryassociation.org/a-bold-decadal-vision-for-fusion-energy-fia-participates-in-white-house-fusion-summit/.

Fusion Industry Association. 2023. Congress provides record funding for fusion energy. Retrieved July 14, 2023 from https://www.fusionindustryassociation.org/congress-provides-record-funding-for-fusion-energy/.

Hibbs, M. 2018. The future of nuclear power in China.

Johnson, C. 1982. *MITI and the Japanese Miracle: The Growth of Industrial Policy, 1925-1975.* Redwood: Stanford University Press.

Ketels, C.H. 2007. Industrial policy in the United States. *Journal of Industry, Competition and Trade,* 7: 147–167.

Kim, L. 1997. *Imitation to Innovation: The Dynamics of Korea's Technological Learning.* Harvard Business School Press.

Lawrence Livermore National Laboratory. 1974. Lasers join the quest for fusion energy. https://www.llnl.gov/sites/www/files/1974.pdf (Accessed July 14, 2023).

Mosk, M. and Greene, R. 2011. Obama Fundraiser Pushed Solyndra Deal from Inside (2023).

National Academies of Sciences, Engineering, and Medicine. 2021. *Bringing Fusion to the US Grid.* Washington, DC: National Academies Press.

Ping, Z. 1987. Nuclear power development in China: The country is seeking to develop a diversified energy base. *IAEA Bulletin,* (2): 43–46.

Plumer, B. and Davenport, C. 2017. Trump budget proposes deep cuts in energy innovation programs. Retrieved July from https://www.nytimes.com/2017/05/23/climate/trump-budget-energy.html.

Reich, R.B. 1982. Why the US needs an industrial policy. *Harvard Business Review(United States),* 60(1): 74–81.

Romer, P.M. 1990. Endogenous technological change. *Journal of Political Economy,* 98(5, Part 2): S71–S102.

Sakoh, K. 1984. Japanese economic success: industrial policy or free market. *Cato Journal,* 4: 521.

Schrank, A. and Whitford, J. 2009. Industrial policy in the United States: A neo-Polanyian interpretation. *Politics & Society,* 37(4): 521–553.

Schumpeter, J. 1942. *Capitalism, Socialism and Democracy.* New York: Harper & Brothers Publisher.

Seife, C. 2000. Will NIF live up to its name? *Science,* 289(5482): 1128.

The People's Daily. 2021. The Central Economic Work Conference was Held in Beijing. Retrieved July 14 from http://finance.people.com.cn/n1/2021/1211/c1004-32305339.html.

Wade, R. 2004. *Governing the Market: Economic Theory and the Role of Government in East Asian Industrialization.* Princeton: Princeton University Press.

Wan, A. and Scott, K. 2014. National Ignition Facility Experiments in Support of Stockpile Stewardship Program (SSP), Lawrence Livermore National Laboratory, LLNL-TR-658691.

World Bank. 1993. *The East Asian Miralce: Economic Growth and Public Policy.* Oxford: Oxford University Press.

Zheng, J., Qin, J., Lu, K., Xu, M., Duan, X., Xu, G., Hu, J., Gong, X., Zang, Q., and Liu, Z. 2022. Recent progress in Chinese fusion research based on superconducting tokamak configuration. *The Innovation,* 3(4): 1–12.

https://doi.org/10.1142/9789819815241_bmatter

INDEX

E

S

www.ingramcontent.com/pod-product-compliance
Lightning Source LLC
LaVergne TN
LVHW010635300926
849161LV00005B/948